SECRET
TOMB
OMEGA

MICHAEL RAPHAEL THOMAS

Order this book online at www.trafford.com
or email orders@trafford.com

Most Trafford titles are also available at major online book retailers.

Print information available on the last page.

ISBN: 978-1-6987-0667-2 (sc)
ISBN: 978-1-6987-0669-6 (hc)
ISBN: 978-1-6987-0668-9 (e)

Library of Congress Control Number: 2021907310

Because of the dynamic nature of the Internet, any web addresses or links contained in
this book may have changed since publication and may no longer be valid. The views
expressed in this work are solely those of the author and do not necessarily reflect the
views of the publisher, and the publisher hereby disclaims any responsibility for them.

Any people depicted in stock imagery provided by Getty Images are models, and such images
are being used for illustrative purposes only.
Certain stock imagery © Getty Images.

Scripture taken from The Holy Bible, King James Version. Public Domain

Disclaimer:

This book is not a theological treatise; it is rather an historical inquiry
in the tradition of the Quest for the Historical Jesus.

As such, this work is not intended as a discourse upon
religion, theology, philosophy, or metaphysics.

Furthermore, there is no political agenda herein; neither should any statement be
construed as implying the superiority or inferiority of any racial or ethnic group.

Neither the author nor the publisher can be held legally or morally liable for
any psychological reactions experienced by those who read this text.

Trafford rev. 04/08/2021

 www.trafford.com
North America & international
toll-free: 844-688-6899 (USA & Canada)
fax: 812 355 4082

Contents

Acknowledgements

I would like to thank and express my appreciation towards Kara Cardeno, Fresno Factor, Mark Francis, and all the teams working at Trafford Publishing and Author Solutions who made this book possible.

Introduction

J esus Christ is the great mystery of Western civilization. Even in the East the name of Jesus is greatly revered as that of a great Master of wisdom, and efforts have been made to link the historical Jesus with Buddhism. Christians claim that Jesus Christ is the very Son of God, born of a virgin, and that he was crucified on the cross as the perfect, final sacrifice for sins once and for all, after which he miraculously rose from the dead. In most branches of Christianity Jesus is regarded not merely as the Son of God, but as God the Son, fully equal in Divinity with God the Father. In Islam Jesus is regarded as a true prophet, and even born of a virgin.[1] Western culture is pervaded by an implicit reverence for Jesus Christ, which is seldom violated. And any violation thereof is inevitably accompanied by a reactionary backlash from the more conservative elements of Western society, and particularly from evangelicals and fundamentalists. True there are currently many theories respecting Jesus that are not in accord with traditional orthodoxy, but in almost all cases there is an unspoken, unwritten law that Jesus is placed upon a pedestal of untouchable sacro-sanctity, like a sacred cow. Even those who claim that Jesus was married and had children nevertheless implicitly uphold the very same

---

[1] Although what purpose such a virgin birth could serve within Islam is a mystery, unless it is merely another dogma to subjugate women to the brutality of an unbridled patriarchy. By contrast, in Christianity the virgin birth is both a logical consequence of the Divine Sonship of Christ, and even has the precedent of biblical prophecy; cf Isaiah 7:14 (LXX).

aura of sacrosanctity and refer to the postulated bloodline as a "Holy Bloodline" or a "Grail Dynasty" or even as "God Kings". Why "God Kings"? And why the gratuitous capitalizations, unless to maintain the cultural fiction of Jesus as untouchably holy, sacred, and divine? True it is that a precious few authors have bravely deviated from the cultural norm, and more radically questioned, not only the alleged ontological status of Jesus Christ as the Son of God, but his very character, morals, motivation, and even his very existence. I refer to the cultural taboo against critical scrutiny of Jesus Christ as the Jesus Christ barrier. The Jesus Christ barrier is ubiquitous throughout Western culture. It denotes more than the dogmatic religious orthodoxy vis-à-vis the ontological status of Jesus Christ; although this is the ultimate basis for it: rather it denotes the cultural inertia that implicitly upholds Jesus Christ as an icon and a cultural archetype of all that is good, holy, righteous, sacred, just, noble and true.

Herein I strive to break through the traditional Jesus Christ barrier. This is not done in a spirit of gratuitous iconoclasm or wanton irreverence; rather it is done in the pursuit of truth. Western society prides itself on diversity, equality, tolerance, openness, liberty, opportunity, democracy, free inquiry, and many other positive principles. The unstated subtext being that such principles are lacking in the East; particularly in communist China and the Islamic world. And while to a large degree this narrative may be true, nevertheless we must continue to strive forward to manifest our lofty ideals in the real world. Oftentimes we fail. We are only human. But these facts should not be excuses for failing to try to live according to our noble ideals. There has certainly been a strong backlash against Islam in the West, and especially in America. Some politicians have even called for a ban on the building of any more mosques in America.[2] The forces of reaction are growing strong in America today, and the prospects appear grim and bleak.[3] Nevertheless the thrust of this book is not political.[4] My interest is to inquire into the mystery of Jesus Christ.

---

[2]   Despite the obvious fact that any such ban would be blatantly un-Constitutional.

[3]   Unless decent Americans can stand up against the forces of cultural, social, and political reaction and affirm the true ideals of the Founding Fathers against those who seek to usurp such ideals and distort them to their own twisted and nefarious ends.

[4]   Although neither does it exist in a political, cultural, historic, or social vacuum.

As such, my inquiry is primarily an historical inquiry.[5] I will make no apologies for any controversial statements contained herein; the very nature of our inquiry is controversial to the utmost degree, and only those with a genuine interest in truth will be at home herein. Neither are any statements made for a calculated and gratuitous shock value; everything must be read in context.

The reader would be well advised to bear in mind that I am an independent researcher, and as such I will not necessarily parrot the general consensus of academic orthodoxy, even in terms of critical biblical scholarship. I am beholden to no such "experts" or "authorities", particularly when they merely pontificate, and give no reasons whatever for their views. They are content upon their Mount Olympus, and we are merely illiterate monkeys in their eyes. So be it. I will give reasons for my opinions herein, and while there may be much speculation herein, you will not find pontification.[6] I am open to any genuine, legitimate criticism of my work.[7] I will gladly correct any mistakes herein. I will admit to any errors, if any can be found herein. It should also be noted that I do not write this to gratuitously insult anyone's religious faith. I have made no misrepresentations herein, and I have been eminently fair to the evidence, such as it is. There is nothing unreasonable or dishonest herein.

There is something that the reader should perhaps know beforehand about my background. As a college freshman I had a born-again religious experience, and it was not until fourteen years later that I finally rejected the Bible-based belief-system. So it should be clearly evident that I am no longer a Bible believer and therefore my position vis-à-vis the resurrection of Christ is one of positive rejection. But this ought to come as no surprise to the reader, since the title of

---

[5] Albeit I do not want to give the impression that I take the alleged historicity of Jesus Christ for granted; any such *a priori* assumption on my part would be a mere acquiescence to the academic orthodoxy of our *zeitgeist* and would only subserve the implicit assumptions of the Jesus Christ barrier. But any inquiry into the alleged historicity of Jesus Christ is in itself an inherently historical inquiry.

[6] At least on my part, although I may quote such from other authors, to show what their views are on certain points.

[7] But I have no interest whatever in the gratuitous threats of the religious rabble, who will gladly assure me that I am damned because I have incorrect beliefs, etc.; such things do not interest me or terrify me.

the present work, as well as the table of contents, as much as disclose the same. So there is no intent to keep the reader in suspense on this score. Indeed, a perusal of the table of contents will suffice to disclose the position taken herein; but only a perusal of the entire text will present the entire case justifying that position. Furthermore I feel that I have been completely fair to all the evidence, and much more so than any number of Christian authors, whom I would rather not mention. Indeed, I have been far more honest than certain Christian authors, who have sought to infiltrate the New Age/alternative paradigm movement by their deceptive promotional tactics and product packaging, etc. We would rather not name such persons, not out of any fear of legal sanctions, but rather because they do not merit any further publicity, however odious. I have written a book about my life as a born-again Christian, entitled *Born Again Nightmare,* which I plan to make available, either as a book, an e-book, or as a website or weblog. I felt that it was important for me to share this personal testimony, not only for the sake of honesty, but also as a credential *in lieu* of a more formal academic credential.[8] In other words, as a result of my born-again religious experience, I became much more familiarly acquainted with the Bible and cognate literature than I otherwise would likely have been. I am well aware of the odium often attached to the work of an *autodidact;* nevertheless I dare say that what will be found herein will rival, if not exceed, much of what is frequently written within this *genre* of literature. Indeed, my very lack of any formal academic credential forces me to be that much more careful and diligent in my research and presentation. I do not claim infallibility. Neither do I make a false pretence to knowledge which I do not possess. My work must speak for itself. I have some knowledge of *Koine* Greek, as well as some Latin and Hebrew. Nevertheless I do not claim to be a Greek scholar, or a biblical scholar in the technical sense.[9] I fully anticipate harsh ciriticisms of my work, both from the academic community, and also from religious quarters. The fact that I do not subscribe to the current academic orthodoxy in terms of critical biblical scholarship will leave me quite unshielded from unwarranted

---

[8]   Although I attended college for three years, I did not graduate.

[9]   Since this requires an intimate knowledge of Hebrew and Greek, in terms of literacy and fluency which is otherwise quite uncommon. Nevertheless I am competent to correct false readings, and to suggest alternate readings, in some instances.

attacks upon both me and my work from religious bigots, and those who are offended that I have not unquestioningly endorsed their pet academic theories. But I will offer the reader something that these other people never do: reasons. I will not insult the intelligence of the reader with mere pontifications. One further point of clarification regarding my perspective I would like to offer: I am not an atheist or an agnostic; and while I do not particularly care for labels, I suppose if pressed I would say that my philosophy is closest to Deism. Therefore I have no *a priori* objection against the supernatural, the miraculous, the spiritual, or the paranormal. Indeed I strongly suspect that a genuine paranormal phenomenon is the key to the motivations of Jesus and the Apostles, and that the knowledge of this phenomenon was the great secret that had to be protected at all costs. This is the ultimate answer to the objections of those fundamentalists who point out that no one will die for a lie. True enough; but one may die to preserve a great secret, especially when held as a sacred trust. But such persons appear congenitally unable to comprehend the rationale of esotericism. The evidence suggests that the outer form of the religion was merely an exoteric shell to protect the inner, esoteric doctrine of Christ. Even the New Testament itself provides some evidence of this principle of esotericism.[10] Men will not die for a complete lie; but nevertheless men may die to protect a great secret; the outer form of Christianity being the parabolic shell of the true inner teaching. I do not claim to have any divine revelation explicating any such esoteric doctrine in detail; I can only speculate. Nevertheless such speculation is not altogether vain, but rather based upon the available evidence, such as it is. It is really more a matter of logical inference, and quite a reasonable inference at that. Furthermore as we will see, there are in some cases discrepancies between accounts of the martyrdoms of certain Apostles, and therefore some reasonable degree of suspicion is attached to the exact circumstances of their deaths. As such, we cannot be altogether certain as to what exactly their dying testimony was. We have only one example from the New Testament itself, namely the case of Stephen.[11] The martyrdom of the Apostle James is recorded, but no final words of testimony.[12] Other than this we have the mention of

---

[10]   Mt 7:6; Mk 4:34; Jn 16:25 cf 1 Corinthians 2:7.

[11]   Acts 7.

[12]   Acts 12:1-2.

the martyr Antipas, but once again no final words of testimony.[13] And if we are correct in assuming an esoteric doctrine within original Christianity, then these men would not have divulged it to the profane in their dying testimony in any case; they instead would have uttered words testifying to the exoteric, parabolic form of the religion; and in this way would have protected and perpetuated the secret doctrine.[14]

Having said these things, we ought to proceed with our study without further ado.

---

[13] Revelation 2:13.

[14] It should also be kept in mind that not all martyrs would necessarily have been privy to the secret doctrine, assuming there was one.

How Many Gospels?

C hristians and most other people in Western society take it for
granted that there are four Gospels: Matthew, Mark, Luke and
John. True it is that these four alone are regarded as Canonical[15] but
there are a host of others, some surviving only in small fragments,
which at one time and by some branches of the early Christian
movement were regarded as divinely inspired.[16] To some degree there
is a greater knowledge of these other texts in our day and age, as
opposed to the prevailing ignorance of former times. But while the
bare existence of such texts cannot be denied, what will no doubt be
denied by Christian fundamentalists is that any of these other Gospels
could predate or even be contemporary with the "genuine" Gospels.
Even many with a more skeptical stance towards Christianity may be
somewhat inclined to such views, since it is so strongly entrenched

---

15   Canonical. In other words, they are accepted as divinely inspired by
     Christians.

16   Of course even this statement is somewhat controversial, and likely to be
     contested by evangelicals and fundamentalists. We are not claiming that
     any of these other texts necessarily ever had universal acceptance among
     Christians, but rather that some persons within the early messianic
     movement associated directly with Jesus Christ used texts other than those
     now commonly esteemed as canonical as actual Gospels of Jesus Christ.
     While many of these may postdate the Canonical Gospels, some may be
     coeval with them, and some may even predate them.

in our culture that the four Gospels esteemed as Canonical are the originals.[17] And there can be little doubt that the four Gospels found in the New Testament do predate *most* texts in the Gospel *genre*. However we will find evidence, even from at least one of the Canonical Gospels, that, in all likelihood, there were other Gospels, which predated said Gospel, but which have not been included in the Canon of the New Testament, and, are no longer extant.[18]

The opening verse of the Gospel of Luke refers to "many" other written accounts of the Gospel commonly accepted by the earliest Christians.[19] It is important to note that Luke specifically refers to written accounts, rather than merely oral traditions. And he speaks of "many" of them. If Luke were the third Gospel to have been written, would it not have been quite an exaggeration for him to speak of only two earlier Gospel texts as "many"? And if we suppose that, quite possibly Luke may not have been the third, but rather the fourth of the Gospels to have been written, would it still not seem to be an exaggeration to speak of three earlier Gospels as "many"? The only justification that springs readily to mind is Luke's reference to the many contradictions between the other three accounts, but this is a point that will hardly be conceded by evangelicals. It is also worth noting that, however many accounts may have already been written, Luke still felt that there was some degree of deficiency in them, inasmuch as he felt justified in writing one more account to "many" already circulating in his time. But unless we justify the apparent exaggeration of Luke speaking of "many" earlier accounts by reason of the large number of contradictions between Matthew and Mark, or between Matthew, Mark and John, then we must concede that Luke must have been referring to other Gospels as well as those that are now found within the New Testament.[20] Of course it would be reckless to indiscriminately accept all those documents in the Gospel *genre* as

---

[17]   Or at least based upon originals. Few today would deny a long scribal history of editing and re-editing such texts over centuries of time.

[18]   I.e., except possibly as fragments, in some cases.

[19]   Luke 1:1.

[20]   And this latter interpretation appears more justified by the fact that Luke proceeded to contradict both Matthew and Mark, and also John as well (assuming John predates Luke, which, while possible, seems somewhat unlikely).

necessarily predating Luke on this account; there are certain features that can help to identify various texts as relatively early or late. For example, the Gospel of Nicodemus appears to be a fairly late text.[21] The same is also true of the Protevangelion of James.[22] But if we take the "many" of Luke literally, then there must have been many Gospel texts in the time in which he wrote his Gospel. I strongly suspect that most of these have not survived. Some few exist merely in very fragmentary form.[23] Other Gospel texts may be contemporary with the Canonicals, and may be of equal merit historically. And even those that postdate the Canonicals are not necessarily altogether without value for a historical reconstruction of early Christianity.

There is another source that also points towards some earlier Gospels, and indeed helps us to identify some of the very earliest Gospels. This is not found in the text of the New Testament, but rather in early Christian tradition. According to such tradition, the Apostle Matthew wrote his Gospel in Hebrew.[24] This is in stark contrast to the academic orthodoxy that preaches to us an original Greek text of Matthew. However, most likely the Greek text of Matthew is largely a translation from an earlier Hebrew text attributed to the Apostle Matthew, with a few notable additions and alterations.[25] The earlier text is also known as the Gospel of the Nazoraions.[26] The

---

[21] Which probably dates to no earlier than the latter half of the third century. This work is also otherwise known as the Acts of Pilate.

[22] The exaltation of Mary, and her alleged perpetual virginity, being taught in later orthodoxy, this work appears to have been written to accommodate the same notions, and to account for those passages in the Canonical Gospels that spoke of the brothers and sisters of Jesus (i.e., Mt 12:46-50; 13:54-56; Mk 3:31-35; 6:2-3; Lk 8:19-21; Jn 7:1-5 cf Acts 1:14; cf Mt 1:25; Lk 2:7; Galatians 1:19; 1 Corinthians 9:5).

[23] It is also just barely possible that the Gospel of Thomas may be one of these "many" texts spoken of by Luke.

[24] See Foxe's Book of Martyrs, and also the Aethiopic text known as *The Mysteries of the Heavens and of the Earth*. Also consult the works of Jerome, and many other early sources.

[25] I.e., the account of the virgin birth, the royal genealogy and the account of the flight into Egypt being later additions.

[26] The Nazoraions also are known as *Notzrim,* Nazarenes, Nazaraeans, Nazars, Nazarae, Nasarae, Nazaraei, Nasaraei, Nasraye, and also possibly *Ebionim,* Ebionites, and *Minim.*

Hebrew Gospel of Matthew, otherwise known as the Gospel of the Nazoraions, was translated by Jerome into Greek. However only very small fragments of this text survive today. But it is the closest in form, structure and content to the Canonical, Greek Matthew of any of the Gospels attributed to Matthew. In fact, one could look upon this other text of Matthew as a manuscript variant of Matthew, albeit originally in Hebrew. The point that is perhaps most pungent in historic terms is the rather blatantly obvious fact that Jesus and the Apostles spoke Hebrew rather than Greek.[27] Therefore it is absurd to suppose that Matthew would have written his account in Greek, rather than Hebrew.[28] Common sense would lead one to believe that the Hebrew text predated the Greek. For the sake of convenience we may refer to the Gospel of the Nazoraions as MtN. But there are also two other Gospels ascribed to Matthew: one is otherwise known as the Gospel of the Ebionites, and the other as the Gospel according to the Hebrews. For the sake of convenience these two texts can be referred to as MtE and MtH, respectively. Greek Matthew can be designated either as MtGk or simply Mt. All three of these earlier Gospels attributed to Matthew exist only in very small fragments. They were used by the *Ebionim,* who were early Hebrew Christians who did not acquiesce to later church orthodoxy. They were opposed to sacrifices in the temple in Jerusalem. But despite the fact that the *Ebionim* may very well have represented the very earliest stream of genuine Christian tradition, they were esteemed as heretical according to later church orthodoxy. As such their writings were suppressed, and the group apparently became extinct. We will have more to say of the *Ebionim* hereafter.

An opposite extreme from the *Ebionim* was found in the teachings of Marcion. Marcion was a cleric of the second century who embraced a more Gnostic version of Christianity. Marcion grouped

---

[27] Or Syriac, as is so commonly supposed today. Syriac (Aramaic, Chaldee) was not commonly spoken by postexilic Palestinian Jews; neither was Greek; cf Acts 21:37. This point will be clarified in more detail later. Jews in Syria spoke Syriac, and those in Alexandria spoke Greek. Most Palestinian Jews spoke Hebrew, at least until the third century.

[28] Of course the consensus of critical biblical scholars today is that Matthew the Apostle was not in fact the author of the Gospel bearing his name. I concur in this view. Nevertheless we may speak of Matthew, Mark, Luke, John, etc. as the authors of the respective Gospels written in their names for the sake of euphony and convenience, rather than as an endorsement of fundamentalism.

certain early Christian texts together into the very earliest Canon of Christian Scripture. The irony is that this Canon was later deemed heretical. Marcion found the character of the Old Testament God to be irreconcilable with the message of Christ, and therefore he rejected that God as a subordinate power, and not the true Father of Jesus Christ, the Supreme Being *par excellence.*

Marcion accepted the Gospel of Luke[29] together with ten[30] epistles of Paul as his very circumscribed Canon of Scripture. But notwithstanding his apparent heterodoxy, Marcion was the first to establish any Christian Canon of Scripture. The New Testament Canon that emerged as a reaction to Marcion is thus deuterocanonical in more than one sense of the term.[31] Marcion was an early Gnostic, but there were many others in early Christianity who advocated a Gnostic interpretation of Christianity. But Gnosticism, like Ebionism, became labelled a heresy by the emerging orthodox church. As such, many early writings of these heretical groups became suppressed.[32] There are many Gnostic Gospels, and other Gnostic texts. Most of these had been so ruthlessly suppressed by the orthodox church that they had been entirely lost until the fortuitous discovery of the Nag Hammadi Codices in Egypt in 1945. A great wealth of such texts were discovered all together at that time, and our knowledge of Gnosticism has been greatly enhanced thereby. We will have more to say regarding both Ebionism and Gnosticism hereafter.

As already noted, there were also other, more traditional Gospels, written to accommodate the emerging orthodoxy. But these for the most part postdate the Canonical Gospels. However there are a few other Gospel texts, or rather fragments of texts, which may be among

---

[29]   I.e., minus the royal genealogy and anything else too "Jewish".

[30]   I.e., the Pauline corpus, minus the Pastorals and Hebrews. Indeed, the pastoral epistles are almost certainly pseudepigraphal, and possibly the entire Pauline corpus also is. See discussion below.

[31]   First, in relation to the protocanonical Old Testament Scriptures; secondly, in relation to the earlier Canon of Marcion.

[32]   This is especially the case with the Ebionites. There may be a two-fold reason for this: first, the Ebionites may have genuinely represented a greater threat to the emergent orthodoxy by reason of their greater antiquity and genuine traditions about Jesus; secondly, because the Ebionites were exclusively Jewish, and therefore smaller in numbers, than the many branches of Gnosticism.

the very earliest. One of these is known as Papyrus Egerton 2, and the other is known as the Gospel of Peter.[33] Altogether this would give us seven Gospels predating Luke.[34] Seven is more reasonably described as "many", and indeed there may have been many others that are no longer extant, even in fragments.

But before moving on I first want to debunk a common fallacy that many biblical scholars are guilty of perpetuating. Critical biblical scholars are no less guilty in this respect than conservative biblical scholars. The fallacy is the implicit assumption that, if a given text has any material in common with any unique portion of one of the Canonical Gospels, then it must necessarily postdate that Gospel. But common sense should be enough to dispel any such notion. The Gospel of Peter will serve as a perfect example, since even the small remaining fragment contains some material that is otherwise unique to each one of the four Canonical Gospels. Bible Scholars, and even critical biblical scholars, who should know better, interpret this as evidence that the Gospel of Peter must postdate the four Canonical Gospels. It is easy enough to demonstrate the literary parallels; but such parallels in no way prove the priority of the Canonical texts. If, for example, we find some "Johannine" style content in Peter, does that automatically mean that Peter must postdate John? How do we know that John did not derive that content from Peter? Or from some earlier source, either written or oral? Therefore the mere fact of commonality with Canonical sources does not indicate dependence upon those sources; the information could have flown in the very opposite direction, for all we know to the contrary. Or both sources could be dependent upon some older tradition common to both. Therefore it is erroneous and misleading to speak of such texts "having knowledge of" the Canonical texts, when in fact those Canonical texts may have been made up from these other, earlier texts.

Appeal may be made, in theory, to a supposed democratic process whereby those Gospels that were written earliest were most likely to have been copied and preserved, read, and used more frequently,

---

[33] The Gospel of Peter, of which remaining fragment contains an account of the passion and resurrection of Christ, has both traditional and Gnostic elements; and also both archaic and seemingly "late" aspects; therefore it is difficult to date, but it seems like an early text to me, or at least one that incorporates early traditions.

[34] MtN, MtE, MtH, MtGk, Mk, Papyrus Egerton 2 & Peter.

and therefore had a greater chance of attaining Canonicity, all other things being equal. This superficially appears to be a sound argument, but in fact, not all other things were equal. As the proponents of religious orthodoxy accrued more authority unto themselves, they became very heavy-handed towards their flock, and insulting and abusive towards any dissidents, quickly labelling them as "heretics". This tendency became especially pronounced after the feigned conversion of the Emperor Constantine in the fourth century. And for those fundamentalists who might argue that orthodoxy was motivated by an adherence to the Scriptures, one has but to point to the many examples of how clear Scriptures were ignored in favour of ecclesiastical orthodoxy, such as the dogma of the perpetual virginity of Mary, the immaculate conception, calling priests "father", bowing down before statues, prayers for the dead, prayers to saints, etc., etc., *ad nauseum, ad infinitum.*

Marcion was at least somewhat justified in making a sharp distinction between God as depicted in the Old Testament Scriptures, and as depicted in the New Testament, as the Father of Jesus Christ.[35] The Old Testament frequently depicts God as commanding certain atrocious actions, such as the slaughter of the Amalekites, the Jebusites, the Girgashites, the Canaanites, the Hittites, the Amorites, the Midianites, the Kenites, the Kenizzites, the Kadmonites, the Perizzites, the Philistines, and the Rephaim.[36] This is clearly in stark contrast to the depiction of God as the Father of Jesus Christ in the New Testament.[37] One other class of contradictions between the Old and

---

[35] Although it must also be admitted that there are many references to and quotations from the Old Testament Scriptures scattered throughout the New Testament, and often the appeal to fulfilled prophecy is made on behalf of Jesus as being the long-awaited Messiah of the Jews.

[36] Genesis 15:18-21; Exodus 17:14; Numbers 21:1-3,21-35; 25:6-15; Deuteronomy 11:24; 20:10-17; 25:17-19; Joshua 6:21; 8:18-26; 10:17-42; 11:21-22; 1 Samuel 15:1-3; 27:8-11; 1 Chronicles 20:1-3 cf Leviticus 25:44-46, where "God" promises the Israelites that they have his permission to enslave the surrounding populations; but only after they have completely exterminated all those who inhabit the Promised Land. Note also Genesis 22, where "God" tests Abraham, by asking him to sacrifice his son Isaac as a burnt offering.

[37] Although some might argue that the New Testament God is infinitely more cruel, since he threatens people with everlasting hellfire; cf Revelation 14:10-11; 20:10,14-15.

New Testaments is the fact that the New Testament declares that no man has seen God,[38] but the Old Testament has many passages in which God appeared to men.[39] Such contradictions and many more besides no doubt suggested to Marcion that the "God" of the Old Testament Scriptures was not the true God at all, or the Father of Jesus Christ, but instead a mere demiurge; an inferior power. This doctrine became common to all the Gnostics, who called this inferior deity Ialdabaoth.[40] One other kindred discrepancy between the Old and New Testaments is somewhat illuminating in relation to this point. In the New Testament, there are a few otherwise seemingly inexplicable verses that speak of the law as being instituted by angels,[41] while in the Torah itself it says that God himself revealed his law.[42] The watchers of Daniel[43] spring to mind as precedents of this new angelology. One suspects that this innovation was a result of Persian influence upon pre-Christian Judaism, as also evinced in the Kabbalah and the angelology of the book of Enoch.

But the Canon of Marcion became supplanted by the orthodox Canon, which, according to some sources, may have been the work of Polycarp.[44] This thesis appears to be sound, at least in principle. Polycarp may have been the author of the pastoral epistles.[45] What

---

[38] John 1:18; 6:46; 1 John 4:12; 1 Timothy 6:15-16.

[39] Genesis 17:1; 18:1; 26:2; 32:30; Exodus 24:11; 33:11; Numbers 12:6-8; 23:4,16; Judges 13:22; 1 Kings 22:19; 2 Chronicles 18:18; Job 42:5; Daniel 7:9-13; Ezekiel 1; Isaiah 6:1-5; Amos 7:7; 9:1.

[40] Otherwise also known under other appellations, but commonly esteemed as a "blind idiot god", far inferior to the true Supreme Being.

[41] Acts 7:53; Galatians 3:19. The same Greek root-word occurs in both instances; being *diatagas* in the former verse, and *diatageis* in the latter; cf Nestle-Aland., NOVUM TESTAMENTUM GRAECE., (© 1979 Deutsche Bibelgesellschaft Stuttgart) (26th critical edition of the Greek New Testament); pgs. 341 & 497.

[42] Exodus 20:1ff.

[43] Daniel 4:13,17,23.

[44] See Trobisch, David., *The First Edition of the New Testament.* (© 2000 Oxford University Press). An epitome of this may be found at http://www.robertmprice.mindvendor.com.

[45] Most critical biblical scholars are in agreement that the pastoral epistles are pseudepigraphal. In fact, some critical scholars have postulated that the entire Pauline corpus is pseudepigraphal.

I have read upon this theme so far appears to be sound, based upon the available evidence. However I would sound a note of caution: the orthodoxy found within the epistles ascribed to Polycarp and Ignatius is not the orthodoxy of the New Testament. There is a detectable difference of dogma to be found between the two respective corpii; the New Testament clearly being somewhat more archaic.[46] Yet it should also be clearly noted that those epistles ascribed by tradition to Ignatius and Polycarp may themselves be pseudepigraphal. Furthermore the orthodoxy of such epistles is also somewhat different from the later orthodoxy of Irenaeus and Tertullian. There is a discernable progression[47] or rather rigidification of dogma from one generation to the next, in a process culminating in a form of ecclesiastical orthodoxy more akin to that of mediaeval times.[48] But in the meantime those "heretical" branches of Christianity known as Ebionism and Gnosticism became pruned from the main tree, as it were. As such, the emerging Catholic and Orthodox Churches claim to represent the original historical tradition, manifested in a supposedly immaculate and indisputable apostolic succession. However it is questionable how valid this claim is in strictly historic terms. The Churches in question were themselves hardly disinterested parties. And the political machinery of the Empire became subordinate to the decrees of the Church after the time of Constantine. These are simply facts. Therefore a genuine inquiry into the true historical circumstances of the origination of Christianity as a religion are cloaked in a veil of obscurity, not only due to the relative antiquity of the times, but also due to the vested interests at stake from such antiquity.[49] But enough clues are in place for at least a tentative reconstruction of likely events. But first we need to become more intimately acquainted with the evidence, such as it is.

In a general sense we can say that the Canon of Marcion became supplanted by that of Polycarp. But the Marcionites did not vanish overnight. Neither did the many other sects of Gnosticism. The Ebionites seemed to have vanished more quickly from the pages of history, and their legacy has been much more thoroughly eradicated,

---

[46] And hence more ambiguous on certain doctrinal points.

[47] Or regression, depending on one's point of view.

[48] Or rather the Dark Ages.

[49] And up to the present day, to some degree.

probably because they were Jewish. If they were not altogether exterminated by the Romans themselves, then what the Romans failed to do was finished by the Roman Catholic and Greek Orthodox Churches. Nevertheless we would be well advised to take a closer look at this supposedly "heretical" branch of Christianity.

Ebionism

E bionism was apparently an early branch of the messianic movement that eventually became known as Christianity. What is uncertain is whether or not the *Ebionim* themselves represented the very earliest, original branch of the movement, directly from Jesus himself. In an earlier work[50] I argued that this may very well have been the case, and that both Christ and his brother James were *Ebionim*. I still believe that this is a reasonable position, however I must admit I wish that the evidence was more conclusive. The chief point of controversy between Ebionism and normative Judaism[51] was an opposition to all blood sacrifices. In this respect the *Ebionim* differed from the Sadducees, the Pharisees, the

---

50   JESUS 100 B.C.

51   If indeed we can speak of a "normative" Judaism of the first century; critical-historical research discloses a fairly heterogenous Judaism in the Near East at that time.

Essenes,[52] and the Zealots.[53] It is questionable precisely when and where such an aversion to blood sacrifices arose. According to some sources, it was due to the "fulfilled messianism" of the *Ebionim,* inasmuch as they believed in Jesus as the Messiah, and that he had died a sacrificial death, and thereby brought the necessity for such blood sacrifices to an end.[54] But such an interpretation requires that Ebionite opposition to blood sacrifices and consequent vegetarianism had to date to no earlier time than the supposed time of Christ's passion. As we will see, even according to those small but surviving fragments of genuine Ebionite texts, this interpretation is excluded. For in the very Gospel of the Ebionites[55] Jesus himself declares "I have come to abolish the sacrifices; and if you do not cease to offer sacrifice, the wrath of God will not cease afflicting you." Not only that, but according to the same text, Jesus also answered his Apostles, saying "I

---

[52] Although traditionally scholars have tended to identify, or at least closely associate, the Essenes with the *Ebionim.* While it is true that in practical terms, neither the Essenes nor the *Ebionim* partook of any temple sacrifices, the difference was that the Essenes disassociated from the temple cultus due to perceived corruption of the priesthood, including accommodation with Roman occupation; while the *Ebionim,* by contrast, were inherently opposed to all animal sacrifices on principle alone. In my earlier work I speculated that the Jewish temple in Leontopolis, Egypt, may have been a place where the *Ebionim* may have worshipped God without any bloody animal sacrifices. This temple was in use from shortly after the invasion of Jerusalem by Antiochus until the fall of Masada. Therefore even if Jesus actually lived in the first century, rather than the first century B.C., as I postulated in my earlier work, he, his brother, his family, and their coreligionists could have worshipped freely at the Leontopolis temple, if they had been *Ebionim.*

[53] There is no evidence to suggest that the Zealots were inherently opposed to blood sacrifices on principle; and if the Dead Sea Scrolls are ascribed to Zealots, Zadokites, or Sicarii, rather than to Essenes, then those texts, such as they are, still envision a future restored temple, wherein such blood sacrifices would once again be offered, in accordance with Ezekiel 40-48. Therefore the *Ebionim* are in this respect deviant from all other extant forms of Judaism at the time that I have any knowledge of.

[54] Ehrman, Bart D., *LOST SCRIPTURES.* (© 2003 Oxford University Press, Inc.); pg. 12. Ehrman also takes the position that the vegetarianism of the *Ebionim* derives from their belief in Jesus as the "perfect and final sacrifice for sins" (Hebrews 9:24-28; 10:1-10). But as we will see, this view is probably incorrect.

[55] Designated as MtE herein, for the sake of convenience.

have no desire to eat the flesh of this Passover lamb with you." While the first saying can be reconciled with a dispensational interpretation,[56] the latter saying cannot, since, there could *at that time* have been no legitimate objection against partaking of the flesh of a Passover lamb, on the grounds cited by Ehrman, *before Jesus had been crucified.* In other words, Jesus had not yet been "offered up" in sacrifice, and therefore there was no basis for strict vegetarianism and/or an absolute rejection of all animal sacrifices at the time depicted in the text in question. Indeed, the very text belies the interpretation offered by Ehrman, who cites no confirming source for his speculation. If the *Ebionim* were vegetarian *before* the time of Christ's passion, then that passion[57] cannot be the basis for such vegetarianism. And there is independent evidence that confirms that these partisans otherwise called *Notzrim* were strict vegetarians even before the time of Christ:

"There was, he says, a sect of Nasaraei before Christ; these he has already described, calling them, however, Nazaraei. He treats of them in connection with the Daily Baptists, who, like the Essenes and allied communities, baptized or washed themselves in water every day; they were Jews, and lived in the same districts as the Essenes. They observed the law of circumcision, the Sabbath and the appointed feasts, and especially reverenced the ancient patriarchs and sages of Israel, including Moses; they however, rejected the canonical Pentateuch, and said that the real Law was different from the one in public circulation. They apparently also rejected all the prophets after Moses. Moreover, they refused to have anything to do with the blood sacrifices of the Temple and abstained from eating flesh. They contended that the books which laid down the rules of these sacrifices were inventions of later times, and that their true ancestors from Adam to Moses did not perform such bloody rites; all the accounts of such sacrifice in the popular scripture were later inventions of scribes who were ignorant of the true doctrine."[58]

---

[56]   I.e., in which Jesus announces beforehand his intent to abolish the temple sacrifices, presumably in an effort to fulfill the prophecy of Daniel 9:27, which is at least a possible, and even probable, origin of the Ebionite objection against all blood sacrifices. However see the remaining discussion in the text.

[57]   Or rather the theological interpretation thereof as a "perfect and final sacrifice for sins once and for all" (Hebrews 9:24-28; 10:1-10).

[58]   Mead, G.R.S., *DID JESUS LIVE 100 B.C.?* (University Books, 1903); pgs. 345-346. Mead is quoting from Epiphanius.

While some may object that the testimony of Epiphanius is untrustworthy, in this instance at least the circumstance of the case seems to favor his position; because it would have been contrary to his interest, as an apologist for Christianity, to admit to such a pre-Christian "heresy" within Judaism. Notwithstanding this we may hesitate to credit his account in all details. Nevertheless Epiphanius confirms the pre-Christian vegetarianism of the *Ebionim,* which undercuts the interpretation proposed by Ehrman. So the testimony of Epiphanius and the surviving fragment from MtE both mutually confirm one another, and refute Ehrman's interpretation.

In my earlier work I speculated that possibly the vegetarianism of the *Ebionim* and their objection against blood sacrifices may have been due to Buddhist influence, but upon due consideration this interpretation does not seem as realistic as my alternate theory that it was based upon Daniel's prophecy of the seventy weeks.[59] This is based upon the simple principle of congruence. In other words, the motivations of a Jewish cult are more likely to be found within an interpretation of the Jewish Scriptures, rather than from a completely foreign influence. And furthermore it is too much to suggest that Daniel 9 could have been inserted into the text of Daniel by such a "heretical" cult. It is much more believable that the *Ebionim* interpreted Daniel 9:27 to mean that the Messiah would be the one to "cause the sacrifice and the oblation to cease", and that therefore, for whatever unknown reason, this was the will of God. The Ebionites may have inferred from this that all such animal sacrifices were displeasing to God,[60] and therefore sought to abolish them, and to practice a strict vegetarianism among themselves. And while it is still possible that there may have been some Buddhist influence upon Ebionism, any such influence would have been of secondary importance.

But what makes me now hesitate to identify the *Ebionim* with the earliest disciples of Jesus is that certain accounts from both the Gospels and the book of Acts seem to belie any such notion that those disciples

---

[59]   Daniel 9:24-27.

[60]   Cf Isaiah 1:10-15; 1 Samuel 15:22; Micah 6:6-8; Hosea 6:6; Jeremiah 7:22; Ecclesiastes 5:1; Psalms 40:6-8; 50:7-15; 51:16-17; 107:22; 116:17; Proverbs 15:8; 21:3,27.

condemned the temple cultus of Jerusalem.[61] And in this regard one cannot appeal to the fallacy of a later orthodoxy obscuring the original historical circumstances, since, as we will see when we examine the passages in question, those very passages inadvertently *subvert* the New Testament orthodoxy of Christ as the "perfect and final sacrifice for sins once and for all." Therefore it is at least *possible,* if not *probable,* that the *Ebionim* may *not* have been part and parcel with the original Jesus movement, but instead merely co-opted it to further their own agenda. And this is really no more unreasonable a position to take than to recognise the very same thing of the *plethora* of Gnostic sects and cults that sought to associate themselves with the name of Jesus. Or are we rather to suppose that all these many cults and sects all arose from the same small group of Apostles and disciples, as so many branches of a single tree? In a strictly historic sense, such a position appears to be untenable. This is not intended to turn a blind eye to the cross-fertilizations that no doubt took place in philosophical terms between such diverse groups. But we ought also to realise that there may have been several distinct Ebionite sects, just as there were so many different Gnostic cults. But if we are to thus identify the earliest post-passion disciples of Jesus with any branch of *Ebionim,* then we would have to posit a branch of *Ebionim* lacking the most distinctive feature that they have been associated with. While strictly speaking this is not impossible, it seems highly improbable, and one wonders if to even speak in such terms is even meaningful.

The chief point of controversy between Ebionism and New Testament orthodoxy revolved around the question of Christology.[62] According to the New Testament, Jesus was the Son of God,[63] but the *Ebionim* esteemed Jesus as merely a righteous but mortal man.[64] They

---

[61]   In my earlier work I went so far as to suggest that the reference to the temple in Luke 24:53 may have been to the Leontopolis temple. But clearly this is contrary to the context of the verse, so I was wrong. Furthermore the accounts from the book of Acts are if anything even more explicit as identifying the temple as none other than that in Jerusalem.

[62]   I.e., the presumed ontological status of Jesus Christ.

[63]   But not necessarily God the Son, despite what orthodox Trinitarians may insist to the contrary.

[64]   Although they accepted Jesus as a true prophet and as the promised Messiah.

denied the virgin birth of Christ.[65] Although Mead speaks of a twofold Ebionism hypothesis,[66] in which by the third and fourth centuries, there are some Ebionites who acknowledge the virgin birth, while others still deny it, yet according to Irenaeus, all the Ebionites rejected that dogma. This is merely an illustration of the marginalization and ultimate assimilation of the *Ebionim*. Those who were not killed in battles with the Romans, were later assimilated into either Judaism or Catholicism.[67] Furthermore it is questionable whether or not the *Ebionim* ever believed in the supposed vicarious atonement of Christ on the cross.[68]

---

[65]   Recall that the virgin birth is absent from MtN. The probability is that MtN predates and is the primary source for the Greek version of Matthew. So in this respect at least the *Ebionim* do seem to have a legitimate claim to priority.

[66]   Mead., op. cit., pgs. 352-353.

[67]   Or Greek Orthodoxy, or possibly some branch of Gnosticism. But it is also possible that the *Ebionim* may have practiced esotericism. In light of some of the evidence I am tempted to postulate that those instances of sacrificial observance on the part of Christian disciples *after Christ's alleged passion,* may possibly be blinds intended to further obscure the truth of the Ebionite origin of the religion. However I fear that this explanation may be too convenient. Part of the problem, or perhaps the very crux of it, is on how precisely we define the Ebionites. Due to the paucity of surviving material, much of what we can say about the Ebionites is merely speculation.

[68]   Or even, for that matter, the crucifixion itself.

Esotericism

Esotericism is the principle of secrecy, particularly in the sense of having an inner, secret teaching within a religious tradition that is withheld from the ordinary adherents of the religion in question. It is the secret teaching reserved for the elect. In fact, in secret societies, there is often an ascending series of secret grades of initiation, before one is fully illuminated into the deepest mysteries of the cult. In ancient times mystery schools flourished in Greece and Rome. In the days of the Roman empire, many citizens thereof became obsessed with Egyptian cults devoted to Isis and Serapis. The Persian cult of Mithras became popular among Roman soldiers. There are some significant parallels between the cult of Mithras and certain forms of Christianity, particularly Roman Catholicism.[69] I will not go so far as to say that Christianity is essentially derived from the cult of

---

[69] See *The Mysteries of Mithras,* by Payam Nabarz. (© 2003 by Payam Nabarz, Ph.D.) Inner Traditions One Park Street Rochester, Vermont 05767. http://www.InnerTraditions.com. For additional information, see *The Gnostics and their Remains,* by C.W. King. (first published in 1887). An online version of this work can be found at http://www.sacred-texts.com/gno/gar/index.htm. There is also some good insight to be gleaned from *The Worship of Augustus Caesar,* by Alexander Del Mar. (first published in 1900). This is available from Kessinger Publishers. www.kessinger.net. Additional information on this theme may be found by consulting the works of Acharya S. Her material is available at http://www.truthbeknown.com.

Mithras. Nevertheless there are some highly significant parallels that prove some degree of influence. And those features in common to both Christianity and the cult of Mithras are archaic features of the latter religion, and so could not have been the result of Christian influence upon Mithraicism. For proof of this consult the works of Tertullian. Tertullian was forced by circumstances to contrive that the devil imitated the mysteries of Christianity by way of anticipation. Thus the devil becomes a rather convenient prop for Christian faith. But this admission of Tertullian is worth taking some note of, since it is an illustration of a point I made earlier vis-à-vis the various stages of orthodoxy. Lest I be accused of a mere pontification, I will here offer some justification of the comment made earlier to the effect that those epistles attributed to Ignatius and Polycarp were not of the same class or phase of orthodoxy as that of the New Testament texts, and that those epistles were also distinct from the later orthodoxy of Irenaeus and Tertullian. A clear example is to be found in the Epistle of Ignatius to the Ephesians:

"Now the Virginity of Mary, and he who was born of her, was kept in secret from the prince of this world; as was also the death of our Lord: three of the mysteries most spoken of throughout the world *now,* but done in secret by God."

Ignatius to Ephesians 4:10.[70]

Clearly this declaration is contrary to Tertullian's explanation that the devil knew beforehand the complete mystery of Christ, which to lead astray the Gentiles he devised a religious system in imitation thereof by way of anticipation. Therefore the "orthodoxy" of Tertullian was a different orthodoxy from that of Ignatius[71] and in this instance at least we will find that Ignatius more closely follows Pauline orthodoxy. In fact, it fairly closely follows the Pauline-Johannine orthodoxy, as spoken of in my previous work. By the "prince of this world" Ignatius undoubtedly refers to Satan, since Jesus himself uses the very same expression in the Gospel of John.[72] What is particularly

---

[70] I am using the numbering system found in *The Lost Books of the Bible.*

[71] Or whoever wrote in Ignatius' name, assuming the Ignatian corpus is pseudepigraphal.

[72] John 12:31; 14:30: 16:11. The context leaves no doubt as to the infernal identity of the one whom Jesus is speaking of.

interesting is that in the original Greek,[73] the word translated as "prince" is *archon,* and can just as readily be translated as "ruler." But this term *archon* is a highly significant term in Gnosticism, as we will see hereafter. What is of further interest in this context is that there is also a very similar passage within the Pauline corpus to what we find above in Ignatius:

6 Howbeit we speak wisdom among them that are perfect: yet not the wisdom of this world, nor of the princes of this world, that come to nought:

7 But we speak the wisdom of God in a mystery, *even* the hidden *wisdom,* which God ordained before the world unto our glory;

8 Which none of the princes of this world knew: for had they known, they would not have crucified the Lord of glory. (1 Corinthians 2:6-8)

The above passage is highly significant, and we will no doubt return to it when we come to examine the use of Gnostic nomenclature within the Pauline corpus. The significance of a number of terms becomes much more clearly evident in the original Greek. But for now it is worth pointing out that not only is the above passage a good example of the very principle of esotericism that we are here discussing, but the two occurrences of the word "princes" are also the very same Greek root-word, but this time the plural *archonton.*[74] While it will become evident that here the men who wrote the epistle[75] probably had intended the word *archonton* to be interpreted according to the nomenclature of Gnosticism, the English translation is ambiguous on this point; "Paul", the assumed author of the epistle, could as readily have intended Pilate and Herod, rather

---

[73] Nestle-Aland., op. cit., pgs. 292, 300, 302.

[74] Ibid., pg. 443.

[75] I.e., Stephanas, Fortunatus, Achaicus & Timotheus. See colophon to the epistle. In my former work I claimed to have *proven* that Paul was a mere *chimera;* while I am somewhat more willing to concede the historicity of Paul (based upon evidence to be presented later), at least as a possibility, or even a probability; nevertheless I still hold that the Pauline corpus is probably either mostly or entirely pseudepigraphal.

than any incorporeal beings. In fact, even in the original Greek, the passage is equivocal, without an accompanying knowledge of Gnostic nomenclature, and the fact that these epistles were circulating at the very time and place when such nomenclature was also widely in use. Therefore Ignatius makes explicit that which is merely implicit within the Pauline corpus, in this instance. In this we can see some development of orthodoxy. But we can also discern a distinction between the assumed orthodoxy of Ignatius and Polycarp and that of the New Testament. There are no less than five distinct differences to be noted by the careful reader: First, the Trinitarian dogma and the Deity of Jesus Christ is very explicit within the epistles ascribed to Ignatius and Polycarp;[76] Secondly, Ignatius protests against the observance of the Sabbath by Christians;[77] Thirdly, Ignatius condemns Christians who assemble without a bishop;[78] Fourthly, Ignatius declared "For I know [sic] that even after his resurrection he was in the flesh; and I believe that he is still so.";[79] Fifthly and finally, Ignatius upholds a literal interpretation of the eucharist as the flesh and blood of Jesus Christ.[80] So it is fair to say that those epistles ascribed to

---

[76] By contrast, the New Testament may allow for these interpretations, but it does not require them. In fact, a more natural, straightforward reading of the New Testament, together with the context of the Old Testament, tends to favor the Arian as opposed to Trinitarian interpretation of theology. But to prove this would require an additional 200 pages to this book. It is a fallacy to suppose that the original Greek of the New Testament somehow "proves" the Deity of Jesus Christ; the bishops who lived in the eastern half of the Roman empire in the days of Arius were fluent and literate in Greek. Neither is it permissible to say that those epistles ascribed to Ignatius and Polycarp somehow "prove" the orthodoxy of the Trinitarian interpretation of the New Testament; already those very texts warn of corruptions of the original faith once and for all delivered unto the saints.

[77] By contrast, see Mt 24:20; 28:1; Mk 16:1; Lk 23:56; Jn 20:1; Acts 1:12.

[78] Compare this with Mt 18:20: "Where two or three are gathered together in my name, there I am in the midst of them." Jesus did not specify the necessity for a bishop to be present.

[79] Smyrnaeans 1:9. Compare this with 1 Corinthians 15:45,50: "The first man Adam became a living soul; the last Adam *became* a life-giving spirit... flesh and blood cannot inherit the kingdom of God; neither does corruption inherit incorruption."

[80] Smyrnaeans 2:16-17; cf Ephesians 4:16 (Ignatius). Compare this interpretation with both Christ's declaration in John 6:53-54 and also

Ignatius and Polycarp are deviant from New Testament orthodoxy, and are also clearly later; probably much later.

But to return to the question of esotericism, we can see some clear evidence thereof even within the New Testament itself. Christ said "Give not that which is holy unto dogs, neither cast your pearls before swine, lest they trample them under their feet, and turn again, and rend you."[81] We are also told of Jesus that he always taught the common people in parables: "But without a parable he spake not to them. But when they were alone, he explained all things to his disciples."[82] Sometimes, at least up until towards the very end of his prophetic ministry, Jesus even kept secret certain teachings from his own Apostles: "These things I have spoken to you in parables; but the time is coming when I will no longer speak to you in parables, but

---

what is written in 1 Corinthians 10:15-22; 11:17-32. By Christ's words "Truly, truly I say unto you, Unless you eat the flesh of the Son of man, and drink his blood, you have no life in you. *But* whoever eats my flesh, and drinks my blood, has eternal life, and I will raise him up on the last day." If Catholics would carefully read these words, they would clearly see that therein Christ is making an absolute declaration respecting both a *necessary* and *sufficient* condition of salvation. In fact, this passage alone is sufficient to dispel the false interpretation of transubstantiation, which led to the untimely and horrible deaths of so many people. Whatever Jesus is talking about here is both *necessary for* and also *sufficient for* salvation. Protestants should take note of the fact that the second birth, while a *necessary* condition of salvation, is *not* a *sufficient* condition of salvation, as this is. Therefore what is being spoken of is something so absolute that it must be essentially spiritual, rather than physical. Because if you satisfy the condition, you will go to heaven; but if you fail to satisfy it, you will not go to heaven. There is no equivocation in the text. You are either saved, or not. In Mark 16:16 Christ says "He that believes and is baptized shall be saved." That is a *sufficient* condition of salvation. Therefore for there to be harmony between Mark and John, the condition mentioned by Christ in Mark 16:16 must inherently *include* the requirements of John 6:53-54. This interpretation, which is based upon impeccable logic, excludes the traditional Catholic interpretation of transubstantiation. Furthermore when we look at the relevant passages from Corinthians this becomes even more evident; for how could a person eat and drink *damnation* unto themselves, as per 1 Corinthians 11:29, if, according to a literal interpretation of Christ's words in John 6:53-54, they would be guaranteed eternal life in heaven by partaking of Christ's flesh and blood sacramentally.

[81] Mt 7:6.

[82] Mk 4:34, according to the Greek text.

will plainly show you *the things* of the Father."[83] Of course Christians will say that, even though Jesus may have taught his Apostles many secret things during the time of his earthly ministry, that now there is no longer any secrecy; everything necessary for salvation has been made known openly in the New Testament. And indeed there is even a "proof" text that supports this exoteric interpretation of Christianity: "What I tell you in darkness, preach in the light; and what ye hear in the ear, proclaim upon the housetops."[84] But the Gnostics claimed to have secret knowledge that was important in the spiritual realm. Perhaps this is the real key to the saying attributed to Christ in Matthew 10:27; it may have been an effort to deny the constant claims of the Gnostics to important secret spiritual knowledge.

The Pharisees also practiced esotericism. In fact, even the Mishnah was not codified in a written form until the dawn of the third century. The Pharisees also kept the secrets of the Kabbalah. The Kabbalah was no doubt of Persian or Chaldean origin; it was brought back by certain *cognoscenti* from the Babylonian Captivity. As such, it preceded the Mishnah. But traditionally it is reserved for the final stage of Jewish illumination. First one must learn the *TaNaKh,*[85] then the *Mishnah,*[86]

---

[83] Jn 16:25.

[84] Mt 10:27 cp Lk 12:3. The corresponding verse in Luke presents a completely different meaning, despite the similarity of the saying. This at least casts some suspicion upon what we find written in Matthew. Or at least we would have the right to question why things so preciously secret during Christ's incarnation would become public knowledge after his passion. Furthermore it seems contrary to Christ's injunction in Mt 7:6 about casting pearls before swine. Perhaps it was intended to keep the curious satisfied with the exoteric teaching, until or unless they were proven worthy of the true esoteric teaching. In any case we can be sure that "true believers" have an inexhaustible capacity for rationalization. If not, they eventually become unbelievers.

[85] TaNaKh. An acronym for the three traditional divisions of the Hebrew Scriptures: the Law, the Prophets, and the Writings (ha-Torah, ha-Nehevim, ha-Kethuvim, respectively). Sometimes the Writings are called the Hagiographa (Holy Writings) (Greek).

[86] Mishnah. A commentary upon the Torah, compiled from the return from Babylon, and finally codified by Rabbi Judah the Prince, the last of the *Tannaim,* towards the close of the second century. The Mishnah is the foundation of the Talmud.

then the *Gemara,*[87] and then the *Kabbalah.*[88] But the Kabbalah almost certainly preceded the Mishnah, at least in embryo. The Persian origin of Pharisaic teachings can be found even in the very word *Pharisee* itself. It is a word resembling *Farsi,* the word for the Persian language. It is also akin to *Parsee,* a term that is used to denote devotees of Zoroaster. The dualism of Zoroastrianism can be found in texts of postexilic Judaism, including Daniel and the Dead Sea Scrolls. Even Ezekiel evinces some Persian influence, inasmuch as the four beasts of his vision correspond to the four fixed signs of the Zodiac.[89] The Zoroastrian influence upon pre-Christian Judaism also exerted an indirect influence upon Christianity.[90]

We can also find another instance of esotericism in an apocryphal Jewish religious book, the Apocalypse of Ezra. Some might claim this as a Christian work, but it seems far more likely that it was originally a Jewish work, which was expropriated by the Christians. Towards the end of the book, God tells Ezra to fast and pray, and he will reveal to him all that had been lost. So Ezra receives a divine revelation, his words written down by scribes. The relevant portion of the book is as follows:

44 In forty days they wrote ninety-four books.

45 And it came to pass, when the forty days were fulfilled, that the Highest spake, saying, The first twenty-four books that thou hast written publish openly, that *both* the worthy and the unworthy may read it;

---

[87] Gemara. An expansion upon the Mishnah, made by the *Amoraim.* Mishnah and Gemara together constitute the Talmud. But there is a Palestinian Talmud, and also a Babylonian Talmud. The Gemara were codified around 600 C.E.

[88] Kabbalah. This is the true mystical teaching of postexilic Judaism. But aside from these four corpii, Orthodox Jews are also expected to know Tosephta, Baraitoth, Siphra, Siphrei, and other Halakhic Midrashim. They must also know Haggadah. Hasidic Jews also have their own special holy books, such as *Tanya.*

[89] I.e., Aquarius, Leo, Taurus, Scorpio.

[90] The story of the *Magi* is an obvious example.

46 but keep *secret* the seventy *written* last, that thou mayest deliver them only to such as be wise among the people:

47 For in them is the spring of understanding, the fountain of wisdom, and the stream of knowledge.

48 And I did so. (IV Ezra 14:44-48)

Notice that it is the seventy *secret* books that are more exalted than the twenty-four *open, canonical* books used by the Jews. This passage is very much in accord with Christ's injunction against casting pearls before swine, and verse 47 is reminiscent of the language of the book of Enoch (which was probably considered one of the seventy *secret* books by the author of IV Ezra). Furthermore Orthodox Rabbis have been very scrupulous about keeping their secret teachings secret, especially from Gentiles. So we can see a common practice of esotericism in early Judaism and Christianity. This must be taken into account in any historical inquiry respecting the origin of Christianity. Gnosticism also employed esotericism, and might even be said to have exploited it, to some degree. Hopefully this is sufficient to establish that esotericism was indeed practiced by Jesus himself, and therefore possibly (even probably) by his Apostles, and by later disciples. One must understand that esotericism, by its very nature, would be particularly difficult to prove, using the very Canonical Scriptures of the exoteric form of the religion in question. But there are sufficient traces of it to be found to settle the point, in my view. Of course this situation facilitated the opportunity for persons unaffiliated with either Jesus or the Apostles to make false claims respecting secret teachings and divine revelations in their names. Paul, if we take him as historical, may have been the first of these charlatans. On the other hand, he may not have been the cynical culprit he is often portrayed to be in various critical reconstructions of early Christianity. In fact, his portrayal in the role of villain itself seems predicated upon an intrinsic cynicism based upon strictly materialistic conceptions of reality. This default paradigm will continue to be the basis for a rejection of such critical-historical scenarios by more orthodox Christians, and also to any number of independent researchers as well, due to the inherent weaknesses of some of the fundamental assumptions thereof. Cynical interpretations of Paul disregard completely his great physical suffering due to fierce persecution by both Jews and Romans.[91] Such sufferings and a martyrdom syndrome cannot be realistically ascribed to cynical motivations. Therefore evangelicals and fundamentalists, however misguided they may otherwise be, at least have a reasonable objection against cynical theories on these grounds. And I trust that my theory, when given a fair hearing, will not be regarded as cynical.[92]

---

[91] 2 Corinthians 11:23-27; Galatians 6:17. Although the Pauline corpus may be pseudepigraphal, we can reasonably accord credence to these reports, due to the harsh nature of the times. Indeed, the extreme persecution suffered by the earliest Christians from both the Romans and the Jews strongly undercuts the phantom Christ theory. Because if Christianity was so highly objectionable to both the Jews and the Romans, would not the movement have been traced back to the very originators thereof, who would have been dealt with very harshly and summarily by the Romans?

[92] Although it will no doubt be rejected as heretical by the vast majority of fundamentalists and evangelicals.

Gnosticism

The origin of Gnosticism is shrouded in as much mystery as the origin of Christianity. But much of the mystery seems to be due to a vague, nebulous definition of Gnosticism. As in the case with Ebionism, Gnosticism can be identified quite distinctively once a clear, unambiguous definition is in place. Of course it would be a mistake to think of Gnosticism in monolithic terms; there was not a strong, homogenous "orthodoxy" of Gnosticism, but rather a considerable heterogeneity of Gnostic cults and sects. Nevertheless Gnosticism, when properly understood, has certain unique characteristics that are not to be found elsewhere. We ought to first distinguish Gnosticism from mysticism and esotericism; not because Gnosticism lacks mystical or esoteric traits, but because to make Gnosticism merely synonymous with either mysticism or esotericism deprives it of any distinctive identity. Gnosticism, while it could be described as a form of mysticism, or of esotericism, is very distinct unto itself. In fact there has been nothing else quite like it in the history of religion on this planet. Gnosticism can be best understood by way of contrast with that which it is not. Gnosticism is most definitely not to be equated with Ebionism, for example. In fact, the two systems could hardly be more mutually opposed. The *Ebionim* may have practiced an esoteric mysticism, perhaps akin to the *Kabbalah,* but this should not be at all confused with Gnosticism. And to speak of a "Judaeo-Gnosticism" is really an oxymoron.[93]

Traditional ecclesiastical heresiology traces Gnosticism back to Simon Magus.[94] This pedigree is suspect, not only due to the polemic nature of the apologetics involved, and the lateness of the sources, but also because there are those who might prefer to esteem Simon Magus as a merely legendary character. Notwithstanding this, Simon may have been a historic figure nonetheless. Simon is associated with one Dositheos, but the sources are divided as to whether Dositheos was Simon's *protégé* or predecessor. Simon claimed to have suffered his passion in Judaea as the Son, appeared among the Samaritans as the Father, and dwelled among the Gentiles abroad as the Holy Ghost.[95] This claim will become significant later when we consider the substitution theory in greater detail. Simon Magus has thus been equated by some scholars[96] with Simon of Cyrene, who, according to some Gnostic traditions, was crucified as a substitute in place of Jesus. There is even a Gnostic text that explicitly states that Simon of Cyrene was the one who was really crucified instead of Christ.

"And I was in the mouths of lions. And the plan which they devised about me to release their error and their senselessness-I did not succumb to them as they had planned. But I was not afflicted at all. Those who were there punished me. And I did not die in reality but in appearance, lest I be put to shame by them because these are my kinsfolk. I removed the shame from me and I did not become fainthearted in the face of what happened to me at their hands. I was about to succumb to fear, and I suffered according to their sight and thought, in order that they may never find a word to speak about them. For my death, which they think happened, (happened) to them in their error and blindness, since they nailed their man unto their death. For their Ennoias did not see me, for they were deaf and blind. But in doing these things, they condemn themselves. Yes, they saw me; they punished me. *But* it was another, their father, who drank the

---

[93]   Despite what C.W. King may have written to the contrary in his work on Gnosticism. Aside from this, however, his work appears to be a good pre-Nag Hammadi source on Gnosticism.

[94]   I.e., the Simon mentioned in Acts 8:9-24.

[95]   King., op. cit., pg. 69.

[96]   Notably Barbara Thiering.

gall and vinegar; it was not I. They struck me with the reed; *but* it was another, Simon, who bore the cross on his shoulder. It was another upon whom they placed the crown of thorns. But I was rejoicing in the height over all the wealth of the archons and the offspring of their error, *and* of their empty glory. And I was laughing at their ignorance."[97]

The Synoptic Gospels record that Simon of Cyrene was compelled by the Roman soldiers to bear the cross of Christ.[98] The Gospel of John, by contrast, does not mention Simon at all, but only tersely states that Jesus bore his own cross.[99] The inference to be drawn from this is that even before the time when the Gospel of John was first penned, already there had been rumors that Simon of Cyrene had been crucified in place of Christ. In fact, Christ showing his wounds to the Apostles in the Johannine version of the post-passion appearance may have been a further effort to squelch such rumors.[100] But it also seems fairly evident that such rumors were based upon the written narrative of the Synoptics, rather than upon any actual historical circumstance; otherwise we would have expected any such rumors to be laid to rest (or at least an attempt to do so) by the time of the first written form of the narrative. Aside from this, there is also the monumental improbability of Simon having been crucified in place of Jesus. Those who opt for this are either daft or have not thought through the entire scenario in any realistic way. We would have to assume any number of extremely improbable things, all working simultaneously to bring about such a strange substitution. We would have to suppose, for example, that Jesus had such an incredible hypnotic power over both Simon, the Roman soldiers, and the surrounding throng of onlookers, that he was able to simultaneously hypnotize them all into believing that Simon was really him, and to slip away unnoticed, and to so keep them under his spell long enough that Simon was nailed to the cross in his stead. A cynical interpretation might be that the Roman soldiers were bribed by Christ's disciples, but then what of the surrounding blood-thirsty throng of Jews? And what of Simon

---

[97]   Second Treatise of the Great Seth. From the Nag Hammadi library. This can be found online at http://www.gnosis.org/naghamm/2seth.html.

[98]   Mt 27:32; Mk 15:21; Lk 23:26.

[99]   Jn 19:17.

[100]   Jn 20:19-27.

himself, who would presumably not be eager to suffer such a brutal fate? Therefore any substitution theory involving Simon of Cyrene is untenable and absurd. It reflects upon the weakness and ineptitude of those Gnostics who seized upon whatever they could in the earliest Gospels to twist and distort beyond recognition. That is not to say that other substitution scenarios were completely out of the question. But we will discuss these in greater detail later. As to the Gnostics, some of them postulated a different, more nuanced, version of a substitution theory:

"When he said those things, I saw him seemingly being seized by them. And I said "What do I see, O Lord? That it is you yourself whom they take, and that you are grasping me? Or who is this one, glad and laughing on the tree? And is it another one whose feet and hands they are striking?" The Savior said to me, "He whom you saw on the tree, glad and laughing, this is the living Jesus. But this one into whose hands and feet they drive the nails is his fleshy part, which is the substitute being put to shame, the one who came into being in his likeness. But look at him and me.""[101]

Here the fleshly body of Christ is regarded as a substitute for the real "living Jesus", a purely spiritual being. This leads to a consideration of Docetism. Docetism is a subset of Gnosticism. As such it is distinct from Gnosticism, but not in the absolute sense. Docetism is the doctrine that Christ only appeared to suffer his passion, and indeed that the entire incarnation was merely an illusion. This was based upon the Gnostic idea that matter is inherently evil, and therefore a pure spirit could never enter into a carnal body. Not all Gnostics were Docetists, but all Docetists were Gnostics. But we still have to clarify Gnosticism more explicitly and show wherein it is unique. Elements of Gnosticism may be traced back to many different sources, including Judaism, Christianity, Zoroastrianism, Platonism, Greek mysticism, and even Hinduism, but Gnosticism itself is distinct from all of these. It is not merely the sum of its parts. In fact, Gnosticism is probably best understood as a distinctly Christian heresy, just as Ebionism was a distinctly Jewish heresy. And the circumstances of the case are such that only within the context of Christianity could

---

[101] Apocalypse of Peter. From the Nag Hammadi library. This is available online at http://www.gnosis.org/naghamm/apopet.html. Those familiar with my earlier work may note the potential significance of the reference to "tree" rather than "cross" here.

such a unique system of thought as Gnosticism have arisen. This will become evident once the essence of Gnosticism is clearly understood.

In a very real sense, Marcion was the first Gnostic. All other systems of Gnosticism seem to be mere embellishments upon his central idea: that although Jesus was the Son of God, the Father of Jesus was *not* the God of the Old Testament; the God of the Jews was merely a subordinate power and ultimately a false God. Nowhere else in the history of religion was there ever such a radical rejection and reinterpretation of what, to all intents and purposes, appears to be the primary source and root of the new religion.[102] This and this alone is what makes Gnosticism unique in the history of religion. This is the essence of Gnosticism; every other consideration is subordinate to this one ruling idea. For this reason, we can see at once that Gnosticism is the antithesis of Judaism and Ebionism. This is why it is oxymoronic to speak of a "Judaeo-Gnosticism"; such a *chimera* simply does not exist, despite the unconvincing arguments of Friedlander to the contrary. For Friedlander to cite Gnostic cults and texts based upon Cain, Seth, Shem, Melchizedek, or the Ophites is fruitless and bootless; the Old Testament Pseudepigrapha also includes many Christian texts based upon Old Testament figures. And while there may have been dissenting "antinomian" Jews before Paul, there is no convincing evidence that they were distinctly Gnostic in character. But there may be any number of quasi-Gnostic writings and cults that are not genuinely Gnostic in character, but which have become thus labelled. Gnosticism is not necessarily synonymous with all that is strange, esoteric, mystical, or anti-Semitic. Although Gnosticism does share these traits to varying degrees. And this notwithstanding the sometimes unmistakable Jewish influence upon Gnosticism. Consider the following excerpt from the Gospel of the Hebrews:

"When Christ wished to come upon the earth to men, the good Father summoned a mighty power in heaven, which was called Michael, and entrusted Christ to the care thereof. And the power came into the world and it was called Mary, and Christ was in her womb seven months."[103]

---

[102] I.e., the Jewish Scriptures, and therefore necessarily the Jewish God.

[103] Schneemelcher, Wilhelm., *NEW TESTAMENT APOCRYPHA: Volume One: Gospels and Related Writings.* (© J.C.B. Mohr (Paul Siebeck) Tubingen, 1990) (English Translation Copyright © James Clarke & Co. Ltd. 1991) Westminster/John Knox Press Louisville, Kentucky 40202-1396.; pg. 177.

The passage is certainly strange, or at least unfamiliar, to most readers. But is it Gnostic? No; the "good Father" mentioned therein is presumably the same as the God of the Jewish Scriptures. Thus Gnosticism can be partially illustrated by way of contrast with Ebionism. Ebionism itself is unique, not due to vegetarianism and opposition to animal sacrifices; the same can also be found in Jainism, Buddhism, and Vaisnava Hinduism; but precisely because these beliefs of the Ebionites exist in the context of an otherwise scrupulous observance of the Torah. Thus Ebionism is quite distinct, as is Gnosticism, although there were a proliferation of various Gnostic sects in the early centuries of Christianity. The various church documents on Ebionism from the third century on are unreliable; for already towards the end of the second century the ill-informed apologists of orthodoxy postulated a mythical "Ebion" as the supposed founder of the sect.

If I may be permitted a slight digression, I would here like to qualify and clarify some points made earlier respecting the various Gospels attributed to Matthew, and the relationship of the Canonical Greek Matthew to MtN, MtE, and MtH. This will hopefully not put the reader off, but will serve to further illuminate the subject under discussion, since Gnosticism can to some degree be illustrated by Ebionism, by way of contrast and comparison. First is the rather obscure point that, according to some scholars, none of these earlier Matthew Gospels were actually written in Hebrew, but in Greek. This point is debatable, but even if the point is conceded in the case of these extant texts, there still remains the fact of early Christian traditions to the effect that the Apostle Matthew wrote his Gospel in Hebrew. Therefore even if all three of these texts had been composed in Greek rather than Hebrew, it is still possible, nay probable, that the Greek Matthew is based upon an earlier Hebrew original.[104] And to early Christian tradition can be added testimony from the text of Matthew itself; for therein we see ascribed to Christ the saying "Do not think I have come to abolish the law, or the prophets; I have come, not to abolish, but to fulfill *them*. For truly I say unto you, Until heaven and

---

Originally taken from E.A.W. Budge., *Coptic Apocrypha in the Dialect of Upper Egypt,* London 1913); Coptic p. 60; English p. 637.

[104] And presumably the original, Hebrew Gospel of Matthew omitted the story of the virgin birth. In any case the Gospel of Mark has not the slightest hint of the virgin birth.

earth pass *away,* not one yod or one tittle shall by any means pass *away* from the law, until all be fulfilled."[105] Even in the Greek text, it is evident that it was intended to refer to the Hebrew letter *yod,* which implies, that Jesus not only first spoke such words in Hebrew,[106] but that he had specific reference to the Hebrew Scriptures in the original tongue, rather than the Greek Septuagint translation. And from this it may be further reasoned that the Gospel of Matthew itself had also originally been written in Hebrew.[107] It is interesting to compare and contrast this saying of Christ with that found in MtE: "I have come to abolish the sacrifices; and if you cease not from offering sacrifice, the wrath of God will not cease afflicting you." The two sayings are in stark contrast. However if by "fulfilling the law and the prophets" Jesus had intended a messianic interpretation of Daniel's prophecy of the seventy weeks,[108] then the two sayings are not *necessarily* in opposition. However a sober assessment leads me to believe that the Greek edition of Matthew *was* to some extent, a refutation of Ebionism. Superficially Matthew 5:17-18 seems to favor Ebionism; but a comparison with another passage from Canonical Matthew will serve to illustrate the post-Ebionite, anti-Ebionite character of the text:

"And, Whosoever shall swear by the altar, it is nothing: but whosoever sweareth by the gift upon it, he is guilty. Ye blind fools! For which is greater, the gift, or the altar that sanctifieth the gift?"[109]

Since animals were still offered in sacrifice on the altar at the presumed time when Jesus (supposedly) spoke these words, then the anti-Ebionite character of the Greek Gospel of Matthew is clearly evident. As such it seems to have been written to refute the claims of the *Ebionim* to represent the original messianic tradition.

---

[105] Mt 5:17-18.

[106] I.e., assuming he spoke them at all, and they were not a later invention ascribed to him. In any case we are expected to believe this by the Evangelist.

[107] Or at least that this saying of Jesus was first spoken and transmitted in Hebrew.

[108] I.e., that Prince Messiah would be the one to "cause the sacrifice and the oblation to cease" in the midst of the final, seventieth, week. See my earlier work.

[109] Mt 23:18-19.

But to return to Gnosticism. There is some degree of anti-Gnostic polemic within the New Testament corpus, but generally in the later portions thereof. For example, we have the anti-Docetic declarations of the Johannine epistles.[110]

"By this you know the Spirit of God: every spirit that confesses that Jesus Christ has come in the flesh is of God; and every spirit that confesses not that Jesus Christ has come in the flesh is not of God: and the same is the spirit of the antichrist, of which you have heard that it would come; and already now is it in the world." (1 John 4:2-3)

"For many deceivers have entered the world, who confess not that Jesus Christ has come in the flesh; this is the deceiver and the antichrist." (2 John 7)

Note well that this is directed specifically against the Docetists, who denied the physical incarnation of Christ. It is not *necessarily* directed against a spiritual interpretation of Christ's resurrection. On the other hand, one cannot help but suspect that possibly the reference to the nail-wounds and spear-wound in John 20:19-27 had an anti-Docetic intent. The twenty-first chapter of John's Gospel also appears to be a later addition, which apparently had an anti-Docetic intent. Some[111] have hypothesized that the scene of a Roman soldier piercing Christ's side with a spear in John 19:34 and some manuscripts of Matthew 27:49[112] had an anti-Docetic intent.

In the pastoral epistles we have some anti-Gnostic polemic as well. As mentioned above, most critical biblical scholars believe that the pastoral epistles are pseudepigraphal. It has recently been suggested[113] that they are the work of Polycarp. This judgment appears to be sound, based upon the available evidence. As such these pastorals must be sharply distinguished from the remainder of the Pauline corpus, which seems to be pervaded by a Gnostic nomenclature. Indeed, one suspects that the liberal use of the Pauline corpus by Gnostics was the prime motivation of Polycarp in forging the pastoral epistles. In 1 Timothy 6:20, we have the following anti-Gnostic proclamation:

---

[110]   1 John 4:1-3; 2 John 7-11.

[111]   Notably Bart Ehrman.

[112]   Codices Sinaiticus, Vaticanus, C, L, and some other early sources. Cf Nestle-Aland., op. cit., pg. 84; apparatus.

[113]   By David Trobisch.

"O Timothy, keep what is committed to thy trust, and avoid profane and empty babble, and antitheses of the falsely-called "knowledge", which some professing, have erred from the faith."

The Greek word for knowledge is *gnosis*.[114] The Gnostics were people who claimed to possess unique spiritual knowledge that would set the spirit free from the bondage and corruption of matter, which they held to be evil, and the creation of a lesser deity. We find a similar denunciation in 2 Timothy 2:16-18:

"But shun profane and empty babble; for they will increase to more ungodliness. And their word will eat away as gangrene, of whom are Hymenaeaus and Philetus, who concerning the truth have erred, saying that the resurrection is already past, and *thereby* overturn the faith of some."

It is interesting that there are some passages from the Gospel of Philip that seems to correspond to this:

"Those who say they will die first and then rise are in error. If they do not first receive the resurrection while they live, when they die they will receive nothing."[115]

"Those who say that the Lord died first and (then) rose up are in error, for he rose up first and (then) died. If one does not first attain the resurrection, he will not die. As God lives, he would *remain dead.*"[116]

I believe that my emendation of the textual reading above is justified on the basis of the following passage from the same text:

"A Gentile does not die, for he has never lived in order that he may die. He who has believed in the truth has found life, and this one is in danger of dying, for he is alive."[117]

We can clearly see that the kind of interpretation of the resurrection, both of Christ and of the individual believer, as espoused in the Gospel of Philip, is what is being refuted in 2 Timothy 2:16-18. Therefore Gnosticism was in full bloom when the Pastorals were written. As far as the epistles of John are concerned, even Christian tradition concedes that they were written as late as the last decade of

---

[114] Compare the Sanskrit *jnana,* which has the same meaning.

[115] The Gospel of Philip; from the Nag Hammadi library. An online version of this is available at http://www.gnosis.org/naghamm/gop.html.

[116] Ibid.

[117] Ibid.

the first century.[118] The very fact that Gnosticism and Docetism are such palpable realities in the Pauline and Johannine corpii may suggest a second-century origin for those texts. It is debatable to what degree Gnosticism and Docetism flourished in the first century, but I suspect that deference has been shown towards Christian tradition, inasmuch as it would have been an embarrassment to admit that these "apostolic" texts are actually pseudepigraphal.[119] On the other hand, the writers of the various New Testament texts appear to have been very scrupulous about avoiding any obvious anachronisms that would betray a second-century origin.[120] Therefore it remains unproven that the references to Docetism and Gnosticism in the Pauline and Johannine corpii are anachronisms betraying a second-century origin for those texts. The Gospel of Peter seems to have some Docetic elements, which may be why it was excluded from the Canon of Scripture.

In my earlier work I suggested that Jesus may have been more commonly known under the Greek form of his name, rather than the Hebrew Yeshua. There is a passage from the Gospel of Philip that seems to support this view.

""Jesus" is a hidden name, "Christ" a revealed name. For this reason "Jesus" is not particular to any language; rather he is always called by the name "Jesus". While as for "Christ", in Syriac it is "Messiah", in Greek it is "Christ". Certainly all the others have it in their own language."[121]

Although the Gospel of Philip probably dates to the second century or later, still this passage seems evidential in terms of specifying the Greek form of the name *Jesus* being more commonly used, rather than the Hebrew *Yeshua,* which militant messianics insist upon today. As I pointed out in my earlier work, many Jewish men had Greek names during the period in question, even in Palestine.

---

[118] Which implies that they are at least this late, if not later. The same also holds true for the Gospel of John.

[119] Which they would have to be if they were of such late origin.

[120] And I suppose I could be accused of special pleading and begging the question on this score, if it were not for some apparent literary dependence on Josephus and Suetonius, as well as the shared suspicions of some critical biblical scholars.

[121] Gospel of Philip, from the Nag Hammadi library. An online version of this may be found at http://www.gnosis.org.naghamm/gop.html. This text can also be found in *The Nag Hammadi Library,* edited by James Robinson.

And if Jesus and his family were originally Alexandrian Jews, as I speculated in my earlier work, then this would be even more probable. From the Gospel of Philip we can see that there was not the slightest hint that Jesus had been known as Yeshua, or that there was even any controversy about this. But if such had been the case, we would expect at least some hint or trace of such a point of dispute between Jewish Christians and Greek Christians. There is another interesting passage from the Gospel of Philip, that is worth taking notice of:

"Some said, "Mary conceived by the Holy Spirit." They are in error. They do not know what they are saying. When did a woman ever conceive by a woman? Mary is the virgin whom no power defiled. She is a great anathema to the Hebrews, who are the apostles and the apostolic men. This virgin whom no power defiled [...] the powers defile themselves. And the Lord would not have said "My Father who is in heaven" (Mt 16:17) unless he had another father; but he would have said simply "My Father"."[122]

This is a strange passage, and one that appears self-contradictory. It at first seems to uphold the virgin birth dogma, which was rejected by the *Ebionim*. As such, the statement that "She is a great anathema to the Hebrews, who are the apostles and the apostolic men" seems to imply an identification of the Apostles as Ebionites. While this seems reasonable in and of itself, then the passage seems to deny the virgin birth, by implying that Joseph really was the father of Jesus.[123] Of course it is not difficult to find Scriptural examples that belie the example that forms the premise.[124] Therefore it is uncertain what point was intended here in Philip. We can really only speculate. Perhaps Mary was not intended in the literal sense, but rather as an archetype; possibly corresponding to the constellation *Virgo*. It also seems just barely possible that the "other father" referred to was not meant to be Joseph, but the demiurge Ialdabaoth. One possible solution[125] is that the latter portion of the above passage was the work of a later hand,

---

122   Ibid.

123   I.e., of his fleshly body.

124   Luke 2:49; 22:29; John 15:1,8. In all these verses Jesus refers to God as "my Father" without the further qualification "heavenly" or "in heaven", etc., therefore the point that the author of Philip was trying to make has counter-examples from the very Scriptures he quotes from.

125   Although likely to be rejected by critical scholars.

who sought to "correct" the implication of a virgin birth according to a more Ebionite orthodoxy.[126]

There is another fascinating passage from another Gnostic work, entitled simply the Testimony of Truth. It is as follows:

"I will speak to those who know to hear not with the ears of the body but with the ears of the mind. For many have sought after the truth and have not been able to find it; because there has taken hold of them the old leaven of the Pharisees and the scribes of the Law. And the leaven is the errant desire of the angels and the demons and the stars. As for the Pharisees and the scribes, it is they who belong to the archons who have authority over them. For no one who is under the Law will be able to look up to the truth, for they will not be able to serve two masters. For the defilement of the Law is manifest; but undefilement belongs to the light. The Law commands to take a husband (or) to take a wife, and to beget, and to multiply like the sand of the sea. But passion, which is a delight to them, constrains the souls of those who are begotten in this place, and those who defile and those who are defiled, in order that the Law might be fulfilled through them. And they show that they are assisting the world; and they turn away from the light, who are unable to pass by the archon of darkness until they pay the last penny. But the Son of Man came forth from imperishability, being alien to defilement. He came to the world by the Jordan River, and immediately the Jordan turned back. And John bore witness to the descent of Jesus. For it is he who saw the Power which came down upon the Jordan River; for he knew that the dominion of carnal procreation had come to an end. The Jordan River is the power of the body, that is, the senses of pleasures. The water of the Jordan is the desire for sexual intercourse. John is the archon of the womb. And this is what the Son of Man reveals to us: It is fitting for you to receive the word of truth, if one will receive it perfectly. But as for the one who is in ignorance, it is difficult for him to diminish his works of darkness which he has done. Those who have known imperishability, however, have been able to struggle against passions [...]. I have said to you, "Do not build nor gather for yourselves in

---

[126] And this despite the apparent opposition between Gnosticism and Ebionism. In some cases Gnostics have used Ebionite sources. For example, Carpocrates used MtH; while Cerinthus used one of the Jewish Christian Gospels attributed to Matthew, although it is uncertain whether it was MtN, MtE, or MtH, or possibly some earlier prototype.

the place where the brigands break open, but bring forth fruit to the Father." The foolish, thinking in their heart that if they confess "We are Christians", in word only (but) not with power, while giving themselves over to ignorance, to a human death, not knowing where they are going nor who Christ is, thinking that they will live, when they are (really) in error-*they* hasten towards the principalities and authorities. They fall into their clutches because of the ignorance that is in them. For (if) only words which bear testimony were effecting salvation, the whole world would endure this thing and would be saved... But when they are "perfected" with a (martyr's) death, this is the thought that they have within them: "If we deliver ourselves over to death for the sake of the Name we will be saved." These matters are not settled in this way."[127]

The mention of the "leaven of the Pharisees" brings to mind certain passages from the Synoptic Gospels, where Jesus warns his disciples against this leaven.[128] In Luke Christ identifies this "leaven" as hypocrisy; this implies that the above passage was written as a rebuke to the hypocrisy of the orthodox Christians. There is also an interesting passage from a text called simply "Melchizedek", which was also found in the codices at Nag Hammadi. Superficially the text almost appears to be anti-Gnostic, or at least anti-Docetic; but it also contradicts Nicene orthodoxy.

"Furthermore, they will say of him that he is unbegotten,[129] though he has been begotten, (that) he does not eat, even though he eats, (that) he does not drink, even though he drinks, (that) he is uncircumcised,[130] though he has been circumcised,[131] (that) he is

---

[127] Testimony of Truth, from the Nag Hammadi Library, edited by James M. Robinson. An online version of this is available at http://www.gnosis.org/naghamm/testruth.html.

[128] Mt 16:6,12; Mk 8:15; Lk 12:1.

[129] I interpret this as being more in accord with Arian theology, albeit the text was probably written before the time of Arius. However it is possible that this was intended as a rebuke to Patro-passionism (i.e., the doctrine that the Father suffered on the cross in the person of the Son).

[130] This is highly significant, inasmuch as it proves that there must have been those who claimed that Jesus was really a Gentile and hence was uncircumcised.

[131] This states no more than what we otherwise read in Scripture; Luke 2:21. However the Epistle of Barnabas correctly pointed out that not only are

unfleshly, though he has come in the flesh,[132] (that) he did not come to suffering, though he came to suffering, (that) he did not rise from the dead, though he arose from the dead."[133]

There are many other such interesting passages to be found in the various texts of the Nag Hammadi library. One of such texts, while not necessarily Gnostic in character, is still somewhat interesting in shedding some light upon a verse found in the Pauline corpus. The verse in question is Romans 2:24, which reads "For the name of God is blasphemed among the Gentiles through you, as it is written." Some Bibles cross-reference the verse with Isaiah 52:5, which reads "Now therefore, what have I here, saith the LORD, that my people is taken away for nought? *and* they that rule over them make them to howl, saith the LORD; and my name is every day blasphemed continually." Some Bibles also cross-reference Ezekiel 36:20, which reads "And when they entered unto the heathen, whither they went, they profaned my holy name, when they said to them, These *are* the people of the LORD, and are gone forth out of his land." But neither of these two Scripture verses are as similar to what we read in Romans 2:24 as the following, taken from the Sentences of Sextus:

"Those on account of whom the name of God is blasphemed are dead before God."[134]

This is indicative of the fact that the Greek New Testament must be understood as a species of Greek literature; such an understanding gives an appropriate context to the provenance of the New Testament texts. In fact, the Jewish Scriptures had already been translated into Greek centuries before, and exerted their own influence upon Greek literature. And as we will see, it was not only the Hebrew originals

---

the Jews circumcised, but so are the Syrians, Arabians, Egyptians and Aethiopians. Circumcision doesn't prove the alleged "Jewishness" of Jesus.

[132] Cf 1 John 4:1-3; 2 John 7-11.

[133] Melchizedek, from the Nag Hammadi library. An online version of this can be found at http://www.gnosis.org/naghamm/melchiz.html. The final portion does not *necessarily* denote a carnal resurrection as opposed to a spiritual resurrection.

[134] Sentences of Sextus, 175, from the Nag Hammadi library. An online version of this text is available at http://www.gnosis.org/naghamm/sent.html. Cp Luke 20:38.

of those texts that were used as sources for the New Testament, but recourse was had to the Greek Septuagint translation as well.[135]

Towards the close of the first century and the beginning of the second, there arose a group that shared the Ebionite rejection of animal sacrifices, a group known as the Elchesaites. They had their own sacred book, the Book of Elchesai. The Elchesaites advocated a second baptism for the remission of sins. They seemed to be somewhat apocalyptic in their beliefs and may have been a branch of the Ebionites. However eventually the movement died out.

Another group was the Encratites. In some cases the Encratites shared Docetic beliefs. The Encratites were very strictly ascetic in practice, and forbade conjugal relations. Encratites used such texts as the Acts of John, the Acts of Thomas, the Acts of Andrew, the Acts of Peter, the Acts of Philip, and the Acts of Paul and Thekla. Traces of Encratism may also be found in other apocryphal texts. The Encratites also enjoined fasting, and probably also forbade certain foods. Most likely the rise of Encratism was the origin of the following anti-Encratite passage from Scripture:

"Now the Spirit speaks clearly, *saying* that in the latter times some shall depart from the faith, giving heed to seducing spirits, and doctrines of demons; speaking lies in hypocrisy; having their conscience seared *as* with a hot *branding* iron; forbidding to marry, *and commanding* to abstain from meats, which God has created to be received with thanksgiving by them that believe and know the truth." (1 Timothy 4:1-3)

Above we briefly discussed the possibility that Polycarp wrote the Pastorals in the second century. The evidence seems to support this position, especially vis-à-vis Encratism. But what may be even more disturbing to some is that there appears to be a seed of Encratism even within the Canonical Gospel of Luke. If we examine the Lukan version of Christ's response to the Sadducees on the question of the resurrection, we find a reading somewhat variant from what is otherwise found in Matthew and Mark, and which, if interpreted literally, seems to support the position of the Encratites:

"But they which shall be accounted worthy to obtain that world, and the resurrection from the dead, neither marry, nor are given in marriage: neither can they die anymore, for they are equal

---

[135] Probably more often than not, although not exclusively, as we have seen already.

unto the angels; and are children of God, being the children of the resurrection."[136]

The passage, taken in isolation from the other two Synoptics, seems to say that in order to attain the resurrection from the dead, one must abstain from marriage, and the attendant pleasures of the flesh.[137] If Marcion shared the Encratite disdain for the flesh,[138] then this may be why he chose the Gospel of Luke as the "purest" Gospel. By contrast, what we read in Matthew and Mark is much simpler than what is found in Luke, and has no trace of Encratism:

"For in the resurrection they neither marry nor are given in marriage, but are as the angels of God in heaven."[139]

For people reading the text of Luke by itself, without being able to compare it with the parallel passages in Mark and Matthew, it probably seemed as if Jesus was saying that conjugal bliss would forfeit heaven. It is strange that the reading of Luke has survived the editing of scribes, who might otherwise have sought to bring the passage into greater conformity with anti-Encratite orthodoxy. Does this mean that the reading found in Luke is more likely genuine than the form found in Matthew and Mark? Maybe. Maybe not. It depends upon whether one looks upon the passage as possibly an Encratite corruption of Luke's text, or a genuine tradition recorded by the Evangelist. If the former were the case, then it is amazing that the text was never restored to conformity with Matthew and Mark. If the latter is the case, then the passage, although deviant from later anti-Encratite orthodoxy, is still suspect, since it conflicts with the simpler forms found in Matthew and Mark. As such I have excluded it from the corpus of "fossil" passages.[140] In fact, the form of the passage in Luke actually obscures the reference to a spiritual resurrection, which was the criterion I used

---

[136] Luke 20:35-36.

[137] I.e., conjugal bliss.

[138] Which seems to have been the case.

[139] Mt 22:30; cf Mk 12:25, which has essentially the same meaning. Matthew's reading includes Mark's.

[140] See discussion below vis-à-vis Forensic Literary Archaeology. One of the canons I used to determine the corpus of "fossil" passages was internal self-consistency, since any implicit historical subtext would be vitiated by contradiction.

to include the parallel passages in Matthew and Mark in the corpus of "fossil" passages.[141]

While on the subject of possible Encratite corruption of the New Testament text, I strongly suspect that Matthew 19:12 may be an example of an Encratite interpolation into the text, although there are apparently no manuscript variants which omit the verse.[142] Astute critical scholars know that the absence of such manuscript variants does not automatically rule out the possibility of an interpolation. The strange verse, which seems so out of place, not only in Matthew, but even within the entire context of the New Testament, evokes a sickly celibate monasticism of extreme asceticism. Shades of possible Buddhist influence are evident here as well. But then again many of the Essenes were also celibate.[143] So it is also just barely possible that we have in this verse a reference to a custom of the Essenes.

Cerinthus was another early Gnostic teacher of some prominence. Cerinthus was starkly antinomian, and according to some rumors he was the real author of the book of Revelation. However I suspect that Cerinthus probably wrote a different *Apokalypse;* possibly a parody of the biblical book of Revelation. On the other hand, suspicions of Cerinthian authorship may have been one of the factors that kept the book of Revelation from being accorded Canonical status for such a long time. Even as late as the latter half of the fourth century there were doubts as to the Canonicity of Revelation, and in fact the book never was accepted as Canonical by the Syrian Orthodox Church.

Aside from Cerinthus and Marcion, there was a great profusion of Gnostic teachers; Valentinus, Basilides, Bardesanes, Ptolemy, Heracleon, and many others, with their various disciples. But the very

---

[141]   And this on the basis of preemptive contradiction of the later orthodoxy of a carnal resurrection. But some portions of the Lukan passage conform to a spiritual resurrection.

[142]   "For there be some eunuchs, who were so born from their mother's womb; and there be some eunuchs, who were castrated by men; and there be some eunuchs, who have made themselves such for the sake of the kingdom of heaven. He that it able to receive it, let him receive it." This verse has been used by the Roman Catholic Church to justify the unbiblical doctrine of mandatory priestly celibacy. Peter, the so-called "first Pope" was married, according to Scripture; Mt 8:14; Mk 1:30; Lk 4:38. Due to this consideration, I include these three verses in the corpus of "fossil" passages.

[143]   Jos. War. 2.8.2.

heterogeneity of the many Gnostic sects only serves to prove that they could not all have been legitimately entrusted with an original esotericism traced back to Jesus and the Apostles. Therefore the different Gnostic systems were in competition with one another, albeit generally on cordial terms. By contrast, the more "orthodox" church took a dim view of Gnosticism, condemning the entire movement as a "damnable" heresy. The original messianic movement was no doubt immersed in apocalyptic Judaism, but this apocalypticism may have been an exoteric, parabolic shell of an esoteric Kabbalism. Indeed, there may have been successive layers of secret teachings. There are varieties of esotericism, but essentially there are two distinct forms of esotericism. A mild version of esotericism is one in which the secret teachings are merely a more detailed explanation of the exoteric teaching, much as a parable hints at the central point thereof; a radical version of esotericism is one in which the secret teaching is strikingly different from, and even sometimes in stark opposition to, the exoteric teaching. Most Christians may allow for a mild version of esotericism in Christ's teachings; but they would regard as heresy any suggestion that the true secret teaching could have been radically different from the familiar exoteric teaching found in the New Testament texts. But Christians, particularly fundamentalists, would do well to question whether or not a parable is a lie. Is a parable a lie? The Gospel parables are introduced by Jesus as if he were simply narrating true-life events, but even the staunchest fundamentalist can readily recognize that these are stories being told with a moral point. We are not expected to believe that these are historical events; they are simply short stories that illustrate certain points. Therefore why is it so hard to believe that there may also be extended, historical parables within the text of the Gospels? Two obvious examples come to mind: first, the reference to the "leaven of the Pharisees, and the leaven of Herod" mentioned in Mark 8:15.[144] The very fact that Jesus is here speaking in parabolic terms implies that the stories of the miraculous multiplication of food earlier in the text were simply historical parables.[145]

---

[144]   For the entire context, see Mark 8:14-21.

[145]   Mark 6:35-44; 8:1-9. The reference to the symbolic numbers seven and twelve, both in the stories, and also in Christ's later conversation with his Apostles underscores the parabolic nature of the stories themselves.

Another example is the miracle of Jesus turning water into wine at the wedding in Kana.[146] The entire story strikes me as a historical parable. Therefore when the master of the feast says to the bridegroom "Thou hast kept the good wine until now" the meaning is evidently "Thou hast kept the good *teaching* until now". Jesus is *symbolically* the bridegroom in the story, not literally, as some would have it. But the parabolic nature of the story is brought out by comparison with Christ's earlier parable of new wine being placed in new wineskins.[147] John's story of the marriage at Kana is his answer to the Synoptic Gospels' parable of the new wine in new wineskins; the point to the story being that the teaching offered in his Gospel is superior to that found in the earlier Gospels.

In my earlier work I speculated that Jesus may not have been ethnically Jewish, but actually a Canaanite. If he was native to Galilee, known famously in Scripture as "Galilee of the Gentiles"[148] then his family may have been descendants of those whom John Hyrcanus forcibly converted to Judaism generations before.[149] If so, then although they may have outwardly embraced Judaism, they may have inwardly harbored resentment against the religion, and secretly held different beliefs. In fact, as I speculated in my earlier work, this may have been one reason why a heretical version of Judaism, such as Ebionism, was adopted by Jesus and his family and associates, assuming such had been the case. If Jesus was not ethnically Jewish, then he may also have secretly taught a radical Gnostic esotericism. This is admittedly a somewhat wild speculation, but not entirely unthinkable. The chief reservation I have about this reconstruction is the fact that the reference to Galilee in Matthew explicitly harks back to Isaiah, and therefore it is arguable that it was merely a more-or-less convenient gratuitous "fulfillment" of prophecy as required by a narrative based upon a hypothetical *Testimonia* of Old Testament prophecies requiring messianic fulfillment. In other words, the passage is of questionable historical value, and we should be cautious not to base too much upon it. But the alleged Jewishness of Jesus ought not to be taken for

---

[146] John 2:1-11.

[147] Mt 9:14-17; Mk 2:18-22; Lk 5:33-39.

[148] Isaiah 9:1; Mt 4:14-16 cf 1 Maccabees 5:15.

[149] Jos. Ant. 13.9.1-3 & 10.1-3.

granted,[150] because that assumption also fits in nicely with the required messianic credentials.[151] In fact, in my earlier work, I pointed out evidence that Jesus and his brother James were really of the priestly tribe of Levi, rather than the royal tribe of Judah.[152] Although therein I postulated that Jesus could only have been of one tribe or the other, I would now say that it is just barely possible that he may have been a descendant of both tribes.[153] Although Numbers 36 does seem to explicitly prohibit intermarriage between the twelve tribes, this was only instituted to prevent the inheritance of one tribe from passing to another. The Levites had no land inheritance in Israel, but God himself was their inheritance.[154] Furthermore Judges 21:1 refers to the possibility of intermarriage between tribes, and the context does not seem to refer to this as an act of lawlessness. Therefore it is conceivably possible that Jesus may have been a descendant of both Levi and Judah. But prophetic Scripture would require Mary herself to be a descendant of both Judah and Levi.[155]

In my earlier work I pointed out that there are two distinctly different doctrines of salvation taught in the New Testament: the doctrine of salvation through works apart from faith, as taught in the Synoptic Gospels and the Apocalypse; and the opposite doctrine of salvation through faith apart from works, as taught in the Pauline and

---

[150]　Despite the vehement protests of those misguided by pseudo-political correctness.

[151]　And a non-Jewish Messiah would have been as much of an embarrassment to the early messianic movement as a Jewish Adolf Hitler would have been to the Nazi Party. However I do not think that this fact makes it impossible to suppose that Jesus was really a Gentile; instead it presupposes that if so, this would have remained one of the most closely-guarded secrets of the inner circle of the movement.

[152]　And therefore this would also be an embarrassment for the messianic movement. The very fact that the two royal genealogies, found in the Gospels of Matthew and Luke respectively, contradict one another, also casts serious doubt upon Christ's alleged descent from King David.

[153]　I.e., assuming that he was even Jewish at all.

[154]　Deuteronomy 10:9. This refers to the privilege of the priesthood.

[155]　Or rather simply Judah. But we "know" from the Gospel of Luke that she was a descendant of Levi. This may be why evangelicals insist that the genealogy of Luke is really that of Mary, even though the text says it is that of Joseph.

Johannine corpii and the book of Acts. For this reason I postulated that the author of Acts was not Luke, but some pseudo-Luke, who wrote in imitation of the Evangelist. The epistle of James seems to be an attempt to reconcile the two opposing systems of salvation, in one requiring both faith and works.[156] Likewise the second epistle of Peter appears to be an attempt to co-opt the Pauline corpus into a works-based salvation scheme.[157] The general picture that emerges is of two distinct factions[158] within the messianic movement, each striving for supremacy, which are both in turn subsumed and co-opted by a pseudo-Petrine faction. I still believe that this analysis is generally sound, although it may be somewhat of a simplification.

There is also a corresponding distinction between the Synoptic and Pauline definitions of the word "apostle". The Synoptic definition is circumscribed to the Twelve Apostles of the Lamb,[159] or in other words, the original twelve Apostles.[160] By contrast, the Pauline definition of the term extends to anyone who witnessed the risen Jesus. On this basis Paul claimed apostleship. In this text I will observe the distinction by using a capital "A" in the first meaning of the term, and a small "a" in the latter meaning.

C.W. van Manen held the entire Pauline corpus to be pseudepigraphal.[161] He also postulated that Marcion was the author of Galatians.[162] I must admit that this is a tempting attribution, but what I have read of Marcion makes me think otherwise. Marcion seems to have been a simple, unassuming (but rigidly logical) man who was led to question and finally reject the proposition that Jesus was the Jewish Messiah. One of his lost works was called *Antitheses*,[163]

---

[156] James 2:14-26.

[157] 2 Peter 3:14-16.

[158] Which I generally designate the Synoptic faction and the Pauline-Johannine faction, respectively.

[159] Revelation 21:14.

[160] I.e., the original eleven Apostles, plus Matthias, who replaced Judas Iscariot; cf Acts 1:15-26.

[161] Mead., op. cit., pg. 38.

[162] http://www.robertmprice.mindvendor.com.

[163] Jonas, Hans., *THE GNOSTIC RELIGION*. (© 1963 by Hans Jonas) Beacon Press books, published under the auspices of the Unitarian Universalist Association. 1970 edition.; pg. 141.

which brings to mind 1 Timothy 6:20, which specifically condemns such "antitheses" by name. This dovetails nicely with the paradigm of Polycarp as the author of the Pastorals and editor of the remainder of the Pauline corpus. As such, Polycarp would have created a distinctly anti-Marcionite context for the Pauline corpus.

Some hold that Marcion's teaching was anti-Semitic. However I strongly disagree. In fact, had the emerging "orthodox" church embraced Marcion's teaching, then the Jews would have had nothing to fear from Christians. Marcion agreed with the Jews that Jesus was not their promised Messiah, who was still to come;[164] the revelation of Jesus had nothing to do with the Jewish Scriptures or the God of the Jews. In practical terms, this attitude is not that different from that of those Christians who, in the days of Manasseh ben Israel, allowed that the Jews would have their own Messiah distinct from Jesus. Notwithstanding this, Jonas refers to Marcion as a "lesser mind"[165] but as far as I am concerned Hans Jonas was a far lesser mind to Marcion.

---

[164]   Ibid., pg. 140.

[165]   Ibid., pg. 141.

Gnostic Nomenclature in
The Pauline Corpus

I would now like to briefly survey some examples of the use of Gnostic nomenclature within the Pauline corpus. But before I do, a few words are in order respecting my position on Paul's historicity and how that may impinge upon the question of the authenticity or otherwise of the Pauline corpus, or portions thereof. This is only fair, since in my former work I claimed to have disproven the historicity of Paul on the basis of the pseudonymous nature of the Pauline corpus. In that text I took the position that the historicity of Paul was so inextricably bound together with an assumption of the authenticity of the Pauline corpus[166] that without the latter the case for the historicity of Paul vanishes like a puff of smoke. The context of my previous work was one in which I was arguing in favor of the postulate that Jesus lived a century before the commonly-accepted time. Therefore the historicity of Paul in the first century was an obstacle to the theory proposed, and accordingly I dealt rather harshly with the evidence, disposing of Paul rather conveniently and hopefully with sufficient *aplomb* to garner the confidence of my readers. Hopefully they will not feel betrayed if I have changed my position somewhat, but I assure the reader that at the time of writing, I was fully convinced of my line of

---

[166] Or some core portion thereof.

argument. No author should feel that he or she is perpetually bound by opinions expressed in previous writings. Furthermore it takes some character to admit one might have been wrong. And, although I still feel that my arguments in my earlier work vis-à-vis Paul were reasonably sound, I may have been wrong on a few points. Chiefly, that Paul was unquestionably *chimerical* I now withdraw, despite my confident assertions to that effect in my earlier work. I will give the specific reason why I am seriously reconsidering the historicity of Paul in a later section on Paul, where evidence of his historicity shall be presented. But an assumed historical Paul once again opens up the question of the authenticity of the Pauline corpus, or at least of some "core" portion of it.

One thing that I am reasonably confident that I was correct about in my earlier work is that the Pastorals are pseudepigraphal.[167] However, I fear that I may have been mistaken about one of the key points I used as evidence of this therein. My argument turned on a reference to 2 Timothy 4:13 in the original Greek, where the word *membranas* was used; a word signifying sheepskin. I argued that sheepskin rather than papyrus was used for codices, rather than scrolls, and that codices did not come into use until the second century, thus "proving" (or so I thought) that the epistle could date no earlier than the second century, in which case it must have been pseudepigraphal. But I am no longer so confident that this is the case. In fact, from a rather obscure text, I suspect that codices may have been used as early as the third century B.C. The text in question is the Letter of Aristeas. The account of Aristeas has also been recorded in Josephus, at least in *epitome*.[168] Although most critical scholars place the writing of *Aristeas* in the middle of the second century B.C., the history narrated took place in the early third century B.C.; more precisely 270 B.C. I personally see no reason to discredit the report by positing over a century of time intervening between the events narrated and the writing of the epistle. In either case, the point I was striving to make regarding the use of books in codex form beginning no earlier than the second century C.E. would definitely be refuted by the text, unless we insist upon an impossibly late date for it, such as the second

---

[167] Most likely they were forged by Polycarp.

[168] Jos. Ant. 12.2.1-15.

century C.E.[169] There are actually a few points that we can learn from Aristeas, and they are relevant to some of the other evidence we will be discussing. First we will get to the point about codices and scrolls. The relevant portion of Aristeas is as follows:

"When they entered with the gifts which had been sent with them and the valuable parchments, on which the law was inscribed in gold in Jewish characters, for the parchment was wonderfully prepared and the connexion *between the pages* had been so effected as to be invisible, the king, as soon as he saw them, began to ask them about the books. And when they had taken the rolls out of their coverings, and unfolded the pages, the king stood still for a long time, and then making obeisance about seven times, he said..." (Aristeas, 7:6-7)[170]

The corresponding passage from Josephus is as follows:

"But as the old men came in with presents, which the high priest had given them to bring to the king and with the membranes, upon which they had their laws written in golden letters, he put questions to them concerning those books; and when they had taken off the covers wherein they were wrapt up, they showed him the parchment. So the king stood admiring the thinness of the pages, and the exactness of the junctures, which could not be perceived (so exactly were they connected one with another)"[171]

Although the reference to "rolls" in Aristeas presumably is to scrolls, both passages also have clear, unmistakable references to what can be none other than a codex, or codices. Interestingly, the English translation of Josephus refers to "membranes", which I am reasonably certain in the original Greek is the very same *membranas* found in 2 Timothy 4:13. But what else can be meant by "the connexion *between the pages* had been so effected as to be invisible", even admitting that the *italicized* words were supplied by the translators? And, as if this is not enough, by a comparison with what is written in Josephus, the case is clinched. It says "the king stood admiring the thinness of the pages, and the exactness of the junctures, which could not be perceived (so exactly were they connected one with another)". How

---

[169]   But then we would also have to insist upon such an absurd date for the works of Josephus, since he refers back to the letter of Aristeas in the *Antiquities*.

[170]   I am using the numbering system of *the Forgotten Books of Eden*.

[171]   Jos. Ant. 12.2.11; 89-90a.

could this possibly refer to anything but a codex? It certainly could not refer to a scroll. And yet even critical scholars place the writing of Aristeas in the second century B.C. And there is no contest that Josephus wrote his *Antiquities* before the close of the first century. So the codex form of books can be traced back at least to the second century B.C., if not actually all the way back to the late third century B.C. Therefore it cannot be argued that 2 Timothy is pseudonymous on that basis. Ironically, 2 Timothy 4:13 is a key verse by which David Trobisch identifies Polycarp as the author of the epistle. Carpus, who is mentioned in the verse, happens to be a variant on the name Polycarp. But the complete work of Trobisch will have to be consulted to appreciate his full case. Sparing that, one ought to at least read the epitome thereof.[172] But this may be unwelcome news in some quarters, since this is contrary to a lot of more commonly-accepted information. I prefer to believe the ancient sources, rather than bogus pseudo-explanations offered by self-appointed "experts". And I would rather admit that I was wrong than carry on a pointless charade.

But before moving on from the letter of Aristeas, there are still a few other things that we can learn from it, which impinge upon our current inquiry. It is a question with which I plan to deal in greater detail in a later section, but since we are here on the topic of *Aristeas,* and there is some relevant evidence to be found therein, we might as well investigate it now. The question has to do with whether postexilic Jews spoke Syriac or Hebrew. My contention is that postexilic Palestinian Jews spoke Hebrew, rather than Syriac, as is otherwise commonly supposed today. Many people today think they are sophisticated by proclaiming that Jesus and the Apostles spoke Aramaic, rather than Hebrew. In fact the use of the term "Aramaic" is part of the problem, since it serves to obscure the actual provenance of the language. Aramaic and Syriac are the same language, which is also sometimes called Chaldee, or even Aramaean. The Greek term for the language is *Syristi,* while the Hebrew term is *Aramiyth.* But the legend is that the Jews somehow forgot or lost their native Hebrew tongue during the Babylonian Captivity. Presumably due to the similarity of the languages, the sister-tongue Syriac was adopted. But this is a myth. Even evidence from the Dead Sea Scrolls serves to refute this particular pseudo-scholarly myth. The relevant evidence from the

---

[172] Available at http://www.robertmprice.mindvendor.com/reviews/trobisch first.htm.

letter of Aristeas, and also from the corresponding passage in Josephus, will help to clarify the issue, which is also relevant to the antiquity and authenticity of the Samaritan Pentateuch, and also the later use of the Syriac Peshitta text of the Bible by the Syrian Orthodox Church. I did not go into very much detail about this in my earlier work, since I wanted instead to focus on a tightly-argued position that Jesus may have lived in the first century B.C., rather than the commonly-accepted time. So let us proceed without further ado. The relevant passage from *Aristeas* is as follows:

"They need to be translated, answered Demetrius, for in the country of the Jews they use a peculiar alphabet (just as the Egyptians, too, have a special form of letters) and speak a peculiar dialect. They are supposed to use the Syriac tongue, but this is not the case; their language is quite different." (Aristeas 1:15-16)

The corresponding passage in Josephus, while superficially seeming to contradict what is written above, really does not, once one understands the true circumstances of the case. The passage is as follows:

"But, he said, he had been informed that there were many books of laws among the Jews worthy of inquiring after, and worthy of the king's library, but which, being written in characters and in a dialect of their own, will cause no small pains in getting them translated into the Greek tongue: that the character in which they are written seems to be like to that which is the proper character of the Syrians, and that its sound, when pronounced, is like to theirs also; and that this sound appears to be peculiar to themselves. Wherefore he said, that nothing hindered why they might not get those books to be translated also; for while nothing is wanting that is necessary for that purpose, we may have their books also in this library."[173]

These two passages, though in some respects seemingly contradictory, are actually in complete harmony with one another; there is no contradiction between them, and they actually serve to supplement and complement each other. It is very important to pay very careful attention to exactly what is being said. The passage from *Aristeas* itself very clearly says that the Jews did not speak Syriac.[174] It is true that Hebrew is "quite different" from Syriac, being a distinct

---

[173] Jos. Ant. 12.2.1; 14-15.

[174] Otherwise also known as Aramaic or Chaldee.

language unto itself. But they are both Semitic languages, and are similar in a general sense. They are in the same family of languages. As such, it is also true that the sound of Hebrew is similar to Syriac, certainly to Greek ears. Greek is in a completely different language family, the Indo-European family of languages. Hebrew and Syriac, by contrast, are both in the Semitic family of languages. When the Jews returned from Babylon, they still spoke Hebrew, but the old palaeo-Hebrew script was replaced by the square Aramaic script which became much more commonly used thereafter. So even the passage from Josephus is not incorrect, although what we find in the letter of Aristeas is more accurate. Critical scholars may scoff at this, but I am only reporting what these ancient texts themselves say about the language spoken by the postexilic Jews. But critical scholars parade around under the false pretence that they know better. I would sooner believe Aristeas and Josephus. As far as I am concerned, the evidence from Aristeas is conclusive, but I will present even more evidence that postexilic Jews spoke Hebrew in a later section.

Finally, critical scholars posit a late date for Aristeas, probably out of habit, but also because the work supposedly serves as Jewish propaganda, explaining why certain Greek authors did not mention Moses. As such it is speculated that it was a piece of propaganda written by a Hellenistic Jew. But without denying the propagandistic aspects of *Aristeas,* one could argue for a much earlier date, and even for the essential authenticity of the story narrated therein. Not even any miracles are narrated, so it can hardly be objected to on such grounds.[175] Some have claimed that the story relates some outrageously unlikely circumstance, namely that all seventy-two interpreters made the same exact *verbatim* Greek translation from the original Hebrew. Well neither my edition of *Aristeas* nor of Josephus relate any such absurd tale. But interestingly *Aristeas* does mention earlier Greek translations of the Torah. But these earlier translations of the law are said to be unreliable.[176]

But now we should return to the Pauline corpus. The pastoral epistles are probably pseudepigraphal. In my earlier work I took the position that the various Pauline epistles, although ostensibly written

---

[175] I.e., assuming that miracles must be an objection to the historian, a position I do not necessarily hold.

[176] Aristeas 11:30.

by Paul, were actually written by those persons identified as such in the respective colophons to the epistles. I still think that this is a sound position to take, although some may carp against it on the grounds that these people were merely acting in the role of secretaries, recording *verbatim* what Paul dictated to them. I pointed out that it would have been unlikely for an intelligent, educated man, such as Paul was supposed to have been,[177] to have merely dictated letters, as if he were illiterate, but rather have written them himself. Of course the alleged authenticity of some core of the Pauline corpus still functions as a strong "anchor" for the alleged historicity of Paul himself. This cannot be denied. But aside from the Pastorals, which are almost certainly pseudonymous, only Galatians and the Thessalonian epistles have no contrary ascription of authorship within the respective colophons. But, as I pointed out in my earlier work, even these colophons do not explicitly name Paul as the author; Pauline authorship is merely assumed in the absence of any other identified author. Of all the Pauline epistles, aside from Galatians, the Thessalonian epistles have the greatest chance of being genuinely Pauline, in my view. But this is not to say that they necessarily are genuine. I pointed out in my earlier work how the Thessalonian epistles seem to betray a carnal conception of the resurrection, which is contrary to what we find elsewhere within the Pauline corpus. This may or may not indicate genuine Pauline authorship; those texts might still be pseudonymous productions that are deviant from typical Pauline eschatology. But they were close enough in other respects to Pauline orthodoxy to be accorded canonical status. But this feature of the *Thessalonians* hints at a commonality with the texts of Luke and John, which makes me suspect that, rather than being very early letters, these epistles may be among the latest, almost in the neighborhood of the Pastorals. Notably, Elaine Pagels, in her work, *The Gnostic Paul*,[178] does not discuss the Thessalonian epistles or the pastoral epistles, since apparently these works were neglected by most of the Gnostics. They were included in the Canon of Marcion, however. Pagels' work is particularly illuminating, and I found it to be

---

[177] Acts 22:3.

[178] Pagels, Elaine., *THE GNOSTIC PAUL*. (© 1975 by Elaine Pagels); Trinity Press International 3725 Chestnut Street, Philadelphia, PENNSYLVANIA 19104. ISBN: 1-56338-039-0.

one of the most lucid treatments on the subject of Gnosticism.[179] But unlike the implication of the book's title, the work does not claim that Paul himself was necessarily a Gnostic.[180] Instead the book focuses on Gnostic interpretations of key Pauline epistles.[181]

According to the respective colophons, the various Pauline epistles were written by the following authors: Romans was written by Phoebe, a woman; 1 Corinthians was written by Stephanas, Fortunatus, Achaicus, and Timotheus; 2 Corinthians was written by Titus and Lukas; Ephesians was written by Tychicus; Philippians was written by Epaphroditus; Colossians was written by Tychicus and Onesimus; Philemon was written by Onesimus; Hebrews was written by Timothy. 1 Peter was written by Silvanus.[182] Then again Silvanus is mentioned as a co-author of each of the Thessalonian epistles,[183] together with Timotheus, so perhaps the mystery of the authorship of Thessalonians is solved. Or not. Timotheus is also listed as one of the writers of 1 Corinthians, which clearly teaches a spiritual resurrection, in stark contrast to the teaching of the Thessalonian epistles. Furthermore Tertius claims to have written Romans.[184] But to me this only serves to prove that Phoebe really is the true author of Romans, rather than Paul. Tertius was merely the secretary.[185] Silvanus can be tentatively identified as the author of the Thessalonian epistles, in the absence of any other name. Some may object to my analysis on the basis of the fact that the men (and woman) named in the colophons are also otherwise mentioned in the Pauline epistles, and/or the book of Acts. On this basis it may be urged that said epistles are at least tacitly genuine, if not absolutely authentic. But this is not necessarily the case. It is possible that the narrative of Acts was constructed around the genuine names of the writers of the epistles; those who are otherwise to be identified as members of the Pauline faction. It cannot be proven with certainty whether the book of Acts

---

[179] I would highly recommend all her works.

[180] Which was the impression I had, until I actually read her book.

[181] I.e., Romans, 1 Corinthians, 2 Corinthians, Galatians, Ephesians, Philippians, Colossians, and Hebrews.

[182] 1 Peter 5:12.

[183] 1 Thessalonians 1:1; 2 Thessalonians 1:1.

[184] Romans 16:22.

[185] How's that for a switch?

or the Pauline corpus[186] was written first. However I will add to the arguments made in my earlier work the fact that none of the famous epistles of Paul are mentioned anywhere in the text of Acts. This fact in itself seems to imply that the book of Acts actually predates the Pauline corpus, or even any portion thereof, as I speculated in my earlier work. Of course if Paul had been merely an invented character, as I postulated therein, then he would have to have first been "introduced" to the reader through the book of Acts; after this, then the character of Paul could then have been used as the basis for pseudonymous texts promoting the new, sectarian interpretation of soteriology advocated by the Pauline faction. However if Paul really existed as a historical person then this changes the equation dramatically. In strictly literary terms, it does seem much easier to imagine the book of Acts as predating the Pauline corpus, since it would have been comparatively easier to use the single text of Acts as a sort of "springboard" and pseudo-historical context from which to write the various epistles attributed to the legendary figure. By contrast, it would have been much more difficult to take the Pauline corpus, or some core thereof, and from that to construct a pseudo-historical narrative surrounding the same legendary character. But the vast majority of biblical scholars, both critical and conservative, hold the Pauline corpus as primordial in relationship to Acts. Interestingly, the respective colophons in the various epistles starkly yet implicitly outline a historical framework; this may have been of some help to the author of Acts, assuming Acts postdates the Pauline corpus. Of course it is uncertain whether or not the implicit historical outline is in any way accurate, even assuming Paul's historicity. But if Paul was a genuinely historic figure, then it is at least possible that the outline is accurate. One interesting thing I have noticed is that in the various Pauline epistles, the person (or one of the persons, as the case may be) mentioned in the colophon as the author (or one of the authors) is "sent" by Paul to the church in question. For example, Phoebe is sent to the Romans,[187] Tychicus is sent to the Colossians[188] and the

---

[186]   In whole or in part.

[187]   Romans 16:1–2.

[188]   Colossians 4:7.

Ephesians,[189] Timothy is sent to the Corinthians[190] and the Hebrews, Titus is sent to the Corinthians,[191] Epaphroditus is sent to the Philippians,[192] Onesimus is sent to Philemon.[193] Of course one could take the position that these are merely literary artefacts, and do not necessarily bear any relationship to historical reality, being merely part of the implicit pseudo-historical timeline supposed. But one could take the opposing view, and suppose that these various people approached the respective churches with epistles which they themselves wrote, but which, having been ascripted to the legendary apostle Paul, had a much greater impact upon the impressionable sheep, who would much more readily submit to the teachings that supposedly emanated from such a legendary figure. Of course this view is not also without certain historical problems; it presupposes, for example, that these texts were either written within the lifetime of the apostle Paul, or shortly thereafter. But this does not seem to be an insurmountable problem. And I must admit that this view seems somewhat more attractive to me now. It seems more dynamic.

The persons mentioned within the respective colophons all had Greek names, which, while it implies that they were Greek, may simply point to Hellenistic Jews, in some cases. But in my former work I pointed out how certain passages from within the Pauline corpus betrayed Gentile authorship, which I interpreted as evidence of pseudonymous authorship. I still think that this is a more economical explanation than the supposition that Paul lied about his ethnic status.

But now that these preliminary points have been discussed, we should move on to a discussion of the use of Gnostic nomenclature within the Pauline corpus. One of the difficulties involved has to do with the fact that Gnostic literature uses common Greek words to denote highly specific concepts within a Gnostic framework of thought, and hence there must be some degree of distinction between an otherwise ordinary usage of common Greek words, into which Gnostics could read by *eisegesis* whatever esoteric Gnostic dogma they

---

[189]   Ephesians 6:21.

[190]   1 Corinthians 4:17; 16:10; Hebrews 13:23.

[191]   2 Corinthians 8:23; 12:18.

[192]   Philippians 2:25. It is uncertain whether this is the same as Epaphras; Col 1:7; 4:12.

[193]   Philemon 10-12.

chose to see there, and an implicit reference to the Gnostic denotations to such words by way of usage. But first we also need to explore, at least to a rudimentary degree, the Gnostic *mythos*. This *mythos* was not shared by Marcion, whose severance of Christianity from Judaism was much more simple and straightforward.

Our study shall now take on some interesting philological implications. Because the Gnostic *mythos,* which I here treat of only in the merest skeletal terms, impinges upon the Greek genders of certain Greek words. We will find the very same phenomenon in Hebrew as well. For example, the Greek word for wisdom is *Sophia.* We all know that Sophia is a woman's name, and therefore the Greek gender is feminine. In Gnosticism, as also in the Kabbalah and Jewish wisdom literature, Wisdom is personified as female, since the Hebrew *chokmah* is also feminine. Furthermore on the Kabbalistic Tree of Life, *Chokmah* is second only to *Kether,* the Crown. But according to the Gnostic *mythos,* the Supreme Father emanated many other beings from himself, beings known as *aeons.* The same Greek word, however, also means *ages* or *worlds.* The *aeons* of Gnosticism were spawned in successive generations, each one less spiritual and exalted than the preceding. Finally one of these *aeons,* being spiritually blinded, proclaimed himself the supreme power in ignorance, and created (or formed) matter into the *cosmos.* But this being, the demiurge, otherwise also known as Ialdabaoth, or by other names, was reproved by a higher being, namely Sophia, one of the higher emanations. Ialdabaoth was identified by the Gnostics with the God of the Old Testament. He was also called *Samael.* Some systems of Gnosticism posited a son of Ialdabaoth, namely *Sabaoth,* who is venerated in some Gnostic systems, notably that of the Ophites and Naasenes. But Sophia herself fell from grace, either because she desired to glimpse the invisible glory of the Supreme Father, or because she sought to create without her spiritual consort. In either case Sophia fell down through the aeons, into the densest matter, from which she must be delivered. In the Gnosticism of Simon Magus his companion Helena was supposed to be the incarnation and personification of Sophia, and also the reincarnation of Helen of Troy. The dilemma of souls or rather spirits who have fallen into matter is that only knowledge of spiritual reality will free them from the bonds of matter. Samael and his angels are the real rulers, the *archonton* of Gnosticism. They are the ones who supposedly keep souls or spirits bound to matter.

There is definitely more than a tinge of Kabbalism in Gnosticism. The four worlds of the Kabbalists correspond to the *pneumatic, noetic, psychic,* and *somatic* aspects of existence, in "descending" order. So the Kabbalistic paradigm also shared an outlook similar to that of some Greek philosophers. The same fourfold system of symbolic attribution is commonly found in the Western mystery tradition.

Wisdom is a key word within the Pauline corpus. It occurs no less than 29 times. Therefore we need to question whether, when the word occurs within that corpus, is it being used merely as an ordinary Greek word, or in such a way that lends distinctively Gnostic connotations to the term. We also have to ask the same of other such terms, as fullness,[194] perfect,[195] mystery,[196] rulers,[197] and abortion.[198] Somewhat of a case may be made for distinctively Gnostic usage of such terms within the Pauline corpus, but the strongest example comes from a passage in first Corinthians. Paul refers to himself in the passage, the context of which is his claim to have seen the risen Jesus, as to "the abortion". Some English translations (or perhaps most of them) have "an abortion"[199] But the presence of the Greek article is what makes all the difference here. It transforms an otherwise innocuous reading into something suggestive of an explicitly Gnostic reference. Indeed, this is the only thing in the entire Pauline corpus that I could find to "nail down" any hard evidence of genuine use of Gnostic nomenclature within the Pauline corpus. This may sound disappointing to some, but in a sense it is a very real victory. All other examples one could give could ultimately be interpreted as merely within an Enochian tradition of Judaism, with the many fallen angels, and evil spirits being the so-called "rulers" of spiritual wickedness in the heavenly regions, Mastema being the lord among them.[200] But this reference to Christ showing himself to Paul as "to <u>the</u> abortion" implies reference to an entity also otherwise spoken of in Gnosticism, namely "the

---

[194] Greek *pleroma.*

[195] Greek *teleios.*

[196] Greek *mysterion.*

[197] Greek *archonton.*

[198] Greek *ektromati.*

[199] The King James has the more modest but misleading "one born out of due time".

[200] Mastema is the name for Satan in the book of Jubilees.

abortion". Some take this as an alternate description of Ialdabaoth. The term was also used by the Mandaeans. The reference may be to when Ialdabaoth became aware of those beings higher in station than himself, and he glimpsed some of the luminous light from above. In any case it is highly suggestive for the men who wrote the epistle to have used such a strange term, unless it had specific reference to this very teaching.[201] Mead pointed out the distinction of this term with the Greek article.[202] According to Mead, the term "the abortion" refers to "the crude matter cast out of the Pleroma"[203] which chaotic matter was then shaped into the *cosmos* by the *Logos*.[204]

We read also in Ephesians of "the ruler[205] of the power[206] of the air"[207] which presumably refers to Satan; and towards the end of the epistle Tychicus writes "For we wrestle not against flesh and blood, but against the rulers,[208] against the powers,[209] against the overlords[210] of the darkness[211] of this world[212]"[213] which the uninitiated reader could assume refers to the host of fallen angels. But the passage is also prone to a Gnostic *exegesis* as well. An interesting variant reading occurs in the Syriac Peshitta text; therein it reads "For we wrestle not only against flesh and blood, but also against ...", which also implies a less pacifist attitude to what we read in the common Greek text.

---

[201] The key point to this discussion is the presence of the Greek article, which requires a reading of "the abortion"; the translation "an abortion" is both false and misleading. It was not as "to an abortion", as some might read the text, but rather as "to the abortion", denoting something definite but unspecified in the context of first Corinthians.

[202] Mead., op. cit., pgs. 354-355.

[203] Ibid., pg. 355.

[204] Ibid.

[205] Greek *archonta*. Nestle-Aland., op. cit., pg. 505.

[206] Greek *exousias*. Ibid.

[207] Ephesians 2:2.

[208] Greek *archas*. Nestle-Aland., op. cit., pg. 513.

[209] Greek *exousias*. Ibid., pgs. 513-514.

[210] Greek *kosmokratoras*. Ibid., pg. 514.

[211] Greek *skotous*. Ibid.

[212] Greek *aionas*. Ibid. See apparatus.

[213] Ephesians 6:12.

It is virtually impossible to be certain that the Pauline faction wrote their texts with a deliberate Gnostic interpretation, either explicitly or implicitly, since most likely, Polycarp and/or others edited the texts so thoroughly that any hint of such is virtually nonexistent. But even Polycarp did not erase the strange reference to "the abortion" in 1 Corinthians 15:8. This could hardly have been because he did not understand the Gnostic implications of the term. But if we assume that Polycarp is the true author of the pastoral epistles, then by ascribing such works to Paul, Polycarp was able to create an anti-Gnostic filter of interpretation as applied to the Pauline corpus, once those Pastorals became widely accepted as genuine.

Elaine Pagels pointed out that the Gnostics did not use historic but rather doctrinal criteria to determine the "genuine" Pauline corpus. And while this may be true as far as it goes, the very fact that the Pastorals were not even mentioned by the Gnostics, not even to point out their spurious character, serves to identify them as later productions; in a way, the preference of the Gnostics for certain Pauline epistles functions as a form of evidence in favor of a relatively earlier dating for those texts.[214]

It is worth pointing out, however, in the interest of full disclosure, that Marcion himself included the two Thessalonian epistles in his corpus, as well as Philemon, but excluded the book of Hebrews. We also read in Ephesians that the gospel had been a hidden mystery until the time Christ came in the flesh, and that through this mystery "now the rulers[215] and powers[216] in the heavenlies might be known

---

[214] Romans, 1 Corinthians, 2 Corinthians, Galatians, Ephesians, Philippians, Colossians, Hebrews. Notably the Thessalonian epistles are absent, together with the Pastorals. As I pointed out earlier, the Thessalonians (written by Silvanus) may have been almost as late as the Pastorals. Silvanus also wrote first Peter (1 Peter 5:12). By default I regard Silvanus as the author of 2 Peter as well. Both Petrine epistles, as well as both of the Thessalonian epistles, deal with eschatology. All four epistles also seem to be efforts at harmonization of the different factions or teachings. There is also a text from Nag Hammadi called the Teaching of Silvanus, which is at least quasi-Gnostic, and also within the Jewish wisdom literature tradition.

[215] Greek *archais*. Nestle-Aland., op. cit., pg. 507.

[216] Greek *exousiais*. Ibid.

through the church the manifold wisdom[217] of God"[218] but this is nowhere hinted at anywhere in the Gospels. Why would fallen angels be impressed with the whole mystery of Christ? Is it even proper to think of fallen angels as being "in the heavenlies"? Of course Job 1:6 speaks of Satan joining with the sons of God, but even in the text of Job, when God asks Satan where he had been, Satan answered that he had been "going to and fro in the earth, and walking up and down in it."[219] This is no heavenly sojourn for the devil. Therefore when we read of these rulers and powers in the heavenlies, the overlords of the world of darkness, and such expressions, the implication is that this is a reference to something other than your standard contingent of fallen angels.

We find similar language used in some of the other epistles as well. In Colossians we read that Christ "spoiled rulers[220] and powers,[221] having made a public spectacle of them, triumphing over them in it (the cross)."[222] The context of the verse is a diatribe against the Torah, which is characterized by Tychicus and Onesimus as "the handwriting of ordinances that was against us, and that was contrary to us", which Christ took out of the way, by "nailing it to his cross"[223] and that this is all the rationale for believers no longer to be subject to any dietary restrictions, or the observance of any religious holy days, or of the Sabbath, because such things were merely "a shadow of things to come; but the body is of Christ."[224] So the context seems to be Gnostic, and also anti-Ebionite, and also anti-Judaic, or at least anti-Torah. But this once more brings to mind an association of angels with the institution of the law, spoken of briefly earlier.[225] We read the very same thing in Hebrews; for therein we read "For if the word spoken by angels was steadfast, and every transgression and disobedience received

---

[217] Greek *sophia*. Ibid.

[218] Ephesians 3:10.

[219] Job 1:7.

[220] Greek *archas*. Nestle-Aland., op. cit., pg. 527.

[221] Greek *exousias*. Ibid.

[222] Colossians 2:15.

[223] Colossians 2:14.

[224] Colossians 2:16-17.

[225] Cf Galatians 3:19 & Acts 7:53.

a just recompense of reward, how shall we escape, if we neglect so great a salvation?"[226] The implication is that God had nothing to do with the giving of the law; it was instead instituted by angels, according to these texts.[227] Of course this is in stark contrast with what we read in Exodus and the rest of the Torah, but this is only to be expected. But these things seem to be strangely invisible to the majority of Christians, who blithely ignore these passages of the New Testament, that clearly point to some major divergences between the Old and New Testaments. It seems highly significant that the reference to the law having been instituted by angels in Stephen's speech in Acts was left intact. None of these things are clearly explained anywhere in the New Testament itself. That only proves that there was some additional teaching given, which *would* presumably explain such things. Such an esotericism, whether originally Kabbalistic, or related to the teachings of some unknown mystery school, lent itself by default, if not by intent, to Gnostic interpretations.

Some conservative biblical scholars say that the use of Gnostic nomenclature within the Pauline corpus was merely Paul's ironic method of using such terminology against the Gnostics. But this seems to be a begging of the question, and an example of special pleading to boot. If so, why then do we not have a much more explicit refutation and repudiation of Gnosticism within the Pauline corpus?[228]

Elaine Pagels wrote[229] that Gnostics interpreted Paul's epistles as written on two levels: one level for the *psychics,* and another level for the *pneumatics.* The *pneumatics* were the *spirituals,* i.e., the elect, who were chosen in Christ before the foundation of the world.[230] The Gnostics naturally claimed to be this spiritual elite, while the deluded *psychics* were just sheep, like little children. But much of the Pauline corpus lends itself to just such an esoteric interpretation.

"However we speak wisdom among the perfect; yet not the wisdom of this world, nor of the rulers of this world, that are perishing; but we speak the wisdom of God hidden in a mystery,

---

[226] Hebrews 2:2–3a.

[227] Fallen angels, by Gnostic *exegesis;* or rather, those lesser emanations who formed the world and rule over it in darkness and ignorance.

[228] For obvious reasons the Pastorals would be excluded from consideration.

[229] Pagels., op. cit.

[230] Ephesians 1:4 cf Revelation 13:8; John 6:44,65.

which God ordained before the world for our glory; which none of the rulers of this world knew: for had they known, they would not have crucified the Lord of glory."[231]

Who are these "perfect" ones, spoken of in this passage? Those initiated into the true mysteries? The Cathars had an order called the perfect, the *Parfait*. Within the Pauline corpus there is a distinction made between "babes in Christ" who need "milk", and those who are more mature, and can be given the "strong meat".[232] Could it be that the real "strong meat" was that the Old Testament God was a false God, a mere demiurge, and not the Supreme Father and Lord of Jesus Christ? What else are we to infer from the relevant evidence? Those same angels who instituted the law,[233] are no doubt the very same rulers and powers whom Christ spoiled on the cross, triumphing over them openly through it, having made a "public spectacle" of them.[234] As a direct result of this, believers are to disallow anyone to judge them on account of dietary restrictions, or the observance of a new moon, a holy day, or of the Sabbath.[235] Further on in the same passage we read "Let no man beguile you of your reward in a voluntary humility and worship of the angels, intruding into those things he has not seen, being vainglorious in his carnal mind"[236] which strikes me as a characterization of Judaism, and specifically Ebionism. In other words, the God of the Jews was really only an angel; not the true God, according to this teaching.

By contrast we have a much different attitude expressed in some of the non-Pauline, non-Johannine epistles. The starkest contrast can be found in the Epistle of Judas, and also in 2 Peter. Judas, more commonly known as Jude, strongly rebukes the irreverent attitude towards angels expressed in the Pauline corpus:

---

[231] 1 Corinthians 2:6-8.

[232] 1 Corinthians 3:2; Hebrews 5:12-13. Cp 1 Peter 2:2: "As newborn babes, desire the sincere milk of the word, that you may grow thereby". Nothing too meaty in Peter.

[233] Acts 7:53; Galatians 3:19 cf Hebrews 2:2.

[234] Colossians 2:15. The "public spectacle" seems to refer to the spiritual realm, in which these entities were defeated by Christ's passion, according to Pauline eschatology.

[235] Colossians 2:16-17.

[236] Colossians 2:18.

"Likewise these dreamers defile the flesh, despise dominion, and speak evil of dignities. Yet *even* Michael the archangel, when disputing with the devil about the body of Moses, dared not to bring against *even* him a railing accusation, but *only* said, the Lord rebuke thee."[237]

The reference to this controversy between the devil and the archangel Michael must have been part of a lost oral tradition; some scholars speculate that there may have been a written form of the story, somewhere in the lost portions of the Old Testament Pseudepigrapha. Usually the Assumption of Moses is assumed to be the text that originally contained this story. But in any case, the point of what Jude is saying here is that even the exalted archangel Michael did not rail against the despicable devil, but only said "the Lord rebuke thee", giving believers an example to respect the superior station even of fallen angels.[238] The context of Judas is one in which he himself rails against certain "licentious" teachers who have sought to "pervert" the faith "once and for all delivered unto the saints". It is not too much of a stretch to say that Judas was talking about the Pauline school, who seemed to disrespect angels. There is at least a contrast between what we read in Colossians and what we read here in Judas. And second Peter also echoes the same sentiments found in Judas. The passage from 2 Peter is as follows:

"The Lord knows how to deliver the godly from temptation, but to reserve the unjust till the day of judgment to be punished; but chiefly them that walk according to the flesh in the lust of uncleanness, and despise government. Presumptuous, self-willed, they are not afraid to speak evil of dignities. Whereas angels, which are *far* greater in power and might, bring not railing accusation against them before the Lord."[239]

Once again we see a completely different and opposing attitude towards angels in the two distinct corpii. Peter and Judas [Jude] both strenuously disagree with the Pauline attitude towards angels. I suppose it is equally possible that Colossians was written against 2 Peter and Jude as to suppose that Peter and Jude wrote in response to Paul.[240] It is uncertain whether 2 Peter was based upon the epistle of

---

[237] Judas 8-9.

[238] Of course one never hears sermons on such texts.

[239] 2 Peter 2:9-10.

[240] I am here speaking of authorship in a general, rather than specific, sense.

Judas, or vice-versa, but most critical biblical scholars believe Judas predates 2 Peter. However one of the chief reasons given I feel is dead wrong. Supposedly the author of 2 Peter sought to "correct" the implicit Canon of Scripture of Judas, since that short epistle quotes from the Book of Enoch, and also refers to the story of Michael disputing with the devil over Moses' body. But such scholars have completely overlooked the fact that both Petrine epistles are very Enochian in character, and furthermore we would have a right to expect a much more explicit "refutation" of any misguided Canon of Scripture implied in the epistle of Judas.[241] For all we know to the contrary, it is just as likely that Judas is an *epitome* of 2 Peter as that 2 Peter is an expansion upon Judas. However there is one other consideration that does make me suspect that second Peter really does postdate the epistle of Judas; in the latter epistle Judas raves against certain persons who are unnamed, but presumably we can infer that the Pauline faction was meant. By contrast, in 2 Peter we have a blatant attempt to co-opt the Pauline corpus into a Petrine dialectic which subsumes also the earlier, Ebionite traditions as found in Judas and James. This appears to be a slightly later stage of orthodoxy, or what soon became such. In other words, the inference is that, to cast aside the Pauline corpus, and to disassociate completely from the Pauline school and their disciples, would be too costly; there were simply too many people who were followers of the Pauline and Johannine schools, compared with the *Ebionim*. Both of the Petrine epistles actually seem to be efforts at harmonization, but this is especially the case with 2 Peter. Therefore it seems more probable that Judas predates 2 Peter. In fact, the very same argument can also be applied to Judas to come up with the same result: had second Peter been written first, then we would have expected a much more explicit refutation of the Pauline school in Judas, and it would have been unlikely that Judas would have modeled his epistle on one

---

Tychicus and Onesimus wrote Colossians, while Judas was probably the author of his own epistle; 2 Peter being the work either of Silvanus, or some unknown scribe of the Petrine school.

[241] Judas. Obviously not Judas Iscariot. Judas is more commonly known simply as Jude, but in the original Greek of the New Testament, the name *Ioudas* (*pronounced YOU-das*) appears in the text. The name was shortened to Jude in English translations to avoid association with Judas Iscariot. But I think we're all big enough to put such niceties aside once and for all.

that accommodated his enemies. In other words, to claim that Judas "silently corrected" Peter is as absurd as to claim that Peter "silently corrected" Judas. To claim such "silent corrections" is to assume too much. The very same principle also applies to the same assumptions applied to the three Synoptic Gospels. Arguments to the effect that Matthew and Luke "silently corrected" Mark are weak and are no better than counterarguments that refute them.

Galatians is unquestionably the boldest of the Pauline epistles. Marcion has been suggested as the author.[242] Without knowing precisely what Van Manen's arguments were for his position, I cannot judge the merits of such an ascription. However Marcion seems unlikely to me; he was too honest a man. It is tempting to posit that Galatians was written as an open rebuke to 2 Peter 3:14-16. At least this seems easier to believe than the contrary assumption, namely that the author of 2 Peter boldly subsumed and co-opted even the virulently anti-Petrine diatribe of Galatians 2:1-11. Of course the editing of Polycarp, together with his own forged Pauline epistles, was sufficient to create a bogus New Testament "orthodoxy" by which we are given to understand, that, although the apostles and early disciples may have had their own petty squabbles, they all finally got along and proclaimed the same gospel message after all. It is like a tale told to children at holiday seasons.

Admittedly a later date for Galatians is also cordial to Marcionite authorship. Once again I do not know but in the absence of any definite name I will tentatively speculate that Silvanus wrote Galatians. It certainly wasn't Phoebe, who was very conciliatory in Romans. Romans also sought to harmonize the Ebionite and Pauline factions, or to at least offer the olive branch of ecumenical peace.[243] Robert Eisenman has rightly pointed out that the one called "weak in the faith" who eats only "herbs" in Romans 14:1-2 is almost certainly James the Just, the brother of Jesus Christ. No doubt it was a gratuitous barb at James, but this serves as yet another item of evidence in favor of the thesis that James was an Ebionite.[244] A strictly vegetarian diet is pre-Noachian in character;[245] but this ought not to

---

[242] By C.W. van Manen.

[243] Romans 14.

[244] An important point in my earlier work.

[245] Cf Genesis 9:1-4.

be too surprising, considering the veneration the patriarch Enoch was accorded by the *Ebionim*. Phoebe, as a liberated woman of the first century, did not share the dietary scruples of the *Ebionim,* nor the otherwise strict observance of the Torah.[246] Likewise first Corinthians 8 takes a rather cosmopolitan attitude towards cuisine; it is only those who are "weak" who create a problem by their superstitious taboo against food offered to idols.[247] But in the *Apokalypse* we are back to the legalistic, condemnatory attitude towards food offered to idols, expressed by none other than the risen Jesus himself.[248] The risen Christ also condemns the deeds and doctrines of the Nicolaitans,[249] whom I strongly suspect are the partisans of the Johannine school. In my earlier work I wrote that I thought that the reference to "that woman Jezebel" was a code, since it seemed unlikely that any woman would pretend to be a prophetess, and call herself by the name of such an infamous woman in the Jewish Scriptures. But now I'm not so sure. Some Gnostics radically reversed things found in the Jewish Scriptures, and those cast in the role of villains are heroes in some schools of Gnosticism.[250] But there is also something else noteworthy about Revelation. In Revelation 21:14, we have the gratuitous anti-Paulinism of the reference to "the names of the twelve Apostles of the Lamb." Obviously this harks back to the original twelve chosen by Jesus, minus the traitor Judas Iscariot, who was replaced by Matthias. Paul, even if he is an apostle in some expanded sense of the term, is not in their class, who are thereby eternally exalted, since their very names are inscribed on the twelve foundations of the eternal city of the New Jerusalem. What is Paul compared to that? But it gets worse for Paul and his faction: earlier on, the risen Jesus says to the Ephesians: "I know thy works, and thy labor, and thy patience, and how thou canst not bear them that are evil: and thou hast tried them

---

[246]   Cf Romans 10:4.

[247]   This attitude is at least more in accord with common sense ideas about such questions, particularly in the postmodern world. The same would also be true of Greco-Roman society. As such, it is easy to see why these attitudes supplanted the overscrupulous attitudes of the Ebionites.

[248]   Revelation 2:14,20.

[249]   Revelation 2:6,15.

[250]   Notably that of the Cainites.

that say they are apostles, and are not, and hast found them liars"[251] which, coupled with Revelation 21:14, seems to entirely exclude Paul and his school from genuine apostleship. Revelation is in accord with the Synoptic soteriology, as opposed to the Pauline-Johannine soteriology. But the use of the name John was probably a deliberate attempt to co-opt the Johannine legacy, subsuming it into a works-based salvation scheme, just as 2 Peter was a shameless attempt to co-opt the Pauline corpus, and Polycarp also sought to reinvent Paul by way of forgery. Once again we have a discussion of food offered to idols in 1 Corinthians 10:25-32. The true believer is exempt from any such dietary restrictions, but the men who wrote the epistle urge caution for the sake of the fragile consciences of those who are less informed. Such flouting of the Torah would not do for the *Ebionim*. Hence the *Apokalypse*.

At the very least we see unmistakable signs of an esotericism within the Pauline corpus. This esotericism may have been influenced by Platonism, Kabbalism,[252] and possibly Gnosticism, as well as the writings of Philo. It is well documented that many Gnostics eagerly embraced the Pauline corpus,[253] Paul being the favorite apostle of the Gnostics. From this we can at least safely assume that the Pauline corpus was more congenial to Gnostic *exegesis*.

Epaphroditus wrote that there were "saints"[254] in Caesar's household.[255] This at least evokes an image of prestige for the early messianic movement, or at least for the Pauline school thereof. It is too easy to dismiss as propaganda; more likely it hints at a pro-Roman agenda within the Pauline corpus. Of course Romans 13:1-7 is an obvious example of gratuitously pacifying the Romans preemptively by inculcating the payment of tribute, etc. That at least insured the survival of the epistle, and possibly of the entire corpus, by extension. The Founding Fathers knew better than to put too much stock in

---

[251] Revelation 2:2.

[252] Albeit the Greek Kabbalah.

[253] I.e., the pre-Polycarp Pauline corpus; Romans, 1 Corinthians, 2 Corinthians, Galatians, Ephesians, Colossians, Philippians, Hebrews.

[254] I.e., believers.

[255] Philippians 4:22. It is uncertain whether this reference is merely to servants, or family. If the latter, this puts a dramatic spin on Nero's persecution of Christians.

it. Before closing this chapter it may be worth pointing out at least one more example of a possible link between the Pauline corpus and Gnosticism, and even Docetism. In the original Greek, there are no less than four instances, in the second chapter of Galatians, where the Greek root-word from which the term Docetism is derived occur.[256] The respective Greek words are *dokousi, dokounton,* and *dokountes.* The author of Galatians is speaking of those who "seemed" to be pillars of the church. While most conservative biblical scholars would likely maintain that this is merely an innocuous use of an ordinary Greek word, which it might very well be, it is at least worth pointing out, in relation to what has just been presented, as possible further evidence of a Pauline link to both Gnosticism and Docetism.

---

[256] Green, Jay P., Sr. (ed., trans.), The Interlinear Greek-English NEW TESTAMENT. © 1985 Jay P. Green, Sr. Hendrickson Publishers., pg. 509. Galatians 2:2,6,9.

The Diatessaron

The Diatessaron was a Gospel harmony written in the latter half of the second century by Tatian, a student of Justin Martyr. *Diatessaron* is Greek and literally means "Through the Four" and so is a synopsis of the four Canonical Gospels. Actually the Diatessaron contains almost all of the text of the four Canonicals, except for the two royal genealogies, and the story of the woman taken in adultery in John 8. Because Tatian was an Assyrian, scholars are uncertain whether or not the Diatessaron was first written in Greek or Syriac. The preponderance of evidence suggests that, despite the Greek title, it was originally written in Syriac. It became very popular in the East, being the standard Gospel text of the Syrian Orthodox Church until it was finally supplanted by the Syriac Peshitta text in the fifth century. I briefly discussed the Diatessaron in my earlier work, but I fear that I may have overestimated its importance, so I wanted to clarify my position here, or rather to correct what I had written earlier. The Diatessaron was composed sometime between 160 and 175 C.E., and therefore the implication is that only the four Canonical Gospels were extant at that time, or so I thought when I wrote *JESUS 100 B.C.* However this is not necessarily the case; as I pointed out in an earlier section, there were probably at least seven distinctly different Gospel texts in circulation by the time Luke began writing his Gospel. It is certainly worth questioning why Tatian used only the four Gospels that later attained Canonicity, but we need to be cautious not to be guilty of the anachronism of supposing that the four Canonicals had already achieved a unique status by the time of Tatian.[257] In other words, I am urging caution in the interpretation of the evidence. The Diatessaron is an important part of the evidence, and it deserves to be mentioned more often; however I do not want to oversimplify the situation. In my earlier work I took the position that, since the Diatessaron was written so early, it precluded the prestige, if not the very existence, of any Gospels other than the four canonical texts in the latter half of the second century. But then what are we to make of Luke 1:1? And what of the various Jewish Matthew Gospels, used by the *Ebionim?* Not only that, but the mere existence of the Diatessaron was not an obstacle to the composition of numerous Gospels, both "orthodox" and "heterodox" in orientation. Why would any evangelists have bothered with any such enterprise, if all other gospels had thus become superfluous? The Diatessaron may serve as evidence that the four familiar Gospels were the most commonly used and known, that they may have been the most prestigious, and possibly among the oldest, but it did not shut the door to further writing of Gospels, at least in Greek and Coptic. But even in Syriac there was a great profusion of religious texts, including Gospels. Were they all considered merely harmless religious fiction? It seems unlikely. So an appeal to the Diatessaron may represent an oversimplification of the actual state of affairs. If not, we would expect Christian apologists to appeal to it more often. But one reason why the *Diatessaron* may be avoided is because Tatian was, according to some accounts, a heretic. Tatian was suspected of being an Encratite. This may be one reason why conservative biblical scholars avoid the example of the Diatessaron as a "proof" of the early Canonicity of the four Canonical Gospels. Another reason may be that such an appeal would be too easily overturned by contrary evidence, known to specialists in the field.

We also might want to consider the Diatessaron as an early form of Christian *apologia,* or apologetics. Already it appears to have been an attempt to bind together in a single codex the four most popular accounts of the life and ministry of Jesus. The very harmonizing rationale behind the text is a tendency of an apologetics

---

[257] On the other hand, if we suppose that Polycarp acted as the editor of the New Testament, then the arrangement of the four most popular Gospels within a single Codex might have functionally secured the Canonicity of such texts for all future generations.

that is all too painfully aware of the discrepancies between the Gospels. Tatian's effort was to minimize or eliminate all such discrepancies. For example, by omitting the two genealogies supplied by Matthew and Luke, Tatian avoided at least one embarrassing contradiction.[258] The same policy was followed throughout the text; by making such an arrangement, Tatian was able to avoid the many embarrassing contradictions between the various Gospel accounts.[259] In fact, one suspects that this was the primary intent behind the writing of the Diatessaron. Another implicit intent may have been the marginalization of those Gospels that had already fallen out of favour with the custodians of "orthodoxy" in the emergent church. This would have especially been the case with those Jewish Gospels ascribed to the Apostle Matthew.

We can thus see the Diatessaron as a link in a chain of self-justifying orthodoxy. An ecclesiastical consensus having been reached on which Gospels are to be most favored, a selection process ensued, with appropriate editing procedures to insure that the new reality would become accepted as the only legitimate reality. Perhaps this is an overly cynical interpretation of events; but there do seem to be aspects of the evidence that lend themselves to such an interpretation. I do not want to be guilty of oversimplifying what was no doubt a fairly complex historical process. In fact I suspect that the sense of "orthodoxy" was internalized on a subconscious level by the clergy involved. For example, most born-again Christians are Trinitarian not because that is what Scripture itself teaches, but because they have been indoctrinated into believing that that is what Scripture teaches, in the original Hebrew and Greek. One can hardly find a text on *Koine* Greek that does not implicitly, more often explicitly, proclaim that the Deity of Christ and the Trinity are inherent to the Greek text of the New Testament, despite the fact that no such thing is true, by any stretch of the imagination. This is a contemporary example of self-justifying orthodoxy. Once one has accepted a certain dogmatic interpretation, one will begin to see it everywhere in the

---

[258] It is also worth briefly noting that these royal genealogies were thus considered easily expendable; a position quite contrary to what our Grail-conditioned populace has been led to believe by numerous pseudo-scholarly treatises.

[259] Contrary to the implications of the term, the Synoptic Gospels contain many embarrassing contradictions between themselves.

text, by a process of *eisegesis*.[260] The very same thing can happen with historical evidence. Once a given theory has been accepted, even a critical one, a person has a tendency to see the postulates of the theory reflected in the available evidence. Whatever doesn't fit the pattern is filtered out, usually subconsciously. We all have a tendency to do this, to some degree. We cannot help it, because it is part of our biological imperative of survival. We need to recognize meaningful patterns because they help us to interpret reality and to survive. So we tend to oversimplify data. Even great, brilliant minds do this, to some degree.[261] So perhaps men like Marcion, Polycarp, Tatian, Ignatius, Irenaeus, Tertullian, Origen, Jerome, Augustine, and so on, oversimplified things a bit. I am not seeking to be an apologist for the apologists; I am merely pointing out the subtleties often overlooked in the historical process. It is impossible to know with certainty the motivations of men who lived so long ago. So my point is that the *Diatessaron* does not preclude the prior existence of Gospels other than the four commonly accepted as Canonical. Neither does it diminish the potential importance of such texts to the communities that used them. But in the case of the Gnostics, this would have been well outside the circle of orthodoxy. The same is equally true of the Ebionites and the Encratites. Perhaps in Syria or Assyria the Diatessaron had a large role in establishing evangelical orthodoxy. To some degree this may have been true throughout the Roman and Byzantine empires as well, but the Diatessaron never supplanted the four canonical Gospels in those regions. Even in Syria the four Canonicals emerged supreme over the Diatessaron from the fifth century on.

---

[260] *Eisegesis*. Greek; reading into the text what is not there.

[261] Although I suppose that, the greater the mind, the more complex the pattern of data it can recognize.

The Anti-Gospels

There was a huge profusion of Gospels, aside from the four most popular Gospels, which eventually became regarded as exclusively Canonical. Many of these Gospels were written to accommodate later notions of orthodoxy, such as the Protevanglion of James, or the Infancy Gospels. Some, like the Gospel of Nicodemus, were written to fill in historical gaps, such as the absence of any genuine Roman records of the trial and crucifixion of Jesus Christ. A number of others were written to promote a specific interpretation of Christ and his teachings, such as the various doctrines of the Gnostics, the Docetists, the Encratites, the Elchesaites, and the Ebionites. As the Christian movement grew, so did those who sought to reinterpret or co-opt the messianic legacy; and in some cases, to oppose the movement by rewriting the history thereof, or making a parody of it. We have so far barely scratched the surface of available texts; we have merely hinted at a huge iceberg underneath the visible unsubmerged "tip" of such texts. We have yet to describe, much less detail, the various texts which could be referred to as "anti-Gospels". These are texts that are so radical in orientation that there really is no better way to characterize them. We shall briefly consider three examples of such texts, although there may be more.

All three texts radically reinterpret Jesus Christ, and the significance of his life and ministry. Even key events in the drama of Christ are rewritten in such a way as to serve the interest of the person or party behind the writing. One of these three texts, the Toldoth Yeshu, I included in my earlier work, together with my notes and commentary, since it was a key part of the evidence that Jesus may have lived a century earlier than the commonly-accepted time. This work repudiates Jesus and denies his messianic status. It is a classic and clear-cut example of an "anti-Gospel". It appears to be a parody, written in imitation of the New Testament Gospels, or at least of the key claims being put forward on Christ's behalf by Christians, and serves to repudiate such claims by way of mockery. As such, it is Jewish propaganda, but it expresses the feelings of Orthodox Rabbis and their disciples.[262] The Toldoth Yeshu still has much to teach us. And while I no longer regard it as providing particularly strong evidence in favor of a first century B.C. date for Jesus, it is still worth examining once again in some detail, since it impinges upon our central thesis herein, in a very important way. As such I reproduce a truncated version of it herein, divested of my notes and commentary.

But there are also two other Gospel texts that we ought to examine. One is the very controversial text of the recently-discovered Gospel of Judas. This is a radical Gnostic text, which portrays Judas Iscariot in a more favorable light than what is found in the New Testament Gospels. Judas is praised by Jesus therein, and said to be secretly blessed, even though his name would be outwardly cursed for ages. The discovery of this text has raised some very important questions about the nature of Christianity, and the precise details surrounding Christ's alleged passion. It is a theological hot potato. Controversy surrounds this text, like flies around a fresh corpse. But the voice of Judas rises up from the sands of the desert, like the voice of the dead from the dust. Or so some would have it. We will see.

Another "anti-Gospel" worth briefly discussing is the Gospel of Barnabas. This text, which was mentioned in certain early Christian texts and decrees, has apparently been reworked into an Islamic form, and therefore holds a special interest for our day and age. Many devout Muslims believe that the text of Barnabas as it has come down to us is the very same as that written by the disciple of the same name. This text functions as a sort of "Old Testament" text in relation to the Koran, inasmuch as therein Jesus foretells the coming of the Prophet

---

[262] At least of mediaeval Rabbis and Jews. Jews today would be considerably more sophisticated, yet would just as strenuously reject the messianic claims made by Christians on behalf of Jesus Christ, their Greek Messiah.

Mohammed, and upholds circumcision as essential for salvation,[263] and generally upholds a form of the gospel message that is cordial to Islam. Of course the vast majority of non-Muslim scholars reject the text as a forgery, either based in part upon the earlier text of Barnabas,[264] or written as a gratuitous exploitation of the reference to such a lost text in the Gelasian decree of forbidden texts.[265]

It will be illuminating to briefly examine these three Anti-Gospels, in order to acquire an appreciation for the great diversity of responses the archetypal figure of Jesus Christ brought forth over time. Such strong reactions were no doubt a response, not so much to the historical Jesus,[266] but rather to the extreme claims put forward by those speaking in his name. So let us proceed without further ado.

---

[263] Shades of Ebionism. This aspect of the text just might be historically accurate.

[264] I.e., the Gospel of Barnabas. This should not be confused with the Epistle of Barnabas, which was

[265] Indeed if there is anything surviving of the original Gospel of Barnabas in the current text of that name, it is impossible to discern from the Islamic overlay. Perhaps an original Ebionite text lay beneath; one in which Jesus affirmed the necessity of circumcision for salvation. Of course this would have been enough to have the book banned (and burned) by the "Catholic" Church.

[266] I.e., assuming that there ever was a historical Jesus as such.

The Gospel of Judas

The Gospel of Judas has aroused as much controversy in recent times as it no doubt did in ancient times as well. A Gospel sympathetic to the despised traitor of the Messiah was no doubt calculated to elicit the most visceral reactions from orthodox Christians; no doubt the anonymous evangelist took secret delight in knowing the vexations and frothing at the mouth of hidebound ecclesiastics his work would evoke. Perhaps it was written by a disillusioned Christian, one who felt betrayed by his faith for some unknown reason. What vengeance he wrought with his time-spanning pen! Of course traditional clergy would characterize the writing of the Gospel of Judas as an act of betrayal akin to that first betrayal by the historical Judas.[267] Others have attained new insights, and have even questioned the historicity of Judas.[268] Students of Gnosticism in particular have been rewarded with yet another gem from the desert sands of Egypt.[269] Antiquarians are naturally fascinated by the text, and the story of its discovery and eventual publication is fascinating in itself.[270]

---

[267] I.e., a Judas whom they are obliged by their faith to esteem as historical.

[268] Notably Robert Eisenman, among others.

[269] Thus the Gospel of Judas supplements the great historic find of Nag Hammadi.

[270] See Krosney, Herbert., *The Lost Gospel.* (© 2006 Krosney Productions, Ltd.)

More recently some have expressed doubts as to the authenticity of the text.[271] Since there have recently been some notorious religious frauds, both archaeological and literary, it is wise to at least approach such controversial texts and discoveries with a note of caution. I suppose one legitimate ground for suspicion is that the Gospel of Judas appears to be a Sethian text, when we would have expected it to be Cainite. Aside from this, the skeptic cites certain philological issues with the Coptic as grounds for suspicion. In any case it is wise to proceed with caution, rather than to construct an elaborate edifice of radical theology upon the controversial text. On the other hand, it seems unlikely that a forger would go to such lengths with no guarantee that his work would attain its desired end. Coptic is much more obscure than *Koine* Greek. The story told of the survival of this text, if it is not complete fiction, belies the work of a forger. What forger with the requisite knowledge of Coptic would have squandered his efforts on a fraud that had so many possible miscarriages? It would have taken almost a miracle to survive. So I provisionally accept the Gospel of Judas as authentic. Others have raised controversy over the accuracy of the initial translation.[272] Aside from these criticisms, there has been a predictable barrage of indignant declamations by furious fundamentalists and outraged evangelicals, frothing at the mouth over the fact that this long-lost Gospel has finally once again seen the light of a better day. The Dark Ages are finally over.[273] Of course the

---

Published by the National Geographic Society. ISBN 1-4262-0041-2.

[271] There are some legitimate objections expressed against the alleged authenticity of the text available at http://www.journal.uts.edu/volume-ix-2008/290-the-gospel-of-judas-is-it-a-hoax.htm. This is not gratuitous fundamentalist ranting but legitimate criticism.

[272] http://www.geneveith.com/the-gospel-of-judas-hoax/ 732/.

[273] Or are they? One must hope so, but with self-professed "Christians" threatening to burn copies of the Koran, one is not so sure. How would Christians feel if Jews threatened to burn copies of the New Testament publicly? And if they truly believe that Jesus was and is the Son of God, and that he also said, as recorded in the Gospel of Matthew "Whatsoever ye would that men should do unto you, that likewise do ye also unto them; for this is the law and the prophets." (Mt 7:12); and also, "Whoever shall smite thee on the right cheek, turn to him the left also." (Mt 5:39), then it behooves them to act accordingly. Furthermore as loyal Americans, they ought not to endanger the lives of American troops or civilians. Another relevant verse is "Blessed are the peacemakers; for they shall be called the

discovery was shamelessly hyped and sensationalized in the media. But such is the nature of capitalism. At least the general public has the right to know of such a discovery, although such a find is likely to be of much greater interest to specialists in the field. But the time is past when such discoveries would be conveniently swept under the rug of academic obscurity, leaving traditional Christianity unscathed. Yet a text like the Gospel of Judas is unlikely to "convert" anyone from traditional Christianity to Gnosticism, or even to agnosticism. But it may serve, in an oblique and parabolic way, to raise certain pertinent issues, such as the relationship between Christianity and Judaism, and also how those two faiths interact and coexist in the postmodern world.

In the wake of the initial fanfare, certain sharply pointed questions have been raised by critical scholars. One of these is whether the figure of Judas Iscariot himself was not merely a convenient fiction, invented to play an unenviable role in a drama of Christ's betrayal and crucifixion.[274] The darker subtext to this speculation is that there was a specifically anti-Semitic intent behind the fabrication; Judas himself being a personification and representation of the Jews as a people, whom the Gospels thus depict as the collective betrayers of Jesus. Robert Eisenman has gone further, and speculated that Judas may represent the *Ebionim,* who are thereby symbolically portrayed as betraying the legacy of Jesus.[275] It must be admitted that this is a reasonably plausible scenario, despite the heavy implications thereof. If Jesus was merely a phantom, then of course Judas himself also was. But even if we accord historicity to Jesus, there is no specific

---

children of God." (Mt 5:9); another is "Blessed are the merciful; for they shall obtain mercy." (Mt 5:7). There are many other appropriate verses scattered throughout the New Testament.

[274] If Jesus Christ himself was merely a *chimera,* then it follows as a matter of course that the twelve Apostles, including Judas Iscariot, were also likewise *chimerical;* however, as I pointed out in my earlier work, in respect to the apostle Paul, so also likewise in the case of Judas Iscariot; Jesus may have been a real, historic person, while Judas was invented to fill the role of traitor. This interpretation is suggested by the fact that in John 13:18, Jesus refers back to the necessity of fulfilled prophecy, quoting from Psalm 41:9. This strongly suggests the possibility that the role of Judas was gratuitously invented, merely as a function to provide a gratuitous "fulfillment" of Scripture prophecy.

[275] See http://www.roberteisenman.com.

logical contingency in place that would *require* the historical existence of Judas Iscariot.[276] In fact, the very fact that several Old Testament prophecies[277] were supposedly directly or indirectly fulfilled by Judas Iscariot, albeit unconsciously and unintentionally, this is an argument *against* his alleged historicity, rather than the reverse. A critical appraisal of the Gospel texts discloses that Judas Iscariot was not necessarily essential to Christ's cruel fate.[278] It certainly heightened the drama, and added a deeper dimension to the story, and also provided gratuitous examples of providentially fulfilled prophecies, but we need not require a Judas Iscariot for Jesus to have sooner or later fallen afoul of the Roman overlords.[279] On the other hand, Herod Antipas may have been a greater threat to Jesus than the Roman procurator.[280] This is not to say that Judas did not exist; merely that he might not have existed. Much is made of the fact that, outside of the Gospels and the book of Acts, Judas Iscariot is not so much as mentioned. But this is not really significant; the epistles and the *Apokalypse* are concerned with other themes. Those who raise the issue of Anti-Semitism within the New Testament, particularly in the figure of Judas Iscariot, are certainly raising a delicate and controversial issue, fraught with emotional dynamics. But they have a right to do so; maybe even a moral obligation to do so, in their own minds. And while I personally

---

[276] As I also noted about the relationship between Jesus and the apostle Paul in my earlier work. Jesus may have been real, while Paul was merely a *chimera;* however if Paul was real, then Jesus also definitely was. So likewise is the case with Judas Iscariot.

[277] Psalm 41:9, referred to in John 13:18; Zechariah 11:10-14, alluded to in Mt 26:14-16 & 27:3-10; Psalms 69:25 & 109:8, referred to in Acts 1:20. There may be others, but these suffice to prove the point.

[278] I.e., assuming that Jesus Christ was crucified, a point as yet unproven herein.

[279] And this would especially be the case if Jesus was really a militant Zadokite, a distinct possibility obscured by later orthodoxy. There is a certain irony in this; for assuming Judas was historical after all, his cognomen *Iscariot* may have been a corruption for the *Sicarius,* meaning a dagger-wielding assassin. Could there be a hint here that, it was Christ's militant associations that ultimately led to his tragic passion?

[280] We will briefly discuss this possibility in another section, when we speak of the Gospel of Peter and literary fossils.

feel that this issue is often exaggerated,[281] I feel out of respect for the persons involved that it ought not to be blithely dismissed. It is too big of a question, and too important a question.

But having said that, there are a few observations I would like to make that alleviate such charges of anti-Semitism in the figure of Judas Iscariot. Robert Eisenman is likely to be scandalized by what I am about to write, but this can't be helped, if he chooses to be hypersensitive about such issues. If he is man enough to make such charges, then he should be man enough to be schooled in counterarguments, without gratuitously lashing out at me, and labeling me as an anti-Semite or latter-day Nazi, simply because I do not agree with all his theories.[282] One of the key points made by Eisenman and other critics alleging this anti-Semitic theory vis-à-vis Judas Iscariot, is that the name Judas is the Greek[283] form of the name Judah, the patriarch of the tribe of Judah, from which we also derive the same root-words as Jude, Jew, and Judaism. As such, Judas is supposed to represent the Jews as a people generically in the text of the Gospels, especially the Gospel of John, which is frequently pointed to as the most anti-Semitic of the four Canonical Gospels.[284] The subtext being that Judas Iscariot the traitor was a personalization of the Jews as a people, who betrayed Jesus to the Romans, who killed him on the cross. The real betrayal in the minds of the Christians was that the Jews (as a people) rejected the messianic claims of Jesus. In any case, the crux of the argument hinges, to a large degree, upon the

---

[281] After all, the New Testament was ostensibly written primarily by Jews, who claimed that Jesus was the Jewish Messiah. And the Old Testament, which they frequently quoted from and venerated as the Word of God, are the Jewish Scriptures; written by Jews, about Jews, and for Jews. As such they believe in the Jewish God, and that Jesus is the Jewish Son of the Jewish God. You can't get much more Jewish than that.

[282] To be fair, Robert Eisenman has suffered abuse from genuine anti-Semites. And I certainly do not want to be equated with such despicable men, who shall remain unnamed herein.

[283] Technically Judas is Latin; Ioudas (pronounced YOU-das) is the Greek form of the name, which is more akin to the Hebrew *Yehudah (Judah)*. But Judas and Judah are the anglicized forms of the name, based upon English transliterations of the respective Greek and Hebrew forms of the same name.

[284] Although the Gospel of Nicodemus is far more anti-Semitic or anti-Jewish.

very name of Judas, rather than his alleged betrayal of Christ. But the problem with this philological argument is the fact that one of the <u>other</u> twelve Apostles is also named Judas.[285] Not only that, but also one of the brothers of Jesus was also named Judas.[286] So here was have two counterexamples to the implied argument based upon the name "Judas"; neither of these other two men[287] betrayed Jesus. So the argument based upon the name of Judas falls to the ground. As such, the charge of anti-Semitism in the case of Judas Iscariot is based on quicksand. If Judas Iscariot had been the only character in the Gospels with that name, then there might be some possible case for the charge of anti-Semitism, however tenuous; but since there are two other men, who are depicted as righteous, noble men worthy of respect and honor, who share that same name, the argument based upon the mere name Judas is proven false. As such, the charges should be withdrawn, with apologies to Christians and other Gentiles. But of course this will never happen; it is merely an example of the constant double-standard in place within the arena of critical biblical scholarship. Christian faith can be gratuitously insulted, mocked, criticized, scandalized, and ripped to shreds, but it is taboo to speak too harshly of Judaism, lest Jews be offended thereby. Christians can be routinely accused of anti-Semitism, both gratuitously and posthumously, but no one dares to charge Jewish critics with an anti-Gentilism, or even anti-Hellenism. But if the Jesus Christ of John's Gospel is merely a ventriloquist-dummy for Anti-Semitism, why then is he quoted as saying "Salvation is from the Jews."?[288] It is time for more honesty in critical scholarship. I am not an Anti-Semite, and I resent any implication that I am, or

---

[285] Judas Alphaeus, the brother of James. Cf Luke 6:16; John 14:22 cp Mark 3:18 & Mt 10:3, where this Judas is called Thaddeus, and Lebbeus, with the surname Thaddeus. This may or may not be the same Judas who wrote the epistle of Judas in the New Testament.

[286] Matthew 13:55; Mark 6:3. This may or may not be the same Judas who wrote the epistle of Judas in the New Testament. See previous note.

[287] And they are two distinct men in the context of the New Testament, notwithstanding Eisenman's efforts to prove that they are one and the same man in his works. The name Judas was very likely a common name in first century Palestine. So was Jesus.

[288] John 4:22. Literally "the salvation"; the one and only.

the implied threat that I might be labeled as such, due to controversial opinions.[289]

One of the corollaries to the charge of anti-Semitism[290] in the New Testament is an implicit pro-Roman bias therein.[291] But even this is exaggerated by the same critics. For example, Luke 13:1 draws attention to the fact that Pilate had brutally slaughtered some Galileans, a fact that the other Evangelists remain silent about. Why, if the New Testament is pervaded by such a ubiquitous pro-Roman bias, would this unsavory item be obtruded to the reader, when Luke could have just as silently passed over the incident without mentioning it at all? This is a definite example of a clear counterargument against the assumption of such a strong pro-Roman bias. Furthermore the entire *Apokalypse* is ridden with anti-Roman imagery throughout. One would have to be blind not to see it for what it is. In fact, first Maccabees is more friendly towards the Romans than anything we find in the New Testament.[292]

But let us now proceed with a closer examination of the Gospel of Judas itself. The text was probably written sometime in the second century. It does not claim to have been written *by* Judas; instead it is a text *about* Judas. As such, it is likely to be somewhat of an anticlimax compared to the many fictional works written about the long-lost Gospel of Judas. I remember years ago I saw a book in the Salem library with the title *The Judas Gospel* and out of curiosity I took it out and read it. I knew that there had been a "Gospel of Judas" back in ancient times, but it had long been lost, probably forever (or so I then thought), so I read the story as the next best thing. In the story, the lost text *was* written by Judas, and it depicted a more natural, believable image of Jesus. Somehow the ancient text is discovered in modern

---

[289] I.e., such as that Jesus might not have been ethnically Jewish, or other controversial views expressed in my works. Neither am I any kind of "National Socialist" or Nazi.

[290] I am not going so far as to say that there is no trace of anti-Semitism in the New Testament; I am merely saying that I feel that this has been exaggerated by some critics.

[291] We have already noted some examples of this, namely Romans 13:1-17, 1 Peter 2:13-17, Titus 3:1, and of course the famous line "Render unto Caesar that which is Caesar's", attributed to Christ in Mt 22:21, Mk 12:17, & Lk 20:25.

[292] Cf 1 Maccabees 8:1-30; 12:1-23; 14:24; 15:15-21.

times, but before it can be published, a Catholic priest is told of the danger if the text ever comes to light, and he is instructed to prevent this from happening. So the plot turns on this theme, predictably enough, with people being murdered by a fanatical priest.[293] But now the long-lost Gospel of Judas has finally been found. Is this the "black sheep" which the Shepherd left the ninety-nine white sheep behind for, in order to seek it out and save it?[294] It is like finding a long-lost brother or sister, only to be disappointed that they are not as perfect as you imagined them to be. So it is with the Gospel of Judas. But it is still priceless.

In the wake of the initial fanfare,[295] we can by now approach the text with greater caution and sobriety. The text is distinctively Gnostic, but this was only to be expected. Some may be disappointed because Jesus does not command Judas to "betray" him, as expected, according to some interpretations of Gnosticism. Of course that would not be a real act of betrayal, but merely a charade. And we would have a right to ask why Jesus would ask Judas to allow the other Apostles to falsely think that he had betrayed Jesus, if that had not been the case. Nevertheless Judas is exonerated, and portrayed in a favorable light. This is chiefly because he alone, of the twelve, has insight into the greater mystery of Jesus, and the spiritual realm. This is why Jesus calls Judas especially blessed.

It is worth commenting that there is a brief passage within the text that lends itself to an Ebionite interpretation; unfortunately the reading is obscure, possibly due to a lacuna in the text. The relevant portion is "Jesus said [to them], "Stop sac[rificing...] which you have [...] over the altar, since they are over your stars and your angels and have already completed their courses there." This is at least faintly

---

[293] Shades of *The Da Vinci Code*. The story also has elements in common with the infamous *Jesus Scroll,* by Donovan Joyce.

[294] Cf Luke 15:4-6.

[295] Aside from Krosney's book, two others were released simultaneously: *The Gospel of Judas*, edited by Rodolphe Kassner, Marvin Meyer, and Gregor Wurst; with additional commentary by Bart D. Ehrman. (© 2006 National Geographic Society); and also *THE SECRETS OF JUDAS,* by James M. Robinson (© James M. Robinson); HarperCollins Publishers, 10 East 53rd Street, New York, NY 10022. There was also a television special on the National Geographic Channel, aired several times. Since then a number of books and articles have been written, as well as gratuitous internet chatter.

reminiscent of the line from MtE, in which Jesus says "I have come to abolish the sacrifices; and if you do not cease from making sacrifice, the wrath of God shall not cease afflicting you." Perhaps the Gospel of Judas was tinged with some Ebionite influence. Of course even if the missing word were supplied after "sacrificing" it would still leave us in the dark, to some degree; suppose the reading were originally "Stop sacrificing *cattle* which you have offered over the altar" would this mean literal cattle, or be a symbol of something else, such as people? Neither do I want to be guilty of an *eisegesis* by insisting upon an Ebionite connotation, when the meaning may be quite unrelated. This instance in the text of Judas is preceded by a vision of priests sacrificing in the temple, who are interpreted to be the Apostles. The relevant section is as follows:

"They [said, "We have seen] a great [house with a large] altar [in it, and] twelve men-they are the priests, we would say-and a name, and a crowd of people is waiting at that altar, [until] the priests [... and receive] the offerings. [But] we kept waiting." [Jesus said], "what are [the priests] like?" They [said, "Some ...] two weeks; [some] sacrifice their own children, others their wives, in praise [and] humility with each other; some sleep with men; some are involved in [slaughter]; some commit a multitude of sins and deeds of lawlessness. And the men who stand [before] the altar invoke your [name], and in all the deeds of their deficiency, the sacrifices are brought to completion [...] After they said this, they were quiet, for they were troubled. Jesus said to them, "Why are you troubled? Truly I say to you, all the priests who stand before that altar invoke my name. Again I say to you, my name has been written on this [...] of the generations of the stars through the human generations. [And they] have planted trees without fruit, in my name, in a shameful manner." Jesus said to them, "Those you have seen receiving the offerings at the altar-that is who you are. That is the god you serve, and you are those twelve men you have seen. The cattle you have seen brought for sacrifice are the many people you lead astray before that altar [...] will stand and make use of my name in this way, and generations of the pious will remain loyal to him. After him another man will stand there from [the fornicators], and another [will] stand there from the slayers of children, and another from those who sleep with men, and those who abstain, and the rest of the people of pollution and lawlessness and error, and those who say, 'We are like angels'; they are the stars that bring everything to its conclusion. For to the human generation it has been said, 'Look, God has received your sacrifice from the hands of a priest'–that is, a minister of error. But it is the Lord, the Lord of the universe, who commands, 'On the last day they will be put to shame.'"'"

Later on in the text, Jesus says to Judas "You thirteenth *daimon*, why do you try so hard? But speak up, and I shall bear with you... Judas, your star has led you astray." Based upon these words, some have criticized the initial translation, saying that it is misleading and falsely gives the impression of a more favorable impression of Judas than otherwise warranted. But later on, Jesus says to Judas "You will become the thirteenth, and you will be cursed by the other generations–and *[but?]* you will come to rule over them. In the last days they will curse your ascent to the holy [generation.]" The latter portion of this passage almost seems like a prophecy of the fate of the Gospel of Judas itself; for if "in the last days they {traditional Christians} will curse your ascent to the holy [generation]" by an "exoneration" through the discovery of the long-lost text of the Gospel of Judas, then this is confirmed by the fundamentalists who assure us all that we are living in the "last days".[296] Later on in the text, Judas asks Jesus "Does the human spirit die?" Jesus answers him, saying "This is why God ordered Michael to give the spirits of the people to them as a loan, so that they might offer service, but the Great One ordered Gabriel to grant spirits to the great generations with no ruler over it–that is, the spirit and the soul." Further on, Jesus declares to Judas: "But you will exceed all of them. For you will sacrifice the man that clothes me." But this is a prophecy, not a commandment. The conclusion of the text ends thusly: "Their high priests murmured because [he {Jesus}] had gone into the guest room for his prayer. But some scribes were there watching carefully in order to arrest him during the prayer, for they were afraid of the people, since he was regarded by all as a prophet. They approached Judas and said to him, "What are you doing here? You are Jesus' disciple." Judas answered them as they wished. And he received some silver and handed him over to them." It is worth noting the similarity of this scene with that depicted in the Toldoth Yeshu, in which one of Christ's disciples, namely Gaisa, betrays Jesus into the hands of the Rabbis; in both texts,

---

[296] This is the irony of a self-fulfilling prophecy.

it is not in the Garden of Gethsemane that Jesus is arrested, but in a synagogue. A complete translation of the extant Gospel of Judas is available online.[297] I am sure new insights will continue to be gleaned from this strange and fascinating text for years to come. In any case, the Gospel of Judas is a clear example of what is aptly described as an "anti-Gospel".

---

[297] Available at http://www.nationalgeographic.com/lostgospel/ pdf/ GospelofJudaspdf.
A complete translation is also available in the book *The Gospel of Judas,* edited by Rodolphe Kasser, Marvin Meyer, and Gregor Wurst (with additional commentary by Bart D. Ehrman). There is also now available a book entitled *READING JUDAS,* co-written by Elaine Pagels and Karen L. King. This book also inlcudes a complete translation of the controversial text.

The Gospel of Barnabas

The Gospel of Barnabas is another "anti-Gospel" inasmuch as it is a complete rewriting and reinterpretation of the person and teachings of Jesus Christ; one that gratuitously accommodates Islam in such a shamelessly obvious way that it is a transparent forgery, similar to the many forged *apokalypses* and *apocrypha* written to promote or defend neo-orthodoxy, or some heretical interpretation of Christianity or Judaism. A critical appraisal of the text discloses a fourteenth century origin as the most likely date of origin. However there was a Gospel of Barnabas listed in the Gelasian Decree of prohibited books; this decree was issued by Pope Gelasius toward the end of the fifth century. Therefore there must have been an ancient text attributed to Barnabas, and some Muslims claim that the current text under the title "Gospel of Barnabas" is none other than the original Gospel cited in the decree. However, some Muslim scholars take a more critical view of the text, and reject it as inauthentic. This is a safe conclusion, and indeed the only sane conclusion, based upon the available evidence, unless we are to embrace Islam. My interest in the Gospel of Barnabas was aroused by a note in a translation of the Koran by George Sale, which quoted from this little-known text. For several years I sought to find this text, to no avail. Then finally I was able to locate a copy of an English translation of the entire text.[298] I was fascinated by the

---

[298]   There are a number of different editions of the English translation available

novelty of it all. But by then I had already rejected both Christianity and Islam as viable alternatives for spirituality/religion. So I did not become completely intoxicated. Nevertheless the text is fascinating, and it is worth reading, if you have never read it.

The Gospel of Barnabas is either a complete reworking of the earlier, original Gospel of Barnabas, or instead a completely independent text, doubtless inspired by the knowledge that there had been a Gospel attributed to Barnabas. It is impossible to determine with certainty which is the case here, although the latter seems more probable, all things considered. There is at least a slight hint of Ebionism or at least of Judaism in the text, inasmuch as therein Jesus insists upon the necessity of circumcision for salvation. Of course we do not know for sure if the historical Jesus took this position, but we can be certain that at least some *Ebionim* did take this position; the New Testament itself tells us that there were some early believers who insisted upon circumcision and observance of the Torah for salvation.[299] In fact, this was a major controversy in the early Christian community, and Paul the apostle and his companion Barnabas are depicted in the book of Acts as being vehemently opposed to this requirement.[300] The same chapter narrates how Paul and Barnabas went to Jerusalem to defer to the Apostles on this question.[301] James, who apparently was the head in Jerusalem, concurs in the same judgment, according to the text.[302] But critical scholars[303] take exception to this portrayal of James. Nevertheless the Pauline school wrote against the faction of the circumcision.[304] Circumcision really

---

today, and possibly different translations as well. One can find a complete online English translation at http://www.answering-christianity.com/barnabas.htm. There are quite a few websites devoted to the Gospel of Barnabas, or that discuss it, both critically and uncritically. Most of these sites are either Islamic or Christian. A complete English translation of the Gospel of Barnabas is also available from A&B publishers in Brooklyn, New York.

[299]   Acts 15:1.

[300]   Acts 15:2.

[301]   Acts 15:2–12.

[302]   Acts 15:13–31.

[303]   Most notably Robert Eisenman.

[304]   Romans 2:28–29; Galatians 5:2–6; 6:12; Philippians 3:2–3.

only became an issue because most Greek and Roman men were uncircumcised. But circumcision was commonly practiced by Syrians, Arabians, Egyptians, and Aethiopians.[305] In any case Paul and Barnabas were opposed to laying the heavy yoke of circumcision upon the Gentiles as a requirement for salvation.[306] The Epistle of Barnabas, as distinct from the Gospel of Barnabas, is generally Pauline in character. In fact, if anything, it could be regarded as super-Pauline. Therefore it is reasonably clear that the person who wrote the original Gospel of Barnabas was not same person as the author of the Epistle of Barnabas. On the contrary, the very fact that the Gospel has become lost belies the assumption that they were either written by the same person or expressed similar religious views. Likewise the Gospel of Thomas may have been written by a different person than the author of the Acts of Thomas. The Epistle of Barnabas is even included in some early New Testament codices. By contrast, the original Gospel of Barnabas has disappeared without a trace, except possibly buried under layers of obfuscation in the text now claiming to be that very Gospel of Barnabas.

But just as there were Pauline texts and Gnostic texts, so there may have been a variety of Ebionite texts, aside from those we already know about. It is possible that the original Gospel of Barnabas was such an Ebionite text, which became lost for that very reason. If so, then we would expect the Gospel of Barnabas to uphold the unity of God, and the observance of the Torah,[307] including circumcision. These traits can also be found in the Islamic Gospel of Barnabas, but, even assuming that this is based in part upon the original text of Barnabas, it has been so overlaid with blatant Islamic imagery that it cannot be taken seriously. Nevertheless, it is accepted as a powerful testimony by some Muslims.

One of the key points of the Gospel of Barnabas is that Jesus himself was never crucified. But this is no more than what we also read in the Koran: "God hath sealed them up for their unbelief, so that but few believe. And for their unbelief, and for their having spoken against Mary a grievous calumny; and for their saying, "Verily we

---

[305] Those thus denoted as Aethiopians by the Greeks were really Nubians, whom today we would call Sudanese.

[306] And in this respect the Pauline corpus and the book of Acts are in accord.

[307] Minus the offering of animal sacrifices.

have slain the Messiah, Jesus the son of Mary, an Apostle of God." Yet they slew him not, and they crucified him not, but they had only his likeness." (Koran Sura IV: 155-157)

And in turn this passage is similar to some of the earlier Gnostic texts we have already examined, which also deny that Jesus was crucified. This might be seen by some as historical evidence that Jesus himself was never crucified, but a substitute was crucified in his place. We will consider this theory in greater detail when we consider the substitution theory. But the Islamic Gospel of Barnabas[308] almost appears to be a sort of *midrash* upon the Koranic passage above. In Barnabas, four archangels are sent by God to rescue Jesus, and to take him up to heaven, so that he might escape the cruel fate planned for him by the Pharisees. But Judas Iscariot, who betrayed him, is miraculously transformed by God to look exactly like Jesus, so that he is crucified in his stead. After this farce is over, the archangels return Jesus to his beloved disciples and relatives, who had been mourning, thinking that he had been truly crucified. In fact the Islamic Gospel of Barnabas even goes so far as to say that some impious men stole the body of Judas from the tomb and spread the rumor that Jesus was risen from the dead. But God allows Jesus to return to visit his mother and disciples, and to explain to them what really happened. Barnabas then asks Jesus why God allowed his mother and closest companions to believe that he had been dead, and to mourn in such grief. Jesus answers by saying that even slight sins are grievous to God, and that, since his mother and other companions had loved him with an earthly love, they were punished for it by this means, rather than by the flames of hell. And that God had decreed that Jesus would in this world be mocked with the death of Judas (as being his own; crucifixion), so that on the day of judgment no demons could mock him, since he had unrighteously been called "God" and the "Son of God" in this world. Although the New Testament calls Jesus the "Son of God", nowhere is he called God outright, and it seems unlikely that anyone would have placed him upon an equality with God, either in his lifetime, or shortly thereafter.[309]

---

[308] In distinction from the original, now lost, Gospel of Barnabas.

[309] On the other hand, this ought not to be hastily ruled out as a distinct possibility; see discussion on the Melchizedek Scroll below, in the chapter on the Dead Sea Scrolls.

The Islamic Gospel of Barnabas has a number of anachronisms, and it also conflicts with both the Bible and the Koran on a number of key points. For example, even though Jesus is called "Christ" in the text, the same text denies that Jesus is the Messiah, even though the two words mean the same thing, in Greek and Hebrew, respectively. Mohammed is called the Messiah in the Islamic Gospel of Barnabas, but nowhere in the Koran is Mohammed called the Messiah; the term is uniformly applied to Jesus therein. This is just one of many examples. But this text is a curiosity, and it may be worth reading by the curious. It would be quite an embarrassment to those Islamic apologists[310] who advocate the Islamic Gospel of Barnabas as the authentic, original Gospel of Barnabas if the latter text were to somehow be rediscovered, just as the long-lost Gospel of Judas has finally come to light. No doubt hardcore Islamists would insist that it was all a Western conspiracy, or even a Judaeo-Christian conspiracy, or a Judaeo-Masonic conspiracy. Such a find could have truly incendiary consequences. Nevertheless it would be a priceless treasure, and it would finally lay to rest any scholarly pretensions of the legitimacy of the text obtruded under that name today. In fact, the Islamic Gospel of Barnabas may be more of an embarrassment to astute Muslims than anything they would want to draw attention to. In the same way, much of the New Testament Apocrypha is a distinct embarrassment for many Christians. But in a sense, these texts act as literary fossils, preserving the religious beliefs of people in the time in which they were written. We will have more to say of literary fossils hereafter.

---

[310] As noted above, not all Muslims accept the Gospel of Barnabas as authentic.

The Toldoth Yeshu

The Toldoth Yeshu (Jeschu) is a classic example of an "anti-Gospel"; it parodies the Christian Gospels, and portrays Jesus as an illegitimate child who acquired magical powers by means of a secret knowledge of the *Shemhamphorasch,* or secret name of God. In my earlier work I pointed to this text as a prime witness to Jesus having lived in the first century B.C. However, I now feel that the evidence from the Toldoth in that regard is not nearly so strong as I then thought. In fact, even then I pointed to Daniel's prophecy of the seventy weeks as a much stronger form of evidence in favor of my theory, as well as the chronological falsifications evident in the Massoretic texts of Ezra and Nehemiah, by substituting the name Artaxerxes for Xerxes in those texts.[311] But even before I finished that work, I realized that the original form of the Toldoth, in all likelihood, was one in which the corpse of Jesus[312] was dragged by the Rabbis through the streets of Jerusalem triumphantly, as the final climax of the story. This of

---

[311] I still feel that this aspect of my earlier research is strong.

[312] Called Yeshu in the Toldoth. This was transliterated as "Jeschu" by German scholars, and the unfortunate transliteration has stuck. As I have pointed out in my earlier work, and also herein, most likely the historical Jesus was known as Jesus, rather than any Hebrew equivalent of his name. For this reason, I have emended the name to "Jesus" in the text of the Toldoth below.

necessity changed my outlook on the entire text; with this as a necessary climax to the story, the form of the story required a Jewish monarch to have held sway at the time; historical considerations were completely secondary. Therefore the placement of Jesus in the reign of Queen Alexandra[313] was merely a function of the necessity of the final outcome. As noted in my previous work, the Talmud is filled with all kinds of anachronisms, particularly in relation to Mary and Jesus. And, despite the fact that Mead spoke of a distinctly Karaite Toldoth,[314] without being able to examine it at first hand, I cannot trust his highly questionable scholarship in the matter. As such, I now esteem the Toldoth as a much younger document than I had formerly supposed; I suspect in fact it may be mediaeval in origin. In any case it is very difficult, if not impossible, to imagine a "distinctly Karaite Toldoth" since the Toldoth reproduced in Mead's book is thoroughly Talmudic. In fact, taking Mead at his word, I attempted to isolate the Talmudic portions of the text from the remainder, but the result was a very fragmentary text; too much would have had to have been removed from the text to leave very much remaining. The incident of Jesus and Judas flying in the air, for example, would have had to have been excluded; but this would also require other large portions of the text to be removed. So it seems more realistic to regard the text as being essentially an Orthodox Rabbinical text with a very Talmudic context. This is not to say that there may not have been relatively early versions of the story that may have predated the rise of Karaite Judaism; in fact the synagogue in Cairo in which Solomon Schechter discovered the Codex described by Mead as "distinctly Karaite" was a Karaite synagogue.[315] From what I can

---

[313] This in itself may be an unwarranted interpretation; for the Queen mentioned in the Toldoth is named Helene therein; as such, she seems to be a composite between Queen Salome (otherwise also known as Alexandra) and Queen Helena of Adiabene; cf Jos. War 1.5.1-4; Ant. 13.16.1-6 & 20.2.1-5.

[314] Mead., op. cit., pg. 316.

[315] Mr. Schechter made his discovery within the *Genizah* of the synagogue; it was the very same place where he also discovered fragments of the famous Damascus Document, later also found among the Dead Sea Scrolls. The Codex of the Toldoth discovered by Schechter was written in Syriac. But my comment about the story of Judas and Jesus flying in the air is based upon the observation that the whole point of the story was to uphold an obscure Talmudic argument regarding the flow of impurity back upstream, from an unclean vessel to a clean vessel; the inherent mockery of Jesus was

discern, the story originally culminated with the dragging of Jesus' body through the streets of Jerusalem. This was almost certainly the original oral and written form of the story. Later on several chapters were added to account for the great "Gentilization" of the messianic movement. Most likely even the story of the finding of Yeshu's body, and of the dragging of it through the streets of Jerusalem, was intended as more of a historical parable, rather than as being literally true.[316] The message instead was that "wise" Israelites know that the claims of the Christians are false with such a degree of certainty, that it is as if Christ's corpse had been dragged through the streets of Jerusalem, in a visible, tangible demonstration of the fact that he was dead. The story also shows in a dramatic way the degree of hostility that existed between these two mutually antagonistic groups of Jews.[317] It is also possible that an early, primordial form of the Toldoth Yeshu may have originated within Rabbincal Judaism but that copies of the text had been acquired by Karaite Jews, who thereafter proceeded to edit the text according to their own doctrinal preferences. But the version reproduced in Mead's book, as well as my earlier book, and also below, is thoroughly Talmudic; the reference to the teact *Nezekin* {Damages} is a dead giveaway to the Talmudic character of the text. Another indication of lateness, as well as the Rabbinical character of the text, is the reference to the wearing of a head-covering. Despite the nearly ubiquitous ignorance concerning this, the practice of wearing a *kipporah* or head-covering by males in Judaism does not date back to the first century, much less the first century B.C.; see the section on Philo below. Furthermore, there is nothing within the pages of *TaNaKh* that mention the necessity for Israelite males to wear any kind of head-covering.

---

merely a gratuitous part of the context, and vice-versa. In other words, Karaites would not have incorporated a story that upheld a Rabbinical interpretation of uncleanness contrary to their own. Therefore any genuinely Karaite version of the Toldoth would exclude the story of Jesus and Judas flying in the air. The version included in Mead's book includes the story. Neither are there any notes given, to help delineate the Karaite version from the Talmudic, in Mead's work.

[316] Otherwise we would have to regard the authors of the story, and their intended audience, as the most fatuous of imbeciles; since, had that been the case, no such religion as Christianity would ever have originated.

[317] The first disciples of Jesus Christ were ostensibly ethnically Jewish.

The Toldoth Yeshu

1. The beginning of the birth of Jesus. His mother was Maryam [a daughter] of Israel. She had a betrothed of the royal race of the House of David, whose name was Yohanan. He was learned in the law and feared heaven greatly. Near the door of her house, just opposite, dwelt a handsome [fellow]; Joseph ben Pandera cast his eye upon her.

It was night, on the eve of the Sabbath, when drunken he crossed over to her door and entered in to her. But she thought in her heart that it was her betrothed Yohanan; she hid her face and was ashamed.... He embraced her; but she said to him, Touch me not, for I am in my separation. He took no heed thereat, nor regarded her words, but persisted. She conceived by him....

At midnight came her betrothed Rabbi Yohanan. She said to him: What meaneth this? Never hath it been thy custom, since thou wast betrothed to me, twice in a night to come to me.

He answered her and said: It is but once I come to thee this night. She said to him: Thou camest to me, and I said to thee I was in my separation, yet heed'st thou not, but did'st thy will and wentest forth. When he heard this, forthwith he perceived that Joseph ben Pandera had cast an eye upon her and done the deed. He left her; in the morning he arose and went to Rabbi Simeon ben Shetach. He said to him: Know then what hath befallen me this night with my betrothed.

I went in to her after the manner of men...; before I touched her she said: Thou hast already this night come once to me, and I said to thee I was in my separation, and thou gavest no ear to me, [didst] thy will and wentest forth. When I heard such words from her, I left her and [went forth]. Rabbi Simeon ben Shetach said to him: Who came into thy mind? He answered, Ben Pandera, for he dwelleth near her house, and is a libertine. He said to him: I understand that thou hast no witness for this thing, therefore keep silence. I counsel thee, if he have come once, then can he not fail to come a second time; act wisely; at that time set witnesses against him.

Some time after the rumour went abroad that Mary was with child. Then said her betrothed Yohanan: She is not with child by me; shall I abide here and hear my shame every day from the people? He arose and went to Babylon. After some [time she bore] a son, and they called his name [[Yeshua after his mother's brother; but when his corrupt birth was made public they called him Yeshu]] Jesus.

2. His mother gave him to a teacher, so that he might become wise in the *Halacha,* and learned in the *Torah* and the *Talmud.* Now it was the custom of the teachers of the law that no disciple and no boy should pass on his way by them without his head being covered and his eyes cast to the ground, from reverence of the pupils towards their teachers.

One day that rogue passed by, and all the wise were seated together at the door of the synagogue-that is, they called the school-house synagogue; that rogue then passed by the Rabbis, head on high and with uncovered pate, saluting no one, nay, rather, in shameless fashion showing irreverence to his teacher.

After he had passed by them, one of them began and said: He is a bastard (*mamzer*). The second began and said: He is a bastard and son of a woman in her separation (*mamzer ben ha-niddah*). Another day the Rabbis stopped in tractate *Nezekin;* then began that one to speak *Halachoth* before them. Thereupon one of them began and said to him: Hast thou then not learned: He who giveth forth a *Halacha* in the presence of his teacher, *without being asked,* is guilty of death? That one answered and said to the wise ones: Who is the teacher and who the disciple? Who of the twain is {was} wiser, Moses or Jethro? Was it not Moses, father of the prophets and head of the wise? And the *Torah,* moreover, beareth witness of him: And from henceforth there ariseth no prophet in Israel like unto Moses. Withal Jethro was an alien,... yet taught he Moses worldly wisdom, as it is written: Set thou over them rulers of thousands, and of hundreds. But if ye say that Jethro is {was} greater than Moses, then would there be an end to the greatness of Moses.

When the wise heard this, they said: As he is so very shameless, let us enquire after him. They sent to his mother, [saying] thus: Tell us, pray, who is the father of this boy? She answered and said:..., [[but they say of him, that he is a bastard and son of a woman in her separation.]] Then began Rabbi Simeon ben Shetach: Today is it thirty years since Rabbi Yohanan her betrothed came to me; at that time he said to me: That and that hath befallen me. He related all that is told above,... how Rabbi Simeon answered Rabbi Yohanan, and how when she was with child, he [Rabbi Yohanan] for great shame went to Babylon and did not return; but this Mary gave birth to this Jesus, and no death penalty awaits her, for she hath not done this of her own will, for Joseph ben Pandera laid wait for her... the whole day.

When she heard from Rabbi Simeon that no death penalty awaited her, she also began and said: Thus was the story; and she confessed. But when it went abroad concerning Jesus, that he was called a bastard and son of a woman in her separation, he went away and fled to Jerusalem.

3.   Now the rule of all Israel was *then* in the hand of a woman who was called Helene. And there was in the sanctuary a foundation stone-and this is its interpretation: God founded it and this is the stone on which Jacob poured oil-and on it were written the letters of the *Shem,* and whoever learned it, could do whatsoever he would. But as the wise feared that the disciples of Israel might learn them and therewith destroy the world, they took measures that no one should do so. Brazen dogs were bound to two iron pillars at the entrance of the place of burnt offerings, and whosoever entered in and learned these letters-as soon as he went forth again, the dogs bayed {barked} at him; if he then looked at them, the letters vanished from his memory.

This Jesus came, learned them, wrote them on parchment, cut into his hip and laid the parchment with the letters therein-so that the cutting of his flesh did not hurt him-then he restored the skin to its place. When he went forth the brazen dogs bayed at him, and the letters vanished from his memory. *But when* he went home, *he* cut open his flesh with his knife, took out the writing, learned the letters *by heart, and* went and gathered three hundred and ten of the young men of Israel.

4. He said to them: Behold then those who say of me *that* I am a bastard and son of a woman in her separation; they desire power for themselves and seek to exercise lordship in Israel. But see ye, all the prophets prophesied concerning the Messiah of God, and I am the Messiah. Isaiah prophesied concerning me: Behold the virgin shall conceive, bear a son, and he shall be called Emmanuel. Moreover, my forefather David prophesied concerning me and spake: The Eternal [Y.H.V.H.] said to me: Thou art my son; this day have I begotten thee. He begat me without male congress with my mother; yet they call me a bastard! He further prophesied: Why do the heathen rage, and the kings in the country [nations] rise up against His Anointed? I am the Messiah, and they, so to rise up against me, are children of whores, for so it is written in the Scripture: for they are children of whores.

The young men answered him: If thou art the Messiah, show us a sign. He answered them: What sign do ye require that I should do for you? Forthwith they brought unto him a lame man, who had never yet stood upon his feet. He pronounced over him the letters, and he stood upon his feet. In the same hour they all made obeisance to him and said: This is {Thou art} the Messiah. He gave them another sign. They brought to him a leper; he pronounced over him the letters, and he was healed. There joined themselves apostates from the children of his people.

When the wise saw that so very many believed on him, they seized him and brought him before Queen Helene, in whose hand the land of Israel was. They said to her: This man uses sorcery and seduces the world.

Jesus answered to her as follows: Already of old the prophets prophesied concerning me: And there shall come forth a rod out of the stem of Isai (Jesse), and I am he. Of him saith the Scripture: Blessed is the man that walketh not in the counsel of the ungodly.

She said to them: Is this truly in your law, what he saith?

They answered: It is in our law; but it hath not been said concerning him, for it is said therein: And that prophet *that seeketh to lead thee astray to worship false gods, shall be put to death; so shalt thou* put the evil away from the midst of thee. {Deut. 13:1-5}. But the Messiah for whom we hope, with him are [greater] signs, and it is said of him: He shall smite the earth with the rod of his mouth. With this bastard these signs are not present.

Jesus said, Lady, I am he, and I raise the dead. {*In some editions of the Toldoth, there is here recounted an episode of Jesus raising someone from the dead*}

In the same hour the queen was affrighted and said: That is a great sign.

Apostates still joined themselves to him, were with him, and there arose a great schism in Israel.

5. Jesus went to Upper Galilee. The wise assembled together, went before the queen and said to her: Lady, he practiseth sorcery and leadeth men astray therewith. Therefore sent she forth horsemen concerning him, and they came upon him as he was seducing the people of Upper Galilee and saying to them: I am the Son of God, who hath been promised in your law. The horsemen rose up to take him away, but the people of Upper Galilee suffered it not and began to fight. Jesus said to them: Fight not, *but* have trust in the power of my Father in heaven.

The people of Galilee made birds out of clay; he uttered the letters of the Shem and the birds flew away. At the same hour they fell down before him. He said to them: Bring me a millstone. They rolled it to the sea-shore; he spake the letters, set it upon the surface of the sea, sat himself thereon, as one sits in a boat, went and floated on the water. They who had been sent, saw it and wondered; and Jesus said to the horsemen: Go to your lady, tell her what you have seen! Thereupon the wind raised him from the water and carried him onto dry land. The horsemen came and told the queen all these things; the queen was affrighted, was greatly amazed, sent and gathered together the elders of Israel and spake unto them: Ye say he is a sorcerer, nevertheless every day he doeth great wonders. They answered her: Surely his tricks should not trouble thee! Send messengers, that they may bring him thither, and his shame shall be made plain. At the same hour she sent messengers, and his wicked company also joined itself unto him, and they came with him before the queen.

Then the wise men of Israel took a man by name Judas Ischariota, brought him into the Holy of Holies, where he learned the letters of the *Shem,* which were engraved on the foundation-stone, wrote them on a small [piece of] parchment, cut open his hip, spake the *Shem,* so that it did not hurt, as Jesus had done before.

As soon as Jesus and his company returned to the queen, and she sent for the wise men, Jesus began and spake: For dogs *have* compassed me. And concerning me he [David] said: Tremble not before them. As soon as the wise men entered and Judas Ischariota with them, they brought forward their pleas against him, until he said to the queen: Of me it hath been said: I will ascend to heaven. Further it is written: If he take me, Sela! {Psalms} *Then* he raised his hands like unto the wings of an eagle and flew, and the people were amazed because of him: How is he able to fly twixt heaven and earth?!

Then spake the wise men of Israel to Judas Ischariota: Do thou also utter the letters and ascend after him. Forthwith he did so, flew in the air, and the people marvelled: How can they fly like eagles?!

Ischariota acted cleverly, flew in the air, but neither could overpower the other, so as to make him fall by means of the *Shem,* because the *Shem* was equally with both of them. When Judas perceived this he had recourse to a low trick; he befouled Jesus, so that he was made unclean and fell to the earth, and with him also Judas. It is because of this that they wail on their night, and because of the thing which Judas did to him. At the same hour they seized him and said to Helene: Let him be put to death! If he be the Son of God, let him tell us who smote him. So they covered his head with a garment and smote him with a pomegranate staff. As he did not know, it was clear that the *Shem* had abandoned him, and he was now fast taken in their hands. He began and spake to his companions before the queen: Of me it was said: Who will rise up for me against the evil doers? But of them he said: The proud waters. And of them he said: Stronger than rocks make they their countenances. When the queen heard this she reproved the apostates, and said to the wise men of Israel: He is in your hand.

6. They departed from the queen and brought him to the synagogue of Tiberias and bound him to the pillars of the ark. Then there gathered to him the band of simpletons and dupes, who believed on his words and desired to deliver him out of the hand of the elders; but they could not do so, and there arose great fighting between them. When he saw that he had no power to escape, he said: Give me some water. They gave him vinegar in a copper vessel. He began and spake with a loud voice: Of me David prophesied and said: When I was thirsty they gave me vinegar to drink. On his head they set a crown of thorns. The apostates lamented sore, and there was fighting between them, brother with brother, father with son; but the wise men brought the apostates low.

He began and spake: Of me he prophesied and said: My back I gave to the smiters, *and my cheeks to them that plucked off the hair: I hid not my face from shame and spitting.* Further of these the Scripture saith: Draw hither, sons of the sorceress. And of me *it* hath been said: But we held him *smitten by God, and afflicted.* And of me he said: The Messiah shall be cut off and he is not. When the apostates heard this, they began to stone them with stones, and there was great hatred among them.

Then were the elders afraid, and the apostates bore him off from them, and his three hundred and ten disciples brought him to the city of Antioch, where he sojourned until the rest-day of the Passover. Now in that year the Passover fell on the Sabbath, and he and his sons came to Jerusalem, on the rest-day of Passover, that is on the Friday, he riding on an ass and saying to his disciples: Of me it was said: Rejoice greatly, Daughter of Zion, *shout, O Daughter of Jerusalem: Behold, thy King cometh unto thee: he is just, and having salvation; meek, and riding upon an ass, and upon a colt, the foal of an ass.* In the same hour they all cried aloud, bowed themselves before him, and he with his three hundred and ten disciples went into the sanctuary.

Then came one of them, who was called Gaisa [that is, Gardener], and said to the wise men: Do you want the rogue? They said: Where is he to be found? He answered: He is in the sanctuary; that is to say, in the school-house {synagogue}. They said to him: Show him unto us. He answered them: We, his three hundred and ten disciples, have already sworn by the commandments, that we will not say of him who he is; but if ye come in the morning, give me the greeting, and I will go and make obeisance before him, and before whom I make obeisance, he is the rogue. And they did so.

The disciples of Jesus gathered together, went and gave their fellows the greeting, for they were come from all places to pray on the Mount of Olives on the Feast of Unleavened Bread. Then the wise men went into the sanctuary, where those were who had come from Antioch, and there was also the rogue among them. Thereupon Gaisa entered with them, left the rest of the company, made an obeisance before the rogue Jesus. Whereupon the wise men saw it, arose against him and seized him.

7. They said to him: What is thy name? he answered Mathai. They said to him: Whence hast thou a proof from the Scripture? He answered them: When (*mathai*) shall I come and see the face of God? They said to him: When (*mathai*) shall he die, and his name perish? Further they said to him, What is thy name? He answered Naki. They said to him: Whence hast thou a proof from the Scripture? He answered: With pure (*naki*) hands and a clean heart. They said to him: He remaineth not unpunished (*nakah*). Further they said to him: What is thy name? he answered: Boni. They said: Whence hast thou a proof from *the* Scripture? He answered: My first-born son (*beni*) is Israel. They said: Of thee it was said: Behold, I will slay thy first-born son. Further they said: What is thy name? he answered: Netzer. They said: Whence hast thou a proof from the Scripture? He answered them: A branch (*netzer*) shall spring up out of his roots. They said to him: Thou art cast forth from thy sepulchre, like an abominable branch (*netzer*). *Then they said to him, What is thy name? he answered them, Todah. They said, Whence hast thou a proof from Scripture? He answered: A Psalm for Todah. But they answered him, saying: Whoso offereth Todah honoureth me.* And thus still more, as he gave himself many names.

Forthwith they seized him, and his disciples could not deliver him. When he saw himself brought to death he began and spake: Verily hath David prophesied of me and said: For thy sake are we smitten every day. And of you said Isaiah: Your hands are full of blood. And of you said the prophet before God: They slew the prophets with the sword.

The apostates began to lament and could not deliver him. At the same hour was he put to death. And it was on Friday the rest-day of Passover and of the Sabbath. When they would hang him on a tree *(Holz),* it brake, for there was with him the *Shem.* But when the simpletons saw that the trees brake under him, they supposed that this was because of his great godliness, until they brought him to a cabbage-stalk. For while he was yet alive he knew the custom of the Israelites, that they would hang him, he knew his death, and that they would *try to* hang him on a tree. At that time he brought to pass by means of the *Shem,* that no tree should bear him but over the cabbage-stalk he did not utter the pronounced name, for it is not "tree" but green-stuff, and so *also plentiful, for in the sixth year there are* in Jerusalem cabbages with more than a hundred pounds [of seed] unto this day.

When they would hang him until the time of afternoon prayer, they took him down from the tree, for so it is written: His body shall not remain all night upon the tree, *but thou shalt in any wise bury him that day, that thy land be not defiled, which the LORD thy God giveth thee for an inheritance.* They buried him on [Friday] and the apostates of his people wept over the grave.

8. Some of the young men of Israel passed by them. They spoke to them in the Aramaic tongue: Why do the foolish ones sit by the grave? Let us look! The foolish ones said in their heart, that they [the young men] would see him in the grave, but they found him not. Thereupon the foolish ones sent to Queen Helene, saying, He whom they put to death was a {the} Messiah, and very many wonders did he show while *still* living *in the flesh,* but now after his death they buried him, but he is not in the grave, for he is already ascended to heaven, and it is written: For he taketh me, Sela! Thus did he prophesy concerning himself.

She went to the wise men and said: What have ye done with him? They answered her: We put him to death, for that was the judgment concerning him.

She said to them: If ye have put him to death, what have ye done then? They answered her: We have buried him. Forthwith they sought him in the grave but found him not. Thereupon she said to them: In this grave ye buried him; where is he therefore? Then were the wise men affrighted and knew not what to answer her, (for a certain one had taken him from the grave, borne him to his garden, and stopped the water which flowed into his garden; then digged he in the sand and buried him, and let the water flow again over his grave.)

The queen said: If ye show me not *the body of* Jesus, I will give you no peace and no escape. They answered her: Give us an appointed time and terms. When she had granted them an appointed time, all Israel remained in lamenting and fasting and prayer, and the apostates found occasion to say: Ye have slain God's Anointed *Prince!*

And all Israel was in great anguish, and the wise men and all the land of Israel hurried from place to place because of the great fear. Then went forth an elder of them, whose name was Rabbi Tanchuma; he went forth lamenting in a garden in the fields. When the owner of the garden saw him, he said to him: Wherefore lamentest thou? He answered: For this and this; because of that rogue who is not to be found; and lo, already is it the appointed time which the queen granted, and we are all in lamentation and fasting. As soon as he heard his words, that all Israel is as them who mourn, and that the rogues say: He is gone up into heaven, the owner of the garden said: Today shall joy and gladness reign in Israel, for I have stolen him away because of the apostates, so that they should not take him and have the opportunity for all time, *to claim he has ascended to heaven,* and thereafter make trouble for the Israelites. Forthwith they went to Jerusalem, told them the good tidings, and all the Israelites followed the owner of the garden, bound cords to his [Christ's] feet, and dragged him {*his body*} to the queen and said: There {This} is he who is ascended to heaven! They departed from her in joy, and she mocked the apostates and praised the wise men.

[This is almost certainly where the original edition of the Toldoth ended; the rest being a later addition.]

Forensic Literary Archaeology

F orensic literary archaeology is a term I use to denote the critical study of literary documents, and the effort to determine which portions are most ancient and authentic. Critical literary scholars employ the principle, albeit without the use of the term. In my former work I briefly discussed the existence of certain "fossil" passages in the New Testament, which served to indicate a historical subtext to the narrative. Even earlier in this work, I briefly discussed observable distinctions in respect to "orthodoxy" in relation to various religious texts. I pointed out the example of how the orthodoxy of those epistles ascribed to Ignatius and Polycarp was not the same orthodoxy that one finds in the New Testament, for example. I further distinguished this intermediate stage of orthodoxy from the later stage of orthodoxy as evinced in the writings of Tertullian and Irenaeus. As applied to the texts of the New Testament, forensic literary archaeology seeks to discern the distinction between those texts which are more likely to preserve genuinely archaic traditions from those which are more likely interpolations. The former verses and passages I refer to as "fossil" passages, since they preserve a phase of orthodoxy which later became outmoded. As such, those passages implicitly point to an underlying historical subtext. But it is also important to realise that there is a distinction between the passages themselves and the underlying subtext; a subtle but important distinction. The key distinction of such "fossil" passages being that they are relatively older than the general corpus of the New Testament.[318] As such they are the *antipodes* of passages identifiable as later interpolations into the text. Of course there are also a large number of "neutral" passages, which cannot necessarily be distinguished as either "fossils" or interpolations; or at least passages which I have not been able to classify as falling into either category. Some may also disagree with some of my classifications. But the general principle is sound.

There are several criteria which I have used to determine "fossil" passages. One criterion is that a given verse or passage preemptively contradicts later orthodoxy. This is the golden rule of discerning literary fossils within the New Testament. By a preemptive contradiction is meant anything that, if taken literally, would be a source of embarrassment for later orthodoxy. A prime example is the mention of brothers and sisters of Jesus in the New Testament.[319] As such, these passages became a source of embarrassment after the false doctrine of the "perpetual virginity" of Mary was inculcated by the Roman Catholic Church. As a result, fables such as those found in the *Protevangelion* were fabricated, to make it appear as if Joseph had been an elderly widower, who already had children fully grown, by his first wife; conversely, Mary was depicted as a very young girl, something that there is no warrant for in Scripture.[320] As such, those passages that speak of the brothers (and sisters) of Jesus are perfect examples of literary fossils, or "fossil" passages, as I call them; they almost certainly point to the underlying historical subtext that Jesus actually had brothers and sisters, who were the children of Mary and Joseph. In turn, such passages strongly testify to the historicity of Jesus Christ. Such passages are never addressed by advocates of the phantom Christ theory.[321] If Jesus was really the incarnation of the Sun

---

[318] I.e., that they are older in origin; either being derived from older written texts, or from older oral traditions.

[319] Mt 12:46-50; 13:54-56; Mk 3:31-35; 6:2-3; Lk 8:19-21; Jn 7:3-5; Acts 1:14; Galatians 1:19; 1 Corinthians 9:5 cf Mt 1:25; Lk 2:7 cf Mt 2:13-21.

[320] Unless it is the use of the Hebrew word *almah* in Isaiah 7:14. the term in Hebrew denotes a young woman, rather than specifically a virgin. I now strongly suspect that the use of *parthenos* in the Greek Septuagint translation of the Hebrew Scriptures was probably because it was the closest-corresponding term in Greek.

[321] I.e., the theory that Jesus Christ never existed as a historical person, but was a completely invented character or *chimera*.

God, as many of these mythicists claim, why then would the writers of the Gospels have given him brothers and sisters? Would that not make the Sun God too human? Such things are overlooked by such persons. Of course others of this persuasion might argue in a more subtle strain that, albeit Jesus was an invented character, as the Messiah it would not have been altogether improbable for him to have had siblings. Therefore such persons could argue that brothers and sisters were introduced to present an element of realism into the narrative, to give it a greater sense of historicity. But to argue along such lines is the *epitome* of special pleading. One potential variation on this theme would be that those persons who invented Jesus as the Jewish Messiah were themselves Jews,[322] and not only wrote the various New Testament texts, but also later came forward as the very *Desposyni* or relatives of the Master whom we here about in some sources. This is a clever line of argument, but I feel that there are too many distinctive traits within the Gospel texts, and even scattered throughout the New Testament, that definitively point to a historical subtext in the case of Jesus. A criterion related to the first one mentioned is that of embarrassment; namely, that there are preserved in certain verses and passages actions, sayings, or circumstances that would be embarrassing to ecclesiastical orthodoxy in a general sense, rather than anything specifically dogmatic. Mark 3:21 springs to mind as a good example. In this verse the relatives of Jesus say that he is out of his mind.[323] No doubt such a verse would only be somewhat of an embarrassment to the Catholic and Orthodox Churches, or to any Christians. It almost appears as a sort of disclaimer by Christ's relatives, to make an excuse for him, and thereby possibly protect him from the wrath of Herod or the Romans, and themselves as well.[324]

A third criterion for literary fossils is anything that points distinctively to a genuine historical subtext. A fourth criterion is anything that is anomalous, deviant, or unexplained elsewhere in the text. Gnostic nomenclature within the Pauline corpus is an example of this, or rather, a whole set of examples. Baptism for the

---

[322] Rather than Romans as usually alleged by this school.

[323] When correctly translated from the original Greek.

[324] Because if they openly endorsed his messianic claims, they also could bear the wrath of Herod and the Romans.

dead is nowhere explained in the New Testament.[325] Neither is "Paul's" reference to "the abortion" in the famous passage on the resurrection.[326] Neither are those passages that speak of the law as having been instituted by angels.[327] Neither is the reference to Peter's "angel" in Acts 12:15. Clearly there is a great deal of overlapping of these criteria in many cases. In some cases I have classified passages as "fossil" passages due to the general character of the passage in question, rather than a specific reason. In some cases it may be legitimately argued that such literary fossils in the text of the New Testament prove no more than an earlier stage or phase of orthodoxy, rather than necessarily pointing to an unmistakable historical subtext. We already saw the example of how the orthodoxy found in those texts ascribed to Ignatius and Polycarp was different from that of the New Testament proper, but also was more archaic than that of Tertullian or Irenaeus. So the astute observer may be able to cite certain examples that lend themselves to such an interpretation; and while recognizing this, I nevertheless contend that there are some passages that by their very nature point definitively to a historical subtext. Indeed, one could argue that the very fact that such layers of "orthodoxy" or proto-orthodoxy in themselves presuppose an actual historical subtext; otherwise would not the inventors of the Christ character have made a much simpler literary creation? If Christ were a mere *chimera,* invented by the caprice of men, why would they labor so over texts that no longer suited their fancy? Why would they not instead have begun afresh to write new Gospels, epistles, acts, revelations?

Although I feel that I have given some explanation and examples of what I mean by literary fossils, and forensic literary archaeology, the technique is best illustrated by way of example. Therefore I will give more examples, but space does not permit for me to explain in detail the rationale behind every possible case; however I will provide a table of all those passages which I regard as fossil passages herein. But first I feel that it is very important for me to make a clear distinction in respect to applications of the principle involved. Protestant Christians often use, and have used, the example of the brothers and sisters of

---

[325]   1 Corinthians 15:29.

[326]   1 Corinthiasn 15:8.

[327]   Acts 7:53; Galatians 3:19-20; Hebrews 2:2.

Christ as a refutation of Romanism. And while they may be perfectly correct in this, there would still remain any number of other New Testament passages that would be an embarrassment or at least a problem, for all Christians. Therefore evangelicals and fundamentalists may rejoice that there are passages that testify to the historicity of Jesus Christ in the New Testament, yet they conveniently overlook the fact that many of these passages belie any supposition of the Divine Sonship of Christ.

What I am attempting to clarify here is a distinction between a literary and a critical-historical application of the principle of forensic literary archaeology. The former application is invalid, while the latter application is valid. I will explain why presently. A strictly literary application of the principle would insist that, since no passage of any document can possibly predate its immediately surrounding context, then the document in question (as a whole) must be regarded as just as old and therefore just as genuine and historic as any literary fossil found within it. Therefore there would be a *holistic* judgment placed upon such texts by reason of such fossil passages, and an unwarranted antiquity would be placed upon them, to subserve the invalid assumptions of biblical fundamentalism. Such a procedure would implicitly disregard contradictions and other problems within the text in question. In such a scenario, the literary fossils would function as "pillars" of the entire text, and ultimately of the entire New Testament, since these literary fossils are scattered throughout the New Testament text. But this would be a fallacy and the height of folly. The internal evidence of any document only proves that the document was written no earlier than the time indicated in the text;[328] it cannot prove that any given text was written earlier than the latest possible feature of the text as a whole. Therefore a strictly literary application of the principle is prohibited. But a critical-historical application is permitted. A critical-historical application would recognize that, while the text as a whole may date to a fairly late date,[329] it may nevertheless contain certain archaic features which are evidence of a genuine

---

[328]   This principle qualifies what I wrote earlier about the Gospel of Peter being an early text; since there are some seemingly "late" features therein, the text as a whole must be fairly late; nevertheless I still believe that it *contains* certain archaic features, which we will examine hereafter.

[329]   Possibly as late as the second century.

historical subtext, or at least of an earlier tradition, whether passed down orally or in written form.[330]

Of course forensic literary archaeology need not necessarily be limited to the New Testament itself; any ancient set of documents could be thus analyzed.[331] In my earlier work I gave as examples five verses that spoke of Jesus being hanged on a tree, rather than a cross, as evidence in favor of my theory.[332] But regardless of the question of chronology, these five examples remain good examples of the principle of literary fossils, since they are deviant from the New Testament norm. One final criterion for New Testament literary fossils is that the passages deviate from what is otherwise standard New Testament orthodoxy. Not all criteria need to co-exist; any one of them is sufficient to classify a verse or passage as a literary fossil.

---

[330] This really is the crux of forensic literary archaeology; no insistence upon written texts is necessary or even desirable; what is sought is instead that which is most authentic in strictly historic terms.

[331] Such as the works of Homer, Hesiod, Livy, Plato, etc.

[332] Acts 5:30; 10:39; 13:29; Galatians 3:13; 1 Peter 2:24.

Literary Fossils

Having introduced the concept of forensic literary archaeology, I will now proceed to further illustrate the principle by more examples. Space will not permit me to go into detail of every example; an entire book would have to be written on the subject for that. But I will give a sufficient number of examples, and I will also provide a table of all those passages that I regard as literary fossils. Such literary fossils may occur in individual cases, or they may be parts of a set or cluster of such cases.

One pungent set of literary fossils is that having to do with the disciples of John the Baptist. When scrutinized, these passages are downright embarrassing to Christian orthodoxy. If we regard John as merely the herald of the Messiah, as Christian tradition assures us, then we would expect both John and all his disciples to immediately submit to Jesus as the Promised Deliverer, once he had been proclaimed as such by John.[333] But what then are we to make of the following passage of the Synoptics:

14 Then came to him the disciples of John, saying, Why do we and the Pharisees fast often, by thy disciples do not fast? (Matthew 9:14 cf Mark 2:18; Luke 5:33)[334]

---

[333] John 1:29-36 cp Matthew 3:13-17.

[334] I quote the text as it stands written in Matthew, because the form of the

The appropriate critical question to ask is: Why, if John the Baptist has already clearly identified Jesus as the Son of God and the Lamb of God, are there still any disciples of John at all? Should not John himself have bowed down in homage to Jesus, if he truly believed that he was the chosen Messiah, for whom he was sent to prepare the way? And would not John have immediately directed all his disciples to go to Jesus, and be his disciples, rather than to continue with him? If the normative picture of John as being merely the herald of Christ were true, then we would expect John to bow down before Jesus in reverent homage, and have directed his own disciples to do likewise. But this is not what we see in the New Testament; instead we find such thorny passages, that speak of John still having his own distinct disciples, even after Jesus had begun his own prophetic ministry. Why? How could this be, if the traditional portrayal of events were true? How could such passages be anything but an embarrassment to astute Christians? Such passages put the lie to the traditional portrayal of events. But as such, the very passages in question clearly point to a genuine, historical subtext; one that differs from traditional Christian orthodoxy. True it is that in the Gospel of John we see some disciples of the Baptist following Jesus as a result of John's proclamation,[335] but this is still far less than what we would expect. It would have been more concordant with the Christian paradigm to see John depicted as bowing down in reverent adoration of Jesus as the Son of God, and immediately all his disciples immediately following suit. But this is exactly what we do not see; we read much contrary things in the narrative. In the Synoptic Gospels, Jesus takes the opportunity to respond to the inquiry with a parable about a bridegroom and a bridechamber, and placing new wine in new wineskins, which parable is answered in the Fourth Gospel with the story of the wedding at Kana.[336] But this is not the only example of an anomalous passage[337] respecting the disciples of John the Baptist. There are a few others. For example, the following:

---

passage in Matthew is actually the most pungent; in Mark and Luke, the disciples of John have been changed to a more innocuous "they", albeit questioning Jesus about the fasting habits of John's disciples nonetheless.

[335] John 1:35–42.

[336] Matthew 9:15–17; Mark 2:19–22; Luke 5:34–39 cp John 2:1–11.

[337] Technically three passages, albeit parallel passages.

"Now when John had heard in the prison the works of the Messiah, he sent two of his *own* disciples, and *they* said unto him, Art thou he that should come, or do we look for another?"[338]

This passage is usually rationalized by Christians as John having doubts due to his own fiery trial of persecution in unjust imprisonment. But not only does this passage belie the supposed supernatural manifestations attending Christ's baptism, such as the visible apparition of the holy spirit as a dove and the voice from heaven,[339] but John still has his own disciples. Why? Unless the traditional story is both incomplete and inaccurate? We see the very same thing narrated on the sad occasion of John's martyrdom.[340] It is John's own disciples who bury his decapitated body, and tell Jesus about what had happened. But why would John even still have his own disciples, if he had already openly proclaimed Jesus as the Messiah? We even see some lingering disciples of John long after the passion of Christ.[341] In fact Apollos, even though he is said to have been "instructed in the way of the Lord" knew only the baptism of John.[342] Of course the text goes on to say that Aquila and Priscilla expounded to him the way of God more perfectly. But this does not answer the question of why John would still have had his own disciples after he had already supposedly proclaimed Jesus as the Messiah and the Son of God. In my former work I speculated that John and Jesus were not contemporaries; John living a century after the time of Jesus. This is a possibility, but it is not the only explanation, or even necessarily the best explanation of the evidence. The general picture that emerges is somewhat different. People have long been speculating over whether John the Baptist may have been an Essene. Some[343] have even equated him with the Teacher of Righteousness. I would not go that far, but I would tentatively say that John may have originally been an Essene, but that at some point he broke away from the sect, and gathered his own disciples around himself. Jesus may have been one of John's disciples. But at some point Jesus broke away from John's

---

[338] Matthew 11:2-3 cf Luke 7:19-20.

[339] Matthew 3:16-17; John 1:31-34.

[340] Matthew 14:12; Mark 6:29.

[341] Acts 19:1-3.

[342] Acts 18:24-26.

[343] Notably Barbara Thiering.

group, and gathered disciples around himself, including some of John's disciples. This could possibly account for the Mandaean vilification of Jesus as a betrayer of secrets.

Another strong literary fossil is the following passage from Luke:

"And it came to pass afterward, that he went throughout every city and village, preaching and showing the glad tidings of the kingdom of God; and the twelve were with him, and also certain women, which had been healed of evil spirits and diseases; Mary called the Magdalene, out of whom went seven demons, and Joanna the wife of Chouza, Herod's steward, and Susanna, and many others, who ministered to him from out of their substance."[344]

This one is a real gold-mine. Not only does this passage belie the notion that Jesus was routinely multiplying food and turning water into wine, by reason of the fact that Jesus and the Apostles are being ministered to by these women, but the very fact that these women are even mentioned at all is somewhat notable; it is in stark contrast to the otherwise ubiquitous patriarchy we see throughout the Bible. But one other thing is also notable here; Joanna is the wife of Chouza, who was the steward of Herod. The Greek word *epitropou* rendered as "steward" above could also be translated as *commissioner, domestic manager, guardian,* or *tutor.*[345] What is notable here is the deviation from an anti-Herodian ethos that otherwise pervades the New Testament.[346]

Another example is that of married Apostles.[347] The Catholic Church maintains that priests must be celibate, even though there are four verses in the New Testament that all clearly state that Peter, the so-called "first Pope" was married. Not only that, but first Corinthians 9:5 also speaks of other apostles being married, and even also the brothers of Jesus being married. That one verse packs a double whammy for the Roman Catholic Church. Supposedly priests

---

[344] Luke 8:1-3.

[345] ABINGDON'S STRONG'S EXHAUSTIVE CONCORDANCE OF THE BIBLE WITH HEBREW, CHALDEE & GREEK DICTIONARIES.

[346] The only other exception I have noted so far is Romans 16:11, where "Paul" refers to his kinsman Herodion. Robert Eisenman has argued on this basis that Paul may have been related by blood to the infamous family of the Herods. This is a distinct possibility, notwithstanding the probable pseudonymous nature of the epistle.

[347] Mt 8:14 cf Mk 1:30; Lk 4:38; 1 Corinthians 9:5.

are to imitate the example of Christ, who was purportedly celibate. But how do we know for sure that Jesus really was celibate? Because Church tradition tells us so? By now we have seen how unreliable such tradition is. For all we know to the contrary, Jesus may have been married, and had children.[348]

I love the next set of examples. Needless to say, it is not exactly congenial to the religious right in America. The examples are those proving that the Apostles and other earlier disciples of Christ practiced a communist economy among themselves, after Christ's alleged passion.

"And all that believed were together, and had all things in common; and *they* sold their possessions and goods, and distributed them to all *the believers,* as every one had need."[349]

"And the multitude of them that believed were of one heart and soul; neither did any claim that anything was his particular possession; but they had all things in common… neither was there any among them that lacked; for as many as possessed lands or houses sold them, and brought the price of the things that were sold, and laid them down at the Apostles' feet: and distribution was made to every man according to his need."[350]

Such passages also belie the idea that the New Testament was written by a wealthy Roman family.[351] They also provide a link

---

[348] However this statement is not intended to endorse any particular Grail theory.

[349] Acts 2:44-45. This is the essence of communism.

[350] Acts 4:32,34-35. Once again, this is essentially communism. Pre-Marxist communism to be sure, but still communism, pure and simple. Such passages clearly prove the blatant hypocrisy of those who co-opt the Bible to promote capitalism and condemn communism; the fact is, communism is blessed by God, while capitalism is condemned. But the religious right in America constantly turn a blind eye to such passages, in their blind hypocrisy, greed, and malignant ignorance. Such passages also belie the common misconception that a communist economic system is inherently opposed to religious liberty. But it seems one will never convince *neanderthalensis ignoramus*. There is a Liberation Theology, but it appears comparatively weak, since the advocates of such lack the blind faith and zeal of evangelicals and fundamentalists. The Qumranites also practiced communism.

[351] One of the phantom Christ theories claims that the New Testament was written by the Pisos, a wealthy Roman family.

with the Essenes, whom Josephus says also practiced a similar type of communist economy among themselves.[352] Likewise the saying ascribed to Christ that "It is easier for a camel to pass through the eye of a needle, than for a rich man to enter the kingdom of God"[353] belies the idea that such a saying could have been penned by some cynical wealthy Roman.

Next there are those passages that suggest that Jesus was not quite the pacifist he is often portrayed to be. We have already seen that Jesus was normatively depicted in the New Testament as a pacifist, particularly in relation to the Romans.[354] But these passages are unquestionably an overlay upon an earlier, non-pacifist Jesus; there can be no doubt of this, once the relevant passages are examined. One incident which is narrated in all four Canonical Gospels flashes a bright spotlight on the fact that neither Jesus nor his Apostles were absolute pacifists. We are told that, when the temple guard sought to arrest Jesus in the Garden of Gethsemane, the Apostle Peter cut off the right ear of Malchus, the servant of the high priest.[355] This proves that Peter had to have had a sword in the first place; why would a pacifist have a sword? Would a modern-day pacifist own a gun? The Gospel of Matthew tries to clumsily overlay the embarrassing incident, by making it another opportunity for Jesus to make another pacifist statement, "Sheath your sword; for all they that take *up* the sword shall perish by the sword."[356] But to the observant reader, the literary tactic does not work; for one is still left wondering why Peter would even have had a sword in the first place, if Jesus had already given such pacifist teachings as "Resist not evil; whosoever shall strike you an your right cheek, turn to him the other."[357] But there is more also. In the Gospel of Luke, Jesus, just before his arrest, tells his Apostles to buy swords: "But now, he that hath a satchel, let him take it, and likewise also his scrip; and he that hath no sword, let him sell his

---

[352] Jos. War. 2.8.3.

[353] Mt 19:24; Mk 10:25; Lk 18:25.

[354] Mt 5:39-48; 22:21; 26:52; Mk 12:17; Lk 6:27-37; 13:1-3; 20:25.

[355] John 18:10 cf Mark 14:47; Matthew 26:51; Luke 22:50.

[356] Matthew 26:52.

[357] Matthew 5:39. A truly suicidal teaching.

garment, and buy one."[358] This is exactly the opposite from what Jesus is made to say in Matthew 5:39 and 26:52. Why? It is certainly a source of embarrassment to Christians.[359] But making a comparison between the two sets of passages, we can clearly see that they are not both equally indifferent, but that the pacifist, pro-Roman passages are clearly an overlay upon an earlier, more archaic, non-pacifist, militant Jesus. In other words, these non-pacifist passages depict an alternate image of Christ, and one that is more in accord with probable historical reality. Even if we do not go so far as to say that Jesus was a Zealot or Zadokite, still he was not an absolute pacifist, which the more normative New Testament passages would lead us to believe. The popular image of Jesus is one in which he is a very calm, peaceful person, akin to Martin Luther King, Jr., or to Mohandas Gandhi. But that apparently was not the case. This is not an attempt to smear Jesus; if anything, I think it is a far more reasonable image of Christ, which portrays him as much more believable, much more human, and much more intelligent. After all, the radical pacifism associated with the popular image of Christ is essentially a suicidal ideology. It is unreasonable to say that there can never be a righteous use of force. But most Bible believers are brainwashed by a completely pacifist image of Jesus, and those who are, are invariably persecuted and taken advantage of by less scrupulous persons.[360] Other Bible believers may make an exception of a "just war" waged by a supposedly righteous nation against another.[361] And being blindly misguided by a false sense of patriotism and a biblical prescription of obedience to the authorities,[362] they unthinkingly support a war waged by their nation, whether it is right or wrong.

Then there is the highly controversial verse where Jesus says "Think not that I have come to send peace on earth; I came not to send peace, but a sword."[363] This verse also contradicts the various pacifist verses. Some Christians try to rationalize these verses away

---

[358] Luke 22:36.

[359] Christians should be embarrassed by such contradictions, although they may make a false pretense to the contrary.

[360] And I know this from bitter personal experience.

[361] And invariably the "righteous nation" is the believer's own nation.

[362] Romans 13:1-7.

[363] Matthew 10:34.

by saying that Christ was speaking of the "sword of the Spirit, which is the word of God."[364] But the context of the verse in Matthew does not support this explanation; Jesus goes on to speak of deadly divisions within families amongst the Israelites.[365] Furthermore, earlier on in the very same chapter, Jesus is speaking of the disciples being persecuted, telling them that, when they are persecuted in one city, they should flee to another.[366] So the context belies any such spiritualizing hermeneutic. Furthermore, when we recall the context of the passage from the Gospel according to Luke, cited above, the scene is such as to belie any such convenient interpretation. In the same passage, Jesus continues, saying "For I say unto you, that this that is written of me must yet be accomplished in me, 'And he was reckoned among the transgressors' for the things *written* of me have their fulfillment."[367] In other words, Jesus is advising his Apostles to purchase swords, because they may be hunted down as criminals. There is nothing mystical in the passage. And the ordinary, down-to-earth, common-sense interpretation of the passage is also confirmed by the response of the Apostles to Jesus: "Lord, behold, here are two swords."[368] Once again, the fact that the Apostles already had two swords proves that they were not all pacifists. We know that Peter was one of the men with a sword. I think I can guess which one of the others also had a sword.[369] Perhaps these two men had the role of bodyguards for Jesus.

So here we have a clear example, by way of comparison between two distinctly different and mutually opposed sets of passages, of a set of contradictions. And not merely an indifferent set of contradictions, but one which also discloses an underlying historical subtext; one in which Jesus was not an absolute pacifist, as we are otherwise given the impression by the Sermon on the Mount, and other verses.

A comparison between the two sets of passages also makes it very clear, in critical-historical terms, that the pacifist passages are definitely the overlay, rather than the reverse. It is inconceivable that an originally pacifist Jesus was overlaid with a quasi-Zealot Jesus, but

---

[364] Ephesians 6:17.

[365] Matthew 10:35-36 cf Micah 7:6.

[366] Matthew 10:23.

[367] Luke 22:37.

[368] Luke 22:38.

[369] Simon the Zealot. Cf Luke 6:15 cp Mark 3:18; Matthew 10:4.

the reverse is quite possible. And indeed, it definitely appears to be the case here. The implications of this are quite far-reaching. For one thing, this is overwhelmingly strong evidence in favor of the historicity of Jesus. Because if Jesus was merely an invented figure, we would not expect to find a militant Messiah overlaid by a pacifist Son of God. If Jesus was merely a *phantom,* then we would expect a much simpler, harmonious text of the Gospels. The text of such an invented Messiah should be seamless, without any discernible layers of proto-historical or proto-orthodox teachings or circumstances. Phantom Christ theorists have to posit an overwhelmingly great talent, ingenuity, and cleverness to the writers of the Gospels and other New Testament texts. Quite frankly, it is overkill. As we have seen already, some of these fossil passages are such that they could not have been written at all, unless either Jesus truly did exist as a historical person, or that those men who wrote the texts in question had a protocol that required the historicity of Jesus be given preference to his supposed ontological status as the Son of God. Of the two possibilities, the first is definitely preferable in terms of economy of thought.

Then there is also the incident of Jesus overturning the tables of the moneychangers in the temple.[370] In John's account we read that Jesus even went so far as to make a scourge of small cords (a whip), by which he drove out those whom he felt were violating the sanctity of the temple. In my earlier book I speculated that possibly the incident of overturning the tables of the moneychangers in the temple was an effort to fulfill Daniel's prophecy of the seventy weeks, which said that the Messiah would "cause the oblation and the sacrifice to cease" in the midst of the final, seventieth week of the prophecy.[371] I still feel that this is a fairly plausible explanation of Christ's actions. Unfortunately this incident is linked with a gratuitous fulfillment of yet another prophecy by John,[372] which casts some degree of suspicion on whether or not the incident was truly historical, or merely was written into the narrative to provide another gratuitous fulfillment of prophecy. But even taking a critical view of the text, it seems more likely that John has merely placed a prophetic overlay on an actual historical event, to smooth out what might otherwise be an

---

[370] Mt 21:12; Mk 11:15-16; Lk 19:45; Jn 2:13-16.

[371] Daniel 9:27. See my earlier work.

[372] John 2:17 cf Psalm 69:9.

embarrassing incident. Even in the Synoptics Jesus is quoted as making reference to passages from TaNaKh[373] in justification of his actions. But it is uncertain whether Jesus actually spoke the words attributed to him on that occasion, or they were provided for him after the fact by some proto-evangelist. I am willing to concede that Jesus may have spoken the words in question; no doubt he was very skilled in the Scriptures, and sought a justification of his actions therein. As to whether or not this was an anti-Roman activity, as some have speculated, remains another matter entirely. For one thing, it is at least possible that Jesus may have lived a century before the commonly accepted time,[374] in which case the cleansing of the temple would have had nothing whatever to do with the Romans, since it was before the time of the Roman occupation of Judaea. On the other hand, even if Jesus lived in the first century, his actions in the temple would not seem to have been calculated to injure the Romans in any way, but rather to disrupt the sale of sacrificial animals. Once again this ties in with the theme of Jesus as an Ebionite. Furthermore the question of the moneychangers is particularly interesting in light of the famous "Render unto Caesar" passage, since those moneychangers would exchange Roman coinage for one acceptable to the temple. They may have charged unfair profits for the exchange of coinage. This once again places Jesus as a champion of the poor, as do very many other passages.[375]

In the light of these passages, I feel the need to modify what I wrote earlier about an exception to pro-Roman bias in the New Testament. I gave the example of Luke 13:1, where Jesus is told about the bloody fate of certain Galileans at the hands of Pilate. My point was that Luke, rather than passing over the incident in silence, as did Matthew and Mark, mentioned it. However the entire context of the passage puts another color on it. After Jesus is told about this incident, he says "Do you suppose that those Galileans were worse sinners than all other Galileans, because they suffered so? I tell you no; but unless

---

[373] Isaiah 56:7; Jeremiah 7:11.

[374] See my earlier work.

[375] Mt 11:5; 19:21; Mk 10:21; 12:42-43; Lk 4:18; 6:20; 7:22; 14:13,21; 19:8; 21:2-3; Jn 13:29. In fact one sees the poor championed throughout the Bible.

you repent, you shall all likewise perish."[376] The response of Jesus is such that it implies that the men involved were guilty of sedition, and therefore were "sinners" and worthy of punishment. Therefore the context of the passage does provide a pro-Roman paradigm. As such, it is not really an exception to the general rule of a pro-Roman ambience to the New Testament. However in the case of the *Apokalypse,* the symbolism is definitely anti-Roman. But the passage in Luke hints at a genuine historical subtext; one in which Jesus may have been informed of some incident in which unfortunate Galileans, who may or may not have been involved in seditious activities, were slaughtered by the agents of Pilate.[377] The warning may have been intended either to dissuade Jesus from militant activities against the Romans, or to tell him that he must protect himself, and should probably flee to safety, at least temporarily. But the incident has been reworked in Luke's narrative of the events.

Another interesting passage that I also classify as a fossil passage is the following one from Mark's Gospel:

22 And he comes to Bethsaida, and they bring a blind man to him, and asked him to touch him, *that he might be healed.*

23 And he takes him by the hand, and leads him out of the town; and when he had spit on his eyes, and laid his hands on him, he asked him if he saw anything.

24 And he looked up, and said, I see men as trees, walking.

25 After that he laid his hands on his eyes, and made him look up. And he was restored, and saw every man clearly.

26 And he sent him away to his house, saying, Go neither into the town, nor tell it to anyone in the town. (Mark 8:22-26)

This passage is interesting for a number of reasons, and there are several reasons for classifying it as among the fossil passages. First of all, such a strange passage would seem to almost be an embarrassment for later orthodoxy, especially the orthodoxy upholding the alleged

---

[376] Luke 13:2-3.

[377] This might possibly correspond to what is narrated in Jos. Ant. 18.3.1-2.

Deity of Christ. Why would God the Son need to lay hands on a blind man twice to restore his sight? For that matter, Why would the Son of God need to lay hands on a blind man twice to restore his sight? The passage predictably is found in no other Gospel. There are several reasons why this passage is definitely a literary fossil. For one thing, it depicts Jesus using a shamanistic healing method.[378] Secondly there is the embarrassment factor: Why does Jesus Christ, the very Son of God, need to lay hands on a man twice to heal him? Thirdly is the fact that this places Christ in a position of subordination to the Father. Fourthly is the fact that this depiction of Christ is contrary to later orthodoxy, and hence an embarrassment on that account. Fifthly is the strange and unaccountable fact that Jesus tells the man to remain silent about his healing. The only valid explanation for this is that the miracle never occurred; by placing such words in the mouth of Jesus, the Evangelist provides an implicit disclaimer for why nobody can be found who testifies of being healed by Jesus, the great wonder-worker. Sixthly is the halting way that the miracle allegedly occurred; this parallels, as we will see, a passage in Suetonius respecting the Emperor Vespasian, suggesting literary influence.[379] So we can see that in some cases, there may be an overlapping of criteria for the classification of a verse or passage as a literary fossil.

Another classic example is the verse where Jesus tells the people to "Call no man on earth your father; for One is your Father, who is in the heavens."[380] Obviously this is a fossil, since it preemptively contradicts the Roman Catholic custom of calling a priest "father". There is a certain twisted irony in celibate men being addressed as "father". But this unbiblical custom is so ingrained in our culture that even non-Catholics are expected to conform to it. And if Jesus did not mean those words, why then are they written in the Gospel? Also the anti-Encratite passage of 1 Timothy 4:1-6 I have included among the literary fossils, because even though in all probability the text was written by Polycarp in the second century, it is still a clear example of a New Testament text preemptively contradicting later Catholic

---

[378] The very same thing is found in a few other passages; Mark 7:32-36; John 9:6-7.

[379] And the overwhelming probability is that Mark was either directly or indirectly influenced by Suetonius, rather than the contrary. This places Mark no earlier than the early second century.

[380] Matthew 23:9.

orthodoxy.[381] There are also those passages that depict both Jesus and the Apostles as upholding and observing the Torah and the Sabbath.[382] Then there are those verses that speak of living saints.[383] Then there are all those passages where Jesus employs secrecy, either telling his Apostles not to disclose his messianic status, or telling recipients of his healings not to tell anyone about them, or teaching in parables, or generally employing secrecy.[384] Then there are those verses that speak of apostles other than the Twelve Apostles of the Lamb.[385] Then there are those passages that depict a spiritual rather than a carnal resurrection from the dead.[386] Then there are those many passages that clearly depict the Son as being subordinate to the Father, both before, during, and after the incarnation.[387] Then there would be all

---

[381] I.e., mandatory celibacy for priests and mandatory abstention from meat during the Fridays of Lent. It does not matter if the Roman Catholic Church may have since relinquished some of the former constraints placed upon both the clergy and laity; the very fact that such unbiblical, anti-biblical doctrines and practices were ever inculcated is an illustration of the principle in question here. In other words, even if Polycarp was the author of 1 Timothy, it still predates the later "orthodoxy" of Roman Catholicism.

[382] Mt 5:17-18; 8:4; 19:16-24; 23:23; 24:20; 27:57-61; 28:16-20; Mk 1:44; 10:17-25; 16:1; Lk 5:14; 18:18-25; 17:14; 24:53; Acts 1:12.

[383] Romans 1:7; 1 Corinthians 1:2; 16:1; 2 Corinthians 1:1; Philippians 1:1; 4:22; Colossians 1:2. Verses that speak of living saints are contrary to the later Roman Catholic orthodoxy of "saints" being certain dead, "canonized" people, in a special class; this is all foreign to the New Testament proper.

[384] Mt 7:6; 8:4; 16:20; Mk 1:44; 3:12; 4:2,33-34; 7:32-36; 8:26,30; Lk 5:14; 9:21; Jn 16:25,29.

[385] Romans 16:7; 1 Corinthians 15:7-9; 2 Corinthians 11:5,13; 12:11; Galatians 1:1; Ephesians 1:1; Colossians 1:1; 1 Timothy 1:1; 2 Timothy 1:1; Titus 1:1. These examples are all from the Pauline corpus; hence the Pauline definition of "apostle" is deviant from the New Testament norm. Traditionally most people only think of the twelve Apostles.

[386] Mt 17:1-8; 22:30; Mk 9:1-8; 12:25; Lk 16:19-31; 20:38; 23:43; Jn 3:1-6; Acts 12:15; 1 Corinthians 15:44-50; 2 Corinthians 5:1-4; 12:2-5; Philippians 1:23; Hebrews 12:22-23; 1 Peter 3:18; Revelation 6:9-11; 20:4. This concept is contrary to later Christian orthodoxy.

[387] There are so many verses and passages in this class that I despair of placing them all in a footnote. But see the table of all the fossil passages.

those passages that are contrary to later Roman Catholic orthodoxy.[388] Obviously this latter class would subsume all those in the former class, as well as many we have already discussed. Aside from these, there are miscellaneous verses and passages that, by their nature, I have classed as literary fossils for one reason or another, or due to their general character.

The literary fossils essentially indicate an earlier phase of orthodoxy, or rather a collection of texts exhibiting certain general characteristics that are more archaic than what is found even in such relatively "early" texts as those epistles attributed to Ignatius and Polycarp, to say nothing of later orthodoxy. Of course phantom Christ theorists could argue that this earlier stage of orthodoxy does not in and of itself prove the historicity of Jesus Christ; however we have already examined certain passages that, by their very nature, suggest an actual historical subtext, since otherwise they would have been contrary to the intent of men inventing a Messiah out of the blue. The same mythicists could further argue that such passages were added to the text to provide a greater degree of realism to their creation. But one would counter that such an argument is merely special pleading and begging of the question.

Once again we must acknowledge that there is a distinction between evidence and the interpretation of evidence. The fossil passages of the New Testament are an important part of the total evidence, in my view. But there is still much more evidence yet to be presented and considered. The following section will offer significant evidence that will serve as a counterpoise to what has been considered here. Therefore it is wise to at least suspend final judgment on the question of the historicity of Jesus Christ. There are some truly brilliant scholars who have come to the conclusion that Jesus was a mere *chimera,* and their evidence ought not to be lightly or hastily dismissed, due to cultural inertia.

But before moving on, I would like to also offer an example of literary fossils from outside of the New Testament proper. I have two examples, both from the Gospel of Peter. Although the text of the Gospel of Peter as a whole may be comparatively late, it still seems to contain certain archaic features, which may hark back to genuine traditions or earlier texts. As such they are worth looking at.

---

[388]   These would of necessity include many we have already considered.

The first example is that, when Jesus is hanging from the cross, he cries out "My power, my power, thou hast forsaken me. And when he had said this, he was taken up."[389] The saying "My power, my power, thou hast forsaken me" obviously is a parallel to the more familiar "My God, my God, why hast thou forsaken me?" of the Gospels.[390] But it is a strange and deviant parallel. If Peter's Gospel had been included in the New Testament, I undoubtedly would have included this as one of the fossil passages. The reason why the reading found in Peter seems more archaic is the fact that it does not conform to the messianic prophetic scheme that we find depicted in Matthew and Mark; instead we have something much more immediate; something that seems much more genuine, rather than something that could be said to have been written to conform to a supposed messianic scheme of required prophetic fulfillment. Could Jesus have uttered a saying from the cross[391] such as we read in the Gospel of Peter, but which was later reworked into a more acceptable messianic framework by the later Evangelists? I think so. In fact, such a saying seems more in accord with what we would expect Jesus to cry out if his passion was more in accord with what we read in the Toldoth Yeshu.[392] In any case, using the very same principles I used to determine the fossil passages of the New Testament, I would definitely also classify this passage from Peter as a literary fossil. The very fact that it deviates so glaringly from a pristine messianic scheme evokes a pungent aroma of authenticity.[393]

The second example is actually earlier in the text. It is the very first verse.[394]

"But of the Jews none washed his hands, neither Herod nor any one of his judges. And when they had refused to wash them, Pilate rose up. And then Herod the king commandeth that the Lord be taken, saying to them, What things soever I commanded you to do unto him, do."

---

[389] Peter 5. I am using the numbering of *The Lost Books of the Bible*.

[390] Mt 27:46; Mk 15:34 cf Psalm 22:1.

[391] Or tree; see my earlier work.

[392] And although the Toldoth Yeshu, as it has come down to us, seems to be a fairly late production, it still may contain old traditions.

[393] And therefore historicity.

[394] I.e., the first verse of that small fragment of Peter that has survived.

The main reason why this verse is anomalous is that it depicts Herod as being more directly responsible for Christ's passion than Pilate. This is in stark contrast to what is written in all four Canonical Gospels. It also depicts Herod as a king, which may be an anachronism.[395] If this is interpreted as an anachronism, then it could be further interpreted as inadvertent evidence that Jesus really lived in the days of the first Herod, who was the King of Judaea and Galilee. This would not be quite so far back in time as I postulated in my earlier work, but it would be a chronological anachronism.[396] But the apparent error may not be an anachronism, or even strictly speaking an error at all. Herod Antipas, though he was merely the *tetrarch* of Galilee, no doubt probably styled himself a king in his vain conceit. After all he was the son of a king, and he would have impressed his royal descent upon all and sundry. What is astonishing is that the passage depicts Herod as exercising such prerogatives in the very presence of Pontius Pilate himself. It is hard to imagine him thus lording over his servants in the presence of his own overlord. But the key point to the passage seems to be that Herod had a greater culpability in the fate of Jesus than did Pilate. This could be an example of whitewashing the Romans, in which case it is wise to look on the verse as an overlay, rather than a literary fossil. But one suspects that the real intent was to place blame upon Herod in particular. And Herod may have felt more threatened by Jesus than Pilate ever did. After all, the people were proclaiming Jesus as the "King of Israel" or "King of the Jews", a title expressly held by his father, and one he no doubt aspired to, or pretended to. As such, Herod may have been the one to decree the fate of death for Jesus, rather than Pilate.[397] The very fact that this passage is deviant from the four New Testament Gospels, and in such a strange way, makes it a literary fossil.[398] On the

---

[395] But if so, then Mark and Matthew are guilty of the very same anachronism; cf Mk 6:14-27; Mt 14:9. Herod Antipas had the title of tetrarch of Galilee; his father was a king.

[396] And it is at least possible that Jesus may have lived at this earlier time; it would also notably be within the era of Roman occupation of Judaea, and hence would conveniently fall within the days of the fourth beast/kingdom depicted in Daniel's visions.

[397] But if so, we would expect that this took place in Galilee, rather than Jerusalem.

[398] This is distinct from the way that the epistles ascribed to Polycarp and

other hand, it is also just barely possible that the entire passage can be traced back to Mark's Gospel, which explicitly calls Herod Antipas a "king" throughout the narration of John the Baptist's martyrdom.[399] This may have been carelessness on Mark's part, but I suspect there was an underlying literary reason for it. Mark records that Herod had promised the daughter of Herodias anything she wanted, up to "half the kingdom."[400] In Esther, the king promises Esther three times to grant her whatever she wished, up to "half the kingdom."[401] What seems most probable to me is that Mark wrote his account as a literary parallel to what we find in Esther; with the obvious ironic distinctions, of course; Herod being merely a vassal of a relatively small tetrarchy of Palestine, while King Artaxerxes reigned over a huge empire of one hundred and twenty-seven provinces. As such, Mark may have sought to show the vanity and conceit of Herod. Matthew no doubt copied his account from that of Mark and due to scribal fatigue, fell into the "error" of calling Herod Antipas a "king".[402] I put "error" in parentheses because it may not have been an error at all, strictly speaking; the Romans may have allowed Herod Antipas to call himself a king over Galilee. In any case Herod I was called a king, even though he himself was also under the dominion of the Roman overlords. Therefore Roman domination is not sufficient reason to deny the title of "king" to Herod Antipas, even though his more proper title was tetrarch.[403]

Ignatius deviate from New Testament orthodoxy. There would have been no reason for some later scribe to place greater blame upon Herod than upon Pilate; both men would have been long dead. And furthermore the Gospel of Peter itself was later rejected as heretical.

[399]   Mark 6:14-27.

[400]   Mark 6:23. Matthew omitted this from his version of the story; cp Mt 14:1-11.

[401]   Esther 5:3,6; 7:2. In my earlier work I noted that the king in question was probably Artaxerxes, rather than Ahasuerus, as narrated in the Hebrew Massoretic text.

[402]   Matthew 14:9.

[403]   The Greek word *tetrarch* means ruler of a fourth part; therefore were not the four men who divided Alexander's empire into four parts literally *tetrarchs* according to the same strict meaning, even though they styled themselves kings? And the Ptolemies pharaohs?

The Fossil Passages

MATTHEW 1:25 + #

MATTHEW 2:13-21 + #

MATTHEW 5:17,18 cp LUKE 16:17 >

MATTHEW 7:6 []

MATTHEW 8:4 cp MARK 1:44; LUKE 5:14 [] >

MATTHEW 8:14 cp MARK 1:30; LUKE 4:38 & #

MATTHEW 9:14 cp MARK 2:18; LUKE 5:33 ★

MATTHEW 10:5,6

MATTHEW 10:34-36 z

MATTHEW 11:2,3 cp LUKE 7:19,20 ★

MATTHEW 11:11-15 cp LUKE 7:28

MATTHEW 11:27 cp LUKE 10:22

MATTHEW 12:46-50 cp MARK 3:31-35; LUKE 8:19-21 + #

MATTHEW 13:54-57 cp MARK 6:1-5 + #

MATTHEW 14:1,2 cp MARK 6:14

MATTHEW 14:12 cf MARK 6:29 ★

MATTHEW 15:24 cp JOHN 10:16

MATTHEW 16:14 cf MARK 8:28; LUKE 9:19

MATTHEW 16:20 cp MARK 8:30; LUKE 9:21 []

MATTHEW 16:23 cf MARK 8:33

MATTHEW 17:1-8 <

MATTHEW 17:10-12 cp MARK 9:11-13 [cp PISTIS SOPHIA]

MATTHEW 18:8,9 cp MARK 9:43-48

MATTHEW 18:20

MATTHEW 19:16-24 cp MARK 10:17-25; LUKE 18:18-25 ^ > #

MATTHEW 20:23 cp MARK 10:40 ^ #
MATTHEW 22:30 cf MARK 12:25 cp LUKE 20:38 <
MATTHEW 23:9 #
MATTHEW 23:23 > #
MATTHEW 24:15 cf MARK 13:14
MATTHEW 24:20 > #
MATTHEW 26:6-13 cp MARK 14:3-9; JOHN 12:1-8
MATTHEW 26:24 cf MARK 14:21 {cf ENOCH 38:2}
MATTHEW 26:51 z
MATTHEW 27:16,17 {JESUS BAR-ABBAS}
MATTHEW 27:32 cf MARK 15:21; LUKE 23:26 {SIMON of CYRENE}
MATTHEW 27:39,40 cp JOHN 2:19
MATTHEW 27:46 cp MARK 15:34
MATTHEW 27:57-61 cp MARK 15:43-47; LUKE 23:50-56 cf JOHN 19:38-42 >
MATTHEW 28:16-20 ^ > #
MARK 1:1-6
MARK 1:9-11
MARK 2:27 {cf II MAKKABEES 5:19 cp DEUTERONOMY 5:14}
MARK 3:12 []
MARK 3:21
MARK 4:2,33,34 []
MARK 6:5 ^ #
MARK 7:32-36 ~ []
MARK 8:22-26 ^ [] #
MARK 9:1-8 <
MARK 9:38-40 cf LUKE 9:49,50 cp MATTHEW 12:30; LUKE 11:23 {Suetonius}
MARK 10:12
MARK 12:29 cf DEUTERONOMY 6:4 ^ #
MARK 12:35-37 cf MATTHEW 22:41-45; LUKE 20:41-44
MARK 13:32 cf MATTHEW 24:36 ^ #
MARK 14:27 cf MATTHEW 26:31 cp ZECHARIAH 13:7 {CD 19:7-9}
MARK 14:47 z
MARK 14:50-52
MARK 14:58 cp MATTHEW 26:61 cf JOHN 2:19
MARK 15:23 cp MATTHEW 27:34

MARK 16:1 >
MARK 16:5-7 cf LUKE 24:4-11 cp MATTHEW 28:5-8
LUKE 1:5-9,36 cf NUMBERS 36
LUKE 2:1-7 cp MATTHEW 2:1 + #
LUKE 2:52 ^ #
LUKE 3:15
LUKE 6:15 z
LUKE 7:28 cp MATTHEW 11:11
LUKE 8:1-3 ^ #
LUKE 9:28-36 <
LUKE 11:27,28 #
LUKE 16:19-31 <
LUKE 17:14 > #
LUKE 19:14
LUKE 22:36-37 z
LUKE 22:49-50 z
LUKE 23:43 <
LUKE 24:53 > #
JOHN 1:1-3 ^ #
JOHN 1:14 #
JOHN 1:35-48
JOHN 3:1-6 <
JOHN 4:22-24
JOHN 5:18,19 ^ #
JOHN 5:30 ^ #
JOHN 6:57 ^ #
JOHN 7:3-5 + #
JOHN 8:41
JOHN 8:42 ^ #
JOHN 9:1-3
JOHN 9:6,7 ~
JOHN 10:16 cp MATTHEW 15:24
JOHN 10:22,23 {cf I MAKKABEES 4:52-59}
JOHN 12:49,50 ^ #
JOHN 13:16 ^ #
JOHN 14:28-31 ^ #
JOHN 15:10 ^ #
JOHN 16:25,29 []
JOHN 17:3 ^ #

JOHN 17:21-25 ^ #
JOHN 18:10-11 z
JOHN 20:17 ^ #
ACTS 1:12 > #
ACTS 1:13 z
ACTS 1:14 + #
ACTS 2:44-46 %
ACTS 3:1 > #
ACTS 4:32-35 %
ACTS 5:30 t
ACTS 7:53
ACTS 10:39 t
ACTS 12:15 <
ACTS 13:1
ACTS 13:6
ACTS 13:13 cp COLOSSIANS 4:10
ACTS 13:29 t
ACTS 14:14 @
ACTS 15:37-39
ACTS 18:1,2 {cp Suetonius; Claudius, 25}
ACTS 18:18 >
ACTS 18:24-26 ★
ACTS 19:1-3 ★
ACTS 21:9 #
ACTS 21:23-24 > [v HEBREWS 9:24-27; 10:1-10]
ACTS 21:37
ROMANS 1:7 / #
ROMANS 15:6 ^ #
ROMANS 16:1
ROMANS 16:7 @
ROMANS 16:11
ROMANS 16:13
I CORINTHIANS 1:2 / #
I CORINTHIANS 2:6-8 []
I CORINTHIANS 8 [v REVELATION 2:14,20]
I CORINTHIANS 8:6 ^ #
I CORINTHIANS 9:1 @
I CORINTHIANS 9:5 & + #
I CORINTHIANS 11:3 ^ #

I CORINTHIANS 15:7-9 @
I CORINTHIANS 15:24-28 ^ #
I CORINTHIANS 15:29
I CORINTHIANS 15:44,50 <
I CORINTHIANS 16:1 / #
II CORINTHIANS 1:1 / #
II CORINTHIANS 1:3 ^ #
II CORINTHIANS 5:1-4 <
II CORINTHIANS 11:5,13 @
II CORINTHIANS 11:31 ^ #
II CORINTHIANS 12:2-5 <
II CORINTHIANS 12:11 @
GALATIANS 1:1 @
GALATIANS 1:11-2:2 [v ACTS 9:1-30]
GALATIANS 1:19 + #
GALATIANS 2:11-20 #
GALATIANS 3:13 t
GALATIANS 3:19
GALATIANS 4:4 #
GALATIANS 4:10
EPHESIANS 1:1 @
EPHESIANS 1:3 ^ #
EPHESIANS 1:7
EPHESIANS 2:2
EPHESIANS 4:4-6 ^ #
EPHESIANS 6:10-17
PHILIPPIANS 1:1 / #
PHILIPPIANS 1:23 <
PHILIPPIANS 2:5-11 ^ #
PHILIPPIANS 4:22 / #
COLOSSIANS 1:1 @
COLOSSIANS 1:2 / #
COLOSSIANS 1:14
COLOSSIANS 1:15 ^ #
COLOSSIANS 1:19 ^ #
COLOSSIANS 2:5 cp I CORINTHIANS 5:3
COLOSSIANS 2:9 ^ #
COLOSSIANS 4:10 cp ACTS 13:13, 15:37-39
II THESSALONIANS 2:1-4 #

I TIMOTHY 1:1 @
I TIMOTHY 2:5 #
I TIMOTHY 3:2-5 #
I TIMOTHY 4:1-3 #
II TIMOTHY 1:1 @
II TIMOTHY 1:2 ^ #
II TIMOTHY 3:12
II TIMOTHY 2:18 <
II TIMOTHY 3:8
II TIMOTHY 4:14
II TIMOTHY 4:20
TITUS 1:1 @
TITUS 1:6,7
HEBREWS 2:2
HEBREWS 6:4-6
HEBREWS 7:27 #
HEBREWS 9:12 #
HEBREWS 9:24-28 #
HEBREWS 10:10-14 #
HEBREWS 12:22,23 <
JAMES 1:1 ^ #
I PETER 1:3 ^ #
I PETER 2:24 t
I PETER 3:18 <
I PETER 3:19 {ENOCH}
I PETER 5:13 #
II PETER 1:1
II PETER 1:2 ^ #
II PETER 2:4 cf JUDAS 6 {ENOCH}
II PETER 2:10,11 cf JUDAS 8,9
I JOHN 2:22,23
II JOHN 9
JUDAS 1
JUDAS 3 cf DANIEL 9:24
JUDAS 14,15 {ENOCH 2 [1:9]; 26:2}
REVELATION 1:1 ^ #
REVELATION 1:6 ^ #
REVELATION 2:13
REVELATION 3:12 ^ #

REVELATION 3:14 ^ #
REVELATION 4 ^ #
REVELATION 6:9-11 <
REVELATION 7:1-8
REVELATION 11
REVELATION 12
REVELATION 13
REVELATION 14:1 ^ #
REVELATION 15:3,4 ^ #
REVELATION 16
REVELATION 17 #
REVELATION 18 #
REVELATION 19:11-21 z
REVELATION 20:4 <
REVELATION 21:1,2
REVELATION 22:8,9

The Testimonia

The Testimonia are something we very rarely hear about anymore, although discussion of the Testimonia was common coin in biblical scholarship in former times. The Testimonia, as used in relation to Jesus Christ and the New Testament, and as distinct from testimonia in the more general sense of the term, denotes a hypothetical document or set of documents used by early messianic Jews or proto-Christians, which listed and quoted passages from the Jewish Scriptures that were supposedly fulfilled by Jesus. There has been a similar document discovered from Qumran, although of course it does not mention Jesus. But it is a classic text of Testimonia, in the sense that it relates scriptural prophecies directly related to the expected Messiah. The text is known as 4QTestimonia or 4Q175. This proves that the Dead Sea community were eagerly awaiting the Messiah, and were compiling documents that wrote down in anticipation those prophecies that the Messiah was expected to fulfill. As I noted in my earlier work, the Dead Sea community may have been awaiting two Messiahs.

But as applied to Christianity, the Testimonia refers to a hypothetical, as yet undiscovered document, that the early disciples composed as a set of "proof" texts that Jesus really was the Messiah, since he supposedly fulfilled all the requisite prophecies. An alternate and more critical theory is that early messianic Jews first compiled such lists of messianic prophecies, and based upon such lists, the writers of the Gospels constructed a narrative around the prophecies. In other words, Jesus fulfilled all the prophecies because he was merely a literary creation, and therefore was made to fulfill all the requisite messianic prophecies in the texts written about him. In other words, according to this theory, the Testimonia, rather than the fossil passages, are the real core of the New Testament; everything else was a mere embellishment.

One alternate critical-historical interpretation is one in which while Jesus was historical, he was nonetheless motivated by a conscious desire to fulfill the requisite prophecies, and therefore acted out a scenario which in his mind would fulfill all the necessary prophecies. This theory is perhaps best expressed in the classic work by Hugh Schonfield known as *The Passover Plot*. Even if we do not agree with all details of Schonfield's thesis, nevertheless if we accord historicity to Jesus then no doubt he was a student of the Hebrew Scriptures, and if he truly believed that he was the Messiah, then he would have conducted himself in such a way as to seek to fulfill all the necessary messianic prophecies. We have already seen an example from the Gospel of Luke,[404] and there are certainly many others clearly expressed throughout the Gospels. In my former work I wrote at length of how Jesus may have sought to specifically fulfill Daniel's prophecy of the seventy weeks.[405] I focused on that prophecy in particular since it is the only Old Testament prophecy to provide a specific timetable for the appearance of the Messiah. My case that Jesus may have lived a century earlier than the commonly-accepted time was largely based upon the chronology of Daniel's prophecy.[406] Daniel's prophecy of the seventy weeks is a key prophecy, since it is the only prophecy in the Jewish Scriptures to provide a clear timetable for when the Messiah was supposed to come. It could be argued that Jesus was merely a phantom created by the exigency of the necessary fulfillment of this key messianic prophecy. If in fact Jesus was a mere *chimera* then Daniel's prophecy of the seventy weeks would have been the text used to determine just when the Messiah was supposed to come, and hence Jesus would have been cast at the appropriate

---

[404]   Luke 22:36–37.

[405]   Daniel 9:24–27.

[406]   Although there was also presented a considerable body of other evidence as well; too much to briefly summarize here. See my earlier work.

time.[407] Of course it should not come as a surprise that a man would make messianic claims at the appropriate time, according to messianic prophecy. Indeed, Josephus writes of many messianic pretenders around the time of Jesus, as well as before and after. Therefore the precise chronology of Christ cannot legitimately be used to subvert the historicity of Christ. Neither can any degree of controversy respecting the chronology of Christ rule out the historicity of Christ.

There are many passages in the Gospels, especially in Matthew and John, that declare very explicitly that Jesus fulfilled this or that prophecy. Or that the circumstances of his life were such as to fulfill this or that prophecy. But of course we do not know for sure if in fact the events took place just as they are narrated, or if the narrative was in fact constructed around a required fulfillment of such prophecies. One thing that Schonfield does not address in his book is the fact that, even if we assume that Jesus acted out prophecies, or arranged circumstances to be or appear to be fulfillments of messianic prophecies, the interpretation of what was required was an eccentric one. In other words, reading the Jewish Scriptures by themselves, without any prior knowledge of the New Testament,[408] one would not necessarily map out a course of action as laid out in the New Testament Gospels. Any number of alternative interpretations would have been possible. Why did Jesus choose such an eccentric interpretation? Or conversely, how were so many other possible interpretations ruled out? The same question applies to those who may have invented Jesus, if we assume he was a mere *chimera*. It is not as if all the messianic passages of *TaNaKh* are clearly set forth in a concise order, which one could follow, as of necessity. One related question is: Could Jesus have in fact have planned a different course of messianic

---

[407] Those familiar with my earlier work will know that the commonly accepted time was just as good as, and in some ways better than, the Hasmonean era. Therefore the chronological markers of the Gospels and other New Testament texts do not act as literary fossils in this respect. Of course 46 B.C., which was the *terminus ad quem* of the seventy weeks, with the *terminus a quo* being the decree of Cyrus, falls within the time of Roman occupation of Judaea, and hence fulfills the further prophetic condition of the Messiah coming in the days of the dreaded fourth beast/fourth kingdom, which the Jews of those times interpreted as being none other than Rome, or the Roman empire.

[408] Something that, strictly speaking, is not possible today. But we can use our imagination.

fulfillment, one that was frustrated by human circumstances? If we picture Jesus as a Zealot then this becomes a distinct possibility, if not a probability. The 4QTestimonia document from Qumran refers to Deuteronomy 18:18-19, which is the implicit subtext of John 1:21 and 6:14, and is explicitly quoted from and referred to in Acts 3:22-23 and 7:37. John 6:15 says that as a result of the miracle Jesus performed, the people would have forcibly crowned him as king, and that for this reason, Jesus withdrew from the crowds. We may surmise from this that the role of Prophet and King were united in the minds of the common people at the time.[409] And both titles were Messianic titles.

In Matthew 26:31 and Mark 14:27, Jesus refers to a prophecy of Zechariah as referring to himself.[410] The Damascus Document, one of the Dead Sea Scrolls, also makes reference to the same prophecy of Zechariah:

"When the oracle of the prophet Zechariah comes true, "O sword, be lively and smite my shepherd and the man loyal to Me–so says God. If you strike down the shepherd, the flock will scatter. Then I will turn my power against the little ones." But those who give heed to God are "the poor of the flock": they will escape in the time of punishment, but all the rest will be handed over to the sword when the Messiah of Aaron and of Israel comes, just as it happened during the time of the first punishment…"[411]

So we have here a clear illustration of a messianic proof-text shared by the community of Qumran and the Evangelists. In fact, although no distinctively Christian document of *Testimonia* has ever yet been discovered, the 4QTestimonia text from Qumran serves as a sort of "missing link" document, in the sense that here we have a sectarian Jewish text, used by a group of messianic Jews, who began to collate the various messianic passages from *TaNaKh* and place them together

---

[409]   Or at least that the Evangelist would so have us believe. But it seems like a reasonably safe assumption.

[410]   Zechariah 13:7; "Awake, O sword, against my shepherd, and against the man that is my associate, saith the Lord of hosts: Smite the shepherd, and the sheep shall be scattered, and I will turn my hand against the little ones." The Syriac Peshitta text has "against the great ones" in the verse.

[411]   Wise, Michael, with Martin Abegg, Jr. & Edward Cook., *THE DEAD SEA SCROLLS: A NEW TRANSLATION.* (© 1996 by Michael Wise, Martin Abegg, Jr. & Edward Cook) HarperCollins Publishers, 10 East 53rd Street, New York, NY 10022. http://www.harpercollins.com ; pg. 58.

in a single text. And we have already noted some linkage between the Essenes and the early Christians, of the fact that they both practiced a communist economy among themselves.[412] This tends to reinforce the impression that possibly John the Baptist was originally a member of the Essene order, but eventually broke away and gathered his own disciples around himself. And very likely Jesus himself was one of John's early disciples, until he himself also broke away from John's group and gathered disciples around himself, taking some of John's disciples along with him. This scenario would explain why Jesus was baptized by John, and also why John still had his own disciples, even after he supposedly proclaimed Jesus as the Lamb of God and the Son of God. This scenario at least has a greater degree of realism than a fundamentalist interpretation of the Gospels.

Robert Eisenman has written extensively on the Dead Sea Scrolls, and his books are among the most interesting and illuminating on the theme of the relationship between the Dead Sea Scrolls and the New Testament, and between the Qumran community and the earliest Christians. He has pointed out that oftentimes the biblical texts that most interested the Dead Sea community also were those most frequently quoted from in the New Testament. A number of other authors, most notably Barbara Thiering and Robert Feather, have also written on the relationship between the Dead Sea Scrolls and the New Testament. It is certainly a rich and suggestive theme, and one that deserves greater attention. But while one can see some parallels between the Essenes and the first Christians, there are also significant differences as well. This is why I feel it is unwise to make an absolute identification between the two groups, but if we postulate a scenario of the Apostles being a third remove from the Qumran community, then this seems more plausible.

But the Testimonia also raise the question of how much of the New Testament narrative is historical, and how much is invention. For those who claim Jesus himself was a mere fiction the Testimonia can provide a convenient rationale for the invention of a biblical Messiah out of the Testimonia. In other words, it could be argued that the ideal Messiah was a literary creation, modeled on the Testimonia.

---

[412] Of course I am here speaking of the very earliest Christian community of the Apostles and the very earliest disciples, who, according to the testimony of the book of Acts, practiced a communist economy among themselves; cf Acts 2:44–46; 4:32–35 cp Jos. War. 2.8.3.

The narrative was built around the core of the Testimonia, in such a scheme. And this is a tempting idea. The Gospels frequently quote from various prophecies, saying that Jesus fulfilled them by his words, actions, or that they were providentially fulfilled by the circumstances surrounding him. Matthew and John in particular make a point of bringing the reader's attention to such fulfilled prophecies. Mark and Luke also do, but not quite as often as Matthew and John. And we should also realise that the narrative may not necessarily draw our attention to a supposedly fulfilled prophecy, but that still a text of prophecy may function as the implicit subtext to the narrative. In fact a person could argue that Mark and Luke function as more advanced specimens of writing on this account. Even if we do not go quite so far as to say that Christ was merely an invented figure, still the question of the Testimonia raises a red flag in terms of questioning how much of the Gospel narrative is merely a gratuitous pandering to the requirements of messianic prophecy. For example, we read that Jesus was born in Bethlehem.[413] Yet in the Gospel of Matthew, attention is drawn to the fact that the Messiah was supposed to be born in Bethlehem.[414] So this raises a cloud of suspicion as to whether or not Jesus was actually born in Bethlehem or not. Furthermore both Matthew and Luke, who narrate the birth of Christ, also each claim that he was born of a virgin.[415] Not only this, but Matthew once again draws attention to a messianic prophecy as a justification for this claim.[416] And while Luke does not explicitly refer to any prophecy still the declaration of Gabriel corresponds to several messianic prophecies.[417] So the Evangelists and/or their sources were very familiar with the Jewish Scriptures. But Matthew and Luke also each provide a royal genealogy for Jesus, and one can only suspect that this was once more a gratuitous provision of yet another messianic credential. So one can only have a healthy dose of skepticism towards

---

[413]   Mt 2:1-15; Lk 2:1-15.

[414]   Mt 2:3-6 cf Micah 5:2 cp Jn 7:42.

[415]   Mt 1:18-23; Lk 1:26-35.

[416]   Mt 1:22-23 cf Isaiah 7:14 (LXX).

[417]   Lk 1:32-33 cp Isaiah 7:14; 9:6-7; 11:1-5; Daniel 7:13-14; 1 Chronicles 17:11-14.

not only the claim of the virgin birth of Christ, but also his supposed royal descent.[418]

Mathew also recounts a tale of a flight into Egypt to escape the wrath of Herod.[419] We are told that Herod slaughtered all the male babies in the region of Bethlehem, from two years old and under. In my former work I speculated that this tale may have been a literary parallel with the account of Herod killing off the last two male heirs of the Hasmonean line.[420] While this is still a valid comparison, it is also notable that the Indian deity Krishna has a similar tale told about his infancy; one that more closely parallels what is found in Matthew. According to the Bhagavata Purana, when Krishna was still an infant, the jealous King Kansa wanted to eliminate him, and ordered all the boys in the region slain. Of course the baby Krishna miraculously escaped, just as the baby Jesus does in the Gospel of Matthew. Some phantom Christ theorists have drawn attention to this interesting parallel. It is just barely possible that the Evangelist may have deliberately ascribed this same tale to Christ's infancy. None of the other Evangelists share the tale, or the account of Herod slaughtering male babies in Bethlehem. Neither does Josephus record any such thing, and as far as I know, neither does the Mishnah. But I suspect that the story was invented to provide two more gratuitous fulfillments of biblical prophecy. We read that Joseph took Mary and the baby Jesus to Egypt to hide from the wrath of Herod, but afterwards he is instructed by an angel in a dream to return to Israel, since Herod had died. This provides Matthew with two more prophecies that were supposedly fulfilled in this instance.[421] We read further in Matthew that Joseph brought Mary and the baby Jesus to Galilee, but this also becomes a pretext for claiming yet another set of fulfilled prophecies.[422] Therefore these details of the life of Christ are subject to grave doubt.

---

[418] Today this latter proposition is taken for granted in any number of Grail theories, despite the tenuous nature of the claim.

[419] Mt 2:3-18.

[420] Jos. Ant. 15.3.3-4; 15.6.1-4.

[421] Mt 2:13-19 cf Hosea 11:1; Jeremiah 31:15.

[422] Mt 2:19-23; 4:12-16 cf Isaiah 9:1-2 cp Isaiah 11:1-5; Zechariah 3:8; 6:12-13; Jeremiah 23:5-6; 33:15-16.

Of course the miracles claimed for Christ are also gratuitous examples of supposedly fulfilled prophecy.[423] Of course Isaiah 53 and Psalm 22 are prime examples of scriptures that Christians claim as fulfilled prophecy in the case of Christ. Some may argue against the use of Psalms as prophecies, saying that when first composed they were not written as prophecies; and while strictly speaking this may be true, nevertheless from a study of the Dead Sea Scrolls it is evident that many devout Jews did interpret the Psalms prophetically, especially in the messianic sense. So the Dead Sea Scrolls at least provide a literary precedent for the practice; it was not something novel to the New Testament. We see towards the end of the Gospel of Luke that Christ also directly claims that many Scripture prophecies foretold his passion and resurrection:

"And he said unto them, These are the words that I spoke unto you, while I was yet with you, that all things must be fulfilled, which were written in the law of Moses, and *in* the prophets, and *in* the psalms, concerning me. Then he opened their understanding, that they might understand the Scriptures; and he said unto them, Thus it is written, and thus it behooved the Messiah to suffer, and to rise from the dead the third day"[424]

So we have here a clear and unmistakable reference to the necessity of the fulfillment of scriptural prophecy. This is why there is a fine line in respect to the use of Testimonia as a criticism of the New Testament; after all, Bible believers can simply claim that there is nothing mysterious or underhanded about the use of Old Testament Scripture, since the New Testament is very straightforward about the claim that many prophecies were fulfilled by Christ. So merely pointing to how a text may have an underlying subtext of Old Testament Scripture is not necessarily a valid criticism in and of itself. But the critical scholar would point to the fact that we have no assurance that such claims of fulfilled prophecy are in fact true historically. If we take Jesus as a historical figure, then it stands to reason that he was a student of biblical prophecy, and sought to fulfill whatever prophecies it was in his power to fulfill. Beyond that, any number of things would have been beyond his control,

---

[423] Luke 7:19-23 cf Isaiah 35:5-6; 61:1-2 cp Luke 4:16-21; John 9:1-7; Mark 10:46-52.

[424] Luke 24:44-46.

aside from the providence of God. But would it be too far fetched to suggest that, quite possibly, certain circumstances surrounding Jesus may have appeared to have been a providential fulfillment of messianic prophecy, and that this provided a boost to the faith of his devout disciples? We must also take into account the fact that many prophecies of *TaNaKh* are incredibly obscure, and subject to various interpretations. It is also worth pointing out that Isaiah 53, perhaps the most famous of all messianic prophecies associated with Jesus, was not necessarily interpreted as a messianic prophecy during the time of the Apostles. This is brought out, apparently inadvertently, in a passage from the book of Acts:

26 And an angel of the Lord spake unto Philip, saying, Arise, go toward the south, unto the way that goeth down from Jerusalem unto Gaza, which is a desert.

27 And he arose and went. And behold, a man of Aethiopia, a eunuch of great authority under Kandakayce Queen of the Aethiopians, who had charge of all her treasure, who had come to Jerusalem to worship,

28 was returning, and sitting in his chariot read Isaiah the prophet.

29 Then the spirit said unto Philip, Go near, and join thyself to this chariot.

30 And Philip ran thither unto *him,* and heard him reading the prophet Isaiah, and asked, Dost thou understand what thou readest?

31 But he said, how can I, unless some man should guide me? Then he asked Philip to come up and sit with him.

32 But the place of the Scripture which he read was this, He was led as a sheep to the slaughter; and like a lamb dumb before his shearer, so he opened not his mouth:

33 in his humiliation his judgment was taken away: and who shall declare his generation? For his life is taken from the earth. [Isaiah 53:7-8]

34 But the eunuch answered Philip, and said, Of whom doth the
prophet speak? Of himself, or of some other man? (Acts 8:26-34)

Christians have always interpreted the prophecy of Isaiah 53 as
applying prophetically to Jesus Christ. This is their prerogative, but
the passage above inadvertently reveals that the prophecy was not
originally interpreted as a messianic prophecy. In fact, the Ethiopian
eunuch thought that the prophet Isaiah may even have been speaking
of his own martyrdom, since there was a tradition that Isaiah was
martyred by King Manasseh. If Isaiah 53 had always been interpreted
as a messianic prophecy, then it would have been needless for the
Ethiopian to ask Philip of whom the prophet was speaking. So the
Jews were not expecting a dying Messiah, much less a crucified
Messiah. This is at least a potential example of an exception to the
rule that the narrative of the Gospels were based upon some text or
tradition of Testimonia; the contrary possibility exists that it was only
after the fact, that the texts of *TaNaKh* were scoured over by the
Apostles and Evangelists, to see if they could find prophetic references
to key events in the life and ministry of Jesus Christ. Such would seem
to be the case with Isaiah 53, if we assume that Jesus was crucified,
or that the Apostles believed this.[425] Psalm 22 and Isaiah 53 both lend
themselves admirably to a claim of prophetic fulfillment in the case of
a crucified man. In that way the Apostles could overcome the "curse"
of a crucified Messiah.[426] Of course we cannot be absolutely sure if this
was the work of the Apostles themselves, or of some later generation of
believers, who wrote the New Testament texts. We must be careful of
begging the question. It is the truth we are seeking.

In my former work I noted that the Habakkuk pesher from
Qumran spoke of a "delay" in the time of the fulfillment of prophecy,
and I interpreted this as evidence that the Habakkuk pesher was
written some time after 46 B.C., which would have been the expected
time of the Messiah, based upon Daniel's prophecy of the seventy
weeks.[427] The Habakkuk pesher proves that the Dead Sea community

---

[425] Or that they wanted other people to believe it. We must bear in mind the
principle of esotericism.

[426] Deuteronomy 21:22-23 cp Galatians 3:13.

[427] I.e., with the further assumption of the decree of Cyrus as the *terminus a
quo* of the timetable of the prophecy. The further assumption being that the
Jews of that time also used the same system of chronological reckoning as

had a special interest in the book of Habakkuk. There is some controversy among Scroll scholars as to whether the Habakkuk pesher speaks of the invasion of Judaea by the Romans in 63 B.C. or in the time of Titus. Robert Eisenman has adopted the latter interpretation, although in this he is outside of the general scholarly consensus.[428]

Mark wrote that the chief priests offered Judas Iscariot silver to betray Jesus to them.[429] But Matthew specifies thirty silver pieces, since it provided another gratuitous fulfillment of prophecy.[430] So it is very difficult, or even impossible, to determine with certainty how much of the story of Jesus as found in the Gospels is actually true.[431] It is tempting to reject the entirety of what we are told about Jesus, and to say that he was merely a *chimera* invented to supposedly "fulfill" the requisite messianic prophecies; and this is a challenge that the Testimonia pose for the critical student of the Bible. Interestingly, the general definition of Testimonia also holds some interest for our study; it denotes references to the earliest written quotations from a given written work.

---

the standard chronology used today, an unproven point, as I noted in my earlier work. But I still think it is reasonably safe to say that the Habakkuk pesher was probably written sometime after 46 B.C. I also speculated that the Hebrew Massoretic texts of Ezra and Nehemiah were likewise written after 46 B.C., to artificially extend the time of fulfillment of Daniel's prophecy of the seventy weeks.

[428] Which is not to say that he is necessarily wrong.

[429] Mark 14:11, according to the original Greek.

[430] Matthew 26:14-15; cf Zechariah 11:12-13 cp Matthew 27:3-10.

[431] I.e., for those without the luxury of blind faith.

Testimonia

Daniel 9:26,27 abomination of desolation cf Mt 24:15; Mk 13:14

Daniel 11:31; 12:11 abomination of desolation

Daniel 11:36 cf II Thessalonians 2:4

Daniel 8:11-14 cf I Makkabees 1:54

Daniel 7:13,14 son of man cf Mt 26:64; Mk 14:62 cp Lk 22:69 cp Revelation 1:13

Daniel 12:1 cf Mt 24:21; Mk 13:19 cp Revelation 12:7-9

Daniel 12:2 cf Jn 5:28,29 cp Revelation 20:12,13

Daniel 12:3 cf I Corinthians 15:50 cp Philippians 3:21

Isaiah 6:1-10 cf Jn 12:39-41 cp Mt 13:15; Acts 28:27

Isaiah 7:14 cf Mt 1:23

Isaiah 9:1,2 cf Mt 4:15,16 cp Mt 2:22 cf Lk 1:26

Isaiah 9:6,7 cf Lk 1:32,33

Isaiah 28:16 cf I Peter 2:6 cp Romans 9:33; 10:11

Isaiah 40:3-5 cf Mt 3:3; Lk 3:4-6 cp Mk 1:3

Isaiah 41:4 cf Revelation 1:8,11,17; 2:8; 22:13

Isaiah 42:1-4 cf Mt 12:18-21

Isaiah 44:6 cf Revelation 1:8,11,17; 2:8; 22:13

Isaiah 48:12 cf Revelation 1:8,11,17; 2:8; 22:13

Isaiah 53:1 cf Jn 12:37,38

Isaiah 53:4 cf Mt 8:17

Isaiah 53:5,6 cf I Peter 2:24,25

Isaiah 53:7,8 cf Mt 26:63; 27:12-14; Mk 14:61; 15:3-5 cp Acts 8:32-33

Isaiah 53:9 cf Mt 27:57-60; Mk 15:43-46; Lk 23:50-53; Jn 19:38-42

Isaiah 53:12 cf Lk 22:37 cp Mk 15:27,28 cf Mt 27:38; Lk 23:33

Isaiah 53:12 cf Lk 23:34

Isaiah 59:17 cf Ephesians 6:13-17

Isaiah 59:20,21 cf Romans 11:26,27

Isaiah 65:17,18 cf II Pet 3:13 cp Rev 21:1,2 cf Gal 4:26; Hebrews 11:16; 12:22

Isaiah 65:1,2 cf Romans 10:20,21

Isaiah 66:22-24 cf Mk 9:43-48

Hosea 1:10 cf Romans 9:26

Hosea 6:2 cf Mt 12:38-40 cf I Corinthians 15:4.

Hosea 6:6 cf Mt 9:13; 12:7

Hosea 10:8 cf Lk 23:30 cp Revelation 6:16

Hosea 11:1 cf Mt 2:15

Amos 9:11-12 cf Acts 15:16,17

Micah 5:1 cf Luke 22:63-64; Mark 15:19; Matthew 27:30; Peter 9
Micah 5:2 cf Mt 2:6 cp Jn 7:42 cf Lk 2:4,11
Micah 7:5-6 cf Mt 10:34-36
Joel 2:28-32 cf Acts 2:17-21 cp Romans 10:13
Jonah 1:17 cf Mt 12:38-40
Habakkuk 1:5 cp Acts 13:41
Habakkuk 2:4 cf Romans 1:17; Galatians 3:11
Haggai 2:6,7 cf Hebrews 12:26
Zechariah 4 cf Revelation 11:4
Zechariah 9:9 cf Mt 21:5; Mk 11:1-7; Lk 19:29-35; Jn 12:14,15
Zechariah 11:10-13 cf Mt 26:15; 27:3-10
Zechariah 12:10 cf Jn 19:37 cp Revelation 1:7 cf Mt 27:49 (Vaticanus)
Zechariah 13:7 cf Mt 26:31; Mk 14:27
Zechariah 14:4,5 cf Acts 1:9-12 cp Mt 24:16; Mk 13:14 cf Lk 21:21
Malachi 3:1 cf Mk 1:2 cp Mt 11:10
Malachi 4:5,6 cf Lk 1:17 cp Mt 11:14; 17:1-13 cf Mk 9:11-13
Jeremiah 31:15 cf Mt 2:18
Jeremiah 31:31-34 cf Hebrews 8:8-12; 10:16-17
Ezekiel 34 cf John 10
Ezekiel 36:16-28 cf Acts 1:6,7 cp Romans 11:1,2,15-24
Ezekiel 37:11-14 cf John 5:28,29
Ezekiel 38 & 39 cf Revelation 20:8-9
Deuteronomy 18:18,19 cf Acts 3:22,23
Deuteronomy 32:21 cp Romans 10:19
Numbers 24:17 cp Matthew 2:2
Genesis 3:15 cf Mt 1:18-25; Lk 1:26-38 cp Galatians 4:4 cf Revelation 12:1-5
Genesis 22:8 cf John 1:29,36
Exodus 12:46 cf John 19:36 cp I Corinthians 5:7
Psalms 2:1-3 cf Acts 4:25,26
Psalms 2:7 cf Acts 13:33; Hebrews 1:5
Psalms 2:9 cf Revelation 12:1-5
Psalms 2:12 cp Luke 7:45
Psalms 8:2 cf Matthew 21:16
Psalms 16:8-11 cf Acts 2:25-28
Psalms 22:1 cf Matthew 27:46; Mark 15:34
Psalms 22:16 cf Luke 24:40 cp John 20:20,24-27
Psalms 22:18 cf Mt 27:35; Jn 19:23,24 cp Lk 23:34; Mk 15:24
Psalms 23 cf John 10
Psalms 34:20 cf John 19:36

Psalms 40:6-8 cf Hebrews 10:5-7
Psalms 45:6,7 cf Hebrews 1:8,9
Psalms 69:8 cf John 7:3-5 & Mark 3:21
Psalms 69:9 cf John 2:17 cp Romans 15:3
Psalms 69:21 cf Mt 27:34,48; Mk 15:36; Lk 23:36; Jn 19:29,30 [Peter 16]
Psalms 69:22,23 cf Romans 11:9,10
Psalms 69:25 cf Acts 1:16-20 cp Mt 27:3-5
Psalms 91:10-13 cf Matthew 4:6; Luke 4:10,11
Psalms 109:8 cf Acts 1:20
Psalms 110:1 cf Mt 22:41-45; 26:64; Mk 12:35-37; 14:62; Lk 20:41-44; 22:69
Psalms 110:4 cf Hebrews 5:6,10; 6:20; 7:1-22
Psalms 118:22,23 cf Mt 21:42; Acts 4:11 cp Ephesians 2:20
Proverbs 30:4 cf Mt 1:18-25; 3:17 cp Mk 1:11 cf Lk 1:26-35 cp
Philippians 2:9-11

The Logia Kyriou

The *Logia Kyriou* are also another topic that is rarely discussed nowadays, at least under that appellation. *Logia Kyriou* is Greek for "Words of the Lord" and denotes a hypothetical document that critical biblical scholars postulated as the source of the sayings of Jesus common to both Matthew and Luke. Today there is no longer much use of this term, but rather the more abbreviated "Q", which is derived from the Greman *Quell,* meaning *source.* Q is a somewhat expanded idea, inasmuch as it incorporates not only sayings of Christ but also the narrative structure common to both Luke and Matthew. There are even hypothetical layers of the hypothetical Q document, such as Q1, Q2, Q3, etc. But so far neither the *Logia Kyriou,* nor Q, nor any distinctively Christian *Testimonia* texts have been found.[432] This is certainly a great weakness to this critical textual theory. The theory further presupposes that, not only were such texts as Q used as a basis for Matthew and Luke, but, once used, they were thereafter destroyed. This is almost impossible to believe. We would expect on the contrary that any such texts would have been esteemed as very holy and sacred and would have been diligently preserved and copied.

Furthermore, since Jesus and the Apostles spoke Hebrew, rather than Greek, we would also expect any genuine document written

---

[432] But as noted in the previous section, a 4QTestimonia document was discovered among the Dead Sea Scrolls.

down either at the time Jesus first spoke his teachings, or shortly afterward, would have been written in Hebrew, rather than Greek. Therefore there should instead be a hypothetical *Doberim Adon* text, which later became translated into the Greek *Logia Kyriou*. This is not impossible, but so far no such texts have been discovered.[433]

Not all critical scholars accept the Q hypothesis.[434] In fact, Mr. Goodacre makes a fairly cogent case that Mark was the basis of both Matthew and Luke, without recourse to any hypothetical secondary document such as Q. I would go further and suggest that Mark is the template for not only the Synoptics, but even for John as well. Most likely, the Gospels were not written to supplement one another, but rather to supersede one another. Luke is the only one of the canonical Gospels that makes any reference to any other Gospels; but the implicit subtext to his introduction is that all these "many" earlier written accounts were somehow deficient, and still one more, better account was both desirable and necessary. None of the other Gospels makes any explicit mention of any other Gospels. Matthew was almost certainly written to replace Mark; Luke was written to replace both Mark and Matthew; John was written to supersede, if not replace the three Synoptics. But by that time it had probably become apparent to the Evangelist that the earlier Gospels were impossible to get rid of; they were already too popular, and too widely distributed. So John filled his text with gratuitous one-upmanships that would make the earlier Gospels seem to pale by comparison. The theory of supersession as opposed to supplementation is the only theory that accounts for the numerous contradictions between the four Gospel accounts. Otherwise why would not any subsequent Evangelist have not slavishly copied and followed in minute detail the specifics of any

---

[433] Although in his controversial book *The Jesus Papers*, Michael Baigent claims that ancient Aramaic texts containing a legal defense of Jesus before the charges of the *Sanhedrin* exist, and that he has seen these documents. This is certainly possible, but Monsieur Baigent is, as far as I know, not an Aramaic scholar, and therefore could not translate such texts. Furthermore even if such texts exist, there is no guarantee of their authenticity. Nevertheless it would be a fascinating and potentially important scholarly discovery.

[434] See, for example, *The Case Against Q: Markan Priority and the Synoptic Problem,* by Mark Goodacre; Harrisburg, Pennsylvania; Trinity Press International; 2002. Further information is available at http://www.markgoodacre.org/Q/.

earlier Gospel text that he used?[435] The Evangelists never imagined that their texts would be gathered together and bound together within the binding of a single codex. Each Gospel was written to stand alone. Indeed, it would have been objectionable to any pristine community of messianic believers to use a multiplicity of Gospels, since this would only be a source of doubt and confusion. Because such a multiplicity of texts would only function as a redundancy, or would create doubt and suspicion by reason of discrepancies between the various accounts. Therefore it is fair to say that each Gospel[436] would have originated in a unique provenance. In other words, assuming that the Gospel of Mark was the first Gospel, then it would have enjoyed the greatest popularity and loyalty of support in the region where it was first written, read, distributed, and used by Christians. Matthew may have been written to supersede Mark, but it did not succeed in entirely eradicating it.[437] Mark may have survived due to its genuine antiquity, and the reluctance of early Christians to relinquish it. Matthew survived for a number of reasons. Not only because, despite Luke's efforts to supersede both Mark and Matthew, the latter Gospel contained too much material that was unique to it, which too many Christians were unwilling to sacrifice; but also because of the popularity of the other early Matthew Gospels, such as MtN, MtE, and MtH. But my point is that each Gospel was probably most popular among a given community or region of believers. One can only speculate as to the provenance of each Gospel. But Christian tradition assigns Ephesus in Asia Minor to John, which seems fairly plausible. Luke may have been written somewhere in Greece or Asia

---

[435] And adding either gratuitous embellishments, or supplementing the earlier account with other traditions which he had heard. But as it is, we must concede that no Evangelist thought any earlier Evangelist was infallible; since each one often "corrected" the testimony of those who wrote earlier accounts. This was either done by *caprice,* or because they heard conflicting details from persons whom they considered to be more reliable sources. This is a standing rebuke to those fundamentalists who insist upon biblical inerrancy. Why should we accept the Gospels as the Word of God, when even the Evangelists themselves did not consider pre-existing Gospels to be such?

[436] Those later deemed apocryphal as well as those later deemed canonical.

[437] Although according to some accounts, Mark was a rare Gospel for a long time and almost became a lost Gospel.

Minor; Mark was probably written in Alexandria; Matthew was probably written in Antioch or Caesarea. Of course these Gospels were also distributed to other areas, and even translated into different tongues, early on. Most likely the four most popular Gospels eventually attained Canonicity. But it is also important to realise that no evangelist writing a Gospel could have had any assurance that the text he wrote would eventually become esteemed as "Canonical" as opposed to "apocryphal"; such categories of distinction did not even exist at the time the earliest Gospels were written. They were written to be definitive texts; they were not a species of religious fiction.[438] Of course this is not to turn a blind eye to the use of esotericism, and extended historical parables. But even granting an esotericism to the Gospel texts, it should be recognized that even the exoteric shell would most likely have been taken literally by the vast majority of early believers.[439]

I personally am very skeptical of the Q hypothesis, mostly because not only has no fragment of any such text ever yet been discovered, but the reconstructions of Q are so arbitrary and highly questionable as to be quite unconvincing. Burton Mack has written somewhat on the Q theory, but he postulates that the apocalyptic element of the Gospels is not in the primary layer of Q.[440] Although initially I disagreed with him about this, I now believe that he may be essentially correct about this. However, I remain skeptical of the Q hypothesis in terms of a <u>written</u> document. This is due to Marc Goodacre's incisive research. But despite the fact that Burton Mack's book on Q begins with an enormous amount of begging the question, as well as a protusion of logical non-sequiturs, which I find ultimately vitiate his entire argument, nevertheless the latter portions of his book may have more merit, at least in terms of different "Jesus" communities and "Christ" communities; it is at least worth

---

[438]   I.e., they were not written as examples of religious fiction, but as factual, historical texts. This is not to say that they were actually historically or factually true; but rather that they were intended to be taken as such. There is no credible evidence to the contrary, notwithstanding Barbara Thiering's dubious theories.

[439]   And indeed even the recognition of a deeper layer of esoteric teaching within a given text would generally not be interpreted as the negation of the literal meaning by most adherents of a given religion.

[440]   Q1.

reading in terms of food for thought. But the main reason why I now acquiesce in this view is because I have discovered no less than three distinct eschatologies within the New Testament. There is first of all what I call the "imminent" escatology, represented by passages where people are told that the "time is at hand" and the kingdom of God is imminent. These portions include places where Jesus describes John the Baptist as the return of the Prophet Elijah. These may very well be authentic passages in the sense that they were the genuine teachings of Jesus. The second eschatology is what I refer to as a Danielic "signs" eschatology. This latter eschatology was probably introduced by the writer of 2 Thessalonians. This is also why I now consider all of the "Son of Man" passages suspect; because almost invariably, especially within the synoptic Gospels, the term "Son of Man" is strongly linked to this Danielic eschatology. The third eschatology is the "fulfilled" eschatology, mostly found in the Gospel of John. But I still think far too many critical biblical scholars are too eager to accept the questionable Q hypothesis. But I still feel domr degree of reservation about all this. Most likely this aversion to apocalypticism arises from a suspicion of the use of messianic prophecy, and the implication that those messianic "proof" texts are therefore secondary and gratuitous embellishments, written into the text to provide messianic credentials for Jesus. In this respect I can understand the rationale, but I would say that, assuming the historicity of Jesus, no doubt Jesus himself was a student of biblical prophecy, and impressed these things upon the minds of his Apostles. It would have been absurd to transform a wandering Cynic into the Jewish Messiah. As noted above, not all critical Bible scholars accept the Q hypothesis.

Some fundamentalists use the dubious Q hypothesis as a sort of "straw man" that they can easily knock down, and thereby speciously claim that the historical accuracy of the Gospels has been vindicated. A case in point is that of one Lee Woodard, who claims that the Washington Codex contains actual first century Gospels.[441] Mr. Woodard positively rants against "Q", implying that it is the only source of Christian apostasy. He waxes poetic about the "mercy killing" of "Q" and how the "funeral dirge" is already sounding. As I pointed out in my earlier work, there are other legitimate objections against the alleged divinity of the Bible, and to posit "Q" as the source of all apostasy is merely a "straw man" argument. In fact critical

---

[441]   http://www.washington-codex.org.

scholars such as Mark Goodacre write against the "Q" hypothesis, without resorting to fundamentalism as the only alternative. While Mr. Woodard's material seems remotely intriguing, it is not congenial to his credibility that he claims that the artwork on the cover of *Codex Washingtonensis* was executed by the Jewish Christian Barnabas, and that they are probably accurate likenesses of the four Evangelists. Mr. Woodard claims to have discovered Aramaic alphanumeric codes inscribed on some pages of the Gospels of the Codex that supposedly "prove" a first-century provenance for them. Mr. Woodard is at least straightforward about the ulterior motive of his research; to uphold the reliability of the Gospels, and in turn to provide powerful testimony to the truth of the Christian faith. In my earlier work I answered Mr. Woodard's claims by saying that even second-century authors who sought to create the impression that the Gospels dated to an earlier time could have placed such obscure alphanumeric codes in the text, to create such an impression. However in a spirit of fairness I must withdraw one statement that I had made before; I falsely assumed that the codex could not have dated to any time earlier than the second century. But based upon what we learned above from the Letter of Aristeas, I would no longer insist upon this. Nevertheless in a holilstic sense, I find his material to be essentially unconvincing.

Crisis Passages

The diligent reader may have noticed that the Testimonia passages and the Fossil passages are not completely discrete; in some instances there is an overlapping of passages, which are included in both categories. This of necessity forces a crisis of interpretation, and I refer to these overlapping passages as crisis passages. The crisis has to do with whether to regard such passages as functioning more as legitimate literary fossils, which point to an underlying historical subtext, or to dismiss them as artefacts of a narrative requiring gratuitous fulfillments of messianic prophecies. The answer is not always clear, but in general I would say that in most cases, the passages lend themselves more to an interpretation of them as literary fossils, rather than mere gratuitous embellishments. Of course there may be a twofold aspect to such passages, or to some of them, which would reflect the underlying aspects of such a divergent analysis. I will take a few examples to illustrate the point. First, we have a passage from John's Gospel that speaks of the brothers of Christ:

"His brothers therefore said to him, Leave here and go to Judaea, so that your disciples may also see your works. For no man works in secret, if he seeks to be openly known. If you do such things, show yourself to the world. For neither did his brothers believe in him." (John 7:3-5)

I included the above passage because the fact that Jesus had brothers was a fact contrary to the later orthodoxy that sought to exalt

Mary as a "perpetual" virgin. But I also grouped the above passage in with the Testimonia passages of the New Testament because it harmonizes with the following verse from Psalms:

"I am a stranger unto my brethren, and an alien unto my mother's children." (Psalm 69:8)

Although the Psalm in question is nowhere quoted from in the passage from John, as being fulfilled in the circumstance of his brothers' unbelief in him, nevertheless it is still possible that it may have served as a literary subtext to the narrative; we know that the very same Psalm is quoted from elsewhere in John's Gospel, as having been fulfilled in the circumstances of Christ's ministry.[442] Mark 3:21 is another verse that lends itself to the interpretation of accommodating Psalm 69:8.[443] So the question then becomes, were the brothers of Jesus invented to provide a ground for a gratuitous fulfillment of a supposed prophecy? I'm sure that the phantom Christ theorists would love to argue in this vein, but it is a vain argument. For one thing, even if one were inclined to so argue, this does not account for the sisters of Jesus.[444] It would have been overkill to write sisters into the narrative, if such was not required by the expediency of messianic prophecy. Furthermore nowhere is the verse from the Psalm in question anywhere explicitly quoted in the text as having been fulfilled on this occasion. This makes it seem extremely unlikely that the brothers of Jesus were merely a gratuitous literary invention suiting the messianic dictates of the narrative. Therefore those passages still function as literary fossils testifying to the probable historicity of Jesus Christ. If they were a mere literary invention, then we would expect that there would have been far less written about them, and also that the one or few instances in which they were mentioned it would be brought out quite clearly that this verse of this psalm was

---

[442] Psalm 69:9, quoted in John 2:17, in relation to Christ casting the moneychangers out of the temple precincts. Furthermore Psalm 69:21 is the narrative subtext to Jesus being served gall mixed with vinegar; Mt 27:34,48; Mk 15:36; Jn 19:28-30. The point being that the Scripture need not be explicitly quoted from in the New Testament to provide the underlying narrative subtext to the messianic scheme thereof.

[443] The meaning of relatives is more evident from the underlying Greek.

[444] Matthew 13:56; Mark 6:3. Since Matthew 13:56 says "Are not all his sisters here with us?" it is evident that, according to the narrative, Jesus had at least three sisters.

being fulfilled in a very specific circumstance; such is not the case. But there is something else worth noting about the passage in John. While it may be implied, the passage does not explicitly state that none of the brothers of Jesus believed in him. The plural is used, so we can be sure that at least two brothers[445] were skeptical of Christ's claims at that time. Robert Eisenman has suggested that the two Apostles named James and Judas[446] were actually brothers of Jesus. If so, then John 7:3-5 could still be true, being a report about Simon and Joseph. In fact, I suspect that Jesus may have had, not four, but five, brothers; his other brother being none other than the Apostle also called Matthew or Levi the son of Alphaeus.[447] Levi being a tax collector may have become the "black sheep" of his family, and so was not mentioned with the other brothers. But this would make three out of five of Christ's brothers chosen Apostles. Alphaeus may have been an alternate name for Cleopas[448] or Clopas,[449] mentioned in Luke and John, respectively. In the latter verse Mary is named as the wife of Clopas, so it may be suggested that this was also another name for Joseph. On the other hand, the woman is said to be the sister of Jesus' mother, so this has puzzled scholars. But if men can have more than one name, then so can women. On the other hand, it may be that John was referring to Elizabeth, the mother of John the Baptist, but left her unnamed, and the other woman was another Mary, married to a man named Clopas. Kamal Salibi has pointed out that John nowhere names the mother of Jesus in his Gospel.[450] So it is just barely possible that Mary was really the name of Christ's maternal aunt, rather than that of his mother. But then what was his own mother's name? Could it have been Elizabeth? Maybe Luke got the names reversed? But this is not really a satisfying solution, since most likely Mark and Matthew were both written before Luke. We see the

---

[445] Out of four named: James, Joseph, Judas, and Simon; Mt 13:55 cf Mk 6:3.

[446] Those listed as the sons of Alphaeus.

[447] Mt 9:9 cp Mk 2:14; cf Mk 3:18; Lk 6:15; Mt 10:3; Acts 1:13.

[448] Greek *Kleopas*. Cf Nestle-Aland., op. cit., pg. 243. Luke 24:18.

[449] Greek *Klopa*. Cf Nestle-Aland., ibid., pg. 313. John 19:25.

[450] Salibi, Kamal., *CONSPIRACY IN JERUSALEM: WHO WAS JESUS?* (© 1998 by Kamal Salibi); I.B.Tauris & Co. Ltd. 6 Salem Road, London W2 4BU 175 Fifth Avenue, New York, NY 10010 www.ibtauris.com ISBN: 978 1 84511 314 8. ; pg. 77.

same confusion evident also in Foxe's Book of Martyrs, which names Simon, Jude and James the younger all as sons of Mary Cleophas and of Alpheus, but then why would the cousins of Jesus have the very same names as his own brothers? It is no more likely than two sisters each having the same name. And if one brings in the explanation of levirate mariage, with Mary as a widow, Alphaeus-Cleophas being Joseph's brother, this "explanation" also falls to the ground, since, regardless of whatever precise circumstances may have precipitated the pregnancy of Mary, Jesus would no doubt have been raised as the son of Joseph and Mary, and the common people would have thought as much.[451] And since Jesus was evidently the son of Joseph, then there would have been no duty of a brother to marry his widow; the law of levirate marriage was specifically for widows without children.[452] So even if Joseph had a brother, and Joseph died at an early age, there would have been no obligation for his brother to marry his widow, since he already had a son by her. Furthermore the language of Matthew 1:25 and Luke 2:7 proves that Mary herself bore other sons to Joseph, notwithstanding the carping of closet Romanists to the contrary.[453] So wise is he who can solve this great conundrum. But just such a circumstance argues against a mythical Jesus: otherwise why would the inventors of a mythical Messiah have not been more concise and simple in their literary creation? Likewise the circumstance of the duplication of names argues <u>against</u> the phantom Christ theory; anyone writing a fictional story is unlikely to so duplicate names; but names that were common historically would likely have been shared by any number of actors in a true[454] story. But since John left the mother of Jesus unnamed in his Gospel, so he likewise may also have left her sister unnamed; the reference to "his mother's sister" may not be further qualified by the name "Mary" as most scholars assume; it may have been simply to another woman named Mary. Why is this such a difficult supposition? Admittedly I am not a Greek scholar, yet I still cannot imagine that the rules of *Koine* Greek grammar are

---

[451] Luke 2:41-48. Some early manuscripts of Luke 2:43 have "his father and mother" rather than the more familiar "Joseph and his mother". Cf Nestle-Aland., op. cit., pg. 159.

[452] Deuteronomy 25:5-6.

[453] Including those who may pose as critical Bible scholars.

[454] Or rather one with a genuine historical subtext.

so constrained as to *require* that the reference to "his mother's sister" in John 19:25 be further qualified by the name "Mary". If so, then Greek grammar is far more constrained than English grammar, and I doubt this very much. But then common sense seems to be *anathema* to biblical scholars.

Another example is the saying of Jesus that he has not come to bring peace, but a sword.[455] While it is true that in the passage Jesus alludes to Micah 7:5-6, and hence one could argue that it serves as an important example of one of the Testimonia passages, still the passage underscores the potential militancy of Jesus, and as such the passage serves as an important literary fossil. Granted because of the clear reference to Micah this passage is not quite as pungent an example as Luke 22:36-37, which also happens to be another crisis passage; but still the various "Zealot" passages are important precisely because they betray a proto-orthodox image of Jesus as a militant Messiah, and hence more historically credible. Jesus may have been astute enough to know that open defiance of the Romans was unrealistic; but he may still have sought to portray such an image of militant defiance to certain persons who would admire him for it. Jesus may have been more of a politician than most people realise.

The crisis passages serve to illustrate the subtlety necessary in approaching a critical-historical analysis of the relevant evidence vis-à-vis Jesus Christ. It is not all black and white. The issues are subtle and complex. At least many aspects of the evidence are subtle and must be approached from a number of different angles to get a clearer view. It is easy to get lost by focusing too closely on only one aspect of the evidence. But one is likely to get only a distorted view of Jesus that way; one will "fill in the blanks" with ingenuity and innuendo. But these are not substitutes for a more complete historical analysis of all the available evidence, approached from a number of different perspectives. Most theorists ignore all evidence contrary to their own pet theory. Or they offer only the lamest pseudo-explanations that satisfy only those with a strong "will to believe" the proffered theory. As such, even many critical theorists are "preaching to the choir", just as the Christian apologists themselves are. They are only singing a different chorus.

---

[455] Matthew 10:34-36.

Crisis Passages

Matthew 1:25
Matthew 2:13-21
Matthew 10:34-36
Matthew 11:11-15
Matthew 17:1-8
Matthew 24:15 cf Mark 13:14
Matthew 27:57-61 cp Mark 15:43-47; Luke 23:50-56 cf John 19:38-42
Mark 1:1-6
Mark 3:21
Mark 12:35-37 cf Matthew 22:41-45; Luke 20:41-44
Mark 14:27 cf Matthew 26:31 cp Zechariah 13:7 {CD 19:7-9}
Luke 1:5-9,36
Luke 22:36-37
John 1:35-48
John 7:3-5
John 10:22-23 {cf 1 Makkabees 4:52-59}
Acts 1:12
1 Corinthians 15:44,50
Galatians 4:4
Ephesians 6:10-17
Philippians 2:5-11
2 Thessalonians 2:1-4
Hebrews 12:22-23
1 Peter 2:24
Revelation 11:4
Revelation 12:1-5
Revelation 21:1-2

The Books of Enoch
and Jubilees

The books of Enoch and Jubilees are of great interest and relevance to our inquiry, and deserve some degree of scrutiny. These two books attained canonicity in the Ethiopian Orthodox Church. Even the Ethiopian Jews accepted these works as sacred Scripture. Therefore it is evident that they enjoyed a sufficient degree of popularity and esteem among both early Christians and Jews as to attain such heights of acceptance. The Ethiopians converted to Christianity *en masse* in the fourth century. This proves that *Enoch* and *Jubilees* had to have been not only sufficiently popular, but also held in high enough esteem, by a large enough number of Christians, for the Ethiopians to accept such works as Canonical Scripture. This is saying a lot. The Ethiopians were not likely to arbitrarily attribute Canonicity to works that other Christians esteemed as non-Canonical at the time. In other words, the evidence is such that, many Christians must have accepted these books as Canonical holy Scripture before and during the time when the Ethiopians first embraced Christianity. Otherwise it would have been impossible for the Ethiopians to accept such books as divinely inspired Scriptures. Fragments of both Enoch and Jubilees have been discovered among the Dead Sea Scrolls, and Enoch is quoted from in the New Testament.[456] This is more than can be said for some of the books of TaNaKh.[457]

Although there is only one sole quotation from the book of Enoch in the New Testament, there are nevertheless dozens, if not hundreds, of literary allusions to Enoch scattered throughout the text of the New Testament. Literary influence from Jubilees is more modest, but still discernible in a few texts.[458] Jubilees mentions earlier books written by Enoch,[459] so it must postdate either the book of Enoch or at least those portions of Enoch that predate it, supposing a composite authorship of the latter text.[460] Enoch[461] appears to have been written sometime in the reign of Herod I and most likely some time after 37 B.C. If the book of Jubilees was written after this, then this in turn makes the Damascus Document[462] a relatively "young" text, since it refers unmistakably to Jubilees. And most Scroll scholars believe that the Manual of Discipline[463] was written some time after the Damascus Document.[464] Not only does the Damascus Document refer to the book of Jubilees, but it does so in such a way as to imply that the latter book was regarded as Canonical Scripture by the Qumranites.

---

[456] Judas 14-15.

[457] Esther, Ezra, Nehemiah, Lamentations, Zephaniah, Obadiah, Ecclesiastes, and the Song of Solomon are never quoted from directly or referred to in the New Testament. Chronicles is debatable, since it is uncertain whether Chronicles or Samuel is quoted from in Hebrews 1:5. It is also uncertain whether Jesus was referring to Chronicles in Matthew 23:35.

[458] Most notably the reference to the "sin unto death" or *mortal* sin, mentioned in 1 John 5:16, and implied in James 5:20. This expression occurs frequently in Jubilees.

[459] Jubilees 4:16-23.

[460] This is the position favored by most critical scholars.

[461] I.e., considered as a whole, rather than a composite text. Or rather, the Canonical version of Enoch dates to no earlier than this time.

[462] One of the key Dead Sea Scrolls.

[463] Another Dead Sea Scroll.

[464] The Damascus Document apparently went through several revisions. Fragments of this text were discovered about fifty years before the Dead Sea Scrolls themselves by Solomon Schechter, in a *genizah* of a synagogue in Cairo, Egypt, in 1897. Cf Shanks, Hershel., *UNDERSTANDING THE DEAD SEA SCROLLS*. (© 1992 Biblical Archaeology Society); pgs. 63-78.

I strongly suspect that both Enoch and Jubilees were regarded as Canonical Scriptures by the Dead Sea community. Yigael Yadin has offered some technical evidence from the texts that the Dead Sea community esteemed the Temple Scroll[465] as a Canonical sacred Scripture.[466] The very same technical point may also serve as evidence in favor of the Canonical status of Enoch and Jubilees among the Essenes. The technical point in question is perhaps best explained in Mr. Yadin's own words:

"Hebrew was originally written in a script scholars refer to as Old Hebrew, or Palaeo-Hebrew. When the Jews returned from exile in Babylon, they brought with them a square "Aramaic" script that gradually replaced the previously used script. However, the earlier Old Hebrew script continued to be used in certain archaizing contexts... In the Dead Sea Scrolls, the tetragrammaton is sometimes written in Palaeo-Hebrew in the midst of a text otherwise written in the square Aramaic text that was in common use at the time. In the Dead Sea Scrolls, the archaized, Palaeo-Hebrew tetragrammaton generally occurs in noncanonical, that is, nonbiblical, texts. In the books of the Bible preserved at Qumran, the tetragrammaton is written, by contrast, in the square Aramaic script, just like the rest of the text. In the Temple Scroll, when the tetragrammaton is used, it is written in the square Aramaic script, as in the biblical books found at Qumran. This is another reason to believe that the Temple Scroll was considered by the Essene community as biblical or canonical."[467]

So if those fragments of Enoch and Jubilees discovered at Qumran have the tetragrammaton[468] written in the square Syriac script, then this proves that the Qumranites held these texts to be Canonical Scripture. It is just a matter of scrutinizing the facsimile edition of the Dead Sea texts. But to someone unfamiliar with Hebrew it may be difficult to detect such subtleties. It will be well to keep in mind what Yigael Yadin has written respecting Hebrew and the use of the square Aramaic script; he did not say that the postexilic Jews spoke Aramaic as their language. They still spoke and wrote in Hebrew; it was the

---

[465]   The longest Dead Sea Scroll.

[466]   Shanks., op. cit., pgs. 87-112. (Hershel Shanks acted as editor and contributor to the work; Yigael Yadin wrote the article cited).

[467]   Ibid., pg. 97.

[468]   Tetragrammaton. The sacred, four-letter Hebrew name of God; YHWH.

script that was different, not the language. According to the same book a complete scroll of the book of Enoch was discovered among the Dead Sea Scrolls, but was hidden away in a private collection.[469] Hopefully it is being carefully preserved, and will eventually be published, together with translations in critical editions. I strongly suspect that this will serve to vindicate the Ethiopic text of the book of Enoch as fundamentally accurate. The books of Enoch and Jubilees were among the most popular books of the Essene community, judging by the fragmentary discoveries made.

The book of Enoch was no doubt first written as a *midrash* on the following passage from Genesis:

And it came to pass, when men began to multiply on the face of the earth, and daughters were born unto them,

2   that the sons of God beheld the daughters of men, that they were fair; and they took wives of them of all which they chose.

3   And GOD said, my spirit shall not always strive with man, for he is also flesh; yet *from henceforth* his days shall be *but* a hundred and twenty years.

4   There were giants in the earth in those days, and also after that, when the sons of God came in unto the daughters of men, and they bore unto them the mighty men of old, men of renown. (Genesis 6:1-3)

Most manuscripts of the Greek Septuagint have the reading "angels of God" rather than "sons of God" in the above passage.[470] Philo Judaeus also agrees with the reading "angels of God"; see Philo, *On the Giants,* section II, or verse 6. Therefore there can be no doubt as to how this strange passage was interpreted by Jews from the third century B.C. on.[471] We can see this clearly by the following passage from the book of Enoch:

---

[469]   Ibid., pg. 262.

[470]   SEPTUAGINTA., (© 1979 Deutsche Bibelgesellschaft Stuttgart); Alfred Rhalfs, ed.; pg. 8 (volume one; Duo volumina in uno).

[471]   There is some evidence for this interpretation in the Talmud, although the Talmud may also incorporate the contrary interpretation of the "sons of God" being the descendants of Seth, who were corrupted by the beautiful

It happened after the sons of men had multiplied in those days, that daughters were born to them, elegant and beautiful. And when the angels, the sons of heaven, beheld them, they became enamoured of them, saying to each other, Come, let us select for ourselves wives from the progeny of men, and let us beget children.

Then their leader Samyaza said to them; I fear that you may perhaps be indisposed to the performance of this enterprise; and that I alone shall suffer for so grievous a crime. But they answered him and said; We all swear; and bind ourselves by mutual execrations, that we will not change our intention, but execute our projected undertaking. Then they all swore together, and all bound themselves by mutual execrations. Their whole number was two hundred, who descended upon Ardis, which is the top of Mount Armon. That mountain was therefore called Armon, because they had sworn upon it, and bound themselves by mutual execrations.

These are the names of their chiefs: Samyaza, who was their leader; Urakabarameel, Akibeel, Tamiel, Ramuel, Danel, Azkeel, Saraknyal, Asael, Armers, Batraal, Anane, Zavebe, Samsaveel, Ertael, Turel, Yomyael, Arazyal. These were the prefects of the two hundred angels, and the remainder were all with them.

Then they took wives, each choosing for himself; whom they began to approach, and with whom they cohabited; teaching them sorcery, incantations, and the dividing of roots and trees. And the women conceiving brought forth giants, whose stature was each three hundred cubits. (Enoch VII:1-12a)[472]

There is also a parallel verse in the book of Jubilees:

And it came to pass when the children of men began to multiply on the face of the earth and daughters were born unto them, that the angels of God saw them on a certain year of this jubilee, that they were beautiful to look upon; and they took themselves wives of all

---

daughters of Cain. The latter interpretation could serve as a moral warning against intermarriage with non-Jews. Some Christians also adopt this latter interpretation; however both Enoch and Jubilees favor the angelic interpretation. The mediaeval *incubi* and *succubi* may also possibly be corrupt forms of the same tradition. One might also consult the book *Heavenly Bridegrooms,* by Ida Craddock and Theodore Shroeder.

[472] As translated by Richard Laurence. The numbering system used by Mr. Laurence is also somewhat different from that used by R.H. Charles, in respect to chapters and verses.

whom they chose, and they bare unto them sons and they were giants. (Jubilees V:1)[473]

In the book of Enoch I would say that some degree of Greek influence is evident; the Greek tales of the Titans no doubt inspired the exaggerated stature of the giants.[474] So we have also in the books of Enoch and Jubilees yet another *mythos* of fallen angels. This is one less familiar to most Western readers, but it was common coin among the messianic Jews and earliest Christians. Despite the probable Greek influence upon Enoch, it could hardly be described as a Hellenistic work. It is much different in character from the Hellenistic Judaic literature of the period. And Jubilees is pervaded by what one can only suspect is an anti-Hellenistic *ethos*. At least it is suspected by some biblical scholars to have been written to counteract the influence of Hellenism upon Jewish life and culture, and this seems likely to be true. The fall of the angels as narrated in Enoch and Jubilees is of course not a negation of the fall of Lucifer;[475] it rather supplements and complexifies the scenario. Most Christian exegetes[476] assume that a third of the angels in heaven joined Lucifer in his initial rebellion against God, based upon no more than an obscure verse in the *Apokalypse*[477] but I can think of no more glaring an example of *eisegesis,* which Christians constantly rail against on the part of occultists and heretics.[478] This all may seem quite superfluous and tedious to those who do not believe in such things, but we need to at least imaginatively enter into the belief-system of the people who wrote these texts with some degree of sympathy if we are to ever hope of understanding such texts. Thus angelology and demonology are informed by these texts of Enoch and Jubilees, both of which are eminent examples of literary fossils.

The book of Enoch ascribes a harsh punishment to those angels who fell from heaven by lusting after mortal women:

---

[473]   As translated by R.H. Charles.

[474]   Compare the three hundred cubits of the Enochian giants with Goliath's "six cubits and a span." cf 1 Samuel 17:4.

[475]   Cf Isaiah 14:12–15; Ezekiel 28:12–19 cp Genesis 3.

[476]   Whether Orthodox, Catholic, or Protestant.

[477]   Revelation 12:4.

[478]   According to their own arbitrary and often ignorant definition of heresy.

15. To Michael also likewise the Lord said, Go and announce his crime to Samyaza, and to the others who are with him, who have been associated with women, that they might be polluted with all their impurity. And when all their sons shall be slain, when they shall see the perdition of their beloved *sons,* bind them for seventy generations underneath the earth, even to the day of judgment, *the effect of* which will last forever, be completed. (Enoch X:15)

This verse clearly corresponds to the following verse from second Peter:

4　For if God spared not the angels that sinned, but cast them down to *Tartarosas,* and delivered *them* into chains of darkness, to be reserved unto judgment... (2 Peter 2:4)[479]

Thus these fallen angels are not those who tempt man, according to these Scriptures. But what of the sons of these fallen angels? What was their fate? According to the text of Enoch:

8. Now the giants, who have been born of spirit and of flesh, shall be called upon earth evil spirits, and on earth shall be their habitation. Evil spirits shall proceed from their flesh, because they were created from above; from the holy Watchers was their beginning and primary foundation. Evil spirits shall they be upon earth, and the spirits of the wicked shall they be called. (Enoch XV:8)

Such a class of evil spirit was no doubt Asmodeus, who in the book of Tobit strangled seven bridegrooms of Sarah on their wedding night, probably out of jealousy.[480] No doubt the story narrated in Tobit also was the literary basis for the Sadducees' question directed towards Jesus, about a woman who had been married to seven husbands, and had no children by any of them, and to whom would she be married

---

[479]　This proves the absurdity of an anti-Enochian interpretation of 2 Peter.

[480]　Tobit 3:8.

in the resurrection.[481] But we also find another passage in Jubilees that further clarifies the punishment of fallen angels and evil spirits:

X.   And in the third week of this jubilee the unclean demons began to lead astray the children of the sons of Noah, and to make to err and destroy them.

2.   And the sons of Noah came to Noah their father, and they told him concerning the demons which were leading astray and blinding and slaying his sons' sons.

3.   And he prayed before the Lord his God, and said:

God of the spirits of all flesh, Who hast shown mercy unto me,
And hast saved me and my sons from the waters of the flood,
And hast not caused me to perish as Thou didst the sons of perdition;
For thy grace hath been great towards me, and great hath been
Thy mercy to my soul;
Let Thy grace be lift up upon my sons,
And let not wicked spirits rule over them,
Lest they should destroy them from the earth.

4.   But do Thou bless me and my sons, that we may increase and multiply and replenish the earth.

5.   And Thou knowest how Thy Watchers, the fathers of these spirits, acted in my day: and as for these spirits which are living, imprison them and hold them fast in the place of condemnation, and let them not bring destruction on the sons of thy servant, my God; for these are malignant, and created in order to destroy.

6.   And let them not rule over the spirits of the living; for Thou alone canst exercise dominion over them. And let them not have power over the sons of the righteous from henceforth and for evermore.

7.   And the Lord our God bade us to bind all *the evil spirits*.

---

[481]   Mt 22:23-28; Mk 12:18-23; Lk 20:27-33. The literary parallel is still valid even if we assume that the incident narrated in the Synoptics was historical; for the Sadducees no doubt were familiar with the book of Tobit.

8.   But the chief of the *evil* spirits, Mastema, came and said:

Lord, Creator, let some of them remain before me, and let them hearken to my voice, and do all that I shall say unto them; for if some of them are not left to me, I shall not be able to execute the power of my will on the sons of men; for these are for corruption and leading astray before my judgment, for great is the wickedness of the sons of men.

9.   And He said: Let the tenth part of them remain before him, and let nine parts descend into the place of condemnation. (Jubilees X:1-9)

So according to the book of Jubilees, nine-tenths of all evil spirits are bound in a spiritual prison, while only one-tenth were allowed to remain free to lead astray mankind. I strongly suspect that the author of the *Apokalypse* also had the abyss implied here as the place from which these evil spirits would be released during the time of God's outpoured wrath.[482] We must face the fact that, most likely, Jesus and the Apostles shared these same kinds of beliefs. Even assuming a practice of esotericism, the secret doctrine was not likely to be more akin to postmodern rationalism, but if anything, even more *phantastic* than the apocalypticism of such Enochian works. We are not greeted by any more rationalism in the world of the Gnostics, for that matter.[483] In any case Enoch and Jubilees provide a greater context for much that is found in both the Bible proper and the Apocrypha. At the very least, the text of Enoch provided material for at least the exoteric, parabolic shell of the messianic teaching. Besides the core of Enoch, which is the story of the fall of angels through lust for earthly women, we also have a number of prophetic embellishments of a messianic character. In fact we find a very exalted concept of the Messiah as a preexistent celestial being:

---

[482]   Revelation 9:1-12.

[483]   Except possibly for the sole truism of the irreconcilability of the Old Testament God with the God and Father of Jesus Christ. But against this the entire messianic scheme of the New Testament is based on the Jewish Scriptures.

1. Thus the Lord commanded the kings, the princes, and those who dwell on earth, saying, Open your eyes, and lift up your horns, if you are capable of comprehending the Elect One.
2. The Lord of spirits sat upon the throne of his glory.
3. And the spirit of righteousness was poured out over him.
4. The word of his mouth shall destroy all the sinners and all the ungodly, who shall perish at his presence.
5. In that day shall all the kings, the princes, the exalted, and those who possess the earth, stand up, behold, and perceive, that he is sitting on the throne of his glory; that before him the saints shall be judged in righteousness;
6. And that nothing, which shall be spoken before him, shall be *spoken* in vain.
7. Trouble shall come upon them, as upon a woman in travail, whose labour is severe, when her child comes to the mouth of the womb, and she finds it difficult to bring forth.
8. One portion of them shall look upon another. They shall be astonished, and shall humble their countenance;
9. And trouble shall seize them, when they shall behold this Son of woman sitting upon the throne of his glory.
10. Then shall the kings, the princes, and all who possess the earth, glorify him who has dominion over all things, him who was concealed; for from the beginning the Son of man existed in secret, whom the Most High preserved in the presence of his power, and revealed to the elect. (Enoch LXI:1-10)

The above passage proves that at least some pre-Christian Jews held to a very high concept of the Messiah as a greatly exalted, pre-existent celestial being. This is contrary to what some pseudo-scholarly Grail authors have written on the subject. It only proves that one must be sufficiently acquainted with one's subject-matter to write intelligently on it. Then again I realise that such a high messianism no doubt also co-existed with a lower messianism that saw the Messiah as no more than an earthly deliverer. Yet it almost seems like a form of internalized anti-Semitism to assume that the Jews could not conceive of spiritual redemption, but only of an earthly kingdom over which God's chosen vicar would reign in the person of the Messiah. There is yet another messianic passage that also clearly depicts the Messiah as a preexistent celestial being:

1. In that place I beheld a fountain of righteousness, which never failed, encircled by many springs of wisdom. Of these all the thirsty drank, and were filled with wisdom, having their habitation with the righteous, the elect, and the holy.

2. In that hour was this Son of man invoked before the Lord of spirits, and his name in the presence of the Ancient of days.

3. Before the sun and the signs were created, before the stars of heaven were formed, his name was invoked in the presence of the Lord of spirits. A support shall he be for the righteous and the holy to lean upon, without falling; and he shall be the light of nations.

4. He shall be the hope of those whose hearts are troubled. All, who dwell on earth, shall fall down and worship before him; shall bless and glorify him, and sing praises to the name of the Lord of spirits.

5. Therefore the Elect and the Concealed One existed in his presence, before the world was created, and forever. (Enoch XLVIII:1-5)

Another powerful messianic passage is the following:

1. In those days shall the earth deliver up from her womb, and hell deliver up from hers, that which it has received; and destruction shall restore that which it owes.

2. He shall select the righteous and holy from among them; for the day of their salvation has approached.

3. And in those days shall the Elect One sit upon his throne, while every secret of intellectual wisdom shall proceed from his mouth; for the Lord of spirits has gifted and glorified him.

4. In those days the mountains shall skip like rams, and the hills shall leap like young sheep satiated with milk; and all *the righteous* shall become angels in heaven.

5. Their countenance shall be bright with joy; for in those days shall the Elect One be exalted. The earth shall rejoice; the righteous shall inhabit it, and the elect possess it. (Enoch L:1-5)

The righteous becoming angels in heaven seems to correspond to Acts 12:15 and Revelation 22:8-9. But it is absurd for a person posing as a historical critic to make a false pretence that the Jews before

Christ's time had no conception of a heavenly, exalted Messiah, but only one of a purely earthly king or deliverer. Consider the following passage:

1. After that period, in the place where I had seen every secret sight, I was snatched up in a whirlwind, and carried off westwards.

2. There my eyes beheld the secrets of heaven, and all which existed on earth; a mountain of iron, a mountain of copper, a mountain of silver, a mountain of gold, a mountain of fluid metal, and a mountain of lead.

3. And I inquired of the angel who went with me, saying, What are these things, which in secret I behold?

4. He said, All these things which thou beholdest shall be for the dominion of the Messiah, that he may command, and be powerful upon earth.

5. And that angel of peace answered me, saying, Wait but a short time, and thou shalt understand, and every secret thing shall be revealed to thee, which the Lord of spirits has decreed. Those mountains which thou hast seen, the mountain of iron, the mountain of copper, the mountain of silver, the mountain of gold, the mountain of fluid metal, and the mountain of lead, all these in the presence of the Elect One shall be like a honeycomb before the fire, and like water descending from above upon these mountains; and shall become debilitated before his feet.

6. In those days men shall not be saved by gold and by silver.

7. Nor shall they have it in their power to secure themselves, and to fly.

8. There shall be neither iron for war, nor a coat of mail for the breast.

9. Copper shall be useless; useless also that which neither rusts nor consumes away; and lead shall not be coveted.

10. All these things shall be rejected, and perish from off the earth, when the Elect One shall appear in the presence of the Lord of spirits. (Enoch LI:1-10)

Anyone who reads such passages can clearly see a very high messianism expressed; the Messiah is second only to God himself.

This is really no more than a development of what can be found within *TaNaKh* itself.[484] But of course there can be no doubt that this high messianism also coexisted with a lower messianism among other Jews, who may have feared that such an exaltation of the Messiah was flirting with idolatry. In Jubilees the messianic element is entirely absent. Perhaps it was an instinctive reaction against the extreme exaltation of the Messiah found in Enoch. Some may posit that the messianic passages are not even Jewish at all, but are merely Christian inventions that were interpolated into the text of Enoch. But that would be like sewing a new piece of cloth onto an old garment.[485] Although some biblical scholars may have held this position in the past, today it is even less popular than it formerly was, and it was never a consensus view. The Dead Sea Scrolls seem to belie such an interpretation; but the decisive answer will be found when the complete scroll of Enoch discovered at Qumran is finally published. I am confident that the Ethiopic text will be vindicated, and then such claims can finally be laid to rest.[486]

Enoch would have appealed more strongly to Christians than Jubilees; the latter work would likely have been less esteemed as being too legalistic, and less important in a dispensation of grace. By contrast, the messianic passages of Enoch must have been very comforting and inspiring to Christians. In fact, it is possible that the messianic passages are what appealed to Judas to such a degree that he openly quoted from the work in his short epistle. Some have attempted to date Jubilees to 100 B.C. on a palaeographic basis. Some have even dated it to as early as 150 or 160 B.C. Possibly it may be even earlier than that. Of course any dating of Enoch or Jubilees for now must be tentative and speculative. Both Enoch and Jubilees have a spiritual as opposed to carnal conception of the resurrection:

31. And their bones will rest in the earth. And their spirits will have much joy. And they will know that it is the Lord who executeth judgment, and showeth mercy to hundreds and thousands and to all that love Him. (Jubilees XXIII: 31)

---

[484] Proverbs 30:4; Isaiah 7:14; 9:6-7; Psalms 2; 45:1-11; 110; Daniel 7:13-14.

[485] Mt 9:16; Mk 2:21; Lk 5:36.

[486] Perhaps one reason why the scroll is still hidden away is fear that the publication of its contents would wreak havoc in contemporary Judaism.

2. *I have seen* that all goodness, joy, and glory has been prepared for you, and been written down for the spirits of them who die eminently righteous and good. To you it shall be given in return for your troubles; and your portion shall far exceed the portion of the living.

3. The spirits of you who die in righteousness shall exist and rejoice. Their spirits shall exult; and their remembrance shall be before the face of the mighty One from generation to generation. Nor shall they now fear disgrace. (Enoch CIII:2-3)

The importance of the books of Enoch and Jubilees can hardly be overstated; and the fact that fragments of these texts have been discovered among the Dead Sea Scrolls provides yet one more link between the Qumran community and the proto-Christian messianic community of Jesus and his disciples. Both Enoch and Jubilees are apocalyptic in style and content; apocalyptic literature being distinctively distinguished by the author narrating visions and conversations with angels. Often the apocalyptic author has a vision, which is then interpreted by an angel. Such distinguishing apocalyptic traits can be found in both Daniel[487] and Zechariah.[488] I would only distinguish between apocalyptic literature and prophetic literature by saying that the former is a subset of the latter, just as Docetism is a subset of Gnosticism. Critical scholars would insist that the apocalyptic mode of writing is strictly postexilic, but in this they beg the question of Daniel's pseudonymity.[489] There is of course a clear literary influence from Daniel upon both Enoch and Jubilees. And in this case there can be very little doubt that the latter works

---

[487] Daniel 7-12.

[488] Zechariah 3-6.

[489] And while judging the matter *holistically* I feel that Daniel is almost certainly pseudepigraphal, I also feel that this question has not been dealt with adequately by critical scholars. There is a fairly simple solution to this question but the ostentatious erudition of academia is not congenial to such simple explanations; critical scholars would rather make a shameless pyrotechnic display of their scholarship to impress their fellow academicians, but in the process they leave such questions unanswered in any satisfactory way. And their pseudo-scholarly imitators are content to parrot them, or even to fabricate evidence, if the mood suits them.

postdate Daniel, even if we assign a very late date to Daniel.[490] Daniel is the only book within *TaNaKh* to mention the Watchers, which are frequently mentioned in both Enoch and Jubilees. In the latter works the Watchers are fallen angels. An interesting point in relation to this is the fact that the Egyptian word most commonly translated as "gods" by Western scholars more literally means watchers.[491]

While both Enoch and Jubilees are exemplary examples of literary fossils, there is a passage in Enoch that is particularly so. It is a prime example of the principle, since it preserves what is an otherwise anomalous or inexplicable teaching, without a larger context of esotericism. As we have seen, Enoch is pervaded by a high messianism, with the Messiah frequently spoken of as either the "Son of Man" or the "Messiah" or "the Elect One" or "the Concealed One" or even "Son of Woman". The "Son of Man" title was no doubt a development from the reference in Daniel's vision to "one like unto a son of man"[492] meaning one with a human appearance. This Messianic figure is greatly exalted in Enoch. There is a curious passage in Enoch in which it appears that Enoch himself is being addressed as the Son of man. The passage is as follows:

11. Michael, Raphael, Gabriel, Phanuel, and the holy angels who were in the heavens above, went in and out of it. Michael, Raphael, and Gabriel went out of that habitation, and holy angels innumerable.

12. With them *was* the Ancient of days, whose head *was* white as wool, and pure, and his robe *was* indescribable.

13. Then I fell upon my face, while all my flesh was dissolved, and my spirit became changed.

---

490   In my former work I did not dwell on the question of the date of Daniel, but I pointed out that, even accepting a second-century B.C. date for the book, it still foretold the destruction of the temple in Jerusalem, and the rise of the Roman empire.

491   The Egyptian word being *neteru*.

492   Daniel 7:13. In the King James Bible this is mistranslated as "one like the Son of man" but the article is absent in the Hebrew; furthermore this is the first literary instance where this figure is introduced; as such it is merely a descriptive term, rather than definitive.

14. I cried out with a loud voice, with a powerful spirit, blessing, glorifying, and exalting.

15. And those blessings, which proceeded from my mouth, became acceptable in the presence of the Ancient of days.

16. The Ancient of days came with Michael and Gabriel, Raphael and Phanuel, with thousands of thousands, and myriads of myriads, which could not be numbered.

17. Then that angel came to me, and with his voice saluted me, saying, Thou art the Son of Man, who art born for righteousness, and righteousness has rested on thee.

18. The righteousness of the Ancient of days shall not forsake thee.

19. He said, On thee shall he confer peace in the name of the existing world; for from thence has peace gone forth since the world was created.

20. And thus shall it happen to thee for ever and ever.

21. All who shall exist, and who shall walk in thy path of righteousness, shall not forsake thee for ever.

22. With thee shall be their habitation, with thee their lot; nor from thee shall they be separated for ever and ever.

23. And thus shall length of days be with the Son of Man. (Enoch LXX:11-23)

In this passage the seer is identified with the preexistent Son of Man. The Ethiopians are to be commended for preserving this passage as it was written, and we can be quite sure that this is the original reading of the passage, since no later Christian scribe would have identified the Son of Man with Enoch. Jesus was preeminently the Son of Man in the Synoptics; would it not have seemed to be heresy, or at least a very strange teaching, to equate Jesus with Enoch? Then again Jesus himself identified John the Baptist with the prophet

Elijah.[493] Of course Christians have long since interpreted such passages in a way as to preclude any hint of reincarnation. And neither the book of Enoch, nor Jubilees, nor the New Testament generally lend themselves to an interpretation amenable to reincarnation in the general sense, as understood in Hinduism or the New Age movement. But once again we must remember the principle of esotericism. Furthermore the exalted figure of the Son of Man, and the exceptional figure of a prophet who was purportedly taken up to heaven alive in a chariot of fire,[494] might constitute exceptions to the general rule of the fate of souls. Enoch was also said to have been taken up to heaven alive, without ever tasting of death.[495] As I noted in my former work, the Pharisees believed in reincarnation.[496] The Talmud also speaks extensively of reincarnation, and there is also a passage within the Apocrypha that implies a belief in reincarnation.[497] But other than these few notable instances, most biblical literature is filled with a notorious heaven and hell dichotomy, and/or the concept of a corporeal resurrection from the dead, to be attended by a final judgment.[498] In fact the passage from Enoch is so strange and potentially controversial that both Richard Laurence and R.H. Charles balked at the idea that the antediluvian patriarch could have been in any way identified with the promised Messiah.[499] Laurence uses the less committal "offspring of man"[500] and while Charles translates the term more accurately as "Son of man" he placed numerous unwarranted "emendations" into the text, changing the reading from the second to the third person no less than nine times, all based upon his further supposition of a lacuna in the text, which is

---

[493]   Mt 11:12-15; 17:10-13; Mk 9:11-13.

[494]   2 Kings 2.

[495]   Genesis 5:21-24; Hebrews 11:5 cp Sirach 44:16.

[496]   Jos. War. 2.8.14.

[497]   Wisdom 8:19-20.

[498]   With ominous implications for whoever does not subscribe to a sectarian interpretation of Christianity that assures the believer of a blessed hereafter.

[499]   I.e., Jesus Christ, according to a Christian interpretation of the text.

[500]   Which I have taken the liberty of emending to the more correct "Son of Man" since that is exactly what the text says in the Aethiopic.

also unwarranted.[501] Neither man could imagine that there had been an intent to identify the prophet Enoch with the expected Son of man. But that is what the text actually does. The implication of this is that for those Christians who read and used the book of Enoch, Jesus himself must have been the reincarnation of Enoch.[502] One suspects that this may have been the reason, or at least one of the reasons, why the book of Enoch fell out of favor in the Byzantine empire. Fortunately for us it was preserved intact in Abyssinia.[503] One alternative interpretation to the reincarnation scenario vis-à-vis Enoch and Jesus would be that both men were merely vessels of a celestial Son of Man, perhaps along the lines of a proto-Nestorian interpretation. This is just food for thought.

---

[501] It was rather a weakness of his scholarly integrity and the virulence of his theological prejudice that produced such unnecessary gyrations. What the Aethiopians themselves did not do, two Western scholars did do, in far less time; and it is all the more shocking that such Western scholars typically pride themselves on their alleged objectivity. Thus the book of Enoch has once again become the victim of Eurocentrism.

[502] One further implication of this in turn is that Jesus may also have been married and had children, just as Enoch became the progenitor of all later generations, according to the biblical text. After all, if Enoch himself, who was married and had children, and yet was said to have "walked with God", and against whom no sin is recorded in Scripture, and who was taken up alive to heaven, why could not Jesus himself also have been married and had children? His exalted ontological status would be no barrier if he was the reincarnation of Enoch, who was married and had children.

[503] Ethiopia.

The Dead Sea Scrolls

The Dead Sea Scrolls are perfect examples of literary fossils. The advantage of these texts is that we know that they have remained unchanged for approximately the past two millennia, and so when we read them, we can be sure we are reading the very same things read by the Dead Sea community.[504] As such, these texts are of inestimable value. In a very real sense, this cache of scrolls functions as a sort of "missing link" between *TaNaKh* and cognate literature[505] on the one hand, and the New Testament texts, on the other. Scroll scholars are divided over the dating of the scrolls; many have tended to favor a second century B.C. provenance, although now it is clear that at least some of the scrolls date from the first century B.C.[506] Some Scroll

---

[504]   Albeit in translation, unless we are able to read them in the original Hebrew.

[505]   Such as the Apocrypha and the Old Testament Pseudepigrapha.

[506]   Two scrolls that had long been suppressed from publication, namely the Nahum *pesher,* and also one dubbed "In Praise of King Jonathan" (4Q169 & 4Q448, respectively) prove by internal evidence to date from no earlier than the first century B.C. The "Jonathan" of the latter text is none other than the notorious Alexander Jannaeus. And King Demetrius is mentioned by name in the Nahum *pesher.* This in itself is a rarity; often the villain of the scrolls is not named, but merely described. This may hint that some of the other scrolls are of an even later date of origin.

scholars[507] have argued that the scrolls date to the first century C.E. As I noted above and also in my former work, the Habakkuk *pesher* speaks of a "delay" in the time of fulfillment; most specifically, that "the last days will be long, much longer than the prophets had said" which indicates to me that most likely the Habakkuk pesher[508] was written sometime after 46 B.C., which would have been the *terminus ad quem* of Daniel's prophecy of the seventy weeks, assuming the famous decree of Cyrus as the *terminus a quo*. And in my earlier work I argued that a straightforward reading of Daniel implies that the decree of Cyrus was indeed the intended starting-point for the prophecy. In this connection it is interesting to note that Jesus is recorded as saying that God would "shorten those days" for the sake of the elect.[509] But the Habakkuk pesher is instructive in the sense that we learn from it that, from the perspective of the person writing it, there had been a definite delay in an expected fulfillment of prophecy. There was a delay in the eschaton. This would no doubt have created a crisis for the true believers. In the wake of unfulfilled prophecy there is invariably a time of reflection, followed by reinterpretation. A sense of desperation pervades the faith of those who have been thus disappointed. And a desperate faith can take on extreme and mutated forms.

One of the most interesting of the Dead Sea Scrolls is the Damascus Document.[510] This text had already been discovered, at least in fragmentary form, fifty years before the first Dead Sea Scrolls had been discovered.[511] The Damascus Document is probably older than most of the other Dead Sea Scrolls; in any case it seems to predate the Manual of Discipline, another key text from Qumran. There can be no doubt that the Damascus Document was known to the author of 2 Thessalonians, whether it was the apostle Paul or someone else writing in his name. It is certainly a key text, yet in a certain sense,

---

[507] Most notably Robert Eisenman. It is worth noting that a first century origin for the Dead Sea Scrolls, or even for some of them, tends to push the New Testament documents into the second century. And this seems highly probable to me, all things considered.

[508] 1QpHab.

[509] Mk 13:20 cf Mt 24:22.

[510] CD.

[511] In the genizah of a Cairo synagogue by Solomon Schechter. Schechter published his discovery under the title *Zadokite Fragments*.

all of the scrolls are; they all must be studied to get a more complete view of the Dead Sea sect.[512] I certainly do not claim to be an expert on the scrolls, and I can only write about them here in the most cursory manner. But I reject the view of the scrolls as being merely an arbitrary collection of diverse religious literature, taken from the temple in Jerusalem.[513] While there is variety in the scrolls, they are also pervaded by a sort of organic unity in respect to themes, attitudes, nomenclature, and often even the unnamed characters are the same in various scrolls. They are all too similar to be merely a haphazard eclectic collection of Jewish religious texts. And even the variety we encounter between various texts from Qumran can be best accounted for by differences of literary *genre,* and also by different generations of the sect. The Damascus Document in particular can teach us a lot about the Qumran sect. For one thing, they were not *Ebionim.* In fact, it quotes from Ezekiel 44:15, which speaks of the Zadokites offering fat and blood to God approvingly. As we have already noted, the Ebionites were opposed to all animal sacrifices. The text also speaks of a "teacher of righteousness" whom many scholars have sought to identify historically. But most Scroll scholars have abandoned the chronological key provided by the text of the Damascus Document. I still fail to understand why they do this, unless the chronology spoken of in the text is inconvenient for their pet theories. This is especially the case for those who seek to identify the Teacher of Righteousness either with Jesus,[514] John the Baptist,[515] or James the Just.[516] But the problem for all these identifications is that the chronology of the text is all against it. Even Eisenman's own translation of the Damascus Document points rather clearly to a much earlier date than the alleged time of Jesus, to say nothing of the later days in which James flourished as bishop of the Jerusalem church. I find it irksome, to say the least of it, that so many scholars prefer to sabotage the clear reading of the text in favour of their own perverse interpretations. Indeed, an interpretation akin to the consensus of

---

[512] Of course even this "more complete view" will still be fragmentary, just as most of the scrolls themselves are.

[513] As advocated by Norman Golb. See his book *Who Wrote the Dead Sea Scrolls?*

[514] Edgar Cayce, Alvar Ellegard, etc.

[515] Barbara Thiering.

[516] Robert Eisenman.

Scroll scholars is an act of sabotage, and a turning away from the available information, simply because it is not in conformity with their expectations or preferences.[517] The relevant passage from the Damascus Document is the only text that gives us a clear account of exactly when this legendary Teacher of Righteousness actually lived. And, lest it be thought that I may somehow be seeking to "boost" my theory that Jesus lived a century earlier than the commonly-accepted time, by making a bone of contention of the Damascus Document, let it be clearly understood that according to the chronology of that text, the Teacher of Righteousness appeared in the early second century B.C., rather than the first century B.C. The relevant passage is as follows:

"In the era of wrath-three hundred and ninety years *from* the time that he handed them over to Nebuchadnezzar king of Babylon, he cared for them and caused to grow from Israel and from Aaron a root of planting to inherit his land and to grow fat on the bounty of his soil. They considered their iniquity and were convicted in conscience, knowing they were guilty men, and were like the blind and like those groping for the way for twenty years. But God considered their deeds, that they sought him with a whole heart. So he raised up for them a Teacher of Righteousness to guide them in the way of his heart."

Nebuchadnezzar attacked Jerusalem in 606 B.C., taking many people prisoner with him to Babylon; he installed a vassal king on the throne of Jerusalem. He returned in 597 B.C., due to a rebellion, this time taking more people prisoner and deporting them to Babylon. Zedekiah was another vassal king, who rebelled in his ninth year; finally in 587 B.C.[518] Nebuchadnezzar sent his armies again, who burned down the temple in Jerusalem. One of these three dates must have been the *terminus a quo* of the "three hundred and ninety years of wrath" spoken of in the Damascus Document. That gives us the results of 216 B.C., 207 B.C., and 197 B.C., respectively as the possible *terminus ad quem* of the prophecy. To this 390-year period must be added the twenty years that the men were "blindly groping" for the way of righteouness, until God sent them "a teacher in righteousness"; this gives us the results of 196 B.C., 187 B.C., and 177 B.C., respectively. It is very simple mathematics. All of these dates are

---

[517] Or rather prejudices.

[518] Or possibly 586 B.C.; exact precision in chronology in respect to such distant times is very difficult, and often impossible.

far too early to refer to either Jesus or any of his contemporaries, or near-contemporaries.[519] I am truly puzzled as to why so many Scroll scholars insist on disregarding this crucial chronological passage of the Damascus Document. They interpret it into oblivion. Or rather misinterpret it into oblivion. Even admitting that the Hebrew may be obscure here, and may allow for their equivocal reading of the text, why prefer it to a reading that is more clear? Because they can find no historical personages to whom they may ascribe identity with the characters mentioned in the scrolls? But in this they lack honesty. They lack integrity. Why not rather admit that one cannot find a definitive correspondence? Indeed, there is as yet no scholarly consensus to the identity of either the "Teacher of Righteousness" or the "Man of the Lie" or the "Wicked Priest". So why assume that they must be easily identifiable historical figures? No doubt they were historical figures, but any identification of who they were or may have been must remain tentative and speculative. Neither do I find such arguments sufficiently enticing to relinquish the more clear declaration of the Damascus Document. Indeed, the very interpretation of a period of 390 years as being a "period of wrath" leading up to the Babylonian Captivity is belied by the clear Scripture passages that say that it was because the Israelites had failed to observe the practice of a Sabbath rest for the land that they were sent into captivity in Babylon.[520] By the implicit logic[521] of the Scroll scholars the passage in the Damascus Document should read 490 years, rather than 390 years.[522] In fact, the very fact that the text reads "390 years" rather than "490 years" is virtually proof *against* the interpretation[523] of the Scroll scholars on

---

[519] Even if we assume that Jesus lived in the early first century B.C.

[520] 2 Chronicles 36:21; Leviticus 25:1-7 cp Jeremiah 25:8-12; 29:10-14. Thus this implies a term of 490 years of wrath, rather than 390 years of wrath, as mentioned in the Damascus Document.

[521] If indeed one can call it logic.

[522] Since the Jews were captive in Babylon for seventy years, this implies a period of 490 years in which they violated the promise to observe the Sabbath of the land agriculturally. Seventy being the seventh part of 490. Note also the clear parallel with Daniel's seventy weeks of years, or 490 years.

[523] Or rather non-interpretation; misinterpretation.

this point.[524] Why would there even be a point of mentioning such a period of 390 years? Possibly some scholars may posit that it refers back to the accession of Rehoboam to the throne of Judah, and thus the "time of wrath" would have begun with him. But does not the Bible also say that Solomon went astray to idols, being led astray by his many foreign wives? So any "time of wrath" in this sense would have to also include the latter part of his reign. But the problem once again is that such a lax interpretation of the text destroys its chronological value completely. This is the fatal weakness of all those theories that try to expropriate the Teacher of Righteousness, and to claim an identity between him and whomever they have decided he must have been, such as Jesus, John the Baptist, or James the brother of Jesus. Sorry but the Damascus Document proves all such theories wrong. The Teacher of Righteousness lived two centuries before the alleged time of Jesus. That is still a century too early for a Jesus who lived in the first century B.C.[525] But here I find yet another argument in favor of the historicity of Jesus Christ. Since the Teacher of Righteousness is not readily identifiable from historical records, and yet he no doubt existed as a historical person, then by way of analogy, we can say that here we have a precedent of a person who was very important in the eyes of a given religious community, and yet is all but invisible in history. The historical silence surrounding the Teacher of Righteousness can be no legitimate argument against his onetime historical existence; therefore why do we concede the propriety of such arguments when applied to Jesus Christ? There is no question of miracles; the miracles attributed to Christ are very likely later inventions, to provide gratuitous messianic credentials for him.[526] Therefore why is an appeal to the silence[527] of historians respecting Christ considered such a potent argument against his historicity? Was the Teacher of Righteousness merely a *chimera?* I know of no Scroll scholar who would say so. Common sense would disallow such a supposition. As

---

[524] It is perhaps worth pointing out the fact that the Scriptures cited in note [17] above suggest the burning of the temple in 587 B.C. as the *terminus a quo* of the 390 years of wrath.

[525] Neither do I consider that theory to be proven by any means, despite the evidence I presented in my former work.

[526] And there are specific albeit oblique disclaimers within the Gospel texts.

[527] Or supposed silence.

yet it is unclear what man, living in the early second century B.C., could have been this legendary Teacher of Righteousness. But this is no legitimate argument against his historicity. Against notoriety in his own time, maybe, but not against his historical existence, or his importance to his own religious community. So it is also reasonable to apply the same situation to Jesus. The argument from silence is thus muted.[528] Finally, I would also like to point out that, according to a strict reading of the chronology of the Damascus Document, even the much-touted "consensus" view of Scrolls scholars is refuted; the group, and even the Teacher of Righteousness himself, arrived on the scene _before_ the time of the Maccabean uprising; hence, they were not a protest movement against the Hasmonaean dynasty of priest-kings; more likely, they were protesting some of the earlier, Hellenizing high priests mentioned in 2 Maccabees.

The "Man of the Lie" or the "Man of Mockery" mentioned in the Damascus Document has been identified by some scholars[529] with the apostle Paul. But once again we run up against the chronological impossibility of this identification, so we can rule out this interpretation. There is another interesting passage in the text, which I find significant due to a literary parallel in the New Testament:

"Moses and Aaron stood in the power of the Prince of lights but Belial raised up Yannes and his brother in his cunning when seeking to do evil to Israel the first time."

8 Now as Jannes and Jambres withstood Moses, so do these also resist the truth: men of corrupt minds, reprobate concerning the faith. (2 Timothy 3:8)

Jannes is just another transliteration of Yannes; they are the same name. But what is curious is that, nowhere in either _TaNaKh_, the Apocrypha, nor the surviving portions of the Old Testament Pseudepigrapha do we read these names, or that these two magicians were brothers.[530] Therefore one wonders where Polycarp would have discovered these obscure names, unless he was conversant with

---

[528] And mooted.

[529] Particularly Robert Eisenman.

[530] These two magicians are mentioned in the Talmud; _Sotah 11a; Sanhedrin 106a; Men. 85a;_ and also the _Zohar._

Jewish oral traditions, or possibly some now-lost texts.[531] But the irony is that such a reference seems to undermine the admonition to discountenance Jewish fables in those epistles, unless this is a reference to some other class of Jewish fables.[532] Once again the New Testament remains ambiguous and obscure.

Another passage from the Damascus Document is similar to a passage from second Thessalonians:

"But Strength, Might, and great Wrath in the flames of fire with all the angels of destruction shall come against all who rebel against the way of righteousness and who despise the law, until they are without remnant or survivor, for God had not chosen them from antiquity. Even before they were created, he knew what they would do."

6   Seeing it is a righteous thing with God to recompense tribulation to them that trouble you,

7   and to you who are *now* troubled rest with us, when the Lord Jesus shall be revealed from heaven with his mighty angels,

8   in flaming fire taking vengeance on them that know not God, and that obey not the gospel of our Lord Jesus Christ;

9   who shall be punished with everlasting destruction from the presence of the Lord, and from the glory of his power;

10   when he shall come to be glorified in his saints, and to be admired in all them that believe (because our testimony among you was believed) in that day. (2 Thessalonians 1:6-10)

---

[531]   I.e., assuming that Polycarp, rather than Paul, wrote the pastoral epistles.

[532]   Kamal Salibi has suggested that Paul was referring to the miracle stories attributed to Jesus, such as those now found in the Gospels. This would seem to be a viable option if we credit Paul as the author of the Pauline corpus, including the Pastorals. Admittedly this is an attractive alternative, despite the problems that it evokes. But assuming the contrary, Why would Polycarp condemn Jewish fables if he cited Jewish fables? For that matter, Why would Paul? The problem is that these Jewish fables are not clearly identified in the text, so it is unclear what is being spoken of. This question is particularly vexing to the Bible believer. I remember it always was to me. Now it is merely a curious conundrum.

To me the similarity of the two passages is quite striking. To be sure, there are passages within *TaNaKh* that speak of God bringing vengeance in flaming fire,[533] but none of the biblical passages have as close of a conformity with what we read in the Damascus Document; angels are not mentioned in any of the passages from *TaNaKh,* for example.[534] Note also that in the latter portion of the passage from CD it says that God foreknew the evil of the wicked; this is a theme we also find elsewhere in the Pauline and Petrine corpii.[535] What is truly strange and noteworthy, in my view, is that this passage occurs in an epistle ascribed to Paul. If we saw it in a text ascribed to Peter or James or Judas or John then there would at least be a reasonable supposition that perhaps they had read the Damascus Document, assuming Jesus was a third remove from the Essene sect. But Paul would have had no occasion for knowing of any such text, presumably. Even being a student of the illustrious Gamaliel[536] would not account for it, since Gamaliel was a Pharisee, and the Pharisees as such would not have known the secret texts of the Essenes. And there is an even greater difficulty, if anything, in supposing that Silvanus wrote the Thessalonian epistles.[537] This is unless we suppose two things: first, that the Damascus Document was not as secret as we may imagine it to have been; secondly, that there was circulating a Greek translation of the text, to which Silvanus had access. It is not altogether unthinkable that there may have been a Greek translation of the Damascus Document, since some of the Dead Sea Scrolls were written or copied in Greek.[538] And while the Damascus Document was probably a fairly closely-guarded text, it is possible that a few rare copies were circulating outside of the Qumran community. Otherwise we would have to ask how fragments of the text were discovered in a Cairo genizah. It was a Karaite synagogue where Solomon Schechter discovered the fragments of the Damascus Document. In

---

[533] Psalms 18:8-13; 29:7; 50:3; 97:3; Isaiah 30:30; 66:15-16,24.

[534] Although Isaiah 66:15 does mention "his chariots", implying an angelic entourage.

[535] Romans 8:29-30; 11:2; Ephesians 1:4-5,11; 1 Peter 1:2.

[536] Acts 22:3.

[537] As speculated above. Silvanus was either a Greek or a Greek-speaking Jew. Many Jewish men had Greek names at that time.

[538] Wise, Abegg & Cook., op. cit., pg. 10.

the same genizah Mr. Schechter also discovered an Aramaic text of the Toldoth Yeshu; one which G.R.S. Mead has described as "a distinctly Karaite Toldoth."[539] So there seems to be some link, however tenuous, between the Qumranites and the later Karaites. This also suggests some degree of a common heritage between the Karaites and the proto-messianic Christian movement. Jesus is recorded as being very much opposed to the traditions of the Pharisees.[540] In this rejection of Pharisaic tradition there is a commonality. The Sadducess, the Essenes, the Karaites, and the Ethiopian Jews and Ethiopian Christians also more strictly follow(ed) certain injunctions and interpretations of the Torah than that advocated by Orthodox Rabbis, the heirs of the Pharisees. One other possible solution to the conundrum of the close and undeniable literary parallel between the Damascus Document and 2 Thessalonians is that the latter text may have been written by an Essene convert to the Messianic movement, who sought to "correct" the "imminent" eschatology with a Danielic "signs" eschatology. This seems more probable in view of the fact that 2 Thessalonians seems to contradict 1 Thessalonians, in terms of eschatology.

There is another Dead Sea Scroll that is noteworthy, and somewhat similar in content to the passage from the Damascus Document quoted above. It is the Melchizedek Scroll. The reader may recall that there was also a codex from Nag Hammadi entitled simply "Melchizedek" which was also briefly quoted from. Melchizedek is only mentioned twice in TaNaKh,[541] but is spoken of more extensively by Timothy in Hebrews.[542] Melchizedek, like Enoch, being a figure of whom very little was said within TaNaKh, became a figure of great speculation within Jewish mysticism. And among the Qumranites he seems to have been identified with the Messiah, and perhaps even placed upon an equality with God:

"He shall proclaim this decree in the first week of the jubilee following *the* nine jubilees. Then the Day of Atonement shall follow after the tenth jubilee, when he shall atone for all the sons of light

---

[539]   Mead., op. cit., pg. 316. The Karaites also shared with the Orthodox Jews the tradition of Ben Pandera.

[540]   Mt 12:1-13; 15:1-20; 23:1-35; Mk 2:15-28; 7:1-23.

[541]   Genesis 14:18; Psalm 110:4.

[542]   Hebrews 5:6-10; 6:20; 7:1-21. The Melchizedek Scroll is otherwise designated 11Q13.

and the people who are predestined to Melchizedek's *grace.* ... For this is the time decreed for the year of Melchizedek's favor; and by his might he will judge God's holy ones and thereby establish a righteous kingdom, as it is written about him in the psalms of David, "God sitteth in the council of *Elohim;* in the midst of *elohim* he holds judgment. Scripture also says of him, "Over *them* take your seat in the highest heaven; God will judge the peoples." Concerning what Scripture says "How long will you judge unjustly, and show favor to the wicked? Selah." the interpretation applies to Belial and the spirits predestined to him, because all of them have rebelled, turning from God's precepts and so becoming utterly wicked. Therefore Melchizedek will thoroughly prosecute the vengeance required by God's statutes. Also he will deliver all the captives from the power of Belial, and from the power of all the spirits predestined to him... this visitation is the day of deliverance that he has decreed by Isaiah the prophet concerning all the captives, inasmuch as *the* Scripture says, "How beautiful upon the mountains are the feet of the Angel who announces *Shalom,* who brings *the* gospel, who announces salvation, who says to Zion, "Your God reigns *supreme."* This Scripture's interpretation *is* "the mountains" are the prophets; they who were sent to proclaim God's truth and to prophesy to all Israel. "The Angel" is the spiritual Messiah, of whom Daniel spoke, "After sixty-two weeks, Messiah shall <u>make a covenant</u>."[543] The "Angel who brings *the* gospel, who announces salvation" is the One of whom it is written, "to proclaim the year of GOD's favor, the day of vengeance of our God; to comfort all who mourn."[544] This Scripture's interpretation *is* he is to instruct them about all the *jubilee* periods of history for eternity ... and in the statutes of truth... "Your God" is Melchizedek, who will deliver them from Belial."

Needless to say, the Melchizedek Scroll is highly controversial. It clearly contains a Divine Messianism, which naturally is a theological

---

[543] Hebrew *karath.* In my former work, I spoke at length of this Hebrew word, and how specifically in this prophecy of Daniel the more appropriate reading is "make a covenant" rather than the more traditional "be cut off"; the very same situation applies here, especially since the very same verse is being quoted from. The context of the Melchizedek Scroll also supports my reading of *karath* here. Scroll scholars can fume against me all they want, but so be it.

[544] Cf Isaiah 61:1-2 cp Luke 4:16-21.

precursor to later Christian thought. Christians can now point to such a text and truthfully claim that a fully Divine Messiah was expected in at least some branches of pre-Christian Judaism.[545] So much for the pseudo-scholarly Grailmongers. It is also notable that the scroll speaks of a day of atonement after the tenth jubilee; this clearly corresponds to the 490 years or seventy weeks of years of Daniel's famous prophecy. This is also confirmed by the fact of a quotation taken directly from that vey same prophecy in Daniel in the Melchizedek Scroll. So it is fair to say that the chronology of the prophecy was very important to the Qumranites.

The Damascus Document also says "They must keep the Sabbath day according to specification, and the holy days and the fast day according to the commandments of the members of the New Covenant in the land of Damascus, offering the holy things according to their specifications." The reference to "the New Covenant" is notable.[546] There is also another text from Qumran[547] known as "The Sage to the "Children of Dawn"". What is remarkable about this text is that it was written in a cryptic script that substituted symbols for letters.[548] This is an example of the practice of esotericism, discussed above. The Qumranites probably had several layers of secret teachings. Other than this, the text uses the term "Sons of Dawn", which is at least somewhat similar to the following verse from first Thessalonians:

5   You are all sons of light, and sons of *the* day; we are not of the night, nor of darkness. (1 Thessalonians 5:5 cp Luke 22:53)

---

[545]   Despite the best efforts of some translators to obscure the full meaning of the text. And it should be very clear from the context and content of my work that I am not hereby seeking to play the role of apologist for Christianity; see especially below. Besides, I was surprised at the content of the Melchizedek scroll myself. Now I will have to modify my views respecting the possibility that Jesus may have been esteemed as fully Divine by his Apostles and other disciples. Now Trinitarians can claim that at least the faint lines of their theology are anticipated in that of the Qumran community. And we would have to concede the point, lest we be guilty of a shameless Talmudic revisionism.

[546]   Cf Hebrews 8:6-13; 10:1-14; Jeremiah 31:31-37.

[547]   4Q298.

[548]   Wise, Abegg & Cook., op. cit., pg. 294.

In the King James the correspondence is obscured by the reading "children of light" and "children of the day", but in the original Greek, the word for "sons" is used.[549] While considered in isolation, such terms are likely too generic to be significant, but when collated with many other literary parallels a significant pattern emerges: one which suggests that the Qumran corpus predates, and also to some degree influenced, that of the New Testament. There is also another noteworthy scroll called the War of the Messiah.[550] Some Scroll scholars believe that this fragment may preserve the end of the famous War Scroll.[551] Initially scholars were uncertain as to whether the Scroll indicated that the Branch of David would be put to death by his enemy, the king of the *Kittim,* or if he would execute the enemy. Obvious parallels with Jesus sparked great interest in the text as a result, but since the initial flurry of excitement most Scroll scholars have decided upon an interpretation in which it is the Branch of David (the Messiah) who is victorious, who executes the king of the *Kittim.* One reason why I find this particular controversy relevant is because it ties in directly with the interpretation of *karath* in Daniel 9:26 and the Melchizedek Scroll.[552] If scholars are so determined that the reading of *karath* in Daniel 9:26 means "shall be cut off" rather than "shall make a covenant", then how can they be so sure that the text of this Messianic War Scroll does not also indicate that the Messiah (the Branch of David) shall be slain by the king of the *Kittim,* rather than the reverse? Or conversely, if scholars are so confident of their current reading of the text of the Messianic War Scroll[553] then why are they so complacent to accept a completely contrary interpretation of the Messiah in Daniel 9:26 and the Melchizedek Scroll? In this we can see the inconsistency of these Scroll scholars. In fact, the very arguments used to justify the current interpretation of the Messianic War Scroll are equally valid against a supposition that *karath* signifies "shall be cut off" either in Daniel 9:26 or in the Melchizedek Scroll, where the verse is quoted. So which is it? Are we to believe that Daniel 9:26 was uniquely anomalous in predicting the untimely death of the

---

[549]   Greek *uioi.* Nestle-Aland., op. cit., pg. 536.

[550]   4Q285, 11Q14.

[551]   1QM, 4Q491-496. Cf Wise, Abegg & Cook., op. cit., pg. 292.

[552]   11Q13.

[553]   4Q285, 11Q14.

Messiah?[554] At the very least this should have shaken these scholars awake enough to at least see the problem with the traditional reading of *karath* in Daniel 9:26. But on the other hand, if that reading is so sound, then why is it so unacceptable to envision a slain Messiah? If the current reading of *karath* was indeed accepted by the Qumranites, then there at least would have been a precedent for expecting that the Messiah would be slain in an untimely manner, possibly to be resurrected; but in that case the original reading ascribed to the Messianic War Scroll would seem to be more justified; i.e., the Branch of David is slain by the king of the *Kittim*. I fear we are seeing far too much politics in Scroll scholarship. Is the new reading merely due to a fear that one in which the Branch of David is slain would be perceived as too Christian?[555] Was it out of a fear of offending Jewish sensibilities that the new reading was adopted?[556] Are we still children? Do we need to be "protected" from the truth, whatever it may be? I doubt very much that astute and intelligent Jews would be in any way offended by either reading of the text.

But the depiction of a militant Messiah no doubt fueled the flames of messianic zeal. The Jews were not expecting a pacifist Messiah. The very concept of a pacifist Messiah is an anomaly, and even an oxymoron. Such a pathetic figure would no doubt have been pitied as a madman, possibly stoned, or even sent to be a jester in the court of Herod. The pacifist image of Jesus in the Gospels is almost certainly an overlay upon a more militant personage. However Jesus may have been discreet enough to realize that open opposition to the Romans was likely to be futile. At least if only the Jews revolted. What was needed was an international resistance movement, working secretly underground, until the right time; if the Jews had been able to network with such an underground resistance movement throughout the Roman empire, then it would have spelled the certain doom of

---

[554] And this anomalous reading is thus read into the Melchizedek Scroll by a process of unconscious *eisegesis* by the Scroll scholars, who have not yet come to grips with the dilemma posed by their reading of *karath* in Daniel 9:26. Even in the Melchizedek Scroll, fragmentary as it is, this reading of *karath* seems discordant from the context of the scroll.

[555] I.e., by way of anticipation.

[556] While I doubt that Christian sensibilities would be offended by the original reading, there may be those who would fear too close a linkage between Qumran and earliest Christianity.

the empire; because the Romans, even as mighty as they were, could not simultaneously crush revolts throughout all their territories. But the cultural xenophobia of the Zealots spelled their doom. It was not possible for them to form any such international network of an underground resistance movement. I personally think it's too bad; I can't help but think that the course of history would have been not only different, but better. But we do see not only hints of the more militant Jesus in the Gospels, but he is unabashedly depicted as a victorious, conquering King in the *Apokalypse.*[557]

One of the theories I did not discuss in my last book was that Jesus was a rival to Alexander Jannaeus. Most specifically, that he was a brother to Alexander Jannaeus, and therefore had a stake in the government. Because there were unnamed brothers who also had been imprisoned by Aristobulus,[558] and Jesus, if he really lived in the first century B.C., may have been one of them. This would also make sense of the Talmudic tradition that Jesus was close to those in power.[559] It would also harmonize with those strange passages and traditions that ascribe Levitical descent to Jesus.[560] If Jesus had been one of the unnamed brothers of Aristobulus and Alexander, then it is easy to see where he could have had a dispute with his brother over the throne. Why this drama was suppressed in the history of Josephus is a question that naturally springs to mind as an objection against it. But possibly Jesus was slain by Alexander, and not only that, but for some reason, a messianic following sprang up around him, transforming his legacy into one of truly superhuman proportions. As such, the movement would have been too much of an embarrassment for Josephus.[561] This is one possible explanation; another is admittedly exotic, if not quixotic. Perhaps Jesus is mentioned after all, but under another name; that of a foreign king. If Jesus was in favor of Hellenization, in opposition to his brother, then maybe Jesus appears in Josephus as King Demetrius himself. I realise that this is going out on a limb; but I merely offer it as food for thought. Another theory is

---

[557] See especially Revelation 19:11-21.

[558] Jos. Ant. 13.11.1.

[559] Mead., op. cit., pg. 180.

[560] See, for example, Luke 1:5,36.

[561] After all, Josephus wrote nothing of the Christians, unless we admit the authenticity of the infamous *Testimonium Flavium.*

that Alexander Jannaeus himself was the original of Jesus Christ. In this scenario, opponents of the Pharisees, who gained the ascendancy under the reign of Alexander's widow, Alexandra Salome, would have kept the legacy of Alexander alive as a memory of happier days. There are some Dead Sea Scrolls that celebrate Alexander Jannaeus as a righteous "Lion of Wrath", after all. Eventually Alexander would become so transformed as to be the awaited Messiah, who will return again in power and glory to conquer the unrighteous. In the final metamorphosis, Alexander Jannaeus (as Jesus) is crucified at the behest of the very party of men whom he had crucified.[562] Admittedly this is also highly speculative, but it is likewise offered merely as food for thought. In this vein, however, it is instructive to compare the instructions that Jannaeus gives to Salome concerning how to conduct herself before the Pharisees, and that if she offers them his body, to do with as they will, they will provide him with a far better funeral than they could have afforded themselves.[563] The reason I find this so evocative is the comparison with the disgraceful treatment meted out to the corpse of Jesus in the Toldoth Yeshu, on the one hand, and the mysterious disappearance of the body of Jesus from the tomb reported in the Gospels, on the other. No doubt Alexander Jannaeus feared that the Pharisees would have wanted to do dishonorable things to his body after his death, by way of revenge; so he gave clever advice to Alexandra to pacify their fury, by which he would be honorably buried. The link in all three accounts being the fate of a corpse. The Toldoth reveals what the Rabbis would have wanted to do to Jesus (or Alexander Jannaeus); the Gospels report an empty tomb, together with messengers who proclaim the resurrection of Jesus, as well as various apparitions of Jesus; and the account we read of Alexander Jannaeus in Josephus is a more prosaic yet believable account of a controversial monarch and how he came to be honorably buried by his worst enemies.[564] Both Alexander Jannaeus and Jesus were called "King of Israel" and "King of the Jews". Both men were also accused of illegitimacy by their enemies.[565] Jesus was crucified; Alexander

---

[562] I.e., the Pharisees. Cf Jos. Ant. 13.14.2.

[563] Jos. Ant. 13.15.5.

[564] Jesus was also buried by men of the *Sanhedrin,* according to the Gospels of Mark & Luke.

[565] Jos. Ant. 13.13.4; John 8:41; Luke 19:14. See discussion in my earlier work.

was a crucifier. Jesus is portrayed as the meek Lamb of God, while Alexander was a conquering king; but Jesus shall return (according to the New Testament) as a conquering King from heaven. Both men were enemies to the Pharisees. Once again this theory is only offered as food for thought.

The Dead Sea Scrolls offer a rich field for research into the possible origin of Christianity. But now we must move on.

The Septuagint

The Septuagint is the ancient Greek translation of the Hebrew
Scriptures. However the Septuagint codices also include a number
of other religious books of the Jews, besides those contained within
TaNaKh. These other books are generally referred to as *apocryphal*
by Protestants and *deuterocanonical* by Catholics. More precisely, seven
books are classed as *deuterocanonical* by the Roman Catholic Church:
Tobit, Judith, the Wisdom of Solomon, the Wisdom of Jesus the son
of Sirach,[566] Baruch,[567] 1 Maccabees, 2 Maccabees.[568] Aside from these
seven books, more complete editions of Esther and Daniel are also
regarded as canonical by the Catholic Church.[569] Aside from these

---

[566] Otherwise known simply as Sirach or Ecclesiasticus; the latter name ought
not to be confused with the Canonical book of Ecclesiastes. Orthodox Jews
generally refer to the book as Ben Sirah.

[567] Together with an epistle ascribed to the prophet Jeremiah.

[568] Makkabees in Greek. Machabees in old Catholic Bibles. Tobit is also called
Tobias in old Catholic Bibles.

[569] In the case of Daniel, those portions not found in the Massoretic text
are probably later additions. See my earlier work. The chronology of the
Massoretic text of Esther is different from that of the Greek edition, which
is also in accord with what we find in Josephus; in these latter sources, the
events narrated are said to have occurred in the reign of Artaxerxes; in the
Massoretic text of Esther, the events are set in the time of Ahasuerus, an
untenable chronology. See my earlier work.

books, there is also one called Esdras[570] that, while it is not esteemed as strictly canonical or deuterocanonical, is nevertheless included in the Latin Vulgate Bible as an appendix.[571] All of these books are included in the Septuagint, as well as the third and fourth books of the Maccabees.[572] The book known as IV Ezra[573] is not included in any current codices (or known codices) of the Septuagint, but it is included in the Latin Vulgate Bible, as an appendix.[574] I strongly suspect, however, that very early codices of the Septuagint included this text, as well as the books of Enoch and Jubilees. But most Bible scholars will not broach this topic or will seek to casually dismiss it like a bunch of nervous nellies, out of a fear of controversy.

Another thing they probably won't tell most people is that the most ancient codices of the Septuagint contain the Greek New Testament. Modern editions of the Septuagint exclude the Greek New Testament, but this is an illusion created by the artifice of the editors of such texts, whom I suspect have some very political motives.[575] Even the quality of the script used is inferior to that used in a standard Greek New Testament. But no doubt students of *Koine* Greek would naturally be inclined to an interest in the Greek text of the Old Testament as well.[576] It almost seems as if students are

---

[570] Otherwise known as I Esdras. See the Apocrypha.

[571] BIBLIA SACRA VULGATA. (© 1969 Deutsche Bibelgesellschaft Stuttgart) (IUXTA VULGATAM VERSIONEM); pgs. 1910-1930.

[572] SEPTUAGINTA., op. cit., pgs. 1139-1184. (volume one; Duo volumina in uno). III & IV Makkabees are included in codices of the Septuagint, although they are not generally regarded as strictly canonical by either the Roman Catholic or Greek Orthodox Churches; nevertheless they are highly esteemed by Eastern Orthodox Churches. Some sources claim that they are accepted as Canonical Scripture by the Ethiopian Orthodox Church.

[573] Also otherwise known as the Apocalypse of Ezra or II Esdras. See the Apocrypha.

[574] BIBLIA SACRA VULGATA., op. cit., pgs. 1931-1974.

[575] As opposed to purely scholarly or academic motives.

[576] Although admittedly *Koine* Greek is somewhat different from the more archaic Greek of the Septuagint. Nevertheless this should not be so much of an obstacle to a person who has already acquired some degree of facility in *Koine* Greek. Even modern Greek is very similar to *Koine* Greek, and some of the words are exactly the same in modern Greek Bibles as in the *Koine* Greek New Testament.

being discouraged from studying the Septuagint, or from thinking too highly of it. One suspects that this is done to protect the primacy of the Hebrew Massoretic text of the Old Testament. After all, these texts are generally prepared by Protestant scholars; this implies an aversion to Catholicism and a subtle Judaic influence.[577] The implication is that a student of *Koine* Greek would be encouraged to study biblical Hebrew, rather than the Greek of the Septuagint text.[578] In fact, the Greek in question cannot be that different from *Koine* Greek; the very fact that both testaments were bound together in a single codex implies that a person could read both fairly easily. But by such an editing process certain ideas are reinforced and made more palpable. This has a subtle influence upon the consciousness of the Bible student. Certain beliefs are being reinforced; certain dogmas. More curious students are likely to be discouraged from asking embarrassing questions.[579] But these are just a few passing observations.

But I would like to briefly address the question of the origin of the Septuagint. I already touched on this to some degree earlier, in discussing the Letter of Aristeas. I argued that there was no compelling reason to reject an early third century B.C. date for that epistle, which implies the same date for the translation of the Pentateuch. In fact, there was even a reference to earlier, but inaccurate, translations of the Torah therein. I broach this topic because some genius on the internet has claimed that the Septuagint did not exist in the days of Jesus and the Apostles. Most people would probably just laugh this off, but mere scoffing is not an answer, however absurd the allegation. This attitude ought especially to be maintained by those who, like myself, frequently advocate highly controversial positions and theories. Therefore in order to clearly demonstrate the falsehood of such an allegation, I will briefly discuss the evidence brought forward in favor of the position advocated, the rationale or motivation for the

---

[577] As an adjunct to this, one may notice that in scholarly books on the Dead Sea Scrolls, for example, the Protestant Canon of Scripture is the implicit Canon assumed. This is also in deference and preference to Jews as opposed to either Catholics or Orthodox Christians.

[578] Or the latter only as a tertiary study. Which is absurd, considering that a knowledge of *Koine* Greek will facilitate learning Septuagint Greek more quickly and easily.

[579] Lest the entire edifice of Christian faith crumble to dust, right in the classroom.

allegation, and those facts that clearly refute the position advocated. Ironically, the key point on which this person makes his case rest is something that I have already discussed above; namely, that in the Gospel of Matthew Jesus is reported to have said "For truly I say unto you, not one *yod* or tittle shall in any way pass away from the law, until all be accomplished."[580] I discussed this verse in relation to the Jewish Matthew Gospels. My point there had to do with early Christian traditions that the Apostle Matthew had first written his Gospel in Hebrew. My further inference was that possibly some of the other Gospels attributed to Matthew, which were used by such groups as the Nazoraions and the *Ebionim*,[581] may have been earlier than, and therefore more authentic than, the Canonical Greek version of Matthew. And this is certainly an important part of the evidence, and must not be overlooked. But it is only a part of the evidence, not the whole of it. In fact I am glad that I here have an opportunity to qualify and clarify what I had written earlier. While I still feel that my point about the various Matthew Gospels is valid, I nowhere stated nor did I seek to give the impression that either the Septuagint did not exist at that time, or that the Evangelists never used it. The person who advocated that position on the Internet had an ulterior motive in thus asserting the non-existence of the Septuagint at the time of Jesus and the Apostles; he is a Christian fundamentalist, and also a "King James purist" who is convinced that the King James is the only legitimate or trustworthy English translation of the Bible. He also wanted to bolster the Protestant Canon of Scripture by denying the existence of the Septuagint in the first century, since the Septuagint contains the additional books mentioned above; the rationale being that, since Jesus and the Apostles only used and quoted from the Hebrew text of the Scriptures, then only those held as Canonical by the Jews are valid, or were used by Jesus and the Apostles. The position of the King James purists in respect to the New Testament is also based upon a textual theory that I also think I should briefly discuss, just to shed some light on the issue.[582]

---

[580] Mt 5:18.

[581] Which may in fact be two different names for the same group. However there may have been a number of different Jewish Christian cults or sects who had similar beliefs.

[582] I am especially acquainted with such *minutiae* from my days as a born-again Christian.

There are over five thousand extant Greek manuscripts of the New Testament. These manuscripts have been collated and studied, and grouped into various text-types by biblical scholars. In fact, there are not merely text-types, but families of text-types; in other words, groupings that have certain readings in common, etc. There are four families of text-types: the Alexandrian, the Byzantine, the Caesarean, and the Western. The Byzantine textual family of text-types is favored by the King James purists; all others are considered corrupted and impure and untrustworthy. The Byzantine family of text-types is predominant among all the Greek manuscripts, due to the fact that Greek was commonly spoken in the Byzantine empire for over a thousand years; by contrast, in the Western half of the Roman empire (or what was left of it), Latin was more commonly spoken. Furthermore the Roman Catholic Church forbade the laity from possessing the Scriptures in their own tongue. Other areas where Greek had once been a fairly common language eventually gave way to more regional languages and dialects. Therefore the vast majority of surviving Greek manuscripts are of the Byzantine family of text-types. The Byzantine textual family is a highly standardized form of the text. While it is true that many Byzantine readings once thought to be interpolations have been vindicated by discoveries of some very early manuscripts, critical biblical scholars use all available texts to reconstruct what they believe to be the most probable form of the original Greek text of the New Testament. It just so happens that some of the earliest surviving texts are not of the Byzantine family. Critical scholars refer to their method of analysis as a "local genealogical" one in which each individual passage of Scripture is studied independently and judged independently; in other words, the critical text is an eclectic text, which avails itself of all textual families, rather than slavishly following a given text or textual family or text-type as the only correct one. The Byzantine family may be the majority text, but it is not necessarily on that account the best or most authentic text. The issues involved are subtle and complex. It is true that in a general sense, the majority text is most likely to conserve the original text, all other things being equal. The problem is that all other things are not always equal. Once a given textual reading has been compromised by an alteration, a deletion, or an interpolation, then the damage has been done. A falsified reading may be more common due to scribal copying; once a text has thus been compromised then it is very difficult to determine the original reading. If the original, true reading is no longer copied, and the new, false reading is, then the false reading will appear in more copies, and hence the majority of texts will have been compromised. Therefore it is not as simple as merely accepting the readings of the majority text. In fact a reading which some scribes may have thought were embarrassing may have been eliminated and replaced with one thought more proper. This is why critical Bible scholars study all available Greek Manuscripts, as well as citations of the text within Greek patristic writings, as well as old translations of the New Testament. As a general rule, the text of the New Testament was not very standardized in the earliest days of textual transmission; over time, a more conservative approach to copying the text prevailed, and the text generally became highly standardized, particularly in the Byzantine empire. I am not saying that the Byzantine textual family is not good; what I am saying is that all the textual families need to be consulted by scholars to arrive at a realistic appraisal of the Greek text of the New Testament. The advocates of the Byzantine family, to the exclusion of all others, refer to their chosen text as the *Textus Receptus*. This Latin term means "Received Text". The term is likewise applied to the King James Bible as a whole, and also specifically to the Hebrew Massoretic text of the Old Testament, and the Byzantine or majority text of the Greek New Testament. These advocates take a dogmatic position on this point, and make their adherence to the *Textus Receptus* an article of their faith. This is no exaggeration; I've been through this in my own life as well. I am independent in the sense that I neither agree altogether with the advocates of the *Textus Receptus,* nor with critical biblical scholars, in all cases, without considering the evidence independently on my own. In some cases I agree with the readings of the Byzantine text against the critical scholarly consensus; in other cases I take the opposing position; in some cases I disagree with both parties. One problem I see is that often legitimate points brought up by advocates of the Byzantine text are blithely ignored by critical scholars, as if any such discussion were beneath them. But in such cases critical scholars are conceding, by way of silence, ground that ought to be defended. In other cases the critical scholars are simply wrong. But the religious fanaticism of the King James purists not only blinds them to the truth, it also prevents critical scholars from taking them seriously. One would hope that there could be a forum where such questions could be discussed and debated openly, but most likely it would soon degenerate into a shouting-match, with invectives and threats being made by religious fanatics.[583]

What is interesting in relation to the above discussion is that sometimes key issues in a given controversy may hinge upon a contested reading of a biblical text. For example, in some early texts of Matthew 27:16-17, the name "Jesus" occurs in relation to Barabbas; the reading being "Jesus Barabbas", instead of merely Barabbas.[584] Following the Byzantine text, we would have merely "Barabbas"[585] instead of the more potentially controversial "Jesus Barabbas". The question is, which reading is more likely to be the correct, original reading? Here I side with the scholars of the *Deutsche Bibelgesellschaft Stuttgart,* who include the name "Jesus" within the text.[586] Apparently it was thought to be an embarrassment that the notorious criminal had the same name as the Savior, so a scribe removed it from the text. This is a more likely explanation than the contrary assumption that a scribe gratuitously placed the name in the text. The potential controversy runs deep indeed, since a "Jesus Barabbas" could be interpreted as either a rival Messiah,[587] or possibly even a son of Jesus Christ. In this connection it is noteworthy that an early commentary upon MtN interpreted "Bar Abbas" as meaning "Son of our Teacher", which was changed in some readings to "Son of their Teacher".[588] Of course in Syriac Bar Abbas means "Son of the Father", which is also an apt title for the Messiah.

But returning to the question of the origin of the Septuagint, we can find even from within the pages of the New Testament itself that the Septuagint predates the New Testament.[589] The passage I am

---

[583] And possibly by outraged critical scholars as well. No nervous nellies in *that* debate.

[584] Nestle-Aland., op. cit., pg. 81. Greek *Iaesoun.*

[585] Greek *Barabban.*

[586] I.e., and not merely in the textual apparatus.

[587] See discussion below respecting the substitution theory.

[588] See Schneelmelcher., op. cit.

[589] I.e., unless we are going to take the obtuse position that the New Testament arbitrarily deviated from the Massoretic text of *TaNaKh,* and in such a way that the Septuagint also arbitrarily copied the form found in the Greek New Testament. While strictly speaking this is possible, considered in isolation, the other evidence in favor of the antiquity of the Septuagint obviates and

thinking of is Acts 7:44-43, which quotes from Amos 5:25-27. But the form of the quotation found in Acts corresponds to that found in the Septuagint text, rather than the Massoretic text.[590] Stephen was a Greek-speaking Jew,[591] and hence it is only natural that he would be familiar with the Greek Septuagint translation of the Scriptures, rather than the Hebrew text. So here we have evidence that belies the claim that the Septuagint was never used by any early Christian disciples. Of course this is not proof, strictly speaking; one might argue that the Greek Septuagint was a Christian translation of the Hebrew Scriptures, and therefore it would "correct" any readings found in the Hebrew text, based upon what was found in the Greek New Testament.[592] Stated otherwise, the Greek New Testament actually represented the Hebrew text as it then existed, but later on the text was corrupted by the Massoretes. In either case there is no proof that the Greek Septuagint predated the New Testament.[593] But in fact we have sufficient evidence of the prior existence of the Septuagint in the Letter of Aristeas, and also in those portions of Josephus that reproduce the account. Furthermore to so rail against the prior existence of the Septuagint in this raving way is to turn a blind eye to well-known historical realities, such as the spread of Hellenistic culture in the wake of Alexander's conquests. There is indeed such an embarrassment of evidence against the absurd carping theory of this blind religious fanatic that one can only recommend that he actually do some legitimate research and pull his head out of the sand. Most of the Jews who lived in Alexandria spoke Greek as their first language and eventually lost the use of Hebrew altogether. Of course they would have wanted the Scriptures in their own tongue. Furthermore, the very fact that the Jews who overheard Jesus crying out in Hebrew *"Eli,*

---

excludes any such interpretation of the evidence.

[590] Although I would hasten to add that the reference to *Babylon* rather than *Damascus* is an error on the part of either Stephen, Luke, or pseudo-Luke; the Septuagint corresponds to the Massoretic text in this detail.

[591] Cf Acts 6.

[592] Of course this argument requires a further assumption; namely that those instances of disagreement between the New Testament and the Massoretic text are deviations on the part of the New Testament, rather than evidence of tampering with the Hebrew text by the Jews.

[593] Or so such pseudo-scholars would falsely claim.

Eli, lama sebachthani?" did not understand him, and thought he was calling out for Elijah to rescue him,[594] only serves to prove that they knew neither Hebrew nor Syriac, but only Greek. Are we to suppose that such Jews, who made a pilgrimage to Jerusalem to celebrate the Passover, were content without having their sacred Scriptures available to them in their own language? It would be absurd to think so. Even the very fact that the New Testament Scriptures were first written in Greek begs the question of pre-existing Greek translations of the Old Testament Scriptures. Not only that, but there are portions of the New Testament that, in the quotations from the Old Testament, side with the Massoretic text against the Septuagint, as well as vice-versa; and there are also some examples of allusions within the text that are literary parallels with the Aramaic Targums; this proves that all three different text-types predated the New Testament.[595]

It would be absurd to suppose that there was no Greek translation of the Jewish Scriptures even though Greek was commonly spoken throughout the eastern Mediterranean since the conquest by Alexander, up until well into the seventh century at least. Jews did not all live in Judaea and Galilee during this time; many lived in Alexandria, and also were scattered in many cities throughout the Eastern Mediterranean, in Asia Minor, Greece, and even in Rome. These Jews had synagogues in these various cities. We can see, even from the book of Acts, that this was the case. Paul was said to have preached to the Jews in the synagogue in Antioch of Pisidia, for example.[596] This is in the midst of Asia Minor, where Greek would have been commonly spoken, both by Jews and Gentiles. Paul and Barnabas also reportedly preached to the Jews in a synagogue in Iconium.[597] Iconium was likewise in Asia Minor; Greek would have been the *lingua franca* there. Also in Thessalonika there was a synagogue of the Jews.[598] This was in Greece itself. It is unthinkable that Jews living in Greece would have spoken Hebrew to the exclusion of Greek. Do not American Jews speak English? There was also a

---

[594]   Mt 27:46-47; Mk 15:34-35.

[595]   Although strictly speaking there was no Massoretic text until the early seventh century.

[596]   Acts 13:14-15,42.

[597]   Acts 14:1. This is also in Asia Minor.

[598]   Acts 17:1.

synagogue in Berea.[599] Berea is also in Greece, so the same argument applies. There was even a Jewish synagogue in Athens.[600] There was also a synagogue in Corinth.[601] There was also a synagogue in Ephesus.[602] And, although the New Testament does not say so specifically, there was no doubt a synagogue in Alexandria, where many Jews lived. We also learn from Josephus that there was a Jewish temple in Leontopolis, Egypt.[603] These were all regions where Greek was commonly spoken by the majority of the people. It would have been absurd for the Jews to accentuate their differences with their neighbors by refusing to speak their language. And in fact we know that certain prominent Jewish authors wrote in Greek, such as Philo Judaeus and Josephus Flavius. We can also see Hellenistic cultural and philosophical influence in some later religious books of the Jews, such as IV Makkabees and the Wisdom of Solomon.[604] According to some sources, Greek was commonly spoken even in Galilee itself. But apparently Greek was not commonly spoken in Judaea.[605] In any

---

[599]   Acts 17:10.

[600]   Acts 17:16-17.

[601]   Acts 18:1-8,17.

[602]   Acts 18:19; 19:1-8.

[603]   Jos. Ant. 13.1-3; War. 1.1.1; 7.10.3.

[604]   Not to mention the Letter of Aristeas, and many other works.

[605]   Acts 21:37: "And as Paul was being led into the fortress, he said unto the *chiliarch,* May I speak unto thee? Who answered, Knowest thou Greek?" The surprised question uttered by the Roman chiliarch proves that native Palestinian Jews were not expected to know Greek, but the Romans did speak Greek. (Mel Gibson should have known this) The following context of the passage creates another challenge, but not an unanswerable one; the chiliarch says to Paul "Art not thou that Egyptian, who before these days made an uproar, and led out into the wilderness four thousand men that were assassins?" The literal Greek being *Sikarion,* denoting dagger-wielding assassins, such as many Zealots were. But this verse (21:38) implies that Egyptians were not expected to know Greek either. Doesn't that throw a monkey-wrench into the argument cited above? Not really; Alexandrians commonly spoke Greek, where many people of both Greek and Jewish descent lived. But native Egyptians, especially those who may have lived far from the metropolis of Alexandria, may have spoken Coptic instead of Greek. Presumably this would also have been true of some Egyptian Jews as well, since the Egyptian referred to is identified as a false prophet who led people to conquer Jerusalem; the implication being that the man was Jewish as well as Egyptian.

case there can be no doubt that the Hebrew Scriptures had already been translated into Greek. There is also no compelling or legitimate reason to reject the account of the Letter of Aristeas, or of the account of Josephus, on this score. Early Greek translations of the Jewish Scriptures were superseded by that of the Septuagint. Aside from the Septuagint itself, a number of other Greek translations followed, such as those of Aquila, Theodotion, and Symmachus.

But the New Testament quotations from the Old Testament much more frequently agree with the text of the Septuagint than the Massoretic text. For example, aside from the earlier example given above, another one from the book of Acts is apt to the point. Acts 15:17, where James the Just is quoted as quoting from the prophet Amos 9:12, his words correspond not to the reading of the Massoretic text, but to that of the Septuagint. This example is particularly pungent, since James the brother of Christ spoke Hebrew, and would no doubt have been quoting from an extant Hebrew text of the passage in question. This proves that the Hebrew text that then existed was in conformity with the text of the Septuagint, rather than the much later Massoretic text. This is but one example. A few others can be found in Hebrews. Hebrews 1:6 quotes from the Greek Septuagint text of Deuteronomy 32:43; the citation is entirely absent in the Massoretic text. Hebrews 2:7 quotes from the Septuagint version of Psalm 8:5, which reads "For thou hast made him *to be* a little lower than the angels, and hast crowned him with glory and honor." In the Hebrew of the Massoretic text we read *elohim* rather than *malachim*.[606] Hebrews 10:5-7 quotes from the Septuagint form of Psalm 40:6-8, as against the current reading of the Massoretic text. Matthew 1:23 quotes from the Septuagint text of Isaiah 7:14, and Matthew 12:21 quotes from the Septuagint text of Isaiah 42:4. Of all these examples,

---

[606] BIBLIA HEBRAICA STUTTGARTENSIA. (© 1983 Deutsche Bibelgesellschaft Stuttgart) EDITIO FUNDITUS RENOVATA. K. Elliger & W. Rudolph. Textum Masoreticum curavit H.P. Ruger. MASORAM ELABORAVIT G.E. Weil. Editio secunda emendata opera W. Rudolph & H.P. Ruger.; pg. 1092. *Elohim* and *malachim* are the Hebrew words for *God* and *angels,* respectively. Technically *elohim* is a plural form of *El,* a Hebrew word for God derived from Canaanite. However the plural in Hebrew is not always strictly numerical; it may instead be a plurality denoting greatness. In any case there are some clear instances where the "plural" form is used in the Hebrew text, which by grammar and usage, denotes a singular entity. Study the Bible.

that of Acts 15:17 quoting from Amos 9:12 is by far the most pungent, since it virtually proves that the Hebrew text at that time agreed with the reading now found in the Septuagint text. Men like Robert Eisenman can rail against this all they want, and claim that the text in Acts was a falsification and an example of revisionism, but they prove nothing but their own prejudice. It is time that such men were taken to task. In fact, it is a patently absurd argument to claim that such examples of the New Testament quoting from the Septuagint form of the text represent a departure from the original text. The reason why should be fairly obvious; why would anyone quote from a false version of a Scriptural text, when they were trying to prove the truth of their own interpretation of that text? In other words, if the Hebrew text _at that time_ was so different from the Septuagint text, as the much later Massoretic text is, then why did the Jews _of that time_ not simply bring forward the genuine Hebrew text and thus refute the Christians? This is an unanswerable argument. No contemporary Jewish apologist can possibly refute the point made here. If any Jews are going to carp that the translation of the Torah into Greek became an occasion of mourning for the Jews, this custom was not instituted until at least the third century, if not much later. It was certainly not something that happened immediately upon the translation of the text. At that time, there would have been rejoicing among the Jews. Any other interpretation is an absurdity and an impossibility. After all, the men who translated the Hebrew Scriptures into Greek were themselves Jews. Why would they have gratuitously falsified their own religious books? At that time there would have been no motive to do so. But those Orthodox Jews who lived after the time of Christ would have had a strong motive to falsify the text. And this is exactly what the Massoretes did. I will never apologise for writing what is true. Finally, as if to clinch the point, the discovery of the Dead Sea Scrolls has vindicated many of the readings otherwise found in the Septuagint text, as well as the Samaritan Pentateuch. Furthermore, the fact that such texts as Jubilees, Enoch, Tobit, Sirach, and many others existed before the New Testament is also proven by the discovery of the Dead Sea Scrolls.

The Greek Messiah

Jesus is presented to us in the New Testament as the Jewish Messiah. But the Greek word for Messiah, *Christos,* while sharing the same key meaning of "Anointed" nevertheless renders a foreign feeling and ambience to the term. As I have mentioned already, it is quite possible that Jesus himself was not even ethnically Jewish. Of course I fully anticipate being castigated and excoriated as a notorious anti-Semite just for suggesting such an idea. In fact, one reviewer apparently accused me [but without naming me] of being a "National Socialist" on this score. Nothing could be further from the truth. He had apparently forgotten, or chose to overlook, the fact that the region of Galilee had been predominantly Gentile, and that the Galilaeans had been conquered by John Hyrcanus, who imposed his version of Judaism upon them. But here once again we see a notorious double standard at work; it is fully acceptable, even desirable, to question the Jewish ethnicity of Paul, who is typically portrayed as an arch-villain. But to even hint that Jesus may not have been ethnically Jewish is enough to insure that one is beyond the pale of cultural acceptability, and one is suspected of being an anti-Semite for such a thoughtcrime. Even if one is provably not an Anti-Semite, one would still be castigated for seeming to give aid and comfort to those who are Anti-Semites by calling into question the ethnicity of Jesus. But one can gratuitously insult Christians by not only questioning, but outright denying the Jewish ethnicity of the apostle Paul, with apparent impunity. Why? Why such a notorious double standard?

I am not going so far as to suggest that Jesus himself was Greek, although I would not say that such a thing is altogether unthinkable. What I am suggesting is that Jesus was probably most commonly known under the Greek form of his name, and was probably fairly congenial towards Hellenism. He also may have spoken Greek; he certainly had some Greek disciples, even among his chosen Apostles.[607] The very earliest artistic depictions of Jesus render him as a noble Greek youth, without a beard. Jesus certainly became much more popular among Greeks than among most of the Jews. Furthermore the books of the New Testament were written in Greek. As we have seen, even many Jews spoke Greek during the time of Jesus and the Apostles.[608] The very fact that no Hebrew translations of these Greek texts were made in the early centuries of the Christian era is somewhat suggestive, and seemingly significant. Indeed, the very fact that none of the apocryphal texts of the Old Testament were preserved in Hebrew belies the myth of a Jewish Christian "remnant" surviving within the greater Christian church.[609]

But many Jews think of Jesus as a sort of "Greek" Messiah. It is true that the Greeks also had a somewhat similar concept of an anointed deliverer; in fact this theme was common to many cultures, such as the Egyptian, Canaanite, Assyrian, Babylonian, Syrian, Samothracian, Mexican, Indian, Persian, etc. The *mythos* of a dying and rising Savior was common coin to many diverse cultures, and we ought not to be surprised if the Jews, or at least some Jews, likewise incorporated such a theme within their own religious tradition. If we countenance this interpretation of events, then perhaps the traditional reading of *karath* in Daniel 9:26 is valid after all. But if this is so, then it is also valid to assume a similar interpretation for such texts as the

---

[607] John 12:20-22.

[608] Regardless of whether Jesus lived in the first century B.C. or the first century C.E.

[609] I am here speaking of those books that unequivocally had been composed in Hebrew, such as Tobit, Judith, Sirach, Jubilees, and most likely, Enoch. Hebrew fragments of these works have been found among the Dead Sea Scrolls.

Melchizedek Scroll and also the Messianic War Scroll.[610] Of course this information is often appealed to by advocates of the phantom Christ theory.[611] What is interesting is that within *TaNaKh* itself, the *Torah* seems almost completely exempt from this *mythos*.[612] The famous passage from Deuteronomy[613] that speaks of God sending a prophet like unto Moses to the Israelites seems to originally have signified that God would send a prophet, or series of prophets, who would speak in his name, and admonish the Israelites to follow the commandments that God had revealed on Sinai. Only later did this text become interpreted as speaking prophetically of one special Prophet whom God would send to instruct his people.[614] But within *Nehevim* and *Kethuvim* we see much of the Messianic theme, which is further developed in texts like Enoch, the Testament of Levi, the Wisdom of Solomon, and other texts of the Apocrypha and Old Testament Pseudepigrapha. Of course Daniel, Isaiah and Psalms are key texts that treat of the messianic theme. The progressive exaltation of the figure of the expected Messiah may have caused concern among some Rabbis that this was a tendency towards idolatry, and this may be one reason why the *Talmud* concentrates so much more on the *Torah* proper than the other portions of *TaNaKh*. There is a story told by the Rabbis to the effect that there were four men who were granted entrance to Paradise; one of the men died; another man went insane; a third man became a heretic, saying that there were Two Powers in heaven; and the fourth, being Rabbi Akiba, came out unscathed. We have

---

[610] 11Q13 & 11Q14, 4Q285, respectively. See discussion on the Dead Sea Scrolls above.

[611] I.e., the theory that Christ never existed as a historical person. Such theorists typically appeal to the silence of Josephus, Philo Judaeus, Suetonius, and other writers, as well as the ubiquitous transcultural *mythos* of dying and rising Saviors as evidence or even proof of their claim that Jesus was a mere *chimera*.

[612] Except of course Genesis 3:15. But certain critical theories respecting the origin and dating of the Torah make it at least a reasonable possibility that a Canaanite or Syrian *mythos* of a dying and rising Savior may have been incorporated into the text, early on in the textual transmission.

[613] Deuteronomy 18:15–22.

[614] Indeed the Dead Sea text 4QTestimonia proves that pre-Christian Jews had already so interpreted this text of Deuteronomy; the Christians merely followed suit.

already seen that the Melchizedek Scroll seems to place Melchizedek, a celestial messianic figure, upon an equality with God. The Pharisees and Sadducees no doubt considered the Essenes to be heretics.

But to return to my point about Jesus: he was almost certainly most commonly known by the Greek form of his name, but today there is an effort by certain groups of Hebrew Christians[615] to Judaize the image of Jesus beyond all reasonable probability. This is offered as a restoration, but I see it as a form of false revisionism. This is an act of falsification, whether willfully or otherwise. If done in ignorance, it merely spreads such ignorance like a virulent cancer among unsuspecting people; if otherwise, it is merely a cynical attempt to co-opt the image and legacy of the historical Jesus to subserve some unknown and questionable political agenda, and to cash in on the gullibility of Zionist Christians in the process. This is most unsavory. The worst thing about it all is that the ignorance is so toxic and leads to an arrogant malignancy and hostility towards anyone who may be inclined to unmask the fraud. I suspect that cynical hypocrisy lies at the bottom of it all. Either that or an invincible ignorance of historical truth. Such things only create confusion and make it that much more difficult for the genuine seeker of truth.

---

[615] Especially the Jews for Jesus and other militant messianics.

The Samaritan Pentateuch

The Samaritan Pentateuch is of special interest since it predates both the Hebrew Massoretic text of *TaNaKh* and also the Greek Septuagint translation of the Torah-Pentateuch. The Samaritan Pentateuch has certain distinctive features that clearly and unmistakably identify it as the most ancient, authentic text of the Torah. However, due to a convergence of accidental circumstances, this fact is very unlikely to be pointed out by any biblical scholars, either critical or conservative. Having conducted some degree of research on the subject, I must say that, while I have been able to find enough information to verify my position, I have yet to find any truly objective, unbiased, or even reasonably fair source of information respecting the Samaritan Pentateuch. Nevertheless what facts are available militate against the common arguments marshalled against the antiquity and authenticity of the Samaritan Pentateuch by those with vested interests.[616]

Some Jewish critics have alleged that the Samaritan Pentateuch dates to no earlier than the time of Sanballat and Manasseh, in the days of the high priest Jaddua, when the temple on Mount Gerizim

---

[616] This includes not merely or even necessarily primarily financially vested interests, but emotionally vested interests; the true facts about the origin and antiquity of the Samaritan Pentateuch are a threat to Judaism, as well as to evangelical and fundamentalist Christianity, and also to the currently-reigning theories of critical biblical scholarship.

was supposedly built.[617] But this assertion is extremely unlikely, to say the least. A more adequate appraisal would be that such a suggestion is altogether untenable. The reason should be fairly obvious to anyone who has bothered to read the relevant texts. When the Jews returned from their Captivity in Babylon, the Samaritans were already in the land.[618] According to the biblical book of Kings, the Samaritans were descendants of people who had been resettled in the land by the Assyrians after the deportation of the ten northern tribes of Israel.[619] But historically the Samaritans have always claimed to be descendants of the legendary ten lost tribes of Israel. Not only that, but after they offered to help the postexilic Jews rebuild their temple, the Jews rather rudely and unjustifiably rebuffed them.[620] But from that time on, there was so much mutual hostility between the two groups that there was no possibility that the Samaritans would have or could have received their version of the Torah from the Jews. It is unthinkable. It is an insult to the intelligence to suggest such a thing. And this fact throws a huge monkey-wrench into the currently-reigning academic orthodoxy vis-à-vis critical biblical scholarship. This is exactly why we are unlikely to ever hear very much about the Samaritan Pentateuch; and whatever we do hear is likely to be greatly distorted by the vested interests of the person or persons presenting the information.

---

[617]   Jos. Ant. 11.8.1-2. It is at least possible that the temple on Mount Gerizim had been built before this time.

[618]   See the books of Ezra & Nehemiah, as well as Jos. Ant. 11.4.3-4.

[619]   2 Kings 17. Josephus always agrees with this interpretation. It is noteworthy that in the book of Ezra, the Samaritans also agree that they were brought from Assyria, as if they were foreign refugees. However historically the Samaritans claim to be the descendants of the ten lost tribes of Israel. The fact that they are quoted as admitting their supposedly foreign origin in Ezra is another red flag that Ezra is a bogus, late pseudepigraphon, as I argued in my earlier work. The evident chronological doctoring in Ezra is another important piece of evidence. See my earlier work. Furthermore note the comparison and contrast with the account of Christ's conversation with a Samaritan woman, where the woman claims to be a descendant of the patriarch Jacob (John 4:12); Jesus does not contradict nor rebuke her on this point. He instead implicitly accepts her as a daughter of Israel. In any case the passage from John is clear proof that the Samaritans claimed Israelite descent.

[620]   Ezra 4:1-6 cf Jos. Ant. 11.4.3-4. So just to set the record straight, the Jews instigated the hostilities, not the Samaritans.

It is notable at least that Josephus himself does not write that it was in the days of Jaddua and Sanballat that the Samaritans first acquired their Pentateuch.[621] Neither does any biblical text make any such allegation. But it is worth pointing out that, even if the Samaritan text of the Pentateuch dated to no earlier than this time, it would still predate both the ancient Greek Septuagint text and the Hebrew Massoretic text. The Torah was not translated from Hebrew to Greek until the reign of Ptolemy Phildadephus in the third century B.C.[622] The earliest extant text of the Greek Septuagint dates to no earlier than the third century C.E. The earliest Massoretic text of TaNaKh dates to no earlier than about 900 C.E., at the very earliest. The Dead Sea Scrolls reveal that the Hebrew text had not yet attained a high degree of standardization in the first century.[623] Later on, the Massoretes standardized the text; one of the chief points they made was to add a system of vowel points to the text; earlier Hebrew texts of TaNaKh were always left unpointed. This whole process is somewhat parallel to how the Byzantine family of Greek texts of the New Testament became standardized in the Byzantine empire. Once the text of the New Testament had reached a high degree of standardization, the scribes were very conservative in their copying of the manuscripts. But in the Byzantine empire the process seems to have occurred in a more natural manner than the comparatively artificial alteration of the text by the Massoretes. There can be no real doubt that the Massoretic text, as it stands today, is very different in many respects from any Hebrew text of the first three centuries of the Christian era.[624] I touched on this theme briefly above; my point being that those New Testament quotations from the Old Testament that agreed with the Septuagint reading against that of the Massoretic text are almost certainly correct. It is absurd and unthinkable to suppose

---

[621]   Actually the Samaritans have a complete Hexateuch, since they also possess the book of Joshua.

[622]   Jos. Ant. 12.2.1-15 cf Letter of Aristeas (Aristeus). However, as we noted above, it is possible that there were some Greek translations of the Torah before this time, but they were considered defective. But there can be no doubt that the Samaritan text predates even the earliest Greek text. The presumed year of the translation of the Torah was c. 269 B.C.

[623]   Despite unsubstantiated claims of the vindication of the Massoretic text by Jews and evangelicals.

[624]   Otherwise designated as the Common Era.

that those who were trying to prove that Jesus was the long-awaited Jewish Messiah would have misquoted from the very texts that they claimed proved his Messianic status. Many educated and intelligent persons had access to the Jewish Scriptures in the Greek translation, including sharp critics of Christianity, such as Porphyry and Celsus; yet nowhere are Christians ever taken to task for allegedly changing or misquoting the Old Testament Scriptures in any of the old polemics of the time.

When the Jews returned from their Babylonian Captivity, they brought back with them a new, square Aramaic alphabetic script. The Hebrew Massoretic text is written in this later script, while the Samaritan Pentateuch is written in the older, more archaic, palaeo-Hebrew script.[625] The palaeo-Hebrew script was used less and less frequently by postexilic Jews, and eventually was completely replaced by the square Aramaic script.[626] But the Samaritans always preserved their Torah in the ancient palaeo-Hebrew script. These are facts. Facts which are likely to be obscured, ignored, or distorted by Jews, evangelical Christians, and critical Bible scholars. Orthodox Jews and fundamentalist Protestant Christians[627] would be motivated to downplay the facts surrounding the Samaritan Pentateuch because they militate against the assumption of a pristine, original Hebrew Massoretic text of the Torah, which their respective religions are predicated upon.[628]

Critical Bible scholars would be motivated to obscure the evidence of the true antiquity and priority of the Samaritan Pentateuch because

---

[625] These are the two different scripts discussed by Yigael Yadin in his article on the Temple Scroll; see section above on the books of Enoch and Jubilees.

[626] This may be part of the reason why confusion about the language of the postexilic Jews exists, such as the idea that they spoke Aramaic rather than Hebrew. I will discuss this in greater detail in the section below.

[627] Who have a notorious and incestuous relationship to Judaism and Zionism.

[628] Explicitly in the case of Jews; implicitly in the case of Christians, especially evangelicals and fundamentalists, and to a lesser degree, Catholic fundamentalists. Fundamentalist Karaite Jews also uphold the alleged primacy of the Massoretic text of the Torah, despite all the contrary evidence. The same is true, ironically, of Jews who may happen to be critical biblical scholars, but for quite opposite reasons: because the priority of the Samaritan Pentateuch militates against the currently-reigning critical theories vis-à-vis the origin of the Pentateuch.

an acceptance of the priority of that text belies the currently-reigning academic orthodoxy respecting the authorship of the Pentateuch. But such critical scholars are notoriously inconsistent in their theories and are also insufferably arbitrary in their Olympian pronouncements. Their chief weapon is silence. Numerous arguments which they cannot answer or refute are simply ignored, as if beneath contempt. There is an ongoing "cold war" of sorts between critical biblical scholars, who represent the currently-reigning academic orthodoxy in the field of biblical scholarship, and their ideological opponents, conservative biblical scholars, who represent the religious orthodoxy of evangelicals and fundamentalists, and the more conservative theological elements of the more traditional churches.[629] But this "cold war" has seemed to have thawed into a form of détente or at least of mutual acceptance of the inevitability of the continued existence of their opponents positions. But both groups are and would be implicitly opposed to any attention being drawn to the Samaritan Pentateuch, since the facts about the Samaritan Pentateuch are such as to discredit both the currently-reigning academic orthodoxy vis-à-vis critical Bible scholarship, and the assumptions of Massoretic supremacy in popular Protestant Christian fundamentalism.[630]

Today one hears much of the theory that it was in the days of King Josiah that Deuteronomy was written; it being the supposed "book of the law" discovered by the high priest Hilkiah in the temple.[631] The argument being that the reform made by Josiah was in conformity with the text of Deuteronomy. However, we have the statement that even long before this, back in the days of King Jehoshaphat, the Levites had "the book of the law of the LORD" with them.[632] Not only that, but the reforms instituted by Jehoshaphat were also in accordance with Deuteronomy, since he "took away the high places and groves out of Judah."[633] Of course critical Bible scholars can carp that this is merely an example of historical revisionism within the text of Chronicles; but if so, then they are themselves guilty of arbitrariness, since they have accorded historicity to the account in

---

[629] I.e., Catholic and Orthodox Churches.

[630] Not to mention Judaism.

[631] 2 Kings 22:8–12; 2 Chronicles 34:15–28.

[632] 2 Chronicles 17:9.

[633] 2 Chronicles 17:6.

the days of Josiah, but have denied it to the much earlier reign of Jehoshaphat.[634] Likewise in the reign of King Hezekiah, we also see reforms that are in accord with Deuteronomy.[635] If this is another instance of alleged historical revisionism, then why should we accord historicity to the account of the reign of King Josiah? Is it because this would have been the "last chance" for any possible historic reform to have been made in the days of the kings of Judah?

My point is quite simply that the Pentateuch must have existed *before* the fateful Babylonian Captivity. In fact, even taking a highly critical view of the Bible, I think it is justifiable to say that the Pentateuch existed as far back as the eighth century B.C. at least, if not far earlier. The ten northern tribes were deported from their land by the Assyrians in the late eighth century B.C., and were supposedly replaced by foreign refugees from other portions of the Assyrian empire.[636] We are told a quaint story of how God supposedly sent lions among the people of the land, since they didn't worship God properly.[637] As a "solution" to this problem, the king of Assyria sent back a priest from one of the ten northern tribes, to teach the new people of the land how to worship God properly.[638] It is possible, if not probable, that this priest brought back with him a copy of the Torah, which was the original Samaritan Pentateuch.

2 Chronicles 17:9 can be accepted as evidence that the book of the law existed as far back as the days of King Jehoshaphat, which was long before the Assyrian deportation of the ten northern tribes. Jehoshaphat is regarded as having lived in the ninth century B.C., even by critical biblical scholars and archaeologists. And the expression "book of the law of the LORD" probably ought not to be restricted to the book of Deuteronomy; most likely, it referred to the entire Torah. In fact, the assumption of critical biblical scholars that only the scroll of Deuteronomy could have been intended is a result of their own internalized prejudice against the legitimacy of the Samaritan

---

[634] I am sure that Orthodox Rabbis would point out the very same thing.

[635] 2 Kings 18-19; 2 Chronicles 29-32.

[636] 2 Kings 17. However this account is suspect, since it was written by postexilic Jews, who were mortal enemies to the Samaritans.

[637] 2 Kings 17:25-26. But if true, then why didn't God do the same thing to the Israelites?

[638] 2 Kings 17:27-28.

Torah. The Samaritan Torah is inscribed on one very large scroll, unlike the five Torah scrolls common in Judaism. Noteworthy is the singularity of expression "book of the law" found in relevant biblical texts.[639] Only because these men had already been conditioned to always thinking of the Torah as divided into five separate scrolls did the theory arise that it must have been the scroll of Deuteronomy that was the book that had been found. But the Samaritan Pentateuch has all five books inscribed on a single large scroll; the individual books are separated by a few lines of space. Therefore even the actual physical description of the Samaritan Pentateuch more closely corresponds to the biblical description of a single "book of the law", rather than several.[640]

We also should keep in mind the words attributed to Jesus in Matthew 5:18: "For truly I say unto you, not one *yod* or tittle shall by any means pass *away* from the law, until all be fulfilled." This is an endorsement of the Samaritan text of the Pentateuch, if taken literally; since only that text is still inscribed in the original, palaeo-Hebrew script. It is interesting that the Samaritans offered to help the Jews to build a temple in Jerusalem. This shows some degree of magnanimity on their part. And we can hardly doubt the veracity of the report, since it was written by their avowed enemies.[641] We cannot be certain that there was no temple upon Mount Gerizim at that time, despite what was written by Josephus. Josephus himself was hardly unbiased in this respect, and was very much unsympathetic towards the Samaritans. But there seems to be some degree of confusion about the temple in Jerusalem, since it is commonly referred to as the "second temple" and yet there is a discrepancy within Scripture as to how long the temple was under construction. If I may be permitted a slight digression, I would like to discuss the temple or temples in Jerusalem, and other Jewish temples.[642] The Persians were generally

---

[639] Joshua 1:8; 2 Chronicles 17:9; 34:14-15; 2 Kings 22:1-11.

[640] As well as the fact that the Samaritan text is written in the original palaeo-Hebrew script.

[641] Ezra 4:2.

[642] Aside from the Jewish temple in Leontopolis that I have discussed briefly above and in my former work, there had also been a Jewish temple in Elephantine, Egypt. And as we will see, there may also have been yet another Jewish temple in Arabia.

lenient and tolerant of the foreign religious practices of the peoples in their empire; for this reason they allowed the Jews to rebuild their temple in Jerusalem.[643] But according to Kamal Salibi, the Jews returned, not to Palestine, but to a region of Western Arabia known as the *Hijaz*. Salibi further contends that the Jews built their temple not in Jerusalem, but in a city (which is today merely a village) known as *Uri Shalim*. Only later did the Jews migrate to Palestine and build a temple in Jerusalem.[644] Kamal Salibi also points out a notable difference between the current site of the Jerusalem temple and the original temple of Solomon; there is a huge monolith housed directly underneath the famous Dome of the Rock.[645] This notable feature is nowhere mentioned in the biblical description of Solomon's temple.[646] Aside from this evidence, there is still further evidence supporting Kamal Salibi's claim; as noted above, there is a discrepancy in Scripture about how long it took to build the so-called "second" temple. According the Scripture, Solomon spent seven years building the first temple.[647] But the second temple apparently only took four years to build, according to other Old Testament sources. According to Haggai 1:1-8, it was in the second year of Darius the Persian that work began on the second temple; according to Ezra 6:15, the temple was completed in the sixth year of King Darius. That makes four years. But in John 2:20 the Jews say to Jesus that it took forty-six years to build this same "second" temple. What? That is a contradiction. I know that apologists for the standard interpretation of biblical history and chronology will use the excuse that this latter reference was to Herod's many "embellishments" to the "second" temple, but that they were only "embellishments"; the same "second" temple was merely added to, the way some people make additions to their houses. While this explanation seems fairly plausible, it is still not entirely satisfying to me. It implies that the structural embellishments took far longer than the original construction of the edifice. That is a bit much to

---

[643] 2 Chronicles 36:22-23; Ezra 1:1-4; cf Jos. Ant. 11.1.1-3.

[644] Salibi., op. cit., pgs. 53-54.

[645] From which that world-famous shrine of the Noble Sanctuary gets its name. Graham Hancock wrote of this famed *Shettiyah* stone in his popular book, *The Sign and the Seal*.

[646] Salibi., op. cit., pg. 54; 1 Kings 6.

[647] 1 Kings 6:38.

suppose. Not only that, but this "explanation" still does not account for what Kamal Salibi has pointed out about the monolith at the site. Many people today suppose that the Wailing Wall is the only surviving remnant of this so-called "second" temple. But I pointed out in my earlier book that, most likely, the Wailing Wall is the remains of a Roman temple to Jupiter, built by the Emperor Hadrian.[648] According to some new information I have since discovered, the truth may be even more shocking than this. According to some other sources, the Emperor Hadrian had intended to build temples to Jesus Christ, which were, according to those same sources, temples without images. Hadrian was dissuaded from this enterprise by the pagan priests, however, although the same idea was contemplated by the later Emperor Alexander Severus.[649] If the temple built in Jerusalem by the agents of Hadrian was really a temple to Christ, then this creates a distinctively different context to the persecution endured by Jewish Christians at the hands of Simeon Bar Kochbah and his minions.[650] I can imagine no more appropriate poetic justice than the dozens, hundreds, or thousands of devout Orthodox Jews daily and devoutly praying before and venerating the Wailing Wall under the delusion that it is the final surviving remnant of their so-called "second" temple, and millions of Jews falsely believing that it is so, all the while it being a remnant of a temple dedicated to the founder of a religious movement bitterly persecuted by them. Some may object against this interpretation the seeming improbability of Hadrian seeking to erect a temple to Christ, since Christ presumably was still largely unknown to the Romans at that time, other than as possibly a strange curiosity of some strange new cult. While this is one possible view of things, it is reported so of Hadrian by Lampridius, who wrote a biography of Severus Alexander.[651]

---

[648] Although it is uncertain just when this Roman temple was destroyed, and by whom. Possibly by the Arabs, when they conquered Jerusalem in the Mohammedan era, if not earlier.

[649] King., op. cit., pg. 118.

[650] Mead., op. cit., pgs. 122-123.

[651] Who reigned as Emperor in the early third century. Since this was before the time of Constantine, it is unlikely that there would have been any historical revisionism in the account written by Lampridius; therefore it ought to be considered fairly credible. However according to the account, Hadrian had been dissuaded from thus erecting a temple to Christ by the

One suspects that the Samaritan text is being deliberately suppressed by an implicit conspiracy of silence by the adherents of academic orthodoxy, which subserves Judaic orthodoxy. And this same conspiracy of silence also enables the adherents of evangelical Christianity as well. Neither side would want a full disclosure of the true facts surrounding the Samaritan Pentateuch to become widely known, due to their own respective vested interests. But the truth is that the Samaritan Pentateuch, and the facts proving its much greater antiquity, represents a much more formidable challenge to dogmatic fundamentalism than all the vain theories of critical biblical scholars. Because we have in the Samaritan Pentateuch an unanswerable challenge, rather than the often insipid and absurd ideas of critical Bible scholars. In fact, a "critical edition" of the Samaritan Pentateuch may be just the weapon that the *Deutsche Biblegesellschaft Stuttgart* may use to "silence" such dissidents as myself. No doubt reigning critical orthodoxy will be implicitly and explicitly upheld in any such text, while the truth will continue to be suppressed.[652]

But it has been elsewhere pointed out that, if the so-called "Documentary Hypothesis" of the critical biblical scholars were correct, then the Samaritans ought to have only the *Elohist* text of the Torah, rather than a complete Pentateuch. According to critical textual theory, as applied to the Pentateuch, there were no less than five sources or redactions of the text: the *Elohist,* the *Jahvist,* the *Priestly,* and two redactions of the *Deuteronomist,* designated as *Dtr1* and *Dtr2,* respectively. The other sources are typically abbreviated as *E, J,* and *P. Dtr2* and *P* were supposed to be the very last redactions, according to this theory.[653] Therefore the Samaritans ought to have a much earlier redaction of the Torah, and yet they do not. Therefore to protect the precious "Documentary Hypothesis" critical Bible scholars will insist

---

pagan priests, out of a fear that everyone in the empire would turn Christian (which is essentially what happened in the reign of Constantine, at least nominally). But there was a temple built in Jerusalem, reportedly with an image of the Emperor as the representative of Jupiter. This led to the Bar Kochbah rebellion, which was brutally crushed by the Romans.

[652] This situation is further facilitated and exacerbated by the very small numbers of the surviving Samaritan community, who are in no position to strongly protest against such misrepresentations, compared to the much larger numbers of Jews and Christians.

[653] And both are regarded as postexilic redactions.

upon the absurdity that the Samaritans received their Torah from their arch-enemies, the postexilic Jews. Supposedly they then proceeded to alter this text, according to their own inclinations. This is an utter absurdity. Furthermore it is an amusing spectacle to see a Christian apologist writing on his website that the Samaritan text is a deviation from the original, essentially because it is *better*. That does not exactly sound like an endorsement of the alleged divine inspiration of the Massoretic text to me.

Jerusalem is not even mentioned in the Torah; neither the Greek, Samaritan, nor Hebrew Massoretic text so much as mention it. This would seem to virtually strike a death blow to the "Documentary Hypothesis", since that hypothesis alleges that the Pentateuch was written in the days of King Josiah, and the goal was to centralize worship in the Jerusalem temple. If so, then why is Jerusalem not so much as even mentioned in the Torah? True, Salem is mentioned,[654] which is supposed to be the same as Jerusalem. But not even Deuteronomy, which specifies that sacrifices should only be offered in the place specially chosen by God,[655] where "the LORD has chosen to place his name" do we find Jerusalem specifically mentioned as that place. This is rather inconvenient for the "Documentary Hypothesis" of the critical Bible scholars, I dare say. And yet these same scholars, together with Jewish and Christian fundamentalists, find fault with the Samaritan text for specifying Mount Gerizim as the place which God has thus chosen. One incompetent fool at Wikipedia even went so far as to claim a fragment of a Dead Sea Scroll as some kind of valid "evidence" against the legitimacy of the Samaritan reading.[656] If the "Documentary Hypothesis" were valid, then Jerusalem definitely should have been named as the place where God had chosen to place his name. Jerusalem is not exactly centrally located in Israel; it is distinctly in the south, in the land of Judah. By contrast, Mount Gerizim is much more centrally located, being much

---

[654] Genesis 14:18.

[655] Deuteronomy 12:4-6,11,21; 14:23-24; 16:2,5-6,11.

[656] It doesn't exactly take an expert on the value of evidence to see how worthless such supposed "evidence" is; the men who wrote the Dead Sea Scrolls being Jews, rather than Samaritans, and furthermore Jews living long after the Jewish schism with the Samaritans, would obviously have followed that form of the text that was normative to them, namely the Jewish, rather than Samaritan, text. This is hardly valid evidence in such a controversy.

closer to the midst of Israel. Thus the geographical location seems more congenial to the Samaritan text; Mount Gerizim being in the very heartland of Israel. And while the Samaritan text explicitly names Mount Gerizim, rather than Jerusalem, as the place where the temple should be built,[657] while the Massoretic text remains silent as to the location where God will choose to place his name, Mount Gerizim is still nevertheless mentioned as a place of blessing, not only in the Samaritan text, but also in both the Hebrew Massoretic text, and also the Greek Septuagint text of the Pentateuch.[658] Of course the Latin Vulgate text also agrees with the readings of the three earlier texts of the Pentateuch.[659] Although apparently everyone agrees to these other instances where Mount Gerizim is mentioned as a place of blessing, only the Samaritan text names Mount Gerizim specifically as the very place where the temple was supposed to be built.[660] I am not convinced that the disputed reading is an innovation on the part of the Samaritans. It is at least possible that this reference was deleted, either by the Jews who returned from Babylon, or possibly even earlier, in the days of David and Solomon. After David had conquered Jerusalem and decided to establish his capital there, clearly that would thereafter be the place identified as the place where God would choose to place his name, according to all the later accounts. In anticipation of the objection that, had that been the case, then would not all subsequent copies of the Torah have expunged the reference to Mount Gerizim? The answer is first of all, no; not necessarily. Remember that even in the Massoretic text of the Pentateuch there are still two positive references to Mount Gerizim as a place of blessing. Secondly, the Samaritans claim that their Pentateuch was written by Abishua, the great-grandson of Aaron. If so, we must remember that Abishua lived long before the days of King David; therefore it is quite possible that the text written by him did clearly designate Mount Gerizim as the place where God would place his name forever. In fact, the probability is that the Samaritan text, while it may be a copy of a copy of a copy,

---

[657] Which fact is sometimes used against the legitimacy of the Samaritan text.

[658] BIBLIA HEBRAICA STUTTGARTENSIA., op. cit., pgs. 37 & 333. Cf Deuteronomy 11:29 & 27:12.; SEPTAUGINTA., op. cit., pgs. 308 & 334.

[659] BIBLIA SACRA VULGATA., op. cit., pgs. 351 & 371.

[660] And this reading is disputed by everyone except the Samaritans.

etc., still faithfully records the original words written by Abishua.[661] It is not altogether inconceivable that such an early copy of the original Torah was carefully guarded against the changes of government of the Israelites by the priests who had charge of it. It seems to me that only the religious prejudice of the Jews and Christians keeps them from giving the Samaritan Pentateuch a fair hearing.

Of approximately 6,000 instances where the Samaritan text differs from the Massoretic text, the Septuagint text agrees with the Samaritan against the Massoretic text approximately 2,000 times. The Dead Sea Scrolls also vindicate the textual accuracy of the Samaritan text to some degree. Furthermore the Samaritan text, being written in palaeo-Hebrew script, more closely resembles in form what must have been the original text of the Torah.

But returning briefly to the question of Mount Gerizim, there is an interesting passage in Josephus that might possibly vindicate the Samaritan reading, albeit in an oblique way. Josephus, in his *magnum opus, the Antiquities of the Jews,* writes about a dispute that arose between Samaritans and Jews living in Alexandria regarding whether the temple in Jerusalem or that at Mount Gerizim was the legitimate and original temple. Since numerous people have misrepresented the writings of Josephus, and often misquoted him and distorted his writings, I feel that I ought to reproduce the entire passage, which is as follows:

"Now it came to pass that the Alexandrian Jews, and those Samaritans who paid their worship to the temple that was built in the days of Alexander at Mount Gerizzim, did now make a sedition one against another, and disputed about their temples before Ptolemy himself, the Jews saying that, according to the law of Moses, the temple was to be built at Jerusalem; and the Samaritans saying that it was to be built at Gerizzim. They desired therefore the king to sit with his friends and hear the debates about these matters, and punish with death *those* who were baffled. Now Sabbeus and Theodosius managed the argument for the Samaritans, and Andronicus, the son of Messalamus, for the people of Jerusalem; and they took an oath

---

[661] And I am not hereby ruling out the possibility that the Samaritan Scroll of the Pentateuch may in fact be the original Scroll inscribed by Abishua himself. If so, then it is an even more pricelessly precious document. Hopefully it will not be damaged or destroyed by some inflamed religious fanatic.

by God and the king, to make their demonstrations according to the law; and they desired of Ptolemy, that whomsoever he should find that transgressed what they had sworn to, he would put him to death. Accordingly, the king took several of his friends into the council, and sat down, in order to hear what the pleaders said. Now the Jews that were at Alexandria were in great concern for those men, whose lot it was to contend for the temple at Jerusalem: for they took it very ill that any should take away the reputation of that temple, which was so ancient and so celebrated all over the habitable earth. Now when Sabbeus and Theodosius had given leave to Andronicus to speak first, he began to demonstrate out of the law, and out of the succession of the high priests, how they every one in succession from his father had received that dignity, and ruled over the temple; and how all the kings of Asia had honoured that temple with their donations, and with the most splendid gifts dedicated thereto; but as for that at Gerizzim, he made no account of it, and regarded it, as if it had never had a being. By this speech, and other arguments, Andronicus persuaded the king to determine that the temple at Jerusalem was built according to the law of Moses, and to put Sabbeus and Theodosius to death. And these were the events that befell the Jews at Alexandria in the days of Ptolemy Philometor."[662]

It is worth noting that Andronicus lied in claiming that the law of Moses itself said anything about the location of any future temple; as noted above, Jerusalem is not mentioned at all in the Torah proper, or at least not in any of the copies that have come down to us. But the very appeal to the Pentateuch also further proves that there must have been a Greek tanslation of it by that time, in contradiction to what certain *illiterati* have written to the contrary on the Internet. But my chief point in quoting the above passage is that the Samaritans had absolute confidence in their position; so much so, that they unfortunately allowed Andronicus to proceed first.

---

[662] Jos. Ant. 13.3.4. The story implies a Greek text at the time supporting the Samaritan reading. Possibly there was a Greek translation of the Samaritan Pentateuch, and this may have been replaced by the Greek Septuagint text. As noted previously, the letter of Aristeas mentioned earlier Greek translations of the Torah, but it said that they were defective. Quite possibly a Greek translation of the Samaritan Pentateuch may have been referred to. If so, then the carping criticism that such a text was inferior was merely an example of gratuitous bigotry on the part of the Jewish author. The same holds true of Josephus.

This mistake cost them their lives. But the very fact that they had such great confidence in their position means that they must have possessed a copy of the Pentateuch that did clearly speak of Mount Gerizim as the place where God would choose to place his name. The Samaritan Pentateuch clearly says that Mount Gerizim is where the sacrifices are to be offered. It is also worth noting from the passage above that all the men named had Greek names, despite their non-Greek ethnicities. Critics will no doubt point out that this dispute was subsequent to the time when the Samaritan temple had already been built (of course), and therefore also subsequent to the time when, according to the critical theory, the Samaritans wrote their version of the Torah. In other words, the passage does not in and of itself prove that the Samaritan reading is a truly ancient reading, or the original reading. But nevertheless the passage does function as proof of the confidence that such men themselves had in the antiquity and authenticity of the reading; they staked their very lives on it. We cannot ask for a stronger witness. Furthermore we ought to keep in mind those positive references to Mount Gerizim as a place of blessing in all texts of the Pentateuch.

Returning briefly to the "Documentary Hypothesis" it is worth reiterating that the existence of the Samaritan Pentateuch functions as a strong form of evidence against that hypothesis. The Samaritan Pentateuch, being written in palaeo-Hebrew script, exists in a form much closer to what the original Torah must have been. Furthermore the fact that the Samaritan Torah is inscribed on a single large scroll is also in more direct conformity to what is mentioned in Scripture[663] than the five Torah scrolls of traditional Judaism. It is not in the least bit credible that the Samaritans ever received their Torah from the postexilic Jews. Therefore if the "Documentary Hypothesis" were true, the Samaritans ought to only have a text conforming to *E,* rather than a complete Torah text, as they have. Not only is this not the case, but no copies or fragments of any of these other hypothetical texts have ever been discovered; there are no remains of either *E, J, P,* or *Dtr1;* only the final text, which is presumably the "redaction" known as *Dtr2.* The very same parallel problem confronts critical biblical

---

[663] Joshua 1:8; 2 Chronicles 17:9; 34:14-19; 2 Kings 22:8-11. In every instance, the singular "book" is used, implying only one scroll. There is no proof that this was only the scroll of Deuteronomy. This is merely an unwarranted assumption of academic orthodoxy.

scholars in respect to the Gospels; no fragments of the hypothetical documents known as the *Testimonia,* the *Logia Kyriou,* or *"Q"* have ever been discovered. They probably never will be discovered, for the simple reason that they probably never existed. Such texts, if they ever existed, would have been regarded as sacred. They never would have been destroyed, as certain critical Bible scholars have suggested.[664] Quite possibly a time may have come when they[665] were no longer copied, and thereafter would have presumably become increasingly rare. But so far no discovery has vindicated any of these theories; no monastery, no Genizah, no cave, no archaeological excavation has ever yet yielded the slightest hint of a fragment supporting the so-called "Documentary Hypothesis" for the Torah, or the various textual theories for the Gospels. Furthermore no cogent appeal can be made to the supposed extinction of texts due to changing orthodoxy; the discovery of the Damascus Document in the Cairo Genizah dispels any such line of argument. In fact the various literary fossils that remain in the Gospels and other books of the New Testament also serve to dispel any such supposition. The Damascus Document would clearly have been a text that was quite archaic to the Jews who congregated at the Cairo synagogue; it would definitely not have represented a normative version of their own faith. Nevertheless it was not destroyed, but instead reverently placed in the Genizah. Critical scholars can multiply theories, but they offer no definitive proof. And in this case it would seem that absence of evidence indicates evidence of absence.

But the very reverse seems to be the case with much of the circumstantial evidence offered by Israel Finkelstein and Neil Asher Silberman, in their book, *THE BIBLE UNEARTHED: ARCHAEOLOGY'S NEW VISION OF ANCIENT ISRAEL AND THE ORIGIN OF ITS SACRED TEXTS.*[666] I have decidedly

---

[664] Such men don't have a pious bone in their body; they have no concept of piety, and therefore cannot understand such simple things in their profusion of endless theories.

[665] Assuming I am wrong and such texts did exist.

[666] Finkelstein, Israel, with Neil Asher Silberman., *THE BIBLE UNEARTHED: Archaeology's New Vision of Ancient Israel and the Origin of Its Sacred Texts.* (© 2010 by Israel Finkelstein & Neil Asher Silberman) Touchstone 2002. Simon & Schuster. business@simonandschuster.com. ISBN 0-684-86912-8.

mixed feelings about this book.[667] On the one hand the book is very scholarly and professionally written, and is also very readable; one is not bogged down in a highly specialized nomenclature or plagued by an excessively dry, tedious, dull, academic treatment of the subject-matter. Furthermore it is refreshing to finally find some archaeologists offering a viewpoint in opposition to fundamentalism.[668] However the authors, who subscribe to the "Documentary Hypothesis"[669] never provide clear-cut evidence in favor of their position. Much of the evidence is in fact ambiguous, and a matter of interpretation. For example, there is no clear proof that a certain level of depth necessarily corresponds to a given time period. Furthermore there are constant claims that it is "known" that such and such was the case at such and such a time, and there is no clear proof of any of it. Furthermore in the case of literacy, absence of evidence does not provide evidence of absence; the fact that no inscriptions are found at a given site or series of sites does not in fact prove that the people living at that time were illiterate; the opposite can certainly be proven by findings of inscriptions, but the absence of such inscriptions does not negate the possibility that the people in question were literate. The Torah implies literacy from even before the time of Abraham. Throughout the Torah literacy is implied and taken for granted; it was not addressed to a bunch of illiterate nomads. Finkelstein and Silberman note the absence of pig bones from the so-called "Iron Age"[670] which in itself is clear evidence in favor of the antiquity of the Torah. And yet they seem puzzled by this, and speculate that the Israelites stopped eating pork because their adversarial neighbors <u>did</u> eat pork.[671] But this does not explain the taboo against eating pork. Why pork? Why would not the Israelites instead have refrained from eating beef, lamb, or chicken? No doubt the Phoenicians and Canaanites ate these other foods too; yet the Israelites continued to eat these foods. Clearly such

---

[667] Any irony is fully intentional.

[668] Stated otherwise, Near Eastern archaeology has traditionally been ruthlessly exploited by evangelicals and fundamentalists to uphold their own views; the very term "Biblical Archaeology" implies an adherence to the literal truth of the Bible.

[669] Hereafter to be designated as simply *DH*.

[670] Finkelstein & Silberman., op. cit., pg. 119.

[671] Ibid., pgs. 119-121.

circumstantial evidence supports the prior existence of the Torah. But such evidence does not fit their paradigm, so it is reinterpreted. In the same vein, Finkelstein and Silberman draw attention to two inscriptions that speak of Asherah as the consort of YHWH,[672] which they then proceed to interpret as evidence that this was the normative form of worship in ancient Israel, to be later supplanted by the supposed "novelty" of a "YHWH-only" party of priestly puritans. But there is not the slightest scintilla of proof of their position; the Bible speaks extensively of the Asherah, but always and uniformly in a condemnatory manner. Who is really guilty of revisionism? The men who wrote the Scriptures, or Finkelstein and Silberman? A parallel from Egyptian history may help to illustrate my point. Akhenaton is commonly portrayed as a "heretic" king today, because he demanded exclusive worship of only one God. But all the earliest Egyptologists, including no less a scholar than E.A. Wallis Budge, have written that the Egyptians were originally monotheistic in their faith. The oldest books of the Egyptians are most strictly monotheistic. The "YHWH-only" movement in Israel was no innovation; it was strictly a reform movement. The unity of God was not merely another doctrine of the Torah; it is instead the central, foundational doctrine of the Torah. An assertion that Asherah was esteemed as the consort of YaHWeH from antiquity is nothing but blatant and shameless revisionism. My point is that even the archaeological evidence offered in support of the currently-reigning orthodoxy vis-à-vis the origin of the Pentateuch is insufficient to overturn a more common-sense approach to the issue. Thus the *DH* is not strong enough to overturn the primacy of the Samaritan Torah. Neither does anything in Josephus subvert the primacy of the Samaritan text, since he does not state explicitly when the Samaritans first acquired their version of the Torah. And even if he did, we would have to take his word with a grain of salt on this matter, since he was hardly unbiased when it came to the Samaritans.

One other example is at least worth noting before moving on. In their book, Finkelstein and Silberman seem to deliberately omit pertinent information relative to their main argument, since it is damaging to their paradigm. They omit the fact that, according to the biblical text, King Hezekiah had instituted reforms that were exactly in accord with the text of Deuteronomy, which they purport was not written until the reign of King Josiah. This omission is conspicuous

---

[672] Ibid., pg. 242.

by it absence in chapter ten of their book, which speaks of the time period in question.[673] This omission is particularly pungent due to the exclusive use of the book of Kings to recount the narrative of the confrontation between Rabshakeh and the men guarding the wall of Jerusalem.[674] The account in Kings omits certain distinctive features which are found in Isaiah. And there can be no real doubt that Isaiah was the original source for that section of Kings. In the book of Isaiah, we read the following relevant verse:

"But if thou say to me, We trust in the LORD our God: is *it* not he, whose high places and whose altars Hezekiah hath taken away, and said to Judah and Jerusalem, Ye shall worship before this altar?" (Isaiah 36:7, KJV)

This verse unequivocally reveals that Hezekiah had made the very distinctive reforms advocated in Deuteronomy. Furthermore Finkelstein and Silberman also deliberately ignore the biblical testimony that King Jehoshaphat, who reigned much earlier than Hezekiah, also instituted the very same kinds of reforms, by removing the high places and groves from Judah.[675] Of course in this instance they will simply say that the book of Chronicles is guilty of shameless revisionism. They are likely to also assert that the book of Isaiah has also been compromised, and that the verse in question is a late interpolation. Yet such a line of argument appears to be a species of special pleading, and of begging the question. In their own way, Finkelstein and Silberman are every bit as obtuse and myopic as Bible fundamentalists are.

Finally, it doesn't really matter if the alleged final redaction of the Torah is referred to as *Dtr2* or *P;* since the hypothetical text is alleged to be a postexilic production, we are once again confronted with the untenable proposition that the Samaritans must have received their Torah from the postexilic Jews, who were in fact their mortal enemies. It is impossible to picture this happening in any realistic way. It is equally impossible to picture the postexilic Jews receiving their Torah from the Samaritans; but the suggestion is no less probable, all things considered. Critical biblical scholars seem to have the blindest faith in their own dubious propositions. Perhaps Finkelstein and

---

[673] Ibid., pgs. 251–274.

[674] Ibid., pg. 253.

[675] 2 Chronicles 17:6.

Silberman take comfort in the fact that Jewish tradition affords some degree of support for their "Double Redaction" thesis; said tradition teaching that Ezra wrote the Torah. But if the Israelites had always worshipped Asherah as the consort of YaHWeH, then those priests and prophets who insisted upon an exclusive worship of YaHWeH alone were the real heretics. Is this even the least bit credible? If the worship of Asherah as the consort of God were normative, then it is virtually impossible and unthinkable that any prophet or priest would have sought to overturn the original, normative faith and practice of the Israelites. Monotheism does not arise as a "purification" from original polytheism; polytheism itself is a corruption of primordial monotheism. All history testifies to this.

The Samaritan text prohibits polygamy in Leviticus 18:18; this is unlikely to be a gratuitous addition to the text; more likely the prohibition was removed by Jewish scribes in later editions of the text, in order to protect the patriarchs from aspersions cast upon their characters because they were in fact polygamous. Despite the fact that Samaritans were hated by the Jews, Jesus himself depicted a Samaritan in a favorable light, albeit in a parable.[676] In a conversation with a Samaritan woman, Jesus did not dispute or deny her claim to be a descendant of Jacob.[677] In the case of the Samaritan Pentateuch, it seems that the blind faith of both religious fundamentalists and critical Bible scholars has kept them from recognizing something truly ancient. And those who are supposed to live according to the truth seem to have done everything possible to obscure the truth about the Samaritan Pentateuch.

---

[676] Luke 10:30-37.

[677] John 4:12.

Hebrew or Syriac?

Although the reigning academic paradigm insists that Jesus and the Apostles, and even all the Jews in Palestine in the first century, spoke Aramaic rather than Hebrew, a close study of the available evidence reveals that the exact opposite was the case. I would urge the reader to first recall some of the evidence I have already presented above, when I quoted from the Letter of Aristeas, which clearly said that the language of the Jews was distinctly different from Syriac.[678] I would also like to point out at the outset that a huge part of the problem is the use of the term Aramaic as opposed to Syriac; this only serves to cloud the issue, rather than clarifying it. It is very important to realise that Aramaic is merely another term for Syriac; the same language is also sometimes called Chaldee. This can be proven by a comparison of ancient texts. But the term Syriac instantly makes an association with a geographical location (Syria), and this helps people to understand how absurd it is to think that Jews living in Palestine would have spoken this foreign tongue.

Supposedly the Jews lost the use of their native Hebrew tongue during their seventy year Captivity in Babylon. Supposedly the Jews adopted the native tongue of Babylon, which was Chaldean or Chaldee.[679] Chaldean or Chaldee is also otherwise known as Culdee,

---

[678]   Aristeas 1:15-16.

[679]   This may have been a different dialect from Syrian Syriac, but it was still the

Aramaic, Aramean or Syriac. Aramaic is linguistically cognate to Hebrew, being from the Semitic family of languages. Arabic and Geez (old Ethiopic) are other examples of Semitic tongues. But the Israelites were slaves in Egypt for four hundred years,[680] yet in all that time they did not lose the use of their original language. So how could a mere seventy-year captivity make them forget their beloved Hebrew tongue? It doesn't make sense. Upon this basis alone there is reason to doubt the commonly-accepted assumption of Syriac-speaking Palestinian Jews during the postexilic period.

Furthermore, if we were to assume that the Jews lost the use of Hebrew during the Babylonian Captivity, how then did they ever manage to rediscover it? If they had altogether lost the knowledge and use of it at that time, would not the language have become irrevocably lost for all time? Therefore we can see how absurd is the myth that the Jews lost the use of Hebrew during the Babylonian Captivity. And as we will see, there is also a plethora of evidence that proves beyond any reasonable doubt that the postexilic Jews still spoke Hebrew.

First of all, only one out of six of the sectarian documents from the Qumran corpus were written in Aramaic; the vast majority were written in Hebrew.[681] And of course the biblical texts themselves were also almost all completely written in Hebrew. Also, the fragments of such apocryphal and pseudepigraphal books as Tobit, Sirach, and Jubilees were all in Hebrew. Furthermore none of the postexilic texts of *TaNaKh* say that the Jews spoke Aramaic, in preference to Hebrew. Neither does the New Testament say that the Jews spoke Syriac. Neither does the Apocrypha say that the Jews spoke Syriac. Neither does the Old Testament Pseudepigrapha say that the Jews spoke Syriac, rather than Hebrew. Neither do Josephus nor Philo say that the Jews spoke in Syriac; in fact, they wrote in Greek.

Let us consider the New Testament itself in greater detail. Nowhere in the New Testament does it say that the Jews of that time, who lived in Judaea, spoke Syriac. The word "Hebrew" occurs eleven times in the New Testament, but only one of these instances refers to ethnicity; the remaining ten references are to the Hebrew tongue.[682]

---

same language.

[680] Genesis 15:13.

[681] Wise, Abegg & Cook., op. cit., pg. 9.

[682] Lk 23:38; Jn 5:2; 19:13,17,20; Acts 21:40; 22:2; 26:14; Revelation 9:11; 16:16

By contrast, whenever the word "Hebrew" occurs within *TaNaKh,* it always refers to ethnicity, and never to the language spoken by the Jews.

Confusion is also created by the fact that, whenever the term "Hebrew" is used in the New Testament, in reference to the common tongue of the Jews, it is automatically and falsely assumed to mean, not Hebrew, but Syriac.[683] Why? Because people are hypnotized by the implicit authority of academic orthodoxy. However, when we examine these texts with greater scrutiny, we can see that Hebrew proper was intended, not Syriac. The mere fact that Hebrew and Syriac are both Semitic languages ought not to lead us to assume that one means Syriac when writing the proper Greek word for Hebrew, any more than the kindred languages of English and German should be confused by a person writing in French or Arabic.

There are two distinct words for Hebrew and Syriac in Greek, and they are both used in the Greek Bible. The Greek word for Syriac is *Suristi* or *Syristi,* and this occurs in the Greek text of Daniel 2:4.[684] The King James renders this word as "Syriack", and this also corresponds to the underlying Hebrew word *Aramiyth* in the Massoretic text.[685] Therefore if the postexilic Jews of Palestine had spoken Syriac rather than Hebrew, the writers of the Greek text of the New Testament could have, should have, and would have used this Greek word *Syristi,* rather than *Hebraisti, Hebrais,* or *Hebraikos,* which are the Greek words used in the respective verses in the New Testament that speak of the Hebrew tongue. Furthermore we can see from the Greek text of Daniel that *Syristi* was the appropriate Greek translation of the Hebrew term *Aramiyth,* from which we get Aramaic. Therefore Aramaic is the same language as Syriac. This is sufficient to debunk the myth that postexilic Palestinian Jews spoke Syriac rather than Hebrew. In fact, the word *Syristi* never occurs in the Greek New Testament. It only occurs in the Greek translation of the Old Testament.

Devout Orthodox Jews and born again Christians believe that Hebrew was the original language used before the supposed division

---

cp Philippians 3:5, where "Paul" speaks of himself as "an Hebrew of the Hebrews".

[683]   I.e., Aramaic; Chaldee.

[684]   SEPTUAGINTA., op. cit., pg. 874 (vol. 2; Duo volumina in uno).

[685]   BIBLIA HEBRAICA STUTTGARTENSIA., op. cit., pg. 1382.

of tongues at the legendary Tower of Babel. Traditionally, Hebrew had been regarded as the tongue of both God and the angels. However the Syrian Orthodox Church claims that Syriac (Aramaic, Chaldee) was the original tongue, and that all the Scriptures of both the Old Testament and the New were first written in Syriac, and only later translated into Hebrew, Greek, and the various other languages. George M. Lamsa, who translated the Bible from the Aramaic Peshitta text into English, claimed that Jesus and the Apostles all spoke Aramaic, rather than Hebrew or Greek. While such claims may seem outrageous and gratuitously self-aggrandizing, we may nevertheless profit from an examination of some passages from a rare Syrian religious book known as the Book of the Bee.

The Book of the Bee is a Christian religious text written in Syriac in the thirteenth century, by Solomon of Akhlat. It contains many old religious traditions of the Syrian Orthodox Church. It was first translated into English by E.A. Wallis Budge and published in 1886. A new edition of the translation, together with the original Syriac, was published by Gorgias Press in 2006.[686] The book is very rare. Despite the obscurity of the text, I believe that it may shed some light upon the question under consideration.

"Salah begat Eber (Abar), and to Eber were born two sons; the name of the one of whom was Peleg (Palag), because in his days the earth was divided. From this it is known that the Syriac language remained with Eber, because, when the languages were confounded and the earth was divided, he was born, and was called Peleg by the Syriac word which existed in his time. After Peleg, Joktan (Yaktan) was born, from whom sprang the thirteen nations who dwelt beside one another and kept the Syriac language."[687]

Some people might try to confuse the issue under discussion by making a false pretence that Aramaic and Syriac are two distinctly different languages. But there are several passages from the Book of the Bee that dispel that false notion, such as the following:

"From Adam until that time they all spoke this language, that is to say Syriac, which is Aramean; for this language is the king of all

---

[686] Budge, E.A. Wallis., translator and editor., THE BOOK OF THE BEE. (Solomon of Akhlat;

c. 1222 A.D. 1886; 2006; Gorgias Press, New Jersey) http://www.gorgiaspress.com

[687] Ibid., pg. 36.

languages. The early writers have erred, in that they say that Hebrew was the primitive language; and here have they mingled ignorant error with their writings. For all the tongues that are in the world are taken from Syriac, and all the languages in books are mixed with it."[688]

From the above quotation we can see that Syriac is the very same language as Aramaic, otherwise also called Aramean. The same thing is also confirmed in the two following passages as well:

"In the days of Reu the languages were divided into seventy and two; up to this time there was only one language, which was the parent of them all, namely, Aramean, that is, Syriac."[689]

"Touching the writing which was written in Greek, Hebrew and Latin, and set over Christ's head, there was no Aramean written upon the tablet, for the Arameans or Syrians had no part in (the shedding of) Christ's blood, but only the Greeks and Hebrews and Romans; Herod the Greek and Caiaphas the Hebrew and Pilate the Roman."[690]

This is an important testimony; if we accept it as valid, then it proves that the Jews in first-century Judaea spoke Hebrew and Greek, but not Syriac. This is exactly what the New Testament itself confirms by its own testimony. Thus even George M. Lamsa himself is refuted by this Syriac text. According to the Book of the Bee, neither Jesus nor his disciples spoke Syriac, but Hebrew.

"And God said, 'Come, let us go down and divide the tongues there'. The expression 'Come, let us,' resembles 'Come, let us make man in our image and in our likeness,' and refers to the persons of the adorable Trinity. While they were tormenting themselves with that vain labour, their language was suddenly confounded so as to become seventy-two languages, and they understood not each other's speech, and were scattered throughout the whole world, and built cities, every man with his fellow spoke the same language. From Adam to the building of the tower, there was only one language, and that was Syriac. Some have said that it was Hebrew; but the Hebrews were not called by this name until after Abraham had crossed the river Euphrates and dwelt in Harran; and from his crossing they were called Hebrews."[691]

---

[688] Ibid., pg. 39.

[689] Ibid.

[690] Ibid., pg. 99.

[691] Ibid., pg. 42.

As noted above, there is a distinct Greek word for the Syriac language, which is different from the Greek word for the Hebrew tongue. Furthermore this Greek word, *Syristi,* occurs in the Greek text of Daniel, which no doubt was used by the early Greek-speaking writers of the Greek texts of the New Testament. So there is no justifiable reason to suppose that they would not have used this word, rather than *Hebraisti,* which occurs in John 19:20, or *Hebraikos,* which occurs in Luke 23:38, which are the two verses that speak of the inscription placed on the cross. John 19:20 says that it was written in Hebrew *(Hebraisti),* Latin or Roman *(Romaisti),* and Greek *(Hellenisti);*[692] Luke 23:38 has Greek *(Hellenikois),* Latin (or Roman) *(Romaikois),* and Hebrew *(Hebraikois).*[693]

The facts noted above prove that postexilic Palestinian Jews spoke Hebrew, rather than Syriac.[694] Of course Jews living in Syria would have learned to speak Syriac, the native tongue of that country. In fact, at the time Syriac was the *lingua franca* of the Fertile Crescent, just as Greek was the *lingua franca* of the eastern Mediterranean. For the same reason, Jews who lived in Alexandria spoke Greek; Jews in other parts of Egypt may very well have spoke Coptic.[695] But these facts in no way prove that Hebrew had ever become a lost tongue. Some people might seek to confuse the issue by pretending that Syriac and Aramaic are two distinct languages, but the Book of the Bee proves that this is a false assumption. The very same point can be proven by comparing the Greek and Hebrew texts of Daniel 2:4. Some might also seek to further cloud the issue by pretending that Hebrew and Syriac were so closely related linguistically that they were virtually indistinguishable, as if they were merely two different dialects of the same language.[696] But there are some Bible verses that disprove the notion that Syriac and Hebrew are merely different dialects of the same language. For example, the following:

---

[692] Nestle–Aland., op. cit., pg. 312.

[693] Ibid., pg. 240.

[694] I.e., Aramaic; Chaldee.

[695] Coptic was already in use in the first century, and there is also an Aethiopian tradition that the Gospel of Mark was first written in Coptic, rather than Greek.

[696] Much as Mandarin is a dialect of Chinese; but Vietnamese is a distinct language from Chinese, although linguistically similar.

26 Then said Eliakim the son of Hilkiah, and Shebna, and Joah, unto Rabshakeh, Speak, I pray thee, to thy servants in the Syrian [Heb. *Aramiyth*] language; for we understand it; and talk not with us in the Jews' [Heb. *Yehudiyth*] language, in the ears of the people that are on the wall. (2 Kings 18:26 cf Isaiah 36:11)

In the Greek text of both Kings and Isaiah, where the verses in question occur, the Greek words used are *Syristi* and *Youdaisti*, respectively.[697] In the Latin Vulgate, the respective terms are *syriace* and *iudaice*.[698] So the Hebrew, Greek, and Latin texts of the Old Testament all use distinctly different words to denote Hebrew and Syriac, thus confirming that they are in fact two distinctly <u>different</u> languages. Notice also by a comparison of the Greek and Hebrew words used to denote Syriac/Aramaic, that Aramaic and Syriac are the very <u>same</u> language; the term Syriac being derived from the Greek, and the term Aramaic being derived from the Hebrew. Furthermore the verse from Kings[699] proves that a knowledge of Hebrew would not guarantee a knowledge of Syriac, or vice-versa; they were and are two distinctly different tongues.

George M. Lamsa for one has sought to characterize Hebrew and Aramaic as almost merely different dialects of the same language, and that all the Jews could have easily understood both tongues. But the verses above disprove this. This is especially brought out by the context of the verses in question. Sennacherib, the king of Assyria, had sent Rabshakeh his general to Jerusalem with a great army, to intimidate the Jews into paying tribute. Therefore when Rabshakeh proudly boasted of the might of the Assyrian army, and how easily defeated the Jews would be, the scribes on the wall, who understood his native language of Syriac urged him to speak in that tongue, since they understood it (as well as Hebrew); they did not want him to speak in Hebrew in the ears of the guardians on the wall, lest they be discouraged. This would have been a pointless request if those men had understood Syriac. Rabshakeh only turned and mocked the Jews

---

[697] SEPTUAGINTA., op. cit., pg. 735 (vol.1); pg. 613 (vol.2; Duo volumina in uno).

[698] BIBLIA SACRA VULGATA., op. cit., pg. 533. The term used in the Latin of Isaiah 36:11 is *syra lingua;* cf Ibid., pg. 1132.

[699] And the parallel verse from Isaiah.

even more, uttering language that, found anywhere outside of the Bible itself, would send self-righteous pseudo-Christian gatekeepers of "moral majority" American "family values" of the right-wing variety into paroxysms of feigned indignation. In any case, the context only serves to confirm that Hebrew and Syriac are two distinctively different languages.

As we have already noted, the Greek word *Syristi* never occurs even once in the Greek New Testament. This is proven and confirmed by the absence of the word from the Greek Dictionary of the New Testament found in ABINGDON'S STRONG'S EXHAUSTIVE CONCORDANCE OF THE BIBLE WITH HEBREW, CHALDEE AND GREEK DICTIONARIES. Had the word *Syristi* occurred in the Greek New Testament, then it would have been placed between *Syria (4947)* and *Syros (4948)*. But it is not in there, because it does not occur anywhere in the Greek New Testament. It is perhaps also worth noting that, the Latin Vulgate text of John 19:20 confirms the Greek reading, using the term *hebraice* rather than *syriace*.[700] The Latin of Luke 23:38 reads *hebraicis*,[701] which is merely another declension of the same Latin root-word.

There is even a passage from the Talmud which confirms that, even in the late second century, the use of Syriac in Palestine was still fairly rare, being merely a relatively new, encroaching development. The following quote is attributed to Judah the Prince, one of the compilers of the *Mishnah,* who taught between approximately 170 and 200 C.E.

"Rabbi Yehudah haNasi continued to fight against the use of Aramaic, and said: "Why use Syriac in Eretz Israel? Speak either Hebrew or Greek" *Bava Kamma 82b-83a)."*[702]

Although the foregoing ought to be sufficient to prove that the postexilic Jews of Palestine spoke Hebrew, rather than Syriac, as commonly supposed according to antiquated academic orthodoxy, there still remain a few points which I would rather address,

---

[700] BIBLIA SACRA VULGATA., op. cit., pg. 1693.

[701] Ibid., pg. 1655.

[702] Steinsaltz, Adin {Rabbi}, *THE TALMUD. (THE STEINSALTZ EDITION);* Rabbi Israel V. Berman, translator and editor. (1989; The Israel Institute for Talmudic Publications and Milta Books) (New York: Random House); pg. 15.

rather than leave my ideological opponents ammunition by way of negligence.

First of all, some may claim that what I have written above is subverted or at least controverted by the alleged presence of Aramaic words in the New Testament. However I shall briefly dispose of this cavil presently. The most important point to bear in mind is the simple fact that, even though there *might* be Syriac words in the New Testament, this does not in and of itself prove that Hebrew had become a lost language, as commonly supposed. Furthermore some or even all of these supposedly Syriac words may in fact be Hebrew after all.

To the best of my knowledge, there are fifteen instances of Chaldee words in the New Testament. Four instances occur in the Gospel of Mark; two others are in parallel verses in Matthew and John; and nine are in the book of Hebrews. In Hebrews, Melchizedek is spoken of nine times.[703] Melchizedek was the king of Salem in the days of Abraham; he is mentioned twice in *TaNaKh*.[704] Curiously, the Greek Dictionary found in ABINGDON'S STRONG'S EXHAUSTIVE CONCORDANCE TO THE BIBLE declares the name Melchizedek to be of Hebrew origin, and the Hebrew Dictionary confirms this at least implicitly; it omits any contrary declaration that the name is of Chaldee origin. If so, then this would automatically eliminate nine of the supposed occurrences of Syriac words in the New Testament, leaving only six. Let us now proceed to consider those instances.

The term *"Golgotha"*[705] is supposedly of Chaldee origin, according to the same Greek Dictionary. In this instance Strong's Greek Dictionary *may* be correct, but I am not necessarily fully persuaded of that. The proper Hebrew term for skull is supposed to be *gulgoleth*. However I am wondering if possibly this is merely another declension or form of the same root-word in Hebrew. The difference does look like it may be due to the typical differences between Hebrew and Syriac, however. There are also two other instances in the Gospel of Mark where Jesus supposedly speaks in Syriac.[706] But if in fact these

---

[703] Hebrews 5:6,10; 6:20; 7:1,10,11,15,17,21.

[704] Genesis 14:18; 110:4.

[705] Mt 27:33; Mk 15:22; Jn 19:17.

[706] Mk 5:41, *"talitha cumi"*; Mk 7:34, *"ephphatha"*.

are clear examples of Jesus speaking in Syriac rather than Hebrew, we would thereafter have to account for the otherwise strange fact that he spoke a language uncommon from that of other postexilic Palestinian Jews. One possible explanation is that the Galileans, being closer to Syria, may have spoken Syriac, while the Jews of Judaea spoke pure Hebrew. This is possible but unproven so far. But if this is true, then Jesus and the Apostles were at least bilingual,[707] and possibly trilingual.[708] We know from Acts 2:8-11 that Jews would commonly learn to speak the language of the land wherever they settled. But by the same token Hebrew never became a completely lost language. If it is supposed that the Jews lost the use of Hebrew due to the great similarity between the two tongues, as opposed to the difference between Hebrew and Egyptian, then how and why was there ever a Hebrew tongue in the first place? A person reading Genesis carefully can see that frequently Hebrew-speaking nomads would interact with those who spoke Syriac; the Hebrews were ostensibly newcomers to the region, yet they nevertheless retained their own tongue back in those days, when they were vastly outnumbered by those who spoke Syriac, in the region of Haran. Furthermore if Hebrew had become a lost tongue for this reason, then how did the Jews ever manage to reacquire it? Would it not have become lost forever? Furthermore there are significant linguistic similarities between Hebrew and Egyptian, so a settlement in Egypt lasting over four centuries was more likely to erase the Hebrew tongue than a mere seventy years' captivity in Babylon.

We run into a problem again in the final instance of Christ allegedly speaking in Syriac, namely Mark 15:34, where Jesus cries out "Eloi, Eloi, lama sebachthani?" The problem is that, in the parallel verse in Matthew,[709] this is rendered "Eli, Eli, lama sebachthani?"[710] By

---

[707] Speaking both Syriac and Hebrew. Otherwise how could Jesus have conversed with people of Judaea, who definitely spoke Hebrew, rather than Syriac?

[708] Speaking Syriac, Hebrew, and Greek. The presence of Latin on the inscription also implies that the Roman soldiers spoke Latin, rather than Greek. Perhaps it was required that the inscriptions be written in Latin, the official tongue of the Roman empire.

[709] Mt 27:46.

[710] It is worth remarking that the version found in Matthew's Gospel is correct, according to the unpointed Hebrew text of Psalm 22:1. This means that

itself this is not really a problem, since it is only a minor variation from what is found in Mark's Gospel; however, the problem arises when we consult Strong's Greek Dictionary. When we look up the phrase as it occurs in Mark, that Dictionary tells us that the phrase is of Chaldee origin; but when we look up that same phrase as it occurs in Matthew, in that very same Dictionary, we are told that the phrase is of Hebrew origin. But if we compare the two accounts, we can see that the events described are exactly parallel; immediately after uttering this cry, Jesus is offered vinegar on a sponge, and some of the Jews think that he is calling upon Elijah to rescue him.[711] Therefore we can safely conclude that Jesus only uttered the cry once, either in Hebrew or Syriac.[712] Otherwise we would be faced with the absurd improbability of the exact same sequence of events occurring twice in a row immediately, which would strain statistical probability to the breaking-point. So Jesus either uttered this cry in Hebrew, or in Syriac. It could not have been both. So which is it? Was it Hebrew, or was it Chaldee? If it was Chaldee, then it could not have been in Hebrew; if it was in Hebrew, than it could not have been in Chaldee. I suppose if one assumes that Jesus spoke Aramaic rather than Hebrew, and his cry was merely an anguished cry of desperation, then one would suppose that he thus cried out in Aramaic.[713] But we have alredy considered a plenitude of evidence proving that the Jews of first century Palestine spoke Hebrew, rather than Syriac. Not only that, but, assuming that Jesus did indeed so cry out, he was no doubt deliberately quoting from Psalm 22, which opens with those very words. As such, he would have cried out in Hebrew, rather than Chladee. As far as why some Jews did not understand him, this only proves that the Jews in question probably spoke Greek rather than Hebrew; it does not prove that the postexilic Palestinian Jews had abandoned the use of Hebrew in preference for Syriac. As far as the discrepancy between

---

Matthew's version is a correct quotation from the Hebrew, while Mark's is deviant.

[711] Mt 27:46-49 cf Mk 15:34-36.

[712] I.e., assuming he uttered such a cry at all; I personally prefer the version found in the Gospel of Peter; "My power, my power, thou hast forsaken me." This preference is not arbitrary, but due to the fact that this alternate reading is deviant from the Messianic scheme of the New Testament, and therefore more likely to be true.

[713] I.e., Chaldee, Syriac.

the form of words found in Mark and Matthew, it is possible that Mark was originally composed in Coptic, rather than Greek. If so, this may account for the discrepancy. Alternatively, the author may have mistakenly thought that Jesus spoke in Syriac, rather than Hebrew; or he may have deliberately misrepresented Jesus and the circumstances surrounding his life, ministry, and death.

Returning briefly to *Golgotha,* it is notable that John 19:17 says that the place was so called in Hebrew.[714] I suppose that an opponent could use this as evidence that in the Greek New Testament, the term *Hebraisti* was used in *lieu* of *Syristi.* But this would be no more than a shameless example of begging the question, and special pleading. I would instead interpret the evidence as indicating that, notwithstanding what the very fallible Greek Doctionary of Strong's Concordance may say to the contrary, the word used is indeed Hebrew rather than Syriac. Otherwise we are implicitly charging the writers of the Greek New Testament with laziness and laxness in comparison with the translators of the Greek Septuagint text. I find this position unacceptable. Those men knew the proper Greek terms for both Hebrew and Syriac, and we have no reason to suppose that they arbitrarily used the term for Hebrew instead of the correct term for Syriac, had they intended to denote the Syriac tongue. Such a suppostion is entirely unwarranted, and represents nothing but special pleading and a begging of the question on the part of those who claim that the postexilic Jews living in Judaea spoke Syriac, rather than Hebrew. So I hereby rest my case.

---

[714] Greek *Hebraisti.* Nestle-Aland., op. cit., pg. 312.

The Syriac Peshitta Text

I want to speak briefly about the Syriac Peshitta text of the Bible, and most specifically of the New Testament. The Old Testament text of the Syriac Peshitta Bible definitely predates the Massoretic Hebrew text of TaNaKh, but it most likely postdates the ancient Greek Septuagint translation, and certainly postdates the Samaritan Pentateuch. The Syriac Peshitta text of the New Testament was made popular in the West by George M. Lamsa, who translated the text into English. Lamsa also translated the Peshitta text of the Old Testament into English, but unfortunately he did not translate the Peshitta text of the Apocrypha into English. However Mr. Lamsa made some claims for the text that are easily refuted. No critical scholar of any stature concedes that the Syriac Peshitta text predates the Greek text of the New Testament. But rather than appeal to authority, I would rather give reasons to support my views. As noted above, many of the regions where Paul was said to have preached the gospel were inhabited by Greeks and other Greek-speaking peoples. Even the Jews who lived in Asia Minor, Greece, and the general area of the Eastern Mediterranean would have spoken Greek, at least as a second language. Most of the Jews who lived in Alexandria spoke Greek as their first language. Many Jewish men and women adopted Greek names. Greek art, literature, philosophy, sports, culture, and aesthetics greatly influenced the people of the Eastern Mediterranean, and even the Romans themselves. Jews were not immune to this cultural influence. Corinthians, Ephesians, Colossians, Thessalonians, Galatians and even some Romans would have spoken Greek. Paul spoke Greek.[715] Phoebe is a Greek name. So are all the other names found in the colophons of the various Pauline epistles: Fortunatus, Achaicus, Stephanas, Timotheus, Titus, Lukas, Silvanus, Onesimus, Epaphroditus, Tychicus. So whether the Pauline corpus was written by Paul or by the people named as the writers in the respective colophons, there can be no doubt that those epistles were written in Greek.[716] Other Greek names abound in both the Pauline corpus and the book of Acts, most especially of those who are most closely associated with Paul. Sosthenes, Apollos, Andronicus, Junia, Amplias, Stachys, Apelles, Aristobulus, Tryphena, Tryphosa, Persis, Asyncritus, Phlegon, Hermas, Hermes, Patrobas, Philologus, Nereus, Olympas, Jason, Tertius, Sosipater, Erastus, Lucius are all Greek names. But George M. Lamsa would have us believe that such people spoke Syriac, rather than Greek. It is absurd.

George M. Lamsa appeals to certain portions of the epistles to claim that they were addressed exclusively to Jews, who (according to him) spoke Syriac. For example, Mr. Lamsa cites 1 Corinthians 10:1 as an example; "Moreover, brethren, I would not *suffer* that ye be ignorant, how that all our fathers were under the cloud, and all passed through the sea..." the reference is to Moses leading the Israelites through the Red Sea while God miraculously parted the waters, so that they were "as a wall unto them, on their right hand, and on their left."[717] While this is a clear reference to people being of Israelite descent, further on in the very same epistle we also read: "Ye know that ye were Gentiles, carried away unto these dumb idols, even as ye were led."[718] So this proves that at least some of the people addressed were in fact Gentiles, who, living in Corinth, must have spoken Greek, not Syriac. Furthermore we are explicitly told that

---

[715] Acts 21:37.

[716] One possible compromise on the position of who wrote the Pauline corpus is that Paul wrote the epistles, but not without active help from such persons as are named in the colophons; in other words, they were more than merely passive secretaries, recording Paul's word's *verbatim;* instead they had a more active role in the writing process. This is a distinct possibility, in my view.

[717] Exodus 14:22.

[718] 1 Corinthians 12:2.

Titus and Timotheus were both Greek.[719] Reportedly Paul circumcised Timotheus, because of the Jews in the area.[720] But Titus did not submit to circumcision; apparently Paul saw how painful the operation had been for Timotheus, and in compassion decided not to inflict such unwarranted pain upon Titus. It is interesting that Timotheus had not been circumcised as a baby, even though he had a Jewish mother; his father was Greek. This belies the current Talmudic revisionism parading today to the effect that a child born of a Jewish mother is somehow automatically Jewish. The Torah itself does not teach that; in fact, it explicitly repudiates such a concept. Take note of the following passage:

10   And the son of an Israelitish woman, whose father was an Egyptian, went out among the sons of Israel; and this son of the Israelitish *woman* and a man of Israel strove together in the camp;

11   and the Israelitish woman's son blasphemed the name *of God,* and cursed. And they brought him unto Moses (and his mother's name *was* Shelomith, the daughter of Dibri, of the tribe of Dan);

12   and they put him in custody, that the mind of the LORD might be shown them.

13   And the LORD spoke to Moses, saying,

14   Bring forth him that hath cursed without the camp, and let all *them* that heard *him* lay their hands on his head, *to testify against him,* and let all the congregation stone him *to death.*

15   And thou shalt speak unto the sons of Israel, saying, Whoever curses God shall bear his *own* sin.

16   And he that blasphemes the name of the LORD, he shall surely be put to death; and all the congregation shall certainly stone him: as well the stranger, as he that is born in the land, when he blasphemes the name *of God, he* shall be put to death. (Leviticus 24:10–16 cp Matthew 12:31; Mark 3:28–29)

---

[719]   Galatians 2:3; Acts 16:1.

[720]   Acts 16:1-3.

The above passage conclusively proves that simply being born of a Jewish mother is definitely not enough to be considered a true Israelite, according to the Torah itself. This point is sometimes emphasized by the Jews for Jesus.

The Syriac Peshitta text is not even the oldest Syriac translation of the New Testament. But most, if not all, of the books of the New Testament were originally written in Greek, not Syriac. It is just barely possible that the epistles of James and Judas were first written in Syriac, rather than Greek.[721] But once again this is asuming that Galilean Jews spoke Syriac, rather than Hebrew or Greek. I now believe that this is possible, and in fact this may be the *panchreston* that explains so much as yet heretofore unexplained. If the Jews of Judaea spoke Hebrew, while those living to the north, in the region of Galilee, which was much closer to Syria, spoke Syriac, then this would account for certain otherwise inexplicable discrepancies. And the context of Mark 5:41 and 7:34 reveals that Jesus was in Galilee (which borders Syria) in the first instance, and in Syria proper in the latter. Therefore it is probable that the people in the area spoke Syriac, or were bilingual, and spoke Syriac and Hebrew. This is at least a reasonable interpretation of the evidence. But this leads to some other interesting questions. The first one being, why did the Evangelist transliterate, rather than merely translate, the actual words (supposedly) spoken by Jesus on these two occasions? Obviously he didn't do this in every instance, or his Gospel would have been much more bulky and taxing to read. The only other occasion is the famous cry of Jesus on the cross of "Eloi, Eloi, lama sebachthani?", which occurs in Mark 15:34.[722] In this last instance, there is a legitimate reason to transliterate as well as translate the actual words of Jesus; since the Jews surrounding him did not understand him, and thought that instead he was calling upon Elijah to save him. This was the rationale for first transliterating the actual words spoken by Christ, and then interpreting them into Greek, so that the Greek reader could understand them. But on these other two occasions there appears to be no such rationale. I suppose one simple explanation was to simply provide a sense of realism and immediacy to the narrative, or possibly to make his Gospel appear to be more authentic. This

---

[721] The latter epistle was never accepted as Canonical by the Syrian Orthodox Church.

[722] Rendered "Eli, Eli, lama sebachthani?" in Matthew 27:46.

is possible, and may be the best, simplest, and most economical explanation. But I think one alternative possibility is that these words were thought of as a sort of magical formula for curing ills. Words spoken in a foreign tongue associated with miraculous cures could easily become accepted as magical formulae by people of those times.

But the above observations also lead into the realisation that in some cases, false arguments have been used against the Syriac Peshitta text of the New Testament. For example, some have pointed to such passages, and supposing that they represent what is also recorded in the Peshitta text, point out that it would have been both unnecessary and absurd for words uttered in the language of the text to be once again interpreted by the evangelist or scribe. While this is true, I have looked up the relevant portions on an interlinear translation of the Syriac Peshitta text[723] and found that there are no such gratuitous repititions in the text.[724] However a Syriac version of the *Diatessaron* was the most commonly-used text of the Gospels in Syria and Assyria until it was supplanted by the Peshitta text in the fifth century. There is no unequivocal evidence that the Peshitta text of the New Testament is any earlier than the fifth century. One obvious example that the Greek text pedates the Syriac is the instance of a false prophet mentioned in the book of Acts. The man is said to be a Jewish false prophet, with the rather embarrassing name of Bar-Jesus.[725] In the Syriac Peshitta text this rather embarrassing apellation is replaced with the more innocuous Bar-Shuma.[726] Another example is the deletion of the name Jeremiah from Matthew 27:9. These are clear examples of places where scribes sought to emend the text to eliminate unfortunate readings. I am not saying that the Peshitta is not an important text; it is certainly very old, and has great value in textual terms. However it does not predate the Greek text, nor was the New Testament written in Syriac or Hebrew.[727] Old translations can be of considerable value, however, in determining the original text. But no translation can

---

[723] Available at http://www.peshitta.org.

[724] George M. Lamsa's English translation of the text was not necessarily absolutely faithful to the Syriac in every instance.

[725] Acts 13:6.

[726] See George M. Lamsa's translation of the New Testament, or the interlinear translation of the Peshitta text at http://www.peshitta.org.

[727] With the possible [probable?] exception of the Gospel of Matthew.

take the place of the original. Of course those who read the Gospels in an English translation should be fully aware that any conversations narrated between Jesus and others is a translation of a translation of what Jesus *might* have said.[728]

---

[728] Since we have to take it on faith that the Evangelists faithfully recorded Christ's own words.

Philio

●

Philo Judaeus was an Alexandrian Jew who wrote a number of philosophical treatises, based upon an allegorical interpretation of the Jewish Scriptures. The Jewish historian Josephus wrote of him.[729] This was because Philo was the chief representative chosen to lead an embassy to Gaius; Philo himself also wrote of the voyage in his works. This is the Emperor also otherwise known as Caius Caesar and also Caligula. Gaius wanted to have a statue of himself placed within the temple in Jerusalem, which naturally would have been a complete abomination to the Jews. This created a crisis for the Jews, but fortunately disaster was averted, and the cruel emperor was assassinated by his countrymen before he could cause any more havoc.

Philo does not mention either Jesus or any Christians or any messianic movement among the Jews at that time. But we must keep in mind that Philo was not a historian, as Josephus was; furthermore the silence of Philo, as well as that of Josephus, is overestimated in terms of import by phantom Christ theorists. Jesus could still have been an intinerant prophet-preacher, traveling throughout greater Palestine. But what is interesting is that there are some literary parallels between Philo's writings and portions of the New Testament, especially the Pauline corpus. I offer some of these below. These examples are by no means exhaustive, but nevertheless there are a few

---

[729] Jos. Ant. 18.8.1.

juicy morsels. These literary parallels are at least somewhat suggestive of possible literary influence.

"And therefore it is enjoined to the priest and prophet, that is to say, to reason, "to place the soul in front of God, <u>with the head uncovered</u>," that is to say, the soul must be laid bare as to its principal design, and the sentiments which it nourished must be revealed, in order that being brought before the <u>judgment seat </u>of the most accurate vision of <u>the incorruptible God</u>, it may be thoroughly examined as to all its concealed disguises, like a <u>base coin</u>, or, on the other hand, if it be found to be free from all participation in any kind of wickedness, it may wash away all the calumnies that have been uttered against its bringing him for a testimony to its purity, who is alone <u>able to behold the soul naked</u>." (Philo, *On the Cherubim,* 17)

13 Neither is there any creature that is not manifest in his sight; but all things *are* <u>naked and opened </u>unto the eyes of him with whom we have to do. (Hebrews 4:13)

4 <u>Every man praying or prophesying with his head covered dishonors his head</u>. (1 Corinthians 11:4)

3 If so that being clothed we shall not be found <u>naked</u>. (2 Corinthians 5:3)

10 For we must all appear before the <u>judgment seat </u>of Christ (2 Corinthians 5:10a; cf Romans 14:10b)

19 Nevertheless the foundation of God standeth sure, having this seal, The Lord knoweth them that are his. And, Let every one that nameth the name of Christ depart from iniquity. (2 Timothy 2:19 cf the "base coin" reference above; the imagery of 2 Timothy 2:19 seems to be of a two-sided coin, each side having an inscription, as quoted in the verse)

23 And changed the glory of <u>the incorruptible God</u> into an image made like unto corruptible man, and to birds, and four-footed beasts, and creeping things. (Romans 1:23)

"And God created man, taking a lump of clay from the earth, and breathed into his face the breath of life: and <u>man became a living soul</u>. The races of men are twofold; for one is the heavenly man, and the other the earthly man. Now the <u>heavenly man</u>, as being born in the image of God, has no participation in any corruptible or earthlike essence.[730] But the <u>earthly man</u> is made of loose material, which he calls a lump of clay. On which account he says, not that the <u>heavenly man</u> was made, but that he was fashioned according to the imgage of God; but the <u>earthly man</u> he calls a thing made, and not begotten by the maker. And we must consider that the man who was formed of earth, means the mind which is to be infused into the body, but which has not yet been so infused. And this mind would be really earthly and corruptible, if it were not that God had breathed into it the spirit of genuine life; for then it "exists," and is no longer made into a soul; and its soul is not inactive, and incapable of proper formation, but a really intellectual and living one. "For man," says Moses, "<u>became a living soul</u>."" (Philo, *Allegorical Interpretation I, 31-32*)

45 And so it is written, The first man Adam <u>became a living soul</u>; *but* the last Adam *became* a life-giving spirit.

46 However the spiritual *appeared* not first, but the natural; and *only* afterwards, that which is spiritual.

47 The first man is of the earth; earthly: *but* the second man is from heaven.

48 As is the <u>earthly</u>, such are they who are <u>earthly</u>; and as is the <u>heavenly</u>, so are they that are <u>heavenly</u>.

49 And as we have borne the image of the <u>earthly</u>, so shall we also bear the image of the <u>heavenly</u>. (1 Corinthians 15:45-49)

"For this reason all the wise men mentioned in the books of Moses are represented as sojourners, for their souls are sent down from heaven upon earth as to a colony; and on account of their fondness for contemplation, and their love of learning, they are accustomed to migrate to the terrestrial nature. Since therefore having taken up

---

[730] Could this possibly be the origin of Docetism?

their abode among bodies, they behold all the mortal objects of the outward senses by their means, they then subsequently return back from thence to the place from which they set out at first, <u>looking upon the heavenly country</u> in which they have the rights of citizens as their native land, and as the earthly abode in which they dwell for a while as in a foreign land. For to those who are sent to be the inhabitants of a colony, the <u>country</u> which has received them is in place of their original mother country; but still the land which has sent them forth remains to them as the house to which they desire to return. Therefore, very naturally, Abraham says to the guardians of the dead and to the arrangers of mortal affairs, after he has forsaken that life which is only dead and the tomb, "I am a stranger and a sojourner among you"" (Philo, *On the Confusion of Tongues,* 77-79a)

13 These all died in faith, not having received the promises, but having seen them from afar, and *they* were persuaded of *them,* and embraced *them,* and confessed that they were strangers and pilgrims on the earth.

14 For they that say such things plainly declare that they seek a <u>country</u>.

15 And truly, if they had thought of that *country* from where they had come, they might have had an opportunity to return *there.*

16 But now *it is clear that* they desire <u>a better country, namely, a heavenly one;</u> wherefore God is not ashamed to be called their God: for he has prepared a city for them. (Hebrews 11:13-16)

"And even if there be not as yet anyone who is worthy to be called a <u>son of God</u>, nevertheless let him labor earnestly to be adorned according to his <u>first-born word</u>, the <u>eldest</u> of his angels, as the great archangel of many names; for he is called, the authority, and <u>the name of God</u>, and <u>the Word</u>, and <u>man according to God's image</u>, and he who sees Israel." (Philo, *On the Confusion of Tongues,* 146)

15 Who is the <u>image of the invisible God, the firstborn</u> of every creature (Colossians 1:15)

1 In the beginning was <u>the Word</u>, and <u>the Word</u> was with God, and <u>the Word</u> was a Divine Being. (John 1:1)

13 And his name is called <u>the Word of God</u>. (Revelation 19:13b)

29 For whom he did foreknow, he also did predestinate *to be* conformed to the image of his Son, that he might be the <u>firstborn</u> among many brethren. (Romans 8:29)

5 Jesus Christ, the <u>firstborn</u> of the dead (Revelation 1:5a)

<u>The name of the Father is the Son</u>. (Gospel of Truth)[731]

"This now, is our opinion upon and interpretation of this passage. But they who follow only what is plain and easy, think that what is here intended to be recorded, is the origin of the languages of the Greeks and barbarians, whom, without blaming them, (for, perhaps they also put a correct interpretation on the transaction), I would exhort not to be content with stopping at this point, but to proceed onward to look at the passage in a figurative way, considering that the mere words of the scriptures are, as it were, <u>but shadows of bodies,</u> and that the meanings which are apparent to investigation beneath them, are the <u>real things</u> to be pondered upon." (Philo, *On the Confusion of Tongues,* 190)

17 Which are a <u>shadow of things to come; but the body</u> is of Christ. (Colossians 2:17)

6 <u>For the letter killeth, but the spirit giveth life</u>. (2 Corinthians 3:6b)[732]

"Again, the principal and dominant part in an animal is the head, and that has seven most necessary divisions: two eyes, an equal number of ears, two channels for the nostrils, and <u>the mouth </u>to make up seven, <u>through which</u>, as Plato says, <u>mortal things find their entrance</u>, and <u>immortal things their exit. For into the mouth do </u><u>enter meat and </u><u>drink, perishable food of a perishable body; but from out of it proceed</u>

---

[731]   This is a clear example of Philo's influence upon Gnostic literature.

[732]   Note also the allegory made in Galatians 4:22–31 of Genesis 21:6–10.

<u>words of the immortal laws of an immortal soul</u>, by means of which rational life is regulated." (Philo, *On Creation,* 119)

15 There is nothing from without a man, that <u>entering into him</u>, can defile him; but the things that come out of him, those defile him.

16 If any man has ears to hear, let him hear.

17 And when he had entered into a house from the people, his disciples asked him concerning the parable.

18 And he said to them, Are you also without understanding? Do you not perceive, that whatever <u>enters </u>a man from without cannot defile him,

19 because it <u>enters</u> not into his heart, but into *his* belly, and *then it is* purged *from the body as waste.*

20 But he said that which <u>proceeds out from </u>the man, that defiles him.

21 For <u>from within</u>, out of the heart of man, proceed evil thoughts, adulteries, fornications, murders,

22 thefts, covetousness, wickedness, deception, licentiousness, envy, blasphemy, pride, folly,

23 all these evil things come <u>from within</u>, and defile the man. (Mark 7:15-23; cf Mt 15:10-20)[733]

"This is Caesar, who calmed the storms which were raging in every direction, who healed the common diseases which were afflicting both Greeks and barbarians..." (Philo, *On the Embassy to Gaius,* 145a)

---

[733] The fact that there is a reversal between the two examples does not take away from the literary parallel; Plato (and Philo following him) having taught that the mouth speaks immortal truths, while Jesus taught that the wickedness of man's fallen nature proceeds from the heart within.

The literary parallels with Jesus are fairly obvious; he purportedly calmed the waves of the sea, (Mark 4:39) and also healed many people (Matthew 4:23-24).

These are only a few examples. I'm sure that a person could probably easily find many more. Once again while the silence of Philo respecting Jesus is damaging to the image of Jesus as a great miracle-worker, it is not sufficient to overthrow his historicity altogether; most likely, the miracles attributed to Jesus in the Gospels were merely gratuitous inventions to supply him with messianic credentials after the fact. But Jesus may very well have been an itinerant prophet-preacher. Remember too the passage from Luke that says that Jesus and his disciples were supported by certain women.[734] This lends an immense amount of realism to the narrative, and for all intents and purposes virtually proves that Jesus was a historical person.[735]

---

[734] Luke 8:1-3.

[735] Because if we assume the contrary, that Jesus was merely a completely invented figure, then we would have to ask why this anomalous and potentially embarrassing detail was added to the narrative. It certainly undermines the image of Jesus as the wonder-working Son of God, which the general tenor of the narrative purports; and for phantom Christ theorists to insist that the detail was merely added to lend such gratuitous realism to an otherwise unbelievable story, they are merely begging the question, and are guilty of special pleading.

Josephus

J osephus was a first century Jewish historian. His writings are of immense value for supplying many details of Jewish history from the third century B.C. until the time of the Emperor Vespasian. His works are generally highly prized by Christians, but Jews still consider him a notorious traitor to his own people, and only ever side with him against the New Testament, but in no other instance. However a judicious appraisal of his writings shows him to have been a most meticulous historian of the first degree. In fact, I would say that oftentimes Josephus has been unfairly maligned, usually by Jewish sources. As to whether Josephus always is more reliable than the New Testament, I am not necessarily convinced that this is the case, in every instance. And it should be clear from the context and content of my work that I am no apologist for Christianity. Nevertheless in my former work I assumed that Josephus had a reasonably accurate chronology,[736] and based some of my arguments upon this assumption. So I have made significant use of Josephus, as also did G.R.S. Mead.[737]

Josephus is valued by Christians because they believe that he made reference to Jesus Christ.[738] Even some of those who present an alternative image of Christ make use of the same passage.[739] However virtually all critical scholars, historians, and literary critics agree that the passage in question is spurious, being an interpolation into the text originating in the fourth century.[740] Nowhere is this infamous passage, known as the *Testimonium Flavium,* ever quoted by any source before the fourth century. Furthermore the passage only occurs in the *Antiquities,* and is absent from the earlier history of Josephus, the *War.*[741] The passage is also notoriously brief, which also lends suspicion to its authenticity; one would expect that if Josephus were to write about Jesus, he would have written more.[742] There is also a different version of the same passage found in a Slavonic version of Josephus. But we ought to at least take a brief look at the controversial pasage itself.

"Now there was about this time Jesus, a wise man, if it be lawful to call him a man. For he was a doer of wonderful works, *and* a teacher of such men as receive the truth with pleasure. He drew over to him both many of the Jews, and many of the Gentiles. He was *called* Christ. But when Pilate, at the suggestion of the principal men amongst us,

---

[736] Although I also pointed out that there was a large discrepancy between the chronology of Josephus and the standard chronology, and that this discrepancy could perhaps be accounted for by Josephus seeking to place Moses at the most remote antiquity possible, that he might seem more venerable in the eyes of the Greeks and Romans. But Josephus placed both Ezra and Nehemiah in the days of King Xerxes, rather than his son Artaxerxes, as do the biblical books of Ezra and Nehemiah. In this matter I assumed the correctness of the chronology of Josephus, rather than the biblical texts. See my former work.

[737] Mead, G.R.S., *DID JESUS LIVE 100 B.C.?,* op. cit.

[738] Jos. Ant. 18.3.3.

[739] Kamal Salibi, Laurence Gardner, Barbara Thiering, etc.

[740] Eusebius is generally suspected as the most likely culprit.

[741] Although some editions of Josephus' *War* do contain a *verbatim* copy of the *Testimonium Flavium* inserted into the text.

[742] On the other hand, this is not necessarily the case; such an assumption may be more due to cultural Christian conditioning.

had condemned him to the cross, those who loved him at the first did not forsake him; for he appeared alive again the third day, as the divine prophets had foretold these and ten thousand other wonderful things concerning him. And the tribe of Christians, so named from him, are not extinct at this day." (Jos. Ant. 18.3.3)

This passage is so clearly bogus that it hardly even merits a refutation. It is suspiciously terse; even when Josephus writes of lesser-known would-be messiahs, he usually supplies far more in terms of details surrounding their circumstances, and their ultimate fate, if known. For example, compare this with the account Josephus gives us of an unnamed Egyptian false prophet,[743] or of Simon, a Jewish magician from Cyprus,[744] or of Judas the Galilean,[745] whom Josephus called the author of a fourth sect within Judaism; or of Theudas, a false prophet and a magician,[746] or of another Simon, who was also a messianic pretender.[747] All of these men, despite their comparative obscurity, have more space devoted to them than Jesus does. Therefore if Jesus truly was performing many miracles, or even if there was a rampant hysteria among the people of the time to this effect, it is close to certain that Josephus would have written more about Jesus than this short paragraph. Of course this leaves Josephus with no direct mention of Jesus anywhere within his works, which mythicists claim as virtual proof that Jesus never existed. But the evidence does not necessarily have to be interpreted in such a way. It seems more likely that in his own time, Jesus was not as noteworthy as later legend would have us believe. And those men who were more notable in their own time, later faded from importance in the scheme of history. This all has far more to do with the historical accident of Constantine's conversion[748] to Christianity in the fourth century than with events of the first century.[749] I have already noted the parallel with the unknown Teacher of Righteousness of the Dead Sea Scrolls. So far nobody from

---

[743] Jos. Ant. 20.8.6.

[744] Jos. Ant. 20.7.2. Could this have been Simon Magus?

[745] Jos. War. 2.8.1; Ant. 18.1.1-6; 20.5.2.

[746] Jos. Ant. 20.5.1.

[747] Jos. Ant. 17.10.6.

[748] Real or feigned.

[749] And even less with events of the first century B.C., if we believe Jesus lived back then.

the early second century B.C. has been identified as the Teacher of Righteousness spoken of in the Scrolls. Yet we know that such a man must have existed.[750] This parallel example of an unknown and as yet unidentified (not to say unidentifiable) person of the early second century B.C. is a perfect refutation to the phantom Jesus theorists. Jesus, like the Teacher of Righteousness before him, was not notable in his own time, except among his own disciples. We only even know about the Teacher of Righteousness due to the fortuitous preservation and discovery of the Dead Sea Scrolls. The case with Jesus is somewhat different, yet arguably no less accidental, rather than providential.[751] But this presents us with an opportunity to rescue Jesus from the naysayers and self-satisfied mythicists. Stated otherwise, this is yet more circumstantial evidence that constitutes a significant challenge to the phantom Christ theory.

Josephus also contains passages about James the Just,[752] and John the Baptist.[753] However in respect to the former passage, it is possible that the clause containing the phrase "brother of Jesus, called Christ" may have been an interpolation[754] by Christians; and while the latter passage may be, and probably is, authentic, it does not provide conclusive proof of the historical existence of Jesus.[755] I would

---

[750] And furthermore as far as I am concerned the Teacher of Righteousness definitely lived in the early second century B.C.; none of the so-called "scholars" who presume to identify him as either Jesus, or John the Baptist, or James the Just, or any other contemporary or near-contemporary with Jesus, has yet presented any reasonable evidence sufficient to disregard the clear chronology of the Damascus Document. This is a fatal weakness to all such theories.

[751] I.e., whether these circumstances are ultimately merely accidental or providential is a matter of interpretation. While of great philosophical import, there is a clear distinction between history proper and the interpretation of history, or the meaning of history.

[752] Jos. Ant. 20.9.1.

[753] Jos. Ant. 18.5.2.

[754] In much the same way as experts determined that the clause "brother of Jesus" was an inauthentic addition to an ancient ossuary by an unscrupulous antiquities dealer.

[755] Since John the Baptist may have existed as a historical person, while Jesus was a mere *chimera*. Conversely, however, if Jesus was historical then John the Baptist also necessarily was. Compare this with the opposite situation

rather not burden this work with further quotations from Josephus respecting James and John, and I would direct the reader to consult the works of Josephus directly. Some scholars have suggested that the infamous *Testimonium Flavium* is not a complete fabrication, but rather a "touched up" version of what Josephus probably wrote about Jesus, which was probably somewhat less flattering.

---

vis-à-vis Jesus and the apostle Paul. In other words, of the three men, John the Baptist has the highest probability of having been a real, historical person. Paul has the most tenuous claim to historicity, by contrast.

Suetonius

S uetonius was a Roman historian of the late first century. He wrote most extensively on the lives of the first twelve Caesars, in a work of the same title. The most important quotation from his works in relation to the historical Jesus is the following:

"Because the Jews at Rome caused continuous disturbances at the instigation of Chrestus, he expelled them *all* from the city." (Suetonius, *The Lives of the Twelve Caesars; Claudius: 25, paragraph 3)*

I discussed this passage in my former work, where I compared it to a corresponding passage in the biblical book of Acts. For the benefit of those who may not have read my earlier work, I will also reproduce the relevant passage from Acts here.

After these things Paul departed from Athens, and came to Corinth; 2 and found a certain Jew named Aquila, born in Pontus, *who had* recently come from Italy, with his wife Priscilla, since Claudius had commanded all Jews to depart from Rome; and he joined them. (Acts 18:1-2)

What is suspicious about the passage in Acts is that it does not provide a reason for why Claudius had ordered all Jews to leave Rome. I suppose a person could say it was embarrassing to admit that dissensions among the Jews over the messianic question grew so violent and unmanageable that the emperor had expelled tham all from the imperial city. And of course this is an obvious inference, but I suspect more. In my earlier work I suggested that the book of Acts does not supply us with the reason for this decree (which is conspicuous by its absence, in comparison to the more complete account of Suetonius) was because the passage from Suetonius presents the entire messianic movement of the time as essentially a strictly Jewish affair, in contrast to the supposedly large number of Gentiles that had already embraced the movement, according to Acts. And while this is still a good observation, one other rather glaring circumstance is that the passage within Suetonius implies that Chrestus himself was personally instigating seditions among the Jews of Rome. And if this Chrestus was Jesus himself, then this depicts Jesus as being alive in the flesh in a very non-supernatural context, long after the time that he was allegedly crucified. This in turn implies one of three things: 1. Either Jesus lived later[756] than the time reported in the Gospels; or 2. He survived his passion; or 3. He had never actually been crucified. Therefore this passage from Suetonius is potentially of great importance and significance to those who may adovcate either a survival theory or a substitution theory in respect to Jesus. Of course it is also true that the Chrestus *might* possibly refer to some other messianic pretender, although most interpreters have assumed that it speaks of the historical Christ. Another possible interpretation is that it only speaks of Christ in a general rather than a highly specific sense; meaning, that Suetonius only knew that the supposed ringleader of the tumults was commonly called *Chrestus,* and he simply assumed that this "troublemaker" had been personally present in Rome. But he writes nothing of the ultimate fate of this supposed ringleader, so either he escaped, or he had never been in Rome; it had merely been his followers who disputed with other Jews about his supposed ontological messianic status. This is a reasonable interpretation. But the very fact that the book of Acts neglects to mention the reason for why Claudius had expelled the Jews from Rome implies a guilty conscience on the part of the author of that work, as if there were some otherwise embarrassing information contained in the explicit reason for the expulsion. This in turn implies that Jesus really had been in Rome, as a ringleader of a messianic rebellion among certain Jews, and that this fact would have been far too embarrassing, and also contrary to the chronology of the crucifixion/resurrection narrated in the Gospels.

So this short passage from Suetonius is a crucial piece of evidence in the puzzle of the historical Jesus. It certainly could be of prime

---

[756] Rather than earlier, as argued in my former book.

importance to advocates of a survival or substitution scenario.[757] The passage is also generally appealed to by advocates of a historical Jesus, to refute phantom Christ theorists. But of course strictly speaking the passage does not in and of itself *prove* the historical existence of Jesus Christ; it is merely evidential as such. The value and strength of that evidence is debatable, as is the exact meaning of the passage as well. But certainly there is something here to keep in mind as a potentially key piece of evidence in our discussion below. At the very least the passage should be taken notice of, and acknowledged as a potentially important piece of the larger puzzle.

Another interesting and possibly relevant passage from Suetonius concerns the Emperor Vespasian. The strange passage is as follows:

"Vespasian, still rather bewildered in his new role of Emperor, felt a certain lack of authority and impressiveness; yet both *of* these attributes were granted to him. As he sat on the Tribunal, two labourers, one blind, the other lame, approached *him* together, begging to be healed. Apparently the God Serapis had promised them in a dream that if Vespasian would consent to spit in the blind man's eyes, and touch the lame man's leg with his heel, both would be made well. Vespasian had so little faith in his *own* curative powers that he showed great reluctance in doing as he was asked; but his friends persuaded him to try them, in the presence of a large audience, too–and the charm worked." (Suetonius, *Vespasian; 7, paragraph 2*)

It is not too difficult to imagine men hired as actors, to pretend to be blind and lame, and to further pretend that they had been miraculously cured by the Emperor, to puff up his vanity and further establish the imperial cult of Emperor-worship among the Romans. But what is most fascinating about the passage is the clear literary parallel it affords with some of the accounts of Christ's healings. Most notably one can cite the example quoted from above, where Christ likewise spit in a blind man's eyes, and he was healed.[758] A similar method of curing a blind man is also narrated in John 9:6, and a similarly shamanistic type of healing method is also mentioned in

---

[757] Which is not to say that it always is cited by advocates of either of these two theories, but merely that it *could* be cited to support such hypotheses.

[758] Mark 8:22-26. Not only do both accounts narrate spitting in a blind man's eyes to cure blindness, but the halting manner of healing in Mark's account is another literary parallel. Note also the similar shamanistic healing methods narrated in Mark 7:33-34 and John 9:6.

Mark 7:33. These literary parallels strongly suggest a literary influence; and the only realistic literary influence in this case would be the use of Suetonius' work in the writing of Mark and John. Since Suetonius wrote of the reign of Domitian in his *magnum opus,* and Domitian was assassinated in 96 C.E., then *The Lives of the Twelve Caesars* could not have been completed and published until towards the very end of the first century, or early in the second. Therefore most likely even the Gospel of Mark, which most critical biblical scholars believe is the earliest of the Gospels, was probably not even written until the second century.[759]

Yet another example of a literary parallel is to be found in the work of Suetonius. In writing of Julius Caesar, Suetonius wrote the following:

"Nobody can deny that during the Civil War, and after, he behaved with wonderful constraint and clemency. Whereas Pompey declared that all who were not actively with the government were against it and would be treated as public enemies, *Julius* Caesar announced that all who were not actively against him were with him." (Suetonius, *The Lives of the Twelve Caesars, Julius Caesar; 75)*

We have examples of both of these sayings attributed to Jesus Christ in the Synoptic Gospels: "He that is not with me is against me" (Mt 12:30; Mk 11:23); and also "He that is not against us is for us" (Mk 9:40; Lk 9:50). Once again these literary parallels at least suggest some degree of literary borrowing on the part of the Evangelists. Before passing on it is at least worth mentioning that Suetonius does mention Christians being punished in the reign of the Emperor Nero:

"Punishments were also inflicted on the Christians, a sect professing a new and mischievous religious belief" (Suetonius, *Nero; 16, paragraph 2)*

Nero reigned immediately after Claudius. So presumably by then the Christian movement had spread to Gentiles.

---

[759] I.e., unless we are willing to concede a wild coincidence of such close literary parallels. However, it is worth noting that Robert Eisler, in his *magnum opus, The Messiah Jesus and John the Baptist,* would have been congenial to the literary influence flowing in the opposite direction. Thus the text of *Mark* may have been earlier.

The Shroud of Turin

The Shroud of Turin remains an item of great controversy, despite scientific scrutiny. True believers will not be dissuaded from their blind faith in the article as a genuine relic of Jesus Christ. Of course not all Christians believe in the authenticity of the Turin Shroud; Protestant Christians have for the most part neglected the item as being too strongly associated with the Catholic Church.[760] While at first the radiocarbon dating[761] of the Shroud in 1988 seemed to strike a death-blow to any further claims of authenticity, some people still came up with ingenious theories as to how and why these radiocarbon results were wrong.[762] Some of those opposed to the radiocarbon results were surprisingly not Christians, but rather those who held to certain historical theories about Jesus that incorporated the Shroud of

---

[760] See, for example, the writings of Josh McDowell. On the other hand, there are some notable exceptions; some strong evangelicals have endorsed the Shroud's authenticity, and have even claimed it is "proof" of Christ's resurrection from the dead. In this vein are Ian Wilson, Vernon Miller, Gary Habermas, Kenneth E. Stevenson, etc.

[761] The Shroud cloth was independently tested by three different laboratories, who all placed the origin of the Shroud between approximately 1260 and 1390 A.D./C.E.

[762] No doubt because they just didn't like the results. This is not science. But alas, with true believers, faith always trumps science.

Turin as evidence in favor of the theory in question.[763] Therefore new theories were offered to account for the supposedly false radiocarbon results. One such theory was offered by Dr. Leoncio Garza-Valdes, who argued in his book[764] that a *bioplastic coating* accumulated on the Shroud had falsified the radiocarbon analysis. Holger Kersten and Elmar Gruber in their book[765] threw down the gauntlet and charged the Vatican with an international conspiracy to falsify the radiocarbon results, since, according to them, the bloodstains on the Shroud proved that the man wrapped in it was still alive when he was wrapped in it, and therefore, if it was Jesus, Jesus did not die on the cross. Thus an authentification of the Shroud by way of radiocarbon dating would present the unprecedented embarrassment of a potential scientific disproof of Christianity, which naturally the Vatican would want to avoid. It is all a bit much, especially when one considers that long before this there had already been sufficient evidence to dismiss any alleged authenticity to the Shroud of Turin, on both historic and scientific grounds. Fundamentalists for their part had sometimes claimed that the Shroud was a sort of "fifth Gospel" that had supernatural properties that somehow proved that Christ had miraculously risen from the dead. But after the 1988 radiocarbon tests they seemed to quiet down a bit, maybe out of embarrassment. I am really only including this chapter on the Shroud of Turin for the sake of completeness, lest I be accused of omitting a crucial item of evidence, either in favor of the resurrection theory, or the survival theory. The Shroud is more or less irrelevant to all the other theories

---

[763] Specifically a theory that Jesus had survived his crucifixion. Some survival theories had made reference to the *alleged* bloodstains on the Shroud of Turin as *proof* that Jesus did not die on the cross. Notably the books *JESUS DIED IN KASHMIR,* by Andreas Faber-Kaiser, *JESUS LIVED IN INDIA,* by Holger Kersten, and *JESUS DID NOT DIE ON THE CROSS,* by Kurt Berna (alias Hans Naber, John T. Bruknear, John Reban) all made reference to bloodstains on the Shroud of Turin as "proof" that Christ had survived his passion. *JESUS DID NOT DIE ON THE CROSS* was originally published as *JESUS NICHT AM KREUZ GESTORBEN* in German.

[764] *The DNA of God?*

[765] *THE JESUS CONSPIRACY.* (© 1992 Albert Langen/Georg Muller in der F.A. Herbig Verlagsbuchhandlung GmbH, Munchen) (English translation © 1994 Holger Kersten & Elmar R. Gruber) 1995 Barnes & Noble Books, by arrangement with Element Books.

of Christ, but only the phantom theory absolutely excludes the Shroud as completely inauthentic. It should also be clearly understood that neither the resurrection theory[766] nor the survival theory *require* the authenticity of the Shroud; rather an assumed authenticity of the Turin Shroud is more generally congenial to such theories.

The tenacity with which advocates of the Shroud's authenticity cling to such an unwarranted opinion and their desperate search for new explanations as to how and why the Shroud is authentic after all, is only an illustration of their blind faith and prejudiced opinion on this matter. For a while I was taken in by some of the explanations offered, but now I no longer find them convincing at all. While it is true that the Shroud of Turin is an item of some legitimate curiosity, perhaps akin to the mystery of the *Bermuda Triangle* or *Bigfoot,* it does not seem to merit the kind of lavish devotion so many sentimental people pay to it. In May of 1898, Secondo Pia photographed the Shroud for the first time; the negative of the image proved to be far more detailed and interesting than the positive image. It was and is a truly haunting image. But I would not stake my eternal destiny on some quirk of photography. It was not long before religious people saw the new, negative image as a strange "confirmation" of their faith. No scientific testing of the Shroud was allowed until the latter half of the twentieth century. STURP (Shroud of TUrin Research Project) began studying the Shroud scientifically in 1978, and it wasn't long until evangelicals and fundamentalists pounced on some of the quirky results as *"proof"* of the central claim of Christianity: the miraculous resurrection of Christ from the dead. Of course there was nothing in the least bit scientific about such claims, or even claims of the Shroud's authenticity. Early on there had been claims of bloodstains on the Shroud, but Dr. Walter McCrone, an eminent American chemist, found that the supposed blood stains were really only red ochre pigment, as used by mediaeval artists. He announced this result back in 1981, but his proclamation fell on deaf ears, for the most part. Kersten and Gruber for their part dispute this finding in their book, claiming that Baima Bollone was able to *prove* that the stains were not

---

[766] Although embraced as an article of faith, rather than as a scientific or historical theory, we will nevertheless regard the claim of a miraculous resurrection of Christ from the dead as a theory herein, to be compared to other theories.

merely blood, but distinctly *human* blood.[767] And some members of the STURP team are adamant that no trace of any pigment has ever been found on the Shroud, despite McCrone's findings. This has naturally created an atmosphere of confusion about the Shroud.

Since Holger Kersten, in his previous book, had cited the Shroud of Turin, and the alleged blood stains on it, as evidence that Jesus had survived the crucifixion, he did not want to relinquish this piece of evidence without a diligent investigation.[768] This is fair, but we also ought to take this fact into consideration, since it is at least *possible* that his prior endorsement of the Turin Shroud's authenticity, particularly as relating to his central survival theory vis-à-vis Jesus Christ, may have clouded his judgment, either on a conscious or subconscious level of awareness. And while it would neither surprise nor shock me that the Vatican could or would resort to an international conspiracy to falsify scientific results vis-à-vis the radiocarbon testing of the Turin Shroud, such an explanation appears to be unwarranted by the evidence; it is simpler to suppose that the radiocarbon results are genuine and true, and the Shroud is in fact a mediaeval hoax. Joe Nickell has studied the Shroud of Turin quite extensively and has proven that there are no supernatural properties whatever to the Shroud, and that it is almost certainly a mediaeval hoax.[769]

Sometimes Shroud enthusiasts claim that pollen from the Middle East has been found on the Shroud, but this is based upon claims made by Max Frei, an amateur criminologist who also mistakenly authenticated the notorious "Hitler Diaries" which later turned out to be a hoax. When the tapes that supposedly contained the famous Middle-Eastern pollen were examined by Dr. McCrone, he found that the pollen was not of Middle-Eastern origin. McCrone had also found vermillion pigment, as well as red ochre pigment, and tempera

---

[767] Kersten & Gruber, *THE JESUS CONSPIRACY.*, op. cit., pg. 33.

[768] Although it should be clearly understood by the reader that, neither the authenticity of the Turin Shroud, nor the presence of bloodstains upon it, are either *necessary* or *sufficient* evidence in favor of a survival theory. In other words, a survival theory neither requires that such be the case, nor would the actual presence of human bloodstains on an authentic Shroud of Turin prove that Jesus survived the crucifixion *and also* later appeared alive again to his Apostles. This latter stipulation is crucial and precise to the survival theory, as defined herein.

[769] See his book *Inquest on the Shroud of Turin.*

paint on the Shroud; he was also adamant that there was no trace of blood on the Shroud. But one generally hears and sees pro–authenticity arguments in the popular media, since a supposedly "authentic" Shroud makes a better story. But one can find both pro–authenticity and anti–authenticity websites all over the Internet. In a strange way, the Turin Shroud almost seems to function like a Rorschach inkblot test, where everyone sees what they want to see. But the so-called "scientific" results of STURP do not in any way prove that the Shroud of Turin is in any way authentic, much less miraculous. Genuine scientific scrutiny of the item reveals just the opposite. Many members of the STURP team were in fact very religious men, who were guided more by their faith than by a truly scientific attitude. At the very least, the absence of a consensus ought to give one pause, and cause a person to approach the question of the Shroud's alleged authenticity with caution, rather than to just shamelessly exploit, either as an icon of faith, or as a gratuitous article of evidence in a dubious theory.

But as far as I am concerned, the legitimate scientific consensus is against the Shroud's long-assumed authenticity. And not only is there a strong scientific basis to reject the claims to the Shroud's authenticity, but there is also a strong historic basis as well. Way back in 1389 the bishop of Troyes[770] wrote a letter to Pope Clement VII[771] that the Shroud, which had been displayed in a church in Lirey, France, no longer be displayed, because it was a pious fraud. The bishop claimed that a former bishop, namely Henry de Poitiers, had already investigated the matter thirty years earlier, and found it to be a fraud. In fact, the man who had painted the Shroud had confessed to Henry de Poitiers. And we must keep in mind that all this occurred back in a time when a belief in miracles was very commonplace; to paraphrase an earlier writer, "it would have been a miracle, if they had not believed in miracles". And yet even in this time, when France was still in the Dark Ages,[772] such a dark cloud of doubt and suspicion had been cast upon this supposedly "holy" relic, by none other than the clergy themselves. Holger Kersten and Elmar Gruber try to smoothe this over by saying that, in effect, it was due to an

---

[770] Pierre d'Arcis.

[771] Regarded by some as an "Anti-Pope".

[772] The Renaissance had not spread to France until about 1495. The Printing Press was not invented until c. 1437.

association with the dreaded Knights Templar that the Shroud thus became calumniated by Catholic clergy. But this argument is rather thin, and not particularly convincing. The convergence of the historic and scientific evidence instead negates any unwarranted assumption of the Shroud's authenticity. Phantom Christ theorists have nothing to fear from the Shroud of Turin.

One of the arguments we sometimes hear in defense of the Shroud's alleged authenticity is that it is not a very impressive artistic image; the underlying subtext being that an artist would have depicted Christ with much greater *pathos* than the faint image seen on the Shroud. But this argument assumes that the Shroud was merely executed as a work of art, and nothing else. In fact, the evidence suggests that the Shroud had been a hoax that was intended to be believed the actual burial shroud of Jesus Christ. As such, the artists intent was not "art for art's sake" or even "art for devotion's sake", but rather to fool people into believing that they beheld in the Shroud image the literal image of Jesus Christ. This explanation also accounts for the forensic accuracy of the image, such as the nail wounds being evident on the wrists, rather than the palms, of the hands. Although certainly not common knowledge in the middle ages, there were nevertheless students of physiology who would have known that a nail through the palms would not be sufficient to suspend a body from a cross or tree. But even looking at the Shroud as strictly a work of art, it is well known and well documented that artistic works executed in paint eventually lose their lustre and original beauty. The restoration of old art works is an undertaking occasionally undertaken by museums with painstaking care. So the Shroud of Turin can be looked upon as part artwork, part hoax. It is not a burial-cloth, either of Jesus or anyone else. I am reminded of a saying often uttered by some religious people: "Just because you don't believe it, doesn't mean that it's not true." True enough. But the inverse of that saying is equally true: "Just because you do believe it, doesn't mean that it is true." They don't seem able to mentally process the latter statement. It just doesn't register with them. I say let the Shroud of Turin rest in peace, just like Jesus Christ himself.

The Spear of Destiny

●

T he Spear of Destiny, otherwise also called the Spear of Longinus, the Lance of Longinus, the Holy Spear, and sometimes even the Spear of Christ, is another highly questionable relic. The famous Spear is supposed to be the spear that pierced the side of Christ as he hung on the cross.[773] However if anything, the claim of the Spear of Destiny to authenticity is even more tenuous and dubious than that of the Turin Shroud. For while all four Canonical Gospels mention a linen burial cloth,[774] and even at least four apocryphal Gospels do so as well,[775] the alleged piercing of Christ's side with a spear is recorded in only one or two[776] of the Canonical Gospels. Even if

---

[773] John 19:34; Matthew 27:49 (although the majority of Greek manuscripts omit the reference to the piercing of Christ by the spear in the latter instance, some of the oldest and best manuscripts do contain it); cf Nestle-Aland., op. cit., pg. 84, apparatus.

[774] Mt 27:59; Mk 15:46; Lk 23:53; 24:12; Jn 19:40; 20:5-7.

[775] MtN; MtH; Peter 6; Nicodemus 10:14.

[776] I.e., two if we regard the instance as recorded in some copies of Matthew's Gospel as an original reading of that text. While I personally tend to favor this reading, the fact that the incident is omitted from both Mark and Luke is at least somewhat of a suspicious omission, in terms of evidence; any relic that claims to be authentic on such an equivocal textual basis in the Gospels is accordingly suspect to the same degree. Therefore any alleged "relic" based upon such a dubious historical incident is necessarily correspondingly suspect.

we accord the benefit of the doubt to those copies of Matthew that record the incident, there is still a problem of the suspicious omission of the alleged incident from both Mark and Luke. The omission from Luke's Gospel is somewhat troubling; Luke having already examined "many" earlier accounts and inquired as diligently as possible into the actual historical circumstances, presumably omitted such a potentially important detail from his account because he found the report doubtful.[777] Of course this is assuming that the story even circulated before John's Gospel had been written. But when we read the incident as narrated in John's text, we have even more gounds for suspicion. This is because John makes the incident the basis for some supposedly fulfilled Scripture prophecies.[778] This raises a legitimate suspicion that possibly the incident was merely invented by John to provide yet another gratuitous alleged "fulfillment" of biblical prophecies. The latter instance of the appeal to a passage in Zechariah which says "and they shall look upon him whom they have pierced"[779] also corresponds to the Septuagint reading of Psalm 22:16 which says "They have pierced my hands and my feet." Therefore the crucifixion, which involved being nailed to a cross, inherently provided a gratuitous "fulfillment" of this other "prophecy" as recorded in Psalms. A person may use this point to argue that John (or Matthew) would have had no need therefore to add a further detail to provide another gratuitous fulfillment to prophecy; the very fact that Jesus had been purportedly nailed to the cross[780] would have automatically provided the necessary fulfillment of both Psalm 22:16 and Zechariah 12:10.[781] Therefore it would have been a work of supererogation for either John or Matthew to provide yet another instance or circumstance

---

[777] I.e., assuming that Matthew originally had narrated the incident in his text. If on the contrary it had never been narrated anywhere until John's Gospel, then this makes the whole matter even that much more doubtful and suspect.

[778] John 19:36-37 cf Exodus 12:46; Numbers 9:12 cf Psalm 34:20 cf Zechariah 12:10.

[779] Which a diligent comparison proves is the true original reading, rather than the bogus Massoretic reading as it now stands; "they shall look upon me whom they have pierced".

[780] John 20:20,25,27.

[781] Or rather the historic basis for the fulfillment of the latter; cp Revelation 1:7.

that happened to conveniently "fulfill" or seem to fulfill scripture prophecy. On this basis it could be counter-argued that the incident actually was historical, rather than an embellishment. The problem with this line of argument is that Matthew is guilty of such overkill in at least one instance; not being content with Mark's report that Jesus had been offered vinegar on a sponge as he hung on the cross,[782] thus providing an implicit fulfillment of Psalm 69:21, he not only copied Mark's account in respect to the vinegar offered Jesus on the cross,[783] but he also transforms the wine and myrrh offered to Jesus as he was being led away to crucifixion in Mark's account[784] into vinegar mixed with gall.[785] Apparently Matthew was scrupulous that gall definitely be included, which Mark omitted from his account. These incidents are merely implicit examples of supposedly fulfilled prophecy, since no quotation from the Psalms is cited in the Gospel text. But the point stands nevertheless. Therefore Matthew was willing to contradict a presumably earlier historic account in order to provide a more complete "fulfillment" of prophecy. Therefore the detail about Christ being pierced in the side with a spear is also very suspect, on the grounds that the incident may have been fabricated to provide a gratuitous "fulfillment" of prophecy. Therefore the Spear of Destiny is suspect on that basis.

But even if there had been a stronger biblical basis to believe in the historicity of the incident, the Spear of Destiny would still be highly questionable in terms of authenticity. Three or four other lances are claimed to be the original, authentic lance that allegedly pierced Christ's side on the cross. Regardless of whether or not Hitler, or other Nazis, believed in the authenticity of this highly questionable relic, or whether various occultists continue to believe in it as authentic, the facts militate strongly against any such assumption. Even if we accord veracity to the account of Christ having been pierced with a lance or spear as he was crucified, it seems very unlikely in the extreme that such a nondescript item would have been kept track of, long before Jesus himself had become a religious legend. The Romans crucified tens of thousands of people; possibly hundreds of thousands.

---

[782] Mark 15:36.

[783] Matthew 27:48.

[784] Mark 15:23.

[785] Matthew 27:34.

Countless thousands or tens of thousands were no doubt killed by spear-wounds, either in battle, or as some gruesome punishment. Even the traditional name of the centurion who supposedly pierced Jesus with his spear points to the tale and the relic as being legendary. Longinus is the supposed name of the soldier or centurion who pierced Christ's side with his spear. But this name is not recorded in any of the Canonical Gospels. Not only that, but it appears to be merely a nominal form of the Greek word *longche,* which is the proper *Koine* Greek word for lance. This makes it transparently obvious to anyone but the terminally gullible that the extra-biblical tales told about this centurion and his lance are merely quaint religious legends. Hence any lance or spear that is claimed to be the very same as that which supposedly pierced Christ's side is almost certainly a fake. I only made a point of including this chapter for the sake of completeness, lest I be accused of omitting any essential item of evidence. But Longinus is parallel to Veronica, the woman who supposedly wiped Christ's face as he was being led away to crucifixion; Veronica being a contraction of *Vera Icon,* meaning "True Image". Such myths and legends have no legitimate historical value and will not get us any closer to the historical Jesus, but instead will lead us astray into many false paths. So we are better off leaving the Spear of Destiny and the Shroud of Turin behind. They will tell us nothing about the original, historical Jesus.

Three Paradigms

So far in this work I have presented a *plethora* of relevant evidence to the pursuit of solving the great mystery of Jesus Christ. Admittedly much of the evidence has been somewhat obscure, and sometimes highly complex as well. I realise that it might be quite overwhelming, especially to the reader unfamiliar to the material. But I want the reader to have an appreciation for the complexities and subtleties of our subject-matter, and the great depths that must be plunged to fathom what is undoubtedly the single greatest mystery of Western civilization. But now we have reached a turning-point. From here on, our inquiry will become immensely simplified. We will see that in fact our most important question about Jesus Christ only leads to a comparatively small number of answers, and these in turn can be analysed and compared, to find the most probable answer. Hopefully the reader will feel that his or her patience will be adequately rewarded by a clarity that has not yet been found elsewhere. It is a matter of asking the right questions. It is also essential to maintain clarity in one's thinking, writing, and speaking throughout the process. It is a matter of discerning the most essential questions to be asked, and applying a process of critical reductionism to the analysis. We will begin here by reducing all possible theories about Jesus Christ to three discrete paradigms. This will be very helpful, since we can be assured that whatever the final truth about Jesus Christ may be, it will fall within the parameters of one of the three paradigms. The three paradigms are the historical, the ahistorical, and the fundamentalist.

The ahistorical paradigm means that Jesus Christ never existed as a historical person. Although this is only one of six possible theories about Jesus Christ, which I have designated herein as the phantom Christ theory, this is also a pardigm unto itself. It is distinct from all other paradigms and theories. It is important to realise that this is a position taken by quite a few scholars and authors and people, and has been for quite some time. In other words, while this theory is a distinct theory, it can and does often take many diverse forms. It would be a huge mistake to just group all advocates of the ahistorical paradigm together as if they all agreed on every aspect of their collective theory. This is not true at all. While often such theorists have been influenced by the writings and arguments of their ideological predecessors, new ideas and developments frequently arise, and different approaches and interpretations of evidence are sometimes offered. Furthermore and most importantly, this paradigm is not static; it is still unfolding, and even some contemporary critics are advocating this paradigm today.[786] And a perhaps even more obscure point, but one which I personally hold as being even more important, is that we must reckon, not only with what has been offered in favor of this thesis, but rather also with what *could be* offered in favor of it. I feel exactly the same way about any theory discussed herein. A sense of honesty and intellectual integrity compels me to take this attitude. In other words, it would be unfair to judge a paradigm or theory only by the worst possible example of it. This is certainly not the way to pursue truth. The ahistorical paradigm is distinct from both the historical paradigm and the fundamentalist paradigm inasmuch as these latter two require the sometime historical existence of Jesus Christ.[787] The ahistorical paradigm is identical with the phantom Christ theory, and as such it is quite distinct from the remaining five alternate theories of Jesus Christ, which all require a historical Jesus. The ahistorical paradigm ought not to be confused with a hybrid theory, in which Jesus exists as a historical person, but someone

---

[786] Although the idea was more *en vogue* in the Enlightenment era of the latter 1700's, and into the 1800's. But it seems to be once again becoming popular in some circles.

[787] I shall soon explain my reason for sharply distinguishing between the historical paradigm and the fundamentalist paradigm.

else in the New Testament, such as either Paul or Nicodemus, were merely invented characters. Jesus Christ himself is the key. It is our interpretation of *him* that determines the theory or paradigm. The ahistorical paradigm is the antipodes of the fundamentalist paradigm, which, like the ahistorical paradigm, is congruent with one of six possible theories about Jesus Christ; namely, the resurrection theory.[788] That leaves the remaining four possible theories to be circumscribed under the umbrella of the historical paradigm.[789]

I distinguish quite sharply between the historical paradigm and the fundamentalist paradigm because, even though technically the fundamentalist paradigm is a subset of a greater historical paradigm, in the sense that fundamentalists of necessity believe in a historical Jesus Christ, fundamentalism extinguishes all rational inquiry and the "true believer" has no need to integrate Jesus into the fabric of history, but instead proceeds to place all history within a fundamentalist interpretation of divine providence, culminating in an apocalyptic eschaton. Faith replaces the need for any historical inquiry, and the believer instead inquires into the meaning of the biblical text. Therefore the entire attitude and outlook is completely different; faith functions as its own proof.[790] This may be fine for the believer, but it does not satisfy the historian or the critical scholar. Neither is it satisfying to those who may have been believers themselves, but after diligent study have found the biblical text to be too fatally flawed to sustain a belief in it as divinely inspired.[791] Therefore I think it is wise to sharply distinguish the fundamentalist paradigm from the historical paradigm herein.

One other question needs to be addressed before moving on. I spoke above of the importance of clarity. Clarity comes from speaking and writing in precise terms, and maintaining clear thinking in our minds on the topics we seek to address. The very way that questions

---

[788] In other words the fundamentalist paradigm is another designation for the resurrection theory, as defined herein. Likewise the ahistorical paradigm is another designation for the phantom Christ theory, as defined herein.

[789] I.e., the survival theory, the substitution theory, the impersonation theory, the termination theory. All four theories are included within the parameters of the historical paradigm.

[790] Hebrews 11:1.

[791] Such as myself.

are framed will often affect just how correct or precise the answers will be. If our questions are framed in ambiguous terms, we are likely to only find ambiguous answers. Many people appear to be content walking through life in a dense cloud of nebulosity. Some people are even deliberate obscurantists, who prefer ambiguity to clear and precise answers. One thing that I have noticed in pursuing critical research into Jesus Christ is the use of a phrase that I feel only clouds the issue: Christian origins. The problem with the term is the plural "origins" as opposed to the singular "origin". The reader may or may not have noticed that I have deliberately refrained from using the plural form of this word as applied either to Christianity, or to the mystery of Jesus Christ. It may seem like a trivial point, but it's really not. It's important. Because the use of the plural implies a degree of uncertainty about any possible answer; it further implies multiple possible answers as holding equal merit. It seems to further imply that the precise origin of Christianity as a religion can never be known, and therefore all theories on the question have equal merit. But whether the answer is known or unknown, or even unknowable, the origin of Christianity is a singular question requiring a singular answer. The use of the phrase "Christian origins" unfortunately appears to be all but ubiquitous. I hope to change that. If my book does nothing else, it will still have served a worthy purpose. The problem is actually far more insidious than the casual reader is likely to fathom. By the use of the comparatively nebulous term "origins" instead of the more precise "origin", the actual origin of Christian belief in Christ's resurrection is obscured in a haze of multiple possible numbers of unknown answers, which all may hold equal merit, and this in turn creates, either deliberately or otherwise, an impression that the true answer is ultimately unknowable, and therefore all inquiry is ultimately futile. But whose interests does such a state of affairs serve? Does it not ultimately serve the interests of the fundamentalists, and more importantly, the economic industry that Christianity has become? Once again we can see that a genuine answer to the question of precisely how Christianity began is a gigantic threat to a vast economic superstructure and cultural infrastructure of Western society. Knowing this truth, of all truths, is the crucial key to unlocking the collective *psyche* of Western civilization. Is that an overstatement? Hardly. Christianity as a religion had only one origin. Even many of the critical scholars who sometimes appear on television shows discussing obscure topics like the Dead Sea Scrolls, the Nag Hammadi codices, or the Gospel of Judas are guilty of using the loose term "Christian origins" and often speaking in such ways as to imply a great diversity in early Christianity. While as discussed above, there was some diversity in early Christianity, ultimately the precise origin of Christianity had to have been quite singular. This is true even if we adopt the ahistorical paradigm. Then we would have to inquire into the precise origin of the New Testament texts. But we still have yet to more precisely frame our most important question.

The Paradox of Jesus Christos

The paradox of Jesus Christ is what we are seeking to unravel herein. But first we need to understand why there is a paradox, and what exactly is the paradox. In other words, before we can arrive at a clear answer, we first need to ask the right question. In fact, we may need to first ask a series of questions, before we arrive at the crucial key question of all, that must be answered. Briefly put, the paradox of Jesus Christ has to do with the resurrection of Jesus Christ. Or more precisely, with the belief in the resurrection of Jesus Christ. This is the most crucial and distinctive claim of Christianity as a religion. The claim is that Jesus Christ died on the cross and rose from the dead, and appeared alive again to his disciples. Fundamentalists will accept the claim as true in itself, and that is the end of all inquiry along those lines for them.[792] Whether or not one accepts the claim, the fact of the matter is that the claim itself has become an article of faith, or rather the chief article of faith, in the religion known as Christianity. Why? How? These are important questions. Crucial questions. Many questions could be asked about Jesus Christ, but what is the most important question we could ask about him? Was he the Son of God? Was he God the Son? Was he the Messiah? Was he a Levite? Was he an Ebionite? Was he a Zealot? Was he a myth? Was he

---

[792] Their proper line of inquiry being from that point the precise meaning of the Scriptures.

black? Was he a prophet? Was he a magician? Was he celibate? Was he crucified? Was he a mutant? Was he the founder of a Grail dynasty? Was he descended from King David? Was he ethnically Jewish? Was he a false prophet? Was he married? Was he a eunuch? Was he a hypnotist? Was he a Cynic philosopher? Did he take hallucinogenic mushrooms? Did he drink wine? Did he work miracles? Was he psychic? Was he bisexual? All these and many other questions are good questions, and make for interesting answers, depending upon whom you ask them. But what is the really big question? What is the most profound question we could ask about Jesus Christ? What is the most crucial question? What is the most important question?

In my former work[793] I presented evidence that Jesus may have lived one hundred years before the time commonly accepted. I devoted the work exclusively to presenting the evidence in favor of that thesis, and excluded other questions relevant to a more complete picture of the historical Jesus. I still believe that it is *possible* that Jesus may have lived a century earlier than commonly supposed; however even in my earlier book I admitted that my evidence did not constitute proof positive of my theory. Furthermore, it should be clear to the reader that comparatively speaking, this chronological question is far less significant than solving the paradox of Jesus Christ. It pales in comparison. Therefore I do not want to burden the present work with an insistence that my chronological theory was correct, or by a too-frequent reference to it herein. On the other hand, some readers may be disappointed that I do not write more about my chronological theory herein, but I feel that it is both unnecessary to do so, and that the current inquiry is surpassingly important by far. Neither do I cling tenaciously to my former theory, as if I feel it has been proven true without doubt. In fact I will even go so far as to admit that, while still a viable possibility, I am rather disinclined to countenance the theory as true. This is not a betrayal; no author should feel so bound by words written in previous works as to not be able to take a contrary position at a later time. Furthermore I would rather not allow for the current inquiry to be burdened by a necessary association with a theory that may be true or false.[794] I will have a little more to say of

---

[793] JESUS 100 B.C.

[794] In other words, my former work must either stand or fall on its own merits. So also likewise must the present work.

this further on. But first we need to reckon with how to determine and frame the most important question about Jesus Christ. I think it is fair to say that the very most important question we can ask about Jesus Christ is whether or not he actually rose from the dead. Did Jesus Christ rise from the dead? That is unequivocally the single most important question we can ask about Jesus Christ. We're on the same page as the fundamentalists and evangelicals about that, but as far as the answer goes, we're in a different book entirely. The answer, as far as I'm concerned, is an unequivocal NO. Jesus Christ did not rise from the dead.[795] If my answer to that question were YES instead of NO then I would be writing a much different kind of book.[796] But that is a different universe entirely.[797]

Now that we have identified and answered the single most important question about Jesus Christ, we can move on to the second most important question.[798] It is close to the first question, yet still distinct from it. The question is: How did the belief in the resurrection of Jesus Christ first arise? In other words, what was the precise origin of this belief? While the belief may be a false belief, the belief itself is a fact that must be reckoned with. There is really no more crucial question we could ask about Jesus Christ. This is the question we will attempt to answer in the remainder of this book.

---

[795] I.e., at least not in the way that most Christians believe. But as a simple answer we will simply say No, Jesus Christ did not rise from the dead.

[796] I.e., assuming I was writing a book at all.

[797] This is a rhetorical and metaphorical expression; it ought not to necessarily be construed as an endorsement of the Many Worlds interpretation of Quantum Mechanics.

[798] Once again I am struck by the irony of how a YES answer to the first question would also lead to a very different "second most important" question.

Six Theories: One Solution

I n answer to the crucial question of how belief in the resurrection of Christ originated, there are only six possible theories. This may perhaps be somewhat surprising to some people, but once the six theories have been presented, it should be clear to the reader that all possible bases have been covered; no other possible explanations remain. There may be a seventh class of theories, which I have termed *exotic,* but it should be clear that ultimately even these finally fall into one of the six previous theories, and furthermore these exotic theories are so highly improbable as to be virtually impossible.[799] Some critics may seek to combine two or more of the theories into a sort of *hybrid* theory, but once again, ultimately the six theories cover all possible circumstances, or rather the six possible answers to the question posed. I will at first briefly name and describe each of the six theories, and then I will present evidence in favor of each theory, and then I will discuss problems with each theory. Then, after we have some knowledge of the strengths and weaknesses of each theory, we will again start from scratch, as it were, to reevaluate the evidence; because the answer to our question must be found in one and only one of the six theories. So while each of the six theories *could* be true, only *one*

---

[799]   In fact it is not too much to say that they are even more highly improbable than Bible fundamentalism itself, and hence can safely be ruled out. They are included at all only for the sake of completeness.

theory actually *is* true. That means that the remaining five, however otherwise attractive they may be, are necessarily *false*. It also means that, despite whatever objections may be lodged against any one of the six theories, one of them *must* be *true*.

1. The resurrection theory.

Quite simply, the resurrection theory is the theory that Jesus Christ truly and miraculously rose from the dead, in exactly the sense in which the New Testament says that he did. One attractive feature of this theory is its sheer simplicity. One who accepts this theory as true no longer needs to look for any other explanation for a belief in Christ's resurrection. Furthermore it being a miraculous event, it is no longer subject to historical criteria for analysis or evaluation. Faith becomes its own justification, and any paranormal phenomena that occur outside the parameters of the belief-system are interpreted according to the rationale of the belief-system; namely, as being diabolical. So faith becomes a self-justifying form of orthodoxy, wherein all events and circumtances are interpreted in such a way as to reinforce and justify the belief-system. The necessary corollary to acceptance of Christ's resurrection as a historical fact is faith in the Bible as the Word of God.[800] But this becomes a very heavy burden to the honest, moral, intelligent seeker of truth. For as we will see, the Bible is very far from perfect, and in fact there are some very serious problems with the Bible; so much so, that an honest, moral, intelligent person seeking the truth cannot sustain belief in the divine inspiration of the Bible indefinitely. In fact, it is not too much to say that the Bible itself (ironically) disproves any miraculous resurrection of Jesus Christ. This is only due to the manifold and multitudinous imperfections of the Bible.[801] One further observation is in order before moving on:

---

[800] Without this corollary, faith in Christ's resurrection would be a completely anomalous belief, and could not be sustained by any rational person for long. Faith in Christ's resurrection requires the context of belief in the Divine origin and authority of the Bible.

[801] Lest I be misrepresented, I am not here in any way seeking to "trash" the Bible; I consider the Bible a great cultural treasure and I think people should read and study the Bible. Ignorance of the Bible is ignorance of Western culture, and hence of global culture. The problem lies in supposing that the Bible is the infallible Word of God.

the resurrection theory is the only theory that *requires* a belief in the supernatural. Each of the remaining five theories do not so require a belief in the supernatural, although they may allow for such a belief. But only the resurrection theory is logically contingent upon belief in the supernatural.[802]

2. The survival theory.

This is the theory that Jesus did not die on the cross; he survived, and later appeared alive again to his Apostles. These post-passion appearances by Christ to his disciples was the origin of the belief in his resurrection from the dead. One attractive feature of this theory is that it is so "close" to the resurrection theory, in strictly historical terms. It is merely the substitution of a natural interpretation of events for a supernatural interpretation. As such, it commends itself to rationalists. It is also fairly economical in the sense that, it seems to be a fairly straightforward reinterpretation of circumstances narrated in the Gospels, and therefore does not seem to require too many additional assumptions in order to be true. It is economical in the sense of being so seemingly "close" to the resurrection theory, that almost all the essential features of the Gospel narratives are allowed to be true. Therefore superficially it appears to be an eminently plausible theory. But the plausibility breaks down upon a diligent analysis. It should be kept in mind that there are several different versions, or possible versions, of this theory. We will discuss these in greater detail below.

3. The substitution theory.

This is the theory that Jesus Christ himself was never even crucified, but another man was crucified in his place. Perhaps this theory should be called the secret substitution theory, since the substitution had to have been done in secret, and must have remained a secret, for belief in Christ's resurrection to originate. Apparently, according to this theory, Jesus appeared alive again to his Apostles sometime after his alleged crucifixion, and since he allowed them to believe that he had been crucified and died and rose from the

---

[802] I.e., miraculous, magical, metaphysical, paranormal, extraordinary, numinous, transcendent, extramundane, paraphysical, extradimensional, phantastic, etc.

dead, then this was the origin of belief in Christ's resurrection.[803] This theory has some attractive features, but also some problems. It should perhaps be noted that both the survival theory[804] and the substitution theory can be supported by a literal reading of Suetonius' passage about Chrestus[805] being in Rome in the reign of Claudius. The substitution theory lacks some of the disadvantages of the survival theory, but it also has a number of unique problems. We have already briefly discussed some versions of the substitution theory, and we will discuss it in greater detail below. Most versions of the substitution theory do not require a belief in the supernatural, but the version found in the Islamic Gospel of Barnabas, discussed briefly above, does. Below I will present a version of the substitution theory I have not heard of or read about elsewhere.

4. The impersonation theory.

This theory is that after Jesus Christ died on the cross, another man impersonated him, and appeared to the Apostles after Christ's crucifixion, and somehow fooled them into believing that he was Christ risen from the dead. Obviously this theory has some serious problems, but it is included for the sake of completeness. I will discuss this theory in greater detail below.

5. The termination theory.

The termination theory is that Jesus Christ simply died on the cross. There was no miraculous resurrection, no survival, no substitution, no impersonation. This appears to be a very weak theory, since it does not provide for any post-passion appearances (or alleged appearances) of Jesus Christ, which presumably were the basis for the belief in Christ's resurrection. For a long time I considered this theory to be untenable. And stated in simple terms, and considered

---

[803] One possible variation on this theory is that Christ revealed the truth to his Apostles, but asked them to keep it secret; the other disciples (or later disciples) were told a tale of Christ's crucifixion, sacrificial death, and resurrection from the dead.

[804] Or secret survival theory.

[805] Chrestus being Christ according to this interpretation. Christ in Greek is *Christos*. The Latin form could be *Chrestus*.

in isolation from other qualifying information, it does not seem very plausible. But the termination theory lacks problems that are common to every other theory, and also problems that are unique to each other theory. We will discuss this theory in greater detail below.

6. The phantom theory.

According to this theory, also otherwise called the phantom Christ theory, or the ahistorical paradigm, or the mythicist paradigm, Jesus Christ never even existed as a historical person at all. He was merely a completely invented figure. One attractive feature of this theory is that it is no longer necessary to imaginatively "enter into" the minds of Jesus Christ and the Apostles, to try and discern what motivations they may have had for various actions or inactions they supposedly or allegedly did or did not do. But then it would be necessary to imaginatively "enter into" the minds of the men who wrote the New Testament texts, and try to discern exactly why they created such fictional characters as Jesus Christ and the Twelve Apostles, etc. For those unfamiliar with some of the evidence, the phantom theory may seem the most far-fetched and unlikely of theories; it almost appears to be a form of cultural apostasy to say that Jesus never lived as a historical person at all. But there are some strong arguments in favor of the phantom theory. Some very intelligent scholars have given credence to this theory. However this theory is not currently fashionable, particularly in academic circles. Therefore one is unlikely to see it discussed on one of the "educational" channels. This is too bad in a way, because I hate to crush an underdog theory. But I will in due season.

The Resurrection Theory

T he resurrection theory need not detain us for long; although the "simplest" theory in some respects, it also has the most unfortunate baggage attached, which makes the "theory" quite untenable.[806] However, I must admit that, under certain circumstances, the resurrection theory can seem to hold a high degree of realism, or rather surrealism, since I myself believed in Christ's resurrection for ten years of my life.[807] I was caught in a self-repeating loop until I was able to escape while my sanity was still intact. Belief in the miraculous resurrection of Jesus Christ from the dead requires a context and a corollary; namely, that the Bible is divinely inspired. As we will see, this is a complete deal-breaker. The multitudinous and manifold problems with the Bible prove by default that Jesus Christ could not have risen from the dead in the Christian sense. Evangelicals, fundamentalists, and born-again Christians try to reverse this process, by first obtruding a supposedly unanswerable paradox before the unsuspecting victim, and challenging him or her to solve the impossible paradox of Christ's alleged resurrection; the desired result

---

[806] The irony is appropriate, since most people who believe in Christ's resurrection do not hold it as a theory, but rather as an article of faith, which is never challenged.

[807] I plan to discuss my life as a born again Christian in a forthcoming work entitled *BORN AGAIN NIGHTMARE*. Don't miss it.

is that the person will acquiesce in frustration to the proclamation of Christ's literal, bodily, corporeal, carnal resurrection from the dead. All the while the person's emotions are being manipulated as well; tremendous emotional pressure is brought to bear upon the question, if not consciously, then subconsciously. I know this by direct experience. Those who are going through transitions in their lives, or are otherwise emotionally vulnerable, are easy prey for such manipulation, which is insidious. Thank God the resurrection of Christ is an impossible nightmare. Otherwise the vast majority of the human race would be facing annihilation or everlasting torment in the fires of hell. This is the wonderful "good news" these people would like to share with you. If instead they would take a few moments to critically examine their own beliefs, they would find those beliefs to be quite insane. Quite simply the resurrection theory is an impossibility. No other theory, no matter how improbable, has as many potential and legitimate objections against it. To embrace the resurrection theory is to reject both science and logic. It is an act of intellectual suicide. We will thoroughly refute this theory below.[808]

---

[808] While my refutation will be as comprehensive as possible, it will necessarily be greatly abbreviated, rather than exhaustive. A truly exhaustive treatment would require several large volumes.

The Survival Theory

The survival theory has a number of attractive features. Superficially it is probably the single most attractive theory of the six. It was the first theory I embraced in *lieu* of the resurrection theory, when I rejected the Bible in 1993. This is because I had discovered a book[809] in the Salem library that presented evidence in favor of a survival theory, and it seemed more realistic than continuing a dying faith in biblical fundamentalism. But I was soon exposed to a number of other theories, which also seemed to have some degree of merit. However, I always seemed to return to the survival theory as the strongest and soundest historical theory vis-à-vis Jesus Christ. To some degree, there may have been some emotional attachment to this theory, since I adopted it at a very transitional time of my life.[810] But when I applied a diligent critical scrutiny to the theory, I found that it was not nearly as strong as I had thought. I do not wish to be misunderstood: I still consider the survival theory to be a comparatively strong theory; one of the best and strongest of the six.[811] But it is not the strongest or the best theory. One thing that bothers me is that advocates of the theory do not deal adequately or honestly

---

[809]   *JESUS DIED IN KASHMIR,* by Andreas Faber-Kaiser.

[810]   I.e., when I rejected the Bible. Naturally this was a huge psychological transition for me.

[811]   And I am by no means suggesting that the survival theory is untenable.

with potential problems and challenges to the theory.[812] A potential problem with a given theory does not vanish simply because it is ignored. Are these men like overgrown schoolboys, merely trying to win an argument? Or are they trying to increase human knowledge? If the latter, then it behooves them to address any potential problems or objections against the theory they are advocating. And it also further behooves them to be completely honest about these potential objections, and the evidence they cite. Unfortunately, this is not always the case. What I find most lacking is any real comparison made between one theory and another, in any realistic or critical way.[813]

There are several possible variations on the survival theory. One early variation was called the swoon theory. According to this theory, Jesus did not die on the cross, but merely became unconscious, as in a swoon. He awoke out of this swoon in the burial cave, and somehow managed to push the large stone away, and then he appeared alive again to his Apostles. Thus was belief in Christ's resurrection born. While this is a completely naturalistic theory, it does seem highly improbable. However it is not impossible; and considered as the *only* alternative to the resurrection theory, it might seem more realistic. But of course it is not the only alternative to the resurrection theory, nor is it even the only version of the survival theory. Of course when Bible believers discuss the survival theory, they almost inevitably and invariably discuss the outmoded swoon theory, and by a few clever turns of phrase, they seek to make the whole thing seem so ridiculous as to be impossible.[814] But even the swoon theory, naked and without embellishment, is more believable than pure Bible fundamentalism.[815]

Another variation on the survival theory is that Jesus was helped by certain secret disciples, who helped him survive his passion, and nursed him back to health afterwards. After his recovery, Jesus appeared alive again to his Apostles, who knew nothing of these secret

---

[812] Of course this objection can be lodged against advocates of any of the six theories. Although hopefully I will be a happy exception to the rule with this book.

[813] Fundamentalists pretend to do this, while they are merely engaging in apologetics.

[814] However I must admit that I do not always make a point of keeping abreast of Christian apologetic literature, so maybe there are some things slightly more sophisticated than the arguments of a Josh McDowell, but I doubt it.

[815] I.e., with all that that entails. See below.

disciples or their plan to help Christ survive his ordeal, and so was faith in the resurrection of Jesus originated. Joseph of Arimathaea, who buried Christ in his own tomb, was called a "secret" disciple in the Gospel of John.[816] John's Gospel also says that Nicodemus, who came to Jesus secretly at night,[817] helped Joseph bury Jesus.[818] Nicodemus reportedly spoke in defense of Jesus at the *Sanhedrin,* of which he was a member.[819] Joseph of Arimathaea was also a member of the *Sanhedrin.*[820] Even if we assume that Joseph and Nicodemus both took Jesus down from the cross[821] and buried him, most likely they still would have needed the help of at least one or two younger, stronger men.[822] If so, it is at least *possible* that all four men were secret disciples of Jesus. It is at least *possible* that these men helped Jesus survive his passion. But how? According to Mark 15:23, Jesus was offered wine mingled with myrrh as he was led to crucifixion.[823] It is at least *possible* that this soporific potion was mixed with yet a more powerful soporific, which was able to make it appear as if Jesus had died on the cross. The Essenes had intimate knowledge of many substances and concoctions that could do the trick. If these secret disciples had any connection to the Essenes, or to any Essene-like group, or were themselves men with such knowledge, which they kept hidden, as they did their devotion to Jesus, then they could have administered such a potion to Jesus as he was led away to be crucified. While Mark's Gospel says that Jesus refused the soporific, Matthew says that he tasted it, but drank no more. So maybe Jesus drank just the right amount to be placed in a coma, or death-like trance, from which he could be revived, but not enough to become lethal. Maybe. Of course even if we assume such a scenario had been planned, there was no guarantee

---

[816] John 19:38.

[817] John 3:1.

[818] John 19:39–42.

[819] John 7:49–50.

[820] Mark 15:43; Luke 23:50 cp Matthew 27:57.

[821] Or tree. See my earlier work.

[822] Since Joseph and Nicodemus were both members of the Sanhedrin, they were probably at least middle-aged, if not somewhat elderly.

[823] In Matthew 27:34, this has been transformed into vinegar mingled with gall, no doubt to provide a gratuitous "fulfillment" of Psalm 69:21.

that it would work. But apparently it did work. So say the advocates of this version of the survival theory. Currently this version appears to be the most popular. It is a version adopted by Andreas Faber-Kaiser, Holger Kersten, Elmar Gruber, Abubakr Ben Ishmael Salahuddin, Fida Hassnain, and any number of others. This version of the survival theory has some strengths and weaknesses. In some ways it is stronger than the swoon theory, since it accounts more readily for how Jesus may have survived his physical trauma. We will discuss the weaknesses below.

A third possible permutation of the survival theory is that Jesus survived the crucifixion through the phenomenon of astral projection. Astral projection, otherwise known as the out-of-body experience, is an occult phenomenon of the paranormal. But enough people have experienced the out-of-body state to say that it is a genuine phenomenon, rather than a mere superstition or urban legend. It is a real phenomenon. Whether it is defined as natural or supernatural is merely a matter of semantics. Jesus may have been adept at astral projection, and thereby used this method to escape the terrible fate of death on the cross. In other words, according to this version of the survival theory, Jesus faked his own death on the cross by occult means. As surprising and astonishing as this is, it is not impossible; there are men in India called *fakirs,* who can have their flesh pierced, without bleeding at all. Other men, called *yogis,* can hold their breath and stop their heart for much longer than an average person. They can fake death. Not only this, but every year in the Philippines there are men who allow themselves to be crucified, to prove their devotion to God. Typically these men survive.[824] In fact, the first-century Jewish historian Josephus reports in his *Vita* that three men he knew were crucified, and he appealed to Titus on their behalf, and all three men were taken down alive from the crosses. Although two of the men subsequently died, a third man fully recovered.[825] So it is not altogether unthinkable that Jesus may have survived his crucifixion. This is especially the case if he was able to use the technique of astral projection to fake his own death, and afterwards return to his body. Astral projection may also have been the great secret that the Apostles

---

[824] Although as far as I know, in most cases these men are tied to the crosses, rather than nailed to them.

[825] See Jos. Vita. 75.

and other intimate disciples sought to protect at all costs. This provides the rationale for a dichotomy between esotericism and exotericism, as evident in misguided fundamentalism.[826] All three versions of the survival theory have a reasonable degree of probability and plausibility. Yet despite its positive features, the survival theory is neither the strongest nor the best theory. Each theory must be considered not only on its own merits, but also in relation to the other five possible theories. We must compare and contrast.

---

[826] In other words, fundamentalism is exotericism without the crucial key of esotericism.

The Substitution Theory

The substitution theory, as it is popularly expressed, is an incredibly weak theory, and hardly even deserves to be mentioned. But there is a version of the substitution theory that is so much better and stronger than any such popular theory as to be among the best and strongest of theories. It will take some time to detail this theory adequately. But first I would like to briefly recapitulate some of the other versions of the theory that we have already discussed, and a few others.

One of the most popular versions of the substitution theory is that Simon of Cyrene was crucified in place of Jesus. There is even a Gnostic codex that explicitly claims this. But we have briefly discussed the extreme improbability of such a thing above, and we have dismissed it without further ado. There is no need to rehash it here. Another version of the substitution theory is that found in the Islamic Gospel of Barnabas, which we also discussed above. As the reader may recall, the Gospel of Barnabas claimed that God sent four archangels to take Jesus away to Paradise, while Judas Iscariot was miraculously transformed to look exactly like Jesus, and so was crucified in his place. The whole story is unbelievable and without merit. It is tedious to relate or contemplate. Another abortive substitution theory is one in which a twin brother of Jesus is crucified in his place. This version of the substitution theory is taught by the Japanese Mahikari religion. While it is true that according to some apocryphal traditions, Jesus had a twin brother,[827] it is a bit much to expect a brother to make the ultimate sacrifice and give up his life to save that of his brother.[828] In fact the situation is far worse and improbable: we are not just talking about death, but the brutal death by crucifixion. This was one of the most brutal, horrible ways to die imaginable. And, since Jesus was a messianic pretender, he would no doubt have been subject to even more brutal and gratuitous cruelties at the hands of the Romans. This would have been realistically anticipated by any reasonably intelligent man, brother or no. And if we assume that Christ's brother was mentally challenged in some way, and yet his fraternal loyalty was heartlessly exploited by Christ in this way, this leaves us with an enormously cynical portrait of Christ that would put Nietzsche to shame.[829] Presumably, if this theory is countenanced, Jesus and his brother would have exchanged places in the Garden of Gethsemane, or before Christ's arrest in the Garden of Gethsemane. In terms of sheer physical mechanics this is at least more believable than Simon of Cyrene as Christ's substitute; but the psychological dimension, not to mention other variables, makes this version of the substitution scenario untenable.

First of all, we are told that Christ's brothers did not even believe in his messianic claims at the time.[830] Furthermore and more to the point, if Jesus had a twin brother, or even a younger brother who resembled him sufficiently to almost look like his twin, this fact could hardly have remained hidden to the Apostles for very long. Neither was it likely to remain hidden from very many people at all, assuming that Jesus was a celebrity in his own time. And assuming that this had been the case, would not Judas have feared the very sort of thing implied in this version of the substitution theory? Would not fear

---

[827] Judas Thomas, called *Didymus*. *Didymus* is Greek for "twin".

[828] In one bizarre twist on the theme, Jesus is crucified but Judas Thomas, his twin brother, takes his place afterwards, effectively impersonating him. But this would technically fall under the impersonation theory. So the six theories really cover all possible bases.

[829] I am not saying that Nietzsche portrayed Christ as a cynic; quite the contrary, in fact; but I mean that Nietzsche himself was consummately cynical in his outlook. See Nietzsche's *The Antichrist*.

[830] John 7:1-5. We discussed this passage briefly above. While it is *possible* that Judas may have been an exception, it is a weakness to a theory to require a reinterpretation.

of Roman "justice" have made him take special precautions not to become confused with his controversial brother? The problem with the theorists who advocate such theories is that they have not bothered to even think them through very far. If they did, they would see that there are some serious problems with such theories, and either attempt to explain them, or abandon the theory. If Judas had been substituted for his more famous brother in this most important way, ought not Christians to worship Judas as their Savior? After all, he would have been the one who died on the cross.[831] Of course if we accept this scenario, Jesus would have been the one who wrote the Epistle of Judas in the New Testament. It is not credible that Judas would willingly offer himself up as a sacrificial lamb, only to let his brother take all the credit and glory.[832]

Another alternative to the above scenarios is one in which the person crucified was a man who had already been expecting to be crucified anyway: Barabbas.[833] By contrast with the other substitution scenarios, this one seems reasonably plausible. In fact, I would say that, all things considered, this is among the best and strongest of the six theories. Barabbas was already in the custody of the Romans, and he was scheduled for crucifixion. We are told that Christ was crucified in place of Barabbas, but what if the reverse were true? What if it was Barabbas who was crucified, just as scheduled, while Christ was allowed to escape? And this with the connivance of Pilate, no less. Whatever objection a critic may bring against this version of the substitution theory, this version is still a trillion times more believable

---

831   Another spin on the theory is that Jesus impersonated his brother Judas after the passion. But then this leaves unanswered the question of how faith in Christ's resurrection first arose. It would have been too obvious if Jesus was never seen with his brother Judas after the crucifixion. It would not take a brain surgeon to figure it out.

832   I.e., in this world at least. But then again if Judas was a true believer, and he had experienced the out-of-body experience, it is just barely possible that he would relinquish earthly glory for heavenly glory. But once again the theory is strained, to say the least of it. Once again, whom would they be trying to fool? Judas Iscariot? But Judas Iscariot also would have known that Jesus had a twin brother, or a brother who resembled him sufficiently to be a twin or double. If such had been the case, would he not have taken precautions against being deceived? There are far too may problems with this scenario to make it plausible.

833   Jesus Barabbas, according to some manuscripts of Matthew 27:16-17.

than any other version yet proposed. This version of the substitution theory also has some advantages lacking in the survival theory. For example, it does not require any explanation for how Jesus might have survived his passion.[834]

The Barabbas substitution theory also has some considerable Scriptural support, too. For example, in Acts 3:13 it says that "Pilate was determined to release" Christ. The Greek word translated as "determined" is *krinantos,* and it implies that Pilate had already made up his mind to release Jesus. He certainly would have been disinclined to release Barabbas, who was a notorious insurrectionist, murderer, and robber.[835] While it is true that Pontius Pilate was not known for his mercy, if he had a choice between two prisoners, one of whom would be released, while the other would be crucified, which of the two men would he have been more inclined to release? A violent insurrectionist?[836] Or a meek pacifist, who says "My kingdom is not of this world"?[837] The question answers itself. Pilate would have decided to release Jesus as a harmless mystic, and hand Barabbas over to crucifixion. Of course some Jewish critics have carped that there was no such custom of releasing a prisoner on the Passover. But all four Gospels record the custom, and the fact that Barabbas was released, while Christ was crucified. The very fact that all four Gospels agree on this point, while often contradicting one another on so many other points, constitutes an overwhelmingly strong form of historical evidence in favor of the custom having been an actual custom, rather than a mere gratuitous fiction. The silence of Josephus and of the Mishnah is insufficient to outweigh the united testimony of all four Gospels on this point.[838] As far as I am concerned, the burden of proof lies on those who claim that there never was any such custom at Passover. It is eminently plausible that there indeed was such a custom, to placate the Jews, who were so frequently

---

[834] Which involved far more than "just" crucifixion, as brutal as that was.

[835] Mt 27:15-23; Mk 15:7-13; Lk 23:16-24; Jn 18:39-40; Acts 3:14.

[836] Who was probably also a Zealot, who sought to overthrow Roman rule in Judaea. As such, Barabbas may have been one of the notorious *Sikarii,* or dagger-wielding assassins.

[837] John 18:36.

[838] The apocryphal Gospel of Nicodemus also mentions the custom, and the release of Barabbas.

seditious against the Romans. It is unmitigated arrogance for some self-proclaimed "expert" to pontificate that there never was any such custom, merely on account of the silence of the Mishnah, or of Josephus, about such a custom. If the story occurred in only one Gospel, then it would be doubtful. If it was mentioned in two, it would be slightly less doubtful, but still somewhat doubtful. If it were omitted from only one of the four Canonical Gospels, then perhaps some slight degree of doubt might still be attached to it. But the fact that it is mentioned in all four New Testament Gospels eliminates virtually all doubt one could reasonably have about such an incident. Otherwise we would have to ask why the tale was so important as to be included in every Gospel? There is nothing miraculous in it, so there are no "philosophical" grounds for doubting it. Of course those critics who insist that the story is a lie cite it as an example of gratuitous anti-Semitism; because the people ask for a murderer to be delivered to them, while Jesus Christ is a victim of their bloodlust, this is supposed to be another example of ubiquitous anti-Semitism throughout the New Testament.[839] This is a notorious example of begging the question, special pleading, and a shameless exploitation of pseudo-political correctness to rewrite history.[840] One who reads my work should also note that my words are well chosen. If you do not read carefully, you may find that you think I wrote something that I did not in fact write. This is a clue to a qualifying statement that will occur later in the text. Then again it must be admitted that the fact that supposedly the people were crying out for the release of Barabbas instead of Christ is yet another unbelievable aspect to the Gospel narrative. If we assume that the incident occurred at all, then most likely, only some of the people were crying out for the release of Barabbas, while the remainder were pleading for the release of Christ. Another factor that also impinges upon this whole scenario is the distinct possibility that Christ was a militant messianic figure; possibly a Zealot. If so, then Pilate may have been no more inclined

---

[839] Even though the New Testament documents were ostensibly written by Jews about a Jewish Messiah who was the Jewish Son of the Jewish God.

[840] The reader should bear in mind that it would be far easier for me to just parrot the "party line" on this score. Know-nothing knee-jerk liberals will no doubt give me grief over this, but as far as I'm concerned they're a bunch of ignorant baboons. A historical inquiry of this nature is above such vain ephemeral politics.

to release Jesus than Barabbas. But this assumption about Christ is so far unproven, and remains pure speculation. But this version of the substitution theory potentially offers an explanation for why crowds of Jewish citizens would have been crying out for the crucifixion of a Jewish man, if we assume, for the sake of argument, that it was not the man we know as the "historical Jesus" that they were seeking to have crucified. Let's suppose instead that these people were actually crying out for Barabbas to be crucified. Why would they have done that? Was Barabbas [Jesus Barabbas, according to the Caesarean text of Matthew] not a noble Freedom Fighter? Yes; but he was also described as a "murderer" in some of the narrative Gospel texts. If Barabbas had killed a Roman soldier or citizen then there is not the least question of any possibility that he would have been set free: the Romans would eagerly have crucified him in a very merciless way. Crucifixion was regarded as "exemplary" punishment, especially for seditionists. But what if, instead of a Roman soldier or citizen, Barabbas had slain some Hebrew merchant or tax-collector, who had been considered a collaborationist to the Romans? While some, even perhaps many, of the Jewish citizens may have felt sympathy for Barabbas, what about the surviving relatives of the man that had been slain? Is is not rather likely that they would cry out for the man to be crucified by the Romans? Thus we can see that this version of the substitution theory answers at least one otherwise unanswered question about the Gospels. So this must also be taken into account, in terms of the probability of the theory in question.

But, one may argue, if Pilate had determined to release Christ, and to crucify Barabbas, then why did he not do so openly, in utter defiance of the Jews? This is a good question, and deserves at least some kind of answer. Although Pilate was often wanton, cruel, and implacable, there were still limits to how far he could reasonably go in his reckless wantonness. In fact he was recalled to Rome after a procuratorship of ten years. But efforts had been made to placate the Jews. The custom of releasing a prisoner at Passover, if we assume there was such a custom, would have been a prime example. Pilate may have played a charade in order to placate the Pharisees, whom he knew were jealous of Jesus; by doing so, he could have his cake and eat it too: he could preserve Jesus alive, while still killing Barabbas, all the while the Pharisees would be fooled into thinking that Pilate was doing their will. Of course the Pharisees probably also thought of Barabbas as a troublemaker, and also wanted him to be eliminated; but he, being a violent man, would likely have been arrested again at some later time, or he would die in battle with the Romans. But once Christ was in custody, this was their golden opportunity to have him eliminated. If they failed this time, they knew they might never get another chance. They knew that Jesus was clever, and also beloved by many of the common people. They could not afford to let him escape. Christ was dangerous to them because he undermined their authority in the eyes of the people. As such, he was probably a far greater threat in their eyes than Barabbas. So Pilate may have been motivated to concoct a scheme whereby Christ would escape the cruel fate of crucifixion, while the violent insurrectionist was crucified, just as scheduled. Of course he would require the complicity of Christ himself. If Christ was some suicidal maniac bent on violent martyrdom, then his death would have been inevitable. While this is possible, for the sake of argument we will stipulate that Christ was a rational human being who wanted to survive, rather than the contrary. And if anyone thinks that there was a moral dilemma for Jesus in this case, just consider that Barabbas was a violent murderer and thief, whom Christ very likely had little sympathy for. In fact, crucifixion, being a very slow death, would have given Barabbas ample opportunity to repent of his sins while he hung on the cross, and so be forgiven. So it could have been perhaps an act of mercy on Christ's behalf to allow Barabbas to die in such a way, rather than possibly being set free, only to die violently and quickly in some future battle with Roman soldiers, which would not afford him any opportunity to repent of his sins.

So what would have been the mechanics of such a scheme? If we assume that such may have been the case, how was it done? Does Scripture allow for such a scenario? After all, how could Pilate have expected to fool the Pharisees into thinking that the man handed over for crucifixion was Jesus, rather than Barabbas? Would they not have been able to clearly see that it was Barabbas, and not Christ? These are all good questions. And while the question of recognition is a potential challenge to this theory, it is far less of a problem than the idiotic assumption that somehow Simon of Cyrene had been crucified in place of Jesus. First of all, the Pharisees did not enter into the judgment hall.[841] But Jesus himself was in the *praetorium* together with Pilate.[842] None of the other Jews were present; none of the men who accused Jesus were in the same hall. This means that they could not see Jesus at that time. They could not keep their eyes on him constantly. This is a key point. Then there is recorded a conversation between Jesus and Pilate. If we assume that Pilate decided to release Jesus, as Acts 3:13 specifically states that he did, then while there was no guarantee that his scheme would work, he could still try it. We are told that Pilate had Jesus scourged, and then the Roman soldiers crowned him with thorns.[843] Jesus was also beaten. But what if it was not Jesus Christ, but Jesus Barabbas? Remember that some manuscripts of Matthew 27:16-17 tell us that Barabbas also shared the name *Jesus*. If so, and the Evangelists knew of the secret substitution,[844] then technically they would not have been *lying* when they wrote that "Jesus" had been mocked, spit on, beaten with a reed, whipped and crowned with thorns by the Roman soldiers. Notice that none of the evangelists ever say that "Christ" was so abused; they always use only the name "Jesus" in the passion narrative; the appellation *Christ* is conspicuous by its absence from the passion narrative.[845] After Jesus (Barabbas) had received such brutal treatment, he was very likely such a bloody mess that he could not be recognized at all. This was what Pilate was counting on, when he brought Barabbas forth to the Pharisees, saying "Behold the man!"[846] This was the moment of truth. If his plan failed, Pilate would know immediately. But apparently it worked. The Pharisees were fooled. Or if any of them weren't they went along with

---

[841] John 18:28. Judgment hall; *praitorion* in Greek.

[842] John 18:33.

[843] John 19:1-2; Matthew 27:26-29; Mark 15:15-19.

[844] Which is extremely doubtful, even if we assume that there *was* a secret substitution.

[845] The only notable exception being Mark 15:32, where the Pharisees mock Jesus on the cross, by saying "Let Christ the King of Israel descend now from the cross, that we may see and believe." But even this fits the pattern, since they had apparently been fooled by the ruse. The only other times when "Christ" occurs is before Pilate has pronounced judgment. The passion narrative proper excludes the appellation *Christ,* and uses *Jesus* exclusively.

[846] John 19:5.

the charade, for whatever reason. They immediately cried out for the man's crucifixion.[847] We are also told that the female disciples, and other acquaintances of Jesus, beheld the crucifixion from far away.[848] Only John's narrative differs in this detail, and on this account is more suspicious; in such a case of contradiction, it is safer to follow the majority reading. Furthermore it is possible that the incident related in John's text may have been written to dispel rumors that there had been a secret substitution.[849] The same exlanation could also apply to the incident narrated in Luke's Gospel where Jesus, as he is being led away to crucifixion, preaches to the daughters of Jerusalem.[850] But this is not the only possible explanation, as we will see shortly. Pilate may have offered safe conduct to Jesus back to Galilee under cover of darkness. So Jesus may have secretly traveled back to Galilee in disguise, accompanied by a contingent of Roman soldiers, at night, to avoid detection. Presumably Jesus would have made an agreement with Pilate not to stir up trouble in Galilee or Judaea ever again, lest he be dealt with summarily. So in terms of mechanics there is a certain degree of reasonable plausibility to such a scenario. Jesus returning to Galilee under cover of night would have afforded him opportunity to escape crucifixion. This is why Christ sent a messenger back to his Apostles telling them to meet him in a cave inside a mountain in Galilee.[851] It is notable that in Matthew 28:16 it says that the eleven disciples went "into a mountain" in Galilee; and in the original Greek, the word is *eis,*[852] which literally means "into", rather than *epi,* which means "upon"; this implies that it was actually a cave inside of a mountain, which actually makes sense, assuming that Jesus did not want to place his life in jeopardy once more.

---

[847] John 19:6.

[848] Mt 27:55-56; Mk 15:40-41; Lk 23:49 cp Jn 19:25-27.

[849] And this is eminently plausible, since John breathes not a word of Simon of Cyrene, who is mentioned in all three Synoptic Gospels; who was also rumored to have been killed in place of Jesus Christ. Therefore this incident may have been gratuitously added to the narrative in John's version of events, in an attempt to dispel such rumors.

[850] Luke 23:27-31.

[851] Matthew 28:5-17 cf Mark 16:7.

[852] Pronounced like "ice".

It is also interesting in regard to this substitution scenario that neither of the epistles of James or Judas[853] mention any sacrificial death of Christ, or even the passion or crucifixion of Christ. This implies that Christ confided his secret to them.[854] I dare say that this substitution scenario is infinitely more believable than any other ever postulated previously. I am not saying that the theory is without difficulties, but comparatively speaking, it is pretty strong. This version of the substitution theory also is not encumbered with some of the problems with the survival theory. For one thing, Jesus suffered an immense amount of physical trauma, and this would have significantly decreased his chances of survival. Advocates of the survival thesis are seldom honest about just how much physical abuse and trauma Jesus suffered, both before and during his crucifixion. For example, Elmar R. Gruber wrote that as far as the whiplashes were concerned, Jesus was not treated any differently from others. Everyone who was sentenced to death on the cross had to first endure such abuses, according to him.[855] Well aside from the fact that Mr. Gruber proceeds to speak of "Hebraic law", which is either a huge mistake, or a deliberate misrepresentation,[856] it may or may not have been the case that all men condemned to the notorious Roman crucifixion were first whipped, but there would have been no reason for all such men to have been crowned with thorns, for instance. This was no doubt a punishment meted out specifically to messianic pretenders. As such, it is unfair to compare the ordeal of Jesus with that of a common thief. So while it would not have been impossible for Christ to have survived his passion, it would not have been nearly as casual as typical advocates of the survival scenario portray it to be. So we have not the

---

[853] I.e., Judas the brother of James; not Judas Iscariot.

[854] Which he may have done if they were his brothers. Of course this is assuming that there was a secret substitution scenario. But the absence of any mention either of Christ's passion, or of the sacrificial nature of such, or even that Christ died as a martyr, is, at the very least, suspicious, if not evocative. As such those two epistles may be regarded as literary fossils.

[855] Kersten & Gruber., op. cit., pg. 245.

[856] An embarrassment in the first instance, and a crime against truth in the second. It was the Roman soldiers who whipped Jesus, not the Jews. The Romans had no restrictions on the number of lashes that could be meted out. So don't be led astray by Jesus Christ Superstar, as Mr. Gruber apparently was.

sheer improbability of surviving the ordeal of the passion to contend with here. A second problem ignored by advocates of the survival theory is that, assuming Christ survived his ordeal, presumably it should have been fairly obvious to his Apostles that *that* was exactly what happened. How could they suppose that Christ's survival of crucifixion was instead a miraculous resurrection from the dead? Could they have been so easily imposed upon? It is really more of an imposition to suggest that they were so incredibly gullible. But if Jesus appeared alive to them again, after they had thought that he had been crucified, literally without a scratch on his body, then this would have seemed like a miracle. In this connection it is worth consulting a verse from the Gospel of Luke: "And when he had spoken, he showed them his hands and feet."[857] Most people, when they read this verse, assume that it means that Christ showed the scars on his hands and feet; the imprints of the nail-wounds. But it is at least *possible* that instead the verse meant that Christ literally had not a scratch on his hands or feet, which would have seemed miraculous; by contrast, nail-wounds would imply mere survival, rather than a miraculous resurrection.[858] Of course if we assume that Jesus survived his crucifixion, he may have confided this to his Apostles, but required them to keep this a secret from thenceforth.[859] So likewise assuming that there had been a secret substitution, whereby Christ escaped crucifixion, it is at least possible that he may have confided this secret to his Apostles, or to

---

[857]   Luke 24:40.

[858]   We should keep in mind the fact that, in all probability, the Gospel of Luke was written before the Gospel of John; therefore the contrary passage in John, where Jesus shows his nail-wounds to Thomas, ought not to be "read back" into Luke's text, by a process of *eisegesis*. The precise meaning of Luke's text is more ambiguous, and could be interpreted either way. Furthermore John's mention of the nail-wounds, which mention is absent in the other three Gospels, may have been a gratuitous invention on John's part, to discountenance a substitution scenario, as envisioned herein. This explanation would also be in harmony with other aspects of John's Gospel, where avoidance of a substitution theory seems to be the implicit rationale for otherwise contradictory material.

[859]   In which case faith in Christ's resurrection from the dead was not based upon Christ's visitation to the Apostles, but rather to an inherent esotericism whereby the truth of Christ's survival of the passion was overlaid with an exoteric myth of bodily resurrection. This is at least possible. But I do not consider it the best theory.

some of them, or to his brothers, or to some small circle of secret disciples. If so, then in this case too the story of Christ's resurrection was more of a parable, disguising the literal truth of Christ's escape from the fate of the cross.

But while this simple version of the substitution theory is viable, there is another that is perhaps more interesting in some respects. We have already noted several times that Barabbas shared the name Jesus, according to some manuscripts of Matthew's Gospel. What if Jesus Barabbas was not just a man with the same name as Christ, but also another messianic pretender? Surprisingly enough, this supposition accounts for some strange characteristics of some of the books of the New Testament. For example, the character of the sayings attributed to Jesus in the Gospel of John are much different than those ascribed to him in the Synoptics. In fact, the doctrine of salvation presented in John is diametrically opposed to that found in the three Synoptic Gospels. In the former, Jesus claims that whoever merely believes in him will have eternal life in heaven. In the latter, Jesus insists upon obedience to the commandments for salvation. Why? Of course one obvious explanation is that the Gospel of John, postdating the Synoptics, incorporates a sectarian dogma of salvation that is an innovation. But what if the real reason is that John's Gospel records the sayings, not of Jesus Christ, but of Jesus Barabbas? The name Barabbas in Syriac is Bar-Abbas, which means "Son of the Father". In the Gospel of John, Jesus refers to God as his Father no less than 113 times. By contrast, in all three Synoptic Gospels, Christ refers to God as his Father only 62 times.[860] Not only that, but the Gospel of John does not contain any pacifist teachings by Jesus, as are found in Luke and Matthew. So it is just barely possible that the words ascribed to Jesus in John's Gospel are the words of a rival Messiah, namely Jesus Bar-Abbas. Of course this presupposes that there were also two rival messianic movements at the same time, each following a Messiah named Jesus. This might seem too improbable to be realistic, but not if the name Jesus was a messianic name, which it may have been. Aside from this is the fact that Jesus was probably a sufficiently common name that it would not necessarily have been too unlikely for two different messianic pretenders to both share that name in common. The book of Hebrews seems to have been written by a devotee of

---

[860]   43 times in Matthew, 5 times in Mark, and 14 times in Luke.

Jesus Barabbas, rather than a disciple of Jesus Christ.[861] Add to this the strange fact that the Epistles of Judas [Jude] and James do not mention a word about Christ's passion, crucifixion, martyrdom, or supposed sacrificial death, and these add up to further evidence in favor of this interpretation. Furthermore, the passage from Suetonius about Chrestus in Rome is also congenial to both a substitution and survival scenario. I am constrained from fleshing out this substitution theory any further, but hopefully I have not only offered delicious food for thought, but have offered what is undoubtedly the most realistic version of the substitution theory.[862] I will discuss the fatal flaws in this theory below. However, before closing this chapter, I feel that in fairness I must offer some supplemental evidence in favor of this particular substitution theory, which I have more recently discovered inadvertently.

Since I wrote the first edition of my manuscript, a book has been published, that breathes new life into the substitution theory presented above, albeit inadvertently. The very fact that this was unintentional on the part of the co-authors only strengthens, in terms of evidence, the value of the evidence. The book is entitled *THE LOST GOSPEL,* and it was co-written by Simcha Jacobivici and Barrie Wilson.[863]

I want to be very clear that the two co-authors in question were not explicitly advocating any kind of substitution theory in their book. Their book is very interesting and significant, however, and ought to be read and studied. The general thesis of their book is that the text otherwise known as *Joseph & Asenath* is really a coded Gospel

---

[861] I.e., the first twelve chapters. The thirteenth chapter seems to be an interpolation, written to make it appear as if Paul had written it or dictated it to Timothy in Rome. But the body of Hebrews speaks at length of the high priesthood of Jesus, which is spoken of nowhere else. It also focuses at length on the sacrificial death of Jesus on the cross. As such, it is more in accord with what actually happened to Jesus Bar-Abbas, assuming the substitution scenario speculated upon herein actually took place. Furthermore the appellation "Christ" only occurs twelve or thirteen times in the book of Hebrews, which is far less frequently than found elsewhere in the Pauline corpus.

[862] I.e., with or without the additional assumption of Jesus Barabbas as a rival Messiah.

[863] Jacobivici, Simcha, and Barrie Wilson., THE LOST GOSPEL. © 2014 Simcha Jocobivici & Barrie Wilson. Pegasus Books LLC. 80 Broad Street 5th Floor New York, NY 10004.

text, telling of a marriage between Jesus and Mary the Magdalene. The *Joseph & Aseneth* story had been known and is generally included in collections of the Old Testament Pseudepigrapha. What a non-specialist may not realise, however, is that any number of texts included in the Old Testament Pseudepigrapha may actually be Christian in origin, and many are Jeiwsh texts that have been re-edited by Christians. As such, the Old Testament Pseudepigrapha ought not to be confused with the Old Testament proper, or the books of *TaNaKh*. Be that as it may, the authors present circumstantial evidence that Jesus may have been allied with Sejanus, who had imperial ambitions, and very likely was planning to assassinate Tiberius, the Roman emperor at the time. They also point out that both Pontius Pilate and Herod Antipas were politically allied with Sejanus, while Joseph Caiaphas was loyal to Tiberius.[864] Although Simcha Jacobivici and Barrie Wilson both accept the crucifixion of Jesus as a historical fact, the very fact that such behind-the scenes political alliances were (probably) in place makes it at least sllightly more probable that Jesus could have arrived at an "understanding" with Pilate, whereby, both men being loyal to Sejanus, there could have been a secret agreement whereby the two men could assist one another in a new political order. Perhaps Pilate was bribed with a "king's ransom" in gold, silver and jewels. Jesus did have some wealthy disciples, after all. Or maybe Jesus healed Pilate or his wife or mistress or servant or lover.[865] As such, it is at least somewhat more probable that there may have thus been a secret substitution scenario. This is at least worth considering, and weighing in terms of comparative evidence.

---

[864] Ibid., pgs. 238-277.

[865] i.e., assuming Jesus had some such healing ability, however paranormal.

The Impersonation Theory

The impersonation theory is that, after Jesus died on the cross and was buried, another man impersonated him and claimed to be Jesus risen from the dead. Presumably a man impersonating Jesus Christ must have strongly resembled him. But it would be more than a trifle absurd to suppose that Judas impersonated his brother after his untimely death on the cross. If Judas either was a twin, or a younger brother who bore such a striking resemblance to Christ as to be virtually a double or "twin", then this fact would have been fairly common knowledge to all the people who knew Christ, and would have precluded such a charade. Of course the impersonation theory is extremely and incredibly improbable and is really only included for the sake of completeness. But I will do my best to present evidence in favor of the theory nevertheless. Surprisingly each one of the four Gospels does provide some slight evidence, however weak, in favor of the impersonation theory.

First of all, in the Gospel of Matthew, we read that when the eleven remaining Apostles went to the mountain designated beforehand by Jesus, and saw him, they worshipped him, but they doubted.[866] This verse is mistranslated in the King James Version as "some doubted". But in the original Greek it simply says "they

---

[866]   Matthew 28:17.

doubted" meaning all of them.[867] Some Christians might prefer to think that this is a reference to earlier times of doubt, such as are narrated in other Gospels, but there is nothing in the text to indicate this; such an interpretation is completely unwarranted. Why would the Apostles doubt when they saw Jesus before their very own eyes? If they knew him, they knew what he looked like, having spent at least a year of their lives in intimate acquaintance with him. So, unless this was another man impersonating Jesus, perhaps in disguise, why would they doubt? Advocates of a survival or substitution theory could argue that it was Jesus himself, but he was in disguise, lest he be arrested again. But it is also at least *possible* to interpret the evidence as implying that another man completely was now pretending to be Jesus risen from the dead.

The Gospel of Mark reports that Jesus had appeared in "another form" to two of the disciples.[868] Could this not once again imply that another man was masquerading as Jesus, risen from the dead? It is at least *possible,* however highly *improbable.* Once again the explanation of a disguise on the part of Jesus could be used by advocates of a substitution or survival scenario. The same incident is narrated in more detail in Luke's Gospel.[869] Once again Jesus is not recognized by men who should have known him. Why? Unless it was another man impersonating him? Once again Jesus being in disguise is an equally if not more likely explanation.[870] Even in the Gospel of John, Jesus is not recognized by some of the Apostles, when he supposedly appeared to them on the shore as they were fishing.[871] Peter doesn't recognize Jesus at all, and has to be told by John that the man speaking to them from the shore was Jesus. Is this not incredibly strange? Unless we suppose that another man was now impersonating Jesus, pretending to be risen from the dead.[872] We are told that "None of the disciples dared ask him, Who are you? Knowing it was the Lord." But if

---

[867]   Nestle-Aland., op. cit., pg. 87.

[868]   Mark 16:12.

[869]   Luke 24:13–32.

[870]   But this would require either a survival or substitution scenario; the impersonation scenario does not have some of the fatal weaknesses of these two theories.

[871]   John 21.

[872]   Or that Christ was in disguise.

they "knew" it was the Lord, why would the thought even occur to them to ask the man who he was? Unless indeed he was another man impersonating Jesus.[873] Once again Christ being in disguise is a convenient explanation that springs to the minds and lips of advocates of the survival and substitution theories. But it should also be borne in mind that the passage in Suetonius about Chrestus in Rome is also congenial to the impersonation theory. The sheer improbability of the impersonation theory is probably enough to keep most people from taking it seriously. Nevertheless I will discuss problems with the impersonation theory below.

---

[873] Of course the impersonation scenario also implies a more elaborate scenario, in which the impersonator (with or without help from accomplices, for unknown reasons) removed the body of Jesus from his original tomb, and secretly buried it elsewhere, in an unknown location. But what possible motives this man (or men) could have had seem unfathomable.

The Termination Theory

The termination theory is that Jesus died on the cross. There was no miraculous resurrection, no survival, no substitution, no impersonation. The chief weakness of this theory is that there were no post-passion appearances of Christ to his disciples to provide a historical basis for the belief in Christ's resurrection from the dead. Therefore superficially this theory may seem to be the weakest of the six theories. I must admit that, without a great amount of explanation and qualification, this theory appears to be all but untenable. For a long time I did consider the theory to be untenable. But after reconsidering it from a number of different perspectives, and also by comparing it with the other possible theories, and weighing the various probabilities, considering the various strengths and weaknesses of all the theories, I finally came to the conclusion that this theory must be the true one. I only ask the reader to be fair and try to suspend judgment on this question until he or she has read the entirety of my book. If they come to a different conclusion, then so be it. Everyone is entitled to their own conclusions, convictions, beliefs, opinions, and interpretations. But I hope that my book will plant a seed within the minds of those who read it. I would also crave the reader's indulgence for any lack of erudition on my part. Superficially both the termination and impersonation theories appear to be very weak, and virtually untenable. But once again I would remind the reader that each theory must be considered, not merely in isolation, upon its own merits or lack thereof; but also and more importantly in relation to the other five theories. It is important to be honest about both the strengths and weaknesses of all the theories. And we must also bear in mind that one of the theories must be true. The remaining five must therefore all be false. While we may not achieve unalloyed certainty in this matter, we nevertheless may attain a level of reasonable conviction. Whatever the truth is, it must stand up to scrutiny. But there is also another lesson in this: truth may not always seem to be truth, even though it is. And falsehood may seem to be truth, even though it is not. Truth is not a matter of opinion. It is what it is, regardless of anyone's opinion to the contrary. You cannot vote on the truth. Truth is not a matter of popularity. At one time most of the people in Europe thought that the Sun revolved around the Earth. They were wrong. Truth is what it is, despite any opinions to the contrary. There is nothing that can take the place of truth. Truth is truth, whether known or unknown, spoken or unspoken, written or unwritten, concealed or revealed. One other variation on the termination theory is that possibly Jesus *did* appear to his Apostles after his passion, but it was in his astral body or his etheric body. This would at least provide a supernatural/preternatural basis for the Christian religion, but without the baggage of biblical fundamentalism.

The Phantom Theory

T he phantom theory is that Jesus Christ never existed as a historical
person. While the uninformed may ignorantly suppose that
this is a weak theory, it is actually one of the strongest theories, all
things considered. It has certain attractive features. For example, one
is freed from having to speculate upon possible motives of Jesus and
any secret disciples, Apostles, etc. One no longer has to account for
any number of things that need explanation if the historicity of Jesus
is assumed. Then the mystery of Jesus Christ becomes the mystery of
the New Testament texts. In other words, the key question becomes,
Who wrote those texts? And why? Because at bottom this is the one
thing that cannot be denied. In fact, the one and only thing that
can be affirmed of the New Testament documents is the mere fact
that they exist. Somebody had to have written them. Whether those
documents can be more easily accounted for without an assumption
of a historical Jesus or not is another question entirely. I suppose
if one returns an affirmative answer to that query then one is by
default endorsing the phantom Christ theory. The phantom theory
is probably the fifth or sixth theory I encountered, and I believed in
it for a long time. Then after a while I questioned it, and I vacillated
between the historical and ahistorical paradigms for quite some time,
until there was supposedly a discovery that at the time I thought had
settled the issue. I am referring to the now-infamous "James ossuary"
which had been obtruded to the public as the genuine ossuary of James

the brother of Jesus. I was so desperate for a definite answer to my dilemma of whether Jesus existed as a historical person or not that I hastily accepted this evidence as genuine proof that Jesus definitely had been historical.[874] But I had reacted too soon. As it turned out, it was later proven by Israeli experts that the latter portion of the inscription was a recent forgery. This forced me to rethink the question of Christ's historicity. I tried to reevaluate the evidence with an open mind, but in the meantime I had already begun to notice some of the fossil passages in the Gospels and other portions of the New Testament, and I felt that these constituted fairly strong evidence in favor of the historicity of Jesus. Once again, however, the paradox of Jesus Christ must be approached holistically. It is not wise to base a decision about this on only partial evidence; all the relevant evidence must be considered in detail.

Advocates of the ahistorical paradigm could readily point out that, all things considered, it would have been no worse of a lie, morally speaking, to completely fabricate the figure of Jesus Christ, than to ascribe miracles to a person who had never performed miracles. And not only that, but it could also be further argued that, since such incredible miracles are attributed to Christ in the Gospels, it would really have been no "bigger" of a lie to have completely invented such a miracle-working figure, than to attribute such wonders to an actual, historical man, who was otherwise a comparative nonentity.[875] But we know that in some cases at least, men who were actual historical persons were credited with miracles.[876] On the other hand it could be argued that cultural prejudice makes us myopic in the case of Jesus Christ; we tend to assume that Jesus was at least historical, rather than a myth, whereas most people in Western society today would think

---

[874] Since if James the brother of Jesus had been historical, then of necessity so was Jesus.

[875] This latter judgment is based upon the silence of Philo Judaeus, the (assumed) silence of Josephus, and the almost complete silence of Suetonius. Suetonius did not attribute miracles to Chrestus, nor did he even say that any of the Jews thought or claimed that Chrestus had performed miracles.

[876] We have seen the example of the Emperor Vespasian from Suetonius. Others include Pythagoras, Alexander the Great, Apollonius of Tyana, Siddartha Gautama (Buddha), Padmasambhava, Simon Magus, Rasputin, and many others.

of Hercules[877] as a myth. Most people in postmodern society would also doubt the onetime existence of Bacchus, Dionysus, Hermes, Aesculapius, Apollo, Circe, Aphrodite, Athena, Minerva, Isis, Osiris, Horus, Cybele, Krishna, Yama, and many other Gods, Goddesses, Heroes, and legendary figures of "foreign" cultures.[878]

Above we spoke briefly of Jesus Christ as a "Greek" Messiah. We briefly discussed the fact that there was a transcultural *mythos* of a dying and rising savior common to many cultures of antiquity. We have no reason to suppose that the Israelites themselves would have been immune from such a seemingly ubiquitous *mythos*. Indeed, the messianic strain within *TaNaKh* could be readily interpreted as just such a cultural expression of this *mythos* within Judaism. We cited Genesis 3:15 as the only indisputable example of a Messianic passage within the *Torah* proper.[879] Even if we take an extremely conservative view, and accept that Abishua wrote the Torah Scroll held by the Samaritans, it is still reasonable to assume a congruity with the transcultural messianic *mythos* adopted by the peoples of the ancient Levant, even at such an early time. And a more critical approach to the *Torah* makes the assumption that much more congenial.

But as noted before, some Rabbis may have had reservations about the development of the Messianic theme within Judaism, seeing therein the danger of creeping idolatry. This may be one reason why the *Mishnah* and *Gemara* generally focus much more diligently on the *Torah* proper, rather than the other portions of *TaNaKh*. We can also see somewhat of a dichotomy in this regard between the books of Enoch and Jubilees; the latter work being entirely devoid of any Messianic content, while the former work abounds with it. The Essenes and the Sadducees appear to have represented the two extreme positions in respect to Messianisim; the Pharisees striking a balance between the two.

---

[877] *Herakles* in Greek.

[878] But are they really foreign? Are we not all one huge melting-pot? They are the legends of our ancestors. And in the cases of Krishna and Yama, faith in their historical existence has remained unbroken among some for untold millennia.

[879] With the additional observation that both *Nehevim* and *Kethuvim* contained a considerable amount of Messianic content. Deuteronomy 18:55-22 appears not to have originally been a strictly Messianic passage, although it became interpreted as such in postexilic times.

There are a number of books available advocating the mythicist position vis-à-vis Jesus Christ. These may be of varying merit. I have read quite a few. There are also some books that, while not openly advocating an ahistorical paradigm vis-à-vis Jesus Christ, nevertheless present information that is at least congenial to that position. One of these is *THE SIRIUS MYSTERY,* by Robert K.G. Temple.[880] I say this because Mr. Temple discusses traditions of an African tribe known as the Dogon, who claim that in ancient times they were visited by a visitor from another planet, called the Nommo, who was crucified on a tree, dying and being resurrected.[881] Nommo even becomes a Eucharistic meal for the Dogon.[882] The Dogon also speak of Ogo, a figure akin to the Lucifer/Satan of the Bible.[883] I find the analogies fascinating particularly considering the allegedly extraterrestrial context of the beliefs. Predictably, however, most advocates of the phantom theory neglect Temple's research; perhaps it is too controversial and they fear that it would detract from their credibility. But how can we ever expect to arrive at the truth if we are not willing to explore such strange mysteries? One reason I find this particular version of the *mythos* so fascinating is that I suspect that it may be the original form of the *mythos.* The deeper implications are the very real but disturbing[884] possibility that said *mythos* is of extraterrestrial origin. Of course this opens up a huge can of worms that may be most unpalatable to academic orthodoxy. I can only imagine. Possibly there is a more prosaic explanation for the origin of the Dogon traditions, but the search for such a prosaic explanation appears elusive and challenging as of yet, since the Dogon also have some highly specific astronomical knowledge of the Sirius star system.[885] But this information must be kept in mind to qualify statements to be made

---

[880]   Temple, Robert K.G., *THE SIRIUS MYSTERY.* (© 1976 Robert K.G. Temple);

Destiny Books One Park Street Rochester, Vermont 05767. ISBN 0-89281-163-3.

http://www.innertraditions.com.

[881]   Ibid., pg. 32. (pg. 76 in the 1998 edition).

[882]   Ibid.

[883]   Ibid.

[884]   To some.

[885]   Temple., op. cit.

hereafter. I am not gratuitously offering this information in order to boggle the mind of the reader, but because in this instance, the information seems relevant to the question at hand.

Another book of some interest in relation to the phantom theory is *The Great Secret,* by Eliphas Levi. Although not written specifically to debunk or refute the historicity of Jesus Christ, nevertheless Levi does cite an example suggestive of the ahistorical hypothesis; he points out that the story of the slaughter of the boys of Bethlehem is almost identical to a similar tale told of the boyhood of Krishna, whom the jealous King Kansa sought to slay. Of course Krishna miraculously escaped. But of course advocates of the phantom theory could point to this as just one more example, among many others, of parallels between the story told of Christ, and of many other such Savior-Gods of antiquity.

Another valuable book along these lines is *THE WORSHIP OF AUGUSTUS CAESAR,* by Alexander Del Mar.[886] This book gives a huge number of examples of all kinds of highly specific parallels between Jesus and Mary on the one hand, and other similar figures found in many ancient cultures, on the other. While this book seems to be comparatively neglected in contemporary books advocating the mythicist position vis-à-vis Jesus Christ, it would certainly be a goldmine of information for those who advocate this position. In fact, some of what Mr. Del Mar points out even inadvertently answers some possible objections against popular versions of the phantom theory. For example, most mythicists draw a parallel between Christ and Mithras, since both Deities allegedly have December 25th as their birthday. But in the case of Christ, this is not true, strictly speaking. On this point the mythicists have not done their homework. In the Gospel of Luke, based upon the information given about precisely when Jesus was born, in relation to John the Baptist, we can be reasonably certain that, according to that text, Jesus was born, not in December, but approximately three months earlier. This is an obscure but potentially important point. Zechariah, the father of John the Baptist, was said to be of the priestly course of Abijah.[887] We learn from first Chronicles 24 that the course of Abijah was the eighth course, out of twenty-four priestly courses for the year.[888] Twenty-four priestly courses for the year makes each

---

[886] Del Mar., op. cit.

[887] Luke 1:5.

[888] 1 Chronicles 24:10.

course approximately two weeks long. The Israelite calendar began in the spring; Passover being celebrated on the fourteenth day of the first month of the ancient Israelite calendar.[889] Jesus was born approximately six months after John the Baptist.[890] After Zechariah returned from his priestly course, it would have been approximately the middle of the summer; presumably John was born about nine months later, sometime in the following spring; this means that Jesus had to have been born, according to Luke's text, sometime in the autumn. Certainly much earlier than December 25th. So if a person were basing the argument entirely on the coincidence of the "same" birthday attributed to both Mithras and Jesus, a more diligent study of Scripture would dispel any such notion. However, (and this shows the potential value of Del Mar's work), from Mr. Del Mar's book we learn that not all of the Savior-Gods were supposedly born on December 25th.[891] The following two passages from his work dispel any such notion:

"B.C. 1406, Assyria.-Incarnation of Nin-Ies, or Ninus, probably invented during the eighth to fifth century B.C. See B.C. 2064. Ninus was foretold by prophets; his celestial father was Ies; his putative father was Belus of the royal line of Ies; his virgin mother was Semiramis, although Rev. Alex. Hislop says her name was Rhaah, or Rhea, the Gazing Mother; his star was the Messianic; he was born at the Vernal equinox amidst flowers and the sounds of heavenly music; he was recognised as the Messiah by the seers or astrologers; his head was surrounded by a nimbus of light; he performed numerous miracles; his favorite disciple, of whom he had ten, afterwards 12, was Argon or Arjon; and after saving the world from sin he was persecuted and crucified to death at Babylon on the winter solstice; descended to hell; rose again after three days and nights; and finally ascended bodily to heaven. His principal sacrament was baptism, his epigraphic symbols were the + and {cross} and his zodion was the Lamb."[892]

"B.C. 1390, Assyria.-Incarnation of Belus, or Bel-Issus. (See above, years 2235-2064). A small stone cylinder in the British Museum is ascribed to Budi-ela, "king of Assyria," and is dated by the Museum authorities "B.C. 1350." All the dates connected with the worship

---

[889] Exodus 12:1-20.

[890] Luke 1:26ff.

[891] Or the winter Solstice. But many of them supposedly were.

[892] Del Mar., op. cit., pg. 84.

of Belus are anachronical. The cult of Belus is probably not older than the 12th century, B.C. This messiah was variously called Belus, Bel, Bel-Esus, Bala, and Baal. His coming was foretold in the sacred books of Chaldea. The name of his celestial father is given by the Greek writers as Jasus, or else Acrisius. His putative father was Ies; his virgin mother was Semiramis, or Astarte. His birthplace, in Baalbec, was indicated by the Messianic star which stood over it. He was born on the vernal equinox (the festival of Beltane) to the accompaniment of flowers and heavenly music. He was recognized as the Expected One by the astrologers, (belephantes). Accompanied by his faithful disciple, Oannes, one of ten, he performed many miracles, which were recorded in the now lost sacred scriptures of his native country. For preaching strange doctrines he was crucified in his 33rd year, on the winter solstice; descended to hell; whence he rose again and ascended bodily to heaven. His principal sacrament was baptism, both by water and fire; his epigraphic symbol, the cross, which appears on numerous Assyrian and Chaldean cylinders; and his zodions were the Bull and Ram (belier)."[893]

So we can see from the two example given above that not all Savior-Gods were born on the winter solstice; some were born on the vernal equinox. The solstices and equinoxes were important points on the messianic calendars, however. But if Jesus was reputedly born on the autumn equinox then it would also fit into the same messianic pattern, at least in a general sense. So even the more precise dating of Christ's birth according to Luke's Gospel does not automatically refute an association with the ubiquitous messianic *mythos*. This comparatively obscure point has not been covered by contemporary expositors of the phantom Christ theory, however. But from the many clear parallels between what is said of Ninus, Bel, and Jesus Christ, a reasonably strong case could be made that Christ must be equally mythical. One will also find that, according to Mr. Del Mar's research, oftentimes even trivial details of Christ's life are duplicated in some of the legendary accounts of earlier Savior-Gods, and there also notable parallels with Mary the mother of Christ:

"B.C. 1332, India.-Approximate aera of Maryamma, wife of Jamadagni, a village carpenter, and the virgin mother of Ies Chrishna, the ninth incarnation of Iesnu, or Vishnu. The name of this divinity is written Maryamma by Oppert and Mariatala by Noel. The latter

---

[893]   Ibid., pgs. 86-87.

regards her as the mother of Parasurama; the former as the sister of Ies Chrishna. Oppert explains that amma means mother; hence Maryamma means Mother Mary. She is also called Gana-gamma, or Ganga-gamma, Mother of God, and has many other names."[894]

Even the devotional imagery is often parallel to that found in some forms of Christendom:

"At these festivals Maryamma is carried about on a gorgeous car with the same pomp as are the stutues of Vishnu and Iesora, the latter being the god with the Bleeding Heart."[895]

"Mr. Fawcett's account includes the significant circumstance that the services at the annual festival to Maryamma have to be conducted by a carpenter."[896]

Mr. Del Mar admits that, according to some authorities, Jamadagni, the husband of Maryamma and foster-father of Krishna, he was a shepherd; while according to others, he was a carpenter.[897] But even in this respect we have a near-parallel in the instance of the shepherds of Bethlehem, spoken of in Luke 2:1-18. There is also another interesting passage that speaks of the theme of a carpenter's "son", who is really born of a virgin mother:

"B.C. 63, India.-Aera of Salivahana, or Vicramaditya, the reincarnation of Ies Chrishna; these deities being evidently one. [sic] Col. Wilford (Asiat. Res. vol. IX) says that: "In general the Hindus know but one Vicramaditya, but the learned acknowledge four; and when at my request they produced written authorities, I was greatly surprised to find no less than eight or nine.... Every Vicramaditya is made to wage war against an antagonist called Salivahana, Salavan, and often denominated Nrishina, Nagendra, etc., except one, whose name was Maha-Bat, and that of his followers Mahabhatadicas, that is to say Mahomet and the Mahometans." Vicramaditya was granted sway over the entire world for 1000 years; after which Salivahana, "a divine child born of a virgin and the son of Taschaca, a carpenter," would deprive him of his kingdom. In the Cumarica-c'handra it was

---

[894] Del Mar., op. cit., pg. 89.

[895] Ibid. In Roman Catholicism, the Sacred Heart of Jesus is depicted as bleeding.

[896] Del Mar., Ibid., pg. 91.

[897] Ibid., pg. 92.

predicted that this would happen after the expiration of the Calijoga {I.e., Kali-yuga} 3100."[898]

The mention of one thousand years is interesting, since it seems to possibly be a parallel with the millennium of Revelation 20:1-7, and might *possibly* be the basis for the millennium of the *Apokalypse*. It also must be admitted that, if such a seemingly trivial detail of the foster-father of the virgin-born Son of God being a carpenter is duplicated (by way of anticipation) in these "foreign" legends, then it seems to constitute fairly strong evidence that Jesus was merely a *chimera*. However in some cases at least, Mr. Del Mar's accuracy is questionable; for example, he writes of Osiris that "he was crucified on the vernal equinox (probably an altered date;) he descended to hell, where he remained three days and nights to judge the dead, and he rose again and ascended bodily to heaven. His principal sacrament was baptism; his emblems were the "Latin" cross, the crux ansata and the Christian monogram, while his zodion was the Bull or Calf (Apis)."[899]

According to other sources, Osiris was not crucified, but tricked into being locked in a coffin by Set[900] and whose body was afterwards cut into fourteen pieces. Furthermore, Del Mar also wrote of Mithras that he "died a violent death on the vernal equinox; descended to the nether world; remained three days and nights; rose again and ascended bodily to heaven."[901] But Payam Nabarz, in his book on Mithras,[902] wrote nothing of such a violent death, or any such significant parallels as are alleged by Del Mar. In fact Del Mar is even uncertain as to whether Mithras was male or female.[903] So there is some degree of doubt as to the accuracy of much of his information. Nevertheless I still find his book fascinating and would say it is well worth reading. It is really a question of how reliable his sources were. We must also

---

[898]   Ibid., pg. 167.

[899]   Ibid., pg. 89.

[900]   Egyptian *Sutekh*. Also otherwise known as Seth.

[901]   Del Mar., op. cit., pg. 133.

[902]   Nabarz., op. cit. Mr. Nabarz' book is entitled *THE MYSTERIES OF MITHRAS*. The subtitle is *The Pagan Belief That Shaped the Christian World*. Nowhere in his book does Payam Nabarz cite any such highly specific parallels between Mithras and Jesus Christ, which seems strange, considering his whole book is devoted to the topic.

[903]   Del Mar., op. cit.

keep in mind that Christian institutions would have a vested interest in suppressing any information that was subversive of Christianity's claims of uniqueness and exclusivity. I suspect that quite possibly his sources actually were more reliable than many contemporary critics are likely to concede. Unfortunately, in the case of many of the ancient texts, they are now lost in the sands of time. In some cases this may be due to sheer antiquity, while in others due to religious sabotage. For example, the Catholic *conquistadors* destroyed the texts of the Mayans, for the most part.[904] Mr. Del Mar also notes some attempts even by museum staff to vandalize certain ancient sculptures in order to suppress knowledge of the *mythos*.[905] So we must reckon with the fact that our knowledge of the past is only partial, and there are obscurantists who would deliberately seek to cover up certain inconvenient truths.

Aside from these books, and the writings of Aleister Crowley,[906] there are a number of books, both old and new, dedicated to the proposition that Christ was a *chimera*. Among these are *The Diegesis,* by Rev. Robert Taylor; *The Devil's Pulpit,* and *Syntagma of Evidences of the Christian Religion,* by the same author; *The Historical Jesus and the Mythical Christ,* by Gerald Massey;[907] *The Christ Conspiracy,* by Acharya S.; *The Jesus Mysteries,* by Timothy Freke and Peter Gandy; *Jesus and the Lost Goddess,* and *The Laughing Jesus,* by the same authors; and *The True Authorship of the New Testament,* by Abelard Reuchlin. There are a number of other works, by these and other authors; but these are the ones I have read so far on this theme. Another book worth mentioning is *Jesus the Nazarene: Myth or History,* by Maurice Goguel; although the author writes *against* the phantom theory, one still can

---

[904]   Only a few surviving codices, such as the *Popol Vuh,* and the book of *Chilam Balam,* have managed to survive. There is also the *Annals of the Cakchiquels.* The Mexicans also had somewhat of the same ubiquitous messianic *mythos.* One perhaps ought to consult Kingsborough's *Antiquities of Mexico,* a very old and rare book.

[905]   Del Mar., op. cit., pgs. 295–301.

[906]   Who seems to have acquiesced to the ahistorical paradigm vis-à-vis Jesus Christ.

[907]   It is worth noting that while Gerald Massey rejected the historicity of Jesus Christ, at least as far as the first century was concerned, he did acknowledge a historical Jesus who lived in the first century B.C., as spoken of in the Toldoth Jeschu. See my earlier work.

learn of certain French scholars who advocated the phantom Christ theory. One other book that is at least worth mentioning is Godfrey Higgins' two-volume *magnum opus, The Anacalypsis*. Higgins, while not an advocate of the phantom theory, nevertheless provides some information that is at least congenial to that theory. Higgins, Taylor and Massey are all deceased. So also now is (sadly) Acharya S./D.M. Murdock. She was one of the most scholarly, and her books are very readable and interesting. She also incorporates much of the material written by her ideological predecessors in her own work. She makes a compelling case that Jesus Christ was an invented character. But she, like most of the other mythicists, claims that Christ was merely another version of the ancient Sun God. But if this is so, why would Jesus have been given brothers and sisters by the evangelists? That would seem to make the Sun God far too mundane and mortal. This is just one example from the various fossil passages discussed above that are deleterious towards this version of the phantom theory. But since so many ancient religious texts have been destroyed or lost, it is impossible to evaluate, in precise detail, whether or not there were or would have been parallels in terms of potential "fossil passages" in respect to the scriptures that spoke of these earlier Savior-Gods. In other words, each one of these "Saviors" might have had unique elements to his story, which would have made it seem as if he "must" have been a historical person, etc....

Abelard Reuchlin's theory, while weaker in some respects, is actually stronger in others. Reuchlin does not try to depict Jesus as another invented Sun God, but rather as an invented Messiah. His theory, in brief, is that a wealthy Roman family, known as the Pisos, invented Jesus by writing the Gospels and other books of the New Testament, in order to subjugate the Jews to the Romans.[908] But Reuchlin and his imitators are not only notoriously cynical, but there are a number of other untenable aspects to Reuchlin's version of the phantom theory. For example, Reuchlin argues that Christ is depicted as a pacifist in order to pacify the Jews with a soporific opiate of a "pie in the sky" religion, which would (hopefully) keep them from constantly rebelling against Roman rule. But those passages that portray Jesus as not-quite-pacifist in the Gospels put the lie to this interpretation. Furthermore the saying ascribed to Jesus that "It is

---

[908] Or rather to keep them subjugated, by replacing militant Zealot messianic pretenders with an invented "pacifist" Messiah, as depicted in the Gospels.

easier for a camel to go through the eye of a needle than for a rich man to enter the kingdom of God"[909] seems unlikely to have originated with a wealthy man, as Reuchlin's theory requires. Not only that, but Reuchlin also appears to be quite uninformed and historically inept. For example, he wrote that the books of the Apocrypha were written by the same people who wrote the New Testament, or even by their *protégés*. But this is a huge blunder; it is fairly well-known, in fact, that most of the books of the Apocrypha[910] were written before the New Testament. In fact, Hebrew fragments of Tobit and Sirach have been discovered among the Dead Sea Scrolls, as well as fragments of Enoch and Jubilees. Reuchlin should educate himself before seeking to "educate" others.

But Reuchlin's theory is more congenial to Jesus having siblings, since there was no reason to suppose that the Messiah would not have had brothers and sisters, unlike some incarnate Sun God. But of course Reuchlin's theory would have to be seriously modified before it attained any high degree of realism. Nevertheless he has offered some insights. For example, it is quite possible that the first codices or scrolls of the New Testament were first buried in sand, in order to make them seem older than they actually were. From the work of Suetonius we have also seen the possibility of some Roman influence upon the text of the New Testament, but it still seems extremely unlikely that a Roman family would have been sufficiently acquainted with the Jewish Scriptures to write the New Testament, unless they were both Roman and Jewish.[911] Possibly certain aspects of Reuchlin's theory could be combined with the best and strongest arguments of Acharya S. and other advocates of the phantom theory, in order to produce a more compelling version of the theory.[912]

One possible version of the phantom theory involves Jesus Barabbas. We discussed earlier the theory that Jesus Barabbas was secretly substituted by Pontius Pilate for Jesus Christ, to fool the

---

[909] Mt 19:24; Mk 10:25; Lk 18:25.

[910] i.e., with the probable exception of II Esdras (IV Ezrae; the Apocalypse of Ezra) and the *possible* exception of the Wisdom of Solomon.

[911] Which is not impossible.

[912] Once again this is possible, and we are compelled to try to imagine the strongest possible form of the phantom theory, in order to evaluate it as an overall theory.

Pharisees. But what if the reference to Jesus Barabbas in Matthew was really a clue that a substitution of an altogether different kind took place? In other words, the substitution was not literal, but literary; the "pacifist" Jesus Christ being a complete invention by the evangelists, while it was the militant Messiah Jesus Barabbas who was crucified on the cross. But as interesting as this possibility is, it still does not answer the key question of how belief in the resurrection of Jesus first originated. Unless we suppose that even Jesus Barabbas himself was merely a composite of real messianic pretenders who had been crucified by the Romans. Therefore Jesus Barabbas would have been a composite of real men, while Jesus Christ was a falsified composite, of both militant messianic pretenders, as well as the sayings of some Cynic sage or school in a genuine wisdom tradition. This would merely be yet another version of the phantom theory, however. But it is interesting that much of the evidence lends itself to such an interpretation. But of course one possible version of the thesis is one congenial to the termination theory. If Jesus Barabbas was historical, while Jesus Christ was *chimerical,* then in effect Jesus Barabbas was the original of Jesus Christ. Presumably he just died on the cross, but became the occasion of weaving a web of lies and legends to the effect that he was the long-awaited Messiah, and he rose from the dead. If the Gospels were written a century or more after the fact, and in locations far removed from the scene of the crime, who could gainsay them? Who could "prove" they were false?

Another version of the phantom theory, which could also be combined with elements of those detailed above, is one in which Jesus was gratuitously created as the supposed fulfillment of prophecy, and specifically for chronological reasons. This is a theme that ties in with my earlier work. If the *terminus ad quem* of Daniel's seventy weeks had passed without any notable or discernible fulfillment, then, it is at least possible that some "pious" Jews would have invented a Messiah, using their Scriptures as a sort of "blueprint" or "outline" of what the Messiah supposedly said and did. The original *terminus ad quem* of Daniel's prophecy of the seventy weeks would have been in 46 B.C., assuming the decree of Cyrus as the *terminus a quo* of the prophecy.[913] But this natural *terminus a quo* of Daniel's prophecy of

---

[913] As argued in my former book. The Decree of Cyrus was in 536 B.C., give or take a couple of years. I have a deluxe King James Bible that places it in 538 B.C., which would give us a *terminus ad quem* of 48 B.C.

the seventy weeks, having been "corrected" by Ezra to the supposed decree of Artaxerxes, in his seventh year,[914] gives us a *terminus ad quem* of approximately 32 A.D./C.E.[915] Therefore if Jesus Christ was merely a *chimera* he was placed in the messianically appropriate chronological *niche* by whoever first invented him. On the other hand, if we assume on the contrary that Jesus was historical, then he either fortuitously lived at just the right time, or was artificially dislocated from his true historical and chronological *niche* and placed in one more messianically appropriate.[916] But the point that is relevant here is that the mere passing of the time of fulfillment of the messianic prophecy of Daniel with no discernible fulfillment may have been the "trigger" for the gratuitous *creation* of the requisite Messiah in legend and literary texts. Whether or not this is a realistic assessment is a matter of judgment.

Three or four variations on this last scenario should also be at least briefly discussed, before presenting a final variation of the phantom theory. As mentioned earlier, John Hyrcanus had conquered the Galilaeans, Samaritans, and Idumaeans and imposed a version of Judaism upon them. As such, these essentially foreign, non-Judaic peoples werer subsequently under the yoke of the Torah-Pentateuch. Very likely, these people resented their forced conversion to a foreign religion. As such, it is not altogether unthinkable that some secret conspiracy of either Galilaeans, Samaritans, or Idumaeans may have invented a false messiah and started a movement, with the express intent to have this flasely-invented literary messiah abrogate the Torah. The Samaritans already had their own ideas of a Messiah-like figure who was destined to come. Galilaeans and Idumaeans probably had already subsribed to some form of the dying-and-rising Savior-God *mythos*. In ancient times, some Israelite women weeped for Tammuz, a fertility deity of such a mythos. According to some phantom Christ

---

[914] Ezra 7:1-8. In my former work I argued that Ezra and Nehemiah were not written until sometime after 46 B.C., and furthermore that they falsified earlier records, substituting the name "Artaxerxes" for "Xerxes", as found in earlier records. I still stand by this allegation. Nobody has ever proven me wrong on this point, nor are they likely to ever so prove me wrong.

[915] It should be kept in mind that a discrepancy of a year or two in such lengthy chronologies is sufficiently close to be considered "on target" by most chronologists.

[916] And this would be equally true if Jesus lived later than the time commonly supposed, rather than earlier, as I proposed in my earlier work. See below.

theorists, Joshua/Jesus was a Messianic name used in some heretical pre-Christian Judaic cults. These facts must all be taken into account when considering the phantom theory.

One other possible variation has to do with the possibility that Jesus as the Suffering Servant and the Messiah may have been the invention of slaves. In the Roman empire, very often, slaves were literate; they were often used as secretaries. It is at least worth considering that such literate slaves may have conspired to invent a Messiah, possibly in hopes of eventually overthrowing the social order. The more-or-less obvious problem with this scenario is that passages such as Colossians 3:22, Ephesians 6:5, Titus 2:9, and 1 Timothy 6:1 seem to clearly belie it. But then again, there are verses like Ephesians 6:9 and Colossians 4:1, which serve to counterpoise the others. This is simply offered as food for thought.

Finally, there is the mushroom theory. In 1970, John Allegro published a very controversial book with the title *The Sacred Mushroom and the Cross*. In the book he argued that the Jesus of the New Testament was not a historical man, but rather represented a hallucinogenic mushroom, and that the New Testament texts had been written in code. John Allegro had been a well-respected scholar who spent years deeply studying the Dead Sea Scrolls. His position on the Copper Scroll had been considered controversial at the time, but now many scholars take his views much more seriously. But the writing of *The Sacred Mushroom and the Cross* was not some kind of scholarly hoax or stunt; he followed this up with *The Chosen People* in 1971, and *The Dead Sea Scrolls and the Christian Myth*. Both of these latter books supplement and support his earlier controversial book and give additional eviddence in favor of his paradigm. So, all of his books should be taken seriously. He was certainly a brilliant scholar, and we can learn much from his books. But ultimately the mushroom theory is a variation on the phantom theory; it would have been a much different scenario if he had claimed that Jesus and the Apostles used psychedelic mushrooms sacramentally. So while the mushroom theory may be more attractive in some ways than other phantom theories, or could possibly be combined with other phantom theories to produce a more strident form of the phantom theory, ultimately all of the phantom theories must be judged against the available evidence, such as it is.

Hybrid Theories Excluded

H ybrid theories have been excluded from consideration herein. But by "hybrid" we do not mean a theory that, for example, posits a historical Jesus, while assuming or arguing for a *chimerical* Paul or Nicodemus, as I did in my former work. Technically that would be classed as well within the historical paradigm, since it is the historicity or otherwise of Jesus Christ himself that determines the paradigm, rather than any other New Testament figure. By "hybrid" as used in the sense of excluded theories, I mean pseudo-theories that only try to confuse the issue by postulating a pseudosynthetic composite of two or more of the six theories noted above. For example, if a person sought to artificially complexify the issue by arbitrarily manufacturing combinations of two or more of the above theories enumerated above. A case in point may be to Kamal Salibi's theory. His theory of Jesus is particularly complex, and one may at first be confused as to just how to categorize it. He admits a first-century Jesus, whom he calls Jeschu; but he also postulates a fifth-century B.C. Jesus, and that the Jesus of the New Testament is a composite of the two. In fact, his theory is even more complex than that: he also posits that the New Testament Jesus is also a composite of certain Arabian fertility deities as well. So how would we classify his theory? Actually it is quite simple; according to the canons of logic, and the criteria for the six possible theories defined above, his theory would definitely be classed as a termination theory, plain and simple. This is because the actual historical Jesus, who lived in the first century, simply died on the cross, with no resurrection, apparent or otherwise; neither had there been any substitution or impersonation. Neither could Mr. Salibi's theory be classed as a phantom theory, simply because he argues that the New Testament Jesus is a composite; because underneath it all there is a historic core of an original, historical Jesus, who became the basis for all the legends encrusted upon him, albeit from older sources. So even such a seemingly complex theory as Kamal Salibi's falls well within the parameters of just one of the six theories enumerated above. Any genuine theory about Jesus Christ will necessarily fall within one of the six categories enumerated above. They cover all possible bases and cases. While it is true that a comprehensive theory of Christ may incorporate aspects of more than one theory, ultimately all possible theories can be reduced to just one of six; namely, those spoken of above.

However for the sake of completeness, I will not neglect to at least speak briefly of yet another *potential class* of theories, which I label the *exotic class* of theories. But this *class* of theories is entirely excluded on two grounds: First, due to the sheer improbability of the theories; secondly, because most likely, even these very strange theories can probably be ultimately reduced and classified into one of the six classes of theories noted above. I am only even writing about this *class* of *exotic* theory or theories for the sake of completeness. Such bizarre theories should only be resorted to if a more prosaic explanation does not satisfy the relevant evidence. So far I have not found this to be the case, in respect to Jesus Christ. Such theories require both the existence of, and also speculation upon the potential motives of, either extraterrestrials,[917] extradimensionals,[918] subterraneans,[919] vampires,[920] or time-travellers,[921] or some combination thereof. If any such theories

---

[917]   Extraterrestrials. While intelligent extraterrestrials may exist, we would have to further assume that they were capable of interstellar travel, and also that they sought to somehow specifically intervene in human history to create the religion of Christianity. Each assumption requires yet another quantum leap of faith, until we arrive at an incredibly unlikely scenario. While strictly speaking the drama of Jesus Christ may have been the result of extraterrestrial intervention, this seems to be so highly improbable as to remain virtually impossible.

[918]   Extradimensionals. Somewhat of a variation on the extraterrestrial theme. Such interdimensional nomads would apparently also use advanced technology to influence human events, for as yet unknown reasons. On the other hand, the mere quasi-technical terminology only masks what in effect is yet another variation on a supernatural paradigm; as such, this could be classified as but a variation on the miraculous resurrection theory. Or a variation upon Gnosticism, etc.

[919]   Subterraneans. Subterraneans as such would require adherence to the hollow earth theory. A theory of subterranean intervention in the case of Jesus Christ would also require another gigantic leap of faith, with wild speculation upon the possible motives of such hypothetical entities. Once again, as in the case of extraterrestrial intervention, advanced technology is postulated as the explanation for seeming miracles, etc. While possibly appealing to certain science geeks, this theory is too far-fetched to be taken very seriously.

[920]   Vampires. Such as the idea that Jesus Christ was a vampire. Like assumed extra-dimentionals, vampires also bring us back to a supernatural paradigm. The difference being that, while the term "extradimensionals" may have a quasi-scientific veneer, to speak of vampires appears to be downright superstitious. If Jesus Christ was a vampire, and he rose from the dead on that account, then this is no more believable than the resurrection theory spoken of above; it is merely a different contextual interpretation of such.

[921]   Time travellers. Time travel is a fascinating science fiction theme, but backwards time travel is almost certainly impossible. There are a number of logical paradoxes that prove this. But even assuming the contrary, and that it was time travellers who somehow used advanced "future" technology to fake Christ's resurrection, we would still have to reckon with the extreme improbability of such, as well as speculating wildly on the possible motives of such hypothetical time travellers. So this is probably the single least likely theory to be true. It is a variation on the science fiction-like appeal of intervention by extra-terrestrials or subterraneans. The sheer improbability of this theory safely rules it out.

were true, then not only would truth be stranger than fiction,[922] but it would be far stranger, and even almost *infinitely stranger* than the wildest fiction imaginable. They would seem, if anything, to be even more highly improbable than biblical fundamentalism itself. Such theories might make good fodder for science fiction stories, but they are not realistic historical theories, in my view.[923] Possible variations include the cloning of the body of Jesus, either by aliens, subterraneans, or time travellers.[924] Another variation would be that the risen Jesus was some kind of solid hologram.[925] Another variation would be that advanced medical technology was able to revive Jesus from clinical death, or from a coma.[926] We can see that all possible *exotic* theories are ultimately only variations on one or another of the six theories enumerated above, and highly improbable ones, at that. As I have already stated, I have only briefly mentioned such strange theories for the sake of completeness. Before moving on, I would also like to briefly state that all these exotic theories share a weakness common to five out of six of the theories. This particular weakness is especially evident in the resurrection theory, but it is also shared by four of the other theories to some degree as well. Only one theory lacks this particular weakness.[927]

---

[922] Which it sometimes is.

[923] And I think of myself as a very open-minded person.

[924] But if we assume the cloning was done to fake the resurrection of Jesus, then this would fall under the rubric of the termination theory.

[925] Once again this would fall under the rubric of the termination theory, since such a display would only have been used to cover up the fact that Christ's body was still dead.

[926] But this would merely be an exotic variation on the survival theory.

[927] Technically this weakness is a potential problem for all six theories, but one of the six theories MUST be true; this particular weakness is less of a problem for the termination theory than for any of the other theories, but especially the resurrection theory. I will disclose this weakness in another section.

Chronological Considerations

I n my former work I presented evidence in favor of the proposition that Jesus had lived about a century earlier than the commonly-accepted time. Much of the evidence was circumstantial; however, considering the cumulative nature of the evidence, I still feel that I presented a reasonably strong case that Jesus may have lived in the first century B.C. In fact, I presented evidence that had been overlooked by G.R.S. Mead in his book on the same theme, and even Alvar Ellegard, in his book on the same theme, overlooked what I consider to be the most crucial piece of evidence in favor of the theory. My former work must ultimately stand or fall on its own merits. I have for the most part refrained from making any detailed references to my earlier work herein; I have kept any chronological questions very much in the background of my present study. There are several reasons for this. One is that I have not uncovered any additional evidence of any significance to uphold my thesis. This is not to say that there might not be some additional evidence, and it is quite possible that some future researcher may uncover some legitimate and highly significant evidence that Jesus lived a century earlier than commonly supposed. Another reason is because, upon due reflection, I no longer find much of the evidence all that compelling. Perhaps the strongest point in my case was the evident falsification of chronology in the Massoretic texts of Ezra, Nehemiah, and Esther. While I feel that this point is all but irrefutable, it proves no more than that such a falsification took place;

it does not prove that Jesus himself necessarily lived in Hasmonean times. I stated as much in my former work. Stated bluntly, I think it may be more realistic to view Jesus as having lived in the first century, rather than the first century B.C. One reason why is the uniformity of the Gospels on this question. Those texts, which otherwise have so many contradictions between them, all agree that Jesus was crucified in the days of Herod Antipas and Pontius Pilate. In my earlier work I postulated reasons why a messianic *kahal* would have made a decree to dislocate Jesus chronologically, in order to make it seem as if he had come at just the right time, according to the then-current interpretations of the chronological scheme of messianic prophecy.[928] But it might perhaps be simpler to assume that Jesus simply lived at that latter time of messianic expectation, rather than earlier. On the other hand, it is worth pointing out, that in terms of the six theories, aside from the resurrection theory,[929] only the substitution theory[930] *requires* Jesus to have lived at the commonly-accepted time. Any one of the other four theories at least allows for the possibility that Jesus may have lived either earlier or later than commonly assumed. There is nothing about either the survival, impersonation, or termination theories that would inherently require Jesus to have lived at the very time stated in the Gospels. And of course according to the phantom theory, Jesus never even existed anyway, so it is a moot point as far as that theory is concerned. So this is some food for thought. A third reason why I have so far for the most part avoided the chronological theme herein is because I did not want a questionable theory to color the perception of evidence I would offer to solve a much greater mystery; some readers might get the false impression that one theory was contingent upon another, which is definitely not the case. For the same reason I did not want to burden my earlier work with an attempt at a complete historical theory about Jesus Christ, but instead sought

---

[928] In other words, this decision would have been made some time in the Roman era of Judaean occupation, and also after the books of Ezra and Nehemiah had been written, which, as I argued in my former work, had substituted "Artaxerxes" for "Xerxes" in order to artificially extend Daniel's prophecy of the seventy weeks, in order to "legitimize" latter-day messianic pretenders, such as Simeon Bar-Kochbah.

[929] Which assumes the divine inspiration of the New Testament as a necessary corollary.

[930] i.e., as postulated herein.

to offer a tightly-argued case that Jesus *may* have lived in Hasmonean times. I wanted that thesis to be considered discretely on its own terms. So by the same token I feel much more incumbent to present a pristine case in favor of my theory about Jesus Christ. The question we are seeking to answer herein is much more profound and far-reaching. The stakes are far higher. What we are seeking to uncover here is the solution to a mystery of superlative magnitude. The question of how belief in Christ's resurrection first arose is of far greater magnitude and import than whether he may have lived earlier or later than the commonly-accepted time, or other comparatively peripheral considerations. A fourth reason why I have adopted my current tactic is because, upon reflection, I realized that an equally strong, or perhaps even stronger, case could be made that Jesus lived, not earlier than the time commonly supposed, but rather later.[931] I will briefly present some of this evidence, before moving on with my theme.

We have already quoted the passage from Suetonius in respect to Chrestus being in Rome, and stirring up tumults among the Jews to such a degree that Claudius expelled all Jews from Rome. If we interpret Chrestus as being Christ, then this places Christ in the reign of Claudius, who reigned later than Tiberius, in whose reigned he was supposedly crucified. We also noted how, although the book of Acts also makes a reference to the expulsion of all Jews from Rome by the Emperor Claudius, it does not hint at the reason why. This is certainly a suspicious omission in any case, and advocates of either a substitution or survival theory could easily point to this omission as an evident embarrassment that Jesus was still alive in the flesh at the time, in a very non-supernatural sense, which implies that he either survived his passion, or even that he was never crucified. Proponents of an impersonation theory could argue that Chrestus was simply the same man who was impersonating Jesus; he travelled to Rome and one way or another created a disturbance among the Jews resident there, resulting in their expulsion from the city. Advocates of any one of the other three theories could interpret Chrestus as a reference, not to Christ personally, but rather to a general identification of the original ringleader of the messianic movement, who was now deceased.[932] But

---

[931] And this despite whatever I may have written to the contrary in my earlier book.

[932] Or miraculously resurrected and ascended to heaven; or that this "Chrestus" was just another dime-a-dozen messianic pretender who raised a tumult in

an alternative interpretation of the evidence is that Jesus actually lived somewhat later than the time commonly supposed.[933]

We also have a report by Josephus of a false prophet who came from Egypt in the reign of Nero, who gathered multitudes of people to the Mount of Olives, in an apparent effort to perform a miracle of the walls of Jerusalem falling down, at which the people could plunder the city.[934] This same Egyptian false prophet is also mentioned in the book of Acts.[935] In fact, Paul is taken to be this very man by the Roman chiliarch. In fact, the word that is translated as "murderers" in the King James Bible in the original Greek is *sikarion,* a term that denotes dagger-wielding assassins.[936] We have seen that there are passages in the Gospels that inadvertently reveal that Jesus was not a complete pacifist. We also know that Jesus frequented the Mount of Olives with his Apostles. Granted the association may seem a bit thin, but here there is at least a *possible neutral historical source* speaking of Jesus, if we are willing to so interpret the passage. This may be preferable to the complete silence of the historical record with respect to Jesus Christ that we are otherwise confronted with. But of course this would also require somewhat of a chronological relocation of Christ; if we were to account for the identity by virtue of a substitution or survival scenario, then presumably Jesus would have been too elderly to be leading an armed revolt in the reign of Nero.

There is another piece of evidence that places Jesus in an even later timeframe, if we so allow it. In Matthew 23:35, Jesus made reference to "the blood of Zechariah the son of Berechiah, whom

---

Rome.

[933] Of course a theory that Jesus lived later rather than earlier than the commonly-supposed time is likewise burdened with an equal need to explain a deliberate chronological dislocation in all the Gospel texts. But one slight advantage that the "later than" theory has over both the "earlier than" theory, or even the commonly-accepted chronology vis-à-vis Jesus Christ, is that we can find *some possible* neutral historical mentions of a figure who *could be* Jesus Christ, rather than the complete silence in respect to the other two positions. The passage from Suetonius is the first example of such.

[934] Jos. Ant. 20.8.6.

[935] Acts 21:38.

[936] Nestle-Aland., op. cit., pg. 389.

you slew between the temple and the altar."[937] Unless we interpret the reference to "Zechariah the son of Berechiah" as referring to some now-lost tradition of a supposed martyrdom of Zechariah the prophet, who was the son of Berechiah,[938] then we either have an error and a contradiction in Matthew, or Jesus was speaking of a different Zechariah altogether.[939] We would have to assume that Jesus was speaking of a more distant ancestor of the Zechariah whose death is narrated in Chronicles; for he was the son of Jehoiada the high priest. Presumably MtN corrected the text of Matthew, unless we assume that "Zechariah the son of Berechiah" was both the original and intended reading. Some manuscripts of Matthew omit the phrase "son of Berechiah" while some manuscripts of Luke contain it.[940] The reason why the reference to "Zechariah the son of Berechiah" is pertinent to our theme is that it is a possible corruption of "Zechariah the son of Baruch", whom Josephus wrote of, and who was unjustly murdered in the temple.[941] A reference to the prophet Zechariah, the son of Berechiah, who wrote the famous biblical book of Zechariah, seems to be an unlikely explanation for Christ's utterance, because as far as I know, there is no reference within the Mishnah to any martyrdom of that Zechariah, and neither is there any such thing to be found in either the Apocrypha or Old Testament Pseudepigrapha. So it seems unlikely that Jesus could have been referring to that Zechariah. Of course it is possible that either Matthew himself or some later scribe made an error, and supplied the phrase, on the assumption that Christ had been speaking of the more well-known prophet, but this would be a species of special pleading, and begging of the question, on the part of Christian apologists. The "problem" is that Zechariah the son of Baruch, mentioned by Josephus,[942] lived in the reign of Vespasian; his murder occurred around 69 C.E. This is certainly long after the time when Jesus supposedly lived. So unless we were willing to redate

---

[937] MtN reads "Zechariah the son of Jehoiada"; cf 2 Chronicles 24:20-22.

[938] Zechariah 1:1.

[939] Notably the parallel verse in Luke avoids any mention of the paternity of Zechariah, only speaking of the circumstances of his martyrdom.

[940] Nestle-Aland., op. cit., pgs. 67, 199; apparatus.

[941] Jos. War. 4.5.4.

[942] Zacharias in Josephus; but this is merely a transliteration from the Greek form of the same name.

Jesus to much later in the first century, then this verse in Matthew is still somewhat problematical.[943] But if we are willing to suppose that Jesus had referred to this later Zechariah the son of Baruch, which became corrupted in the text to read "Zacharias the son of Berechias" then this verse is accounted for. As to why, assuming this were the case, that Jesus was said to have lived at an earlier time in the Gospels, the very same reason as proposed in my earlier work would suffice: it was more messianically appropriate, according to the scheme of prophecy, especially according to the "corrected" chronology of Daniel's prophecy of the seventy weeks.[944] Once again the advantage of assuming Jesus lived later is that we have at least these few "neutral" passages from various historical documents that speak of him, if we are willing to so interpret them.[945]

There is another possible reference, albeit highly controversial. In 1972 Australian author Donovan Joyce wrote a controversial book entitled *The Jesus Scroll*. In his book Joyce claimed to have discovered an ancient scroll, supposedly written and signed by Jesus himself, in which Jesus claimed to have been the last rightful king of Israel. Joyce's book created a considerable amount of controversy for a while. The scroll was allegedly discovered at Masada, where Jesus supposedly died, according to this theory. While this ties in with the theme of Jesus as a Zealot, the provenance of the scroll is doubtful, to say the least of it. The book is full of cloak-and-dagger mystery, and no realistic answers are offered to legitimate questions. Most objective observers opined that the book was more fiction than fact. Despite being an octogenarian, Jesus supposedly made his last stand at Masada, according to Donovan Joyce. Joyce apparently subscribed to the survival theory.[946] This particular theory is admittedly skating on very thin ice, but I felt that it was at least worth mentioning.

There is still one more possible avenue of evidence that Jesus may have lived later than the commonly-accepted time, albeit this piece of

---

[943] At the very least this suggests that the Gospel of Matthew was written sometime after 70 A.D./C.E.

[944] i.e., "corrected" according to the much later texts of Ezra & Nehemiah.

[945] By "neutral" I mean those that are neither propagandistic, such as the Gospels, nor polemic, such as the anti-Gospels.

[946] But Joyce may have subscribed to a substitution theory, according to alternate sources.

evidence requires a few further assumptions. One assumption is that Jesus travelled all the way to India, presumably in search of the lost tribes of Israel. This evidence is presented in the book *JESUS DIED IN KASHMIR,* although therein it is interpreted differently.[947] The book recounts a conversation that a travelling prophet (presumed to be Jesus) had with a king in northern India. The incident is recorded in the *Bavishyat Mahapurana,* which is a sacred scripture of Hinduism. Holger Kersten, in his first book, *Jesus Lived in India,* also quoted from the same passage of the *Bavishyat Mahapurana,* although it is translated somewhat differently in Kersten's book. The relevant passage is as follows:

"Shalewahin, grandson of Bikramajit, assumed the government, he fought off the Chinese hordes, the Parthians, the Scythians, and the Bactrians. He defined the frontier between the Aryans and the Amalekites, ordering them to keep to the other side of the Indus. One day Shalewahin set off towards the Himalayas, and there, in the middle of the land of the Hun, the powerful king saw a distinguished person sitting near a mountain. The saint had a fair complexion and wore white clothes. King Shalewahin asked him who he was. He replied pleasantly, "I am known as the son of God and *was* born of a virgin." As the king was astonished by this answer the saint added, "I preach the religion of the Amalekites and follow the principles of truth." The king questioned him about his religion and he answered, "Oh king, I hail from a far-away land, in which the truth no longer exists, and in which evil knows no limits. I appeared in the land of the Amalekites as the Messiah. Through me the sinners and the delinquents suffered, and I also suffered at their hands." The king begged him to explain his teaching of his religion more fully, and the saint told him, "Teach love, the truth, and purity of heart. Teach men to serve God, who is at the centre of the sun and *of* the elements. And God and the elements will exist forever." The king returned after having promised obedience to the saint." (Bhavishya Mahapurana, verses 17-32 (Viyas)).

The reference to the "Amalekites" might more accurately be rendered as "Mleccha", being a Sanskrit term for non-Aryan peoples, or those who do not believe in the Vedas or practice Vedic principles.

---

[947] That book presented evidence that Jesus may have survived the crucifixion, including the Shroud of Turin. The book also claimed that Jesus travelled to Kashmir in India, where he is now allegedly buried.

There are a number of different transations of the passage available on the internet. But the obvious parallel of a self-proclaimed virgin-born son of God is at least highly suggestive of Jesus,[948] and it is just barely possible that this could be the historical Jesus. Interestingly, however, this "Shalewahin" is almost certainly a variation on "Salivahana", mentioned above, in the section on the phantom theory. As there were supposedly a series of several such "Salivahanas" and "Vicramadityas", who confront one another, this at least implies that such personages were merely legendary.[949] But if we interpret the incident as historical, and we further assume that the prophet was none other than Jesus, then this would place Jesus in a much later time frame. According to inscriptions on a pillar as to when this King Shalewahin lived, this conversation apparently took place in 132 C.E.[950] That would make Jesus a contemporary with Simeon Bar-Kochbah.[951] Admittedly these last two examples are especially tenuous, doubtful, and highly speculative, but they are at least part of a pattern suggesting that the historical Jesus *may* have lived later than the commonly-accepted time. This is still an important and interesting variable,[952] but throughout the remainder of this text I will proceed under the implicit assumption that Jesus lived during the commonly-accepted time.

---

[948] Although we should also keep in mind that in Zoroastrianism there are said to be a series of virgin-born Saviors. Most likely self-proclaimed holy prophets would frequently claim to have been born of virgin mothers. Others became so exalted by their disciples upon their decease.

[949] And this probability is studiously avoided by those advocates of that version of the survival theory that places Jesus in Kashmir after his passion.

[950] i.e., A.D.

[951] But then this in turn would cause an inquiry into the reliability of those sources that testify that Simeon Bar-Kochbah persecuted Jewish Christians in Palestine. My only source for that allegation is G.R.S. Mead. On the other hand, both accounts could be potentially reconciled.

[952] i.e., chronology.

Evidence for A Verdict

So far we have discussed evidence both in favor of and against various theories in a relatively neutral way; we have not yet applied a ruthless analysis nor a diligent critical scrutiny to the various theories we have been considering. In the case of the substitution theory, I had to present evidence in favor of what I deem to be the strongest possible form of that theory, since it is otherwise generally unknown.[953] While some weaknesses of most of the theories have been briefly touched on above, I have not yet applied the most scorching criticism to such theories. It is now time to unmask the weaknesses of the five false theories, leaving the sixth theory as true by default.[954] But it will not be mere default that defines the termination theory as the true

---

[953] It is possible that another author may have suggested a substitution theory involving Barabbas, but I have not read of any such theory in any book or website, or heard of it anywhere; I deduced it as a distinct possibility from my own knowledge of Scripture.

[954] Hopefully this manner of stating my procedure will not appear to be a begging of the question; I am also sorry for any loss of the potential dramatic effect my work would have had, had I kept the reader in suspense up until almost the very end; but a perusal of the table of contents, as well as prior statements made herein, will no doubt have disclosed the position taken herein. Furthermore it would be the most vain pretence imaginable if I were to effect a literary fiction whereby I seemed to have been undecided as to my conclusion throughout the first 99% of my book.

theory; I will explicate the specific evidence proving that this theory is superior to the other five, by far.

In terms of the three paradigms discussed above, the ahistorical and fundamentalist paradigms will of necessity be excluded, since they are both provably false. That is a statement of fact, not a mere opinion. Just because large numbers of people hold to a given belief does not vindicate the belief, nor give it any more credibility; and just because some otherwise seemingly highly intelligent, erudite, educated people hold to a given belief also does not inherently justify said belief. The truth is to be found neither in biblical minimalism nor biblical fundamentalism.[955] Once the ahistorical and fundamentalist paradigms have been ruled out, then that only leaves the four theories of the historical paradigm to be considered. Three of these are necessarily false, while only one can be true. Once the full evidence has been presented, it should be fairly easy to recognize which are false and which is true. I will begin to debunk the resurrection theory immediately below.

---

[955] The latter term being used as an umbrella term to cover evangelicalism, born-again Christianity, Mormonism, Protestantism, Catholicism, and Orthodox Christianity. This usage is fully justified, despite the vain and hypocritical protests of clueless people who will otherwise insist that they are not "fundamentalists" and yet are somehow "Christians"; you either believe in a religion or you do not; if you do not believe in the Bible, then you are not really a Christian, regardless of whatever you call yourself.

Resurrection Theory
Excluded by The Evidence

The resurrection theory is unquestionably the most popular "theory" since the vast majority of people in the Western Hemisphere subscribe to it.[956] I suppose in global terms the substitution

---

[956] i.e., at least implicitly or nominally. The vast majority of people in the Western Hemisphere being Christians, this is necessarily the case, in demographic terms. A person who does not believe in the miraculous resurrection of Christ from the dead, and yet who insists upon being called a "Christian" is a consummate hypocrite of the very worst variety. As far as the Eastern Hemisphere is concerned, Christians are in the minority, although sizable. Muslims have their own religious beliefs about Jesus, since Jesus is incorporated into Islam in the Koran. They do not believe in the resurrection. Some Muslims believe in a survival theory, but most believe in a substitution theory. Hindus and Buddhists do not have explicit beliefs about Jesus, since he is not an official part of either religion. Most Christians in the Eastern Hemisphere live either in Europe or Australia. While there may be a fairly large number of Christians in many parts of Africa, much of Africa is Muslim, and many native Africans still cling tenaciously to their ancient tribal beliefs. The true beliefs of the vast majority of the people in communist China cannot be accurately determined, for obvious reasons. Japan is mostly Buddhist and Shinto; there are very few Jews or Christians in Japan. Jews may have various beliefs about Jesus, but unless they are Jewish Christians, they would definitely exclude the resurrection theory. Jews are only a tiny, tiny minority in both Hemispheres.

theory would have to be the second most popular theory, since the vast majority of Muslims subscribe to it. A direct corollary of the resurrection theory is the acceptance of the Bible as the Word of God.[957] However a diligent scrutiny of Scripture will disprove any assumption of divine inspiration therein. While many self-identified "Christians" may seek to distance themselves from the perceived cultural odium associated with "fundamentalism", this is really more of an indictment of their own ignorance and unbridled hypocrisy, than anything else. For if the vast majority of so-called "Christians"[958] only go to church and "go through the motions" of supposedly being Christian due to "cultural" reasons, or to please relatives, or some other superficial and unworthy reason, then they are merely vain and shallow hypocrites; if they are constantly plagued by doubt then they should consciously reassess their beliefs, or be content to wallow in the mire of superficiality and lukewarm, half-hearted, double-minded hypocrisy. Such people are the epitome of mediocrity. And those who actually do believe in the Bible can only sustain such an unwarranted belief by a continuous act of intellectual suicide and constant denial of reality at every point; it is a mere sustained ignorance and chronic idiocy. Such "pious" dishonesty is really the very essence of impiety and fraud. Self-delusion is the ultimate form of fraud, deception, and hypocrisy. If these seem like "harsh" words and judgments, the reader ought to keep in mind that most of these "true believers" have far harsher words and judgments for those who do not subscribe to their own delusional belief-system. The threat of eternal torment in a raging inferno for not acquiescing to a highly questionable belief-system seems to be the height of absurdity to anyone rational enough to assess it without bias. This threat alone is a completely irrational and unreasonable belief, that constitutes an unanswerable objection against such a belief and belief-system. It ultimately unmasks the fact that the entire edifice is constructed on fear. And an irrational fear at that. If a person was afraid of a bear in a forest that would at least be a rational fear. But an imaginary hell is somehow supposed to frighten us into accepting Jesus so that we can go to an imaginary heaven?

---

[957] Otherwise belief in a miraculous resurrection of Christ from the dead would be an anomalous belief, without any proper psychological or ontological context. This could only lead to massive cognitive dissonance, or in other words, hypocrisy, or even insanity.

[958] Of whatever denomination: Catholic, Orthodox, Protestant, etc.

This is ridiculous. This is insulting to the intelligence of anyone who is reasonably intelligent. At the very least, this appears to be quite an anachronistic belief within the twenty-first century. But then again the belief never had any validity anyway. It only seemed to, to some people. I must admit that I was one of those people, for quite a few years even. But I once was blind, but now I see. It is not "amazing grace" that reveals the truth, but a modicum of intelligence, logic, reason, common sense, evidence, and critical thinking. Truth must be self-consistent. The Bible is not. Truth bears up under scrutiny. The Bible does not. Truth is consistent with other known facts. The Bible is not.

I will now proceed to prove that the Bible lacks divine inspiration and authority. I do not claim that this will be an exhaustive treatment, since that would probably require several large volumes, or even entire libraries. But nevertheless what I will present ought to be sufficiently comprehensive to prove my point to any unbiased person.[959] Since there are so many classes of objections against the alleged divinity of the Bible, and so many potential examples of some such objections, it will take some time and space to even present a greatly abbreviated summary of such objections. And it should be implicitly understood that an objection against the alleged divinity[960] of the Bible is also necessarily an objection against belief in Christ's resurrection. Either the entire Bible is true in every detail, every "jot and tittle", or Christ's supposed resurrection from the dead comes crashing down to the ground, crumbling to dust.[961] There is no middle ground. This is an "all or nothing" contest. And I would certainly be a great fool if I treated the matter of the fate of my soul recklessly. The same is equally true of every other person. So this is no laughing matter. Since there is so much ground to cover, this will probably be the single

---

[959] It is impossible to "prove" anything to prejudiced religious fanatics, who have already made up their mind to exclude *a priori* whatever is contrary to their beliefs. Their much-vaunted "faith" is nothing but primitive superstition.

[960] Divinity. I.e., in the sense of Divine inspiration and hence Divine Authority.

[961] I fully realise the irony of the fact that many self-identified fundamentalists would delight that I have clearly delineated the argument in such terms, since they insist upon the inerrancy and *plenary* and *verbal* inspiration of Scripture.

longest chapter in the book. So it may be unwise to attempt to read it all in a single sitting. Nevertheless we ought to proceed, without further ado. Generally speaking, there are two different interpretations of the divine inspiration of Scripture; the "strong" version and the "weak" version. The "strong" version of divine inspiration holds that the Bible is inerrant,[962] and also that the Bible is divinely inspired in every part, and even the very words of Scripture are divinely inspired. These concepts are defined as the *plenary* and *verbal* inspiration of Scripture, respectively. The "weak" version of divine inspiration relinquishes both *inerrancy* and the *verbal* inspiration of Scripture, although usually the *plenary* inspiration is acknowledged, for whatever particular Canon of Scripture is being upheld. Others may hold even "weaker" versions of divine inspiration, such as that the Bible *contains* the Word of God,[963] or that it is merely *part of* the Word of God,[964] or that the Bible *becomes* the Word of God, through a divinely–inspired interpretation, etc. Some also claim that the Bible is divinely inspired, but requires a secret esoteric key to interpret it correctly.[965] Of course the latter claim merely turns the Bible into a gratuitous ventriloquist-dummy for whatever cultic or occult teaching is being promulgated by the person making the claim. None of these claims are warranted by the evidence. A person using the Bible in a questionable manner is merely promoting a questionable teaching. This is not to say that an "outsider" may not occasionally have some valid insights into the meaning of portions of Scripture, even in terms of spiritual content, but at the very least, any such claims should be approached with extreme caution.

It is fairly easy to disprove claims to divine authority for the Bible, especially the claims to *inerrancy* and *verbal* inspiration. The Bible contains errors. In fact, Jesus himself made some errors. For

---

[962] i.e., that it contains no errors of fact, whether of history, geography, science, biology, entomology, zoology, chemistry, astronomy, botany, etc.

[963] Rather than actually *being* the Word of God.

[964] The other part being through Tradition, and/or through ongoing revelations, etc.

[965] Occultists and cult leaders generally make such claims. Mary Baker Eddy is a perfect example. But such claims are excluded by Scripture itself; cf 2 Peter 1:20.

example, Jesus said that the mustard seed was the smallest of seeds,[966] yet it is well known to botanists that the mustard seed in fact is not the smallest of all seeds.[967] If Jesus had truly been the Son of God, he should have been infallible, and would have known that in fact mustard seeds are not the smallest of all seeds. To answer the objection, as some inept Christians attempt to do, by arguing that Christ was merely speaking of seeds a farmer in Israel would plant, is no real answer to the very legitimate objection. God is supposed to be omniscient; God would not have allowed Jesus to make such a mistake, if Jesus had been infallibly guided by the Father through the Holy Spirit. Christians often argue, rather obtusely and myopically, that, God would be unjust if he based admission to heaven upon intelligence. While this is true enough, Christians seem to require a lower level of intelligence to attain admission to heaven. After all, if God was so deceptive as to lead more intelligent people astray by having his Son Jesus speak in such loose language as to make those acquainted with the science of botany, or those who might acquire such information, doubt the veracity of a revelation necessary for salvation, then he would be infinitely more unjust than what Christians are wrongfully complaining about.[968] Such a God would be a notorious trickster, more malicious and malevolent than the very devil imagined by Christians. In fact what we have here is actually a far stronger form of evidence against the supposed divine authority of Scripture; because not only was Christ wrong, which clearly proves the absence of his alleged infallibility, but this also points to something else lacking in the New Testament: the potential for Jesus to prove his divinity by disclosing testable information that could be later verified.

---

[966] Mt 13:31–32; Mk 4:31.

[967] See the relevant article on seeds in the Encyclopaedia Britannica. Once again, not the online version, which is terrible. However one may find the right answer to the question "What is the smallest seed in the world?" online. Christian attempts to rationalize Christ's botanical blunder are absurd, ridiculous, and a shameless example of special pleading and begging the question. They are notorious buffoons, and should be ashamed.

[968] No religion claims that only people of a sufficiently high I.Q. will attain "salvation". But if Christianity were true, then the reverse would hold; only those of a sufficiently low level of intelligence would have the hope for salvation, and even then only if they were born in the right place at the right time, etc.

In other words, if Jesus Christ had truly been the Son of God, then he could have, should have, and would have, disclosed scientific secrets as yet unknown, but which could be tested in a later, scientific, age. There is none of this in the New Testament whatever. It only shows more starkly how wrongheaded are such feeble excuses by Christians and how futile is such an apologetics of pure idiocy. And these very same people will assure you that you are headed straight to hell if you do not believe in the same nonsense. There are none so blind as they who will not see.

A further error of such people is the vain assumption that a person has any real choice in respect to belief. While there may be some element of "choice" in respect to various unknown postulates, there are some beliefs that are so far removed from any reasonable reality that it is literally impossible for educated adults to believe them. If I am wrong then I would like the reader to choose to believe in Santa Claus by a sheer act of will. Can you do it? The question answers itself. You might as well try believing in Peter Pan, Snow White and the Seven Dwarfs, Cinderella, Leprechauns, Munchkins, and Unicorns.[969] My point here is simply that belief is not a choice. Or at least not always. To claim that a person can literally *choose* to magically believe in Jesus Christ as the Son of God, with all the attendant baggage, is a fundamental misperception of reality on the part of fundamentalists. Many things that we may have believed as children are no longer believable to us as adults. This is not meant to sound cynical, but it is a fact of life. At some point we must put away childish things.[970] Of course this does not necessarily mean that we must lose our sense of wonder at life, especially in the face of the unknown; but it does mean that we owe it to ourselves not to be taken in by fear-based arguments and circular reasoning. Even children can sometimes see through the lie of Christianity. Many Christians have no clue as to how ridiculous they often sound to other people; they speak glibly of the devil and hell in such an unconscious act of begging the question that they make more rational people think they are like children, telling tales to one another to frighten one another.

Christians never use rational arguments to convince people. There may sometimes be a very thin veneer of such, but generally the

---

[969] With apologies to the Easter Bunny and the Tooth Fairy.

[970] 1 Corinthians 13:11.

arguments are based upon guilt and fear. Such an appeal to the basest of human emotions is unlikely to lead to any genuine spiritual truth.[971] In any case an inquiry into cosmic truth requires a dispassionate attitude, rather than inflamed emotional zeal. This is precisely the opposite from what you will encounter with "true believers"; the problem is that they themselves are completely bound by fear of an imaginary hell. They also fail to grasp that their threat of "hell" is quite hollow to people who do not believe in it. They seem to believe that, at bottom, everyone else is just as superstitious as they are. It is pitiful, really.

Jesus also made another mistake; this one had to do with the earth's relative geography. In speaking of the queen of Sheba, Christ made the following statement:

"The queen of the south shall rise up in the judgment with this generation, and shall condemn it: For she came from the uttermost parts of the earth to hear the wisdom of Solomon; and behold, a greater than Solomon *is* here."[972]

The Ethiopians claim in the *Kebra Nagast* that the queen of Sheba who visited King Solomon was a queen of Ethiopia. Josephus claimed that the famous queen of Sheba was queen of both Egypt and Aethiopia.[973] Some have claimed, even from as far back as the sevententh century, or possibly earlier, that this famous queen was the ruler of southern Arabia, called by some Sabaea or Sabea. But regardless of whether this legendary woman hailed from Aethiopia, Abyssinia, or south Arabia, none of these locales could be realistically described as "the uttermost parts of the earth" from Palestine. If Jesus Christ had truly been the Son of God, much less God the Son, he should have known this; how could he not perfectly know the precise geography of the earth? And God would also have to have foreknown

---

[971] i.e., assuming that there is such a thing as "spiritual" truth. I may believe in a spiritual context to reality, but I do not want to appear to be "begging the question" in that respect, nor do I wish my book to lack utility to atheists and agnostics.

[972] Matthew 12:42. The reference to "the queen of the south" was a distinct Danielism.
Cp Daniel 11.

[973] Jos. Ant. 8.6.5–6. This Aethiopia is Nubia, or Sudan; this is distinct from Abyssinia, or modern Ethiopia. Notably Josephus twice calls her "queen of Aethiopia", which suggests she was of Nubian descent.

that people living in the age of globes would be able to clearly see how foolish it is to describe such a comparatively close location as "the uttermost parts of" the earth. The same mistake is made when Jesus supposedly tells his disciples that they will proclaim him to "the uttermost part of the earth" in Acts 1:8. Did these disciples really go to the South Pole? Did they travel to Japan, or even China? Did they go to the Americas, or to Australia, New Zealand, or Indonesia? Did they go to Hawaii or Polynesia? Of course not. And it would be false for Christians to claim that Jesus had been speaking of later Christian missionaries, since the verse does not allow for such an interpretation. The verse very specifically says that Jesus was speaking to the eleven remaining Apostles themselves. But returning briefly to the *snafu* Jesus had made in respect to the queen of Sheba, it is questionable in exactly what sense Jesus referred to "One greater than Solomon"[974] being present. If it was a reference to wisdom, then this is a contradiction of 1 Kings 3:12, where God himself assures King Solomon that none either before him or after him will ever excel him in wisdom or understanding. If it was a reference to wealth,[975] then this is a contradiction of 2 Chronicles 1:12, where God himself promises King Solomon that no other king, either before him or after him, will ever exceed him in wealth, riches, and honor. So even the Messiah himself, whether it is Jesus or any other man, can never exceed King Solomon in wealth, wisdom, or honor, according to the Jewish Scriptures. These are both embarrassing contradictions for Christians.[976] Even these few examples are enough to demolish any claim to scriptural inerrancy by any honest person. But there is more. Far more.

Proverbs 30:25 says that ants are not strong. In fact, ants are among the very strongest creatures, in proportion to their very small body size, on earth. The God who created ants would have known this, and would not have inspired such fallible and provably false words into his revelation. Ants can lift over twenty times their own body weight. How many men can do that? How many gorillas can do that? How

---

[974]   A clear self-reference, despite the supposed "meekness" of the Lamb.

[975]   And who could have greater wealth than the Messiah in the millennial kingdom?

[976]   Or rather they would be if Christians were capable of embarrassment. Apparently they are not, in matters of their faith.

many elephants can do that? How many bears can do that? What other creature on earth can even come close to doing that? So we once again have here a perfect example of the absence of any real evidence of divine inspiration, which in this case functions as evidence of absence of any such alleged divine inspiration. A man who thought he was clever could have written such a verse about ants. But anyone with real scientific knowledge of just how incredibly strong ants are would never utter such folly. And God would have known such things, and would never have inspired such insipid and false utterances. Otherwise God himself would be party to a lie. And God would be leading astray countless people, especially the most intelligent people, by "inspiring" such provably false nonsense into what fools claim to be his Word. In the Christian paradigm it is a question of whether one can be foolish enough to be "saved". It has nothing whatever to do with morality. There is no question of ethics. It is all purely authoritarian; both the moral sense and the intellect must be subjugated to the will to believe the most utter inanity and insanity. Once again, God is supposed to be supreme and almighty; it is only foolish for believers to make up insipid excuses to justify their belief in such nonsense. God needs people to make excuses for him? Please. Wake up and smell the coffee. God could have, should have, and would have, inspired messages, perhaps even in code, if necessary, which would have contained accurate scientific knowledge that could be verified in a later, scientific, age, by scientific means. But this is found nowhere in the Bible. True some people claim obscure numerical codes supposedly "proving" the divine inspiration of Scripture, but no legitimate mathematician has endorsed any such claims. Such a reality-challenged religion has spawned desperate claims of extraordinary proof. But all such claims fall to the ground.

We would have a right to expect precision in a document that was both *inerrant* and *verbally* inspired. But this can also be proven to be lacking from Scripture. For example, we are told in the Gospel of Luke that shortly after Jesus had been baptized by John the Baptist, as he was about to embark on his prophetic ministry, that he "began to be about thirty years of age"[977] at that time. Why the imprecision? Would not God have known the exact age of his Son, Jesus? Why would the Holy Spirit not have infallibly guided and inspired Luke to write the exact age of Christ at the time? Otherwise, would it not have

---

[977]   Luke 3:23.

been more expedient to omit the detail altogether? But this points precisely to the lack of the requisite precision required in a supposedly "divinely inspired" document. We find yet another example of such imprecision in Luke's Gospel. In respect to the "transfiguration" of Jesus. Luke wrote that "it was about eight days after" Jesus had made a famous saying about those standing there would see the kingdom of God coming with power.[978] Not only is this an imprecision; it is also a contradiction to what both Matthew and Mark wrote about the intervening length of time. And this imprecision that mars the New Testament is also present within *TaNaKh* as well. When Jehu was taking vengeance on the house of Ahab, and the wicked queen Jezebel looked out a window and mocked him, Jehu asked who was on his side; and then the text says "there looked out the window two or three eunuchs."[979] My point is that God would have to have known precisely whether it was in fact two or three eunuchs, and would have infallibly guided and inspired the scribe who wrote the text with the exact number, had the text been *verbally inspired*. As we can see from these few examples, the case for a "strong" version of divine inspiration falls down to the ground. And as if by a domino effect, this spells the doom for the entire superstructure of the belief-system. It all inevitably and irrevocably comes crashing down to the earth, to be scattered as so much dust in the wind. Bible believers may accuse me of being overly scrupulous or even "nit-picky" but these are the very same people who want to legislate morality and determine public policy on a theocratic basis. They want to impose their intolerant attitudes upon the general public by law, if possible. And if not by law, then by social convention. They would even violate the privacy of the bedroom. This is supposed to be a free country but it won't be for long if these people get their way. Please excuse this slight "political" digression, but it is pertinent to our discussion. The Founding Fathers had at least passed "European History 101" and knew enough that there *had* to be a fundamental separation between Church and State if this country was ever to achieve and maintain true liberty and not repeat the bloody lessons of the past. The necessity for a secular state for the maintenance of religious liberty would be a valid principle even

---

[978] Luke 9:28 cp Mt 17:1; Mk 9:2.

[979] 2 Kings 9:32.

if the Bible *were* divinely inspired; but it is abundantly clear that the Bible definitely is *not* divinely inspired at all.

Another problem with the Bible is that it contains anachronisms. There are over a dozen of these in the Old Testament. The first example is Genesis 7:2, where God supposedly commanded Noah to take seven pairs of "clean" animals aboard the ark, but only two pairs of "unclean" animals. This is an evident anachronism, since God did not reveal the distinction between supposedly "clean" and "unclean" animals until it was revealed to Moses, as written in Leviticus 11 and Deuteronomy 14.

The next example of an anachronism in Scripture is in Genesis 23:2, where it says that Sarah, Abraham's wife, died in Kirjath-Arba, which is called Hebron. But in Judges 1:10, we learn that Hebron was called Kirjath-Arba until after the death of Joshua.

In Genesis 28:19 we are told that Jacob had a dream in a place he called Bethel, but that the place had been called Luz before that. But in Judges 1:23-26, it says that the very same place was called Luz "unto this day." So we have another obvious anachronism.

The entire 36th chapter of Genesis is grossly anachronistic. In verse 31 we read "And these are the kings that reigned in Edom, before there reigned any king over the sons of Israel." This proves either one of two things: either the book of Genesis was not written until the reign of Israel's first king, or later; or, the text of Genesis has been interpolated by some later scribe. In either case, the pretence that Genesis has any claim to Divine Authority is vitiated completely. There is another anachronism in Genesis 38:8, where Judah tells his son Onan to marry his brother's widow, to raise up seed for his brother. But the custom of levirate marriage was instituted by Moses, in Deuteronomy 25:5ff. We also have another anachronism in Genesis 38:24, where when Judah was informed that his daughter-in-law was pregnant outside of marriage, he orders he to be burnt alive. But this brutal custom was promulgated by Moses, in Leviticus 21:9.[980]

---

[980] The sheer brutality of such customs is another argument against the alleged divine inspiration of the Bible. It should also be a matter of grave concern to those who realise what a huge threat religious fundamentalism is to religious liberty. The reader should be informed that there are some extreme groups of Christians who want to establish a pseudo-Christian theocracy in America; these people are under the banner of "Dominion Theology" or "Christian Reconstruction".

There is also at least one more passage from Genesis that can be proven to be an anachronism or interpolation. It has been interpreted by both Jews and Christians as a messianic passage. It is a passage within Jacob's parting words to his twelve sons:

8 Judah, thou *art he* whom thy brethren shall praise:

Thy hand *shall be* in the neck of thine enemies; thy father's sons shall bow down before thee.

9 Judah *is* a lion's whelp: From the prey, my son, thou art gone up.

He stooped down, he couched as a lion, and as an old lion; who shall rouse him up?

10 The *royal* sceptre shall not depart from Judah, nor a lawgiver from between his feet, until Shiloh *has* come; and unto him the gathering of the people *shall be.*

11 Binding his foal unto the Vine, and his ass's colt unto the choice Vine; he washed his garments in wine, and his clothes in the blood of grapes;

12 his eyes *are* red with wine, and his teeth white with milk. (Genesis 49:8-12)

Supposedly this was a prophecy or a decree that the Messiah would be a descendant from the tribe of Judah. It also seems to clearly imply that the king of Israel would be chosen from this tribe. But there is a serious problem here; there are no less than three circumstances from within Scripture that belie this supposed decree or prophecy as found in Genesis. First of all, in Exodus 32:9-10, we read the following:

"And the LORD said unto Moses, I have seen this people, and behold, it is a stiffnecked people: now therefore let me alone, that my wrath may wax hot against them, and that I may consume them; and I will make of thee a great nation."

The problem is that Moses himself was of the tribe of Levi, not Judah. If God had destroyed all the other Israelites, as he threatened to do here, then the supposed prophecy or decree of Jacob could never have been fulfilled. So was God making an empty threat, or is Genesis 49:8-12 an interpolation? Or is it an anachronism, proving that the text was not written until long after the reign of King David? No matter what answer is given, the supposed divine authority of Scripture is effectively nullified. Furthermore even had Moses been of the tribe of Judah, how could the prophecy or decree have been fulfilled? How could the other sayings of Jacob have been fulfilled? So there is a definite problem here for Bible believers. But it is actually much worse than this; there is yet another Scripture passage that proves that Genesis 49:8-12 is a blatant anachronism. What is strange is that the Israelites had no king for approximately four hundred years, after they entered the "promised" land. But when they finally decided that they wanted a king, it was somehow displeasing to God and his prophet, Samuel.[981] This also proves that the passage in Genesis is bogus. In first Samuel 8, verse seven, we read: "And the LORD said unto Samuel, Hearken unto the voice of the people in all that they say unto thee: for they have not rejected thee, but they have rejected me, that I should reign over them *as their King.*" So this verse, and even the entire eighth chapter of first Samuel puts the lie to Genesis 49:8-12. In fact, it also puts the lie to Deuteronomy 17:14-20, which gives detailed regulations on the conduct of the future king of Israel. Therefore Deuteronomy 17:14-20 is yet another anachronism. Why would God have inspired Moses to write a detailed list of how the future king should conduct himself, if the very idea of the Israelites even having a king was contrary to God's will? The question answers itself. But not only do these two circumstances prove that Genesis 49:8-12 is an anachronism, but there is a third circumstance, found in Scripture, that clinches the matter. Samuel chose a man, not from the tribe of Judah, but from the tribe of Benjamin.[982] So this proves beyond any shadow of a doubt that the supposed prophecy or decree by Jacob in Genesis 49:8-12 is an interpolation or an anachronism.[983]

We also have two more apparent anachronisms, in Leviticus and Deuteronomy, respectively. The two passages in question purport to be prophecies made by God through Moses, foretelling many of the woes the Israelites would suffer for disobedience to God's law. The

---

[981] 1 Samuel 8.

[982] 1 Samuel 9-10.

[983] i.e., in either case it would technically be an anachronism; but the latter case implies that the entire book of Genesis is a late pseudepigraphon.

two passages are Leviticus 26:14-44 and Deuteronomy 28:15-68. Of course to Bible believers the two passages are prophecies but a critical appraisal of the texts would be that they are anachronistic passages, written after the Assyrian deportation of the ten northern tribes of Israel. Even if a person does not approach the Bible with a particularly skeptical attitude, a diligent reading of the text would lead one to acquire such a skeptical stance towards it.

We also have four anachronisms in the book of Judges. Four times we read that "In those days there was no king in Israel"[984] twice coupled with "every man did that which was right in his own eyes."[985] This proves that the book of Judges was not written in the time of the judges, but in the days of the kings of Israel.

We have yet another anachronism in the account of Joshua's concquest of Jerusalem.[986] If Joshua and the Israelites had conquered Jerusalem, why then did King David have to conquer Jerusalem all over again, four centuries later?[987] At the very least we have here a contradiction, or rather, two contradictions. Because if Joshua had truly conquered Jerusalem, as it is written in his book, then the Israelites would have occupied the city from that time forth, and there would have been no need for David to once again conquer it, centuries later. So either we have an anachronism in the claim that Joshua had conquered Jerusalem, or a silly story that David conquered Jerusalem all over again was invented, to glorify him and flatter him.[988] In either case it proves how historically untrustworthy the Bible is.

Another very strong class of objections against the Bible is that of numerous barbaric passages in the Old Testament. Indeed, this class alone contains such atrocious episodes, with apparent divine sanction, that this would be enough to exclude the Bible from being regarded as any source of moral authority. First we have God commanding Abraham to sacrifice his son as a burnt offering.[989] While Jews and

---

[984]   Judges 17:6; 18:1; 19:1; 21:25.

[985]   The first and last instances, respectively.

[986]   Joshua 10:1-27.

[987]   2 Samuel 5:6-9; 1 Chronicles 11:4-8.

[988]   i.e., assuming that David was still alive when such tales were told.

[989]   Genesis 22:1-2. The text as it now stands reads "Isaac" but Muslims claim that it was Ishmael whom Abraham was to offer. Ishmael was the firstborn son, so there is some basis for supposing that Muslims may be correct about

Christians will hasten to point out that God sent an angel to stop Abraham before he killed his son, this does not really diminish the barbarity of what "God" was supposedly asking Abraham to do. How could the true God[990] command a man to perform an action that, by its very nature, is inhuman, wicked, contrary to nature, and the very antithesis of what distinguishes us as human? What kind of a "test" was this? And while Christians cannot escape this any more than Jews, since they have "inherited" the Scriptures of the Jews as a legacy, in a way it seems even more of a burden for them. For in the New Testament, Christians are told to not trust every spirit, but to "test the spirits"[991] to see whether they are of God. But in the case of Abraham, we are left wondering whether he "tested" the voice that told him to offer up his son as a human sacrifice. Would not the very nature of such a "command" have identified the source as diabolical, rather than divine? What kind of a "God" would "command" such an inhuman atrocity? It would be more believable, at least to people who believe in a devil, to ascribe such an auditory "command" to the devil, rather than to God. Yet Christians and Jews seem blithely oblivious to this moral dilemma.[992] They are so hidebound by an authoritarian belief-system that they cannot either reason for themselves, or listen to their own individual voice of conscience.[993] This is really the fundamental problem. But of course in this example, the crux of the argument for biblical apologists is that God did not allow Abraham to follow through with the action. The argument being that, since God had all along decided that this was merely a "test" of Abraham's faith and loyalty, the intended atrocity is really superfluous, since it was never performed.[994] But there are cases where atrocities were performed,

---

this. Isaac was not Abraham's "only" son.

[990]　i.e., assuming that there is a God.

[991]　1 John 4:1ff.

[992]　The same is also true of Muslims, who also believe in the story, albeit as applied to Ishmael, rather than Isaac. The story is also referred to in the Islamic Gospel of Barnabas.

[993]　i.e., unless they are lucky enough not to be completely brainwashed by a blind belief in the Bible.

[994]　Assuming there was any historicity whatever to the story, the incident was unlikely to foster very much in the way of filial affection; the psychology of such a case could inspire volumes on the subject, as perhaps an example of

not only with apparent divine sanction, but even at divine command. We will get to these examples shortly. But first the reader ought to be informed that, according to the Bible, the "God" of the Israelites allowed them to have foreigners as slaves:

44 Thy bondmen, and thy bondmaids, which thou shalt have, *shall be* of the heathen that are round about you; of them shall ye buy bondmen and bondmaids.

45 Moreover, of the children of the strangers that do sojourn among you, of them shall ye buy, and of their families that *are* with you, which they begat in your land: and they shall be your possession.

46 And ye shall take them as an inheritance for your children after you, to inherit *them for* a possession; they shall be your bondmen for ever: but over your brethren the sons of Israel, you shall not rule over one another with rigor. (Leviticus 25:44-46)[995]

This is both barbaric and unjust, and we would not expect the true God to inspire any such thing. Notice also that such bondage is placed upon a distinctively ethnic basis. If the Bible were truly the word of God, then it would not contain any such glaring barbarities. There is no legitimate excuse for this; if appeal is made to the brutality of antiquity, then would not the divinity of the Bible have been most clearly evident by the tolerance, compassion, and enlightenment that it otherwise could have, should have, and would have displayed, had it been so inspired? In fact, this is another instance in which the distinctly human origin of Scripture is quite self-evident; because, as we will see, the bulk of the most barbaric passages always occur in the oldest books of the Bible. We see a more lofty conception of God and ethics unfolding in the Jewish Scriptures as they approach closer to our own time; it almost seems to be a sort of moral and philosophical evolution, discernible right in the "sacred" pages of "holy" writ. This moral, philosophical, and theological evolution can also be further

---

a "dysfunctional" family. So much for the so-called "family values" of the religious right wing.

[995] Such a notoriously shocking passage is printed right in the Bible for everyone to see and read, yet if anyone dares to call Judaism a racist religion, they are castigated as an Anti-Semite. What unmitigated *chutzpah!*

traced in the Apocrypha and the Old Testament Pseudepigrapha, and finally in the New Testament.[996] This last statement is by no means intended to place the New Testament upon a pedestal above the Old Testament. In fact, the Old Testament is the necessary foundation for the New, and if the Old Testament lacks divine inspiration, then the New Testament also falls into quicksand.

But we may also notice that the Israelites are only allowed to enslave the surrounding people, rather than the native Palestinians. Why? Because "God" commanded the Israelites to completely exterminate the latter. This statement is so incredibly shocking that the reader may not believe it. But it is right there in the Bible itself:

10 When thou comest nigh unto a city to fight against it, then proclaim peace unto it.

11 And it shall be, if it make thee answer of peace, and open unto thee, then it shall be, *that* all the people found therein shall be tributaries unto thee, and they shall serve thee.

12 And if it will make no peace with thee, but will make war against thee, then thou shalt besiege it:

13 And when the LORD thy God hath delivered it into thine hands, thou shalt smite every male thereof with the edge of the sword:

14 But the women, and the little ones, and the cattle, and all that is in the city, *even* all the spoil thereof, shalt thou take unto thyself; and thou shalt eat the spoil of thine enemies, which the LORD thy God hath given thee.

15 Thus shalt thou do unto all the cities *which are* very far off from thee, which *are* not of the cities of these nations.

---

[996] However there is one notable but explainable exception to this process of moral evolution; I am speaking of the concept of everlasting torment, which does not explicitly occur anywhere within *TaNaKh*. But this circumstance can be accounted for on quite human grounds. See discussion below.

16 But of the cities of these people, which the LORD thy God doth give thee *for* an inheritance, <u>thou shalt save alive nothing that breathes:</u>

17 But thou shalt <u>utterly destroy</u> them; *namely,* the Hittites, and the Amorites, the Canaanites, and the Perizzites, the Hivites, and the Jebusites; as the LORD thy God hath commanded thee. (Deuteronomy 20:10-17)[997]

This passage clearly and unmistakably advocates, nay, even commands, with alleged divine authority, the slaughter, nay the very extermination, of the native Palestinians.[998] This cannot be merely a matter of translation either. However the passage is translated, the underlying meaning is still the same. It is not one that inspires confidence in the Bible as the word of God. This would seem to make the position of Bible believers untenable, especially in the moral sense. And yet these very same people want to "legislate" morality and determine public policy. The strange thing we also find in the Bible is that, although the Israelites were sometimes lax in carrying out such a program of extermination, their "God" would be very angry with them for such laxness. In other words, oftentimes because the Israelites were reluctant to kill the Palestinians, "God's" prophets would denounce them for such a lapse of faith. Whether this "laxness" was due to sheer laziness, fear, or possibly a sense of common humanity, or perhaps the perceived difficulty of overcoming the will of their opponents to live, in any case the "God" of Israel was most disappointed with such deviations from his intended program. Can anyone imagine a more malevolent deity? Is this the "God" we are expected to believe in? The very fact that both intelligence and morality are subjugated to the authoritarianism of blind faith among such people is what makes the whole thing so potentially dangerous.[999]

---

[997] Notice that the Hittites are also under the ban of extermination. So David's murder of Uriah the Hittite could not have seemed to be too much of a moral problem, presumably.

[998] In view of this text the current Israeli policy vis-à-vis Palestinians is understood, but not condoned. Such policy being one of *apartheid* and ultimately *genocide*.

[999] And this includes Christianity, Judaism, and Islam. Remember 9/11/2001?

But we can see this program or *pogrom* spoken of frequently within the *Torah*.

24 Every place whereon the soles of your feelt shall tread shall be yours; from the wilderness and Lebanon, from the river, the River Euphrates, even unto the uttermost sea shall your coast be. (Deuteronomy 11:24)

Obviously such conquest would only be possible by the subjugation, if not extermination, of the indigenous peoples of the land. We find the seeds of this even in Genesis:

18 In that same day GOD made a covenant with Abram, saying, Unto thy seed have I given this land, from the river of Egypt unto the great river, the River Euphrates;

19 the Kenites, and the Kenizzites, and the Kadmonites,

20 and the Hittites, and the Perizzites, and the Rephaim,

21 and the Amorites, and the Canaanites, and the Girgashites, and the Jebusites. (Genesis 15:18–21)

All these peoples were targeted for extermination. But this program of genocide was also expanded, to include the Amalekites:

14 And the LORD said unto Moses, Write this *for* a memorial in a book, and rehearse *it* in the ears of Joshua: For I will utterly blot out the remembrance of Amalek from under heaven. (Exodus 17:14)

17 Remember what Amalek did unto thee by the way, when ye were come forth out of Egypt;

18 how he met thee by the way, and smote the hindmost of thee, *even* all *that were* feeble behind thee, when thou *wast* faint and weary; and he feared not God.

19 Therfore it shall be, when the LORD thy God hath given thee rest from all thine enemies round about, in the land which the LORD

thy God giveth thee *for* an inheritance to possess it, *that* thou shalt blot out the remembrance of Amalek from under heaven; thou shalt not forget *it*. (Deuteronomy 25:17-19, KJV)

Sometimes Christians and Jews try to defend such a proposed atrocity by alleging that the people in question performed human sacrifices; therefore it was a matter of rescuing harmless infants from this terrible danger. But a diligent scrutiny of Scripture dispels any such pretence; for "God" even commanded the Israelites to murder innocent little babies. This is so shocking that only a direct quotation from Scripture will do:

2   Thus saith the LORD of hosts, I remember *that* which Amalek did to Israel, how he had laid *wait* for him in the way, when he came up from Egypt.

3   Now go and smite Amalek, and utterly destroy all that they have, and spare them not; but slay both man and woman, infant and suckling, ox and sheep, camel and ass. (1 Samuel 15:2-3, KJV)

So the false pretence that infants, toddlers and young children were being rescued from a brutal culture is belied by this text. What kind of a "God" would order people to kill innocent little babies? As far as I'm concerned the true God would never order any such thing. I don't expect anyone to "take my word" that the passage is in the Bible; I urge the reader to look it up for himself or herself. Once again I do not believe that the problem lies with the translation. Regardless of what translation you consult, the meaning will remain the same. Furthermore the reader should also be aware of the fact that the King James translators would have wanted to put the best possible "spin" on such embarrassing passages as possible; but without falsifying the text altogether, we are left with some pretty barbaric conceptions of God and the will of God. Christians might attempt to rationalize the passage away by appealing to how the "carnal mind" cannot be subject to God, and therefore cannot judge such things.[1000] But this lame excuse is hardly satisfying to anyone objectively looking at the evidence. Some Christians and Jews also try to justify the intended genocide of the Amalekites by appealing to God's foreknowledge that

---

[1000]   Romans 8:5-8.

a Hitler–like persecutor of the Jews would have been born from among them.[1001] But once again this is a dubious argument, and in the very nature of the case, can never be proven. What strikes me as worst of all is that I know of no group of either Jews or Christians who have repudiated the passage in question as uninspired.[1002] Even the Koran contains nothing quite as barbaric as this.[1003] Neither does the Law of Manu, which is quite barbaric.[1004] Is it not time for us to put such archaic, antiquated things behind us?

We see yet more brutality and slaughter in the so–called "holy" Bible:

And *when* King Arad the Canaanite, which dwelt in the south, heard tell that the Israelites came by the way of the spies, then he fought against Israel, and took *some* of them prisoners.

2 And Israel vowed a vow unto the LORD, and said, If thou wilt indeed deliver up this people into my hand, then I will utterly destroy their cities.

3 And the LORD hearkened to the voice of Israel, and delivered up the Canaanites; and they utterly destroyed them and their cities: and he called the name of the place Hormah. (Numbers 21:1-3)

We also read of similar inhuman barbarities perpetrated by the Israelites, with apparent divine sanction; when the Israelites began to mingle with the Midianites, and were supposedly led astray into idolatry, severe measures were taken:

[1001] In fact some Rabbis believe that Hitler was an Amalekite. The arch-fiend Haman of the book of Esther was an Amalekite, according to Josephus; cf Jos. Ant. 11.6.12.

[1002] Of course by doing so, the *plenary* inspiration of Scripture would fall to the ground; nevertheless in my view they would have been taking the moral high ground.

[1003] But it does say of "infidels" to "kill them wherever you find them"; Koran Sura 2:191. Ironically, some Christian ministries try to use this verse from the Koran as a basis for polemics against Islam, and to promote Christianity; but they will blithely ignore the far worse things found in the Bible.

[1004] The Law of Manu is a sacred scripture of the Hindus. It disallows the equality of women, and speaks of cutting off a person's fingers for theft, etc.

4   And GOD said unto Moses, Take all the heads of the people, and hang them up before the LORD against the sun, that the fierce anger of the LORD may be turned away from Israel. (Numbers 25:4)[1005]

Then in the same chapter we read that one of the sons of Israel brought a Midianite woman to his brothers in the sight of Moses, while the people were mourning over the supposed "sin" of Israel. The sequel to this is perhaps best told in the words of Scripture:

7   And when Phinehas, the son of Eleazar, the son of Aaron the high priest, saw *this,* he rose up from among the congregation, and took a javelin in his hand;

8   and he went after the man of Israel into the tent, and thrust both of them thrugh, the man of Israel, and the woman, through her belly. So the plague was stayed from the sons of Israel. (Numbers 25:7-8)

And "God" responded to this action by granting Phinehas a covenant of an everlasting priesthood.[1006] So we can clearly see that the Old Testament God was a brutal God of vengeance. The Israelites often carried out the brutal pogrom against the native Palestinians.

21   And they utterly destroyed all that *was* in the city, both man and woman, young and old, and ox, and sheep, and ass, with the edge of the sword. (Joshua 6:21)

How is it that we almost never hear about this holocaust of Palestinians? Neither do we typically hear very much[1007] about the current Israeli policy of Palestinian *apartheid* and *genocide*. This is no doubt partly do to the incestuous relationship between Jews

---

[1005] George M. Lamsa, in his translation of the Bible from the Syriac Peshitta text, tried to obscure the innate brutality of this verse by his translation. But if one reads his entire translation, one will see that he could not eliminate every instance of such atrocities in Scripture. Since there are so many other passages that display an inhuman brutality, there is no reason to doubt it in this instance.

[1006] Numbers 25:13.

[1007] At least not in American media.

and Christians in America and the West.[1008] After all, the Christians hold the Jewish Scriptures sacred as their Old Testament. And the millennial fascination with biblical prophecy has been a boon to Dispensational Premillennialists, who have vigorously promoted their literal interpretation of Scripture, and virtually "cornered the market" on Protestant interpretations of eschatology. This has resulted in the explosion of Christian Zionism, which gives the current Israeli regime the façade of legitimacy through entrenched political support. Perhaps this *status quo* is subconsciously guaranteed by the guilty consciences of so many Americans, since white Europeans have in effect perpetrated a similar policy of *apartheid* and *passive genocide* upon the indigenous peoples of the Americas.[1009]

We can see that the Israelites sometimes eagerly followed through with the bloodthirsty pogrom against the Palestinians.[1010] Of course we cannot be sure whether or not these things literally happened, despite the often cynical assessment of human nature. Nevertheless what we do read of is so horrible that we fail to see how anyone could derive legitimate spiritual edification from such things. Furthermore we can be reasonably certain that there was some degree of bloodshed and brutality. To blame it on the brutality of the times is no excuse. God is supposed to be morally perfect from all eternity. Why did he not display that moral perfection by inculcating the highest possible model of morality in his revelation from the very beginning? How were the Israelites supposed to be a beacon of light to the world, if they slaughtered the Palestinians, and enslaved the surrounding peoples? Neither Christians nor Jews can provide a reasonable answer to this question, without abandoning the false pretence of biblical inspiration.

And what of David, so beloved by both Jews and Christians? He is upheld as a hero, a prophet, and a saint. Yet we read some things of him in Scripture that are not too salubrious. We read that "God" was

---

[1008] And this in spite of the age-long persecutions of Jews by so-called "Christians".

[1009] I hope the reader will pardon my indulgence in this brief political digression; but this shows one of many ways in which our discussion is relevant to current events. We need to first become aware of the problem, before we can fix it. We can choose to be part of the problem, or part of the solution. Sorry if this sounds a bit "preachy", but I would rather be part of the solution, than part of the problem.

[1010] Joshua 11:21-22.

disappointed with King Saul because he did not slaughter all of the Amalekites,[1011] so he sent Samuel to anoint David to be king,[1012] even calling David "a man after his own heart"[1013] apparently because David was not so squeamish about killing men, women, and children.

8   And David and his men went up, and invaded the Geshurites, and the Gezrites, and the Amalekites; for those *nations were* of old the inhabitants of the land, as thou goest to Shur, even unto the land of Egypt.

9   And David smote the land, and left neither man nor woman alive, and took away the sheep, and the oxen, and the asses, and the camels, and the apparel, and returned, and came to Achish.

10 And Achish said, Whither have ye made a road today? And David said, Against the south of Judah, and against the south of the Jerahmeelites, and against the south of the Kenites.

11 And David saved neither man nor woman alive, to bring *tidings* to Gath, saying, Lest they should tell on us, saying, So did David, and so *will be* his manner all the while he dwelleth in the country of the Philistines.

12 And Achish believed David, saying, He hath made his people Israel utterly to abhor him; therefore he shall be my servant forever. (1 Samuel 27:8-12, KJV)

Although the text does not mention it, presumably David killed all the children, as well as both the men and the women, to prevent his atrocities from becoming known to the Palestinians. These are clearly inhuman acts of barbarity, and today would be considered war crimes. Consider also this brutal treatment:

And it came to pass, that after the year was expired, at the time that kings go out to battle, Joab led forth the power of the army, and wasted the country of the sons of Ammon, and came and besieged

---

[1011]   1 Samuel 15.

[1012]   1 Samuel 16.

[1013]   1 Samuel 13:14.

Rabbah. But David stayed at Jerusalem. And Joab smote Rabbah, and destroyed it.

2 And David took the crown of their king from off his head, and found it to weigh a talent of gold, and there were also precious stones in it; and it was set upon David's head: and he brought also exceeding much spoil out of the city.

3 And he brought out the people that were therein, and cut them with saws, and with harrows of iron, and with axes. Even so dealt David with all the cities of the sons of Ammon. And David and all the people returned to Jerusalem. (1 Chronicles 20:1-3)

We can hardly imagine a worse manner of execution than what is described here, with apparent divine sanction. Any person with a shred of human decency would be utterly revolted by such passages.[1014] From the perspective of a universal ethics, it is unreasonable to grant any moral authority whatever to the Bible. But although these brutal passages are found in the Old Testament, this is not strictly a problem for Jews; Christians also are burdened with the weight of this unanswerable moral objection against the Bible. Jesus himself is reported to have quoted from the Jewish Scriptures as the absolute word of God, on many occasions. He explicitly acknowledged the alleged Divine Authority of TaNaKh. This is brought out especially by the "every yod" passage.[1015] So Christians cannot escape the moral culpability of felony genocide without violating the integrity of Scripture. The Israelites also had apparent divine sanction to rape women captured in battle.[1016] We should also keep in mind that the Bible also sanctions slavery.[1017] Because of this, during the days of

---

[1014] This was one of the things I struggled with in my life as a born-again Christian. Finally I could no longer rationalize such things away any longer.

[1015] Matthew 5:17-18; cf John 10:35.

[1016] Deuteronomy 21:10-13. Some apologists might point out that "God" allowed the women thus captured to mourn for their parents a full month, before being sexually violated. I suppose that this is supposed to prove how "enlightened" the Israelites were.

[1017] Leviticus 25:44-46; Ephesians 6:5; Colossians 3:22; 1 Timothy 6:1; Titus 2:9. In all four instances from the New Testament, in the original Greek the proper word for *slaves* or *slave* are used, being *douloi* and *doulous,* respectively;

the American slave trade, many southern preachers sought to justify that horrible practice by an appeal to the Bible. So we can see that these questions are more than just theoretical. Unfortunately, this brutal legacy is like a poison root that pervades the whole of Scripture; however otherwise lofty and noble are some of the sentiments expressed in certain portions of the Bible, the context of Scripture, and especially the fact that the very earliest, most foundational portions of Scripture, are filled with such inhuman, unmitigated brutality and barbarity vitiate any claim to divine inspiration or moral authority. One must also note that the point here is not that the Bible merely records instances of barbarity, which any number of historical records may do; but rather that such barbarity is actually inculcated as righteousness therein. It was as if the more brutal, barbaric, and inhuman the Israelites could be, the more that "God" was pleased with them. How could this be the true universal God? How could this be the Supreme Being? How could this be the Creator? The answer should be obvious. The "God" of the Old Testament was merely a tribal deity of an ignorant, superstitious people.[1018]

We mentioned in a footnote above that the only exception to the moral evolution otherwise apparent throughout Scripture is the case of the concept of eternal torment. There is no explicit reference to a state of eternal torment anywhere within TaNaKh.[1019] But the concept of eternal torment is found in the Apocrypha, the Old Testament Pseudepigrapha, and the New Testament.[1020] So in this respect we

---

cf Nestle-Aland., op. cit., pgs. 513, 529, 548, 558. The King James softens this to *servants.*

[1018] i.e., unless we were to acquiesce to the teaching of Scientology that it was a malevolent extraterrestrial. But this seems too far-fetched to be true; besides, this is merely a materialistic variation on Gnosticism.

[1019] On this basis certain Christian cults, like the Seventh-Day Adventists, the Jehovah's Witnesses, the Christadelphians, and others, postulate such doctrines as *soul sleep* and *annihilationism.* The former doctrine is that the soul is unconscious until the final day of judgment and resurrection; the latter doctrine is that the unsaved will not be eternally tormented in a fiery inferno, but will instead by completely destroyed (annihilated) by God; in other words, completely erased and uncreated. While these ideas may be morally superior to more traditional interpretations of judgment in Christianity, they will not bear up under the scrutiny of a critical-historical appraisal, in terms of the roots of Christianity within apocalyptic Judaism.

[1020] And there can be no real doubt that the Dead Sea community believed in a

find a counter-example to the moral evolution otherwise evident. But this circumstance may be readily accounted for in critical-historical terms. It was not any lack of brutality on the part of the Israelites that kept them from postulating a state of endless torment hereafter for their enemies; it was merely a lack of imagination. What is notable is that none of the Jewish religious books dating to before the second century B.C. contain any explicit reference to a possible state of eternal torment for the wicked; the concept can only be found in those texts dating to the second century B.C. or later. This is the key. What happened in the second century B.C.? During that century, the Jews were bitterly persecuted by Antiochus Epiphanes and his minions, and were brutalized in the most barbaric ways imaginable,[1021] in an effort to make them forsake their ancestral religion. The brutal treatment that the Jews received at the hands of Antiochus Epiphanes and his minions was unprecedented. Finally Antiochus was overthrown, but the emotional scars upon the Jewish people remained. They must have mused upon the justice of God, and what the ultimate fate of the wicked would be. This had not been clarified in any of their earlier Scriptures. So some Jews, at least, adopted the idea that the justice of God could only be vindicated if such wicked men were tormented forever in some afterdeath realm.[1022] Other Jews rejected the idea. These latter came to be called the Sadducees.[1023] But the Sadducees also rejected any resurrection, either carnal or spiritual.[1024] Apparently this was done to maintain consistency. But their view was not without precedent within the Jewish Scriptures.[1025] The Sadducees rejected the

---

state of everlasting torment for infidels, since they held such books as Enoch and Judith as authoritative.

[1021] Cf II Maccabees 6-7; IV Maccabees.

[1022] Cf Judith 16:17 cp Isaiah 66:24; Mark 9:43-48; cf IV Maccabees 5:34; Enoch 22:14;
II Esdras 7:56; 9:9-12; Luke 16:19-31; Revelation 14:9-11; 19:20; 20:10-15 cp Malachi 4:1; Ezekiel 28:17-19.

[1023] Both the Pharisees and the Essenes accepted the idea of eternal torment of the wicked. The Talmud also speaks of a state of everlasting torment. I am uncertain as to whether or not Karaite Jews also believe in a state of eternal torment for the wicked.

[1024] Acts 23:8; Jos. War. 2.8.14.

[1025] Isaiah 38:18; Ecclesiastes 9:5; Psalms 6:6; 88:5; 115:17; 146:4.

divine authority of both *Nehevim* and *Kethuvim;* they held only the *Torah* as strictly Canonical. In any case the majority of Jews living after the second century B.C. believed in hell, or a place of everlasting fiery torment, for unbelievers. This is the necessary historical context that must be acknowledged when studying the Gospels and other books of the New Testament. Cults that teach soul sleep and annihilation are ignoring the historical context from which Christianity emerged. This results in an arbitrary, artificial interpretation of Scripture.[1026] They are just as guilty of begging the question in respect to the Canon of Scripture as all the other Protestant groups are.[1027] So it must be admitted that, in all probability, an assumed state of eternal torment was at least the exoteric form of earliest Christian teaching.[1028] So the moral atrocity of such a barbaric concept as that of everlasting torment is easily explained by recourse to historical circumstances. Once again this points to the purely human origin of Scripture. And such a grotesquely barbaric idea is also another huge and ultimately unanswerable objection against the pretended divine authority of the New Testament.[1029] So both the Old Testament and the New are morally unacceptable. They are uninspired. Therefore any miracles that they relate remain unproven and incredible fables; and this also necessarily includes the supposed miracle of Christ's resurrection from the dead. Indeed, the fables of the New Testament are not even cunningly devised.[1030] If God performed all the miracles narrated in the Bible, then he could have, should have, and would have, performed the final miracle of preserving his Word intact, in a state of pristine

---

[1026] However otherwise pleasing their interpretations may seem to be.

[1027] It is quite evident on critical-historical grounds that the books of Enoch, Jubilees, as well as several books of the Apocrypha were accepted as Canonical Scripture by the earliest Christians. This fact vitiates all the arguments of such cults in favor of their invented doctrines of soul sleep and annihilationism. In fact it is not going too far to say that the New Testament is not fully understandable without reference to these other books. But Protestant fundamentalists would sweep this all under the rug.

[1028] It is possible, if we assume an esotericism within original Christianity, that this is not what Jesus and the Apostles themselves believed. But we can really only speculate on this.

[1029] The same objection is equally valid against the presumed divine inspiration of the Koran.

[1030] Cp 2 Peter 1:16.

perfection. The manifest imperfection of Scripture is proof against any presumption of divine inspiration. And this evident imperfection also necessarily casts reasonable doubt upon the alleged miracles recorded in Scripture. We can only maintain the gravest suspicion upon such dubious matters; and the only reasonable option is to positively reject all such claims as preposterous.

Before moving on to the next subsection, there is an important point I would like to make, lest my words be misconstrued or taken out of context. Nothing I write herein is in any way intended to denigrate or insult people who may be ethnically Jewish. Nobody can choose what racial or ethnic group they may be born into, nor do I wish to imply that Jews as an ethnic people are in any way responsible for what their ancestors may have done, written, or believed. There are some brave Jews of conscience who are also speaking out against the Israeli policy of Palestinian *apartheid*. There are some Jews critical of Israeli foreign and domestic policy.[1031] There are some American Jews who have spoken out against the oppression of people in Gaza. There are also some very brave Israeli Jews who have protested against the unjust policies of the Israeli government. I fully acknowledge all this. So I do not want certain critical statements made herein to be taken out of context, or blown out of proportion by intolerant demagogues and pedagogues. Furthermore it should be quite clear that I haven't exactly given Muslims or anyone else a "free pass" herein.

Another problem with the Bible is the grave uncertainty surrounding the Canon, text, and interpretation of Scripture. Different Christian denominations disagree about these three crucial questions. A person examining the religion objectively can see a great deal of ambiguity, which is not what we would expect of a divine revelation. We have only very briefly touched upon legitimate doubts as to the delineation of the Canon of Scripture in some of our discussions above. In fact there are eight distinct Christian Canons of Scripture: the Greek Orthodox, the Syrian Orthodox, the Coptic Orthodox, the Ethiopian Orthodox, the Russian Orthodox, the Nestorian, the Roman Catholic, and the Protestant. The Protestant Canon of the New Testament is identical with that of Roman Catholicism, Greek Orthodoxy, and Russian Orthodoxy.[1032] The Protestant Canon of the

---

[1031] Such as Norman G. Finkelstein.

[1032] I am uncertain as to whether or not the Nestorian Canon of the New

Old Testament is congruent with the holy Scriptures of the Jews, otherwise known as TaNaKh.[1033] The Syrian Orthodox Church excludes five books from its Canon of the New Testament.[1034] The Coptic Orthodox Church includes a secret book of Mark as part of its New Testament Canon.[1035] The Ethiopian Orthodox Church includes threeor four books not included in the more "standard" canon in its Canon of the New Testament.[1036] The Ethiopian Orthodox Church also includes a number of books in its Old Testament Canon of Scripture not included in the Protestant Canon.[1037] The Greek Orthodox Church holds as sacred all the books included in the Ethiopian Orthodox Old Testament, except for Enoch, Jubilees, Baruch, IV Baruch, IV Ezra, I Maccabees, II Maccabees. The Russian Orthodox Church holds a Canon identical to that of the Greek Orthodox Church, to the best of my knowledge.[1038] The Roman Catholic Church includes all the books found in the Protestant Canon of Scripture, as well as Tobit, Judith, Wisdom, Sirach, I Maccabees II Maccabees.[1039] A person with a personal faith in Jesus Christ as the Son of God would thereby be confronted with seven possible choices in respect to the Canon of Scripture; and while an individual Christian might have his or her own opinion as to what the most correct or appropriate Canon of Scripture is or should be, the different

---

Testament is any different from this.

[1033] However the Ethiopian Jews also hold other Scriptures as Canonical, such as the books of Enoch, Jubilees, Baruch, and IV Ezra.

[1034] i.e., II Peter, II & III John, Jude & Revelation.

[1035] See the 1971 printed edition of the Encyclopaedia Britannica.

[1036] i.e., I Clement, Hermas, Sinodos, and possibly the Epistle of Barnabas.

[1037] i.e., Enoch, Jubilees, Baruch, IV Baruch, IV Ezra, Judith, Tobit, Wisdom of Solomon, Sirach, I Maccabees, II Maccabees, III Maccabees, IV Maccabees. Although the Kebra Nagast is not held as strictly Canonical, in functional terms it is; it is implicitly believed by all the Aethiopian Christians. The African Orthodox Churches also have a very high veneration of Mary, the mother of Christ, in common with the Roman Catholic Church.

[1038] However the Russian Orthodox Church is autocephalous, and in this respect is independent in determining its own Canon of Scrpiture.

[1039] As well as the more complete texts of Esther and Daniel, found in the Septuagint, which texts are also standard in all the Orthodox Churches as well.

Canons of the different churches could only create reasonable doubt in respect to any Canon of Scripture; and this in turn would only lead to greater doubt about other things, including ultimately the whole of the Christian faith.[1040] Uncertainty in respect to the text of Scripture is a related but somewhat more technical issue, which may not come up in a Christian's life, unless it is in the case of those King James purists who uphold the Byzantine textual family as superior to the other three families.[1041]

Uncertainty with respect to the interpretation of Scripture is a relevant issue, however; and this uncertainty can be traced back to the inherent ambiguity of the meaning of Scripture, which in turn is based upon the false premise of the unity of Scripture, which in turn is based upon the false premise of the divine inspiration of Scripture. Since the Bible contains numerous and manifold contradictions, the meaning thereof in a holistic sense is ambiguous. Why else would there be so many different Christian denominations, churches, cults, and sects? Of course part of the problem is the copious volume of Scripture. Even stripping the Bible down to the Protestant Canon of Scripture, it is still a book composed of many different books, written by different men at different times and places. There is also the fundamental distinction between the Old Testament and the New Testament. The various books of the Bible also comprise a number of different literary *genres,* which necessarily must be approached somewhat differently, in terms of interpretation. But even taking all these things into account, there still remains a much larger degree of ambiguity and uncertainty to the meaning of the text, by reason of multitudinous contradictions; this is not what we would expect of a document or set of documents comprising a divine revelation. Various attempts at reconciliation of discordant passages result in several different sets of interpretations, each one favored by a particular denomination or sect of Christianity. As a person who has been there, I can vouch for the fact that this situation creates an immense amount of confusion and doubt in the mind of the serious seeker of truth; these are not mere

---

[1040] I am not saying that uncertainty with respect to the Canon of Scripture would in and of itself necessarily be sufficient to overturn a person's faith; but we must consider this question in relationship to all the other problems with the Bible touched on herein.

[1041] i.e., the Alexandrian, the Caesarean, and the Western. See the discussion above on the text-types and textual families.

gripes of scorners, mockers, iconoclasts, or cynics. These are problems confronted by the sincere seeker of truth.[1042]

Another problem with the Bible is that it is notoriously incomplete. There are at least ten books that are mentioned in the Bible that are no longer found anywhere in the Bible; neither are these books to be found in the Apocrypha or the Old Testament Pseudepigrapha. These are the lost books of the Bible.[1043] From the very context of Scripture, and the way that these books are spoken of, as well as the fact that in most cases, the authors are otherwise identified in Scripture as men who were true prophets, we have every reason to expect that these books would have been considered divinely inspired by the Israelites, and would have been preserved in the Canon of Scripture, but unfortunately they did not survive the ravages of time and history. The following is a list of ten of these books, and where in the Bible references to them may be found:

1. The book of the Wars of the LORD.[1044]
2. The book of Jasher.[1045]
3. The book of Samuel the Seer.[1046]
4. The book of Gad the Seer.[1047]
5. The book of Nathan the Prophet.[1048]
6. The book of Ahijah the Shilonite.[1049]
7. The vision of Iddo the Seer.[1050]

[1042] Who may hold a sincere faith in Jesus as the Son of God.

[1043] Protestant Christians try to speciously argue that these books were never intended to have been included in the Bible, since they were not divinely inspired. But their arguments are dishonest, ridiculous, absurd, obtuse, myopic, and unconvincing. Once again as usual they constantly beg the question, and are guilty of special pleading.

[1044] Numbers 21:14.

[1045] Joshua 10:13; II Samuel 1:18. Jasher is also called Jashar or Asher.

[1046] I Chronicles 29:29. This book should not be confused with the biblical book of Samuel, which was originally entitled Kings. See the Septuagint.

[1047] I Chronicles 29:29.

[1048] I Chronicles 29:29; II Chronicles 9:29.

[1049] II Chronicles 9:29.

[1050] II Chronicles 9:29; 12:15; 13:22.

8. The book of Shemaiah the Prophet.[1051]
9. The book of Jehu.[1052]
10. The book of the Acts of Solomon.[1053]

Aside from these books, there is also mention made of the chronicles of the kings of Media and Persia.[1054] While we would not expect such a volume to be included in the Bible, nevertheless the work has become lost in the sands of time. As a result, we no longer have this secular historical record confirming what is written in Esther. And this is definitely a problem for the Bible.[1055] The reason why is appeal is being made to a source confirming the story narrated in the text of Esther. God could have, should have, and would have, preserved this chronicle intact, had the Bible been his divinely inspired Word. We at least have a reasonable expectation of such. We're talking about God here. In Christian theological terms, God is defined as omnipotent, omnipresent, and omniscient. Nothing is impossible for God.[1056] References to now-lost books in the Bible is a standing argument against the presumption of the divine origin of the Bible. We are also told that King Solomon wrote three thousand proverbs and one thousand and five songs.[1057] Yet of these only one song of Solomon has survived, and the book of Proverbs contains far less than three thousand proverbs. Furthermore we are told that Solomon spoke of trees, beasts, fowl, creeping things, and of fishes.[1058] Yet there is none of this in Scripture.[1059] We also read of the book of the kings of

---

[1051] II Chronicles 12:15.

[1052] II Chronicles 20:34.

[1053] I Kings 11:41.

[1054] Esther 10:2.

[1055] And the argument in this case applies to the ten books already enumerated, regardless of whether or not they were ever considered divinely inspired.

[1056] i.e., other than a logical self-contradiction.

[1057] I Kings 4:32.

[1058] I Kings 4:33.

[1059] Unless we count the errant verse about ants. Spiders are mentioned in Proverbs 30:28. But it is clearly evident that we only we have a relatively small portion of what Solomon wrote.

Israel and Judah,[1060] and also of the book of the chronicles of the kings of Israel,[1061] and the book of the chronicles of the kings of Judah.[1062] We can be quite sure that the reference to the book of the kings of Israel and Judah is definitely not to the biblical book of Kings; this is proven by the fact that the prayer of Manasseh is said to be written therein.[1063] This is nowhere to be found in the biblical book of kings, although some editions of the Apocrypha contain it. We are also told that more details are to be found in the Sayings of the Seers, another lost work.[1064] The book of the chronicles of the kings of Israel is definitely a lost book of the Bible. The book of the chronicles of the kings of Judah is also definitely a lost book. One may be tempted to identify the latter work with the biblical book of Chronicles, but the problem is that this would presuppose that Chronicles predates Kings, which, although it is possible, is extremely improbable and most biblical scholars reject the idea. But I would also hasten to add that if one were to adopt this position, then one would have to distinguish between the book of the kings of Israel and Judah, mentioned in the text of Chronicles, and the biblical book of Kings. Otherwise one is invoking the paradox of two works that both predate one another.[1065] Of course all these texts were most likely source documents for the biblical books of Kings and Chronicles. But we can see by all this the absence of a providential preservation of texts that would be essential for a complete appraisal and testimony to the supposed divine revelation proclaimed. Of course Christians can no doubt come up with clever excuses, but they prove nothing. Nobody looking at the evidence objectively can be impressed with the emotionally-charged arguments and sentimental appeals likely to be made by such persons. Most likely the book of Jasher was lost during the Assyrian invasion of Israel, or the Babylonian conquest of Judah. The various lost books mentioned in Kings and Chronicles were probably lost during the

---

[1060] I Chronicles 9:1; II Chronicles 16:11; 27:7; 28:26; 33:18; 35:27.

[1061] I Kings 14:19; 15:31; 16:5,14,20,27; 22:39; II Kings 1:18; 10:34; 13:8,12; 14:15,28; 15:11,15,21,26.

[1062] I Kings 14:29; 15:7,23; 22:45; II Kings 8:23; 12:19; 15:6; 16:19; 20:20; 21:17,25; 23:28; 24:5.

[1063] II Chronicles 33:18.

[1064] II Chronicles 33:19.

[1065] And postdate one another as well. This is clearly impossible.

tumultuous battles and hazards of the Maccabean era. Interestingly, we read of yet more lost texts in the books of the Maccabees. The book of the chronicles of the high priesthood of John Hyrcanus[1066] has unfortunately become lost. The five books of Jason of Cyrene, which was the basis for II Maccabees, has also become lost.[1067] It is uncertain exactly how and when these two works were lost, but the former work may have been known to Josephus.[1068] The latter work may have been lost either during the first Roman invasion of Judaea, or during the time of Titus, or Hadrian. Whether it survived beyond this is unknown. Unfortunately the library of Alexandria was burnt during the days of Antony and Cleopatra. But in this we see that these various religious books of the Jews have suffered the same fate as many other works of antiquity; we have only a portion of ancient writings. This is a terrible tragedy, because I feel that we can learn so much from all these things. But once again, the lesson learned is that the Bible, while a great literary treasure, is not the word of God.

Some apologists for the Bible make a huge mistake in thinking that critics of the Bible are somehow out to "destroy" the Bible. They speak glowingly and with admiration of the "survival" of the Bible in the face of centuries of criticism. But no civilized person seeks to "destroy" the Bible in a purely vandalistic sense, as if that would prove anything, other than the ignorance and barbarity of the perpetrator. Criticism of Scripture is instead aimed at the false belief in the Bible as divinely inspired. Of course we recognize that the Bible is the single greatest literary icon of our culture; it is part of our Western heritage. In fact I would say that ignorance of the Bible is ignorance of Western culture, and hence of world culture. A serious critic of the Bible is not seeking to "destroy" the Bible in some crude literal sense. We seek instead to liberate people from a false, delusional, and superstitious belief-system. But as far as "survival" is concerned, it once again proves nothing. The ancient Egyptian Book of the Dead

---

[1066] I Maccabees 16:23-24.

[1067] II Maccabees 2:23.

[1068] Cf Jos. Ant. 13.8.1-4; 13.9.1-3; 13.10.1-7. According to William Whiston, the translator of Josephus, the chronicle of John's high priesthood was still extant until the time of Santes Pagninus and Sixtus Senensis, at Lyons. See note on Jos. Ant. 13.7.4 in the Nelson edition of The Complete Works of Josephus; pg. 421. (Thomas Nelson: Nashville).

has survived for far longer than the Bible.[1069] So has the Avesta. So have the Vedas. Mere "survival" in this sense proves nothing, in terms of alleged divine inspiration. Neither does popularity. On a global scale the Koran rivals the Bible in popularity. This no more proves that the Koran is the word of God than the Bible. I have no doubt that thousands of years from now people will still be reading the Bible and the Koran. But this proves nothing about divine inspiration. Neither do I seek to discourage people from reading the Bible. Far be it from me to do so, or to suggest any such thing. In fact, even my book is not fully understandable without reference to the Bible. So we are not vandals, seeking to "destroy" the Bible. We are instead seeking to place it within a critical-historical context. One that makes more sense than fundamentalism.

Another problem similar to the various lost books of the Bible is that of suspicious omissions. The link with lost books is incompleteness. Incompleteness is a form of imperfection, especially in a purported divine revelation. But the Bible is also riddled with suspicious omissions. For example, we are not told the name of the Pharaoh when Abram and Sarai went down to Egypt in a time of famine.[1070] We are also not told the name of the Pharaoh during the time of Joseph.[1071] We are also not told the name of the Pharaoh who "knew not Joseph" who enslaved the Israelites, and ordered all the male babies of the Hebrews to be drowned in the Nile.[1072] We are also not told the name of the Pharaoh in the days when Moses was a grown man, and fled to Midian; or the name of the Pharaoh who ruled over Egypt in the days when Moses performed all his miracles of the ten plagues.[1073] These are all incredibly suspicious omissions, to say the least. If we had been told the names of these respective Pharaohs, then at least we could attempt to verify, through historical records, whether or not any extraordinary events were reported as occurring during their respective reigns. We could at least attempt to verify (or falsify) the biblical record. But since none of these kings are named, it is impossible for us to do so. This suggests one of two things: either

---

[1069] People still read and study it today. And not just professional Egyptologists.

[1070] Genesis 12:10-20.

[1071] Genesis 37-50.

[1072] Exodus 1; 2:1-10.

[1073] Exodus 2:11ff.

the events did not occur in the way that they are narrated in the biblical text, or the biblical stories are complete fabrications altogether. Some authors have stated erroneously that no Egyptian kings are ever named in the Bible, but this is not true. We are told the names of at least four different kings of Egypt, two of whom are also designated as pharaohs. One of these is Pharaoh Necho, who reigned during the time of King Nebuchadrezzar of Babylon.[1074] Another Pharaoh who is named is Pharaoh Hophra.[1075] At least two other kings of Egypt are also named in Scripture; King So[1076] and Shishak.[1077] What is notable about the distinction is that no miracles are associated with the reigns of these kings of Egypt, who are named in Scripture. This makes the absence of any name for the earlier pharaohs that much more glaring. As to why these last two kings of Egypt are not designated pharaohs in the Bible I suspect that the reason may be because they were foreign kings, who ruled over Egypt. In the case of Shishak, he is otherwise identified historically as Sheshonq, a ruler of a Libyan dynasty, which was the 22nd Egyptian dynasty. It is at least possible that King So was also of a foreign dynasty, and for this reason the Scripture did not accord him the title pharaoh.[1078] We are also not told the name of the Pharaoh whose daughter King Solomon married.[1079] This is also a somewhat suspicious omission, but presumably it was the last native Egyptian pharaoh before the Libyan dynasty, since Sheshonq invaded Jersualem in the days of Rehoboam the son of Solomon.[1080] Another

---

[1074] Jeremiah 46:2; II Kings 23:29-35. Nebuchadrezzar is the Hebrew form of Nabuchadnezzar; the latter being derived from the Greek form of the name.

[1075] Jeremiah 44:30.

[1076] II Kings 17:4.

[1077] II Chronicles 12:1-9. This Shishak is known to secular Egyptologists as Sheshonq.

[1078] In this case most likely the Nubian (Aethiopian, Kushite, Sudanese) dynasty, which was the 25th Egyptian dynasty.

[1079] I Kings 3:1; 7:8; 9:24.

[1080] i.e., this is also assuming that the explanation of the distinction between "kings of Egypt" and "pharaohs" postulated herein is correct. But I can think of no other reason for the distinction. On the other hand, the fact that, according to Josephus, it was the queen of Aethiopia and Egypt who came to visit King Solomon, implies that she ruled over an Aethiopian dynasty, reigning over both her native Aethiopia and Egypt. The Kebra Nagast also claims the queen of Sheba as the queen of Aethiopia. But

foreign king named in Scripture who may also have ruled over Egypt is Tirhaka, the king of Aethiopia.[1081] This is also likely because the time period also corresponds to that of the Aethiopian dynasty. This tends to confirm the rationale for the distinction between pharaohs and other kings of Egypt. Taharqa, who is clearly the Tirhaka of Scrpiture, is also identified by secular sources as a king of the Nubian dynasty. So while there is some degree of correspondence between Scripture and secular records, when it comes to the miraculous, the providential, or the extraordinary, the various pharaohs are suspiciously unnamed. Therefore in some cases it is not too difficult to distinguish between the historical and the legendary in Scripture.

There are also some suspicious omissions in the New Testament. For example, the miraculous resurrection of Lazarus from the dead[1082] is not mentioned in the three Synoptic Gospels. If the events transpired in the way that they are narrated in John's Gospel, then this would have been one of Christ's greatest miracles. It would have been literally impossible for three Evangelists to completely overlook it.[1083] This is a serious problem for fundamentalism. The Gospel of John omits any mention of the "transformation" of Jesus, narrated in the three Synoptics, even though John was purportedly an eyewitness to that

---

various scholars have speculated that she was the queen of Sabea, or Sabaea. It is uncertain which records are the most accurate in this respect. According to secular sources the 25th Egyptian dynasty did not begin until the eighth century B.C. We must also take note of the fact that the queen of Sheba visited Solomon long after he had married Pharaoh's daughter. So there may have been a change of dynasty in the interim. On the other hand, it is also possible that the entire story was only a legend.

[1081] II Kings 19:9; Isaiah 37:9.

[1082] John 11.

[1083] On the other hand, if the incident had involved a secret ritual in which the aspirant would experience an out-of-body state, which would necessarily have been an esoteric mystery, then this could account for the silence of three of the four Evangelists. This would especially have been the case if the ritual somehow went wrong, and perhaps Lazarus slipped into a coma, or some such thing. John's exoteric retelling of the tale portrays it all as a miraculous resurrection from the dead. Presumably any disciples who did not know the esoteric mystery of astral projection would have thought that a real miracle of resurrection had taken place. This explanation is more likely than the fundamentalist interpretation.

event.[1084] Once again this is a highly suspicious omission. Peter makes reference to the incident in his second epistle,[1085] but the Gospel ascribed to Peter has been excluded from the New Testament as non-canonical. This is all very suspicious.

Another serious and suspicious omission in the New Testament is the story of the Roman soldiers guarding the tomb of Christ.[1086] Matthew alone mentions this tale; the other three Evangelists completely overlook it.[1087] This is a particularly serious and egregious omission, and can only arouse the deepest suspicion about such a dubious tale. Because if in fact Roman soldiers (or any soldiers) were guarding the tomb of Jesus, then this would be an important part of the evidence in favor of Christ's resurrection from the dead. As such, all four Evangelists should have included this all-important detail in their accounts. But only Matthew does; the other three remain completely silent about it. This betrays the tale as a completely made up story, invented either by Matthew, or by one of his sources, to bolster the dubious claims of Christ's resurrection. A person could argue on this basis that Matthew was the last of the four Canonical Gospels to have been written.[1088] On the other hand, if we esteem Luke and John as later than Matthew,[1089] then their omission of the story virtually guarantees that it is a gigantic lie. On the other hand, it is quite possible, or even probable, that the earliest text of the Gospel of Matthew may have omitted the story entirely; it may have been something added to the text of Matthew, either in a Hebrew or Greek edition of the text, that became a permanent fixture therein. The structure of the narrative lent itself to such an interpolation [if that is what it is] in the text of Matthew; the reader can test this for himself or herself: read the last two chapters of Matthew, but deliberately "skip" over the relevant portions, which contain this tale; you will find that the text "reads" in a very natural way without this story of men (either the temple guard or Roman soldiers) guarding the tomb.

[1084] Mt 17:1-9; Mk 9:1-9; Lk 9:27-36.

[1085] II Peter 1:16-18.

[1086] Matthew 27:62-66; 28:11-15.

[1087] Although the story is reiterated in Peter and Nicodemus.

[1088] Since otherwise it would have been lax and an inexcusable oversight to neglect so important a detail in the gospel story.

[1089] And there is some textual evidence that this is the case.

None of the other three narrative Gospels lend themselves so readily to any such interpolation. The last few verses of Matthew are also later additions to the text.

Before moving on I want to make a few points. Although sometimes superficial and pseudo-scholarly critics of the Bible may be unfair in their arguments, as well as crude and uninformed, and also sometimes guilty of gross misrepresentations, I feel that my evidence and my arguments have been eminently fair and straightforward. I have not been the least bit dishonest herein. Furthermore I would urge the reader to consider the cumulative nature of the evidence I have presented, and will yet present hereafter. Thirdly I fully realise that some Bible believers may know of some obscure evidence that, in their opinion, strongly supports belief in the alleged divinity of the Bible. And although in some cases there may be some legitimate evidence upholding the Bible, or portions thereof, when the Bible is considered holistically, it must be rejected conclusively. Fourthly I also fully realise that there may be some evangelicals, fundamentalists, or born-again Christians out there who might be thinking to themselves "If he only knew about…, then he would believe in the Bible" or something along those lines. But the chances are, that I already <u>do</u> know of whatever information that supposedly "proves" that the Bible is divinely inspired, etc., at least in embryo. I was a Bible believer for ten years of my life, and even after I rejected the Bible I became aware of some obscure material that supposedly "proves" the divine origin of the Bible. Once again, all this evidence must be considered holistically, and in context. The legitimate problems with the Bible do not just magically disappear because you choose to ignore them. Furthermore, the Bible must be considered holistically; the "good" parts of the Bible do not redeem the "bad" parts. Fifthly and finally, none of those people who claim to have had visions of Jesus or angels can explain away these very legitimate and serious problems with the Bible.

Another serious problem with the Bible, and particularly the Gospels, is the absence of any first-person eyewitness testimony to the events narrated. This is a very serious problem, in terms of a lack of evidence. We are expected to believe, not only some of the most incredible miracles ever recorded in any documents, but also that our eternal fate hinges upon our faith in those very same documents, and what they teach us about salvation. At the very least we would expect a stronger presentation of the purported evidence that the claims made are true. But neither the Gospels nor the book of Acts contains any first-person eyewitness testimony that the things narrated therein are true. The only exception we can find is a few verses from the Gospel of John.[1090] But even these verses are not really an exception, since the Evangelist, who apparently claims to be the Apostle John, speaks, not in the first person singular, but in the first person plural. Neither does he name himself explicitly. Why? This weakens the testimony immensely. The same is also true of Peter's alleged testimony in his second epistle.[1091] While speaking in the first person, Peter speaks in the first person plural, which considerably weakens the testimony, in my view. Why the use of "we" when the use of "I" would be much more called for? Neither Matthew, Mark, nor Luke were present on the mount of transfiguration; Peter, James, and John were. Yet John omits any mention of this event in his Gospel. Why? This is a suspicious omission, as noted above. Even in the opening verses of the first Epistle of John, the first person plural is used, rather than the first person singular.[1092] Why? This weakens the statement immensely. Certainly in psychological terms the statement seems far weaker, and also in terms of testimony as well. Does a person give testimony in a Court of Law in the first person plural? The judge would quickly quash any such presumptuous and pretentious language as unacceptable and lacking in proper decorum. And yet fundamentalists like to claim that there is first person eyewitness testimony in the New Testament. In fact the only place in the entire New Testament where first person singular testimony is offered is in the book of Revelation. But this is precisely where such testimony is least valuable; we would have wanted it in the Gospels, and the book of Acts. But neither does the book of Acts provide such testimony. True the Apostles claim to be witnesses of Christ's resurrection therein; and they also claim that the other Jews living in Jerusalem and throughout Judaea were also witnesses to the miracles of Christ; but once again, this entire account was written by a third party.[1093] In other words, we are only reading

---

[1090] John 19:35; 21:24.

[1091] II Peter 1:16-18.

[1092] I John 1:1-2.

[1093] i.e., Luke or pseudo-Luke. It is possible that the book of Acts may have been written by Luke, since the book of Acts may be interpreted as being under a new dispensation of grace, of the new covenant; by contrast, while Jesus was

what the author wants us to read; it is all third-person narrative: there is no first-person testimony. Neither do we find any such thing in any of the Gospels; not even those allegedly written by Apostles. For example, nowhere in Matthew's Gospel do we read "I Matthew saw the Lord Jesus do such and such" or "I Matthew heard the Lord say..." there is no such thing in any of the Gospels. Likewise nowhere in John do we read "I John saw the Lord raise Lazarus from the dead" or "I John saw Jesus walking on water" or "I John heard the Lord say "I am the bread of life"", etc., etc. There is nothing. Literally nothing. Of course such statements would still be subject to some degree of doubt, but my point is that even these very documents that Christians claim we must hinge our eternal destiny upon in a desperate act of faith do not even go out on a limb and give us any first-person singular testimony to the events narrated. It is all hearsay. Such evidence would never be premitted in a Court of Law, especially when such grave matters are under discussion.

Another issue that has some degree of relevance is archaeology. While the Bible can be neither proved nor disproved by archaeology alone, in recent years the traditional position of archaeology as a bastion of biblical evidence is being challenged by more recent findings. For example, there is the work of Israel Finkelstein and Neil Asher Silberman.[1094] Although I voiced some criticisms of their work above, nevertheless the point still stands that no longer can evangelicals and fundamentalists fall back on the spade of the archaeologist as a species of biblical apologetics. No longer is there a near-unanimous consensus among archaeologists that the biblical record is historically accurate. In fact, Finkelstein and Silberman are comparatively moderate in their views.[1095] There are some archaeologists that are far more minimalist in their views. So archaeology is no longer a refuge for the fundamentalist. Apologists might try to ignore this situation, and to present only the evidence that supports their position, but the tide in archaeology has definitely turned.

---

still alive in the flesh, the old covenant of the Mosaic law was still in effect, according to Pauline theology.

[1094] Finkelstein & Silberman., *THE BIBLE UNEARTHED.*, op. cit.

[1095] e.g., they endorse the historicity of David and Solomon, although they debunk biblical fundamentalism.

Finally the Bible is filled with contradictions. I saved this class of objections for last because it is the one with the largest number of possible examples. Bible believers claim that there are no real contradictions in the Bible, only "apparent" contradictions. Some Bible believers will complain about people who will say that there are contradictions in the Bible, but cannot give any examples. But it is the apologists for the Bible who are the real obscurantists; there are numerous websites that enumerate large numbers of Bible contradictions. And I dare say that the pathetic, lame attempts by Bible believers to reconcile contradictory verses and passages in the Bible is contemptible, pitiful, futile, ridiculous, absurd, clownish, counterproductive, and ultimately self-defeating. Don't these people realise that they are completely crushed and defeated by the Internet? Please. True enough there may be some superficial people who will see contradictions where there are none, giving false examples, or poor examples. But it is also equally true that a favorite trick of fundamentalists is to point out a few examples of "pseudo-contradictions" and then cleverly "reconcile" them, in an effort to "prove" that all such contradictions can ultimately be reconciled. Unfortunately for them and their credibility, this is simply not true. There are definitely examples of real contradictions that by no means of ingenuity can be reasonably reconciled. These are invincible contradictions. They literally cannot be harmonized. To pretend the contrary is merely an assumed air of false pretense. It is no argument; it is merely a tactic of calculated silence about an embarrassing topic. It is essentially an appeal to ignorance.

There are several classes and categories of contradictions. The two most general classes of contradictions are doctrinal contradictions and historical contradictions. Of these two classes, historical contradictions generally make better examples, because historical narrative is generally so straightforward that there is insufficient "wiggle room" for a person to try to cleverly reinterpret the two or more conflicting passages; any unbiased observer could clearly see that the two or more accounts are irreconcilable, if they are truly contradictory.[1096] Doctrinal contradictions generally make poorer examples because a person familiar with the Bible can generally rationalize away contradictions between two sets of passages, by cleverly reinterpreting

---

[1096] Of course in some cases two different passages may merely seem to be contradictory, but ultimately can be reconciled.

one set of passages in a non–literal sense.[1097] This is an important key. Whenever there are two sets of conflicting doctrinal passages, a believer will always embrace one set of passages as literally true, while subjecting the opposing set to a reinterpretation that "spiritualizes" the meaning beyond all reasonable recognition. This is the specious process used to "justify" and "reconcile" various conflicting Bible passages. But if both sets of passages were interpreted literally, the contradiction would become self-evident. But once again these doctrinal passages generally make poor examples because they can be subjected to a clever reinterpretation by Bible believers. It is an absurd process of begging the question. It should also be understood that in the case of born-again Christians belief in the Bible is based upon a traumatic, cathartic experience of deep emotional profundity. This is usually preceded by a personal crisis of some sort, where the person is in search of a new identity on some level, either consciously or subconsciously. And in the wake of the "born again" experience, the person is generally awash with a new set of emotions, and a huge sense of relief and a new personal identity. One can hardly expect such persons to be the least bit objective about the state of the evidence against the Bible. One is not arguing with a rational mind, but with pure emotion. A thin veneer of intellectualism may occasionally (but rarely) be present, but it is only a mask for deeply held and addictive emotional beliefs. I am not saying that no examples of doctrinal contradictions should ever be given, but rather I am merely pointing out that historical contradictions are generally much more straightforward and harder to argue against. Of course one ought not to care about "winning an argument" like some juvenile schoolboy, but rather with what is or is not true. Seeming right is not nearly as important as being right. After all we are talking about the soul and eternal destiny. This is hardly anything to trifle with. Neither is wasting a lifetime on a false belief, such as Bible fundamentalism.

It would be a huge mistake to think that every possible example of a contradiction is equally strong. In fact there is a spectrum of strength of contradictions, from very strong examples, to very weak and poor ones. These can generally be classed within three classes, or rather, two. The weakest examples would be those verses and passages which

---

[1097] But one will also find that the specific way in which this process of reinterpretation is carried out is usually determined by what particular church or denomination the believer goes to.

are not necessarily contradictory at all, but which can be reasonably reconciled. These are really only apparent contradictions, or pseudo-contradictions. Of course there are examples of these, just as Bible believers maintain. So technically these are not really contradictions at all. Then there are any number of passages or examples that may or may not be truly contradictory. Some are more clearly contradictory, while others are more doubtful. But then there are those passages that absolutely cannot be reconciled at all. These are invincible contradictions. These are solid. Bible believers can ignore them, but this does not make them magically go away. They are still there in the Bible. The Bible is what it is. There is no point in trying to pretend that it is something different. To pretend that the Bible says what it does not say, or that it does not say what it does say, is a mere act of false pretense. It does not matter if it is perpetrated by a fundamentalist, an occultist, or someone with a political agenda.[1098] We must proceed with the general assumption that the Bible says what it means, and means what it says.[1099]

There are also distinct categories of contradictions, according to what portion of the Bible they may be found in. For example, contradictions within the Torah would be one category; contradictions within the Gospels would be another. Approaching the Bible holistically, there are three basic categories of contradictions: contradictions within the New Testament, contradictions within TaNaKh,[1100] and New Testament contradictions of TaNaKh. Of course these categories could be potentially expanded to include contradictions within the Apocrypha, contradictions between the New Testament and the Apocrypha, contradictions between TaNaKh and the Apocrypha, contradictions between the New Testament and the New Testament Apocrypha, contradictions between TaNaKh and the Old Testament Pseudepigrapha, and every possible combination of each class and category. But I will only give examples from the Protestant Canon of Scripture, since this Canon functions as a sort of

---

[1098] Whether left-wing or right-wing.

[1099] While the issue of precise interpretation and translation may occasionally crop up, in the case of individual verses and passages, it is only fair and honest to approach the Bible with a literal, straightforward interpretation, according to the plain meaning of words.

[1100] I deliberately prefer this term in lieu of the more nebulous "Old Testament". See discussion above on the Canon of Scripture.

"skeletal structure" of the entire Christian Bible.[1101] There is such a wealth of possible examples that I cannot hope to possibly enumerate them all, so I will only choose several from each category. I will nevertheless append tables tabulating the contradictions by scripture references. Even these tables are not necessarily exhaustive; they are merely representative. More examples can no doubt also be found on the Internet.

Since we are inquiring into the resurrection of Jesus Christ, or more specifically how belief in Christ's resurrection from the dead first arose, I will first offer examples of contradictions surrounding the circumstances of Christ's purported post-passion appearances to his disciples. Some of these are invincible contradictions; they cannot be reconciled by any means.

In Matthew and Mark, we are told that Jesus first appeared alive again to his Apostles in Galilee.[1102] By contrast, in Luke and John we are told that Jesus first appeared alive again to his Apostles in Jerusalem.[1103] Would not the Apostles have remembered exactly where they were when they first saw Jesus alive again after his passion? The question answers itself. Furthermore all three Synoptic Gospels are very clear that the eleven remaining Apostles were all together when Jesus first appeared alive to them after the crucifixion.[1104] But John

---

[1101] In other words, all the books found within the Protestant Canon of Scripture are held as Canonical sacred Scripture by the overwhelmingly vast majority of Christians, especially in the Western Hemisphere, and especially among English-speaking peoples. Therefore nobody can object to my examples on the basis of being outside the Canon of Scripture. But it should be clearly evident that the larger the hypothetical Canon of Scripture, the more examples of contradictions a person could find. Therefore an expanded Canon of Scripture would produce far more examples of contradictions. While the issue of the Canon of Scripture is still a valid issue, as well as a legitimate objection against any unwarranted assumption of the divine authority of the Bible, I am limiting myself only to the Protestant Canon of Scripture for examples of contradictions and other problems for the sake of fairness, and to muzzle those who would otherwise find fault with my presentation of evidence.

[1102] Matthew 28:5-10,16-17; Mark 16:5-7,14.

[1103] Luke 24:33-40; John 20:18-21.

[1104] Mt 28:16-17; Mk 16:14; Lk 24:33-36.

says that Thomas was absent the first time.[1105] Matthew and Mark report only one messenger at the tomb;[1106] but Luke and John both report two messengers at the tomb.[1107] In the Synoptic Gospels, Mary Magdalene is accompanied by at least one or two other women, when she first goes to visit the tomb.[1108] But in the Gospel of John, Mary Magdalene is all alone.[1109] Matthew reports that Jesus himself appeared to the two Marys after they left the tomb, and they touched his feet, bowing down to him.[1110] But according to both Luke and Mark, there was no such appearance of Jesus to Mary Magdalene and the other women at that time.[1111] This is already a mass of contradictions. But it gets worse. No mention of any post-passion appearance of Christ to any women is reported in first Corinthians.[1112] Of course Corinthians does accord with an account that Jesus first appeared to Peter, which is reported in Luke.[1113] But this alleged appearance is nowhere directly narrated. It seems to be yet another contradiction. In any case we clearly have a huge cluster of contradictions here, which cannot fail to cast an immense cloud of doubt and suspicion upon the whole story of the resurrection. Attempts to reconcile these diverse and discordant accounts have been made throughout the history of Christendom, without avail. Some try to pretend that the appearance of Jesus to the eleven Apostles as recorded in Matthew was a later appearance, rather than Christ's first alleged post-passion appearance. But there is a definite problem with this argument; first of all, anyone reading the Gospel of Matthew would assume that the appearance narrated therein was Christ's first post-crucifixion appearance. Secondly, this is confirmed by the fact the text says that the Apostles all doubted

---

[1105] John 20:24-27.

[1106] Matthew 28:5-7; Mark 16:5-7.

[1107] Luke 24:4-7; John 20:11-13.

[1108] Mt 28:1; Mk 16:1; Lk 24:1-10.

[1109] John 20:1-16. Notice also that this lone appearance of Jesus to Mary Magdalene is also included in the longer ending of Mark; cf Mark 16:9-11.

[1110] Matthew 28:9-10.

[1111] Luke 24:1-10; Mark 16:1-8.

[1112] I Corinthians 15:5-7.

[1113] Luke 24:34.

when they saw him.[1114] If Jesus had already appeared to his chosen Apostles several times already, then they would be insane to doubt his fourth or fifth appearance to them. John's Gospel is also very specific that Jesus first appeared alive again to ten of the Apostles,[1115] then to the eleven Apostles together,[1116] and finally a third time to seven of the Apostles, at the Sea of Tiberias.[1117] John is very specific that it was the third time that Jesus made an appearance to his disciples, when he showed himself to them by the Sea of Tiberias.[1118] This would make Christ's appearance in the mountain in Galilee the fourth time, if we were to reconcile Matthew with John. But this is ridiculous, since the Apostles would have been guilty of an almost impossible superhuman doubt if they doubted the fourth time Jesus appeared to them. Besides, anyone reading Matthew's Gospel would never imagine that it was Christ's fourth appearance to his Apostles. That would be anticlimactic and anti-dramatic. If we assume this to be true, then why would Matthew have written about the fourth visitation by the risen Christ? Would he not rather have written about the first? Of course. And is it credible that Luke would have omitted the appearance of Jesus to the female disciples, had it actually taken place, as Matthew says?[1119] We have, in these five different accounts of Christ's alleged post-crucifixion appearances, such a huge cluster of invincible contradictions as to disallow any genuine faith in Christ's resurrection from the dead. Nobody can believe that in good conscience. Not really. Not with such a mass of contradictions as alleged "testimony" to it. That is a joke. It is also notable that here we have a more intensely packed cluster, if you will, of contradictory assertions, than is otherwise typically encountered in the four Gospels. In other words, while contradictions can be found throughout the Gospels, the intensity of contradiction increases dramatically after the passion. This alone suggests that Christ never rose from the dead. This particular cluster of contradictions is absolutely fatal to any genuine conviction that Jesus Christ rose from the dead miraculously. And as we will see,

---

[1114] Matthew 28:17, according to the original Greek [or Hebrew].

[1115] John 20:19-24.

[1116] John 20:24-29.

[1117] John 21:1-14.

[1118] John 21:14.

[1119] Luke 24:1-11 cp Matthew 28:1-10.

this is also a serious problem for several other theories as well, such as the substitution theory, the survival theory, the impersonation theory, etc. We have no agreement among available sources about either the location of where Jesus first appeared to his Apostles after his passion, or of who exactly was present, or even of what precisely was said by Jesus. How could this be? Even if the Gospels were written twenty, thirty or forty years after the events, how could the Apostles have forgotten the most essential details of exactly when, where, and to whom Jesus appeared after his crucifixion? It could not have failed to be a very dramatic experience, had it actually happened. And human experience teaches us that dramatic events tend to etch details indelibly into our consciousness; it would have been impossible for the Apostles to disagree so much about the exact details of Christ's first post-passion appearances to them. While insignificant details may escape memory, the broad outlines of an important event cannot fail to register. For example, whether it was in Galilee or Jerusalem where Jesus first appeared to them. Or whether Thomas was present or absent the first time. Or what exactly Jesus said at the time. For the sake of illustration, let us imagine a hypothetical example. Suppose a mother and father had lost their son or daughter some day. The child simply disappeared without a trace. But the parents wanted to hope against hope that their child was still alive. Then suppose that, three or four years later, the child is miraculously found again. Of course this would be cause for great rejoicing to the father and mother of the boy or girl. But my point is this: Would not the father and mother remember whether it was at an airport, or a police station, or in a park, or at their own home, when they were first reunited with their long-lost child? Of course; the question answers itself. So likewise if the Apostles had thought that Jesus was dead, but then he appeared alive again to them in some cicumstance, it would have been equally impossible for them to forget exactly where it was that he first appeared to them again. They would certainly have remembered whether it was in Jerusalem, or Galilee. You don't forget something like that. And even if some of them maybe remembered certain details a little bit differently, they had over twenty years to get their story straight. There should have been no discrepnacies of details, much less the gross contradictions we encounter in the Gospels.

According to Mark and Luke, Jesus appeared in another form to two disciples.[1120] But Matthew and John are completely silent about this. These contradictions are irreconcilable; they are invincibly contradictory. A person could go insane trying to reconcile these contradictory passages, and a person who claims to have reconciled them is certifiably insane.[1121] Any attempt to reconcile these passages will only result in a falsification of at least some of them, if not all of them. Nobody can read all four accounts according to the plain meaning of words and see them all as literally true. Not if one is a careful and diligent reader, with a good memory. But it is a matter of honesty and intellectual integrity. People enslaved by emotion will not be able to reason clearly. And when the dominating emotion is one of fear (as it necessarily is in the case of Christians) then it is almost impossible to break through that barrier. That's the real Jesus Christ barrier. It almost takes a miracle to break through it.[1122] Such people are content to wallow in invincible ignorance. Blind faith is a form of invincible ignorance.

Another invincible contradiction occurs between John and Matthew. Because it would have been literally impossible for John the Baptist to both know, and also not to know, who Jesus was, before he baptized him.[1123] There is nobody in heaven or earth who can reconcile these two passages. They are absolutely and invincibly contradictory. There is no doubt about it. In the Gospel of Matthew, John the Baptist protests his unworthiness to baptize Jesus; he says "I have need to be baptized by thee, and *yet* comest thou to me?" and Jesus answers him, saying "Suffer it to be so for now; for thus it becometh us to fulfill all righteousness." But in John's Gospel, John the Baptist says of Jesus "And I knew him not. But he that sent me to baptize in water said to me, He upon whom you see the Spirit descending, and remaining upon him, he it is that baptizes with holy spirit."[1124] So either he knew Jesus, or he did not. It cannot be both. And ignoring the contradiction doesn't make it go away.

[1120] Mark 16:12; Luke 24:13–33.

[1121] Or at least should be held for observation at the nearest sanitarium.

[1122] If one will pardon the irony here.

[1123] Matthew 3:13–15 versus John 1:33.

[1124] John 1:33, according to the original Greek.

Another invincible contradiction is that of two mutually exclusive accounts of Jesus' arrest in the Garden of Gethsemane. According to all three Synoptic Gospels, Judas Iscariot enters the garden with a contingent of the temple guard; he stealthily approaches Jesus, and betrays him with the infamous "Judas kiss".[1125] But the account in John's Gospel is completely and invincibly contradictory; in that narrative, Judas leads the temple guard to the Garden of Gethsemane, but he has no opportunity to kiss Jesus; instead, Jesus asks the men whom they are seeking. They answer "Jesus the Nazoraion". Jesus answers them "I am he". This happens twice; the first time the men fall back. The text explicitly states that Judas stood with the men while this was happening.[1126] It is literally impossible to reconcile these two mutually contradictory accounts. The *Diatessaron* attempts to reconcile the two accounts, by having Judas kiss Jesus before the incident narrated in John. While this may be a noble attempt at a reconciliation, it ultimately fails; if the purpose of Judas in kissing Jesus was to identify him to the temple guard in the darkness of night, then the incident as narrated in John becomes superfluous, since Jesus would have been already identified by Judas. On the other hand, John may have wished to depict Jesus more heroically and therefore dispensed with the kiss of Judas, having Jesus proactively confronting the men from the temple guard and proclaiming his identity to them. If Judas had already kissed Jesus, this "heroic" incident would have been superfluous; it would be nothing but a charade and mock bravery. On the other hand, if Jesus had already boldly identified himself to the men, then the kiss of Judas narrated in the Synoptics becomes superfluous; there would no longer have been any need to thus identify Jesus. Tatian opted for the kiss of Judas preceding rather than following the incident narrated in John, but once again, it does not hold up to scrutiny. Tatian's Diatessaron also says that Judas stood with the other men while Jesus twice proclaimed his identity as Jesus the Nazoraion. But Judas would have had to have been right next to Jesus to kiss him. So are we to picture Judas first kissing Jesus, and then very quickly moving away from him? It doesn't wash. Furthermore if the entire incident took place as it is narrated in the Diatessaron, then why were all three Synoptic Evangelists silent about

---

[1125] Mt 26:47-50; Mk 14:43-46; Lk 22:47-48.

[1126] John 18:1-8.

the incident narrated in John's Gospel? And why was John silent about the infamous kiss of Judas Iscariot? One may wish to consult the text of the Diatessaron to see how various contradictions between the Gospels are dealt with therein.[1127] Although it cleverly attempts to reconcile contradictions, it usually fails miserably. The point is the Diatessaron was a deliberate attempt to harmonize the four Gospels. But why would this have been necessary, if all four accounts had already been harmonious? It would have been superfluous. It only fools people who are already fooled. And fools for Christ are still fools.[1128]

Another invincible contradiction occurs in two different accounts of James and John seeking future glory. The two accounts are found in the Gospels of Matthew and Mark, respectively.

20 Then came to him the mother of Zebedee's sons with her sons, making obeisance to him, and desiring a boon of him.	35 And James and John, the sons of Zebedee, came to him, saying, Teacher, we would that you would grant us whatever we desire.
21 But he said to her, What do you desire? She answered him, Grant that these my two sons may sit *by you,* in your kingdom, one on your right hand, and one on *your* left. (Matthew 20:20-21)	36 And he said to them, What would you ask *from me?* 37 They said to him, Grant us that we may sit *near you* in your kingdom, one at your right hand, and the other at your left hand. (Mark 10:35-37)

By comparing the two accounts side by side, we can clearly see that they are mutually contradictory. Christians may claim that Matthew's account is more detailed, but a person reading Mark's Gospel would not picture the mother of James and John being

---

[1127] There is an online version of the Diatessaron available at http://www. earlychristianwritings.com/text/diatessaron.html. This may often be vastly superior to more contemporary attempts by fundamentalists to reconcile Gospel contradictions. But the Diatessaron also contains errors; for example, in the account of Christ's betrayal, it says that Judas was also accompanied by Roman foot-soldiers. None of the four Gospels say this.

[1128] I Corinthians 4:10.

present on that occasion. Furthermore Mark says that James and John themselves ask Jesus for prestige in his future kingdom; in Matthew's account, it is the mother of the two brothers who asks this on behalf of her sons.[1129] I suppose if we accord historicity to the incident, Matthew's version might be more credible; but why would Mark's supposedly divinely inspired record be so deficient? Perhaps it is going too far to classify this particular contradiction as "invincible" but I still think it is a very good example of a strong contradiction. One example of a clearly invincible contradiction is one between Matthew and Luke. The contradiction is between two mutually exclusive accounts of Christ healing a centurion's servant.[1130] In this instance we definitely do have an invincible contradiction; Matthew says that the centurion approached Jesus, asking him to heal his servant. But Luke says that the centurion sent the elders of the Jews, to ask on his behalf. In Luke, the elders attempt to persuade Jesus, by pointing out how the centurion built a synagogue; furthermore the message that the centurion sent includes his own sense of unworthiness as to why he did not come personally to ask Jesus. Therefore the absence of the centurion in Luke is a central part of the story. But in Matthew, the centurion himself asks Jesus for the cure for his servant. He is definitely present, in person. And the context and content of the two accounts proves that they are simply different narrations of the same incident. Therefore we have here another clearly irreconcilable contradiction. These examples are really enough to prove the point that there are contradictions in the New Testament. Therefore the New Testament cannot be the word of God, since God would not contradict himself. And these contradictions are undeniable. They cannot be reasonably reconciled. But there are many more examples. As mentioned above, the two royal genealogies of Jesus found in Matthew and Luke contradict one another.[1131] In the two accounts of Christ's temptation in the wilderness, the order of the temptations is different.[1132] In Matthew, the tempter says to Jesus "If thou art *the* Son

---

[1129] At least Zebedee himself had the good taste and class not to be involved in any such petty things.

[1130] Matthew 8:5-13 versus Luke 7:1-10.

[1131] Matthew 1:1-17 versus Luke 3:23-38. These were omitted from Tatian's *Diatessaron*.

[1132] Matthew 4:1-11 versus Luke 4:1-13.

of God, command that these stones be turned into loaves of bread."[1133] But in Luke, the devil says "If thou art *the* Son of God, command this stone, that it be turned to bread."[1134] In Mark, when Jesus sends his twelve Apostles out in pairs to preach the gospel, he allows them to carry a staff; but in Matthew and Luke, he forbids them to carry a staff.[1135] Matthew records two demon-possessed men in the region of the Gergesenes, who were cured by Jesus; but in Mark and Luke, there was only one man possessed by demons.[1136] These were definitely accounts of the same alleged incident; the fact that Mark and Luke use the term "Gadarenes" rather than "Gergesenes" does not distinguish the incidents as distinct. The context and content of the accounts proves that they are parallel passages.

One notably suspicious omission that I forgot to mention earlier was Jesus healing a man born blind, narrated in John's Gospel.[1137] If this really happened, it would have been one of Christ's greatest miracles, and it would have been unthinkable for the Synoptic Evangelists to have overlooked it. But even the context of the story in John's Gospel betrays it as a probable historical parable, similar to the story of Jesus changing water into wine at the wedding in Kana. The resurrection of Lazarus may have likewise been a historical parable, based upon the parable in Luke 16:19-31, which also uses the name Lazarus. But fundamentalists and evangelicals do not interpret the story that way. So if they choose to be bound by the letter of the law, they shall be judged by the letter of the law, and proven to be wrong by the letter of the law.

In the Gospels of Matthew, Luke, and John, Jesus declares at the last supper that, before the cock crows, Peter will deny him three times.[1138] This is contradicted by Mark, who records Jesus as saying that, before the cock crows twice, Peter will deny him thrice.[1139] And of course the narrative of the fulfillment follows the narrative of the

---

[1133] Matthew 4:3, according to the original Greek.

[1134] Luke 4:3, according to the original Greek.

[1135] Mark 6:8 versus Matthew 10:10; Luke 9:3.

[1136] Matthew 8:28-34 versus Mark 5:1-20; Luke 8:26-39.

[1137] John 9.

[1138] Matthew 26:34; Luke 22:34; John 13:38.

[1139] Mark 14:30.

prophecy, in each of the respective Gospels; giving us yet another set of contradictions.[1140] This gives us six contradictions, all based upon this one discrepancy. But there are three more; because the fulfillment narrated in Mark's Gospel is contrary to the prediction Christ made in the three other Gospels.[1141] This gives us nine contradictions, all based upon this single discrepancy.

In Matthew, Jesus has a conversation with the Pharisees in the temple, asking them whose son the Messiah is. They answer him by saying he is David's son. But in Mark and Luke, this dialogue is replaced with pure monologue; it is Jesus alone who speaks.[1142] In the same way, a parable told by Jesus of laborers in a vineyard who killed the servants and the son of the owner of the vineyard is climaxed in Matthew by Jesus asking the chief priests and elders what the owner of the vineyard would do to the laborers. They answer him by saying "He will miserably destroy those wicked men, and will lease the vineyard to others, who will render to him the fruits in their seasons."[1143] But in Luke's Gospel, this is all a pure monologue; Jesus himself supplies both the question and the answer; furthermore this is unmistakable because when the chief priests and scribes heard the judgment pronounced, they said "God forbid."[1144] In Mark's Gospel the text itself is ambiguous as to whether this is monologue or dialogue; but in red-letter editions of the Gospels, all of the words are interpreted as those of Jesus.[1145] If the speech took place at all, it had to have happened in only one way; it was either pure monologue, or there was some dialogue between Jesus and the Pharisees. It is absurd to uphold the *verbal* inspiration of Scripture in the light of such discrepancies. Another similar one is a contradiction between Matthew and Luke; in Matthew, Jesus says to the Pharisees "But if I cast out demons by the Spirit of God, then the kingdom of God is come unto you."[1146] But in Luke, Jesus is recorded as saying

---

[1140] Mark 14:66–72 versus Matthew 26:69–75; Luke 22:54–61; John 18:17–27.

[1141] Mark 14:66–68 versus Matthew 26:34; Luke 22:34; John 13:38.

[1142] Matthew 22:41–42 versus Mark 12:35; Luke 20:41–42.

[1143] Matthew 21:33–45.

[1144] Luke 20:9–19.

[1145] Mark 12:1–12.

[1146] Matthew 12:28.

"But if I with the finger of God cast out demons, then no doubt the kingdom of God is come upon you."[1147] So what did Jesus say? Did he say "Spirit of God" or "finger of God"? Because the content and context of the two passages proves beyond any real doubt that they are parallel passages; Christians might try to weasel out of the dilemma by pretending that these were two separate incidents, but the context and content belies any such assumption. It would be ridiculous to imagine Jesus having the very same conversation with the Pharisees, over and over again. If the dialogue took place at all then Jesus had to have said either "spirit" or "finger"; not both. While such examples may seem trifling, in fact they are good clear examples of contradictions.

Matthew says that Herod wanted to kill John the Baptist, but Mark implies the opposite.[1148] In Mark, when Jesus curses a fig tree, it is not until the next day that any of the Apostles notice that the fig tree has withered away.[1149] But in Matthew, the fig tree withers away immediately.[1150] The Greek word *parachrema,* which is used in Matthew 21:19,[1151] means *instantly.* Matthew tells us that Judas Iscariot went and hanged himself; but in Acts we read that Judas fell headlong, and all his bowels gushed out.[1152] Matthew tells us that the Roman soldiers clothed Jesus in a scarlet robe; but Mark and John say that it was a purple robe.[1153] In Matthew 24:20, Jesus tells his Apostles to pray that their flight not be in the winter, nor on the Sabbath; this implies that Jesus expected his followers to still observe the Sabbath under the dispensation of the new covenant.[1154] But in Colossians 2:16, the Sabbath is set at nought as an irrelevant custom of the old covenant. Try as they might, Seventh-Day Adventists cannot bring

---

[1147] Luke 11:20.

[1148] Matthew 14:5 versus Mark 6:20.

[1149] Mark 11:12-21.

[1150] Matthew 21:19-20.

[1151] Nestle-Aland., op. cit., pg. 59.

[1152] Matthew 27:5 versus Acts 1:18.

[1153] Matthew 27:28 versus Mark 15:17; John 19:2. For what it's worth, the Gospel of Peter agrees with Mark and John against Matthew in this detail.

[1154] And nowhere in the New Testament is the Sabbath changed from Saturday to Sunday.

forward a truly convincing argument that "Paul"[1155] meant only the annual "Sabbath" of the Passover. A straightforward reading of the text implies no more than that the weekly Sabbath was abrogated in Colossians.

In Matthew and Luke, Jesus tells the Pharisees and Sadducees that no sign would be granted to his generation, except the sign of Jonah.[1156] But in the parallel verse in Mark's Gospel, Jesus simply says that no sign would be granted to his generation.[1157] No mention is made of the sign of Jonah. If the sign of Jonah was supposed to be a reference to the empty tomb, then this means that for Mark the empty tomb was not a sign. This may become significant later. But here we have not only three contradictions, since technically the statement attributed to Christ in Mark is, by way of omission, a contradiction to the three other passages, found in Luke and Matthew; but all four passages contradict all those passages wherein Jesus or his Apostles perform miracles.[1158] As mentioned above, and also in my earlier work, there are some passages that teach salvation through works apart from faith,[1159] and others that teach salvation through faith apart from works.[1160] By the same token, some passages seem to teach that a believer can never lose his or her salvation,[1161] while there are others that imply that a person can lose his or her salvation.[1162] So the

---

[1155] Really Tychicus and Onesimus, according to the colophon to Colossians.

[1156] Matthew 12:38-40; 16:1-4; Luke 11:29-30.

[1157] Mark 8:12.

[1158] John 2:11,23; 3:2; 4:46-54; 5:36; 6:2,26; 7:31; 9:3,16; 10:25,38; 11:47; 12:37; 14:10-12; 15:24; 20:30-31; Matthew 11:2,20:20-23; 13:54-58; 14:2; Mark 1:40-44; 6:2,14; Luke 4:36; 9:1; 10:13,19; 19:37; Acts 2:22,43; 4:30; 5:12; 6:8; 8:6,13; 10:38; 14:3; 15:12; 19:11-12; Romans 15:19; I Corinthians 12:10; 14:22; II Corinthians 12:12; Hebrews 2:4; 6:5.

[1159] Mathew 25:31-46; John 5:28-29 cf Galatians 5:19-21; Ephesians 5:5; I Corinthians 6:9-10; Mark 10:17-19; Matthew 5:17-18; 7:15-27; 19:16-19; 24:20; 28:20; Luke 18:18-20 cp James 2:24.

[1160] Mark 16:16; John 3:16-19; 6:29; 11:25-26; Acts 16:30-31; Romans 5:1-10; 10:9-10; Galatians 2:16; Ephesians 1:7; 2:8-9; Colossians 1:14; Hebrews 9:24-27; 10:1-10.

[1161] John 10:27-29; Romans 6:23; 8:38-39; Ephesians 1:13; 4:30; I John 5:13 cf Mt 12:31-32.

[1162] Hebrews 3:6; 6:4-6; 10:26-31; II Peter 2:20-22; Colossians 1:23; II John

various churches that have different interpretations on salvation can find Scriptures to support their positions, but they must ignore or reinterpret into oblivion contrary passages.

I trust that this is a sufficient sample of New Testament contradictions. But the New Testament also contradicts the Jewish Scriptures, upon which it claims to be based. For example, Zechariah 14:21 says that "no longer shall a Canaanite be in the house of the LORD." But despite this, Jesus chose Simon the Canaanite as one of his twelve Apostles.[1163] Jesus laid down a very strict teaching against divorce, even though Moses permitted divorce in the Torah.[1164] For Jesus to say that Moses allowed the Israelites to divorce their wives due to the supposed hardness of their hearts[1165] is a complete cop-out. After all, either Deuteronomy was divinely inspired or it was not. Jesus three times quoted from Deuteronomy when tempted by the devil, each time saying "It is written..." implying Divine Authority. What happened to this attitude of reverence for that Scripture when he was questioned about divorce by the Pharisees? But the situation is actually even worse than this; in Ezra 10 and Nehemiah 13, the Jews are told that they must divorce their foreign wives, in order to observe the Torah. This implies that not only the wives, but also any children that had been born to them, were abandoned by those devout Jews in the days of Ezra and Nehemiah.[1166]

The strange verse about eunuchs for the kingdom of heaven in Matthew[1167] is diametrically opposed to what is written in the Torah.[1168] Although David was all alone when he fled from King Saul, all three Synoptic Gospels say that there were men with him

---

9; Revelation 20:11-15; 21:8; 22:11-15; Galatians 5:19-21; Ephesians 5:5; I Corinthians 6:9-10; John 5:28-29; Matthew 7:21-27; 10:28; Luke 12:4-5; Mark 9:42-48.

[1163] Mt 10:4; Mk 3:18.

[1164] Mt 5:31; 19:3-9; Mk 10:2-12 vs. Deuteronomy 24:1-4

[1165] See Mt 19:8.

[1166] i.e., assuming that this is something that really happened. But see my arguments that Ezra and Nehemiah are both late pseudepigrapha in my earlier work.

[1167] Matthew 19:12.

[1168] Deuteronomy 23:1; Leviticus 21:16-20.

at the time.[1169] Mark's Gospel also wrongly names Abiathar as the high priest of the time; but the high priest was Ahimelech.[1170] These errors are placed in Christ's lips by the Evangelists. Matthew 21:43 implies that the Jews will be abandoned by God, to be replaced by the Christians. But this is contrary to promises made by God within TaNaKh.[1171] Luke 1:6 says of Zechariah and Elizabeth that they were both righteous before God, walking in all the commandments and ordinances of the Lord blamelessly.[1172] But in the Jewish Scriptures we are told that there is no one without sin.[1173] Romans 3:23 agrees with these Old Testament passages that none are without sin before God, but these verses are all contradicted by yet other verses from the Jewish Scriptures.[1174] Isaiah 66:22-23 depicts the perpetual observance of the new moon and of the Sabbath, throughout eternity, in the new heavens and the new earth. But not only does Colossians 2:16 casually abrogate the observance of both the new moon and the Sabbath, but Revelation 21:23 abrogates the need of the sun and the moon, once again implying that any observance of a new moon or a Sabbath would be thereafter superfluous. Isaiah 66:21 says that God will choose Levites from among the Israelites to serve him in the new Jerusalem; but Hebrews 8:13, 9:23-27, 10:1-14 implies that the Levitical priesthood is no longer valid, and superfluous. In fact those very same passages from Hebrews also set at nought all of Ezekiel 40-48.

James 1:13 says that God tempts no man. But Genesis 22:1 says that God tempted Abraham. And this was no caprice of the translators; the very same Greek root-word is found in both James 1:13 and in the Septuagint translation of Genesis 22:1.[1175] In I Corinthians 10:8, we

---

[1169] I Samuel 21:1-6 versus Mark 2:25-26; Matthew 12:3-4; Luke 6:3-4.

[1170] Abimelech in the Greek Septuagint. SEPTUAGINTA., op. cit., pg. 544 (vol. 1; duo volumina in uno).

[1171] Isaiah 54:9-12; 66:21-23; Jeremiah 31:35-37; 33:17-22.

[1172] However this testimony is implicitly contradicted by Romans 3:23. This is another contradiction within the New Testament.

[1173] Ecclesiastes 7:20; I Kings 8:46; II Chronicles 6:36; Psalm 143:2.

[1174] i.e., Job 1:1,8; 2:3; Genesis 5:21-24; I Kings 15:14. No sin is recorded in Scripture against Enoch, Elijah, Elisha, Daniel, Azariah, Mishael, Hananiah, Zechariah, Malachi or Jonathan.

[1175] Nestle-Aland., op. cit., pg. 589; SEPTUAGINTA., op. cit., pg. 29. (vol. 1;

read that 23,000 people died in a plague recorded in the Pentateuch; but in the Pentateuch itself the number is given as 24,000.[1176] Acts 7:14 tells us that the kindred of Jacob numbered 75 souls. But Genesis 46:26-27 tells us that the number was seventy. Acts 7:16 says that Abraham bought a sepulchre from Emmor the *father* of Sychem. But Genesis 23 says that Abraham bought the cave of Machpelah from Ephron the son of Zohar, who was a Hittite. It was Jacob who bought land from Hamor the father of Shechem.[1177] In Acts 7:42-43, Stephen quotes from the Septuagint text of Amos 5:25-27; however, Stephen misquoted the text, because he said "Babylon," while the Septuagint agrees with the Massoretic text in reading "Damascus." But are we not supposed to believe that Stephen was filled with holy spirit, and that he was therefore infallibly guided in his speech?[1178]

Proverbs 16:7 says "When a man's ways please GOD, he makes even his enemies to be at peace with him." But II Timothy 3:12 says "All that will live godly in Christ Jesus shall suffer persecution." Yet we are told that the new covenant is a better covenant.[1179] How is that better? In any case the two verses are absolutely contradictory. Furthermore we are also told that all the promises of God are yea and amen in Christ.[1180] But there is no harmony between the two verses; they are diametrically opposed. There are some verses within TaNaKh that seem to imply the idea of soul sleep.[1181] By contrast, the New Testament depicts a conscious existence immediately after death.[1182] There are some passages within TaNaKh that seem to support the idea of annihilationism.[1183] By contrast, the New Testament disallows the

---

duo volumina in uno).

[1176] Numbers 25:9.

[1177] Genesis 33:18-19. This Hamor father of Shechem is no doubt the same as Emmor the father of Sychem, whom we read of in Acts 7:16.

[1178] Mt 10:16-20; Mk 13:9-11; Lk 21:12-15.

[1179] Hebrews 8:6.

[1180] II Corinthians 1:20.

[1181] Ecclesiastes 9:5; Isaiah 38:18; Psalms 6:5; 88:5; 115:17; 146:4 cf Daniel 12:2; I Samuel 28:15.

[1182] Luke 16:19-31; 23:43; Philippians 1:23; II Corinthians 5:6-8; Hebrews 9:27; Rev 6:9-11.

[1183] Isaiah 66:24; Malachi 4:1; Ezekiel 28:18-19.

concept of annihilationism.[1184] Acts 15:18 says "Known unto God are all his works from the beginning of the world." But there are many verses within TaNaKh that say that God changed his mind.[1185]

Finally, there are contradictions within TaNaKh. For example, Genesis 22:2 says that Isaac was Abraham's only son; but Genesis 16:15 records the earlier birth of Ishmael to Abram by Hagar. In Exodus 6:3, God tells Moses that he did not reveal his name YaHWeH to Abraham, Isaac, or Jacob. But there are many instances where the tetragrammaton occurs in the text of Berashith.[1186] In Exodus 20:4, God commanded the Israelites not to make any graven images. But there are many instances where this commandment was violated, with apparent divine sanction.[1187] In Exodus 20:13, God commanded the Israelites not to kill. But there were many exceptions to this commandment, with apparent divine sanction.[1188] In Exodus 20:15 God commanded the Israelites not to steal. But there are many exceptions to this commandment, with apparent divine sanction.[1189]

[1184] Revelation 14:9-11; 19:20; 20:10; Luke 16:19-31; Mt 18:8-9; Mk 9:43-48; Jude 7.

[1185] Genesis 6:6; Exodus 32:14; Deuteronomy 32:36; Judges 2:18; I Samuel 15:11.35; II Samuel 24:16; Psalms 106:45; 135:14; Joel 2:13-14; Hosea 11:8; Jeremiah 15:6; 18:8-10; 26:19; Amos 7:3,6; Jonah 3:10; 4:2; I Chronicles 21:15.

[1186] Berashith. i.e., Genesis, in Hebrew. Genesis 4:26; 13:18; 15:2,7,8; 18:14; 21:33; 22:14,16; 24:3,7,21,26,27,31,35,40,42,44,48,50,51,52,56; 25:21,22; 26:25,28,29; 27:7,20,27; 28:13,16,21; 29:32,33,35; 30:24,27,30; 31:49; 32:9; 49:18. These instances are not only contradictions to Exodus 6:3, but also can be considered anachronisms on that account. Either these are instances of scribal interpolations into the text of Genesis, or the book dates to a time later than Exodus.

[1187] Exodus 25:8-20; Numbers 21:8; I Kings 6:23-29,35; 7:23-25,29; 10:19-20; I Chronicles 28:11-19; II Chronicles 3:10-13; 4:3-4 cf Ezekiel 40:26,31,34,37; 41:17-20,25-26.

[1188] Exodus 19:12; 21:12,15-17,29; 31:14-15; 35:2; Leviticus 20:2,9-16,27; 24:16-17,21; 27:29; Numbers 1:51; 3:10,38; 15:35; 18:7; 21:1-3,21-35; 35:16-18,21,30-21; Deuteronomy 7:1-2; 13:5,9; 20:10-18; 21:22; 24:16; 25:171-9; Joshua 3:10; 6:21; 8:18-26; 10:8-14,20,26,28-43; 11:1-12,21-22; Judges 1:18-35; 2:1-4; I Samuel 15:1-33; 18:6-8,25-27; II Samuel 12:29-31; I Chronicles 5:18-22; 20:1-3; Jeremiah 48:10.

[1189] Exodus 3:22; 12:36; Numbers 31:9,11-12; Deuteronomy 2:35; 3:7; 20:14; Joshua 11:14; 22:8; II Samuel 12:29-31; I Chronicles 20:1-3; II Chronicles

In Exodus 33:20, God tells Moses that he cannot see the face of God, since nobody can see God, and still live in the flesh. But there are many instances throughout TaNaKh where it is said that men have seen God.[1190] In fact, in Numbers 12:8 God says that Moses shall behold the similitude of God, and that he speaks to him mouth to mouth.

In II Samuel 24:1, we read that God's anger was kindled against Israel, and he moved David to number them. But in I Chronicles 21:1, we are told that it was Satan who stood up against Israel, and provoked David to number them. In II Samuel 24:9, we are told that there were numbered 800,000 men of Israel, and 500,000 men of Judah. But in I Chronicles 21:5, we are told that there were numbered 1,100,000 men of Israel, and 470,000 men of Judah. In I Chronicles 21:12 the prophet Gad came to David, offering him a choice of three calamities; either three years of famine; or three months of defeat by Israel's enemies; or three days of pestilence. But in II Samuel 24:13, Gad offers David a choice of either seven years of famine; or three months of defeat by the Israelites' enemies; or three days of pestilence. In II Samuel 24:24, we are told that David bought the threshingfloor of Araunah for fifty shekels of silver. But in I Chronicles 21:25, we are told that David paid six hundred shekels of gold for the site.[1191]

Numbers 23:19 says that God does not repent, or change his mind. But there are many passages within TaNaKh that depict God changing his mind.[1192] II Samuel 21:8 says that Michal the daughter of King Saul had five sons. But II Samuel 6:23 says that Michal the daughter of Saul had no child unto the day of her death. Deuteronomy 24:16 says "The fathers shall not be put to death for the sons, neither shall the sons be put to death for the fathers: every man shall be put to death for his

---

14:13-14; 15:11; 20:25.

[1190] Genesis 17:1; 18:1; 26:2,24; 32:30; Exodus 24:11; 33:11; Numbers 12:6-8; 23:4,16; Judges 13:22; Isaiah 6:1-5; I Kings 22:19; II Chronicles 18:18; Job 42:5; Amos 7:7; 9:1; Ezekiel 1; Daniel 7:9-13.

[1191] In Chronicles, the owner of the threshingfloor is named Ornan. The reason why God was angry over the census of the Israelites is that David did not also take an offering for the ransom of their souls, as commanded in Exodus 30:11-16.

[1192] Genesis 6:6; Exodus 32:14; Judges 2:18; I Samuel 15:11,35; II Samuel 24:16; I Chronicles 21:15; Psalms 106:45; 135:14; Jeremiah 15:6; 18:8-10; 26:19; Hosea 11:8; Joel 2:13-14; Amos 7:6; Jonah 3:10; 4:2; Deuteronomy 32:36.

own sin." But there are many examples of exceptions to this, with apparent divine sanction.[1193] In II Samuel 18:18 we read that Absalom the son of David erected a memorial pillar, because he had no son. But in II Samuel 14:27 we read that Absalom had three sons. Absalom's sister Tamar was greatly desired for her beauty by Amnon, one of David's sons by another woman.[1194] When Amnon sought to force himself upon Tamar sexually, she pleaded with him, saying he should ask permission from his father King David, who would grant his request to have her in marriage.[1195] But this would have clearly been against the prohibition of fraternal incest.[1196] While strictly speaking this is not *necessarily* a contradiction, it implies one of three things: 1. Either the Torah was generally unknown to the Israelites, even the royal family, whom we would expect to be diligently educated therein; or 2. The royal family felt that they were somehow exempt from the commandments of the Torah; or 3. The Torah postdates the time of King David. None of these alternatives are particularly congenial to a high view of Scripture. In Leviticus 7:23, the eating of fat is strictly prohibited. But in Nehemiah 8:10 it says "Go your way, eat the fat, drink the sweet, and send portions unto whom nothing is prepared: for this is a holy day unto our Lord: neither be ye sorry; for the joy of the LORD is your strength."

I Chronicles 2:15 lists David as the seventh son of Jesse, but I Samuel 16:6-13 depicts David as the eighth son of Jesse. The law of levirate marriage was ostensibly instituted to carry on the name of the deceased, if a man died before begetting a son to carry on his name.[1197] But in Scripture we see a flagrant violation of this principle; Ruth the Moabitess had been married to an Israelite named Mahlon, who died without any children.[1198] Boaz, being a kinsman of Mahlon, married Ruth. In fact, Boaz even says "Ruth the Moabitess, the wife of Mahlon, I have purchased to be my wife, <u>to raise up the dead upon his inheritance, that the name of the dead be not cut off from among his brethren, and from the gate of his place</u>: ye are witnesses this day."

[1193] Joshua 7:24-25; II Samuel 21:1-9; Esther 9:7-10,14,25; Numbers 16:31-33.

[1194] II Samuel 13:1ff.

[1195] II Samuel 13:13.

[1196] Leviticus 18:9.

[1197] Deuteronomy 25:5-6.

[1198] Ruth 1:5; 4:10.

But this is so far from being the case that we no longer so much as read of the name of Mahlon ever again, in either the Old Testament or the New Testament. Instead the line is always traced back to Boaz and his paternal ancestors.[1199] This is not only a contradiction, but an everlasting slap in the face to Mahlon, and his paternal ancestors, who were not immortalized in Scripture, as they should have been, had the stated intent of levirate marriage been observed and upheld therein. This makes the Torah a laughingstock. It is also of some considerable importance, since it concerns the royal dynasty of Judah.[1200]

Proverbs 6:30-31 says that a thief will restore sevenfold, but Exodus 22:1 says a man will restore five oxen for a stolen ox, and four sheep for a stolen sheep. Leviticus 6:5 says that a man will restore whatever amount he has stolen, and add also a fifth part. The repentant Zaccheus tells Jesus that he will restore fourfold to whomever he had defrauded by false accusation.[1201]

Jeremiah rants on and on that from thenceforth, no true prophet will ever use the expression "the burden of the LORD."[1202] But both Zechariah and Malachi, who lived centuries after the time of Jeremiah, used the same prohibited phrase, in their supposedly "divinely inspired" texts.[1203]

In Jeremiah 7:22, God says "For I spake not unto your fathers, nor commanded them in the day that I brought them out of the land of Egypt, concerning burnt offerings or sacrifices." But the Torah is literally filled with so many instances where God gives Moses detailed instructions on exactly how to offer animal sacrifices, including bulls, goats, sheep, rams, and doves, that it would be excessively tedious to even attempt to enumerate them all. Fundamentalists can only reply by saying that the verse in Jeremiah does not mean what it says. But if that verse does not mean what it says, how can we be sure that any other verse means what it says? How can we be sure of the meaning of any verse or passage, if there are verses that do not mean what they say?

Daniel 9:24 seems to indicate an eschaton in which sacrifices will no longer be offered, since there will no longer be any need for them;

[1199] I Chronicles 2:9-12; Matthew 1:2-5; Luke 3:32-33.

[1200] Therefore this is also a matter of potential concern to Grail enthusiasts.

[1201] Luke 19:8.

[1202] Jeremiah 23:33-40.

[1203] Zechariah 9:1; 12:1; Malachi 1:1.

it says "Seventy weeks are decreed upon thy people and upon thy holy city, to finish the transgression, to make an end of sins, to make reconciliation for iniquity, to bring in everlasting righteousness, to seal up vision and prophecy, and to anoint the most Holy." The first four things mentioned all seem to imply the cessation of sacrifices; to "finish transgression" implies that there is no longer any need for sacrifice; to "make an end of sins" seems to imply directly the cessation of sin offering; and in any case, if sins come to an end, sin offerings become superfluous; to "make reconciliation for iniquity" seems to imply a finality to the act of reconciliation; and to "bring in everlasting righteousness" also seems to ratify the finality of the whole scheme. Furthermore as if to even more strongly confirm this interpretation, later on in the very same passage, we read that the Messiah will "cause the sacrifice and the oblation to cease"[1204] which of course confirms the finality of the reconciliation spoken of. The problem is that this is in stark contrast to the prophetic scheme envisioned in Ezekiel, in which sacrifices will be offered in a restored kingdom of Israel, seemingly indefinitely.[1205]

Deuteronomy 15:4 says that a time will come when there will be no poor among the Israelites, due to the future blessing of God. But Deuteronomy 15:11 says that the poor will never cease out of the land.[1206]

Deuteronomy 18:22 says that a false prophet can be recognized by his failed prophecies. Yet Jonah's prophecy of Nineveh's destruction within forty days[1207] failed to come true, and nevertheless he is regarded as a true prophet. Furthermore Jeremiah 18:7-10 provides a loophole for unfulfilled prophecies. This is rather too convenient, and also nullifies the utility of Deuteronomy 18:22. These are both contradictions.

Not only is the Bible filled with contradictions, there are also contradictions between some of the accounts of the Apostles' martyrdoms. For example, according to *Foxe's Book of Martyrs*, the Apostle Matthew was killed by a spear.[1208] But according to Grant

---

[1204] Daniel 9:27.

[1205] Ezekiel 40-48.

[1206] Cf Matthew 26:11; Mark 14:7.

[1207] Jonah 3:4.

[1208] Foxe., op. cit., pg. 9.

Jeffrey's book *The Signature of God*, Matthew was slain by a sword.[1209] According to *Foxe's Book of Martyrs*, the Evangelist Mark was drawn by ropes to a fire and then burned alive.[1210] But according to *The Signature of God*, Mark was dragged by horses through the streets of Alexandria until he died.[1211] According to *Foxe's Book of Martyrs*, the Apostle Bartholemew was beaten and crucified, excoriated, and finally beheaded.[1212] But according to *The Signature of God*, Bartholemew was killed by being flayed to death by a whip.[1213] According to *Foxe's Book of Martyrs*, the Apostle Thomas was slain with a dart.[1214] But according to *The Signature of God*, Thomas was killed by a spear in India.[1215] These examples should suffice to prove the point. I'm sure that more examples could probably be found by further diligent research. One book I read on this subject was even bold enough to say that such and such an Apostle was martyred "either or" one way or another. But common sense ought to tell us that if the circumstances of the case are so uncertain as to be "either or" then they may also be "neither nor" as well. This particular class of discrepancies are especially fatal to the claims made by Christians vis-à-vis the testimony of the Apostles to the resurrection of Jesus Christ. After all, we don't even know for sure the exact circumstances of their alleged martyrdoms, much less what their final words of testimony were.[1216] None of the people who claim to have had visions of Jesus or of angels sent by him ever explain any of these very serious problems with the Bible, or answer any legitimate questions about the Canon, text, or interpretation of Scripture, or resolve any contradictions, or clarify any of these relevant issues.

[1209] Jeffrey, Grant., *THE SIGNATURE OF GOD.*, pg. 337.

[1210] Foxe., op. cit., pg. 7.

[1211] Jeffrey., op. cit., pg. 337.

[1212] Foxe., op. cit., pg. 7.

[1213] Jeffrey., op. cit., pg. 338.

[1214] Foxe., op. cit., pg. 6.

[1215] Jeffrey., op. cit., pg. 338.

[1216] And as has been pointed out above, if there was an esoteric doctrine within proto-Christianity, then this would most likely have remained secret; perhaps the most important secret died with the Apostles. I suspect that the greatest secret was where they buried the body of Jesus.

New Testament Contradictions

MATTHEW 1:1-17 v LUKE 3:23-38/MATTHEW 3:13-14 v JOHN 1:33/

MATTHEW 4:1-11 v LUKE 4:1-13/ MATTHEW 8:5-13 v LUKE 7:1-10/

MATTHEW 5:33-37 v ACTS 18:18; 21:23-24/

MATTHEW 8:28-34 v MARK 5:1-20; LUKE 8:26-39/

MATTHEW 12:28 v LUKE 11:20/ MATTHEW 13:58 v MARK 6:5/

MATTHEW 14:5 v MARK 6:20/ MATTHEW 20:20-21 v MARK 10:35-37

MATTHEW 20:29-34 v MARK 10:46-52; LUKE 18:35-43/

MATTHEW 21:1-7 v MARK 11:1-7; LUKE 19:28-35; JOHN 12:12-16/

MATTHEW 21:33-41 v MARK 12:1-12 cf LUKE 20:9-16/

MATTHEW 21:41 v LUKE 20:16/ MATTHEW 21:19-20 v MARK 11:12-21/

MATTHEW 22:41-42 v MARK 12:35; LUKE 20:41-42/

MATTHEW 24:20 v COLOSSIANS 2:16/ MATTHEW 25:31-46 v MARK 16:16;

JOHN 3:16; 6:29; 10:27-29; 11:25-26; ACTS 16:30-31; ROMANS 5:1,6-10; 10:9-10;

GALATIANS 2:16; EPHESIANS 1:7; 2:8-9; COLOSSIANS 1:14 cp MARK 10:17-19; MATTHEW 5:17-18; 7:15-27; 19:16-19; 24:20; 28:20; LUKE 18:18-20; JOHN 5:28-29; GALATIANS 5:19-21; EPHESIANS 5:5; 1 CORINTHIANS 6:9-10; JAMES 2:24;

REVELATION 2:23; 20:12-13; 21:8,27; 22:14-15/ MATTHEW 27:5 v ACTS 1:18/ MATTHEW 27:28 v MARK 15:17; JOHN 19:2/ MATTHEW 27:34 v MARK 15:23/ MATTHEW 28:5-7 v LUKE 24:4-7; JOHN 20:11-13 cp MARK 16:5-7/

MATTHEW 28:16-20 v LUKE 24:33-50/ MARK 6:8 v MATTHEW 10:10; LUKE 9:3/

MARK 6:8 v MATTHEW 10:10; LUKE 9:3/ MARK 8:12 v MATTHEW 12:38-40; 16:1-4; LUKE 11:29-30 cp MARK 16:17-18; JOHN 2:11,23; 3:2; 4:46-54; 5:36; 6:2,26; 7:31; 9:3,16; 10:25,38; 11:47; 12:37; 14:10-12; 15:24; 20:30-31; MATTHEW 11:2,20-23; 13:54-58; 14:2; MARK 1:40-44; 6:2,14; LUKE 4:36; 9:1; 10:13,19; 19:37; ACTS 2:22,43; 4:30; 5:12; 6:8; 8:6,13; 10:38; 14:3; 15:12; 19:11-12; ROMANS

15:19; 1 CORINTHIANS 12:10; 14:22; 2 CORINTHIANS 12:12; HEBREWS 2:4; 6:5/ MARK 14:30 v MATTHEW 26:34; LUKE 22:34; JOHN 13:38/

MARK 14:66-68 v MATTHEW 26:34; LUKE 22:34; JOHN 13:38/ MARK 14:66-72 v MATTHEW 26:69-75; LUKE 22:54-61; JOHN 18:17-27/

MARK 16:1 v LUKE 23:56/ LUKE 9:28 v MATTHEW 17:1; MARK 9:2/

LUKE 13:31-35 v HEBREWS 13:12-13 cf MATTHEW 23:37-39 cp REVELATION 11:8/ LUKE 23:39-43 v MATTHEW 27:44; MARK 15:32/ LUKE 23:47 v MATTHEW 27:54; MARK 15:39/ JOHN 1:21 v MATTHEW 11:14; 17:12-13; MARK 9:13/

JOHN 2:13-21 v MATTHEW 21:12-13; MARK 11:15-17; LUKE 19:45-46 cf ACTS 3:2 cp EXODUS 34:23 cf MARK 14:55-59; MATTHEW 26:59-61; 27:40/

JOHN 5:18 v HEBREWS 4:15; 2 CORINTHIANS 5:21; 1 PETER 1:19; 3:18;

1 JOHN 3:5 cp NEHEMIAH 13:15-21; JEREMIAH 17:21-27 cf JOHN 5:8/

JOHN 18:3-8 v MATTHEW 26:47-50; MARK 14:43-46; LUKE 22:47-48/

JOHN 19:17 v MATTHEW 27:32; MARK 15:21; LUKE 23:26/

JOHN 19:25-27 v MATTHEW 27:55-56; MARK 15:40; LUKE 23:49/

JOHN 20:11-18 v MATTHEW 28:1-10 cp MARK 16:9 cf LUKE 24:13-31/

JOHN 20:24-27 v MATTHEW 28:16-20; MARK 16:14; LUKE 24:33-36/

ACTS 9:1-30 v GALATIANS 1:11-2:2/ ROMANS 3:23 v LUKE 6:1; MATTHEW 1:19; JOHN 9:3/ 1 CORINTHIANS 8 v REVELATION 2:14,20/

1 CORINTHIANS 12:3 v GALATIANS 3:13/1 CORINTHIANS 14:22 v 1 CORINTHIANS 14:23-25/COLOSSIANS 2:9 v I CORINTHIANS 15:45/ PHILIPPIANS 3:4-5 v GALATIANS 3:13-14; COLOSSIANS 2:13-14 cf ROMANS 9:3-4; 11:1;

II CORINTHIANS 11:22/ HEBREWS 7:14 v LUKE 1:5,36 cp REVELATION 5:5; 22:16; ROMANS 4:3; 2 TIMOTHY 2:8; MATTHEW 1:1-20; LUKE 3:23-38 cf MATTHEW 9:27; 12:23; 15:22; MATTHEW 20:30; 21:9,15; MARK 10:47,48; LUKE

18:38,39 cp MARK 12:35-37; MATTHEW 22:41-45; LUKE 20:42-44 cf NUMBERS 36 cf JUDGES 21:1 cf NUMBERS 18:20-24/ HEBREWS 9:11-28; 10:1-12 v ACTS 18:18; 21:23-24; LUKE 24:53 cf ROMANS 5:1-11; COLOSSIANS 1:14; EPHESIANS 1:7/

New Testament Contradictions of TaNaKh

MATTHEW 10:4 v ZECHARIAH 14:21 cp MARK 3:18/
MATTHEW 19:3-9 v EZRA 10; NEHEMIAH 13 cp MARK 10:2-12/
MATTHEW 19:12 v DEUTERONOMY 23:1; LEVITICUS 21:16-20/
MATTHEW 21:43 v ISAIAH 54:9-12; 66:21-23; JEREMIAH 31:35-37; 33:17-22/
MARK 2:25-26 v I SAMUEL 21:1-6 cp MATTHEW 12:3-4; LUKE 6:3-4/
LUKE 1:6 v ECCLESIASTES 7:20; 1 KINGS 8:46; 2 CHRONICLES 6:36; PSALM 143:2/ LUKE 16:19-31 v ECCLESIASTES 9:5; ISAIAH 38:18; PSALMS 6:5; 88:5; 115:17; 146:4 cp PHILIPPIANS 1:23; LUKE 23:43 cp 2 MAKKABEES 15:12-16/
JOHN 1:18 v GENESIS 17:1; 18:1; 26:2; 32:30; EXODUS 24:11; 33:11; NUMBERS 12:6-8; 23:4,16; JUDGES 13:22; 1 KINGS 22:19; 2 CHRONICLES 18:18;
JOB 42:5; DANIEL 7:9-13; EZEKIEL 1; ISAIAH 6:1-5; AMOS 7:7; 9:1 cp JOHN 6:46;
1 JOHN 4:12; 1 TIMOTHY 6:15-16/ JOHN 3:13 v 2 KINGS 2:11/
ACTS 15:18 v GENESIS 6:6; EXODUS 32:14; DEUTERONOMY 33:36; JUDGES 2:18; 1 SAMUEL 15:11,35; 2 SAMUEL 24:16; PSALMS 106:45; 135:14; JOEL 2:13-14; HOSEA 11:8; JEREMIAH 15:6; 18:8-10; 26:19; AMOS 7:3,6; JONAH 3:10; 4:2;
1 CHRONICLES 21:15/ ACTS 7:14 v GENESIS 46:26-27/
ROMANS 3:23 v JOB 1:1,8; 2:3; GENESIS 5:21-24; 1 KINGS 15:14/
GALATIANS 2:16 v LEVITICUS 18:5; DEUTERONOMY 30:11; NEHEMIAH 9:29/
COLOSSIANS 2:16 v ISAIAH 66:22-23 cp MATTHEW 24:20/
2 TIMOTHY 3:12 v PROVERBS 16:7/ JAMES 1:13 v GENESIS 22:1/
REVELATION 14:9-11 v MALACHI 4:1; EZEKIEL 28:18-19; ISAIAH 66:24 cp LUKE 16:19-31 cf MARK 9:43-48; MATTHEW 18:8-9 cp JUDITH 16:17/
REVELATION 21:23-25 v ISAIAH 66:22-23/ REVELATION 22:8-9 v 1 CHRONICLES 29:20; EXODUS 11:8; ISAIAH 49:23; 60:14/

Contradictions within TaNaKh

GENESIS 16:15 v GENESIS 22:2/ GENESIS 32:28 v GENESIS 35:10/ EXODUS 6:3 v GENESIS 4:26; 13:18; 15:2,7,8; 18:14; 21:33; 22:14,16; 24:3,7,21,26,27,31,35,40,42,44,48,50,51,52,56; 25:21,22; 26:25,28,29; 27:7,20,27;
28:13,16,21; 29:32,33,35; 30:24,27,30; 31:49; 32:9; 49:18/
EXODUS 20:4 v EXODUS 25:8-20; NUMBERS 21:8; 1 KINGS 6:23-29,35; 7:23-25,29; 10:19-20; 1 CHRONICLES 28:11-19; 2 CHRONICLES 3:10-13; 4:3-4;
EZEKIEL 40:26,31,34,37; 41:17-20,25-26 cp DEUTERONOMY 4:15-18,23; 5:8/
EXODUS 20:13 v EXODUS 19:12; 21:12,15-17,29; 31:14-15; 35:2; LEVITICUS 20:2,9-16,27; 24:16-17,21; 27:29; NUMBERS 1:51; 3:10,38; 15:35;
18:7; 21:1-3,21-35; 35:16-18,21,30-31; DEUTERONOMY 7:1-2; 13:5,9; 20:10-18;
21:22; 24:16; 25:17-19; JOSHUA 3:10; 6:21; 8:18-26; 10:8-14,20,26,28-43; 11:1-12,21-22; JUDGES 1:18-35; 2:1-4; 1 SAMUEL 15:1-33; 18:6-8,25-27;
2 SAMUEL 12:29-31; 1 CHRONICLES 5:18-22; 20:1-3; JEREMIAH 48:10 cp DEUTERONOMY 5:17/ EXODUS 20:15 v EXODUS 3:22; 12:36; NUMBERS 31:9,11-12; DEUTERONOMY 2:35; 3:7; 20:14; JOSHUA 11:14; 22:8; 2 SAMUEL 12:29-31;
1 CHRONICLES 20:1-3; 2 CHRONICLES 14:13-14; 15:11; 20:25 cp DEUTERONOMY 5:19/ EXODUS 33:20 v GENESIS 17:1; 18:1; 26:2,24; 32:30;
EXODUS 24:11; 33:11; NUMBERS 12:6-8; 23:4,16; JUDGES 13:22; ISAIAH 6:1-5;
1 KINGS 22:19; 2 CHRONICLES 18:18; JOB 42:5; AMOS 7:7; 9:1; EZEKIEL 1;
DANIEL 7:9-13/ EXODUS 37:1-9 v DEUTERONOMY 10:5/ NUMBERS 22:20 v NUMBERS 22:22/ NUMBERS 23:19 v GENESIS 6:6;
EXODUS 32:14; JUDGES 2:18; 1 SAMUEL 15:11,35; 2 SAMUEL 24:16;
1 CHRONICLES 21:15; PSALMS 106:45; 135:14; JEREMIAH 15:6; 18:8-10; 26:19;

HOSEA 11:8; JOEL 2:13-14; AMOS 7:6; JONAH 3:10; 4:2; DEUTERONOMY 32:36 cp 1 SAMUEL 15:29/ DEUERONOMY 15:4 v DEUTERONOMY 15:11 cp MARK 14:7;

MATTHEW 26:11; JOHN 12:8/ DEUTERONOMY 18:22 v JONAH 3:4 cp JEREMIAH 18:8-10/ DEUTERONOMY 24:16 v JOSHUA 7:24-25; 2 SAMUEL 21:1-9;

ESTHER 9:7-10,14,25; NUMBERS 16:31-33 cp EZEKIEL 18/ JOSHUA 10:1-27 v 2 SAMUEL 5:6-9; 1 CHRONICLES 11:4-7/ JOSHUA 24:19 v EXODUS 34:6-7; DEUTERONOMY 4:31; 2 CHRONICLES 30:9;

NEHEMIAH 9:17,31; PSALMS 36:5; 52:8; 59:16; 69:13; 86:5,15; 89:2,14; 100:5; 103:7-8; 106:1; 107:1; 108:4; 116:5; 117:2; 118:1-4,29; 136; 138:8; ISAIAH 1:18;

JEREMIAH 3:12; JOEL 2:13; JONAH 4:2 cp EXODUS 23:20-21/ JUDGES 14:15 v JUDGES 14:17/ 1 SAMUEL 17:55-58 v 1 SAMUEL 16:14-23; 17:31-39/ 2 SAMUEL 6:23 v 2 SAMUEL 21:8/

2 SAMUEL 24:1 v 1 CHRONICLES 21:1/ 2 SAMUEL 24:9 v 1 CHRONICLES 21:5/

2 SAMUEL 24:13 v 1 CHRONICLES 21:12/

2 SAMUEL 24:24 v 1 CHRONICLES 21:25/ 2 KINGS 8:26 v 2 CHRONICLES 22:2/

1 CHRONICLES 2:15 v 1 SAMUEL 16:6-13/

2 CHRONICLES 15:17 v 2 CHRONICLES 16:1-12/

NEHEMIAH 8:10 v LEVITICUS 7:23/

ESTHER 3:2 v EXODUS 11:8; ISAIAH 49:23; 60:14; 1 CHRONICLES 29:20/

PROVERBS 6:16-19 v JUDGES 4:17-21; 5:24-27; 1 SAMUEL 27:8-11;

1 KINGS 13:18; 22:23; 2 KINGS 10:18-25; 2 CHRONICLES 18:22; JOSHUA 2:4-6 cp PROVERBS 12:22/ PROVERBS 6:30-31 v EXODUS 22:1; LEVITICUS 6:5/

ECCLESIASTES 1:4 v ISAIAH 65:17-18; 66:22; PSALMS 102:25-26/ ECCLESIASTES 7:20 v JOB 1:1,8; 2:3; GENESIS 5:21-24; 1 KINGS 15:14 cp

1 KINGS 8:46; 2 CHRONICLES 6:36/ ECCLESIASTES 9:5 v DANIEL 12:2; EZEKIEL 37:12-14; 1 SAMUEL 28:15 cp ISAIAH 38:18; PSALMS 6:5; 88:5; 115:17; 146:4/

ISAIAH 43:11 v JUDGES 3:9,15; 2 KINGS 13:5; NEHEMIAH 9:27; OBADIAH 21;

ISAIAH 19:20 cp HOSEA 13:4/ JEREMIAH 7:22 v Torah cf 1 SAMUEL 15:22; HOSEA 6:6 cp MATTHEW 9:13; 12:7/ JEREMIAH 23:33-40 v ZECHARIAH 9:1; 12:1; MALACHI 1:1/ DANIEL 9:24-27 v EZEKIEL 40-48/

Objections Against The
Phantom Theory

H aving eliminated the resurrection theory and the fundamentalist
paradigm, it is now time to consider objections against the
phantom theory. As we will see, these objections are sufficiently strong
to effectively rule out the phantom theory. We have already briefly
considered some of the problems with this theory above, but we need
to more critically examine the theory.

The theory is generally predicated upon two or three
circumstances of the available evidence; first, the presumed silence of
contemporary historians respecting Jesus Christ; second, the general
similarity of the central themes and events associated with the life and
ministry of Jesus to an otherwise seemingly ubiquitous cross-cultural
messianic *mythos;* and thirdly, a combination of the two, with an
emphasis upon the Jewish aspects of the case: the absence of historical
proof that Jesus either lived or performed all the necessary messianic
requirements or fulfilled all the necessary messianic prophecies; and
the further presumption that the figure we read of in the Gospels
is merely a literary invention, created to accommodate messianic
expectations of the Jews. Variations on the theme are that the New
Testament texts were not written exclusively or even primarily for
Jews, but rather for Gentiles; the point being that militant resistance
to the Romans is futile, and the promise of heaven is better than

anything in this life anyway. Thus this version of the theory is that those documents were written to pacify Gentiles who may have had inclinations to revolt from Roman rule, by pointing to the example of what had happened to the Jews. This latter explanation would be particularly pungent if we further assume a second-century origin for the Gospels and other New Testament texts. But we would have to also assume that they were written by Romans, or those who had genuine sympathy with the Romans, for this scenario to be true; and that seems very unlikely. Even admitting the whitewash of the Romans evident in the New Testament,[1217] the passages in question do not give me the impression of being one of genuine sympathy with the Romans, but rather of the expediency of wishing not to jeopardize the fate of the documents, or of the persons receiving or sending them. But this brings us to a very strong objection against at least one version[1218] of the phantom theory: it would have been considered an act of treason for any Romans to write texts subverting the Roman religion, and substituting a Jewish God for the Roman pantheon; had this been the case, no doubt the perpetrators would have been sought out, discovered, and beheaded. Why would a wealthy Roman family risk everything on a highly dubious pursuit, which would not bear fruit for centuries? Furthermore it is absurd to imagine a wealthy man writing any such thing as that it is easier for a camel to pass through the eye of a needle than for a rich man to enter the kingdom of God.[1219] Furthermore Abelard Reuchlin, the proponent of this particular version of the phantom theory, made a huge blunder by postulating that the same people also wrote the various books of the Apocrypha. Fragments of some of the books of the Apocrypha were found among the Dead Sea Scrolls, as well as fragments of the books of Enoch and Jubilees. But even if we try to imagine a more intelligent variation on Reuchlin's theory, we would have to assume that the Roman family or group in question had an intimate knowledge of the Jewish Scriptures, since the New Testament is filled with references to, allusions to, and quotations from, those Scriptures. Perhaps they were Roman Jews? But if so, what exactly were they trying to accomplish?

[1217] ,Although I still think that this point is usually greatly exaggerated.

[1218] i.e., the Piso conspiracy; the idea that a wealthy Roman family known as the Pisos wrote the various New Testament texts.

[1219] Mt 19:24; Mk 10:25; Lk 18:25.

This is exactly where the greatest difficulty seems to emerge. Because to assume that the figure of Jesus Christ was merely invented out of pure imagination, for whatever reason, presents us with an immense psychological challenge. Quite simply, what would have been the purpose of it all? The people writing such texts would have known that the whole thing was a complete fabrication; this would seem to be a fatal flaw in any assumption that they could have sustained the necessary motivation to convince any number of people that Jesus had actually existed, and that the events narrated had truly transpired. Of course it is possible that a person could have recourse to any argument involving esotericism; in other words, even though Jesus himself did not exist, he and the religion surrouding him were meant to function as an outer shell for an inner teaching that was to remain secret, except to initiates. But even this seems unlikely; there is simply far too much geographical and historical detail in the Gospels. It would have been complete overkill to include so much gratuitous detail. For phantom theorists to claim that such details had to be included to convince the skeptical is merely an act of special pleading on their part. I challenge them to find any similar example in writings associated with any other such Savior God, such as Krishna.[1220]

While it is true that, in a strictly moral sense, it would have been no more of a lie to completely invent a miracle-working Messiah, than to attribute miracles to a failed messianic figure, this in itself does not justify the phantom theory. Phantom theorists need to show how and why an assumption that Jesus was merely a phantom is more probable than the contrary assumption. They have not done so. One trick they use is to take everything written about Jesus in the New Testament as a package, and then to say that there are no historical records verifying that any such wonder-working person lived at that time. But this is garbage. This is no real argument; it is almost an inverted form of fundamentalism. In other words, the fundamentalist image of Jesus is used as a straw-man for them to debunk as nothing but a complete myth. But of course the fundamentalist version of Jesus is a myth, as we have seen above.[1221] This does not mean that there was

---

[1220] And while the Bhagavata Purana may be highly detailed, it lacks the realism found in the Gospels; it is more akin to a psychedelic experience. There is literally no comparison.

[1221] After all, I just demolished the Bible. Therefore the fundamentalist version of Jesus Christ has no validity or credibility.

no historical Jesus. To present such a false dichotomy to their readers, phantom Christ theorists are playing fast and loose with the facts and the real state of the evidence. Such crudity is no doubt calculated to appeal to the lowest-common-denominator mentality of popular counter-culture. The ahistorical paradigm may have a superficial pseudo-intellectual appeal to effete elites in their smug assurance of ideological correctness and fashionable philosophy, but it is a tedious, masturbatory preaching to the choir. There is no appreciation for subtlety or nuance in such theses. It is absurd to take a holistic fundamentalist image of Jesus from the New Testament, and then use that mythic image as a target to be debunked, and then to claim that one has proven that Jesus never existed as a historical person. That is exactly why I sharply distinguished between the historical and fundamentalist paradigms herein. The ahistorical paradigm may be the polar opposite to the fundamentalist paradigm, but it exists in a state of relative codependency upon it. It is merely an inverted mirror-image of fundamentalism. It is an all-or-nothing proposition. Just as fundamentalists believe that every verse of the New Testament is true in every detail, the mythicists deny historicity to every part of the New Testament; not even the slightest historical subtext is admitted to underlay the text. But mythicists have not adequately addressed the actual historical circumstances of the writing of the New Testament texts. Someone had to have written them, since they exist. Why? In sheer psychological terms, it is easier to believe that miracles were ascribed to a person who never performed them, rather than that the central figure of all those books was a mere *chimera*.

Sometimes mythicists will attack the position of their opponents by criticizing Euhemerus, the Greek who postulated that the various Gods and Heroes of legend were actually men who had lived, and were later deified.[1222] He is singled out for abuse and scoffing. But we know that in some cases, this is exactly what happened. In the case of the Caesars, this cannot be denied.[1223] Vespasian was not only deified, but credited with miracles, even in his own lifetime. Today there are certain cult leaders who are believed by their disciples to be divine. Sabbatai Zevi was credited with miracles, and we know that he was

---

[1222] Euhemerus is sometimes transliterated Everemus. His theory is called *Euhemerism* or *Evemerism,* respectively.

[1223] Consult the work of Suetonius. See also Alexander Del Mar's *The Worship of Augustus Caesar.,* op. cit.

a historical person. Furthermore as I pointed out above, we have in the Dead Sea Scrolls the figure of the Teacher of Righteousness, who undoubtedly was a historical person, but who has so far remained unidentified. And mythicists can hardly fall back on the most popular suggestions offered, since in two out of three cases, they involve the necessary existence of Jesus as a historical figure.[1224] And the chronology we discern from the Damascus Document proves, that the Teacher of Righteousness lived in the early second century B.C. This may be a "good news/bad news" situation for the phantom Christ theorists; while on the one hand it points away from such candidates as John the Baptist, Jesus Christ, and James the Just, it still undercuts one of their chief arguments, namely the argument from silence. In other words, the presumed silence of contemporary historians respecting Jesus presents a reasonable to strong presumption that Jesus never existed, according to them. But if so, then who was this Teacher of Righteousness, who is so prominent in many of the Dead Sea Scrolls? He must have been important to the Dead Sea sect, but he has so far remained unidentified in Jewish history. The parallel with the case of Jesus is too pregnant with the obvious inference that, just as the Teacher of Righteousness was important to the Dead Sea community, but otherwise virtually unknown in his own time, so Jesus Christ likewise was very important to his disciples, even though he was virtually a nonentity in his own time. This may be embarrassing to Christians, but it presents an equal challenge to the phantom theorists as well. Because now we at least have a precedent of a person who actually lived and was vitally important to a religious sect, and yet was not an identifiable historical figure. This could be a description either of the Teacher of Righteousness or of Jesus Christ.[1225] So the discovery of the Dead Sea Scrolls, in an oblique way, has provided us with a precedent that refutes one of the prime postulates of the phantom theorists. Of course this in and of itself does not prove the historical

---

[1224] The three most popular suggestions being James the brother of Jesus, Jesus himself, or John the Baptist. While it is just barely possible that John the Baptist may have existed while Jesus was a *chimera,* at least some mythicists explicitly deny the historicity of John the Baptist (such as Acharya S.).

[1225] And it would be the epitome of absurdity for mythicists to claim that the Teacher of Righteousness himself was merely an invented figure. But now they probably will claim that, since they have nowhere else to go with this dilemma.

existence of Jesus, nor do I claim such. But it does mean that Jesus Christ is not unprecedented in the sense of being a highly venerated religious figure who in his own time was a virtual nonentity, apparently. So this is really a deathblow to the supposed argument from silence. If not, those mythicists better come up with a believable historical identification of the Teacher of Righteousness in 176 B.C. Otherwise they are merely begging the question with their appeal to a supposed argument from silence.

Another item of relevance, although admittedly obscure and oblique, is the position of the Mandaeans vis-à-vis John the Baptist and Jesus Christ. The Mandaeans venerate John the Baptist as a true holy prophet, but they revile Jesus as a false prophet and a deceiver and a revealer of forbidden secrets. This is curious, and more than curious. It seems very unlikely that the Mandaeans could have or would have adopted this attitude if both John and Jesus were merely invented literary figures. After all, John is depicted as merely the herald of Christ in the Gospels. If the Mandaeans were basing their beliefs about Jesus and John on those texts, then their attitude is inexplicable. On the other hand, if we assume the historicity of both John and Jesus, then this attitude is at least amenable to some explanation. We speculated above that quite possibly, John the Baptist himself was a member of the Essene order. At some point he apparently broke away, and gathered disciples around himself. One of his disciples was Jesus. That is why Jesus had been baptized by John. Eventually Jesus broke away from John's group, taking some of John's disciples with him, and gathering other disciples to himself. If this scenario took place, then what the Mandaeans say about Jesus is readily understandable; they presumably are repeating traditions passed down from remnants of John's disciples, to whom Jesus was a traitor who betrayed secrets. This line of tradition would have held John the Baptist as a true messenger of God, but Jesus as a deceiver.[1226] Therefore the attitudes

---

[1226] In fact according to some occult teachings, John the Baptist was a true messenger from the heavenly Father, while Jesus was a servant of Ialdabaoth, the blind idiot-god of the Old Testament. Some Gnostic teachings reverse the picture; depicting Jesus as the true messenger of the Father, while John was the servant of Ialdabaoth. Naturally both sets of teachings were esoteric, and never exposed to the ears of the sheep, who only had the exoteric teachings.

of the Mandaeans towards John and Jesus are only explicable under an assumption of the historicity of both John and Jesus.

As far as the messianic *mythos* is concerned, whether this is looked at from a cross-cultural perspective, or limited to a strictly Jewish cultural viewpoint, the phantom theory wrongly assumes that no actual man would have acted out the messianic drama, in a three-dimensional carnival of life and death, as a supreme rendition of living performance art. But we know that there are men who do this all the time. Every year in the Philippines, men allow themselves to be crucified, to prove their devotion to God. Passion plays are still performed annually in Germany. Of course we are not talking about a mere passion play in the case of Jesus Christ. Nor am I suggesting that Jesus deliberately sought to be crucified.[1227] But what I am saying is that these mythicists are no more justified in tacitly assuming that no man would or could step forward and claim to be the expected Messiah. In fact, the history of Josephus proves that there were many messianic pretenders. Jesus was merely one among many. As far as the possible "passion play" aspect of the *mythos* is concerned, there is abundant evidence that ancient religions abounded with pageantry. Even assenting to a ubiquitous cross-cultural messianic *mythos,* it is not too far-fetched to speculate that sometimes the drama was acted out by real people, putting on a performance with a religious function. Mithraic mysteries are said to have flourished in Asia Minor, and particularly Tarsus, the city of Saul. Could Paul have had such a thing in mind when he wrote to the Galatians "O foolish Galatians, who has bewitched you, that you should not obey the truth, before whose eyes Jesus Christ has been evidently set forth, crucified among you?"[1228] While I suppose that Catholic fundamentalists could use this verse to argue in favor of a first-century use of crucifixes, this does not seem to be the meaning of the verse. But "crucified among you" is admittedly a very strange expression, considering that Jesus was supposedly crucified just outside of Jerusalem. Does this mean that some early Christians performed passion plays? That seems doubtful too, but the verse is certainly provocative. One almost never hears a sermon on it. Bible commentaries typically gloss over it, without any

---

[1227] Although this is a remote possibility. See discussion below on *karath.*

[1228] Galatians 3:1. The point made here is equally valid if Silvanus, or some other person, wrote the epistle to the Galatians in Paul's name.

real digging. In any case the phantom theory assumes that the Jews were very passive in respect to messianic prophecies, an assumption belied by the writings of Josephus. Furthermore the presumed silence of Josephus about Christ, which is pointed to by mythicists as evidence that Jesus never existed, is also equally problematical with respect to the fact that Josephus is also silent about any Christian movement.[1229] And yet most phantom Christ theorists posit at least an embryonic Christian movement sometime in the latter half of the first century.[1230] As far as the argument from silence goes, in respect to the question of Christ's historicity, absence of evidence does not prove evidence of absence. I will always return to the example of the Teacher of Righteousness as an unanswerable refutation to the so-called *argument silentio*.

The Teacher of Righteousness, being a person spoken of in the Dead Sea Scrolls, brings up yet another argument relative to the Dead Sea Scrolls. While I confess that I have not yet studied the Scrolls in the most intimate and minute detail, nevertheless I feel that there are some similiarities between the Scrolls and what is found in portions of the New Testament that are more easily accounted for by an assumption of historicity, rather than ahistoricity. This is a rather subtle point, and I will not press it, but I believe it is something that may bear fruit with research. In the interim I could recommend the works of Robert Eisenman as demonstrating highly suggestive literary parallels, to say the least of it. These literary parallels are more easily accounted for under the assumption of Christ's historicity, in my view. The reason why has directly to do with the secrecy of the scrolls. They were not common property, even among the Jews. As such, it is far less likely that some group of people who were not in any way associated with the Dead Sea community would have been able to write documents with close literary parallels to secret scrolls held by the sect. On the other hand, if we assume that Jesus led a group that

---

[1229] i.e., if we exclude the infamous *Testimonium Flavium*, which virtually all reputable historians and literary critics reject as an interpolation. It is never quoted from earlier than the fourth century.

[1230] In all fairness, however, it is not necessary to adopt this position. One could argue, perhaps more persuasively, that the Christian movement originated in the early to mid-second century. But this evidence could be interpreted as proving, not that Jesus never existed, but that he lived at a later period of time; possibly as a contemporary of Simeon Bar-Kochbah.

was a third remove from the Essenes, then such parallels are much more readily accounted for. Of course there are a number of unknown variables, and I am certainly not making my argument hinge upon this, but this is one more thing that fits into a pattern suggesting a historical rather than an ahistorical, paradigm.

Another problem for the phantom theory is contradictions. If Jesus Christ was merely a completely invented literary figure, why would the men who invented him have not been consistent in their tale? Why would they so frequently contradict one another, if they wanted people to believe their incredible story? In fact, this virtually disproves the phantom theory all by itself. Because if it was nothing but the Gospels written by a conspiracy of men who invented Jesus Christ that was supposed to be evidence in favor of the religion, then the very inconsistency of those texts would have been fatal to any acceptance of the story as true.[1231] In other words, there had to have been some other basis whereby the early Christians believed in their faith. A bunch of mutually contradictory texts would not suffice to establish their faith. The many blatant contradictions between the four Gospels belies any notion that Christianity could have begun as a mere literary movement.[1232] The contradictions are admittedly and paradoxically a potential problem for any one of the six theories;[1233] they are the biggest problem for fundamentalism, and after that, for minimalism or mythicism.[1234] Men who are inventing a story and literary characters whom they want to pass off as historical are not about to jeopardize their credibility by contradicting one another. The New Testament contradictions simultaneously disprove both fundamentalism and the phantom theory. Mythicists never address this problem. It is blithely ignored, together with all the other evidence against their theory.

But the single greatest class of objections against the phantom Christ theory are the many fossil passages. These passages, by their very nature, disprove the phantom theory. This is especially true of

---

[1231] By contrast, the contradictions can be better accounted for in critical-historical terms.

[1232] Which is essentially what the mythicist position amounts to.

[1233] However we must keep in mind that one of the six theories must be true; there are no other theories. Therefore the use of "paradoxically" above.

[1234] The ahistorical paradigm or the phantom Christ theory, respectively.

those passages that speak of the disciples of John the Baptist.[1235] Had the story of Jesus been a complete fiction, then these embarrassing verses would never have been written. The same holds true for any number of other fossil passages as well. The fossil passages are named such because they imply an actual historical subtext beneath the surface of the text. Thus they point to something more archaic and primordial. These are the real roots of the story, around which legendary and mythic layers have been encrusted. If we imagine a scenario in which Jesus had been one of John the Baptist's disciples, then naturally he would have been baptized by John. The baptism is transformed in the New Testament as an opportunity for John's supposed testimony to Jesus as being the chosen Lamb of God and the Son of God.[1236] The baptism of Christ is narrated fairly straightforwardly in Mark,[1237] but this is dealt with rather awkwardly by Matthew, who has John protest his unworthiness to baptize Jesus.[1238] What is merely a subjective experience in Mark becomes objective in Matthew and John.[1239] So what would have been a completely natural occurrence if one assumes that Jesus had initially been one of John's disciples becomes a potential source of embarrassment, which is dealt with better by Mark and Luke rather than Matthew and John. John and Matthew deal with the embarrassing circumstance differently; in John, Jesus had not been recognized as the Messiah by John until he could visibly see the Holy Spirit descending upon him; in Matthew, John already knows that Jesus is the Chosen One, and therefore he protests his unworthiness. Interestingly, MtE contains elements of the baptism scene as found in all four Gospels.[1240] My point here is that, if Jesus and John had been completely invented characters, then the writers who wrote the story would not have written it so awkwardly; there would instead be

---

[1235] Mt 9:14; 11:2–3; 14:12; Mk 2:18; 6:29; Lk 5:33; Acts 19:1–3 cf Jn 1:35–42.

[1236] John 1:29–36.

[1237] Mark 1:9–12.

[1238] Matthew 3:13–17.

[1239] Mark 1:10–11 cp Matthew 3:17; John 1:31–34 cf Luke 3:21–22.

[1240] Which suggests that MtE postdates the four Gospels. A comparison between the accounts in this instance discloses an awkwardness on the part of the text of MtE which seems to be an effort at harmonization, akin to the Diatessaron.

a smoothness to the narrative that is often lacking in the Gospels. I suppose that one hypothetical solution would be to propose that while Jesus was mythical, John was historical. But even this solution does not work; the Gospels, having been written long after the alleged events they purport to narrate, could easily have reinvented John as the herald of Christ in a much smoother way, had Jesus merely been a purely invented character. Furthermore it is unlikely that a historical John would have been eclipsed by a completely mythical Jesus.

The passages mentioning the brothers and sisters of Jesus also belie the Solar God version of the phantom theory.[1241] But if Christ were merely a completely invented figure, then how do we account for Luke 8:1-3, which says that certain women ministered to Jesus and the Apostles out of their own substance? A completely invented miracle-worker, who routinely multiplies fishes and loaves of bread, would have no need of any such assistance. But the passage is credible as a lapse on the part of Luke, where the truth slipped out, in almost Freudian fashion. Or what about the embarrassing instance of Christ's family saying he was insane in Mark 3:21? Would men inventing a Messiah have placed such an embarrassing verse in their text? The question answers itself. The obvious answer is that these quirky verses appear in the text because they point to an actual historical subtext; in other words, some of the real history of Jesus Christ obtrudes upward in the Gospel texts, like stalagmites. In effect the various fossil passages of the Gospels are like stalagmites in a cave, obtruding upward from the legendary palimpsest composed by the Evangelists. These passages prove, as nothing else can, that Jesus was a real person. For mythicists to argue that such passages were gratuitously placed within the Gospel texts to provide more historical credibility and realism to their creation would merely be an outrageous act of special pleading on their part; it would be as much as an admission of defeat. Such convoluted reasoning is more akin to the constant rationalizations of fundamentalists, or the paranoid conspiracy theories of the lunatic fringe. So the phantom Christ theory can be safely ruled out. Ironically the fossil passages, as well as the contradictions, found in the New Testament, rule out both fundamentalism and minimalism.

The phantom Christ theory attempts to eliminate the psychological aspect of the Jesus Christ paradox. But instead it has

---

[1241] Although brothers and sisters are not so far-fetched for an invented Messiah, ala Abelard Reuchlin.

merely relocated it from the person of Jesus to the men and women who wrote the texts of the New Testament. Even assuming an esoteric motivation, there is an immense psychological difficulty in supposing that people would not only invent a literary character, but act out an elaborate charade to convince other people that the events narrated had actually taken place. It is too much. It is not realistic to assume that the origin of belief in Jesus Christ's resurrection from the dead was merely or even primarily due to a literary phenomenon. All the evidence points in the opposite direction: that the literary texts, particularly the Gospels, were the very last phase of an actual historical messianic movement.[1242] They were written after hope had been lost that the Son of man would soon return from heaven to establish the kingdom of God on earth. The contradictions within the New Testament are more easily accounted for in a critical-historical framework, rather than a radically minimalist framework. The fossil passages constitute an unanswerable objection against the phantom theory.

Now we have eliminated both the fundamentalist paradigm, and the ahistorical paradigm. That only leaves the four theories of the historical paradigm. We will now consider them in turn.

[1242] The last phase, i.e., before petrification into a more dogmatic ecclesiastical form; but as Christianity became calcified into a more rigid, authoritarian structure, the original spiritual vitality of the movement subsided. Gnosticism and Montanism may have been attempts to recapture the original flame of true zeal and spirituality, but the glory had departed from Israel, never to return.

Objections Against The Survival Theory

The survival theory seems to be a very strong theory, at least superficially. It is certainly a much stronger theory than either the phantom theory or the resurrection theory. It is also much stronger than the impersonation theory. Admittedly it has advantages lacking in any other theory. But it also has disadvantages. We have briefly discussed some of the advantages of this theory above; now we must consider objections against the theory.

The first objection against the survival theory is the unlikelihood that Jesus could have survived his extreme physical trauma.[1243] This issue is never adequately addressed by advocates of the theory. The chief point is that Jesus was not a typical crucifixion victim. He had also been crowned with thorns.[1244] Only a messianic pretender would

---

[1243] Once again I am not saying that this would have been impossible, but merely unlikely.

[1244] Mt 27:29; Mk 15:17; Jn 19:2,5. Luke omits this detail from his narrative. Possibly this was because his sources did not confirm it, and it is implicitly unbelievable. It is not that the Roman soldiers would have lacked the requisite cruelty to do such a thing; but I could never picture how they could have formed a "crown" out of thorns, without cutting their own hands and fingers. Therefore it is possible, at least, that this detail is a gratuitous invention on the part of the other Evangerlists. I recognize that

have been treated in this way; a typical thief, for example, may have been flogged, but he would not have been crowned with thorns. So it is a lie to say that Jesus suffered no more physical trauma than a typical man condemned to crucifixion.[1245] The very fact that Simon of Cyrene had been compelled by the Roman soldiers to bear the cross of Christ proves that Jesus had endured atypical trauma; most condemned men would carry their own cross to crucifixion. Simon of Cyrene had only been enlisted for the task because it was feared that Jesus wouldn't make it to the place of crucifixion. Jesus had been arrested [preumably] Thursday night, having been betrayed by one of his trusted twelve Apostles; he was brought before Annas first,[1246] then led to Caiaphas.[1247] After Jesus answered the high priest's adjuration as to whether or not he was the Messiah, the Son of God, in the affirmative, sentence of death was immediately passed upon him by the *Sanhedrin,* and Jesus was spat upon, mocked, blindfolded, and slapped.[1248] The trial was a mockery; it was held on Friday, and Jesus had probably gotten very little sleep. We are not told so, but it is possible that the temple guard may have whipped Jesus with forty lashes.[1249] Jesus was led by the chief priests, scribes, lawyers, Pharisees and the temple guard to Pontius Pilate, for execution.[1250] Pilate questioned Jesus at length, and then sent him to Herod for further questioning.[1251] Jesus had also been mocked by Herod's warriors. The emotional trauma that Jesus suffered must also have aggravated any physical trauma he

---

pointing this fact out may weaken, to some degree, some of the arguments presented here; but nevertheless there can be no doubt that Jesus did suffer an immense amount of physical trauma.

[1245] As Elmar Gruber implied in the book he cowrote with Holger Kersten; Kersten & Gruber., op. cit., pgs. 245-246. Gruber also obscured the issue, either deliberately or by mistake, by assuming that Jesus had been whipped by the Jews, rather than by the Romans. The Gospel texts all say that Jesus had been whipped by the Romans, upon Pilate's orders. The Romans had no law against more than forty stripes, as the Jews had.

[1246] John 18:13.

[1247] John 18:24 cf Matthew 26:57; Mark 14:53; Luke 22:54.

[1248] Matthew 26:63-69; Mark 14:61-65.

[1249] Deuteronomy 25:1-3.

[1250] Mt 27:1-2; Mk 15:1; Lk 23:1; Jn 18:28-31; 19:7.

[1251] Luke 23:6-11.

received.[1252] Pontius Pilate had Jesus scourged by his soldiers.[1253] The Romans had no law prohibiting more than forty lashes. Then the Roman soldiers mocked Jesus and spat upon him, and placed a crown of thorns on his head, and hit him on the head with a reed.[1254] Even if we take an extremely critical view and say that these accounts are very much exaggerated, it is reasonable to assume that Jesus suffered an immense amount of physical and emotional trauma during the ordeal. While it would not have been impossible for Jesus to have survived this ordeal, advocates of the survival theory generally tend to understate and downplay this aspect of the situation. I am not saying that this alone is enough to refute the idea that Jesus may have survived his passion, but it is a far more formidable obstacle than most advocates of a survival theory are willing to concede.

Of course, many advocates of the survival theory claim that Jesus was helped through his traumatic ordeal by secret disciples, who helped him survive. But as we will soon see, this assumption rests on a foundation of quicksand. The assumption of secret disciples actually creates further unanswered questions, which are never addressed by advocates of the theory. For example, if we assume that Jesus received assistance from alleged secret disciples, then what precisely were the motivations of these secret disciples? How did they manage to keep their devotion to Jesus a secret, both from the *Sanhedrin* and from the Apostles and other disciples? Furthermore if we assume a scenario in which it was secret disciples who helped Jesus survive the crucifixion, and we further assume that this fact was kept secret from the eleven Apostles and all the other disciples and relatives of Jesus, then this would seem to place these "secret disciples" in a position of unspeakable power over Jesus. In other words, if it was all an elaborate charade designed to fool the Apostles and other disciples into believing that Jesus rose from the dead, then could not these "secret disciples"

[1252] The emotions can have a powerful effect upon bodily health, for better or worse. We are all well acquainted with the phenomenon of psychosomatic illness. When extreme physical and emotional trauma are inflicted the results can be fatal. Sometimes women who are gang-raped die from the trauma. This could not be strictly from physical trauma alone. Cf Judges 19:25-28.

[1253] Mt 27:26; Mk 15:15; Jn 19:1.

[1254] Mt 27:27-30; Mk 15:16-20; Jn 19:2-3. But the crowning with thorns is doubtful.

have held this over Christ's head as an ultimate trump card? Would not Christ have become a mere puppet of such men, who could betray his great secret? But such questions as these are never answered or even addressed by advocates of that version of the survival theory that makes it hinge upon the help of "secret" disciples.

But even the assumption that there were any such "secret" disciples is entirely unwarranted by the evidence. In fact the term "secret disciple" never even occurs anywhere in the Gospels. The closest thing to this is John 19:38, which says of Joseph of Arimathaea that he was "a disciple of Jesus, but secretly for fear of the Jews". The Greek word used here is *kekrummenos,* which signifies "kept hidden."[1255] But this hardly proves that there was an entire class of "secret" disciples. In fact, none of the other Gospels refers to Joseph in this way. Matthew calls him a disciple,[1256] but nothing about being a so-called "secret" disciple. In fact, Jesus uttered a saying that excludes the possibility of "secret" disciples.[1257] So of the four Gospels, only Matthew and John refer to Joseph of Arimathaea as a disciple; and only John calls him what may be the equivalent of a "secret" disciple.[1258] Neither Mark nor Luke say that Joseph of Arimathaea was a disciple of Jesus, although they do mention him as the man who asked for Christ's body from Pilate, and buried him in his own tomb.[1259] Mark and Luke also specify that Joseph was a member of the *Sanhedrin,* which both Matthew and John are completely silent about.[1260] It strikes me as more than a bare coincidence that the two Gospels that happen to say that Joseph was a member of the Jewish *Sanhedrin* say nothing about him being a disciple of Jesus, "secret" or otherwise, while the two Gospels that claim Joseph was a disciple of Christ fail to mention that Joseph was a member of the *Sanhedrin.* Of course it is *possible*

[1255] Nestle-Aland., op. cit., pg. 314.

[1256] Matthew 27:57.

[1257] Matthew 10:32-33: "Whosoever therefore shall confess me before men, him will I confess also before my Father which is in heaven. But whosoever shall deny me before men, him will I also deny before my Father which is in heaven."

[1258] Although the verse implies that Joseph's loyalty to Jesus became known from that time on, when he buried Christ's body.

[1259] Mark 15:42-46; Luke 23:50-53.

[1260] Ibid.

that all four Gospels are correct on this point; after all, this is not a contradiction; Joseph *may* have been both a member of the *Sanhedrin*, and he was also secretly a "disciple" of Jesus, in some sense. This is *possible,* but it strikes me as highly improbable. Joseph may have felt sympathy for Jesus and admired him, but this is not the same thing as being a disciple, or even a "secret" disciple. Most likely, Joseph of Arimathaea was not a disciple of Jesus at all, but merely a sympathetic man who sought to bury a fellow Jew before the Sabbath as an act of righteousness. Comparing all four accounts of Joseph of Arimathaea, those of Mark and Luke seem the most realistic and straightforward. Perhaps in an effort to demonize the entire Jewish *Sanhedrin,* Matthew made no mention that Joseph was a member of that body, and falsely claimed that Joseph had been a disciple of Jesus. But this claim was belied by other textual evidence; the female disciples did not know Joseph at all,[1261] so in an effort to explain, justify, and reconcile the three earlier accounts, John augmented Matthew's fiction about Joseph being a disciple of Jesus by claiming that he had kept his discipleship hidden, for fear of the Jewish elders. Thus the fact that the women did not know Joseph is "explained" by the allegation that he kept his loyalty to Jesus a secret. Thus the myth of "secret" disciples is exposed as being based upon the fig leaves of Matthew and John. Interestingly, in the Toldoth Yeshu, it is the "wise men" who claim to have buried Jesus. This accords with the view found in Mark and Luke. This is actually an immensely important point. If Joseph of Arimathaea had indeed been a member of the *Sanhedrin,* then this fact could not have been hidden. In fact the bare statement of Mark is elaborated upon by Luke, to the effect that Joseph "had not consented to the counsel and deed" of the men who condemned Jesus.[1262] But Mark insisted that the *entire* Sanhedrin voted to condemn Jesus.[1263] Nevertheless, both Mark and Luke speak of Joseph as a good and just man.[1264] Perhaps we see

---

[1261] Which we may readily surmise from what is said of them in relation to Joseph of Arimathaea; that they merely beheld where Joseph had buried Jesus; cf Mk 15:47; Mt 27:61; Lk 23:55. If the women knew Joseph and recognized him as a disciple of Jesus, then they would have also assisted in the burial, anointing Jesus with spices & ointments.

[1262] Luke 23:51.

[1263] Mk 14:64.

[1264] Luke 23:50; Mark 15:43.

a slight hint of sectarianism in Matthew and John, who seek to claim Joseph as one of Christ's disciples. Nicodemus, who is only mentioned in John's Gospel, was also supposedly a member of the Jewish *Sanhedrin*.[1265] In my former work I postulated that Nicodemus may very likely have been a completely invented character.[1266] But even if he was not, it is more realistic to see him as a man sympathetic to Jesus and who may have admired him and his teachings, who merely helped Joseph to give Jesus a proper burial. As devout Jews they would have considered it a duty and a righteous act to bury another Jew. There is no need to postulate that they were "secret" disciples of Jesus on this account. And to further suggest that they hatched a scheme to help Jesus fake his own death on the cross is more than a little far-fetched. It also raises yet more unanswered questions, such as, Was this planned by Jesus all along, as some sort of Passover plot scenario? Or was this a contingency Jesus planned, in case he ever fell into the custody of the Romans? Either scenario creates a huge psychological dilemma that is never even remotely addressed by advocates of this version of the survival theory. This psychological dilemma necessarily involves both Jesus, and any other "secret" disciples who would have been involved in such a scheme. Even as a contingency, Jesus and the other men involved would have to have known that it was not guaranteed to work. But if it was part of some elaborate Passover plot, then that opens up a whole other can of worms.

There are two massively huge problems with a supposed Passover plot on the part of Jesus, either with or without help from supposed "secret" disciples. The first of these is the extreme psychological problem. Unless we are to ascribe a truly superhuman ontological status to Jesus, then presumably his mind could never bear the strain of anticipating an excruciating death (or neath death) by crucifixion. He would have known and anticipated the particularly brutal treatment meted out to messianic pretenders by the Romans. Of course Jesus lived in a dangerous world; there was always risk involved in any great endeavor. But there is a world of difference between taking great risks, on the one hand, and deliberately acting out a course of action that would ultimately lead to a sadistically cruel fate; it would have been suicide by proxy. And the most unimaginably slow, cruel,

---

[1265] John 3:1.

[1266] I will discuss Nicodemus in greater detail below.

brutal, torturous, painful, excruciating, unbearable agony; this is not like a suicide bomber or someone committing "suicide by cop." This is crucifixion. This is being whipped, spat on, mocked, beaten, slapped, nailed to a cross, raised up on the cross, pierced in the side with a spear, and finally dying. Talk about fanaticism! To survive such barbarities would seem to be almost as miraculous as rising from the dead. Jesus would have had to have been not only suicidal and completely fanatical, but insane and masochistic as well. Perhaps he was a mad genius. But I am willing to give him more credit than that. After all, if Jesus was truly insane then this implies that all the Apostles and other disciples were also insane, which in turn implies that all the early Christians were insane, etc., etc. However much one may disdain Christianity as a religion, it is not reasonable or credible to "explain" the origin of the religion as an explosion of insanity. But if Jesus planned to execute this design, with an intent to survive the ordeal,[1267] then he was guilty of unparalleled *hubris*. Such grandiosity and egomania is unbecoming of the meek Lamb of God. This extreme psychological problem, or rather complex of undiagnosed mental illnesses, is an unanswerable objection against any alleged "Passover plot" type of theory. But there is also another huge problem that is never addressed by such persons. It is the bare assumption that Jesus had intended to survive at all.[1268] It would not have been a matter of *hubris* if Christ had no intention of "surviving" the ordeal, but rather of dying and being literally resurrected from the dead, either physically or spiritually. Or at least, it would have been a much different *kind* of *hubris*. Of course if Jesus had been contemplating a martyr's death, or even a "sacrificial" death, especially by the brutal method of Roman crucifixion, then the huge psychological problem remains. But this problem is more explainable in the context of a person who is already committed to dying, *if necessary*. And in this respect there is a definite advantage to the idea that Jesus had intended to die on the cross, rather than somehow fake his own death. This will lead us back to a discussion of the Hebrew word *karath,* which I discussed at length in my earlier work.[1269]

[1267] To what end? To try to fool men who would be so easily imposed upon?

[1268] I.e., assuming that there had been any kind of "Passover plot" in the first place.

[1269] *JESUS 100 B.C.*

The Hebrew word *karath* occurs frequently within *TaNaKh,* and usually signifies to "cut off" or be "cut off" which in turn means cut off by death. Essentially the word, as it is most commonly used, means to kill or be killed, to suffer death or total destruction in some way. However, the root idea has to do with "cutting" and a permissible interpretation of the word in some instances is to "cut" as in making a covenant by way of cutting.[1270] The word is used of the Messiah in Daniel 9:26 and I argued in my earlier work that in that instance it should have been translated as "make a covenant" rather than "cut off." The context of the verse seems to almost require the reading "make a covenant" rather than "cut off", since the latter interpretation implies that the Messiah would die a violent death almost as soon as he appeared. Furthermore there is a reference to the Messiah "confirming the covenant" in Daniel 9:27, which implies the correctness of my reading of *karath* in Daniel 9:26. I argued that it was only subsequent to the time of Jesus that the reading of *karath* was interpreted by *Christians,* or rather Messianic Hebrews, as a supposed prophecy of Christ's supposedly "sacrificial" death on the cross or tree.[1271] I further argued that the Jews acquiesced in this false reading since the prophecy became useless to them after the time of Simeon Bar Kochbah. I also pointed out that, as far as I know, there are no Greek manuscripts of Daniel predating the late first century B.C.[1272] So I felt that I made a reasonably strong case that the original reading of *karath* in Daniel 9:26 not only could be, but probably was, "make a covenant" rather than the contrary "shall be cut off", as most Bibles have it. I still feel that I made a fairly strong case, but let us suppose for a moment that I was wrong. Let us suppose that the true original reading of *karath* <u>was</u> "shall be cut of" rather than "shall make a covenant."[1273] If so, then would not Jesus have planned, not to fake his own death, but to actually die, as prophesied? To postulate that Jesus sought to fake

---

[1270] As in circumcision, or cutting an animal to be slaughtered for sacrifice, etc.

[1271] See my earlier work.

[1272] And therefore after the time of Jesus, according to my earlier chronological theory.

[1273] I hasten to point out here, as I also pointed out in my earlier work, that the Greek texts of Daniel, as found in the Septuagint, support that traditional reading of *karath* as meaning "shall be cut off". SEPTUAGINTA., op. cit., pg. 924. (vol.2; duo volumina in uno).

his own death in order to create the false impression that a prophecy had been fulfilled is to turn Jesus into a completely cynical con-artist. What would be the point of such a charade? Faking his own death would also mean faking the fulfillment of prophecy. Was Jesus trying to fool God? That would have been absurd. If Jesus truly believed in the prophecy, and he interpreted it in a way requiring the death of the Messiah, and he believed that he was that Messiah, then he would have had to submit to death, to fulfill the prophecy. Otherwise he would have been mocking God. The only way out of this dilemma, other than supposing that Jesus did not thus interpret the prophecy, is by recourse to an esotericism in which such prophecies were taken in jest. But this would have been a rather cynical esotericism, to say the least of it. There is no indication that Jesus did not implicitly believe in such prophecies as literally true. So if I was wrong in my reading of *karath,* then this is a standing refutation of the survival theory, or at least of any Passover plot variation thereof. It is also an equal refutation of the substitution theory as well. Thus entire edifices can sometimes hinge upon the meaning of a single word. And the meaning of this word would have been of absolute importance to Jesus, and to anyone else who sincerely believed that he was the promised Messiah. Perhaps the very ambiguity of the Hebrew was a way out of a path that seemed to lead to certain death. On the other hand, assuming that Jesus was a true believer,[1274] then even a brutal, barbaric death may not have frightened him. We must also keep in mind that the prophecy, even if it is interpreted as implying an early death for the Messiah, does not specify the manner of death. It could have meant death in battle, or by a quick martyrdom. Furthermore if Jesus had experienced the out-of-body experience, then death as such would have held no terror for him. Of course that brings us to another variation on the survival theory: that Jesus survived his crucifixion through astral projection.

If we postulate that Jesus survived his crucifixion through recourse to astral projection, this at least removes the spurious "secret disciples" from the scenario. Not only that, but this interpretation potentially reconciles the dilemma of a fatal reading of *karath* with the survival theory; if Jesus interpreted the out-of-body experience as a literal death and resurrection, then he could have used this method

---

[1274] And all the evidence seems to support this assumption.

to literally fulfill Daniel 9:26.[1275] While most people today would probably not interpret astral projection as a death and resurrection, it is at least possible, if not probable, that Jesus may have.[1276] If we further postulate that secret rituals involving astral projection were part of an esoteric practice within the inner circles of the messianic movement, then those fortunate disciples who experienced the out-of-body state may also have interpreted the experience as a death and resurrection from death. The probability that the supposed resurrection of Lazarus may have been a ritual involving the out-of-body experience is enhanced by the use of the name Lazarus itself, since it is a Semitic variation upon Osiris, an Egyptian deity associated with the underworld. Osiris is associated with the Egyptian concept of the resurrection. The Jews were influenced by Egyptian religion and culture, despite the strong antipathy towards Egyptian religion and culture often expressed in early Jewish literature. Some degree of influence was still present, albeit repackaged in Hebrew cultural forms. Of course any degree of real influence upon Jewish society from foreign sources, whether Egyptian, Canaanite, Syrian, Assyrian, Chaldean, Persian, Greek, particularly religious influence, would be submerged in a deep esotericism that would be covered by denials and blatant historical revisionism. Yet these cultural influences can still be detected. The case of Lazarus, if we interpret the story as a historical incident,[1277] may not have been mentioned by the Synoptic evangelists because they themselves may have been unaware of the incident. Or they may have felt it was too sacred a mystery and therefore should be kept secret. This interpretation is reasonably plausible if we further interpret the incident as a secret ritual that apparently went wrong.[1278] Conversely, if these Synoptic evangelists did know of the true circumstances surrounding the incident, they may have chosen silence as the wisest course of action.[1279] By contrast, John chooses to tell us

---

[1275] i.e., assuming that he interpreted *karath* as meaning "shall be cut off" rather than "shall make a covenant."

[1276] i.e., assuming that he was acquainted with the phenomenon.

[1277] i.e., rather than as a historical parable based upon Luke 16:19-31. But this latter interpretation seems more probable, in some respects.

[1278] i.e., Lazarus was in the out-of-body state for too long, and perhaps it was feared that he would never return to his body.

[1279] Although Luke uses it as the basis for a parable he attributes to Jesus.

the tale, but in such a modified way as to make it seem like something it was not: a genuine miracle.

Of course if the story of Lazarus stood alone as the only possible hint of astral projection in the New Testament then we might be skating on thin ice; but there is also an incident reported in Mark's Gospel that at least remotely hints at the possibility of astral projection. The scene is immediately after the arrest of Jesus in the Garden of Gethsemane. The brief passage is as follows:

50 And they all forsook him, and fled.

51 And there followed him a certain young man, having a linen cloth cast about his naked body; and the young men laid hold on him:

52 But he left the linen cloth, and fled from them naked. (Mark 14:50-52)

While admittedly this brief passage ostensibly has nothing to do with astral projection, the very fact that he was wearing only a linen cloth over his naked body suggests that he may have been present to receive an initiation ritual involving an out-of-body experience; a linen cloth would have been a very loose-fitting garment, and even today people who seek to undergo the out-of-body experience are admonished to wear loose-ftting clothes. There are also a few other verses that seem to imply astral projection in the New Testament, but we will look at these later. For now we will assume that secret rituals involving astral projection were at least a reasonable possibility of an esoteric practice among Christ's intimate disciples. After all, astral projection is a truly numinous experience; men and women who had experienced such a thing would have had a taste of transcendence and an assurance in respect to the reality of a spiritual realm. What greater source of faith and motivation could they have had? Such persons would have known directly, by their own personal experience, that the soul could exist apart from the body, and thus would have despised death. And if this was the great esoteric secret of Christ's inner circle, then this could provide the motive basis for all that followed. Possibly such rituals may have involved the use of certain hallucinogens; some people who have taken large quantities of hallucinogens have reported out-of-body and near-death experiences. But all this would have to remain highly secret. Admittedly this is a matter of speculation; but I find it more realistic than pure blind faith as a motive force for willing martyrdom. At bottom there had to be something real that motivated the Apostles and other early disciples. The usual explanations are unsatisfactory. They just do not cut it. Not as far as I'm concerned. But while the out-of-body experience may have been at the heart of proto-Christianity, appeal to astral projection as a technique whereby Christ survived the crucifixion still faces some serious challenges. This is because every possible form of the survival theory has some challenges. First is the sheer improbability that Jesus could have survived his brutal ordeal, even with an ability to consciously astral project at will.[1280] Secondly one would also have to stipulate that Jesus either interpreted *karath* in Daniel 9:26 as meaning "shall make a covenant" or, if Jesus interpreted *karath* in the contrary sense in that passage as meaning "shall be cut off", then he also interpreted astral projection as an actual death-and-resurrection experience.[1281] Thirdly one would also have to stipulate that the Apostles and other disciples would also have had to have accepted Jesus as risen from the dead, despite the absence of any miraculous healing of his wounds. This brings us to another huge objection against the survival theory: Christ's survival would have been far too obvious to the Apostles to be taken for a miraculous resurrection from the dead. Or if not, why not? This is something else that is never addressed by advocates of the survival theory: If Jesus merely survived his passion, either from a swoon, or from deliberate astral projection, would not the fact that Jesus had simply survived his passion been fairly obvious to the Apostles? Why would they think that he was literally risen from the dead? Were they absolute dunces? If Jesus still had wounds from a crown of thorns, from having been whipped, from being nailed to the cross, from being pierced in the side with a spear, why then would the Apostles have interpreted a living Jesus as risen from the dead? Could they not also have reasoned that, perhaps Jesus had merely survived his ordeal? After all, Josephus wrote of three men who had been taken down alive from crosses.[1282] One of the men even made

---

[1280] And it must be remembered and admitted that Christ's alleged ability to astral project is an additional assumption, however justified.

[1281] This is an additional assumption, however convenient.

[1282] See Jos. Vita. 75.

a full recovery. Granted this incident may have been later than the time when Jesus supposedly lived, but even still, there must have been occasional incidents when it was known that a man could survive crucifixion. Of course once again we know that in Christ's case he suffered far more physical and emotional trauma, since the Romans viciously brutalized messianic pretenders, to make examples of them. And yes I know that the Gospel of John reports that Jesus still had wounds from the nails and from the spear that pierced his side,[1283] but John is also the only evangelist who explicitly mentions any such wounds.[1284] Christians never seem to question why these wounds had not been miraculously healed, if Christ truly rose from the dead. Of course mystical reasons are given, such as the wounds of Christ being eternal reminders of the price he paid for our salvation, etc., etc. And I suppose I must admit that the Gospel of John seems to undercut the point I am seeking to make here; it seems to imply instead that Jesus did still have his wounds, and yet the Apostles still accepted Jesus as risen from the dead. And in fact, the Gospel of John is perhaps the Gospel most congenial to the survival theory; it is invariably quoted from by advocates of the theory. But then this implies the primacy of John, which is a dubious proposition at best.[1285]

Despite the appeals made to John's Gospel, I cannot help but reiterate that if Jesus had merely survived his passion, then this fact should have been fairly obvious to the Apostles, and it would have been a wild exaggeration, if not an outright lie, to claim this as a miraculous resurrection from the dead. An assumption of survival as the origin for belief in Christ's resurrection from the dead makes the Apostles either liars or dunces.[1286] In fact according to the united

---

[1283] John 20:19-27.

[1284] It is assumed that Luke does so, in 24:39-40, but that passage mentions no wounds, and instead seems to only have the point of proving Jesus was not a spirit.

[1285] See discussion on the order of the Gospels below.

[1286] Once again appeal may be made to esotericism as the explanation for how a story that is otherwise a lie may be the shell for an esoteric truth. While this is a reasonable principle, the claim made by the survival theorists is that the fact that Jesus appeared alive again after his passion to his Apostles is the very origin of belief in his resurrection. My argument still stands against this as an explanation, since the Apostles could have, should have, and would have known that Jesus had merely survived his passion, rather

testimony of the three Synoptic Gospels, none of the Apostles even witnessed Christ's crucifixion, and the female disciples and other acquaintances of Christ only beheld the scene from far away.[1287] Only John claims that any acquaintances of Jesus were close enough to him to speak to him while he hung on the cross.[1288] But John's Gospel is deviant from the Synoptics in a number of respects,[1289] not the least of which is the fact that John alone mentions any acquaintances standing close enough to Jesus as he hung on the cross to hear his words. Two other highly significant differences are the fact that, as already stated, John alone explicitly mentions any wounds on Jesus,[1290] and also the fact that John alone is silent about Simon of Cyrene, saying that Jesus bore his own cross.[1291] All three of these unique features of John's Gospel bear the stamp of being implicit arguments against a substitution having taken place.[1292] As such they have no evidential value whatever. So any appeal to the supposed wounds on Christ or

---

than being risen from the dead, unless we make the additional assumption that they were dunces beyond all comparison. Furthermore neither any of the Apostles, or any other disciples of Jesus, were close eyewitnesses to the crucifixion. Therefore they could not have even been sure that he was even crucified at all, much less that he was dead as a corpse.

[1287] Mt 27:55; Mk 15:40; Lk 23:49. The verse from Luke could be interpreted as including the eleven Apostles, but we are not told this explicitly. We are told that the eleven Apostles forsook Jesus and fled in the Garden of Gethsemane, when he was arrested; cf Mk 14:50.

[1288] John 19:25-27.

[1289] Hence the term "Synoptic" is one of relative agreement, as against the more deviant Gospel of John.

[1290] John 20:19-27.

[1291] John 19:17 cp Mt 27:32; Mk 15:21; Lk 23:26.

[1292] As the reader may recall one early rumor was that Simon of Cyrene had been crucified in place of Christ. John may have sought to quell such rumors by omitting any mention of Simon of Cyrene in his Gospel, making a point of saying that Jesus bore his own cross. To serve the same end, John may have also added the story of a conversation with Jesus as he hung from the cross, and also the detail about his crucifixion wounds. Since presumably these tales were all gratuitously invented to stifle a rumor that Simon of Cyrene, or possibly some other man, had been crucified in place of Jesus, they do not hold any real evidential value, particularly since they fly in the face of the united testimony of the other three Gospels.

to the supposed conversation between Christ and his mother and the beloved disciple is a hollow appeal, without any strong foundation.[1293]

But aside from all these other problems, the survival theory also has another serious problem. As we have already seen above, all four Gospels present unique and glaringly contradictory accounts of Christ's alleged post-passion appearances. According to Matthew and Mark, Christ first appeared alive again to the eleven Apostles in Galilee;[1294] according to Luke and John, it was in Jerusalem or Bethany.[1295] According to Matthew, Mark, and Luke, all eleven Apostles were together when Jesus appeared alive again to them;[1296] according to John, the Apostle Thomas was absent the first time.[1297] According to Mark and John, Jesus first appeared alive again to Mary Magdalene;[1298] according to Matthew, he appeared to two Marys simultaneously.[1299] According to Luke, Jesus first appeared to Simon.[1300] While such contradictions are clearly fatal to the resurrection theory, they are also a massively huge problem for the survival theory as well.[1301] Because if the theory is meant to give a "natural" explanation to the supposed post-crucifixion appearances of Jesus to the disciples, then the many contradictions are still something that is unexplained by the theory. Admittedly these contradictions are somewhat of a problem for all six theories, but one of the theories *must* be true; for a survival theory, or a substitution theory, or an impersonation theory, these particular contradictions are a very strong and serious objection against the theory. Because if we are to assume that Jesus somehow survived his passion, and then subsequently

---

[1293] In fact it was not really even a conversation, but rather words uttered by Jesus from the cross. Supposedly Jesus entrusted the care of his mother to the beloved disciple. But if this was a true account then why did all three Synoptic Evangelists omit it from their Gospels?

[1294] Matthew 28:16-17; Mark 16:7,14.

[1295] Luke 24:33-43; John 20:19-20.

[1296] Matthew 28:16-17; Mark 16:14; Luke 24:33-38.

[1297] John 20:19-24.

[1298] Mark 16:9; John 20:11-18.

[1299] Matthew 28:1-10.

[1300] Luke 24:34. Presumably Simon Peter is intended; I Corinthians 15:5.

[1301] And for that matter, for the substitution and impersonation theories as well.

showed himself alive again to his disciples, and this was the basis for belief in his resurrection from the dead, then the dilemma of where it happened and who was present is definitely a problem. People do not forget such vital details of a momentous experience.[1302] So we have a right to ask: Assuming that Jesus did survive the crucifixion, and then subsequently appeared alive again to the Apostles, Where did this happen? In Galilee? Or in Jerusalem? Was Thomas present, or absent? Were both Marys present when Jesus appeared to them, or only Mary Magdalene? Did Simon Peter see Jesus before the other Apostles? These are all legitimate questions for proponents of the survival theory. I am not saying that a person could not give possible reasons for preferring one or another Gospel account, in terms of the details surrounding these alleged appearances. But such things are generally left unstated, and the various problems and challenges to the theory are not addressed in any realistic way. So with all these very strong objections against it, the survival theory is not nearly as viable as we once thought. As far as I am concerned it is a theory on life support. It is a matter of grave doubt as to whether the survival theory will even survive.

But I will admit that, the various contradictions between the different accounts of the post-passion appearances of Jesus are not nearly as problematic for the survival theory, the substitution theory, or even the impersonation theory, as they necessarily would be for a miraculous resurrection theory. But even with this qualification, there is still another huge problem for the survival theory: the manner of Roman crucifixion. In Roman-style crucifixion, the man is either tied to the cross, or nailed to it; then he is hoisted up, where he will remain until he dies. Sometimes it would take several days for a man to finally die. But one of the excuciating agonies of Roman-syle crucifixion was that a man would have to periodically lift himself up, pushing himself up, using his arms and feet to raise himself up to breathe. Very often, as such men grew weaker over time, they finally fell unconscious, and thereby became asphyxiated. Therefore, if Jesus became unconscious while he hung upon the cross, he would have

---

[1302] Of course people may forget inconsequential details, but such details as where an important event took place, and who was present, could hardly be considered inconsequential. On the other hand, if these stories were completely made up, then the contradictions may be more readily accounted for.

died. This is a fatal flaw to the survival theory. Even the Essenes, or any supposed "secret" disciples, would likely have known that any man who became unconscious while hanging from a cross or tree would almost certainly die. Therefore if they had secretly given him some kind of soporific, then this would merely have been a mercy-killing, rather than an attempt to rescue him. This problem is not generally addressed by advocates of any version of the survival theory. There are, however, two potential avenues of escape from this knotty little problem. One is that, possibly through the use of astral projection, Jesus *might* have been able to circumvent any such asphyxiation. The other solution is possibly related: in India, certain yogis can slow down their breathing and heartbeats to an incredible degree. Advanced practitioners of Hatha Yoga can perform such amazing feats. Possibly Jesus was such an adept. This would imply that he may have travelled to the East during his so-called "Missing Years". While this is *possible,* it still seems like quite a stretch. Admittedly not nearly as much as biblical fundamentalism, but still it requires quite a few questionable assumptions. Furthermore, we will stipulate that, albeit Jesus may have survived his passion, but it was fairly evident to his Apostles and other disciples that it was a case of survival, rather than a supernatural resurrection from the dead. Therefore the latter story may have been an exoteric shell of the esoteric truth. But even if we do so stipulate, then we would have expected that even the exoteric shell would have greater consistency than it does in the New Testament.

One other possible argument in favor of the survival theory I feel that I must share, for the sake of intellectual honesty and integrity. If we assume, as most of these theories do, that Jesus was actually crucified, then, according to Jewish law, he became ritually dead, simply be virtue of crucifixion.[1303] Even while Jesus was still alive on the cross [or tree], he was already ritually dead and cursed by the Jewish God. This would have been known to the chief priests, scribes, Pharisees, Sadducees, doctors of the law, and all the devout religious Jews. Let us recall that Jesus had some wealthy disciples.[1304] Also recall what was mentioned above of the possibility that Jesus may have been politically allied with Sejanus, as were also Herod Antipas and Pontius

---

[1303] Deuteronomy 21:23.

[1304] e.g., Luke 8:1-3.

Pilate. It is not beyond the realm of possibility that Pilate may have been bribed by some wealthy disciple with a "king's ransom" in gold, silver and jewels, to release Jesus before he died on the cross. This offer may have been made either by Joseph of Arimathaea (assuming he really was a disciple of Jesus, secret or otherwise), or by Nicodemus, or by Zacchaeus, or by Joanna the wife of Chuza, or by Mary the Magdalene, or by some other known or unknown disciple or group of disciples. Pilate may have granted this; Jesus may have been taken down from the cross alive, even though he was already ritually dead, according to the tenets of Judaism. The Pharisees could thereafter claim that Jesus was a false prophet who had been cursed by God. It would have been a huge punishment for Jesus, even if he had survived his ordeal. If this scenario, or something like it, was true, then very likely is would have been the end of any kind of prophetic or messianic career for Jesus, at least in Palestine. While this scenario is possible, in terms of relative probability it must also be compared with all of the other theories. But we could suppose that the story of Christ's purported resurrection was ultimately a parable, to function as an outer "shell" for the esoteric truth. In Hebrews it says that Abraham received his son Isaac "as if" he had been raised from the dead, in a parable.[1305] In the Greek New Testament, the very word *parabolae* is used in that verse.[1306] While this is all interresting food for thought, we still need to compare the various theories, in terms of relative probability and improbability.

[1305] Hebrews 11:19.

[1306] Nesle-Aland., op. cit., pg. 580.

Objections Against The Substitution Theory

The substitution theory, as it is usually presented, or rather the versions that so far have typically been proposed, is a rather weak theory, despite its seemingly wide appeal. However I have proposed to myself, not merely to examine those forms of any given theory that have already been proffered, but even any possible hypothetical variation of a given theory. I am seeking the truth; not merely trying to win some schoolboy argument. As such I have proposed what I consider to be a much stronger form of the substitution theory above, so that the reader can at least take it into consideration as food for thought. Perhaps some might even prefer it to the solution I offer to the paradox of Jesus Christ herein. But once the potential weaknesses of the theory are exposed, it no longer seems quite so attractive.

It should perhaps first be pointed out that the various contradictions between the different post-passion appearances in the four Gospels is as much of a problem for the substitution theory as it is for the survival theory.[1307] This is not necessarily an unanswerable objection however; a proponent of the theory may bring forward reasons in favor of one Gospel account over the others. But whereas a

---

[1307] It is also a problem for the impersonation theory, and for the phantom theory, but most especially for the resurrection theory.

survival theory would probably seek to give the greatest prominence and even primacy to the Gospel of John, a substitution theory would by contrast probably favor the text of Matthew. Matthew's Gospel says that the eleven Apostles first saw Jesus in a cave inside a mountain in Galilee. This would be in accord with a need for secrecy, which is realistic, since Jesus would not have wanted to be arrested again. If we give credence to the cave story, then perhaps this had been a secret meeting place used by Jesus and the Apostles before the crucifixion. A cave is of course another link with Mithraism.

But there are some serious problems with the substitution theory, aside from just Gospel contradictions.[1308] First is the objection that quite possibly there was no such custom as the release of a prisoner on the eve of Passover. While I argued strongly that there probably was such a custom above, I may have been wrong; besides, I was merely responding to a perceived bias in critical biblical scholarship. Furthermore I felt it was necessary to at least strongly advocate for the proposed theory while it was being introduced, lest it die an abortive death. But one must reckon with the fact that this would remain, not only a bone of contention by opponents to the theory, but a very real and legitimate objection against the theory, since in fact those who claim that there was no such custom might be right, despite the apparent weakness of their arguments.[1309] It is a weakness of a theory if it contains a dubious postulate as a necessary variable. While the theory may be of some interest and merit, and may fascinate some due to its relative novelty, I feel that a serious advocate of the theory would be perpetually haunted by the fear that maybe there really was no such custom after all. Of course it is impossible to prove a negative, so a person who only cares about appearing wise might be content in the knowledge that a mere argument from silence is insufficient to overturn the supposition that the united testimony of all four Canonical Gospels must be correct in respect to such a custom.[1310] While he or she may hope that perhaps by some miracle

---

[1308] i.e., specifically Gospel contradictions regarding the post-passion appearances of Christ.

[1309] And the comparative strength of the counterarguments.

[1310] One point that I neglected to mention above is that the appeal to the argument from silence can in this instance be turned on its' head; i.e., the Mishnah may be silent about any such custom by the Romans during Passover, but it is also equally silent about making this an argument against

some ancient text might turn up vindicating this aspect of what we read in the Gospels, there is no possibility of the opposite happening; no textual discovery could "prove" that there never was any such custom of releasing a prisoner on the Passover. Perhaps Josephus had no occasion to mention the custom, or it would have been too much of an embarrassment to him. As far as the Mishnah goes, there would have been no reason for the *Tannaim* to concede any compassion on the part of the Romans; and this sentiment would especially have been evident after the tragic consequences of the Bar Kochbah rebellion. But a person of good conscience could not help but to at least feel some degree of uneasiness, knowing that quite possibly this story might have been another lie common to all four Gospels. So this is an objection against the Barabbas form of the substitution theory. I feel that I have already adequately dealt with the other forms of the substitution theory above.

Another potential objection against the substitution theory is that if Barabbas had never been released, this would have been noticed sooner or later. He must have had either a family, or at least comrades in arms, who would have wondered where he was, if he supposedly had been released, but never was. In other words, if there had been some such substitution initially, it would probably not have remained secret for very long. This is a fatal flaw in the theory. The fact that Barabbas had never been released would have been a sort of "loose end" which turns into a fatal flaw for the theory.[1311] Pilate would have had enough foresight to see that this could turn into a fatal problem to his scheme, had he ever thought of making such a secret substitution. Another "loose end" would have been Jesus Christ himself. Could Pilate have trusted Jesus to keep the secret, and to never be discovered again? Pilate would have discerned that, at the very least, Christ was a religious fanatic. A mystic perhaps, and maybe even a man with some lofty and noble sentiments; but ultimately an untrustworthy religious fanatic with a loyal following. It is doubtful that Pontius Pilate

the accuracy of the Gospels. In other words, nowhere in the Mishnah is this point brought up, in order to refute the Gospels. So Christians and advocates of the Barabbas version of the substitution theory could in turn make their own appeal to an argument from silence.

[1311] Naturally this fatal flaw is predicated upon the assumption of the custom of releasing a prisoner at the Passover, but so is the entire Barabbas version of the substitution theory.

would have considered Jesus merely a harmless mystic, regardless of whatever Jesus had said to him in person. Pilate was probably shrewd enough to know that a man will say anything to save his own life.[1312] Furthermore even if there had been a custom of the Romans releasing a prisoner on Passover or the eve of Passover, in the case of such a notorious prisoner as Barabbas it is unlikely that such a dangerous criminal would have been released under any circumstances. So even if the people had been crying out for the release of Barabbas, as the Gospels affirm, most likely Pilate would have released a less dangerous criminal.[1313] Then again the Gospels all say that Barabbas had been released.[1314] So if we credit the story of Barabbas at all, then it behooves us to believe that Barabbas had been released, while Christ was sentenced to death. At the very least an advocate of this version of the substitution theory would have to address these potential challenges to the theory, if they wanted to be taken seriously.

I feel that it is at least worth briefly pointing out that the story of Barabbas may have been invented, not as a species of gratuitous anti-Semitism, but rather as a historical parable based upon the two goats of Leviticus 16. that chapter of Leviticus deals with the great Day of Atonement, and how two goats are used to ritually purify the people of their sins. One goat is offered up to Yaho [Yahweh], while the other goat is the scapegoat. It says that the high priest will lay his hands uopn the head of the scapegoat, which will bear the sins of the people out to the wilderness.[1315]

Another problem is the question of whether Jesus would have kept the substitution a secret from his Apostles, assuming that he even could. In other words, even if we imagine a scenario in which Jesus had initially escaped crucifixion by virtue of such a fortuitous convergence of circumstances, it is highly questionable as to whether the scheme could have remained a secret indefinitely. If Christ allowed his Apostles to believe that he rose from the dead, after having been crucified, even though he never had been crucified, then we would have to inquire into his moral character and potential motivations for such a fraudulent imposition. Would it not have been a tremendous

---

[1312] And especially to escape the barbaric death by Roman crucifixion.

[1313] i.e., assuming that the custom had been practiced at all.

[1314] Mt 27:26; Mk 15:15; Lk 23:25; Jn 18:39–40.

[1315] Leviticus 16:1–10.

risk on the part of Jesus to gamble that the Apostles would never discover the truth? On the other hand, if Jesus told them what really happened, then once again we cannot use the bare appearance of Christ to his Apostles as the basis for belief in his resurrection from the dead. In that case, we would have to suppose that Christ admonished his Apostles to keep the truth secret, and that the tale of Christ's crucifixion and resurrection from the dead was more of a historical parable, as a moral tale of the victory of good over evil. But then this supposition undercuts the whole reason for supposing that there had even been any secret substitution in the first place. In that case, the substitution theory becomes so much unnecessary baggage. So the substitution theory has too many loose ends, and should be substituted by a better theory.

Objections Against The Impersonation Theory

The impersonation theory is definitely one of the weakest theories, and is really only even included for the sake of completeness. In fact, the impersonation theory is really the weakest of all the theories.[1316] It will not take long to refute it. Once again it should be pointed out that the contradictions between the various accounts of Christ's post-passion appearances to the Apostles is as much of a problem for the impersonation theory as it is for the survival and substitution theories. In other words, even a "naturalistic" interpretation of Christ's alleged post-passion appearances to his Apostles is confronted with a plethora of discrepancies between the Gospel accounts. They cannot all be literally true, even interpreted "naturalistically."

But aside from this gratuitous objection, the impersonation theory is virtually self-refuting in its sheer absurdity. What I find appalling is the spectacle of self-proclaimed critics of the Bible countenancing this theory as if it were in the least bit credible. It is intellectual

---

[1316] Although technically it remains true that the resurrection theory is the theory with the largest actual number of potential objections against it, due to the overwhelming number, variety, and magnitude to the problems with the Bible.

dishonesty to give a "free pass" to a theory simply because it is a critical theory. And just as the Bible cannot be the Word of God by reason of contradictions, so likewise all critical theories cannot be true by reason of mutual contradiction. Only one theory can be true. The others are all false.

The sheer improbability of the impersonation theory serves as a sufficient refutation thereof. We are expected to believe that the Apostles, who spent at least a year in intimate familiarity with Jesus, would have been fooled by some impostor. The man in question would have to have not only looked just like Jesus, but also to have had the same voice, the same mannerisms, the same body language, the same personality, the same charm, the same quality of teachings. We ought not to think so little of the Apostles as to suppose that they would have been fooled by some impostor either from afar, or from someone superficially putting on an act. After all, the man would not merely have been seeking to impersonate Jesus, but to also be Jesus resurrected from the dead. This latter claim makes the whole scenario even more unbelievable. The Apostles would have been suspicious of any such strange character who claimed to be their beloved Lord and Master risen from the dead. The claim is ridiculous. Whoever supposes that the Apostles were such dunces is himself the dunce of all dunces. The impersonation theory is no more credible than that Paul McCartney is an impostor of the original Paul McCartney. In fact, it is less so. It's time to return to planet earth. Furthermore, any similar theory that belief in Christ's resurrection could have been based upon mere hallucinations is equally laughable and contemptible; it is an insult to the intelligence.

Objections Against The Termination Theory

F inally we come back to the termination theory. For a long time I considered this theory to be so weak as to be untenable. Superficially it does seem very weak, since it provides for no tangible basis for the resurrection accounts narrated in the Gospels. But as we have seen, those accounts are wildly contradictory to one another. Aside from this perceived deficit, this theory lacks the objections found in any or all the other theories. It is a matter of comparison. Of course the termination theory in and of itself does not explain the actual origin of belief in Christ's resurrection from the dead. That will require some further explanation. But the termination theory is not burdened with the pitfalls of the other theories, enumerated above. For example, if one were to postulate an impersonation theory, one would have to suppose that the Apostles were so easily imposed upon as to be fooled by a complete impostor. One would also have to speculate upon the possible motives of such an impostor. If one were to suppose that belief in the resurrection was based upon Christ's survival of his passion, then one would have to suppose that the Apostles were sufficiently gullible to mistake Christ's survival for a miracle. If one were to postulate a substitution theory, one would have to assume that somehow the substitution remained a secret against all odds. If one were to accept the resurrection theory, then one would be compelled

473

to also accept the Bible as the Word of God, with all the baggage that *that* entails. If one were to resort to a phantom theory, then one is confronted with the psychological inexplicability of the motives of the persons who wrote the New Testament documents. Comparatively speaking, the termination theory is relatively economical.[1317] It requires further elaboration to be sure, but it is not burdened with the shortcomings of the other theories. So the termination theory seems to have only one real objection against it, which is that it provides no immediate explanation, in and of itself, for the origin of belief in Christ's resurrection. But this can be remedied by further inquiry.

As noted previously, the various contradictions found between the different Gospel accounts of Christ's post-crucifixion appearances are somewhat of a problem for all six theories, yet we know that one of these six theories *must* be true, because there simply are no other theories. What was briefly touched upon above was the fact that, while there are a plenitude of contradictions between the four Gospels, these contradictions seem to multiply in intensity and frequency when we read of the post-passion appearances of Jesus. The contradictions rule out fundamentalism,[1318] and are also a serious problem for the phantom theory as well.[1319] All Bible contradictions rule out fundamentalism, all New Testament contradictions subvert the phantom theory, but only the contradictions between the "resurrection" accounts are a real problem for the survival, substitution, and impersonation theories. I suppose one could argue that they are also a problem for the termination theory as well.[1320] But this would prove nothing, since we know that one of the six

---

[1317] I.e., in terms of economy of thought, or the principle of parsimony.

[1318] And the attendant resurrection theory.

[1319] Since a conspiracy of men inventing a character would not write contradictory accounts if they sought to impose their creation upon the gullible as history.

[1320] Since it could be argued that even if the termination theory were true, there should only have been one version of Jesus' post-passion appearances to the Apostles, to make the story believable. In other words, a person could use essentially the same argument as is used in the case of the phantom theory; i.e., if the resurrection story was completely made up, then why didn't the Evangelists at least follow the same script in recounting it? This is a valid objection, but once again we are confronted with the paradox that one of the six theories must be true, since there is no seventh theory.

theories must be true. In fact, this provides us with a key to prove that the termination theory is in fact the true theory. The essential point to remember in relation to this is the fact that, while there are contradictions scattered all through the four Gospels, these contradictions cluster and multiply in density and intensity precisely after the passion narrative.[1321] This very fact is also further evidence against a phantom theory.[1322] It also functions as circumstantial evidence against the survival, substitution, and impersonation theories.[1323] But the termination theory does not suffer from this one fatal weakness.[1324] It also lacks the specific weaknesses of each of the other five respective theories, or whatever weaknesses they may otherwise have in common. When the full evidence is presented, then the true theory should be clearly evident. I ask the reader's indulgence and patience until I complete my task.

[1321] We should also remember that the passion narrative of John's Gospel is deviant from that of the three Synoptic Gospels, but this is best explained by John's attempt to refute rumors of a substitution. John's Gospel seems far less historically reliable.

[1322] Since if Jesus were merely a completely invented figure, we would not expect the literary narrative to display this feature; even if one concedes that contradictions are inevitable, there should not be such a stark increase in them precisely at the climax of the story.

[1323] Since once again, if Jesus appeared alive again, or some double impersonated him, then we have a right to expect a greater agreement between the four accounts than what we have, if these appearances, either by Jesus, or by an impostor, actually took place.

[1324] And in fact this particular circumstance is more congenial to the termination theory than to any other theory; a historical Jesus who really died on the cross, and really was buried, who was not impersonated by some impostor, but who was said to be risen from the dead. The fact that the latter portion of the story was a fabrication is evinced by the greater number and intensity of contradictions. This theory does justice to the fossil passages, and takes account of the larger number of contradictions per chapter between the post-passion appearances of Jesus.

One Solution Necessary

●

Having now presented the six theories in detail, as well as the objections against them, we are in a better position to reevaluate them in relative terms. Only one theory can be the truth. Just as the Bible fails to display the characteristics of a divine revelation by virtue of multitudinous contradictions, so also likewise all critical theories cannot be true, by virtue of mutual contradiction. For self-proclaimed critical scholars to give a "free pass" to a theory simply because it is a critical theory is neither genuine scholarship nor legitimate criticism. This is particularly the case when the theory is patently absurd.[1325] Some obscurantists who pose as biblical scholars may be content to wallow in the mire of obscurantism and perpetual nebulosity with respect to the historical Jesus, and perhaps even base their careers on such obscurantism. But a genuine scholar will instead seek to resolve historical paradoxes. The paradox we are seeking to resolve herein is the single greatest historical paradox of Western history: namely, How did belief in the resurrection of Jesus Christ originate? As we have seen, this question resolves itself into merely six possible answers, or theories; therefore one of the six theories must be true, and must be the right answer to the question asked. So far we have seen that while there are potential and legitimate objections to each of the six theories,

---

[1325] Such as the impersonation theory.

the termination theory has the least number of objections against it.[1326] Furthermore the single objection against the termination theory can be explained, once all the relevant evidence has been presented. So we can see that the termination theory is comparatively the strongest of the six possible theories, and we have a right to presume that it is the correct theory, merely by default. But I am glad to add that it is not merely by default that the termination theory will be vindicated, but rather by the full weight of the complete evidence, presented in context. In fact I have not yet argued very strongly in favor of this theory but merely presented it as one of six possible theories. But when the remainder of the evidence is presented, together with a diligent comparison with the other five theories, then the termination theory will be seen as the most highly probable theory, and therefore the true theory. Furthermore I am fully confident that what I present will hold up to scrutiny, and stand the test of time. At the very least, anyone contesting my position will have to address the various objections noted above, and answer them in a convincing manner. All of the evidence presented herein will have to be addressed. The question has to do with which of the six theories best accounts for all of the relevant evidence. I have no doubt that the termination theory is the best theory, the strongest theory, and the correct theory. But each reader will have to be their own judge and jury.

[1326] In fact it only has one objection against it; see immediately above.

Evidence Re-Examined

We now need to once again reconsider all the available evidence as well as additional evidence to be sure of the truth. One topic that I would like to return to is that of astral projection, or the out-of-body experience. I presented some evidence above that quite possibly a knowledge of the out-of-body experience may have been the key secret teaching of Jesus Christ, which was the one secret that the Apostles and other early disciples[1327] had to protect at all costs. This theory at least provides a genuine basis for a valid form of esotericism, which in turn provides an explanation for motivations vis-à-vis secrecy in respect to certain otherwise unaccountable circumstances surrounding the paradox of Jesus Christ. This is where fundamentalists have lost the key to explaining so much about the origin of the Christian faith.[1328]

[1327] i.e., those who had experienced this as part of their spiritual training.

[1328] It is possible that some other paranormal phenomenon, such as telepathy, clairvoyance, clairaudience, hypnosis, precognition, or transpersonal phenomena were at the heart of proto-Christian esotericism. My point is that most likely there was something real at the bottom of it all, rather than sheer blind faith. This may not appeal to cynics, atheists, or agnostics, but to me it seems more realistic than supposing such zealous faith was based on pure superstition and nothing else. Even if we assume that the use of hallucinogens was involved in the experience of non-ordinary states of consciousness among these early believers, we still ought to credit them

While it is possible that some other paranormal phenomenon or combination of phenomena may have been the great secret of the messianic movement, we have at least seen that there is some evidence that astral projection was the actual key phenomenon. I said that I would share additional verses that supported this interpretation. While there are really only a few more, they are worth taking a look at.[1329] Some of these verses will be surprising, because of precisely where they are found in the New Testament. Four of these passages occur in the Apokalypse;[1330] three occur in the Pauline corpus;[1331] and one occurs in the book of Acts.[1332] I suppose that in a very real sense it ought not to be any more shocking or surprising than finding such a passage in the Gospel of John.[1333] On the other hand, John the Evangelist may not have known the true secret of ritual astral projection, and for this reason he presented the story of Lazarus as a miraculous resurrection in his Gospel.[1334] The John who wrote the *Apokalypse* was probably not the same person as John the Evangelist, and both men were also probably distinct from John the Apostle.[1335]

---

with a sufficient modicum of intelligence, whereby they would insist upon objective verification of any numinous phenomena experienced. Otherwise we ourselves would be guilty of a cynicism that itself requires blind faith in such arrogant dogmatic myopia.

[1329] The reader would be advised to remember John 11 & Mark 14:46-52 as the passages we examined above in relation to astral projection; as well as my comments upon them.

[1330] Revelation 1:10; 4:1-2; 17:3; 21:10.

[1331] Colossians 2:5; I Corinthians 5:3; II Corinthians 12:2-4.

[1332] Acts 12:15.

[1333] i.e., the Gospel of John being sectarian in character, it seems to be a departure from the original wisdom tradition of the Synoptic Gospels.

[1334] By contrast, the Synoptic Evangelists may have been admonished to keep the story of Lazarus a secret. Alternatively, John's source or sources may have told him the story as one of a miraculous resurrection. On the other hand, it is possible that John's account is merely a historical parable, based upon the precedent of Luke 16:19-31. However even assuming that this had been the case, it is still possible that Jesus and his inner circle may have conducted secret rituals involving the out-of-body experience. The passage from Mark's Gospel is actually somewhat suggestive of this, and is even more highly evidential, in my opinion, than that of John's Gospel.

[1335] Even according to early Christian tradition, the Apokalypse and the Gospel

Assuming that Christ's Apostles were approximately the same age as himself, John would have probably been a centenarian by the latter half of the first century. Of course while it is just barely possible that John may have been a particularly young disciple,[1336] it is still a bit of a stretch to suppose he was still alive in the flesh at such a late time. Furthermore John's Gospel is so contradictory to the other three Canonicals that it only arouses suspicion in respect to authorship, date, and provenance.[1337] The further suspicion is that John's Gospel represents a departure from the original messianic tradition, especially in terms of salvation.[1338] As such, it is challenging to suppose that John the Evangelist would have had any knowledge of esoteric rituals or any important secrets, however veiled. By contrast John the author of Revelation is squarely within the Synoptic tradition, and while it is doubtful that the Apostle John himself wrote the Apokalypse, the text may at least be based upon a legitimate chain of apostolic succession, in terms of tradition. Therefore it is not quite so incongruous to suppose some knowledge of the occult rituals engaged in by the early disciples

---

of John were not written until the last decade of the first century. If John the Apostle was still alive at the time, he would have been extremely elderly. For this reason Christian tradition and Christian artwork have traditionally depicted John the Apostle as much younger than the other Apostles. But there is no real basis for such an assumption in Scripture; the sole passage supporting a very youthful John being John 20:4-8, where John outran Peter to the tomb of Christ. Notice also that in Luke's Gospel, Peter runs to the tomb, but it says nothing about John outrunning him to the tomb; cf Luke 24:12. This is either a suspicious omission, or another contradiction. But a relevant question is: How did either of them know where Jesus had been buried? The answer to this question will become important later.

[1336] In fact some have identified him with the young man of Mark 14:51-52. While this interpretation seems to be precluded by Mark 14:50, still the very fact that Jesus did have some young male disciples, whom he apparently initiated into the out-of-body experience, suggests that possibly John may have been a young man. On the other hand, the position of being an Apostle would seem to entail additional responsibilities, that ordinary disciples would be unqualified to fulfill.

[1337] In other words, it was probably written later than the time claimed by Christian tradition. This would preclude any possibility that the Apostle John wrote it. The same argument applies, albeit to a lesser degree, to the book of Revelation.

[1338] Since the three Synoptic Gospels, especially the Gospel of Matthew, uphold obedience to the commandments of the Torah as essential for salvation.

of Jesus. The passages from Revelation suggestive of the out-of-body experience are as follows:

10   I was in spirit on the Lord's day, and heard behind me a great voice, as of a trumpet. (Revelation 1:10)

After this I looked, and, behold, a door was opened in heaven; and the first voice which I heard, as of a trumpet speaking to me, saying, Come up here, and I will show you those things that must be hereafter.

2   And immediately I was in spirit; and behold, a throne was set in heaven, and One sat on the throne. (Revelation 4:1-2)

3   So he carried me away in spirit into a desert; and I saw a woman sit upon a scarlet-colored beast, full of names of blasphemy, having seven heads and ten horns. (Revelation 17:3)

10   And he carried me away in spirit to a great and high mountain, and showed me that great city, the holy Jerusalem, descending out of heaven from God... (Revelation 21:10a)

I want to quickly point out that while most English Bible translations have the article "the" before the word "spirit" in the translation, and also the word "spirit" is usually capitalized, the original Greek of all four passages lacks that article before the Greek word for spirit, *pneuma*.[1339] Therefore my translation is more correct and accurate. There is also no compelling need to gratuitously capitalize the initial "s" in "spirit", since many early Greek manuscripts were written either entirely in uncials or miniscules.[1340] These are yet more examples of where trinitarians read the "Holy Spirit" into the text by an unwarranted process of *eisegesis*. But when correctly translated, these verses seem to imply some acquaintance with the out-of-body experience. We must remember that, even assuming that these people did experience this phenomenon, they would have filtered their experience through their own cultural and religious beliefs. We should also bear in mind that certain aspects of the experience would

---

[1339]   Nestle-Aland., op. cit., pgs. 633, 639-640, 665, 677.

[1340]   i.e., capitals or small letters, respectively.

have remained a closely-guarded secret. In fact, most likely it was not the experience itself that was so much of a secret, as the means to induce the experience, and to bring back a genuine memory of the experience.

There are also a few verses in the Pauline corpus that seem to be speaking of the out-of-body experience.

5   For though I be absent in the flesh, yet am I with you in the spirit, rejoicing and beholding your order, and the steadfastness of your faith in the Messiah. (Colossians 2:5)

3   For I truly, as absent in body but present in the spirit, have already judged him that has so done this deed. (I Corinthians 5:3)

Both of the two verses above imply some sort of out-of-body experience, however much doctrinaire fundamentalist Christians may seek to deny it. But what strikes me as unusual or even potentially problematic is the fact that these verses occur within the Pauline corpus. Therefore it is a legitimate question to ask where either Paul himself[1341] or those men who allegedly wrote those epistles[1342] acquired a knowledge of the out-of-body experience, or were bold enough to make such claims. Neither Paul himself nor those persons named as the authors of his epistles in the respective colophons would have been in any way associated with the original, proto-Christian messianic movement, presumably. They were outsiders. And, considering the extreme dichotomy between the Pauline and Johannine corpii, on the one hand, and the Synoptic corpii, on the other, it seems very unlikely that the Apostles would have willingly initiated either Paul or any of his disciples into their own esoteric mysteries. Therefore this is somewhat of a mystery and a paradox. However, it is just barely possible that this may be yet another key to explaining how and why the Pauline corpus[1343] was ultimately accepted as canonical scripture. If

---

[1341]   i.e., assuming Pauline authorship of the corpus. But see arguments above, and in my former work.

[1342]   Tychicus and Onesimus in the case of Colossians; Stephanas, Fortunatus, Achaicus, and Timotheus, in the case of first Corinthians, according to the respective colophons of those epistles.

[1343]   And the Johannine corpus. The Johannine corpus as defined herein excludes the Apokalypse; it instead refers to the Gospel and Epistles of John. The

either Paul himself, or his protégés were somehow able to convince the custodians of the original messianic tradition that they also held some genuine esoteric knowledge, such as the mystery of the out-of-body experience, or some other secret knowledge, that would verify that he or they had direct experience of the numinous, and also that they had a legitimate claim to somehow being in spiritual contact with Jesus,[1344] then this may possibly account for the admission of such otherwise extraneous matter into the New Testament. Admittedly this is highly speculative, but something along these lines seems to be implied by the otherwise unaccountable circumstance. As far as how either Paul[1345] or any of those other men acquired a knowledge of astral projection, it is worth at least pointing out that within some ancient Greek literature there are occasional references to phenomena that today would be called either lucid dreaming or astral projection.[1346] So it should not be surprising if various mystery schools conducted secret rituals involving the out-of-body experience. Viewed in this context, our theory vis-à-vis astral projection does not seem so far-fetched. Neither Jesus nor the Apostles would have had a monopoly on such arcana.[1347] There is also a third passage within the Pauline corpus that at least hints of an out-of-body experience:

2   I knew a man in Christ over fourteen years ago, (whether in the body, I cannot tell; or whether out of the body, I cannot tell: God knows;) such a one *was* caught up to the third heaven.

Apokalypse is squarely within the Synoptic tradition; cf Revelation 21:14, "And the wall of the city had twelve foundations, and in them the names of the twelve Apostles of the Lamb." This is a direct rebuke to the presumed apostleship of Paul and his disciples.

[1344] This would also be required, since a mere acquaintance with the supernatural would not have qualified Paul or anyone else as a true messenger of God; cf Mt 24:24; Mk 13:22.

[1345] i.e., assuming that he existed, and also that he wrote or dictated those epistles attributed to him, minus the Pastorals, which were probably written by Polycarp.

[1346] Or astral traveling. Lucid dreaming is a related but distinct phenomenon. There are a plethora of books written on these themes.

[1347] In this connection, however, it is interesting to speculate that possibly Jesus himself may have received knowledge of the out-of-body experience from John the Baptist, who in turn learned of it from the Essenes.

3   And I knew such a man, (whether in the body, or out of the body, I cannot tell: God knows;)

4   how that he was caught up into paradise, and heard unspeakable words, which it is not lawful for a man to utter. (II Corinthians 12:2-4)

This passage is actually even more explicit than either of the others; being "out of the body" is explicitly spoken of, at least as a hypothetical possibility. Of course most contemporary Christians would want to avoid and downplay any association with the contemporary phenomenon of astral projection, but the link seems unavoidable. In this case, however, we may have a description of a near-death experience; the author speaks of the man being "caught up into paradise", which implies that whoever had the experience thought that he had died.[1348] Many Christians suspect that Paul was writing of his own near-death experience, narrated in Acts 14:19-20. Paul was stoned by some Jews in Lystra, and he was thought to be dead. But according to the narrative, he "rose up" and returned to the city. Christians generally interpret this as a resurrection from the dead, but today we would probably classify it as a near-death experience. Of course this once again raises the question of Pauline authorship of the Pauline epistles. This is unresolved, since we do not even know for certain whether the apostle Paul even ever existed; and if he did exist, whether or not he wrote those epistles ascribed to him in the New Testament.[1349] The colophons of most of the Pauline epistles bluntly state that those texts were written by other men.[1350] Second Corinthians was written by Luke[1351] and Titus, according to the colophon. Luke is called a beloved physician and is an associate of Paul.[1352] He is also the presumed author of the Gospel bearing

---

[1348]   And at the very least, the passage proves that the idea of being "out of body" was one that the writer(s) of the epistle had been acquainted with; it was not something inconceivable. This further implies that they either had direct experience of the phenomenon, or knew those who had.

[1349]   Or any core of them.

[1350]   And in the case of Romans, by a woman, Phoebe.

[1351]   Lukas.

[1352]   Colossians 4:14.

his name, as well as the book of Acts. Titus was a close associate and disciple of Paul.[1353] So if we are to credit the colophons as being accurate in terms of authorship, then it coud be argued that this also circumstantially substantiates the historicity of Paul. While this may be a sound line of argument, things are not necessarily that simple. For example, a more critical person may discountenance the colophons as spurious; the argument being that they were no more than an item to further an elaborate historical charade. A modification of this view would be that while the names are accurate, the alleged roles played by such persons within either the narrative of Acts or what might be written in various epistles is at least suspect on critical-historical grounds. Aside from these arguments, as I pointed out in my former work, we have a historical paradox in the fact that Paul apparently never so much as met or saw Jesus himself, even though he had been supposedly taught by Gamaliel in Jerusalem.[1354] This is at least a potential problem for the presumed historicity of Paul.[1355] But this is not nearly so much of a problem if we concede that Jesus was not a famous miracle-worker, as depicted in the Gospels. If instead Jesus had been seen by most of his contemporaries as yet another messianic pretender, then Saul's presumed ignorance of Jesus is not particularly notable. But to return to our point about astral projection, either Paul himself narrated his own near-death experience, or the men who wrote the epistle at least had some knowledge, either directly or by hearsay, of the out-of-body experience. If we assume the former, it is interesting that, most likely, this near-death experience occurred before the writing of any epistles. The implication being that possibly a person who has experienced a near-death experience may be more prone to the out-of-body experience subsequently. The near-death experience may have functioned as a sort of "trigger" to open up a latent ability to consciously, willfully initiate an out-of-body experience. Perhaps the Teacher of Righteousness had a near-death experience, and was subsequently able to willfully and consciously

---

[1353] Galatians 2:1-3; II Corinthians 2:13; 7:6,13-14; 8:6,16,23; 12:18.

[1354] Acts 22:3.

[1355] We have already dispensed with arguments against the historicity of Jesus above. Furthermore Galatians 1:19 and I Corinthians 9:5 create a presumed logical contingency, such that, if Paul existed historically, then Jesus also *necessarily* did; this logical contingency does not function in the opposite direction, however.

initiate the out-of-body experience; later he instructed his own trusted disciples in the technique. Possibly John the Baptist acquired this knowledge through the Essenes, and in turn taught Jesus, who taught his chosen Apostles. Of course this is only speculation, but it seems reasonable to me.

Finally, there is yet another verse that seems to uphold the concept of astral projection in the New Testament. The context of the verse is that the Apostle Peter had been arrested and was probably going to be executed by Herod.[1356] Peter manages to escape, purportedly with the help of an angel; he goes to the house of Mary the mother of John, and knocks on the door; Rhoda reports that Peter is at the door, but is not believed by the other disciples. While she is insistent about it, they finally say "It is his angel."[1357] But the meaning of this expression is nowhere explained in the text. To suppose that it was Peter's guardian angel is not a very satisfying interpretation, since, Why would Peter's guardian angel be wandering around knocking on doors, rather than watching over Peter in prison? Furthermore, why would Peter's guardian angel have Peter's voice? So a quaint old-maid Christian interpretation of it being Peter's guardian angel will not do. Since Peter was scheduled to die, perhaps the disciples thought that it was the spirit of Peter visiting them before he ascended to heaven. On the other hand, they may have surmised that it was the astral double of Peter visiting them from prison. They referred to this as "his angel". In any case the verse is at least suggestive of astral projection.[1358]

All of the above evidence suggests that astral projection was a phenomenon known to the early disciples, or at least to some of them. This is an important point, because it provides a motive

---

[1356] Acts 12.

[1357] Acts 12:15.

[1358] We ought not to let different terminology blind us to the underlying phenomenon being described. If they thought that Peter was already dead, then this implies that a visitation from a departed spirit was acceptable, rather than some abomination, as typically taught in contemporary Christianity. Alternatively, if they thought that Peter himself was visiting them through his "angel", i.e., his astral double or astral body, then this in turn implies that this phenomenon was both known to them, and it was also acceptable, rather than an abomination. Either way, contemporary interpretations of Christianity are refuted by the text of the New Testament itself. We have seen that the "guardian angel" interpretation is untenable.

basis for an esotericism that may have been protected by an outer shell of exotericism. This accounts for things that are otherwise unaccountable. Once again fundamentalists are congenitally unable to understand such fundamental principles, to their own detriment. But this makes their arguments very hollow indeed. Such rigid thinking on their part will keep them trapped in a false belief-system indefinitely. The importance of esotericism will become evident later, when we consider the psychological motivations of the Apostles to keep certain things secret. It also removes the cynical element from such speculations, which constitute an unanswerable argument against them.

As far as the passage about Chrestus in Suetonius goes, we have seen that a literal interpretation thereof is most congenial to either a survival, substitution, or impersonation theory. One alternate theory is that Jesus may have lived later than the time commonly assumed.[1359] Despite the congeniality of the passage to the above theories, it is often ignored as unimportant by advocates of such. Christians and phantom theorists also generally ignore it, or interpret in such a way that it does not require Jesus Christ to have personally been present in Rome at the time. Advocates of a termination theory could take the very same approach.[1360]

As far as the presumed silence of Philo and Josephus respecting Jesus is concerned, this is not really a very strong argument against Christ's presumed historicity; albeit it is injurious to an assumption of his miracle-working prowess. Philo and Josephus are also silent about any Christian or proto-Christian movement, as well; and most mythicists concede that there was a first-century proto-Christian movement, at the very least. We should also take into account the fact that Josephus and Philo may have been motivated to abstain from any mention of Jesus or his movement. This may have been due either to jealousy, opposition, or fear of drawing unwanted attention to yet another militant messianic movement, which the Romans frowned upon. These things are never taken into account by phantom Christ theorists. Rather they are studiously avoided. We have noted some

---

[1359] Rather than earlier, as I argued in my former work.

[1360] i.e., not to ignore the passage, but to interpret it in a general sense, as referring to disputes between Jews and Jewish Christians in Rome. Notably Josephus is silent about the decree of Claudius. So an appeal to the silence of Josephus respecting Jesus Christ is hardly a very strong argument.

literary parallels between the works of Philo and the Pauline corpus. We have also noted some literary parallels between the writings of Suetonius and the Gospels. In my former work I also noted at least one literary parallel between the writings of Josephus and the Gospel of Matthew.[1361] These literary parallels suggest a second-century origin for the New Testament texts, or at least for the Gospels.[1362] We have also ruled out the ahistorical paradigm on the basis of the fossil passages.[1363]

As far as the Shroud of Turin is concerned, we have seen that it is not really an important part of the evidence, since it is almost certainly a mediaeval fake. While it is true that a linen shroud is mentioned in all four canonical Gospels,[1364] as well as three or four apocryphal Gospels,[1365] the problem is that the famous Shroud of Turin is too doubtful to provide any significant evidence in respect to the historical Jesus. It is not genuine criticism to extend an unwarranted "benefit of the doubt" to some dubious relic that some researchers have insisted has distinctive pigments used by artists, and absolutely no bloodstains, as claimed by the advocates of the Shroud's authenticity. Furthermore unbiased experts have determined that there are absolutely no paranormal properties to the Shroud of Turin.[1366] While some advocates of the survival theory have pointed to the Shroud of Turin as providing evidence in favor of their thesis that Jesus survived his passion, the fact that experts who have examined the Shroud insist that there are in fact no blood stains on it rules out this appeal to non-existent "evidence" in favor of a dubious theory. The Shroud of Turin can safely be ruled out, in my opinion.[1367]

We have seen that an assumption of Christ's miraculous resurrection from the dead is unwarranted by the evidence, since

---

[1361] Jos. Ant. 15.3.3-4 cf Mt 2:1-18 cp Jos. Ant. 15.6.1-4.

[1362] It is just barely possible that some of the Pauline epistles date to the first century.

[1363] As well as other reasons given above.

[1364] Mt 27:59; Mk 15:46; Lk 23:53; 24:12; Jn 19:40; 20:5-7.

[1365] MtH; Peter 6; Nicodemus 8:14; cf MtN.

[1366] In contradistinction to claims by some evangelicals and fundamentalists that the Shroud somehow "proves" the supernatural resurrection of Jesus from the dead.

[1367] Despite the convoluted theories of those claiming the Shroud's authenticity.

it entails an adherence to the baggage of biblical fundamentalism, which is untenable. The phantom theory has also been thoroughly refuted above. We have also seen that the survival theory is much less probable than advocates of that theory are willing to concede; the substitution theory is too far-fetched and has too many loose ends; the impersonation theory is wildly improbable and will not hold up to scrutiny. That leaves the termination theory. But, as we will see, the termination theory emerges victorious not merely by default, but also because it is the only theory that satisfies all of the relevant evidence.

Finally, it is important to consider the evidence holistically. While only one aspect of the evidence can be examined at a time, once a person is acquainted with all the key variables, then it is important to step back and consider the whole of the evidence all together, rather than to narrowly focus on only one or two aspects of the evidence. In the next chapter we will examine the probable order of the Gospels, which is an important piece of the complete evidence.

Order of The Gospels

Now we should give diligent consideration to the question of the order of the Gospels. We discussed above the fact that, aside from the four Canonical Gospels, there had also been a number of other early gospels, which did not attain canonicity. It is naturally impossible to analyze texts that are no longer extant; and those that exist merely in fragmentary form will only lend themselves to a partial analysis, in terms of forensic literary archaeology. So we can really only focus on the four Canonical Gospels. However, we should at least briefly address the question of apocryphal gospels as well, lest we leave room for unwarranted doubt in respect to arguments yet to be made. We can state at the outset that the Gospel of Nicodemus and the Protevanglion of James postdate the four Canonicals, by generations, if not by centuries.[1368] The same holds true for the various Infancy Gospels, and those texts that exalt Mary as a "perpetual" virgin. The Gospel of Peter, while possibly including some archaic elements, also possibly postdates all four New Testament Gospels. As far as the various Gnostic Gospels are concerned, I statesd above that the Gospel of Thomas may very well have predated the Gospel of Luke. However we must remember that Luke was speaking of "many" narrative texts of the Gospel, so this may have excluded the Gospel of Thomas, had it

---

[1368] And this judgment holds even if we assume a second-century origin for the four Canonical Gospels.

been extant at the time. But quite possibly the Gospel of Philip could be another early text; maybe even predating the Gospel of Luke. On the other hand, there are certain features of both Thomas and Philip that seem to be very "late" features. In any case, neither text is written in the distinct narrative form of our better-known Gospel texts. That leaves the various Ebionite texts. Most likely, MtN, MtE, and MtH probably all postdate MtGk. But this must be qualified by the further stipulation that MtGk was probably based upon an earlier Hebrew original, which lacked the first two chapters and the last three verses of our familiar Greek Gospel of Matthew.[1369]

Since the Gospel of Luke refers to "many" earlier written accounts, it is unwise to posit Luke as the first of the Canonical Gospels. Despite this, some have proposed this very thing.[1370] Some have argued in favor of the primacy of John.[1371] Traditionally Matthew has been advocated as the earliest Gospel. But most critical biblical scholars deem the Gospel of Mark as the earliest. Arguments for virtually any order could be brought forward, but one desires an analysis that will hold up under scrutiny. The Diatessaron is helpful inasmuch as it proves that all four Gospels had been written sometime before 175 C.E.[1372] It also further proves that either none of the apocryphal gospels had been written, or if they were, they were so lightly esteemed as to be taken no account of. So the Diatessaron is perhaps more important than I stated above. Marcion, who preceded Tatian, chose Luke alone as Canonical. We cannot be sure whether or not Marcion's text of Luke included a reference to many earlier written accounts, but if it did so, then they were regarded as inferior and suspect.[1373] Matthew and Mark may have been regarded by Marcion as too "Jewish", and John may have been rejected because it was simply too different from Luke.

Most critical Bible scholars grant primacy to the Gospel of Mark. However this must be qualified by an understanding that according to such critical scholars, the last twelve verses of Mark are regarded

---

[1369] i.e., MtGk.

[1370] Acharya S., in her book, *THE CHRIST CONSPIRACY.*

[1371] Notably A.T. Robertson and Barbara Thiering.

[1372] This is another point that Acharya S. stumbled on; she postulated that the Gospel of Matthew was not written until 180 C.E., in her first book.

[1373] i.e., in the eyes of Marcion and the Marcionites.

as spurious. This is an issue we will need to discuss at some length, to know exactly what the evidence is in respect to this. While some of the arguments in favor of the priority of Mark do not hold up to scrutiny, considered holistically, the Gospel of Mark does seem to be the most archaic of the four Gospels, or at least of the Greek editions of such narrative texts. The probable order of the Greek Gospels is Mark, Matthew, Luke and John.

We will not be able to deal with this subject exhaustively herein; but hopefully enough evidence will be presented to make a sufficiently strong case for the order proposed above. For a fuller treatment of the subject, one could perhaps consult the work of a specialist, such as Mark Goodacre.[1374] In fact I go a bit further than Mr. Goodacre, since I propose Mark as the template, not only of the Synoptics, but also of the Gospel of John.

The Gospels of Matthew and Mark are the two most similar Gospels, and have the most material in common. It is easier to believe that Matthew expanded upon what Mark wrote, rather than that Mark condensed Matthew's account. It is not that the latter assumption is impossible, but we would have to wonder why Mark omitted so much of what is otherwise found in Matthew, especially in terms of Christ's teachings. We have already seen some evidence of Markan priority above, and I would rather not reiterate it here. But Matthew omits the embarrassing episode of Mark 8:22-26. The cursing of the fig tree is more impressive in Matthew, since the fig tree withers away instantly; in Mark it is not until the next day that any of the Apostles notice that the fig tree has withered.[1375] In Mark 6:5 we are told that Jesus literally "could not" perform any work of power in Capernaum; in the parallel passage in Matthew, it simply says that Jesus "did not" perform many miracles because of the people's unbelief.[1376] In Mark 13:32, Jesus says "But of that day and hour no man knows; neither the angels in heaven, nor the Son, but *only* the Father." But in the parallel verse in Matthew, the clause "nor the Son" is omitted from the majority

---

[1374] Goodacre, Mark; *The Case Against Q: Markan Priority and the Synoptic Problem.*, op. cit.

[1375] Mt 21:17-20 vs. Mk 11:12-14,20-21.

[1376] Matthew 13:58.

of Greek manuscripts.[1377] All of these differences point towards Mark predating Matthew, all other things being equal.

Matthew and Mark both report that when Jesus was arrested in the Garden of Gethsemane, one of the Apostles drew a sword, and cut off the ear of one of the men of the temple guard.[1378] Luke supplies an additional detail, telling us that this man lost his right ear.[1379] John supplies the most detail of all, telling us the name of this man, and also the name of the Apostle who cut off his ear.[1380] This progression of increasing information suggests the order of the Gospels proposed above: Mark, Matthew, Luke, and John.[1381] It almost seems as if the more detailed accounts were written to satisfy inquisitive early Christians. Of course gratuitous additional information does not *always* necessarily point to a later text. But in this instance, it seems to.

Mark and Matthew both tell us about how Simon of Cyrene was compelled to bear the cross of Jesus.[1382] Luke tells us about the

---

[1377] Nestle-Aland., op. cit., pg. 70, apparatus. This is one instance in which I disagree with the proposed reading of the *Deutsche Bibelgesellschaft Stuttgart,* since they include the clause in the text of their critical edition. But it is more likely that the original text of Matthew omitted the clause, which was added by a later scribe, to bring the text into greater conformity with Mark's Gospel. For that matter, some few manuscripts of Mark omit the clause, yet in that instance the critical scholars followed the majority reading. This is yet an instance of where such scholars are notoriously inconsistent. It is much easier to believe that the clause was absent from the earliest text of Matthew, and was later added by some scribe seeking to bring Matthew's text into greater conformity with Mark's, than to suppose the alternative that, while the clause had originally been present in Matthew's Gospel, it was removed by scribes who thought it was injurious to the supposed Deity of Christ. This latter argument is virtually self-refuting; if scribes eliminated the clause from Matthew's text, then why did they not also remove it from Mark's? In this instance critical scholars have robbed themselves of another argument in favor of Mark's priority over Matthew.

[1378] Matthew 26:51; Mark 14:47. The man injured is identified as a slave of the high priest.

[1379] Luke 22:50.

[1380] John 18:10; "Then Simon Peter having a sword drew it, and smote the high priest's slave, and cut off his right ear. The slave's name was Malchus."

[1381] We have already considered some evidence that Mark predates Matthew.

[1382] Mk 15:21; Mt 27:32.

incident, but he qualifies it by saying that Simon bore the cross after Jesus.[1383] From the Greek it is evident that the meaning of the word translated as "after" here does not mean afterwards in time; it rather denotes that Simon carried the latter part of the cross behind Jesus. This precludes an explanation of the verse as an attempt to harmonize Matthew and Mark's accounts with that of John, who wrote that Jesus bore his own cross.[1384] Once again the evidence suggests that John's Gospel postdates the three Synoptics; John omitted any mention of Simon of Cyrene due to the embarrassing rumors that Simon had been crucified in place of Christ. But Luke's supplement of data supplied by Mark and Matthew also suggests that Luke's Gospel postdates their accounts. Mark tells us that this Simon was also the father of Alexander and Rufus, and this detail is omitted by both Matthew and Luke. But this is best explained by the fact that some believers still alive at the time probably knew who this Alexander and Rufus were, who are not mentioned anywhere else in Mark's Gospel, or in any of the Gospels.

Matthew and Mark both tell us that female disciples of Jesus watched his crucifixion from far away.[1385] Luke also tells us that these female disciples watched from a distance, but also adds that "all his acquaintance" also looked on from afar.[1386] John deviates from this united Synoptic testimony, inserting an episode in which the mother of Jesus, as well as Mary Magdalene, and two other women, and the beloved disciple, were all standing close enough to Jesus as he hung from the cross to have a conversation with him.[1387] John's eccentric version of the story can be accounted for as an attempt to squelch rumors that Simon of Cyrene or some other man had been crucified in place of Christ. But once again, we have the same pattern in respect to this detail as well; the proposed order of Mark, Matthew, Luke and John is upheld by this circumstance as well. As a brief digression I want to respond to a potential argument that could be brought forward by advocates of a substitution theory. They could argue that, since there is at least some literary evidence from the Gospel of John that

---

[1383] Lk 23:26.

[1384] Jn 19:17.

[1385] Mt 27:55–56; Mk 15:40–41.

[1386] Lk 23:49.

[1387] Jn 19:25–27.

John the Evangelist was attempting to dispel embarrassing rumors that there had been a secret substitution, that this in itself is a form of evidence that in fact there had been such a substitution. But as I pointed out above, John was responding to rumors about Simon of Cyrene specifically, and most likely those rumors only arose as a response to the verses in the Synoptics about Simon of Cyrene. In other words, the rumors themselves were late rumors, arising as a response to the written form of the *kerygma* or proclamation; presumably had there be any rumors arising directly from the historical incident itself, then the very first written form of the *kerygma* would have answered them, or at least would have attempted to do so. Furthermore we pointed out the fatal weaknesses of the substitution theory above.

Returning briefly to the question of the priority of Mark, a diligent comparison between Mark and the other two Synoptic Gospels provides very strong evidence that Mark was written first. Mark is more generally archaic in character. Mark would have included far more of Christ's teachings that we find in Matthew, had Mark's text postdated Matthew's. Mark would have included far more of Christ's teachings as found in Matthew and Luke, if his Gospel had been an abridgement and conflation of theirs. Mark's Gospel sometimes includes more detail, but once again, those items that are unique to Mark all consistently point to it being an earlier text, rather than a later one.[1388] Mark did include some teaching by Christ, so it is not as if teachings *per se* were of no interest to Mark. But once again, we would have expected Mark to have included more of what is found in Matthew and Luke, had it been written subsequent to them. For the same reason we can clearly see that John postdates the Synoptic Gospels; no Johannine teachings are found in any of the Synoptic Gospels. Furthermore the fact that John's Gospel teaches a completely sectarian, antinomian doctrine of salvation, in contradistinction from the Synoptic doctrine of obedience to the commandments as a necessary requirement for salvation, strongly points to John as being a later literary production than those other Gospels.[1389] At this point I

[1388] The sole exception to this rule is the last twelve verses of Mark's Gospel; but most likely, this portion of Mark was not original to Mark's text. We will discuss these controversial last twelve verses of Mark in another section below.

[1389] Jn 3:16-18; 6:29; 10:1-30; 11:25-26; 14:6 vs. Mt 7:21-29; 10:22,28; 19:16-19;

would like to briefly and preemptively respond to what may be lodged either as a criticism of this analysis, or a veiled act of apologetics on the part of evangelicals. So please bear with me in this brief digression. Some may object to my sharp division of the New Testament into two different "halves", each teaching diametrically opposed doctrines of soteriology. Critics and apologists might be tempted to point out that, while my analysis may hold true in a general sense, there are some exceptions, inasmuch as one can find instances of a "works-based" salvation scheme within the Pauline and Johannine corpii, and also of a "sectarian" salvation scheme within the Synoptic corpii.[1390] While technically there are such exceptions, nevertheless I do not feel that these exceptions completely vitiate the truism of the general analysis. In other words, while Christians might attempt to argue that the New Testament texts are more homogenous than they really are, by pointing to such exceptions, this is merely a species of desperate apologetics. In terms of legitimate criticism, the presence of such exceptions does not vitiate the analysis in forensic literary terms, in my view. In the case of Christians it would be merely an attempt to deny actual contradictions within the text of the New Testament. I suppose I could be accused of special pleading if I suggested that later scribes were responsible for placing these gratuitously "harmonizing" exceptions within these texts. But it is not altogether unthinkable. Nevertheless it is not necessary to insist upon any such thing; the

---

24:20-51; 25:31-46; 28:20; Mk 9:43-48; 10:17-19; Lk 18:18-20. Of course the very same argument could be used to suggest that the Pauline corpus also postdates the Synoptic Gospels, or at least the earliest one of them. But if the Gospel of Mark was not written until the early second century then this argument would also necessarily make the entire Pauline corpus pseudonymous. On the other hand, it is just barely possible that the Gospel of Mark was written as a sort of refutation of the Pauline school. In any case it is evident that the Pauline corpus (minus the Pastorals) predates the Johannine corpus (minus Revelation). This is evident by a process of forensic literary archaeology; the Johannine corpus is far more radical than the Pauline corpus, since the Johannine corpus literally revises the very teachings of Jesus Christ himself, placing a Pauline-type of salvation scheme into the very lips of Jesus himself. This is an outrageous and enormous act of historical and literary revisionism.

[1390] Galatians 5:19-21; Ephesians 5:5; I Corinthians 6:9-10; John 3:19-21; 5:28-29; 15:6 vs. Mt 10:32-33; Mk 16:16. Please note that this last instance falls within the controversial last twelve verses of Mark. See discussion below.

fact is, we do find statements that are diametrically opposed in meaning, according to a straightforward reading of the text, according to the plain meaning of words. And the general thrust of each of these respective corpii can be readily identified in this way. Nobody familiar with the New Testament would classify Matthew or Mark as antinomian in character, nor would they claim that the writings of John or Paul were works-based in character. As a general rule we would expect the ethical teaching to precede the sectarian one.[1391] This does not necessarily mean that every instance of sectarianism or antinomianism postdates every contrary document. Most likely there was a sort of literary polemics involved, going back and forth between the two rival factions. As I speculated in my earlier work, most likely the Synoptic faction and the Pauline-Johannine faction were both probably ultimately subsumed into a pseudo-Petrine faction.[1392]

It is easier to account for Matthew and Luke in literary terms as expansions upon Mark's Gospel, rather than the contrary assumption that Mark was an abridgement of Mathew and Luke. Mark is more archaic than either Matthew or Luke. For example, compare Mark 9:13 with the parallel verse in Matthew; in Mark, Jesus says "But I say to you that Elijah has already come, and they have done to him whatever they wished, as it is written of him." But in Matthew 17:12, Jesus says "But I say to you that Elijah has already come, and they knew him not, and have done to him whatever they wished." Although TaNaKh does foretell the return of the prophet Elijah,[1393] nowhere in either TaNaKh, the Apocrypha, or the Old Testament Pseudepigrapha, does it say that Elijah will be mistreated, as Jesus seems to say in Mark's rendering. Therefore it seems less likely that Mark would have garbled what Matthew had gotten right; it is more likely that Matthew emended what he had found in Mark.

[1391] However this will not always be manifested in the literary unfoldment of the movement. It is important to keep in mind that the movement began as an actual historical movement, rather than as merely a literary movement, as mythicists would have it. Therefore a critical-historical analysis must take this into account; we cannot afford to take a superficial, one-dimensional, strictly literary analysis of the evidence. Instead we need to use the actual documents to discern the underlying history of the movement.

[1392] This faction is most visibly manifested as the Roman Catholic Church.

[1393] Malachi 4:5.

Mark presents the baptism of Jesus by John in more or less matter-of-fact terms; but this becomes virtually a theological dilemma for Matthew, who has John protest his unworthiness to baptize Jesus.[1394] While Luke's narrative follows Mark's more closely here, John deals with the baptism in a different way; it becomes yet another opportunity for John the Baptist to endorse Jesus as the Son of God and the Lamb of God.[1395] Furthermore what is presented as a subjective experience in Mark and Luke is depicted as an objective phenomenon if Matthew and John.

I spoke briefly above on scribal fatigue. This is another phenomenon that further proves the primacy of Mark. I will give a clear example of this presently. The phrase "kingdom of the heavens" occurs frequently in the Gospel of Matthew, and only in the Gospel of Matthew. The other three Gospels always use the phrase "kingdom of God." Nowhere in Mark, Luke, or John does the phrase "kingdom of the heavens" occur, even in parallel verses in the Synoptic Gospels, where Jesus is giving the very same teaching. But there is an instance where the phrase "kingdom of God" occurs in Matthew, and it is in the verse about a camel going through the eye of a needle.[1396] If Matthew had been written first, we would expect Jesus to have used the phrase "kingdom of the heavens" and that we would find the same reading in the parallel verses in Mark and Luke; but instead we have a clear example of scribal fatigue, in which Matthew simply copied *verbatim* what he found written in Mark. And the fact that this is a case of scribal fatigue can be decisively proven by comparing Matthew 13:11 and Mark 4:11; in Mark, Jesus uses the phrase "mystery of the kingdom of God", while in the parallel verse in Matthew, Jesus uses the phrase "mysteries of the kingdom of the heavens." The point is that, while we have an example of Matthew using the phrase "kingdom of God" in one verse otherwise common to the other two Synoptics, nowhere is either Mark or Luke is there a counter-example of Jesus using the phrase "kingdom of the heavens", as is exclusively used in Matthew. Thuis strongly suggests that Matthew was copying from Mark, rather than vice-versa.

[1394] Mark 1:9–11 cp Matthew 3:13–17.

[1395] Luke 3:21-22 cp John 1:29-34.

[1396] Matthew 19:24 cf Mark 10:25; Luke 18:25.

As a general rule, Matthew seems to address his Gospel to Jews, or at least to Jewish Christians. By contrast, Luke seeks to reach out to a wider Gentile audience. This suggests that Luke's Gospel postdates Matthew's. Furthermore, in Matthew John the Baptist calls the Pharisees and Sadducees a brood of vipers, while in Luke it is the entire multitude who come for baptism that he calls a brood of vipers.[1397] This suggests that Luke's Gospel is comparatively more anti-Semitic, which in turn suggests that it is somewhat later than Matthew's. On the same basis the Gospel of John can also be seen as postdating the Synoptics, since it is comparably more anti-Semitic.[1398] The same criterion also places the Gospel of Nicodemus as later than the Canonicals.

The story of Roman soldiers guarding the tomb of Christ is found only in Matthew.[1399] This suggests that Matthew was written last, rather than first, all other things being equal. But we have already seen a number of compelling reasons for supposing that Luke and John both postdate Matthew and Mark. But this still functions as further evidence in favor of the priority of Mark against Matthew. Once again, we need to consider the evidence respecting the relative order of the Gospels holistically. From all of the above evidence, we see a clear pattern that supports the proposed order of Mark, Matthew, Luke, John.

Above I wrote that Mark was the template not only of Matthew and Luke, but also of John. While more difficult to prove, since John does not fit into the Synoptic pattern, there is still nevertheless some oblique evidence of this.[1400] So far I have only found a few passages to support this position in a highly specific way, but they are worth taking a look at.

[1397] Mt 3:7 cp Lk 3:7.

[1398] The only notable exception in John's Gospel being 4:22, where Jesus says "Salvation is of the Jews." Other than this is the fact that Jesus was ostensibly Jewish in the ethnic sense. Furthermore, the use of the term "anti-Semitic" must be understood in relative terms.

[1399] Mt 27:62-66; 28:11-15. The story does occur in various apocryphal gospels, such as MtN, the Gospel of Peter, and the Gospel of Nicodemus.

[1400] In any case we have clear evidence that John postdates all three Synoptic Gospels, so Mark becomes the literary template for all the Gospels by default.

Mark reports that at the trial of Jesus before the high priest, certain false witnesses came forward, saying that they heard Jesus say "I will destroy this temple that is made with hands, and within three days I will build another *temple* made without hands."[1401] Matthew reiterates an abbreviated form of the same testimony. But nowhere in either Mark or Matthew is the incident explained or elaborated upon. But in John's Gospel, when Jesus is challenged by the people to show a sign proving he had the authority to cast the merchants out of the temple, he said "Destroy this temple, and in three days I will raise it up."[1402] It is easier and more economical to suppose that John gratuitously wrote the incident into the narrative of his text, in order to provide a context for what is otherwise found in Mark and Matthew, than to suppose the reverse; i.e., that John's account predates both Mark and Matthew, who have used what John wrote as fodder for their own narratives. It would not have been very clever for both Evangelists to avoid any mention of the incident narrated by John, had his account been earlier. But John seems so eager to surprise us with his clever solution to the false testimony offered by the false witnesses in Mark and Matthew that this may be why he inadvertently committed an anachronism in his placement of the incident of Christ casting merchants out of the temple.

In Mark, when Joseph of Arimathaea asks Pilate for the body of Jesus, Pilate "marveled" that Jesus was already dead, and asked the centurion if Jesus was already dead.[1403] The very next verse says, "And when he knew it from the centurion, he gave the corpse to Joseph."[1404] While the text is somewhat ambiguous, one might picture the events narrated in either of two ways: either Pilate simply asked the centurion, who answered him immediately in the affirmative; or, the centurion deliberately left to make sure that Jesus was really dead. The latter assumption seems to be in accord with what is narrated in John 19:34, which says that one of the soldiers pierced Jesus in the side with a spear. The incident in John seems to be based upon the narrative of Mark; the piercing of Jesus with a spear being a "test" to see if he was already dead, or possibly to insure that he truly was dead. Ironically,

---

[1401] Mark 14:58 cp Matthew 26:61.

[1402] John 2:19.

[1403] Mark 15:44.

[1404] Mark 15:45, according to the original Greek.

there are some survival theorists who insist that the fact that both blood and water came from the side of Jesus after this, it proves that Jesus was not clinically dead at the time.

Finally, John agrees with Mark against Matthew, saying he was clothed in a purple robe, rather than scarlet.[1405] There would have been no reason for him to do this, unless he regarded Mark as more authoritative than Matthew, and hence older.[1406] John never agrees with Matthew against Mark, unless Luke also agrees with Matthew against Mark.[1407]

So based upon all the evidence we have studied, the order of the Gospels is almost certainly Mark, Matthew, Luke, John. Thus in critical-historical terms, this order of the Gospels is potentially significant in terms of evidence. All other things being equal, we would expect the testimony of earlier documents to be more historically reliable. John's Gospel is so highly suspect as to be almost worthless in historical terms. It is both last and least of the Canonical Gospels.

[1405] John 19:2 cf Mark 15:17 cp Matthew 27:28.

[1406] Or as we would say, older, and hence more historically authoritative.

[1407] In fact the only example I can think of is the discrepancy about Peter's denial before the cock crows twice or thrice. In this instance, all three Gospels contradict Mark. But this is the only example that I can think of.

Supplemental Addendum

I beg the reader's indulgence for the addition of this very brief supplement to the chapter immediately above. Much time has passed since I wrote the original edition of this work; as such, I have acquired much relevant knowledge pretinent to the discussion herein. Furthermore, there were really only three choices open to me: either to virtually extinguish all that is written in the immediately foregoing chapter, to be replaced by some ad-hoc and potentially substandard material; or to take an undue amount of time in so thoroughly revising it that I would risk violating a perceived publishing deadline; or to only lightly revise what I had already written, while adding a brief supplementary chapter. I chose this last option, so please bear with me. While for the most part what I wrote above I still believe is generally very good, and I did not wish to sacrifice it altogether, I do want to qualify it by an appeal to evidence I did not have at the time. In the interim I discovered a little-known book which contains a very old Hebrew text of the Gospel of Matthew.[1408] This archaic text of Matthew in Hebrew was part and parcel of a mediaeval Jewish polemic work known as the *Even Bohan,* by Shem Tob. However, Professor Howard presents much detailed, manifold and highly persuasive evidence that the Hebrew text of Matthew found in the

---

[1408] Howard, George., (ed., trans.), *Hebrew Gospel of Matthew.* © 1995, Mercer University Press. Macon, Georgia, USA.

Even Bohan definitely dates back to pre-mediaeval times; in fact, it very well might go back to the third or even the second century, in my opinion. I cannot do full justice to all of the available evidence in this brief chapter. But Mr. Howard has presented evidence of puns within the Hebrew text which lead me to believe that the original Gospel of Matthew *must* have been written in Hebrew.[1409] As such, it is unthinkable that the original, Hebrew text of Matthew could have been based upon a Greek text of Mark. Furthermore, even in the *Even Bohan* version of Hebrew Matthew, the example given above about "the kingdom of God" in Matthew 19:24 is absent; the Hebrew reads "kingdom of the heavens".[1410] So, arguments that may be applicable to the Greek text of Matthew are not necessarily applicable to the Hebrew text of Matthew. Likewise, the clause "nor the Son" is also absent from the Hebrew Matthew in Mt 24:36.[1411] But I also noticed a number of passages where the text of Hebrew Matthew seemed less primitive than what is sometimes found in the Greek. How is this to be accounted for? Probably be the fact that, in both Hebrew and Greek, the texts have undergone a number of different redactions and recensions; Mr. Howard discusses these issues in greater detail in his book. People who found my first book interesting will also find great interest in George Howard's book; he discusses the *Toldoth Jeschu,* as well as many other texts, in relation to the Hebrew Matthew. So I highly recommend his book. Furthermore, some of the quirky features of Mark's Gospel may be accounted for by theories other than primacy. One possibility is that whoever wrote the narrative text we know today as the Gospel according to Mark, wrote it as a coded anti-Gospel. This theory would require a book to provide the evidence in detail. I will admit that Marc Goodacre presents some seemingly overwhelmingly strong evidence in favor of the primacy of Mark, but this evidence is only valid if we limit ourselves to the Greek texts, or at least the extant Greek texts. As far as I'm concerned, the evidence from the Hebrew puns is conclusive; the original, Hebrew text of Matthew must predate both Mark and all the other canonical Gospels. So Mark, whether written as a literary Trojan Horse or not, post-dates [Hebrew] Matthew. One theory is that Mark was written

---

[1409] Ibid., pgs. 184-190.

[1410] Ibid., pg. 94.

[1411] Ibid., pg. 122.

as both a literary abridgement and Greek translation of an earlier, Hebrew text of Matthew. Under the assumptions of this theory, only after the Greek text of Mark appeared did a Greek translation of the entire text of Matthew take place. While this is an attractive scenario, I do not consider it a necessary inference; Greek Mark could have been written subsequently to a Greek translation of Hebrew Matthew. The author of Mark may have wanted to present a more humanistic vision of Jesus, as a prophet and healer, but not as God the Son. Or he may have wanted to deliberately sabotage the Messianic movement with heretical views and a disparaging portrayal of Jesus in his text. In any case I now firmly believe in the primacy of a Hebrew text of Matthew.

Perfect & Final
Sacrifice for Sins?

O ne of the central doctrines of the New Testament is the
atonement, or the idea that Jesus died a sacrificial death on the
cross, to become the basis for eternal salvation. The sacrificial death of
Christ on the cross is said to be the perfect and final sacrifice for sins
once and for all. This teaching pervades most of the New Testament,
although it is most strongly evident within the Pauline corpus, and
particularly in the book of Hebrews. This doctrine is primordial
Christian orthodoxy *par excellence;* it is not merely another dogma of
Christianity, but one of the most central and foundational teachings
of the Christian faith. It is explicitly acknowledged by all branches
of Christianity. It is also inextricably bound up with the theme of
the resurrection of Christ. However there is a set of fossil passages
that belies the idea that this teaching had been uniformly accepted
immediately after Christ's supposed resurrection from the dead. This
same set of passages also casts suspicion upon the supposition that the
original disciples of Jesus were *Ebionim.* This is a conundrum, but it
may also serve as a clue to the beliefs of the Apostles in the immediate
aftermath of Christ's passion. In any case it is a sufficiently curious part
of the evidence that it should at least be taken into account.

First let's look at some passages that clearly teach that Jesus Christ
suffered and died as the perfect, final sacrifice for sins once and for all.

24 For the Messiah entered not into holy places made with hands, *which are* but antitypes of the true *things,* but into the heaven itself, now to appear before God for us;

25 nor yet that he should offer himself often, as the high priest enters into the holy place every year with blood of others;

26 for then must he often have suffered since the foundation of the world:

But now once for all upon ends of the ages has he appeared to put away sin through the sacrifice of himself *on the cross.*

27 And as it is appointed to men to die once and for all, but after this a judgment,

28 so also the Messiah was offered once for all to bear the sins of the many; *but* for those who look for him shall he appear a second time without sin in salvation. (Hebrews 9:24-27)

For the law having a shadow of good things to come, *but* not the very image of the things, can never with those sacrifices, offered continually year by year, perfect those who partake in them.

2 For would they not then have ceased to be offered? Because the worshippers once for all purged should have had no more conscience of sins.

3 But in those *sacrifices is* a remembrance of sins made again every year.

4 For *it is* impossible for *the* blood of bulls and goats to take away sins.

5 Therefore, when he comes into the world, he says, Sacrifice and offering thou wouldst not, but a body hast thou prepared me:

6 In burnt offerings and sin offerings thou hadst no pleasure.

7   Then I said, Behold, I come to do thy will, O God; in the heading of the book it is written of me.

8   Above when he said, Sacrifice and offering and burnt offering and sin offering thou wouldst not, neither hadst pleasure therein; which are offered according to *the* law;

9   then he said, Behold, I have come to do thy will, O God. He takes away the first, to establish the second.

10 By which will we are sanctified through the offering of the body of Jesus Messiah once for all. (Hebrews 10:1-10)

The above passage[1412] clearly teaches that Jesus died as the perfect and final sacrifice for sins once and for all. This theme of blood redemption through Jesus Christ is prevalent throughout the Pauline corpus, and is also found in other portions of the New Testament.[1413]

Justified by faith, we *now* have peace with God through our Lord, Jesus Christ;

2   by whom also we have access by faith into this grace wherein we stand, and rejoice in hope of the glory of God.

3   But not only so, but we glory in tribulations also; knowing that tribulation produces patience;

4   and patience, experience; and experience, hope;

5   but the hope does not shame us; because the love of God has been poured out in our hearts through holy spirit which is given to us.

6   For when we were yet without strength, in due time Christ died for the ungodly.

7   For hardly would one die *even* for a righteous person, yet maybe for a good person one would dare to die.

[1412] In the original Greek it is all one passage; chapter divisions came later.

[1413] With the notable exceptions of the Epistles of James and Judas.

8   But God proves his love to us, inasmuch as, while we were still sinners, Christ died for us.

9   Much more then, having been now justified by his blood, we shall be saved from the wrath *of God* through him.

10 For if when we were enemies we were reconciled to God through the death of his Son, much more, being reconciled, we shall be saved by his life.

11 But not only so, but we also rejoice in God through our Lord Jesus Christ, through whom we have received the atonement. (Romans 5:1-11)

This passage likewise also teaches the blood atonement of Jesus Christ as the basis for salvation. This teaching of blood atonement is most conspicuous within the Pauline corpus, but it is least developed in the Gospels, and it is entirely absent from the epistles of James and Jude. Tychicus or Paul wrote of Jesus "In whom we have redemption through his blood, the forgiveness of sins"[1414]

In Mark, we read the following passage:

22 And as they ate, Jesus took bread, blessed it, and broke it, saying, Take, eat;

This is my body.

23 And he took the cup, and when he had given thanks, he gave it to them:

And they all drank of it.

24 And he said to them, This is my blood of the new covenant, which is shed for many.

25 Truly I say unto you, I will no more drink of the fruit of the vine, until that day I drink it new in the kingdom of God. (Mark 14:22-25)

[1414] Ephesians 1:7; Colossians 1:14.

So we can see that belief in a bood redemption through Christ's sacrificial death on the cross was a normative part of Christian faith, presumably from the very beginning. Yet there are some passages that belie this notion, and present us with a contradictory course of action on the part of the Apostles and other disciples. Mere hypocrisy is not a satisfying explanation; it is not credible that such a fervent messianic movement would have expanded and flourished with no more inspiration than the example of hypocrites. But we read in Luke 24:53 that after Christ's passion, the Apostles were in the temple in Jerusalem continually. What? Why would the Apostles abide continually in the temple, or go there to worship God, if every day bloody animal sacrifices were offered? We can see that this is not just a problem for a supposition that those men were Ebionites; if they truly believed that Jesus had died on the cross as the perfect, final sacrifice for sins once and for all, then it would have been a shameful act of hypocrisy for them to attend vain sacrifices of goats and bulls in the temple. At the very least, the verse from Luke suggests that belief in Christ's sacrificial death was not an article of faith immediately upon his decease.[1415] Acts 3:1 tells us that Peter and John went to the temple at the hour of prayer. Why would they have gone to the temple at all, if they believed that Jesus had already died on the cross as the "perfect and final sacrifice for sins once and for all" as taught elsewhere in the New Testament? Indeed, even Jesus' words as recorded in Mark's Gospel about the blood of the new covenant should have been enough to clue them in about the theme of blood redemption. But the very fact that Acts 3:1 says that they went to the temple belies any supposition that Jesus actually said what he was reported to have said respecting this supposed blood redemption. The same also holds true of Luke 24:53. There is no justification for such conduct on the part of the Apostles, had they truly believed Christ had died as a perfect and final sacrifice for sins once and for all. These verses also prove, or at least

---

[1415] Christians might argue that attendance at the temple was merely an attempt to witness to the other Jews about their messianic faith in Jesus. However this is not an entirely satisfying argument; while Acts 5:25 does say that the Apostles taught in the temple, that was not the first place where they witnessed to Christ's resurrection. The very fact that these men still attended the temple services belied any real belief in the once-for-all atonement through Jesus Christ; after all, actions speak louder than words.

tend to prove, that neither Jesus nor the Apostles were Ebionites.[1416] There is a verse in John's Gospel that contradicts these two verses by the Evangelist Luke, but we have seen that the Gospel of John is not particularly trustworthy.[1417] We also read of the apostle Paul that he himself also attended temple services, and even took part in a vow involving an animal sacrifice.[1418] But Paul supposedly wrote that "Christ is the end of the law for righteousness to every one who believes."[1419] Paul is also the purported author of Hebrews, Ephesians, Galatians, and Colossians. All these epistles teach that Christ has redeemed believers from the "curse" of the law, and that he is the perfect and final sacrifice for all sins once and for all.[1420] As already noted, actions speak louder than words. One is tempted to attribute such conduct to Paul's legendary hypocrisy. After all, Paul supposedly admitted that "to the Jews I became as a Jew, that I might gain the Jews; to them that are under the law, as under the law, that I might

---

[1416] Above I suggested that quite possibly these verses might be blinds, to obscure the fact that the earliest disciples were Ebionites. But this is not a credible supposition, since these verses inadvertently belie one of the central doctrines normative to the New Testament; i.e., that Jesus Christ died on the cross as the perfect and final sacrifice for sins once and for all. As such, these verses are eminent examples of fossil passages. In fact, in an oblique way, these verses uphold my preferred reading of *karath* as meaning "shall make a covenant" rather than the more common "shall be cut off"; more precisely, these verses suggest that Jesus and the Apostles initially interpreted *karath* in Daniel 9:26 in the sense I have suggested, and only some time after Christ's death was that prophecy reinterpreted to read *karath* as "shall be cut off" because this reading supported the novel interpretation of the Messiah as a sacrifice.

[1417] John 9:22; "...for the Jews had already agreed that if anyone confessed that he was the Messiah, he would be expelled from the synagogue." Perhaps this was a clumsy attempt by John the Evangelist to disavow the embarrassing verses from Luke & Acts about attendance at the temple by the Apostles after Christ's death. If so, then this discrepancy also upholds the order of the Gospels postulated above. Despite the dichotomy between the respective soteriologies of Luke and Acts, these two books may nevertheless have been written by a single author; the difference can be accounted for within a dispensational scheme of soteriology.

[1418] Acts 21:21-27; cf Numbers 6:1-21.

[1419] Romans 10:4.

[1420] Galatians 3:13; Hebrews 9:24-27; 10:1-10; Romans 5:1-11; Ephesians 1:7; Colossians 1:14.

gain them that are under the law; to them that are without law, as without law (yet not without law to God, but under the law to Christ), that I might gain them that are without law."[1421] If we assume Pauline authorship of Corinthians, then this looks like an admission of guilt, or rather an attempt at an explanation as to why he conducted himself so apparently hypocritically in Jerusalem. But there is something else that does not quite make sense. In Acts 21:17-27, it is James who advises Paul to partake in a temple vow.[1422] In Acts 21:25, James refers to the instructions to the Gentiles that they eat no food offered to idols, and abstain from partaking of blood, and from strangled food, and from fornication. What doesn't make sense is that this directly refers back to a meeting of the Apostles in Jerusalem recorded in Acts 15:1-29. But both Paul and James were present at this earlier meeting; James seems to have presided over it. Presumably this is the very same James mentioned in Acts 21, since the other James had already been martyred in Acts 12:2.[1423] In Acts 15, after Peter spoke, then Paul and Barnabas told the multitude about the miracles and signs God had performed among the Gentiles through them. Finally, after this, James speaks up and addresses the multitude, referring back to Peter, but ignoring Barnabas and Paul completely.[1424] Either he was being rude or the whole incident is suspect.[1425] But there is another detail that is often overlooked, that may provide a key to understanding the crux of the matter; we need not necessarily relegate the whole story to mere legend or invention. In Acts 15, the issue had to do specifically with Gentiles who entered the messianic movement; in Acts 21:21, James says to Paul that many Jewish believers suspect that he is teaching Jews of the *Diaspora* to forsake the Torah, and to forsake circumcision. So

---

[1421] I Corinthians 9:20-21.

[1422] A contradiction of both Matthew 5:33-37 and James 5:12.

[1423] James the Apostle and brother of John the Apostle; both sons of Zebedee. There was another Apostle named James, however: James Alphaeus, who had a brother named Judas, who was also another Apostle (not Judas Iscariot). There was a third James, however; James the brother of Jesus. This James is often denominated James the Just, and he is presumed to have been the "bishop" of the Jerusalem Church. But if so, we would expect that it was this very same James in both Acts 15 & Acts 21. So the confusion remains.

[1424] Acts 15:7-21.

[1425] Robert Eisenman has rejected the episode as spurious revisionism.

the difference had to do with the conduct of Jewish Christians, as opposed to Gentile Christians. In other words, James seems to have made a concession that Gentile believers need not be circumcised, but believers who were ethnically Jewish should continue the custom of circumcision, as well as other ritual observances of the Torah. What is questionable about the whole thing is the idea that Paul would have gone along with customs that he despised as antiquated and obsolete. But this dichotomy between Paul's purported actions and his purported words argues very strongly in favor of his historicity. This is the single strongest evidence of Paul's historicity, in fact. But ironically this evidence once again casts doubt upon the Pauline authorship of the Pauline corpus. I say ironically because in my former work I argued that an assumption of the authenticity of the Pauline corpus was the single strongest form of evidence in favor of Paul's alleged historicity, and without that, the case for Paul's historicity vanishes like a puff of smoke. However the full magnitude of the implications of the discrepancy between Paul's purported words and his reported actions had not yet registered in my consciousness.

This also once again raises questions about the relative dating of the Pauline corpus and the book of Acts. If Luke, who supposedly was a close associate of Paul, wrote the book of Acts, then it would seem rather shameful for him to portray Paul as such a weakling, coward, and hypocrite. This is another argument in favor of a pseudo-Luke as the author of Acts. But if Acts really postdates the Pauline corpus,[1426] then why would the author of that document seek to weaken the otherwise normative doctrine of Christ as the perfect and final sacrifice for sins once and for all? The actions of Paul and the Apostles as reported therein[1427] create doubt and controversy as to whether or not they truly believed in Christ's blood redemption. At the very least, we have a justified suspicion that this was a later doctrine. I am

---

[1426] Pauline corpus. i.e., some core of that corpus, namely Romans, I Corinthians, II Corinthians, Galatians, Ephesians, Philippians, Colossians, Hebrews.

[1427] And in Luke 24:53. Significantly, some manuscripts omit the clause "in the temple" in that verse. This suggests that quite possibly it was an interpolation into Luke's text by a scribe seeking to harmonize the Gospel with the book of Acts. We can be sure that Marcion's copy of Luke would not have contained the clause. See Nestle-Aland., op. cit., pg. 246, apparatus.

not saying that the Apostles themselves never came to believe this; but what seems doubtful, if we are to credit these verses from Luke and Acts, is that they believed in this blood atonement immediately after Christ's decease. If not, then this suggests that neither Jesus himself taught any such thing, nor had he intended to die a sacrificial death on the cross. This further suggests that such an interpretation of events was made some time after the fact; in other words, it was a reinterpretation of events. Prophecy now became reinterpreted in the light of the Messiah's unexpected martyrdom. Naturally passages were conveniently found to justify belief in the necessity of Christ's passion and death on the cross.[1428] So this evidence at least weighs against the idea of Jesus as a suicidal martyr fixated upon a Passover plot. This also breathes new life into the historicity of Paul. But in all fairness, we must admit that the Apostles may have felt justified in attending services at the temple based upon the last nine chapters of Ezekiel. Those chapters clearly depict a restored temple, wherein sacrifices are offered. Despite all of this, I still believe it is possible that the original disciples of Jesus may have been Ebionites.

[1428] Isaiah 53 & Psalm 22 being prime examples. Daniel 9:26 was reinterpreted to mean that the Messiah would be "cut off" and die, even though this interpretation is belied by Daniel 9:27.

Paul

Paul presents us with a paradox, particularly if we concede his historicity. As noted in the immediately preceding section, the dichotomy between Paul's reported actions and his purported words as read in the Pauline corpus provides us with circumstantial evidence in favor of his assumed historicity. I will not go quite so far as to claim that this is proof positive of his historicity, but if we now insist that Paul was merely *chimerical,* this would strongly undercut our appeal to the fossil passages as proving Christ's own historicity. In fact, the reasons I postulated in my former work as to exactly why the character of Paul was invented[1429] are still viable and strong reasons. Namely, that Paul would first and foremost have been invented to "lock in" claims of Christ's resurrection, by providing an unanswerable argument against those who might otherwise seek an explanation such as that the Apostles either simply reburied Christ's body, or that Jesus somehow survived his crucifixion, or that he had never actually been crucified, etc. If a person advocated any of these explanations, then they would have to further explain how and why Paul, a complete outsider as far as the Apostles and other disciples were concerned, also claimed to have seen the risen Christ. One could argue that this was a completely invented paradox, by virtue of the nonexistence of Paul. The second

---

[1429] i.e., assuming he was invented; or ahistoricity rather than historicity in the case of Paul.

reason why Paul would have been invented was to introduce through the invented character Paul a new, sectarian scheme of salvation that was completely antinomian in character.[1430] Both of these are good reasons for why Paul could have or would have been an invented character, rather than a historical person. And both of these reasons are also mutually harmonious; in other words, they could both be true. But this must be weighed against the evidence we have seen from the book of Acts. Acts depicts Paul acting in a way contrary to what we would expect of a person who truly believed the things written in epistles ascribed to him. As such, the passage in Acts is a fossil passage that provides evidence in favor of Paul's historicity. To this may be added the discrepancy between what Paul supposedly wrote in Galatians and what is narrated in the book of Acts. This kind of discrepancy also points towards a historical Paul.[1431]

But if Paul was historical, and he also wrote the Corinthian epistles, then we are confronted by a dilemma. Unless Paul really had a vision of Jesus, then why would he claim to have had one? In fact Paul claimed to have had ongoing visions of Jesus. But why? What was his motivation? This presents us with a psychological paradox. As far as I am personally concerned, a Nietzschean interpretation of Paul is too cynical to be realistic. And to interpret Paul's vision of Christ as an instance of epilepsy is an insult to the intelligence. Even the accounts of that first vision in the book of Acts are mutually contradictory.[1432] Therefore the experience itself is subject to grave doubt. Only one direct mention of this vision occurs within the Pauline corpus.[1433] I would like to briefly point out, however, that this vision is distinctly different from the post-passion appearances narrated in Luke and John. In those narratives, Jesus is quite tangible, and even eats with the Apostles. With Paul there is merely a vision. This may be a significant

---

[1430] This also further assumes that the Pauline corpus predates the Johannine corpus, which is also congruent to evidence discussed above.

[1431] Although it is uncertain whether Galatians was written by Paul, Silvanus, or some other person. But if Paul existed historically then it is not altogether unthinkable that he may have written Galatians. In fact, Paul may have been the author of the core of the Pauline corpus, if we assume that those persons named in the respective colophons acted merely as secretaries, or possibly secondary writers.

[1432] Acts 9:3-9 vs. Acts 22:6-11 cp Acts 26:13-18.

[1433] I Corinthians 15:8.

point. I must say that advocates of the survival theory have done rather poorly in accounting for Paul's coversion. It is a hard sell to portray Paul's experience as a personal meeting with a flesh-and-blood Jesus who survived the crucifixion. Such an interpretation is entirely unconvincing.

If we assume that Paul had no vision, then his "conversion" could be interpreted as a response to a personal crisis of faith. This need not have been quite as cynical as Nietzsche portrayed it to be. Perhaps Paul saw something in the new messianic movement lacking in his own Pharisaic Judaism. Then again, it is often argued that Paul's brand of Christianity was heretical in respect to the original messianic movement. Yet Paul himself was never regarded as a heretic, as was Marcion. Paul is depicted rather heroically in the book of Acts, and there is no other canonical text narrating the early history of the Christian faith. And although the Pauline corpus was highly esteemed by the Gnostics, those writings were not rejected as heretical on that account. Nevertheless the Pauline corpus is deviant from the Synoptic tradition, inasmuch as it inculcates an antinomian, sectarian scheme of salvation. Perhaps Paul had delusions of grandeur. Perhaps he had grown disillusioned with Judasim, and sought an ingenius form of revenge through the new messianic movement. But of course Paul was not about to subjugate himself to mere fishermen from Galilee; he was an expert in the Scriptures, and thereby constructed his own edifice of messianic interpretation. Presumably the Apostles were claiming that Jesus was the Messiah, and that he had ascended to heaven in some sense; either spiritually or carnally. If Paul came along and claimed to have had a vision of the risen Jesus, how could they possibly contradict him? If they knew that Jesus had either survived his passion, or that a secret substitution had been made, or that they themselves had secretly reburied Jesus' body elsewhere in a secret tomb, then they could not call Paul's bluff without betraying their own deepest secret.[1434] In effect, by claiming to have had a vision of Jesus, Paul was calling *their* bluff. Does this sound too cynical? I don't think so. Christians may be scandalized, or may feign shock and indignation at any suggestion that Paul or anyone else could have had base motives for proclaiming Christ's resurrection from the dead. Some naïve and ill-informed persons might likewise reject any such interpretation as too cynical.

[1434] And we have effectively ruled out the survival and substitution theories above.

But we do find a passage right in the New Testament itself, in the Pauline corpus no less, where we see that Paul or Epaphroditus wrote that there were in fact some who preached Christ for base motives:

15 Some indeed preach the Messiah through envy and strife, but some also through good will.

16 The one preach the Messiah not sincerely, but out of rivalry, thinking to bring *further* trouble to my bonds;

17 but the other out of love, knowing that I am set for the defence of the gospel.

18 For what then? Notwithstanding yet in every way, whether in pretence, or in truth, Christ is preached, and therein I rejoice, and will yet rejoice. (Philippians 1:15-18)

The Greek root-word translated as "envy" above is *phthonon*, and could also be translated as *jealousy, spite, detraction,* or *ill-will*. The Greek root-word translated as "strife" above is *erin*, and could also be translated as *wrangling, contention, debate, variance,* or *quarreling*. The Greek root-word translated as "rivalry" above is *eritheias*, and could also be translated as *contention, intrigue, faction,* or *party spirit*. The Greek root-word translated as "pretence" above is *prophasei*, and could also be translated as *cloke, colour, pretext, hypocrisy,* or *outward show*. So even Paul himself[1435] claimed that there were those even in his own time who had less than pure motives for proclaiming the *kerygma*. So maybe Paul himself had an ulterior motive or motives. He may have grown disillusioned with the legalistic, Pharisaic Judaism that he had grown up with; at the same time he was unwilling to submit to men whom he esteemed as ignorant fishermen from Galilee. Perhaps Paul

---

[1435] Paul himself. If we assume Pauline authorship of the epistle; however, even assuming that Epaphroditus wrote the epistle, or some other person wrote it, the text was written "as if" Paul himself had written it; we are expected to believe that it was Paul himself who was complaining about false preachers of Christ in his own time. This is a pretty strong argument against an appeal to brutal persecution and martyrdom as guaranteeing the supposedly pristine motives of either the Apostles, or any other early disciples of Jesus Christ.

genuinely felt that God had led him in another direction, and he was sincere in his proclamation of Jesus as the Son of God.

In my former work I alluded to a story told by the Rabbis to the effect that Paul was not ethnically Jewish, but Greek. According to the story, he became enamored of the daughter of the high priest, and sought her hand in marriage. But he could only attain this if he became circumcised. After going through the painful procedure, the woman spurned him (or the high priest disallowed the marriage). As a result, Paul turned in vengeance against Judaism, and used the Christian movement to preach against Judaism and circumcision. While the story itself is suspect, one could point to those instances within the Pauline corpus where "Paul" seems to slip up, and inadvertently admit they he is not ethnically Jewish as evidence in favor of the story.[1436]

One other thing is also worth pointing out. Paul claimed to have been a student of the illustrious Gamaliel.[1437] Earlier on in the book of Acts, Gamaliel swayed the *Sanhedrin* against putting the Apostles to death.[1438] He spoke of earlier messianic movements, that had fizzled out. His argument was that, if this new messianic movement was merely a movement of men, it too would die out eventually; but if it was truly of God, then it would be unwise to oppose God. This comparative open-mindedness may have been passed on to his student Saul, who, upon reflection, may have decided that Jesus must be the promised Messiah. This is a distinct possibility, in my opinion. So while a historical Paul may be somewhat of a challenge, he is not an insurmountable obstacle to my theory. Furthermore, it is only in the Corinthian epistles where the author explicitly claims any actual visions of Jesus. Paul may very well have been historical, but maybe he didn't write the Corinthian epistles, and maybe he never claimed to have had a vision of Jesus.

[1436] Alternatively, this same evidence could be interpreted as signifying the pseudonymous nature of the Pauline corpus; this latter interpretation is also further supported by the fact that all the names of those persons named as the writers of those epistles are Greek names.

[1437] Acts 22:3.

[1438] Acts 5:33–40.

Unfortunately, the historicity of Paul is generally linked with the authenticity of the Pauline corpus.[1439] This inevitably leads critical scholars to assume that the Pauline epistles predate the book of Acts. But I see a potential problem in this. I am not necessarily persuaded that the book of Acts postdates any of the Pauline epistles. For one thing, none of those famous epistles of Paul are mentioned anywhere in the book of Acts. Secondly, in strictly *ergonomic* terms, it would have been much more difficult to write a pseudo-historical narrative around a pre-existing corpus of Pauline texts than to use a pre-existing narrative as a literary basis for such texts. This problem is never grappled with, at least in popular critical literature. I suppose one could answer the first objection by stating that the book of Acts was an attempt to harmonize divergent branches of the early Christian movement, and therefore there was less desire to draw attention to writings that evoked schism. But I am not sure if even this argument is very persuasive; after all, Paul is depicted in very heroic terms in Acts, especially in the latter half of the text. Furthermore the Pauline stand on circumcision is upheld in the book.[1440] So such an argument is not particularly persuasive. As far as the second objection is concerned, it is unanswerable.[1441] And such observations are more congenial to a *chimerical* rather than historical Paul. On the other hand, the dichotomy between Paul's reported actions and his *purported* words functions as evidence in favor of his historicity. The discrepancy between Acts and Galatians is further evidence. But is it proof? That is a matter of interpretation. I refuse to pontificate; it is up to the reader to decide. But one advantage of my theory is that it does not require Paul to be either historical or *chimerical;* either way the termination theory vis-à-vis Jesus Christ is left intact.

For the sake of completeness I would like to offer an anacdote or two from my own personal experience, to help illuminate this thorny question and conundrum. While I was a college student, we had a speaker from the Unification Church address our philosophy class.

[1439] Or rather with some core portion thereof, such as Galatians, Romans, Ephesians, Philippians, Colossians, I Corinthians, II Corinthians, and possibly the Thessalonian epistles or Hebrews.

[1440] Acts 15:1-31; 21:21-25.

[1441] i.e., there is no actual reason that can be offered against my argument. One could nevertheless acknowledge the legitimacy of the argument, but still maintain the primacy of the Pauline corpus on other grounds.

After the talk, I had a private conversation with the man. He told me that Jesus had appeared to him in a vision, and Jesus told him he was on the right path. Was the man telling me the truth? I have no way of knowing the answer to that. Does he deserve any less of a "benefit of the doubt" than any of the Apostles? I was also on a Christian retreat while I was a college student and a woman there also told me she'd had a vision of Jesus. Does she deserve more or less credibility than the man from the Unification Church? Maybe these people both told me the truth. But I cannot base my life on other people's experiences, but only on my own. Should we give greater credence to people who lived in ancient times? Why? They cannot be interviewed, or questioned about their experiences. But many people within contemporary times have had near-death experiences, lucid dreams, and out-of-body experiences.

Finally, we should be brave enough to consider the possibility that Paul was historical and he actually had a vision of Jesus. Of course this is not a concession to the absurd resurrection theory of the Christians; but it is expanding the scope of our inquiry to include the paranormal. We have already spoken of astral projection. Assuming that Jesus truly died on the cross, he still would have been alive in his astral body. It is just barely possible that Jesus appeared to the Apostles and to Paul in his astral body. We must be careful here, however; we have already seen that the various Gospel accounts of the post-passion appearances of Christ are wildly contradictory to one another. Therefore an appeal to astral visions of Jesus should not be construed as a vindication or explanation of those wildly contradictory accounts. This is a very important point, and should be very strongly emphasized. Yet the out-of-body phenomenon implies some form of life after death. The same is true of the near-death phenomenon. Therefore it should not be too shocking to consider the possibility that Jesus appeared in his astral body to his disciples, and to Saul on the road to Damascus. However I want to be very clear that I by no means am insisting upon this interpretation, nor do I by any means make my theory hinge upon this speculation. It is offered as food for thought. Hopefully it will be regarded by intelligent readers as a refreshing alternative to the ubiquitous materialism evident in various treatises of biblical criticism. So much for the apostle Paul.

Nicodemus

Nicodemus is worth discussing, albeit briefly. In my former work[1442] I argued that, most likely, Nicodemus was a merely invented character. While I do not insist upon this interpretation herein, I still feel that the evidence is reasonably strong against any presumed historicity of Nicodemus.

Nicodemus is only mentioned in the Gospel of John. The Synoptic Gospels and the rest of the New Testament say nothing of him. This creates a dark cloud of suspicion around him, since he is mentioned in John as the man who helped Joseph of Arimathaea bury Jesus.[1443] This places Nicodemus in a comparatively important role; therefore it is suspicious that the three Synoptic Evangelists do not mention him. It is not a particularly credible argument that his name was omitted from the earlier Gospels in order to protect him; even the earliest Gospel was probably written at least thirty to forty years after the time of Christ's passion. Most likely, by that time Nicodemus would already have been deceased.[1444] So the argument that he was being protected through the silence of the Synoptic Evangelists does not hold up to scrutiny. Furthermore why would it have been more necessary

---

[1442] JESUS 100 B.C.

[1443] John 19:38–42.

[1444] This is especially likely, considering he was probably at least middle-aged, if not somewhat elderly, being a member of the *Sanhedrin*.

to protect him, rather than Joseph of Arimathaea? If the mere act of burying Jesus was to be considered treason by the *Sanhedrin,* then why would Mark, Matthew, and Luke endanger him by pointing him out as the man who buried Jesus? But there is no real reason to suppose that it was construed as an act of teason or betrayal to bury Jesus. Devout Jews would often feel duty-bound to bury a fellow Jew, no matter how wayward. Furthermore, it was only Matthew and John who identified Joseph as a disciple of Jesus. As far as Mark and Luke were concerned, Joseph of Arimathaea was just a righteous man who happened to be on the *Sanhedrin.* And we have seen above that in this instance, the account of Mark and Luke is more believable than that of John or Matthew. This is confirmed by the scriptural evidence itself. And this is an important point. We will return to this later.

Nicodemus is mentioned only two other times in John's Gospel; we read of him speaking in defence of Jesus in the midst of the *Sanhedrin,*[1445] and also when he came secretly to Jesus at night.[1446] The most significant passage is the one in which Nicodemus is introduced to the reader for the first time. The reason why is because in response to Nicodemus' inquiry, Jesus himself introduces a new, sectarian, antinomian doctrine of salvation.[1447] This is highly significant. The new teaching would have been credible as an esotericism, except for the fact that John cannot contain himself, and has Jesus proclaim this novel teaching to all and sundry in his Gospel.[1448] So this reveals Nicodemus as merely a literary foil for introducing this new sectarian teaching. This interpretation is confirmed by the book of Revelation, in which the deeds and teachings of the Nicolaitans is condemned by the risen Jesus.[1449] As I pointed out in my earlier work, the Greek word *Nikolaitans* is derived from *Nikolaos,* which also has the same meaning as *Nikodemos. Nikodemos* and *Nikolaos* both have essential meanings of "victory over the people" or "conquest of the people". The Greek word *demos* means "people" and is related to our words *democracy, demographics, demonstration,* etc. The Greek word *laos* also means "people" and is also reflected in such words as

---

[1445] John 7:50-51.

[1446] John 3:1-2.

[1447] John 3:3-21.

[1448] John 6:29; 10:1-29.

[1449] Revelation 2:6,15.

laity, lay person, lay minister, layman. Nikos means *victory* or *conquest,* or by extension, *victor* or *conqueror.* I argued in my former work that most likely the occurrence of the word in Revelation was a code to identify the antinomian teaching associated with the Gospel of John and the Pauline corpus. Most likely, the Apokalypse was written as a curative against the leaven of the new antinomian teaching.[1450] This evidence suggests that Nicodemus was merely an invented character. Furthermore we have seen above that John's characterization of Joseph of Arimathaea as a "secret" disciple of Jesus was misleading at best, or a fabrication at worst. So it is doubtful that Nicodemus ever existed.

On the other hand, it is not necessary to rule out the historicity of Nicodemus in order to maintain the termination theory. Furthermore Joseph of Arimathaea most likely would have needed help from some other men to take Jesus' body down from the cross. So assuming that Nicodemus did actually exist, he may have been one of those other men.[1451] But I want to reiterate that even assuming that Nicodemus truly existed, and also helped Joseph take the body of Jesus down from the cross, and bury him, this does not prove that they were somehow "secret" disciples of Jesus. They were unknown to the female disciples of Jesus. So do not be led astray by religious artwork. This is important.

[1450] Although the Apokalypse does have a sectarian teaching and also acknowledges the blood redemption through Jesus Christ; cf Revelation 5:9; 7:14.

[1451] But even assuming that Joseph was helped by Nicodemus, as John 19:38–42 says, these two men would still probably have needed help from at least two other, younger, stronger, men.

The Empty Tomb:
Sign or No Sign?

I n the Gospel of Matthew, a statement is attributed to Jesus that
is generally understood to be a reference to the empty tomb as
the single great "sign" given to his generation that he was and is the
Messiah. The context of the passage is one in which Jesus is asked to
perform a sign by the Pharisees. Jesus answers them, saying: "An evil
and adulterous generation seeks a sign, but there shall be no sign given
to it, except the sign of Jonah the prophet; for as Jonah was three days
and three nights in the whale's belly, so shall the Son of man be three
days and three nights in the heart of the earth."[1452] The presumed
"sign" that Jesus was supposedly referring to must have been that of
the empty tomb, in which he had been buried, after his crucifixion.
But there are two very important observations to be made upon this.
First is the fact that, this statement virtually proves that Jesus never
performed any miracles, as he is supposed to have done, according
to the Gospels. The reason why is because a mere empty tomb, in
which Christ's body was supposedly buried, and simultaneous claims
by devout disciples that Christ appeared to them alive again, is hardly
much in the way of evidence. It certainly pales in comparison to actual
healings of lepers, the lame, the paralyzed, the blind, the deaf, the

---

[1452] Matthew 12:39–40 cf Mt 16:4; Luke 11:29–30.

dumb, the insane, the demon possessed, raising the dead, multiplying fish and bread, turning water into wine, knowing the secret thoughts of men, walking on water, or any of the other miracles that Christ allegedly performed. If these miracles had truly taken place, they would have constituted far greater and more direct proof of Jesus' claim to being the long-awaited Messiah than a mere empty tomb. Christians might say that the resurrection itself was the "sign of Jonah" but the resurrection is merely an inference one could draw from the fact of an empty tomb, unless the risen Christ had appeared to all the people in Jerusalem, which did not happen. People raised from the dead, healed of various diseases, blind men who can now see, deaf men who can now hear, lepers who have been cured of leprosy, paralyzed men who can now walk, make far better witnesses to the messianic claims of Jesus than a mere empty tomb. There is literally no comparison. Had these miracles truly occurred, we would have had a multitude of then-living witnesses who could have, should have, and would have testified to the miraculous power of Jesus Christ. But of course oftentimes in the Gospels we read that Jesus gave the strange admonition to these beneficiaries of his cures to "tell no man" of what he had done. The sole exception that springs to mind is that of the Gadarene demoniac.[1453] But the region was conveniently in Gentile territory; nobody in Galilee, Judaea, or Samaria ever testified to having been healed by Jesus.

The second observation is equally important, if not more so. In the parallel verse in Mark, Jesus says that <u>no sign</u> shall be granted to his generation:

12 And he sighed deeply in his spirit, and said, Why does this generation seek after a sign? Truly I say to you, no sign shall be given to this generation. (Mark 8:12)

In the verse from Mark there is no mention of the supposed "sign of Jonah" that we read of in Matthew and Luke. The "sign of Jonah" was apparently invented by the Evangelist Matthew. This is highly significant because it means that the empty tomb was not regarded as a sign by Mark. The empty tomb was a fact, but not a sign. We have

---

[1453] Mk 5:1-20 cf Lk 8:26-39 cp Mt 8:28-34. In Matthew, Jesus does not tell the man to testify to his deliverance; this could <u>also</u> be interpreted as evincing the priority of Matthew.

the right to say that the empty tomb was a fact, unless we suppose that the account that the women observed where Joseph of Arimathaea buried Jesus was a lie.[1454] But the circumstances of the case argue strongly against this supposition; there would have been far less utility in inventing such a lie than in remaing silent about something that could be strongly urged against the story narrated. In other words, the fact that the female disciples saw the tomb in which Jesus had been buried is a concession to the possibility that the disciples *could have* removed the body of Jesus from the tomb, and then have claimed that he was risen from the dead. It would have been better if Matthew had remained silent about this, since if skeptics claimed that the disciples removed Christ's body from the tomb, the disciples[1455] could claim that the location of the tomb was unknown to any of the disciples, and therefore they could not have removed Christ's body. According to Mark, Joseph of Arimathaea was a member of the Jewish council or *Sanhedrin,* and so if the Apostles had been making false claims that Jesus had risen from the dead in his carnal, fleshly body, then it would have been easy enough for Joseph and other men of the council to refute such claims by producing the body of Jesus from the tomb, had the location of the tomb itself been such a closely-guarded secret that none of Christ's disciples had known exactly where it was. As such, an admission that the women saw where Jesus had been buried can safely be regarded as a "fossil" passage inasmuch as the contrary supposition that it was a lie would have created this obvious dilemma for the disciples. The only potential utility of the claim being a fabrication was to provide yet another gratuitous "fulfillment" of supposedly messianic prophecy.[1456] Yet in comparative terms it would have been much more potentially damaging to fabricate a story that female disciples (or any disciples of Jesus) saw the actual location of the tomb, if that had not been true. The reason why has been stated

---

[1454] Mark 15:47 cf Matthew 27:61; Luke 23:55.

[1455] Or later followers of the Jesus movement.

[1456] i.e., Isaiah 53:9, "And he made his grave with the wicked, and the rich in his death; because he had done no violence, neither *was any* deceit in his mouth." The latter portion of the verse supposedly pointing to Joseph's sympathy, empathy, and admiration for Jesus, and hence his greater willingness to bury him in his own tomb. The reference to the "wicked" is generally not attributed to Joseph of Arimathaea, but to the unrepentant thief.

above; because the fact that the location of the tomb had been known could be used as evidence *against* the Apostles' claims of Christ's resurrection: because it could be objected that the Apostles or other disciples simply removed Jesus' body from the tomb. So we can clearly see that the report that the women had seen where Joseph buried Jesus was an admission and a concession on Matthew's part, albeit possibly unwittingly. And in this he was followed by Mark and Luke, but not by John, who remains silent about this triple admission. Yet even in John's text the fact that Mary Magdalene knew the location of the tomb is taken for granted; it was impossible for John to undo what three other prominent Evangelists before him had already done. The fact that the location of the tomb was known to the disciples also implies that it could have, should have, and would have become a site of pilgrimage to followers of the nascent messianic movement, had Jesus' body still been buried therein. However this never happened.[1457] So we can safely conclude that the empty tomb was a fact. The empty tomb was a fact, but it was not commonly regarded as a sign, even by the earliest Christians themselves.[1458]

Mark does not cite the empty tomb as a sign because it is merely a negative form of evidence. The absence of a corpse from a tomb does not prove a miraculous resurrection from the dead. It does not even come close to proving it. The most natural supposition in such a case is simply that the body had been been removed, and reburied elsewhere. If one exhumes the grave of some long dead person, only to discover that the coffin is empty, does that mean that the person is a vampire? Is that the simplest and most logical explanation? I don't think so.

But it behooves us to be more certain as to exactly what Mark did testify to in his Gospel. If the last twelve verses of Mark's Gospel are spurious, as critical Bible scholars claim, then there is no narrated post-passion appearance by Jesus in Mark's Gospel. Yet, unless we suppose

---

[1457] There is no proof that the contemporary site known as the Holy Sepulchre is really the tomb where Jesus was buried by Joseph of Arimathaea. However the fact that it is a site of pilgrimage by thousands and even millions of Christians only serves to prove the point made above about the original tomb.

[1458] The fact that Mark's Gospel does not so regard it confirms this. Neither is there any such appeal made anywhere in the Pauline corpus, or in any other epistles. Neither does the Gospel of John speak of the so-called "Sign of Jonah".

that Mark wrote his text as a coded anti-Gospel, then it is reasonable to infer that Mark intended us to interpret the evidence as pointing to Christ's resurrection from the dead. According to his account, three women[1459] went to the tomb to anoint Christ's body.[1460] They find that the stone blocking the entrance to the tomb had been moved, and inside the tomb a messenger described as a young man dressed in a long white garment sitting down, who tells them that Jesus was risen, and will meet the disciples in Galilee.[1461] Notably the young man does not state explicitly that Jesus had died; only that he had been crucified, but was no longer present in the tomb.[1462] After this, the women quickly leave the tomb, saying nothing to anyone.[1463] And here the Gospel of Mark ends, according to the critical scholars. At first blush it is almost impossible to believe that the Evangelist would have written such a strange text with such a strange ending; if the critical scholars are correct about the original form of Mark's Gospel, then we have a literary paradox therein. This is something that is hardly ever addressed by such scholars. This is a fatal weakness to their theory, and their theories in general; they never offer any explanation or justification for their postulates, which they dogmatically proclaim, as if from Mount Olympus. It is almost unthinkable that anyone would write a text without a proper ending, as Mark apparently has done, if we acquiesce to the position of the critical scholars. At the very least such a strange ending would seem to require a valid explanation. We should explore the pros and cons of the positions regarding the last twelve verses of Mark. Critical scholars have been somewhat economical with the facts. But then again so have fundamentalists.

The last twelve verses of Mark are as follows:

9   Now when *Christ* was risen, early on the first of the week, he appeared first to Mary the Magdalene, out of whom he had cast seven demons.

[1459] Mary Magdalene, Mary the *mother* of James, and Salome. Mary the *mother* of James might possibly refer to Christ's own mother; cf Mk 6:3.

[1460] Mark 16:1.

[1461] Mark 16:4–7.

[1462] This could be interpreted as evidence in favor of the survival theory. But see objections to that theory enumerated above.

[1463] Mark 16:8.

10 She went and told them that had been with him, as they mourned and wept.

11 But they, when they heard that he was alive, and had been seen by her, did not believe.

12 After that he appeared in another form to two of them as they walked and went into the country.

13 They went and told the rest, but neither did they believe them.[1464]

14 Afterwards he appeared to the eleven as they sat eating, and reproved them for their unbelief and hardness of heart, since they believed not them that had seen him after he was risen.

15 And he said to them, Go into all the word, and proclaim the gospel to every creature.

16 He that believes and is baptized shall be saved; but he that believes not shall be condemned.

17 And these signs shall follow those that believe: in my name they shall cast out demons, they shall speak with new tongues,

18 they shall take up serpents; and if they drink any deadly thing, it shall not harm them; they shall lay their hands on the sick, and they will recover.

19 So then after the Lord Jesus had spoken to them, he was received up into the heaven, and sat at the right hand of God.

20 But they went out, preaching everywhere, the Lord confirming the word with signs following. (Mark 16:9-20)

This longer, more traditional ending of Mark's Gospel is generally regarded as spurious by critical biblical scholars. In fact the Deutsche Bibelgesellschaft Stuttgart goes so far as to say that the passage is "known" not to be part of the original Gospel. What gives them the

---

[1464] This contradicts Luke's account; cp Luke 24:33-35.

confidence of such insufferable and incurable arrogance I do not know. It is nothing but unbridled *hubris,* as far as I can see. At the very least they should be honest about the complete state of the evidence, and they are not.[1465] The excision of Mark 16:9-20 is "justified" by an appeal to the two oldest Greek manuscripts, which omit the verses. But there is a definite problem here, since the evidence from those two manuscripts also proves that the section in question definitely predated those manuscripts. In the Codex Vaticanus, while the last twelve verses of Mark are absent from Mark's Gospel, there is an empty space at the end of Mark's Gospel just large enough for those twelve verses. In the Codex Sinaiticus, while the last twelve verses are missing from Mark's Gospel, the letters strangely expand towards the end of Mark's Gospel; once again it is just enough space for the missing twelve verses. So this evidence proves that the last twelve verses predated those two manuscripts.[1466] Critical biblical scholars never share this information with their students, or with uninformed laymen. But this evidence is strongly in favor of the supposition that the last twelve verses were an original part of Mark's Gospel. The other piece of evidence is the problem of having a seemingly "unfinished" Gospel. But all of the other evidence is against the authenticity of the last twelve verses, in my opinion. Some early translations of Mark also omit the last twelve verses.

Some critical scholars postulate that the original ending somehow became lost. But this is virtually impossible and unthinkable; it is not credible that not even one surviving copy of Mark would have retained the original ending, had it been different from either of those proposed.[1467]

[1465] I absolutely stand by this statement, since the Nestle-Aland omits any reference to the fact that the overwhelming majority of Greek manuscripts contain the reference to "Daniel the prophet" in Mark 13:14. In the Nestle-Aland, not only is the reference to Daniel the prophet excluded from the text, but there is also no reference to this, even in the critical apparatus. This proves dishonesty.

[1466] Green., op. cit., pg.vii. However this does not prove that those last twelve verses were an original part of Mark's Gospel. See further discussion.

[1467] In the interest of completeness, there is a shorter ending to Mark's Gospel, added after Mark 16:8. It is simply "And they reported all the instructions briefly to Peter's companions. Afterwards Jesus himself, through them, sent forth from the east to the west the sacred and imperishable proclamation

Even though the last twelve verses predate Codices Sinaiticus and Vaticanus, there presumably was a legitimate reason why they were removed from texts of Mark. On textual grounds, we can see that the last twelve verses are distinct from the general body of Mark in a number of significant respects. First of all, the appeal to a sectarian, antinomian scheme of soteriology in Mark 16:16 is contrary to what Jesus taught in Mark 10:17-19.[1468] The reference to signs in Mark 16:17-18 is contrary to what Jesus said in Mark 8:12.[1469] The reference to Mary Magdalene having seven demons cast out of her is strange, since none of the three earlier references to her in Mark contain this detail.[1470] The "new tongues" are otherwise only found in the book of Acts and Corinthians, and the reference to taking up serpents might possibly refer to the incident of the viper attacking Paul in Acts 28:3-6. Aside from these observations is the fact that between verse eight and verse nine there is a break in the flow of the narrative; in verse 8 three women flee from the tomb in fear, saying nothing. The narrative is broken at that point; in the very next verse, we are told simply that Jesus first appeared to Mary Magdalene. Nothing is said of the other two women. This was apparently intended to harmonize with John's account. The sectarian soteriology is a key that

---

of eternal salvation." There is also a passage known as the Freer Logion, which is inserted between Mark 16:14 and 16:15. It is extant only in one ancient codex, namely Codex Washingtonensis. It reads as follows: "The eleven excused themselves, saying, This age of lawlessness and unbelief is controlled by Satan, who by means of unclean spirits, does not allow the truth to be known. So reveal your righteousness now" they said to Christ. Christ replied to them, The measure of the years of Satan's power is filled up, but other fearful things draw near to those for whom I was delivered to death for their sin, that they might repent and sin no more that they might inherit the imperishable spiritual glory of righteousness in heaven." The Washington Codex is the Gospel Codex that Lee Woodard claims dates to the first century. Most critical scholars date the Codex to the fourth or fifth century. I personally believe that it may date to the late second century.

[1468] While the discrepancy can be resolved by an appeal to dispensationalism, this is a further requirement; in simple terms, the two statements contradict one another.

[1469] i.e., that no sign would be granted to his generation.

[1470] Mark 15:40,47; 16:1. The first reference to these seven demons occurs in Luke 8:2, where Mary Magdalene is first introduced in Luke's Gospel. This suggests that Mark 16:9-20 was written by another hand.

the last twelve verses of Mark are almost certainly spurious. One could argue that Mark recorded an independent tradition. This is at least possible, but we must acknowledge the complete evidence. The two oldest Georgian manuscripts of Mark omit the last twelve verses. One hundred Armenian manuscripts of Mark omit the last twelve verses. I am uncertain as to whether any Coptic, Syriac, or Latin manuscripts of Mark omit the last twelve verses.[1471] However I feel that it is safe to assume the contrary, since we would most likely be informed of it by the lap-dogs of academic orthodoxy.[1472]

But against all this evidence remains the single strongest objection; namely, that it almost unthinkable that Mark would have written his Gospel with what seems for all the world like an incomplete ending. For a long time I considered this an unanswerable objection against the supposition that the last twelve verses are spurious. One possible solution is that Mark died of a heart attack immediately after writing verse eight of chapter sixteen. Or maybe he was struck by lightning. While such things are possible, such an inauspicious circumstance as either of these things would seem to be gambling most recklessly with the probabilities of the case. It would be absurd to postulate such an extreme improbability[1473] to account for the evidence. It makes any such suggestion itself outrageously improbable.[1474] It is easier to suppose either that Mark wrote the last twelve verses despite the evidence to the contrary, or that he did not, even though we are left with a literary paradox of why the Evangelist wrote his Gospel without a more seemingly proper ending.

Fortunately I have found a literary precedent within Greek literature. I am referring to the *Critias* by Plato. The *Critias* ends

---

[1471] The question of the authenticity of the last twelve verses of Mark is not merely academic; in some parts of the Bible belt, some people handle snakes and drink poison, on the basis of those verses. Thus they are risking their lives as a testimony to their faith.

[1472] Critical scholars themselves remaining arrogantly aloof and silent in their towering Mount Olympus.

[1473] i.e., of either being struck by lightning, or having a fatal heart attack, at the precise moment when he had finished writing verse eight of chapter sixteen. Either circumstance would be incalculably improbable, and would tax the laws of statistical probability. It verges on the preternatural, and therefore is not congenial in critical-historical terms.

[1474] Although still possible, strictly speaking.

with a gathering of the Gods on Mount Olympus, and Zeus is about to give a speech. But then the text abruptly ends. Plato apparently deliberately wrote the *Critias* in just that way, for whatever unknown reason. Perhaps it was for dramatic effect. The same thing is at least *possible* in the case of Mark. But even the shorter ending to Mark leaves no appeal to the empty tomb as a sign of Christ's resurrection. The reference to the disciples seeing Jesus in Galilee in Mark 16:7 implies that the disciples really did see Jesus, according to Mark's text, even without the last twelve verses. So even without the last twelve verses, Mark's Gospel still offers literary testimony to the resurrection of Jesus. Stated otherwise, Mark conveys a tradition that Jesus did in fact appear alive again to his disciples in Galilee.[1475] This in turn implies that the earliest claims of Christ's resurrection were made in Galilee, rather than Jerusalem.[1476] Perhaps Mark omitted any written account of Jesus' appearance to his Apostles because he felt that any written version of such a momentous event would be anticlimactic. Perhaps it was a form of esotericism. But whatever reason or explanation that we can imagine for why Mark would have written his Gospel without a more proper ending, it will still remain unsatisfying to Christians and others as well. If we assume that the last twelve verses of Mark are pseudonymous then Mark's Gospel would have a very suspicious omission. So the bare possibility that Mark actually did write those last twelve verses cannot be absolutely ruled out, in my opinion. Either assumption leaves the termination theory intact. Regardless of whether one esteems the last twelve verses of Mark as genuine or not, in either case the Evangelist did not appeal to the empty tomb as a sign of Christ's resurrection. Whether or no the "sign of Jonah" passages were an original part of the original Hebrew text of Matthew must remain an unknown question. If so, then this makes Mark's "no sign" statement by Jesus that much more pungent, and increases the probability that Mark had been written as a coded anti-Gospel. As such, it may very well have been the case that the Evangelist ended his narrative so abruptly, without any actual appearance by Jesus, as an implicit clue that the resurrection was a hoax. He wanted us to "read between the lines" as it were.

[1475] In fact without the last twelve verses, Mark's Gospel is more amenable to an oral tradition of a post-passion appearance more similar to what is otherwise found in Matthew.

[1476] As reported in Acts, and implied in Luke and John.

But I have neither the time nor the space to provide sufficient evidence to support my theory vis-à-vis Mark as a literary Trojan Horse and a coded anti-Gospel. That theme would require a book in itself. If we assume the absence of the last twelve verses in the original of *Mark,* then this is most congenial to such a theory. But the one remaining problem to this supposition is the fact that, if one carefully reads the last twelve verses, despite the incongruities noted immediately above, there is a strange and almost unaccountable *congruity* in those verses: they depict the eleven remaining Apostles as being very weak in faith, and generally in a very negative light, just as we also read in the body of Mark's text. Luke did not depict the Apostles as being so unbelieving. So, this particular congruity suggests that possibly the last twelve verses might be authentic. However, considered holistically, the weight of the evidence suggests the contrary. What is ironic is that this notable congruity is not the kind of thing that, in the very nature of the case, is likely to ever be pointed out by evangelicals or fundamentalists.

But we have a much different situation with the Gospels of Matthew and Luke. In fact, Matthew elevated the empty tomb to being the single greatest sign, and even the "only" sign, that Jesus was the Son of man. In this we see desperation; people had begun to suspect the true circumstances surrounding Jesus Christ's burial and reburial. Matthew tried clumsily to squelch such rumors by inventing an absurd story about Roman soldiers guarding the tomb. But Mark, Luke and John omit any mention of soldiers guarding the tomb. It is virtually unthinkable that they would have omitted this essential detail, had it been true.

But the reburial theory[1477] may not have been the first alternative theory[1478] to arise in response to the Apostles' claims of Christ's resurrection. There is a slight hint that possibly a survival theory preceded suspicions of a secret reburial, and this is found in the original Greek of Mark's Gospel.[1479] The relevant passage is as follows:

[1477] Perhaps a more apt name for the termination theory. I now generally call it the "Suffering Servant" theory.

[1478] Most likely these theories did not originate as formal theories *per se,* but rather as rumors and suspicions.

[1479] Although it is debatable as to whether the reading in question was the original reading, or a later reading. In either case the argument still stands.

42 And now when evening had come, because it was the preparation, that is, the day before the Sabbath,

43 Joseph of Arimathaea, an honorable counsellor, who also waited for the kingdom of God, came, and boldy went in to Pilate, asking for the body of Jesus.

44 But Pilate marveled that he was already dead; and calling the centurion, he asked whether he had already died.

45 And when he knew from the centurion, he gave the corpse to Joseph. (Mark 15:42-45)

In the original Greek of Mark 15:43, the word I have translated as "body" is *soma,* the common Greek word for body.[1480] But in Mark 15:45, the Greek word I have translated as "corpse" is *ptoma,* which is the Greek word for corpse or dead body. There is some question in respect to the original reading, however, since the majority of Greek manuscripts read *soma* in Mark 15:45, rather than *ptoma.* Not only that, but some few Greek manuscripts read *ptoma* in Mark 15:43.[1481] According to sound textual theory, the majority text is more likely to conserve the original reading, all other things being equal. However as we have seen above, not all other things are always equal, when it comes to the biblical text. But even if the original reading of the text was *soma* rather than *ptoma* in verse 45,[1482] the following point still stands. We must remember that the literary proclamation of the gospel was preceded by an oral proclamation. Therefore the first responses to the message would have been not to the written form of the message, but to that form of it proclaimed by the Apostles and other early disciples. By using the word *ptoma* in Mark 15:45, the Evangelist sought to squelch rumors that Jesus had survived his passion. He wanted to emphasize that the body of Jesus was definitely a dead body when it was handed over to Joseph of Arimathaea. Alternatively, if Mark had used *soma* in Mark 15:45, and it was later changed by some

---

[1480] As in *psycho-somatic* illness.

[1481] Nestle-Aland., op. cit., pg. 146; critical apparatus.

[1482] Which was afterwards corrected back to *soma* in the majority of manuscripts.

anonymous scribe to *ptoma,* then the same point holds, but in respect to the scribe in question. He sought to stifle rumors that Jesus may have survived his crucifixion. But the whole passage looks as if the point was being made that Jesus was definitely already dead; therefore *ptoma* seems more justified as the original reading.[1483]

We should bear in mind that Mark was not one of the twelve Apostles; it is possible that he was numbered among the earliest disciples, but this is unproven. It is uncertain whether the Evangelist Mark is purported to be either John Mark, the associate of Paul and cousin of Barnabas,[1484] or the biological son of the Apostle Peter.[1485] Some have sought to identify Mark the Evangelist with the young man mentioned in Mark 14:51-52 and/or Mark 16:5-7. These are all interesting speculations, but there is no way to make a clear determination. Furthermore the literary evidence that points to Mark having been written in the second century precludes any supposition that Mark was any of these men.[1486] Mark only "knew" what he was told, and possibly from third and fourth-hand sources.

Significantly, the empty tomb, although a fact, was not a sign as far as Mark was concerned. He was apparently persuaded of a tradition that Jesus had appeared alive again to his Apostles in Galilee. As to why Mark omitted any narrative of this in his Gospel,[1487] this remains a mystery but the most likely explanation that springs to mind is esotericism. Mark wrote that Jesus always taught the common people exclusively in parables, and only interpreted the parables privately to his own Apostles.[1488] Furthermore Mark's Gospel frequently has Jesus

---

[1483] But then this interpretation requires an explanation for how and why *ptoma* was changed to *soma* in later texts. The most likely explanation that springs to mind is that some scribes may have felt that the use of the word *ptoma* in relation to Christ's body was disrespectful.

[1484] Colossians 4:10.

[1485] I Peter 5:13 cf Mk 1:30.

[1486] But a person would have to judge the relative weight of the evidence in both directions. I do not consider it altogether unreasonable that Mark may have been written in the first century.

[1487] I.e., assuming that the last twelve verses of Mark are spurious, as critical scholars allege.

[1488] Mark 4:33-34.

urging secrecy upon recipients of his cures.[1489] Furthermore when Peter privately professes his faith in Jesus as the Messiah, Jesus orders the Apostles to tell no man of his messianic identity.[1490] Jesus also tells his Apostles that to them alone is granted the knowledge of the mystery of the kingdom of God.[1491] So it ought not to surprise us too much if the details of the post-passion narrative, and especially the post-passion teachings of Jesus would have been veiled in silence by the Evangelist. But aside from the possibility of esotericism, there also remains the possibility that Mark was written as a coded anti-Gospel, or heretic Gospel. Either that, or his text had been sabotaged by some disgruntled scribe; possibly a slave.

[1489] Mark 1:44; 3:12; 5:43; 7:36; cf 9:30.

[1490] Mark 8:30.

[1491] Mark 4:11-12; cf Isaiah 6:9-10.

Joseph of Arimathaea

Joseph of Arimathaea is a key character in our inquiry, since he is the man who actually buried Jesus.[1492] We have seen above that the accounts of Joseph in John and Matthew are comparatively unreliable, since they portray him as a disciple of Jesus, or even as a "secret" disciple. By contrast, Mark and Luke both portray Joseph as a righteous man who happened to be a member of the *Sanhedrin*. This latter interpretation is more in accord with common sense. Furthermore it also accords more closely to what we find narrated in the Toldoth Yeshu, that says that it was the "wise men" who buried Jesus. In fact, had Joseph been a disciple of Jesus, secretly or otherwise, then this would have been a suspicious circumstance in relation to later claims of Jesus' resurrection. Joseph instead appears to have been a relatively neutral party in respect to Jesus; he was neither an open enemy nor a mesmerized disciple. He was merely a righteous Jew who sought to bury a fellow Jew before the Sabbath. At least this seems to be the most reasonable interpretation, in my opnion. We can also discern that Joseph was not a disciple of Jesus by virtue of the fact that he was unknown to the female disciples. And here I must strongly emphasize the importance of not being led astray by religious art. There are many paintings, sculptures, statues, and stained-glass artworks that depict women together with men with the dead body

---

[1492] Mk 15:42-46; Mt 27:57-60; Lk 23:50-53; Jn 19:38-42.

of Jesus, after he had been taken down from the cross. But it is very important to realise that all this artwork is completely contrary to what we read in the Synoptic Gospels.[1493] The very things that are written reveal, in a very inadvertent and unsolicited way, that the women did not know Joseph of Arimathaea personally, nor did he know them. After the narrative of Joseph burying the body of Jesus, the very next verse says "But Mary the Magdalene and Mary the *mother of* Joses beheld where he was laid."[1494] The other two Synoptic Gospels also confirm what is written in Mark in this respect; in Matthew we read "But there was Mary the Magdalene, and the other Mary, sitting over against the sepulchre."[1495] And Luke also confirms what is written in Mark and Matthew; "But the women also, who came with him from Galilee, followed after, and beheld the sepulchre, and how his body was laid."[1496] This manner of speaking would have been strange and unwarranted if Joseph and these women recognized each other as Jesus' disciples. Instead, the women would have been together with Joseph and the other men helping him, anointing Christ's body with spices and ointments, and mourning and lamenting, in the tomb. But this is not what we read at all. Furthermore I have rendered the Greek more accurately than the King James translators, who have begun each of the three verses with "and" rather than "but". But in the original Greek, the proper Greek word for but, namely *de,* occurs, rather than *kai,* the proper Greek word for "and." This even more strongly illustrates the contrast of circumstances between what is first narrated of Joseph of Arimathaea, and then of the women. This is an important point. It may seem insignificant, but it really is quite significant. For Matthew to claim Joseph as a disciple of Jesus was a massive blunder on his part. Perhaps this was the real reason why John claimed that Joseph had kept his discipleship to Jesus a secret.[1497] For all

---

[1493] And as we have seen above, the Synoptic Gospels definitely predate the Gospel of John.

[1494] Mark 15:47; cf Matthew 27:61; Luke 23:55.

[1495] Matthew 27:61.

[1496] Luke 23:55.

[1497] John 19:38. But this presupposes that Joseph kept his discipleship a secret, not only from the men on the *Sanhedrin,* but also from the female disciples as well.

that, John only adds Nicodemus to the burial party.[1498] John remains completely silent about the women. This betrays a guilty conscience on his part, or at least the fact that he realized how potentially damaging the testimony of the three earlier Gospels was in regard to how the women spied out the sepulchre, unbeknownst to Joseph of Arimathaea, and whoever may have been helping him.[1499] So while John remains silent about the women spying out the location of the tomb, he nevertheless has Mary Magdalene visiting the tomb two days later.[1500] Not only that, but Peter and John also already know the location of the tomb.[1501] This in itself is suspicious; how could Peter and John already have known the location of the tomb, unless the women[1502] showed the Apostles where the actual tomb was? So despite the silence of John about the women, he still admits by default that they must have spied out the location of the tomb, as recorded in the three earlier Gospels. Furthermore the reader of John's text must take it as understood that, for whatever reason, Peter and John both already know the location of the tomb where Jesus had been buried.

My most important point about Joseph of Arimathaea is that he was unknown to the women, and the women were not known to him either. This is very important to remember. It is key. So do not be led astray by religious artwork. Another example of unbiblical religious artwork is Michelangelo's famous sculpture of David. Michelangelo depicted David as a beardless youth; however, in the Bible David is said to have had a beard, even as a young man.[1503] I am not seeking to in any way detract from the aesthetic appreciation of such noble works of art, but what I am pointing out is that in terms of an historical inquiry it is important not to be led astray by artwork executed many centuries or millennia after the fact, rather than the earliest historical documents that we possess.

[1498] John 19:39–42.

[1499] As mentioned elsewhere above, most likely Joseph would have needed help from other men taking the body of Jesus down from the cross, and also moving the body to the tomb. Nicodemus may have been one of these men, assuming he actually existed.

[1500] John 20:1.

[1501] John 20:2–10.

[1502] Or at least one of them.

[1503] I Samuel 21:12–13.

One final point about Joseph of Arimathaea should be cleared up. Some sources have claimed that Joseph of Arimathaea was either the brother or uncle of Jesus, and that he owned a tin mine in England, where he took Jesus as a boy. But there is absolutely no legitimate evidence that any of this is true. These are merely legends, invented in the wake of Christianity's rise as an empire-spanning religion. Naturally every region that later became predominantly Christian would want to boast of some association with some saint or key figure in the drama of Jesus; so we have Joseph of Arimathaea as a wealthy owner of a British tin mine, Mary Magdalene sailing to the shores of France, and inhabitants of Loreto, Italy claiming that the very house where Mary the mother of Jesus lived had been miraculously transported to Loreto. It is similar to the phenomenon of relics in the Dark Ages. None of these legends bear up to critical-historical inquiry. Just as there are discrepancies between various traditional accounts of the Apostles' martyrdoms, so likewise oftentimes there are too many relics claimed to be of the same person, or several different locations are claimed as the final resting place of a given Apostle, disciple, or saint. In addition to the discrepancies between various accounts of the Apostles' martyrdoms mentioned above, there are a few others that I have since learned of. Simon the Apostle[1504] was supposedly killed either by crucifixion, or by being sawn on half. Matthew the Apostle was killed either by being burned, stoned, pierced with a spear, slain with a spear, or beheaded. Philip the Apostle is claimed as a martyr, but there is no specific information on how he actually died.[1505] This only aggravates the problem of discrepancies noted above. It further illustrates the untrustworthiness of legends surrounding key biblical figures such as Joseph of Arimathaea. It is safer to just follow the earliest historical documents we know of. Finally, it may be worth pointing out that, according to the Hebrew Gospel of Matthew, the Joseph in question hailed from a town or village known as Karnasiah.[1506]

[1504] i.e., Simon the Canaanite or the Zealot. Not Simon Peter.

[1505] This information can be found online at http://www.apostles.com/apostlesdied.html.

[1506] Howard., op. cit., pg. 146. In the interest of full disclosure, it is worth pointing out that, according to the Hebrew text of Matthew, the "Simon of Cyrene" mentioned in Mt 27:32 is therein identified as "Simon the Canaanite"; ibid., pg. 144. To some, this may increase the probability of a

The Female Disciples

The female disciples are an important key in our inquiry. They play an important role, since they alone knew the true location of the tomb where Joseph buried Jesus. According to Mark and Matthew, it was the two Marys who saw where Jesus was buried.[1507] Luke merely says it was the women who followed Jesus from Galilee.[1508] John for his part is silent about the women, but he could not hide what had already been written in the three earlier Gospels. In any case he has Mary Magdalene going to the tomb on Sunday morning.[1509] Mark reports the two Marys together with Salome visiting the tomb early on Sunday morning.[1510] Matthew only mentions the two Marys as visiting the tomb early Sunday morning.[1511] Luke once again does not specify the names of the women, but he uses the plural, so there must

---

substitution theory, since Simon the Canaanite is elsewhere identified as one of the twelve Apostles. However, one must bear in mind the evidence against the substitution theory enumerated above; chiefly the "loose ends" such a theory entails.

[1507] Mk 15:47; Mt 27:61.

[1508] Lk 23:55.

[1509] Jn 20:1.

[1510] Mk 16:1.

[1511] Mt 28:1.

have been at least two of them, according to his account.[1512] We should probably credit Mark's account as the most complete and accurate one. In fact, these are not even contradictions, strictly speaking. Matthew may have only mentioned the two Marys, but this does not exclude Salome from having been with them.

But the visitation to the tomb by the women is almost certainly a fiction, in the form in which it is narrated in the Gospels. The more important point by far is the admission that the women saw the tomb where Jesus had been buried by Joseph of Arimathaea.[1513] This is really the key to the whole mystery. Since the women knew where Jesus had been buried, they could then tell the Apostles. In fact, the women would have had to tell the Apostles, since they would have needed men to move the large stone blocking the entrance to the tomb away. Otherwise the women would never have been able to properly mourn for Jesus, and to anoint his body with ointment and spices, and to lament over him. So the story of the women going to the tomb unaccompanied by any men is almost certainly a lie. Even if we assume for the sake of argument that the women had forgotten about the stone blocking the entrance to the tomb, as soon as they returned they would have seen it again and then would realise that they would need help from the male disciples to move it. Furthermore it seems very unlikely that the women would have waited until Sunday morning to visit the tomb; they would have instead most likely waited until sundown on the Sabbath, when the Sabbath ends, according to Jewish custom and reckoning.

We should also expect that the Apostles and other male disciples, as well as the relatives of Jesus, would have wanted to find out what had happened to his body, to pay their final respects. They would have wanted to give him a proper burial, with lamentation and mourning. So all of Christ's disciples would have been motivated to locate his tomb, at the very least.

But the female disciples, who witnessed Christ's crucifixion, albeit from a distance, had the advantage of at least knowing the actual location of the tomb. The fact that the female disciples watched Jesus' crucifixion does not necessarily mean that they were braver or more devout than the men; the fact that they were women made it less

---

[1512] Lk 24:1.

[1513] Mk 15:47; Mt 27:61; Lk 23:55.

likely they they would have been in grave physical danger from the Romans, or from the Jewish elders or Pharisees.[1514] We should not underestimate the importance of the female disciples; they were very important to Christ's ministry. It is questionable whether Mary Magdalene[1515] was the same person as Mary of Bethany, the sister of Lazarus. Mary also had a sister named Martha.[1516] I strongly suspect that the man otherwise known as Lazarus was the same as Simon the leper.[1517] Not only is the location of Simon's house in Bethany, where Lazarus and his sisters lived,[1518] but in three of the four accounts we read that a woman anointed Jesus at the house,[1519] and John specifies that it was six days before the Passover.[1520] This strongly supports the interpretation that Lazaus was a real person, rather than that the account of Lazarus narrated in John's Gospel was merely a historical parable based upon the parable about Lazarus and the rich man in Luke's Gospel.[1521] This in turn implies that the story narrated in John about Lazarus' supposed resurrection was probably an embellished account of a secret initiation ritual gone wrong. Such rituals involved at least a symbolic death and resurection, if not an actual out-of-body experience. And I would personally opt for the latter interpretation as more likely. While it is possible that Mary Magdalene may have been one and the same with Mary of Bethany, this seems unlikely. Luke introduces Mary Magdalene as a woman out of whom went seven

---

[1514] This is due not merely to common human compassion, but because women are generally not perceived as being as great a threat as men. The Romans were not exactly overflowing with compassion, and oftentimes Jewish and Christian women were brutally treat ed, but this generally happened after the time of Jesus.

[1515] Although in common English usage Magdalene sounds like a surname, in the Greek it seems to be more of a title or designation, since it is always "the Magdalene". Also the most literal transliteration of the name Mary from the Greek is Mariam. This was probably derived from Miriam, the sister of Moses. Cf Exodus 15:20ff.

[1516] Luke 10:38-42; John 11:1-46; 12:1-9.

[1517] Mark 14:3; Matthew 26:6-7.

[1518] John 11:1-2; 12:1-3.

[1519] John 12:3; Mark 14:3; Matthew 26:6-7.

[1520] John 12:1-3.

[1521] Luke 16:19-31.

demons,[1522] and there is no hint in the later chapter where he speaks of Martha and her sister Mary that this was the same Mary mentioned earlier.[1523] Mary the Magdalene is always distinctly identified as such in all four Gospels.[1524] Mary was probably a common name in first century Palestine. Aside from these two Marys, there was Mary the *wife*[1525] of Klopa.[1526] As noted above, it is uncertain whether the reference to the sister of Christ's mother in John 19:25 means Elizabeth or another sister named Mary.[1527] Aside from these three, four, or five women named Mary there was also Joanna the wife of Chouza Herod's steward, Susanna,[1528] Salome,[1529] and many other[1530] women among the disciples of Jesus. Aside from the twelve specially chosen Apostles, Jesus also had at least seventy other male disciples, whome he sent out as missionaries throughout Israel.[1531] But we are also told that at some point many disciples abandoned Jesus due to the controversial nature of his teachings.[1532] From John's report we get the impression that only the twelve Apostles remained loyal to Jesus from that time, among the male disciples.[1533] Of these remaining twelve, Judas Iscariot

---

[1522] Luke 8:2.

[1523] Luke 10:38–39.

[1524] Matthew 27:56,61; 28:1; Mark 15:40,47; 16:1,9; Luke 8:2; 24:10; John 19:25; 20:1,18.

[1525] Or sister or mother or daughter; the Greek does not specify the exact relationship; there is merely the Genitive case or declension of the Greek article and name. See *Koine* Greek grammar and syntax.

[1526] John 19:25 cf Luke 24:18, *Kleopas*. In the King James, the name is rendered as Cleophas in John 19:25 and Cleopas in Luke 24:18.

[1527] Possibly Elizabeth was also named Mary; we have seen that Simon the leper was also called Lazarus. Simon the brother of Andrew became also known as Peter and Kephas; cf Galatians 2:9; I Corinthians 9:5; 15:5. Saul became known as Paul; John was also known as Mark; Judas Alphaeus was also known as Lebbaeus and Thaddaeus.

[1528] Luke 8:3.

[1529] Mark 15:40; 16:1.

[1530] Luke 8:3.

[1531] Luke 10:1,17.

[1532] John 6:60,66.

[1533] John 6:67–71.

betrayed him, and Peter denied him. Matthew reports that Judas committed suicide,[1534] but this seems unlikely to me; more likely Judas fled Palestine, never to return. Peter repented, and briefly assumed a leadership role among the disciples, until he was eclipsed by James the Just.[1535] We are also briefly told of a young male disciple.[1536] Some might seek to identify this young man with the Apostle John, but this seems contrary to the declaration that "they all forsook him, and fled" which would seem to include the eleven Apostles. But the most important key in respect to the female disciples is that they saw where Joseph buried Jesus' body, and so they were able to tell the Apostles the location of the tomb.

[1534] Matthew 27:5 cp Acts 1:18.

[1535] Traditionally believed to be the younger brother of Jesus Christ.

[1536] Mark 14:50-52.

No Soldiers Guarding
The Tomb

T here were no soldiers guarding the tomb where Jesus was buried.
It is very important to dispel this myth, since Christians always
resort to this as an essential and powerful part of the "evidence"
in favor of Christ's supposed resurrection. But it is child's play to
demolish the edifice of this monumental lie. First of all, the other
three Canonical Evangelists omit this detail from their respective
narratives. This is more than just a suspicious omission. It is fatal to
any reasonable supposition of the truth of the tale. Matthew alone
breathes a word of this story.[1537] Neither Luke, Mark nor John say
anything about Roman soldiers or any other soldiers guarding Christ's
tomb. So only one out of four Canonical Gospels breathes a word
of this highly suspicious story. That fact alone is a gigantic red flag,
telling us that most likely the tale is a lie. Had there been any soldiers
guarding Christ's tomb, then all four Evangelists should have reported
it. They should have, they could have, and they would have. This is
only reasonable. Christians might argue that there would have been no
need to reiterate every detail of the story in each of the Gospels. While

---

[1537] i.e., in the New Testament proper. But later apocryphal Gospels, such as
Peter and Nicodemus, include it. So likewise do some lame "alternative"
texts.

this is true, oftentimes there is tedious repetition from one Gospel to another. Not only that, but in this case, the sheer importance of these events and circumstances would require a repetition in this case. After all, some people are basing their entire lives on these texts. They are staking their eternal destiny on the supposed veracity of these reports. And these people threaten skeptics with everlasting hellfire for not believing such things. Any prospective convert to Christianity has a right to know the answer to legitimate questions, which are never answered by Christians. And a legitimate question would be, Why was the story of the Roman soldiers guarding the tomb of Christ omitted from three out of the four New Testament Gospels? Christians can offer no reasonable or satisfying answer to this question. They may pull the sheep's wool over their own eyes, but they can't fool everybody. Even though there are reasonable grounds for believing that Matthew had been the first Gospel to have been written, we would still have a right to expect such an important detail of the story to be confirmed by the other Evangelists.[1538] Of course, even had such a detail been repeated in all four Gospels, this would by no means dispel all doubt on the question. But the bare fact that only one out the four Canonical narratives even mentions the story makes it highly suspect. Furthermore, as pointed out above, it is even questionable as to whether or not the story was present in the original edition of Matthew; a person could read the text without the storyline, and it reads quite naturally. So, quite possibly the story may have been inserted into Hebrew and/or Greek editions of Matthew, even after the other three Gospel texts had been written. The story no doubt would have been perceived as an improvement upon the earlier text, and copied by scribes thereafter, in both Hebrerw and Greek editions of Matthew.[1539]

But we can also see from internal inconsistency that the tale is false. Why would the Pharisees have thought that Jesus ever claimed that after three days he would rise from the dead?[1540] Where would they get that idea? True it is that Jesus purportedly predicted his

---

[1538] Of course just because something is found in all four Gospels does not make it "Gospel" truth.

[1539] i.e., assuming that it was in fact an addition to the original text.

[1540] Mt 27:63.

passion, death, and resurrection.[1541] But in every one[1542] of these instances, the context explicitly states that Jesus was speaking privately to his twelve Apostles.[1543] So even in terms of the Gospel narrative, there is no real basis for the Pharisees to have suspected that Jesus ever made any such claim beforehand.

As far as the reference to the "sign of Jonah" is concerned, although in the first passage Jesus is speaking to the Pharisees,[1544] and in the second passage to both the Pharisees and the Sadducees,[1545] as we have seen above, the parallel verse in Mark's Gospel completely omits any reference to the "sign of Jonah" and Jesus simply says that no sign will be granted to his generation.[1546] This creates an overwhelmingly strong presumption that all three references to the "sign of Jonah" are merely inventions attributed to Jesus.[1547] Even if one posits the cryptic reference to destroying the temple and raising it again in three days in John's Gospel[1548] as something that the Pharisees seized on and somehow "correctly" interpreted it as a reference to a claim by Christ of his impending death and resurrection in three days, the evidence we have seen above respecting the relative order of the Gospels comes pretty close to completely vitiating any such appeal; more likely John invented this episode to accommodate the

---

[1541] Mark 8:31; 10:32-34; Mathew 16:21; 17:22-23; 20:17-19; Luke 9:21-22; 18:31-33; 24:6-7.

[1542] The sole "exception" being Luke 24:6-7, where the messengers refer back to Christ's earlier prophecy of his passion, death, and resurrection. But this is to the female disciples, who would have been privy to such things, assuming that there had been any such prediction on Christ's part, which in itself is outrageously unlikely.

[1543] However we should remember that since the Gospels probably were written at least twenty years after the crucifixion, these "predictions" were essentially all post-dictions, written into the Gospel narrative long after the fact by the Evangelists. Most likely Jesus never anticipated his betrayal, arrest, passion, or crucifixion.

[1544] Matthew 12:38-40 cp Luke 11:29-30.

[1545] Matthew 16:1-4 cf Luke 11:29-30.

[1546] Mark 8:12.

[1547] Including the reference in Luke 11:29-30, where Jesus was speaking to a crowd of people.

[1548] John 2:19 cf Mark 14:58; Matthew 26:61.

passages about the false witnesses in Mark and Matthew.[1549] In fact, John may have realised the deficiency of the Synoptic texts in respect to providing a realistic public prophecy by Christ of his approaching death and resurrection; and although neither Luke nor John himself included an account of any soldiers guarding Christ's tomb, John may still have been motivated to provide an oblique form of evidence whereby belief in the story could be maintained, and this was his real motivation for inventing the incident in his version of the cleansing of the temple by Jesus. We ought to take a look at the passages in Matthew that speak of the guards.

62 But the next day, that followed the day of the preparation, the chief priests and the Pharisees came together to Pilate,

63 saying, Lord, we remember that that deceiver said, while he was still alive, After three days I will rise again.

64 Command therefore that the sepulchre be made secure until the third day, lest his disciples come by night and steal him away, and say to the people *that* he is risen from the dead: so the last error will be worse than the first.

65 Pilate said to them, You have a *contingent of* guards: Go and make the *place* as secure as you can.

66 So they went, making the sepulchre secure, sealing the stone, and setting the guards. (Matthew 27:62-66)

11 But as they were going, behold some of the guards came into the city, and told the chief priests all that was done.

12 And when they were assembled with the elders *of the Jews,* and had taken counsel, they gave a large *sum* of silver to the soldiers,

13 saying, Say that his disciples came by night, and stole him while we slept.

[1549] Mark 14:58; Matthew 26:61.

14 And if the governor hears of this, we will persuade [bribe] him, and secure you.

15 So they took the silver, and did as they had been instructed. And this word is commonly reported among the Jews to this day. (Matthew 28:11-15)

While it is not absolutely certain whether we are to understand that it was Roman soldiers, or rather men of the temple guard, in either case we are meant to believe that men hostile to Jesus and his disciples had been guarding the tomb. Pilate's response to the chief priests and Pharisees, saying, "You have a guard" sounds as if he was saying that they already had their own temple guard, who could keep watch over the tomb, if the high priest commanded them so. On the other hand, the very fact that Pontius Pilate himself was approached by these chief priests implies that it was Roman soldiers whom we are to believe were guarding the tomb of Jesus. Furthermore the fact that the guards were not only bribed to lie by the chief priests, but also encouraged and comforted by assurances that, if necessary, Pilate himself would be bribed, and no harm would come to them, further implies that these men were supposed to be Roman soldiers. If it were merely a matter of men of the temple guard, then Pilate could hardly have been overly concerned if the men had fallen asleep on their watch. Furthermore Pilate's only concern in the matter would have been to squelch any possible propagandistic use of a legend of a messianic resurrection to fuel the fires of militant resistance to the Roman occupation of Judaea. This is where the potential zealotry of Jesus becomes a matter of interest once more. While this is something to take into account, we can still safely rule out the story as an utter fabrication. No Roman soldiers or men of the temple guard were keeping watch at the tomb of Jesus. There would have been no need for any such thing; there is no proof that Jesus ever even predicted that he would rise from the dead after three days, either privately or publicly. Neither is there any clear and unambiguous messianic prophecy anywhere within *TaNaKh* that the Messiah would die and rise again after three days.[1550] Therefore there would have been no suspicion or anticipation that there would subsequently be any

---

[1550] Neither is there any such prophecy anywhere in the Apocrypha or the Old Testament Pseudepigrapha.

claims of a resurrection. This is clear as day. The story of soldiers guarding Christ's tomb is a complete lie, from beginning to end. But what is most revealing about all this is the fact that the story was apparently invented in response to suspicions that in fact the disciples *had* removed Jesus' body from the tomb, and apparently reburied it elsewhere, in some unknown location. This means that this suspicion was considered a reasonable supposition to those who rejected the Apostles' claims vis-à-vis Jesus being the Messiah. And this was definitely the vast majority of people living in Judaea and Galilee at that time. Of course we should remember that the Apostles were able to convince a sizable minority of their messianic claims on Jesus' behalf, so we must also factor this in as well. But once again we are not certain as to exactly what was claimed by the Apostles themselves, since all the written documents date to a far later time. Presumably they wanted to perpetuate Christ's legacy in some meaningful way, and this would most likely have involved some claim that he lived on in some sense. But it is unproven that the original Apostles themselves ever claimed that Jesus was risen from the dead in the carnal, bodily sense. While this is possible, even if they did so, it was probably only as an esotericism.[1551] So the evidence from Matthew only serves to strengthen the idea that the disciples removed Jesus' body from the tomb in which Joseph buried it. This was not done to perpetrate a fraud; only cynics believe that. It was instead meant to give a proper burial to their esteemed Lord and Master, and to protect his body from desecration by those Jews who did not believe in his messianic status. In the following chapter I will outline the probable sequence of events, to be supplemented by additional evidence in favor of the reburial theory following.

[1551] i.e., that any claim of a carnal resurrection was only the exoteric shell of the true, inner esoteric teaching of a spiritual resurrection. Therefore strictly speaking the exoteric teaching was not a lie, but a historical parable, meant to protect the inner teaching of Christ's spiritual resurrection. If the Apostles believed in the latter in good conscience, then they cannot be rightly convicted of fraud. It may have been convenient that Christ's body could no longer be found, but the thrust of their message was no doubt more spiritual.

The Secret Burial

O n Thursday evening, Jesus and his disciples began their celebration of Passover, and of the feast of unleavened bread.[1552] The three Synoptic Gospels only mention the twelve Apostles as being with Jesus, but this leaves unanswered the question of where the women celebrated Passover. This question is never addressed, even in the various Grail books that give prominence to female disciples, such as Mary the Magdalene. A Passover Seder is traditionally regarded as a family celebration,[1553] and there can be little doubt that the female disciples were thought of as family by Jesus.[1554] Therefore while it is possible that the women may have celebrated Passover separately, it is also at least possible, if not probable, that they celebrated it together with Jesus and the Apostles. On the other hand, it could be argued that all the relevant texts give the impression that only the twelve Apostles were with Jesus that night. While this is true, we should also remember the exception of the young man mentioned in Mark 14:51-52. We must also remember that the feast of Passover and of unleavened bread was a seven-day feast.[1555]

[1552] Mark 14:1-17 cf Matthew 26:1-20; Luke 22:1-14.

[1553] Much as Thanksgiving and Christmas are regarded as family celebrations by many Christians.

[1554] Mark 3:31-35; Matthew 12:46-50.

[1555] Exodus 12:1-20.

Judas had already agreed to betray Jesus for silver.[1556] According to Matthew's account, the chief priests, scribes, and elders of the Jews were solicitous that Jesus not be killed during the Passover feast, lest there be an uproar among the people.[1557] According to John's account, Judas left the feast while the others were still inside, sitting at the table.[1558] While this is possible, this is suspect, because not only are the three Synoptic Evangelists completely silent about exactly when Judas departed, but thereafter in John's text Jesus proceeds to utter a long discourse to the remaining eleven Apostles, which evidently we are to understand was to remain secret until the writing of John's Gospel.[1559] Not only that, but John and Luke once again contradict Mark and Matthew, inasmuch as the latter two Gospels both say that after Jesus and the Apostles sang a hymn, they went to the Mount of Olives, and it was outside, on the Mount of Olives, that Jesus foretold Peter's triple denial;[1560] while by contrast the former two Gospels both depict Christ's prediction of Peter's denial while they were still inside.[1561] So the earlier Gospels should probably be followed.

Jesus is betrayed by Judas in the Garden of Gethsemane; Judas leads a contingent of the temple guard to arrest Jesus, and identifies Jesus with a kiss.[1562] After this ensued the passion of Jesus, culminating with his crucifixion on Friday. Jesus was buried by Joseph of Arimathaea on Friday, shortly before sundown. We can be reasonably sure that the actual Passover fell on the Sabbath that year. That means that in all probability, Jesus was crucified in 27 C.E.[1563] We know from astronomical records that the Passover fell on the Sabbath that year. This gives us a strong chronological marker for exactly when Jesus

---

[1556] Mark 14:10-11 & Luke 22:3-6, according to the original Greek. Matthew specifies thirty pieces of silver; Matthew 26:14-16; 27:3.

[1557] Matthew 26:3-5.

[1558] John 13:21-30.

[1559] John 13:31-18:1.

[1560] Mark 14:26-31; Matthew 26:30-35.

[1561] Luke 22:31-39; John 13:36-38 cf 18:1.

[1562] Mark 14:43-46.

[1563] i.e., 27 A.D. But according to Gibbon, Jesus was crucified in 29 A.D./C.E. But we should also remember the evidence presented by Jacobivici and Wilson in The Lost Gospel that, most likely, the crucifixion occurred in 32 C.E.

was crucified. All four Gospels converge to confirm this date and interpretation. All four Gospels agree that Jesus was crucified the day before the Sabbath.[1564] John's text says that *that* Sabbath was "a high day", which signifies that it was the very day of the Passover itself.[1565] Matthew's text also confirms this in a strange and unexpected way, since in the original Greek of Matthew 28:1, the plural form of the word for Sabbath is used.[1566] This denotes the weekly Sabbath, and also the annual Passover Sabbath. They both fell on the same day that year.[1567] As already noted, the women saw where Jesus was buried.[1568] The women prepared spices and ointments, with which to anoint Jesus' body.[1569]

But there was a stone blocking the entrance to the tomb; according to Matthew's text, the stone was very large.[1570] The women would remember the stone blocking the tomb and would have sought out help from the Apostles to remove it. More importantly, they knew that the Apostles would also want to know where Jesus' body was. Most likely, shortly after sunset on Saturday the women sought out the Apostles. Even assuming that the eleven remaining Apostles were in hiding, the women were probably sufficiently resourceful and intimately familiar with the customs of these men to know where they likely were. Alternatively, the Apostles may have sent out messengers in search of the women, who presumably were easier to find. In either case it was only a matter of time until the Apostles once again came into contact with the women, who knew where Jesus was buried. Although no doubt the disciples were secretly grateful to Joseph of Arimathaea for burying Christ's body, he was still a member of the dreaded *Sanhedrin*, which had just murdered their beloved Lord and Master. Therefore they did not seek to contact him, at least initially. The disciples would have been in fear, and rightly so, of the Romans

---

[1564] Mark 14:42; Matthew 28:1; Luke 23:56; John 19:31.

[1565] John 19:31.

[1566] Greek *sabbaton*. Nestle-Aland., pg. 85.

[1567] One may recall that the Toldoth Jeschu also says that the Passover fell on the Sabbath the year that Jeschu was crucified. All together, this is strong confirming evidence.

[1568] Mark 15:47 cf Matthew 27:61; Luke 23:55.

[1569] Luke 23:56 cf Mark 16:1 & Luke 24:1.

[1570] Mt 27:60 cf Mk 15:46; 16:3.

and of the Jewish elders, especially the former. Furthermore, they knew that the elders and chief priests had many agents among the people. Most likely, however, the disciples also had their own network of trusted messengers and sympathizers.

Going to the tomb, the Apostles and other disciples were confronted with two choices: either they could anoint Christ's body there, and seek to give him a proper burial service with weeping, lamentation, or mourning; or they could remove the body, and seek to bury it secretly elsewhere, where such rites could be performed. Since the tomb and the land on which it was located were owned by a man they did not know,[1571] they chose the latter option. The disciples also knew the boundless hostility of the scribes, Pharisees, Sadducees, Herodians, chief priests, and Jewish elders towards Jesus and all that he stood for. They may have feared the desecration of the tomb, and even of Christ's body itself, by the unbelieving Jews.[1572] Therefore they took Jesus' body, and secretly buried it somewhere else, in a location known only to themselves. <u>This was not a theft</u>. <u>It was not grave-robbing</u>. Nobody had a greater claim to Jesus' body than his own closest disciples, who were his true family. Neither was this action done to perpetrate a fraud. It was done to protect the body of Jesus from desecration by the Jews. We must remember that in the eyes of his disciples, Jesus was not merely a holy prophet. He

---

[1571] Although we can be certain that Joseph was unknown to both the Apostles and the female disciples personally, it is uncertain whether or not they knew his actual identity, and that he was a member of the *Sanhedrin, at that time,* or whether this information came to light subsequently. If we assume the former, then this would have been an additional reason for them to quickly remove Christ's body from the tomb. But even if they did not know *at that time* who specifically it was who buried Christ's body, or that he was a member of the *Sanhedrin,* this would still have remained a disturbing possibility, and they would have been motivated to relocate Christ's body, and bury it elsewhere.

[1572] Recall that in the Toldoth Yeshu the Rabbis dragged the corpse of Jesus around in the filthy, dirty streets of Jerusalem. And this text was unquestionably written by Jews, and for Jews. Thus they have testified against themselves, respecting their intentions towards Christ's body. This fully justifies the removal of Jesus Christ's body from the original tomb, and a secret reburial in an unknown location elsewhere. And for Jews to turn around and accuse the disciples of "stealing" the body of Jesus, in order to supposedly perpetrate a fraud, is an outrageous calumny against them. Jews should apologise to Christians for this.

was the Messiah. It was through the Messiah that the new covenant would be made.[1573] True Jesus was regarded as a prophet,[1574] but to his disciples he was more than a prophet; he was the Messiah. Therefore typical Jewish customs vis-à-vis burial and mourning may not have been strictly followed in his case. Since Jesus had been buried either in or near Jerusalem, most likely he was also reburied not too far from the original location. The Apostles and female disciples possibly took a blood oath to never reveal the true location of Christ's new tomb. It was left unmarked, at least in the ordinary sense. Possibly they placed a distinctive rock or planted a tree at the spot where they had buried Jesus, so that it would always be known to them. But after reburying Jesus and mourning for him, it was time to carry on his legacy in a positive way. Even if their faith in Jesus' messianic status had been shaken by the events of the passion, their faith in Jesus as the Messiah was ultimately triumphant; it gave meaning and purpose to their lives. Their faith was tested, but ultimately strengthened by the events of Christ's ordeal. After a certain length of time, we cannot be certain how long, they began to proclaim Jesus as the Messiah openly, claiming that he ascended to heaven victoriously. They would have found a scriptural basis for this within TaNaKh.[1575] It is uncertain whether they initially or ever claimed a carnal, bodily resurrection from the dead in the case of Jesus; there is no proof either way, considering the relative lateness of the Gospel texts and the book of Acts. But presumably they did claim that Jesus was still alive in some sense; that he was victorious over death in some real sense.[1576] They could have claimed this in all good conscience, if they themselves had been persuaded from Scripture that Jesus was indeed the Messiah, and had fulfilled the role of the Suffering Servant. After passing through a deep crisis of faith, they concluded that Jesus was the Suffering Servant and also the Messiah. They did not need to see him, either in a vision, or alive in the flesh. It was admittedly convenient for them that now Jesus' body was no longer to be found. But once again we cannot be sure that the Apostles initially or ever claimed a carnal, bodily resurrection for Jesus, as opposed to a spiritual

---

[1573] Jeremiah 31:31-34 cf Daniel 9:26-27 cp Hebrews 8:6-13; 9:1-18; 10:1-18.

[1574] Mt 21:11.

[1575] Daniel 7:13-14 cf Psalm 110:1.

[1576] And not merely in a strictly symbolic sense.

resurrection. If they claimed no more than this, then it was not a lie, but rather a conviction. And there is evidence to suggest that in fact this was the case; the first teaching was of a spiritual resurrection. The concept of a corporeal resurrection was probably a later corruption and carnalization of the original post-passion *kerygma*. It seems to be linked to the "Son of Man" material within the New Testament, as well as the Danielic "signs" eschatology; this material probably being an attempt to bring the movement into greater accord with biblical and traditional Judaism. Perhaps I would be going too far out on a limb if I suggested that it may have been part and parcel with the post-Marcionite reaction of the orthodox catholic church of the second century. But nevertheless I will offer this as food for thought. Finally, I want to offer some insight from the Gospel of John. In that text, Thomas must play the role of being a notorious doubter of Christ's resurrection. But the famous line from that text is when Jesus says to Thomas "Blessed are they who have not seen, and yet have believed".[1577] We speculated above that possibly Jesus did appear to his Apostles and other disciples, and possibly even to Saul/Paul, either in his etheric body or his astral body. While I would still maintain this as a sheer possibility, we pointed out problems with the contradictions in the resurrection accounts. The verse from the Gospel of John suggests that a person who believes in Christ's resurrection is even more blessed than the twelve Apostles, who saw him alive again from the dead, according to those texts. But perhaps this is hinting to us that they too never saw him, but merely were blessed with sufficient faith to believe in his resurrection, at least in the spiritual sense. To some, this may be blasphemy; to others, it may be spiritual insight.

[1577] John 20:29.

Resurrection: Carnal
or Spiritual?

While it is true that some New Testament passages speak of people rising out of their graves,[1578] there are a number of others that depict a more spiritual interpretation of the resurrection.[1579] So there is some degree of confusion about the precise Christian teaching on the afterlife, and different denominations sometimes have somewhat different teachings on this subject. As noted above, some Christian cults teach their own strange doctrines, such as soul sleep and annihilationism. However we have seen above that such eccentric interpretations do not hold up to critical-historical scrutiny. The earliest Christians were influenced by the Jewish Scriptures[1580] in terms of determining such questions.[1581] We have seen above that the

---

[1578] John 5:28-29; I Thessalonians 4:16; Revelation 20:12-15 cf Matthew 27:52-53.

[1579] Mark 12:25; Matthew 22:30; Luke 16:19-31; 20:34-38; 23:43; John 11:26; I Corinthians 15:42-50; II Corinthians 5:1-9; Philippians 1:23; 3:20-21; Hebrews 12:22-23; Revelation 20:4-6. This last passage is admittedly questionable, in terms of interpretation.

[1580] Primarily by *TaNaKh,* but also by the Apocrypha and Old Testament Pseudepigrapha.

[1581] Other than what Jesus himself had taught about such things.

books of Enoch and Jubilees taught a spiritual concept of resurrection. These two books, especially the former, were very important books to the early Christians. The Apocrypha itself contains passages that depict a carnal, bodily resurrection from the dead,[1582] and also those that portray a more spiritual interpretation of life after death.[1583] *TaNaKh* itself depicts a carnal, bodily resurrection from death.[1584] However other portions of *TaNaKh* depict a more spiritual afterlife existence.[1585] Yet other verses of *TaNaKh* seem to imply no belief in any resurrection or afterlife whatever.[1586] We also see the same dichotomy in parts of the Apocrypha.[1587] And from Josephus we learn that the Pharisees, or at least some of them, believed in reincarnation.[1588] There is also a hint of reincarnation in the Apocrypha.[1589] There is even a slight hint of reincarnation in the New Testament.[1590] And of course there is the always implicit and sometimes explicit heaven-and-hell dichotomy all throughout the New Testament.[1591] So confronted with such a mass of contradictory material, it is small wonder that there is much confusion about any clear teaching on the afterlife in Christianity.

Of course we would inquire most diligently into the teachings of Jesus himself, and of the Apostles, inasmuch as they can be determined. But it must be admitted that there can be no clear and unambiguous certainty respecting this matter. If we were to insist, for example, that Jesus taught reincarnation, then it would be all too easy for fundamentalists to point to the many passages where Jesus speaks in terms of a resurrection from the dead, and of judgment, based upon a single lifetime. It would be easy enough for them to find such

---

[1582] II Maccabees 7:9–36; 12:43–45 cf Wisdom 5:1–16; Judith 16:17.

[1583] II Maccabees 15:12–16 cf Wisdom 3:1–8; 4:7–11.

[1584] Ezekiel 37:1–14; Daniel 12:2; Isaiah 26:19; Psalms 16 & 49.

[1585] Genesis 35:18; Deuteronomy 18:11; I Samuel 28:11–19.

[1586] Ecclesiastes 9:5; Isaiah 38:18; Psalms 6:5; 88:10–12; 115:17; 146:4.

[1587] Tobit 3:6; Sirach 10:11; 14:12,17; 17:27–28; 41:4.

[1588] Jos. War. 2.8.14.

[1589] Wisdom 8:19–20.

[1590] Matthew 11:14–15; 17:10–13; Mark 9:11–13; John 9:1–3.

[1591] Mt 5:29–30; 18:7–9; 25:31–46; Mk 9:42–50; 16:16; Lk 16:19–31; 23:43; Jn 5:25–29; Romans 14:12; II Corinthians 5:10; Hebrews 9:27; I John 5:16; Revelation 20:11–15.

passages.[1592] If we were to insist that Jesus taught a strictly spiritual version of the afterlife, then opponents could easily cite any number of passages where Christ speaks of a very carnal conception of a physical resurrection from the dead. There could also be debates about the meaning of various passages as well. So we cannot claim certainty in this matter. But neither can the fundamentalists, either.[1593]

Christians often claim that, while there will be a public, general resurrection of the dead at the *parousia* or *eschaton,* which is typically interpreted as a physical resurrection; that there is also an intermediate spiritual afterlife state for the dead, until that time. This appears to be an effort to resolve the various contradictory passages about this question of the afterlife/resurrection. But one objection against this seemingly clever interpretation is that, if we grant that there actually is a real spiritual existence immediately after death, then any subsequent "resurrection" would seem to be superfluous and redundant. If one attempts to answer this objection by making an appeal to carnal pleasures that only a corporeal body could experience, such as conjugal bliss, then this very answer is refuted by none other than Jesus Christ himself, who clearly said that there would be no marriage in the resurrection:

25 For when they shall rise from the dead, they neither marry, nor are given in marriage; but are as the angels in heaven. (Mark 12:25)

30 For in the resurrection they neither marry, nor are given in marriage, but are as the angels of God in the heavens. (Matthew 22:30)

The absence of marriage in the resurrection implies also the absence of conjugal bliss in the resurrected state.[1594] In Matthew, the

---

[1592] Although Hebrews 9:27 is the most frequently-cited "proof" verse against reincarnation by fundamentalists and born-again Christians.

[1593] They may *claim* certainty, but the fact remains that there are contradictions between various passages on this very topic. We are not obliged to take their claims seriously.

[1594] By contrast, the Koran does offer conjugal bliss in the hereafter. An interesting side point is that some people have claimed to have experienced astral sex.

Greek word for resurrection, *anastasei,* is used.[1595] This proves that Jesus was not discussing some "intermediate" afterlife state, but rather the resurrection itself. His words imply a transcendent state of spiritual bliss, rather than a carnal, bodily resurrection as commonly thought.[1596] Most importantly, these words are attributed to none other than Jesus himself. We cannot be certain that he spoke them, but since they are found within the Synoptic tradition, and especially within the earliest Gospels, they should be given due weight. Such words probably do represent Christ's actual teaching on the resurrection. And we can clearly see that it was a more spiritual conception than what is often found in Christian fundamentalism.

What I find most significant is the fact that, despite the more corporeal concept of the resurrection later taught by most Christian churches, we still find at least a trace of a more spiritual concept within the New Testament itself. Of course a person could argue that the carnal concept of bodily resurrection was the original concept, and a spiritual concept of resurrection was merely a later refinement of the idea, within Christianity.[1597] But there are five facts that point to the opposite interpretation as being true; i.e., that the spiritual concept of the resurrection was the true original teaching, which was later corrupted to a more carnal conception. First is the fact that both carnal and spiritual conceptions of the resurrection can be found within the

---

[1595] Nestle-Aland., op. cit., pg. 63.

[1596] Furthermore it could be argued that sexual pleasure is part of our biological imperative of the survival of the species; therefore such pleasure serves no purpose in an afterlife. On the other hand, I cannot altogether rule out the possibility of astral sex, although I have not yet consciously experienced it myself. Astral sex, assuming it is a real phenomenon, suggests that there will be sexual pleasure (or at least the possibility of it) in the hereafter. But here we are inquiring into what Jesus, the Apostles, and early disciples believed about life after death. If they practiced esotericism, as much evidence suggests, then it may be impossible to determine with certainty what they believed about such things.

[1597] And this argument would tend to coincide with a survival theory, or a substitution theory, or even an impersonation theory. In other words, if belief in Christ's resurrection was based upon his still being physically alive in the Apostles' estimation, then they necessarily would have had a more corporeal concept of the resurrection, which later was corrupted and refined to a more spiritual concept.

Apocrypha.[1598] Second is the fact that the books of Enoch and Jubilees both endorse the spiritual conception of the resurrection.[1599] Third is the fact that the New Testament itself gives robust expression to the spiritual concept of the afterlife; it is arguably equally prominent or even more prominent than the contrary carnal conception therein. Fourth is the fact that explicit faith in a more carnal conception of the resurrection is only found in documents postdating the New Testament. Fifth is the fact that the order of the Gospels also suggests the same thing.

The parable that Jesus told of Lazarus and the rich man[1600] depicts a spiritual existence immediately after death, with both rewards and punishments. Certain cults like the Seventh-Day Adventists, the Jehovah's Witnesses, the Christadelphians, and others insist that the fact that this is merely a parable undercuts any implication of a literal interpretation. They further point out that nowhere in *TaNaKh* is there any explicit threat of a fiery state of torment hereafter, as spoken of in the parable. While this latter assertion is true, this does not in and of itself justify their eccentric interpretations of the parable, however otherwise morally desirable. Though a parable is a story with a single point,[1601] all the details of a parable are expected to reflect an assumed reality; in other words, while the parable may be merely a story, biblical parables are not placed within phantastic settings; people hear of things either from daily life, or what was commonly believed about life in the hereafter. An argument against a literal interpretation of the details of the parable is specious on at least two grounds: First, if Jesus was speaking in terms of the people's common beliefs about the hereafter, and he knew that those beliefs were false, then it was deceitful for him to not correct those false beliefs; such an allegation places Christ's morality into grave question. For Christ to perpetrate false and superstitious beliefs through a parable would have been the epitome of hypocrisy and pure evil. Furthermore the appeal to

---

[1598] This proves that the spiritual concept predated the New Testament itself, and even Jesus and the Apostles.

[1599] Enoch & Jubilees were both highly esteemed by the Essenes and the early Christians. Enoch was even quoted from in the New Testament Epistle of Judas (Jude).

[1600] Luke 16:19–31.

[1601] Proverbs 26:9.

"Moses and the prophets" in the parable ought not to be construed as a circumscription to the current Hebrew Canon of Scripture as denoted by *TaNaKh*. After all, Judas the brother of Christ quoted from the book of Enoch in his short epistle, and in such a way as to clearly indicate his acceptance of that book as Sacred Scripture, fully upon an equality with the *Torah*. And the book of Enoch does clearly depict a state of conscious punishment for the wicked hereafter. The same is also true of the book of Judith. And for such cults to argue that the expression "Moses and the prophets" somehow proves that Enoch is excluded, since he lived before Moses, is merely a false pretense; Abraham is called a prophet by God in the Torah[1602] and he lived centuries before Moses. So it is both false pretense and obscurantism to pretend that Enoch was excluded from "the prohets" in Luke 16:29-31. A genuine critical-historical analysis of the parable will place it within the timeframe, culture, and geography in which it was first allegedly spoken. If anything, the parable strongly confirms that most of the first-century Palestinian Jews accepted a larger Canon of Scripture than what was later circumscribed at the Council of Jamnia.[1603]

While the idea of bodily resurrection was probably acquired from the Persians, many Hellenistic Jews probably believed in a more spiritual conception of the afterlife. This Hellenistic influence is evident in the books of Enoch, Jubilees, and fourth Maccabees.[1604] The last-named book apparently had some degree of literary influence upon Luke's Gospel; we see this reflected, among other things, in words attributed to Christ in his answer to the Sadducees respecting the resurrection. Jesus is reported to have said "For he is not a God of the dead, but of the living; for all live unto him."[1605] This expression occurs several times in fourth Maccabees.

As we already noted, some Jews believed in a bodily resurrection, while others believed in reincarnation. Others believed in a pure

---

[1602] Genesis 20:7.

[1603] Either that or the idea of conscious fiery punishment in a hellish hereafter was commonly accepted. As noted above, the *Talmud* does depict such a state for the wicked hereafter.

[1604] Jubilees 23:31 depicts a spiritual afterlife. In this respect Hellenistic influence is evident, although it must be admitted that the book of Jubilees as a whole seems to have been written as a protest against Hellenistic cultural influence upon Judaism.

[1605] Luke 20:38.

spiritual afterlife. But a common explanation may be found for the otherwise contradictory beliefs in reincarnation and resurrection. The Jews were promised a future time of great prosperity and blessing.[1606] The various passages depicted an earthly kingdom in which these blessings would be enjoyed. So while many Jews accepted the promise of a corporeal resurrection from the dead, in order to enjoy such benefits, others apparently balked at such an idea, and somehow acquired a belief in transmigration.[1607] In either case, those Jews who aspired to the enjoyment of God's promised kingdom pictured it as being right on earth, rather than in heaven. Some Jews imagined that it would be through a carnal resurrection from the dead, while others believed it would be through reincarnating into bodies of children born into that kingdom. Some other Jews also apparently believed in a more spiritual conception of life hereafter, while still others believed in no such thing.

The statement of Jesus to the repentant thief on the cross also depicts an immediate afterlife.[1608] Once again, cults that teach soul sleep try to argue that the fact that the original Greek lacks punctuation gives them license to move the implied comma from after the word "you" to after the word "today", thus changing the meaning. But this is a hollow argument, since common sense dictates that it would have been a redundancy for Jesus to merely emphasize that it was on that day that he was making the declaration; it is insipid and inane to make any such absurd argument. No; the point is that Christ was telling the thief that *that* very day he would be together with him in paradise. In fact, it must have been quite deliberate on Luke's part to place such a declaration into Christ's mouth; the whole point being to retroactively cite a messianic endorsement of his concept of an immediate judgment hereafter, with both rewards and punishments. Luke at least is consistent in this respect. Those cults

---

[1606] Micah 4:3-4; Isaiah 65-66; Ezekiel 40-48; Zechariah 3:10.

[1607] It is uncertain where, when or how exactly this belief was acquired by the Jews. Possibly from the writings of certain Greek philosophers, or from Buddhist missionaries, or from Hindu merchants. But the Pharisees believed in reincarnation; cf Jos. War. 2.8.14. Later on the Jews acquired much more extensive beliefs about transmigration; much of the *Talmud* speaks of such things. See my earlier work.

[1608] Luke 23:43: "And Jesus said to him, Truly I say to you, Today you will be with me in paradise."

who argue against the clear meaning of Luke 23:43 cannot cite even a single example elsewhere of Christ making a similar gratuitous and apparently redundant use of "today" as they vociferously argue is the case in that verse. Thus they are refuted by common sense, and a host of empirical evidence.

The *Apokalypse* also depicts a spiritual resurrection. For example, consider the following verse:

4   And I saw thrones, and they sat upon them, and judgment was given unto them: and I saw the souls of them that were beheaded for the witness of Jesus, and for the word of God, and which had not worshipped the beast, nor his image, nor had received his mark upon their foreheads, or in their hands; and they lived and reigned with the Messiah for a thousand years. (Revelation 20:4)

This verse seems to clearly depict a spiritual resurrection, since it says it was "the souls of them that were beheaded for the witness of Jesus" that "lived and reigned" with Christ "for a millennium." Opponents of this interpretation might say that the usage of the Greek word *psychas* here ought not to be construed in a highly circumscribed sense, but denotes rather that these souls or persons were raised from the dead, to reign with Jesus Christ for a millennium, in an earthly kingdom. But against this argument we have yet another passage from the same book, which also clearly depicts those who have died as martyrs for Jesus as consciously existing in a heavenly state:

9   And when he had opened the fifth seal, I saw under the altar the souls of them that were slain for the word of God, and for the testimony that they held.

10   And they cried out with a loud voice, saying, O Lord, holy and true, dost thou not judge and avenge our blood on them that dwell on the earth?

11   And white robes were given to every one of them; and it was said to them, that they should rest yet for a short season, until their fellow slaves and their brethren also, that should be killed as they had been, would be fulfilled. (Revelation 6:9-11)

Some might argue that this passage does not prove an actual conscious hereafter is being explicitly taught, since the passage could be parabolic. An appeal could be made to Hebrews 12:24, which speaks in a parabolic way of how Christ's blood "speaks better things" than that of Abel.[1609] But any such argument is hollow; any person reading the book of Revelation without any preconceptions or any need to "harmonize" various biblical passages, would interpret the above passage as implying that those who died as martyrs for Jesus would enjoy heavenly bliss immediately upon their mortal decease. This is what we get from a simple, straightforward reading of the text, according to the plain meaning of words. Anything else is a spurious *eisegesis.* On the other hand, the fact that Revelation 20:4 says that those souls who were martyred for Christ's sake "lived and reigned with the Messiah" could be interpreted as implying a corporeal, bodily resurrection from the dead. The Hebrew word *nephesh,* which is generally translated as *psychae* in the Greek Septuagint, is often used in a very bodily sense in the Pentateuch.

The Pauline corpus also strongly supports a spiritual conception of the afterlife. In first Corinthians, we read that Jesus became a spirit.[1610] We also read that "flesh and blood cannot inherit the kingdom of God"[1611] which is much different from what is found in Luke and John.[1612] We can also be quite sure that no "intermediate" state of a hypothetical temporary spiritual existence is being spoken of in first Corinthians; in fact, the entire passage is clearly speaking of the resurrection.[1613] In this connection it is notable that in that famous chapter, an exact correspondence and equivalence between Christ's resurrection and that of the believer is explicitly being made throughout. And in *that* chapter, the resurrection of Christ is depicted as a completely spiritual phenomenon. While "Paul" or whoever

---

[1609] Cp Genesis 4:10: "And he said, What hast thou done? The voice of thy brother's blood crieth unto me from the ground." Abel's blood cried out for vengeance; Christ's blood, by contrast, pleads for mercy. The martyrs of the *Apokalypse* also cry out for vengeance, and therefore this facilitates a potential argument for a parabolic reading of the passage.

[1610] I Corinthians 15:45.

[1611] I Corinthians 15:50.

[1612] Luke 24:36–43; John 20:19–27; 21:1–15.

[1613] I Corinthians 15.

wrote the epistle does speak of a resurrected body, it is a spiritual body, rather than a carnal body of flesh and blood. The term "body" was probably meant to imply no more than that the resurrected person would have a definitely recognizable form, rather than being some amorphous blob, like Casper the friendly ghost. Only by Christians seeking to falsely harmonze incompatible passages does the truly spiritual nature of the spiritual body spoken of in that chapter become obscured. If the text is allowed to speak for itself, then it reveals something much different from what most Christians imagine.

In second Corinthians we read that while we are at home in the body, we are absent from the Lord.[1614] The passage then goes on to say that we shoud be willing to be absent from the body and present with the Lord.[1615] In Philippians 1:23, Paul[1616] wrote that he had a desire to depart, and be with Christ, which was far better than living on in the flesh. This once again teaches us that the earliest Christians believed in an immediate spiritual afterlife upon death. Hebrews 9:27 also implies as much. But there is also another passage from Hebrews that also points to a spiritual rather than a carnal conception of the resurrection.

22 But you have come to Mount Zion, and to the city of the living God, the heavenly Jerusalem, and to *myriads* of angels,

23 and to *the* general assembly and church of the firstborn, which are written in heaven, and to God the Judge of all, and to the spirits of just men made perfect,

24 and to Jesus, the mediator of the new covenant, and to the blood of sprinkling, that speaks better things than that of Abel. (Hebrews 12:22-24)

Note the reference to "the spirits of just men made perfect"; this clearly denotes a spiritual existence in heaven hereafter, as being taught in such texts. Note well that, since these just men have been perfected, there is no need for a carnal, corporeal reasurrection from the dead

---

[1614] II Corinthians 5:6.

[1615] II Corinthians 5:8. It is worth pointing out that this passage also supports the idea that the out-of-body phenomenon was known to the earliest Christians.

[1616] Or Epaphroditus, writing in Paul's name.

to perfect them any further; in that case, they would not be truly perfect.[1617] So we have a *plethora* of evidence from the New Testament in favor of a spiritual concept of the resurrection. This is not to say that there is no evidence of a contrary teaching of a carnal resurrection also to be found therein; but we have already recognized the fact that the New Testament is not an absolute unity, as Christians maintain. But even some of the passages that may be urged against a spiritual concept of the resurrection are invalid, once the concept of a spiritual body is understood. For example, in Philippians we read the following:

20 For our citizenship is in heaven, from whence we look for a savior, *our* Lord, Jesus Christ,

21 who shall change our vile body, that it may be fashioned like unto his *own* body of glory, according to the power he has to subject all things to himself. (Philippians 3:20-21)

This passage does not in the least contradict those others that we have already examined that speak of a spiritual resurrection. Christians only get a false impression because of the lies told in John and Luke, of Jesus being touched by the Apostles, and eating with them. Those things never happened after Jesus died on the cross. Even Colossians 2:9 does not contradict these other verses about a spiritual resurrection; remember we read about a spiritual body in Corinthians. The Thessalonian epistles do seem to deviate from the norm, but this has already been conceded.[1618]

So we have found abundant evidence from within the New Testament itself in support of a spiritual concept of the resurrection.[1619] In fact, it could be argued that the very fact that later texts were written in more explicit support of a more physical concept of

---

[1617] Of course opponents might argue that the perfection spoken of was merely moral perfection, rather than ontological perfection. But once again this is a hollow argument, since the entire thrust of the Pauline corpus is contrary to an imagined corporeal resurrection in carnal bodies of flesh and blood. One has but to consult the famous fifteenth chapter of first Corinthians to find the most definitive Pauline teaching on the resurrection, and it is unambiguously a spiritual conception.

[1618] Although strictly speaking the point is debatable.

[1619] Of both Christ and the individual believer.

the resurrection only serves to prove that the New Testament was ambiguous on the point, and even leaned in the opposite direction. So a spiritual conception of Jesus' own resurrection is also more compatible with all the other evidence we have uncovered herein.[1620]

One more example I would also like to present, for the sake of greater completeness.

18 For even Christ himself suffered, once and for all; the righteous for the unrighteous; that he might bring us to God; being put to death in the flesh, but made alive in the spirit (I Peter 3:18)

The verse above is mistranslated in the King James; it was not "by" the spirit, but rather "in" the spirit, according to the original Greek; furthermore, there is no need or real reason to capitalize the "s" in "spirit"; there is no supposition of it being a reference to some latter-day hypostatic person of a hypothetical trinity, but rather of Jesus' own spirit, being made alive again by God. Remember that Jesus, having been crucified, was ritually and spiritually dead, according to Judaic law. This interpretation is also likewise confirmed by the following verses of the passage, where it says that Christ "in the spirit" visited the "spirits in prison" and proclaimed a message of salvation to them, etc. As noted above, both Petrine epistles are highly Enochian in character.

Of course to Christians the resurrection is a matter of faith. Whether it was a matter of faith or sight to the Apostles must remain an open question for now. It is just barely possible that Jesus may have appeared to them in his astral body.[1621] But as I was at pains to point out above, even if we assume that such an astral vision or visions were the actual basis for belief in Christ's resurrection, we must be careful to not fall into the trap of seeking to harmonize hopelessly

---

[1620] One alternative title for this work was *The Spiritual Resurrection of Christ*. But I felt that this title would have been construed as misleading, especially by Christians. So I opted for a different title, which in turn determined the ambience and tone of the book.

[1621] While the astral body is ordinarily invisible to carnal eyes, on rare occasions it can be seen. There are documented cases of this phenomenon. People have also sometimes had visions of departed relatives. In such visions, typically the deceased person looks as solid as an ordinary person; there is nothing "ghostly" about the apparition. If the Apostles experienced such visions of Jesus after his death on the cross, then this would account for the origin of belief in Christ's resurrection from the dead.

irreconcilable passages on this basis; the four narratives of the Gospels vis-à-vis Christ's post-passion appearances are all hopelessly contradictory to one another. This fact implies that no such astral vision was the basis for belief in Christ's resurrection; otherwise we would expect a uniformity of narrative in this respect.[1622] In that case, it was faith and logic[1623] that produced such an invincible belief in the minds of the Apostles and other early disciples of Jesus. They learned from Scripture that the Messiah was destined to ascend to heaven, and remain there until God sends him back to vanquish all his foes.[1624] It did not matter that his body was secretly buried in a location known only to themselves; Jesus ascended to heaven in his spiritual body, victorious over death and sin. Nothing could shake this conviction from henceforth. They staked their lives on it. They *knew* that it was true; it *had* to be. This is no more than the blind faith evinced by Christians today. In the words of their own Scripture, "Blessed is he who has not seen, and yet has believed."[1625]

While some may still feel somewhat unsatisfied by the evidence I have presented in favor of the reburial theory, we must evaluate this theory in relation to the other theories, and judge it accordingly. We have seen that rumors of a reburial of Jesus' body were circulating fairly early on, which was the motive for Matthew [or some later scribe] inventing the tale of Roman soldiers guarding the tomb. This implies that even fairly early on in the days when the Apostles were proclaiming the resurrection of Jesus many people suspected that Christ's body had simply been removed from the original tomb. It may be a prosaic explanation, but it is also economical. This explanation or theory is not burdened with the various problems associated with each of the other theories noted above. The sole objection to this theory is that it lacks any empirical basis for belief in Christ's resurrection from the dead. But even this is not an absolute, since it is at least possible that the Apostles did see Christ in his astral body. There are also a

---

[1622] But I personally would want to keep the door open to this possibility, however slim.

[1623] Logic. Not ordinary logic, but rather a logical consistency based upon certain assumptions, such as the messianic status of Jesus, the divine inspiration of the Jewish Scriptures, etc.

[1624] Daniel 7:13-14; Psalm 110:1.

[1625] John 20:29.

few other things that must be considered. First is the fact that, with the sole exception of Saul, Jesus only appeared to either people who already believed in his messianic status, or to relatives. If Jesus had truly survived his crucifixion, or escaped it somehow, or if some other man was impersonating him after his death on the cross, then a valid question is: Why were there no appearances to doubters or neutral parties? We have also seen that, although there are contradictions all throughout the Gospels, these contradictions sharply increase in frequency and density precisely in the post-passion narratives. This is suspicious, and points to the reburial theory as the true one. Finally, there is yet another piece of literary evidence confirming the reburial theory. It does so in a very inadvertent way. In Luke's Gospel, when Jesus is talking to the Apostles, he says "These are the words that I spoke to you, while I was yet with you..."[1626] What?! If Jesus was physically present with them, as the narrative claims, how could he have spoken such words as "while I was yet with you"? Would the Apostles not immediately have asked him if he was leaving them? The very words "while I was yet with you" is a key showing us that Jesus in fact *was* no longer with them, in any ordinary sense of the term. He was dead. But this passage once again points towards the Scriptures as the basis for the disciples' messianic faith in Jesus, and hence in his spiritual resurrection from the dead, and ascension to heaven.[1627] Note well also that in the Toldoth Yeshu it is ascension to heaven that is claimed on behalf of Jesus by the disciples. Resurrection *per se* is not mentioned; it is instead implied by default.

[1626] Luke 24:44.

[1627] The verse goes on to cite the law of Moses, and the prophets, and the psalms, as speaking prophetically of Jesus. After the tragic death of Jesus on the cross *karath* in Daniel 9:26 was definitely reinterpreted to mean "cut off" rather than "make a covenant", assuming it had been interpreted otherwise previously. The dead body of Jesus pointed to a spiritual interpretation of the Messiah's exaltation by necessity.

Jesus Christ: Great in Life, Greater in Death

It has been observed that the sum influence of Jesus Christ as a person runs counter to the general flow of history; in other words, his influence has increased, rather than decreased, over time.[1628] Most historical figures, even prominent ones like Julius Caesar, Ghengis Khan, or Alexander the Great, have an influence that subsides over time. Jesus Christ is one of the rare exceptions of men whose influence can legitimately be said to have increased over time, in contrast to the usual flow of history. This is recognized in the East as one of the marks of an *avatar,* or manifestation of God. Of course Christians believe that Jesus was and is the Son of God, and most branches of Christianity acknowledge him as God the Son, fully equal to God the Father in Divinity. We have stripped away the mythical encrustations that have attached themselves to the legend of Jesus Christ, and attempted to pierce the veil of legend itself in an attempt to uncover hints of the historical Jesus. Our goal was to answer the most powerful and relevant question that could be asked about Jesus, namely, How did belief in his resurrection from the dead first arise?

[1628] F. Aster Barnwell, *The Meaning of Christ for Our Age.* (© 1984 by F. Aster Barnwell); Llewellyn Publications, P.O. Box 64383 St. Paul, Minnesota 55164; pg. 18.

We believe that the answer that we were led to is most in accord with the available evidence, critically examined. We have not sought to "humanize" Jesus but rather to uncover his original underlying humanity. Nevertheless Jesus maintains an elusive mytique not found in any other figure, including Moses, Buddha, or Mohammed. One could argue that this is merely a cultural artefact of the Jesus Christ barrier pervasive throughout Western society.[1629] But one could also posit that the mystique and continual popularity of Jesus Christ as an *archetype* in Western culture is more a product of the fact that he is associated with genuinely lofty moral sentiments and noble ideals. Whether this is rightly or wrongly so is debatable, and ultimately a matter of interpretation. From the New Testament, and especially the Gospels, we can discern that Jesus Christ was not the infallible Son of God; but we can also sometimes see an appeal to a universal ethics that rivals any other system of morality inculcated in any system of philosophy or religion. We ought not to reject pearls just because they are found in the mud. On the other hand, we cannot accept the package deal offered us by fundamentalists, evangelicals, and born-again Christians. Intellectual suicide is too high a price to pay for a temporary emotional high. The Bible belongs to everyone, not just to Christians.[1630] You can read it and study it on your own, without "guidance" from people who seek to impose their own beliefs upon you. But I have a few words of advice for anyone seeking to really acquire knowledge of the Bible. First, be aware that not all translations are equally valid or accurate. Do some research on which translations are better, and remember that the original Greek and Hebrew[1631] are more important than any translation. Also avoid all those "read the

---

[1629] Indeed one could also argue in this vein that the above-observed phenomenon of an influence "counter" to the flow of history is due more to accidental historical factors, such as the unique circumstances under which Christianity grew as a religion within the Roman empire, the "conversion" of the Emperor Constantine in the fourth century, etc.

[1630] This statement is not meant to endorse the idea that any casual reader can arbitrarily impose an equally valid subjective interpretation upon Scripture; cf II Peter 1:20.

[1631] Do not be led astray by those who claim that the Hebrew Massoretic text is inviolate, or textually superior to the Greek Septuagint version. While the Greek Septuagint is a translation, it is a translation of an earlier Hebrew text, before the Massoretes altered the text.

Bible in a year" plans; they are guaranteed to keep you ignorant of the Bible. Because you need to know the Scriptures in their original, book-by-book context to really get a grip on the Bible. Do not try to "read into" the text what is not there; just follow the simple, plain meaning of words. Do not assume that the Bible is a unity; it is not, as we have already proven above. On the other hand, do not study individual books of the Bible in complete isolation from one another, as some Christians do in their Bible studies. Do not take someone's word for what is or is not in the Bible; ask for book, chapter, and verse. Do not read the Bible carelessly or superficially. Do not confuse a Bible passage with someone's arbitrary interpretation of it. See what the passage itself actually says. Common interpretations are often wrong. Do not use a paraphrase. Avoid "study" Bibles; they will only push their own denominational interpretation, and give the false illusion of scholarship backing up the interpretation. Do not accept an interpretation simply because it is more pleasing; this is more likely to be a false interpretation. Do not confuse interpretation with belief.[1632]

Jesus Christ, like Jim Morrison, became far more famous after his death than he ever was in his life. Strikingly both men had somewhat mysterious circumstances surrounding their deaths, giving rise to legends.[1633] Jesus Christ has become the predominant *archetype* in Western culture; he is part and parcel of the collective *psyche* of Western society. Despite this, we can pierce the veil of obscurity surrounding him and see that he was just another mortal man.

[1632] Most people misinterpret the Bible out of a desire to justify belief in the Bible, or to comfort themselves with a quasi-biblical or rather pseudo-biblical justification of their own lifestyle choices or personal vices. More often than not, fundamentalists are correct in their interpretation of Scripture, as opposed to occultists, "liberals", or even critical Bible scholars. For example, there is no evidence from within the Bible itself that the first eleven chapters of Genesis were interpreted in any way other than as literal history, even by Jesus Christ himself; cf Mk 10:6-8 cp Genesis 1:27; 2:24. Fundamentalists are usually correct in their interpretation of the Bible; they are simply wrong to actually *believe* it.

[1633] In the case of Jim Morrison there is an undying urban legend to the effect that he faked his own death, and went on to live a secret second life.

The Least Improbable
Theory Must Be True

We have explored in some detail the six possible theories to account for the paradox of Jesus Christ; namely, how and why belief in his resurrection first arose. While the resurrection "theory" is the simplest in many respects, we saw that it was untenable by reason of necessary association with fundamentalist baggage.[1634] Indeed, we only even included any reference to the Christian claim of Christ's miraculous resurrection from the dead as a "theory" for the sake of completeness; in reality any such claim is merely an article of faith.[1635]

[1634] Otherwise belief in a supernatural, carnal resurrection of Jesus Christ from the dead, as it is commonly understood in Christianity, would be a completely anomalous belief, without a proper paradigmatic context. The many serious and fatal problems with the Bible, including barbaric passages, anachronisms, scientific errors, contradictions, suspicious omissions, lacunae in the text, references to lost texts, incompletenesses, imperfections, ambiguities in respect to the Canon, text, and interpretation of Scripture, all militate against any supposition of Divine inspiration in the Bible. Hence the alleged miraculous resurrection of Christ from the dead is excluded as false by default.

[1635] And hence is invalid as a theory or hypothesis. For any given postulate to be considered a valid scientific hypothesis, it must be potentially falsifiable; otherwise it is not a testable theory and instead merely an article of faith,

The survival theory was rejected for several strong reasons; for one, the unlikelihood that Jesus could have even survived his brutal ordeal. Secondly, because even assuming that Jesus did survive his passion, presumably that fact would have been clearly evident to the Apostles, when he visited them again.[1636] Thirdly, the fact that all of the alleged post-passion appearances of Christ to the Apostles recorded in the Gospels are hopelessly contradictory to one another; had Jesus really survived his passion, and then appeared alive again to his Apostles, and this was truly the basis for their belief in his resurrection from the dead, then we would expect a reasonable harmony among the four accounts. But instead they are all wildly and invincibly contradictory to one another. This fact is just as fatal to the survival theory as it is to the resurrection theory. Fourthly is the fact that Jesus only ever appeared either to Apostles, disciples, or relatives, after his passion. Why would this be, if he was a man still living in the flesh? Claims that Jesus traveled to Kashmir after his crucifixion are unwarranted by the evidence; more likely it was some other prophet who is buried in the famous tomb in Srinigar.

We have also seen that any substitution scenario is also hopelessly unlikely. It would have required some absurd acrobatics for Simon of Cyrene to have been substituted for Jesus; to even merely try to picture how it could have happened is sufficient to refute any serious countenance of such a prospect. It is also outrageously unlikely that any twin brother or double would have volunteered to be crucified in place of Jesus as a false Messiah. The story about Judas being crucified in place of Jesus is merely an artefact of Muslim faith, and not even all Muslims believe the story. It is based upon the Islamic Gospel of Barnabas, which probably dates to no earlier than the fourteenth century. Even the most probable of the substitution scenarios, namely that it was Barabbas who was crucified in place of Christ, is not without serious problems. We have seen that, although the mechanics may have allowed for such a scheme, and a case could be made in terms of the motivations of Pilate and Jesus, there are too many loose ends to sustain a belief in this theory for long. For one thing, we are not absolutely sure that there ever even was a custom of releasing a prisoner at Passover, despite the fact that this particular objection

---

superstition, or urban legend.

[1636] Unless we make the additional assumption that they were all dunces.

is likely to be overstated by opponents.[1637] This is one possible legitimate objection to this version of the substitution theory, but it is the single weakest objection. Others include the fact that, even assuming that there had been such a custom, presumably family or comrades-in-arms of Barabbas would have noticed that he never really was released, and they would have grown suspicious, to say the least. This would have been a serious loose end. Another objection is the unlikelihood that Pontius Pilate would have trusted Jesus to no longer stir up trouble, either in Judaea or Galilee. Another objection is that any such scheme was unlikely to have remained secret indefinitely. There would have been at least some Roman centurions or soldiers who would of necessity have known of the actual events. They could have blackmailed Pilate, or revealed the truth to the Jews.[1638] Another possible objection to this scenario is that it would have been too obvious to the Apostles.[1639] Another potential objection is that there is no hint of any such suspicion or any rumors to that effect in early polemic or apologetic literature.[1640] One other potential objection against the substitution theory is the wildly contradictory nature of the post-passion appearances of Jesus.[1641] Had Jesus truly escaped crucifixion somehow, and then appeared alive again to his Apostles, then there should have been a uniformity or at least harmony to the four Gospel accounts about such a momentous occasion. Another objection against the substitution theory is that Jesus only appeared alive again either to the Apostles, disciples, or relatives.[1642] That makes

---

[1637] Because a reasonably strong case can be made that there was in fact such a custom, and the agreement of all four Gospels on the point is very strong evidence in favor of such an assumption. See discussion above.

[1638] Of course in answer to this objection, one could argue that Pilate bribed the Roman soldiers in question, or possibly have threatened them with death, or blackmailed them in some way, or some combination thereof.

[1639] Once again unless we make the additional assumption that they were dunces. The same objection applies to the survival theory, as noted above.

[1640] This same objection may also be lodged against the survival theory, with the possible exception of my interpretation of *ptoma* in the Greek text of Mark 15:45.

[1641] As we have seen this is also a legitimate objection against the survival theory.

[1642] As we have seen this is also a legitimate objection against the survival theory.

no less than eight strong and legitimate objections against the Barabbas version of the substitution scenario, or the substitution theory in general.

The impersonation theory is even weaker and more improbable. It is too far-fetched to think that some other man, regardless of how much he may have resembled Jesus, was able to fool men who were intimately familiar with Jesus, into thinking that he was Jesus risen from the dead. He would have had to have had the very same appearance, the same voice, the same mannerisms, the same body language, the same personality, the same kind of teachings, and everything else, down to the last detail. This is even more far-fetched than Bible fundamentalism itself. This alone is enough to rule out the impersonation theory as untenable. But not only that, but once again, the various contradictions between the accounts of the time and circumstances of Christ's various post-passion appearances in the four Gospels also militates against this theory.[1643] Furthermore the fact that Jesus only allegedly appeared either to the Apostles, disciples, or to relatives, also argues strongly against this theory.[1644] Finally the fact that there is not the slightest hint of any suspicion or rumor that some other man impersonated Jesus in early polemic or apologetic literature is also a strong item of evidence against the impersonation theory.[1645] That makes four legitimate and overwhelmingly strong objections against any impersonation theory.

The phantom theory was also rejected as untenable for a number of good reasons. Most importantly, the many fossil passages found scattered throughout the New Testament point definitively to an underlying historical subtext. We cited a number of specific examples, that were sufficient to disprove any ahistorical hypothesis in the case of Jesus Christ. Even the general character of the Gospels belies any such scenario; they are far too detailed in terms of geographical and historical detail to have been entirely fabulous fiction. To argue that such copious amounts of historical and geographical detail were

---

[1643] As it also does against the survival and substitution theories.

[1644] As is also the case with the survival and substitution theories.

[1645] As is also the case with the survival theory, excepting only the use of *ptoma* in the Greek text of Mark 15:45. And also in respect to the Barabbas version of the survival theory. Early sources did speculate that Simon of Cyrene had been substituted for Christ, but we have seen that any such scenario is untenable.

necessary to create the illusion of historicity is to be guilty of the most shameless special pleading. Furthermore the phantom theory creates a psychological problem in terms of the motivation of the persons who wrote the Gospels and other New Testament documents; it is too far-fetched to suppose that anyone would have been motivated to write completely fictional accounts about an invented character. All the evidence points towards a historical origin to Christianity, rather than a mere literary origin. The Gospels and other texts of the New Testament presuppose a pre-existent messianic movement, rather than an effort to create one, literally out of the blue. Furthermore the phenomenon of contradictions between the Gospels and other New Testament texts also argues strongly against a purely literary origin to Christianity; this is also especially evident in the additional phenomenon of a sharp increase in the frequency and density of contradictions in the Gospel narratives, precisely following the passion narrative. Had Christ been a completely invented figure, we would expect a greater uniformity or at least harmonic unity to all the texts purporting to narrate the life and ministry of some invented character. And furthermore the very climax of the story, namely the resurrection, should have been especially uniform, rather than diverse and disharmonious, which it is. All of this evidence points away from Christ having been completely invented by a literary conspiracy. We have also seen that an appeal to the supposed silence of Josephus, Philo, and Suetonius is specious. We have the earlier example of the Teacher of Righteousness, mentioned in the Dead Sea Scrolls, who has not as yet been accurately identified.[1646] We have also seen that in some cases, actual historical men have been credited with miracles, and even deified.[1647] The supposed similarity of circumstances of Christ's life and ministry with a ubiquitous messianic *mythos* is no real

---

[1646] We are of course excluding those provably false theories that have sought to identify the Teacher of Righteousness with either James the Just, John the Baptist, or Jesus Christ himself, since all three theories violently violate the explicit chronology of the Damascus Document. So the Teacher of Righteousness remains unidentified as yet, leaving a strong example and precedent of a man considered significant by a religious community (as was Jesus among his disciples) but who nevertheless apparently was not historically significant in his own time. This perfectly parallels the case of Jesus, and effectively silences the argument from silence.

[1647] The Caesars, for example.

argument against his onetime historical existence *per se*. Jesus Christ is understandable in the context of first-century Jewish religious beliefs. The Jewish messianic theme is merely a subset of the larger, multicultural messianic *mythos*. This in no way proves that no men ever stepped forward with messianic claims among the Jews. One has but to read Josephus to learn the contrary. As such, the fate of Jesus need not surprise us. But all of this evidence strenuously militates against any supposition that Jesus Christ was a completely invented character. There was a man underneath the myth and legend. Finally, there is not the slightest hint of any suspicion or rumor that Jesus was merely a literary invention in any of the early polemic or apologetic literature.[1648] Finally, there are many instances in the New Testament of multiple persons having the same name; there are at least two or three Marys, at least five Simons; at least three men named James; at least four men named Judas; at least two men named Ananias; at least three or four men named John; at least four men named Joseph; at keast two men who had the name Antipas; at least three men who had the name Philip; at least two men who had the name Mark; at least two women had the name Salome. Writers of fiction do not typically multiply characters with the very same name; the very opposite is the case. The fact that so many people in the New Testament share names in common with other characters is overwhelmingly strong evidence against any phantom theory vis-à-vis Jesus Christ. The only answer that phantom theorists could make to this would be to resort to special pleading, which they invariably do; either that, or to take shelter in a conspiracy of silence.

By contrast, we can clearly see that there were suspicions among many Jews that the disciples of Jesus had removed his body from the original tomb, and buried it secretly elsewhere, in some unknown

---

[1648] Despite what some pseudo-scholars might claim to the contrary by pointing to Gnostic Gospels. In fact the Gnostic Gospels depict Jesus as a historical person; even the Docetist texts acknowledge Jesus as historical, albeit incorporeal. But men like Timothy Freke and Peter Gandy are completely disingenuous in claiming that Gnostic or Docetic texts depict a non-historical Jesus. There is no argument to the effect that Jesus had been merely an invented literary character, in the same vein in which they argue; to construe such texts as teaching any such thing is the epitome of dishonesty.

location. In fact this is clearly stated in Matthew's Gospel.[1649] In fact, such suspicions were clearly the reason why Matthew invented the tale of Roman soldiers guarding Christ's tomb.[1650] This story is not found in any of the other three Canonical Gospels. So early on there were suspicions that the disciples had removed Jesus' body from his original tomb, and reburied it elsewhere. Matthew does his best to squelch such rumors, but he only has recourse to a tale that is easily discerned as false. So much so that neither Luke nor John reiterate a word of it, but follow Mark's text against Matthew's.[1651] Had either Luke or John been able to confirm Matthew's tale then no doubt they would have also incorporated it into their own narratives. The fact that they did not speaks volumes against any supposition that it was a true story. The reburial theory is the simplest, most economical theory in terms of the interpretation of the available evidence; the facts all support it as the most likely inference. The reburial theory is not burdened by any of the problems or objections that any of the other theories are burdened with. The sole objection against the reburial theory is that it leaves no visible basis for Christ's post-passion appearances to the Apostles. But even this objection is not absolute.[1652] Yet even this objection, if allowed to stand as an objection, is not altogether insurmountable. It must be weighed against the objections lodged against each one of the other five theories. Even if the Apostles did not see Jesus alive again after his passion, and they knew that his body was buried in a secret location known only to themselves, and by themselves; still their messianic faith in him could have given birth to an unshakable conviction that Jesus had victoriously ascended to heaven as the Messiah and the Son of man, in his spiritual body. This is not in the least bit far-fetched, in my opinion. The reburial theory is the only theory that fully accounts for all of the relevant facts of the case. It accounts better for the phenomenon of the stark increase in frequency and density of contradictions in the post-passion narratives

---

[1649] Mt 28:13–15.

[1650] Mt 27:62–66; 28:11–15.

[1651] Although the story of Roman soldiers guarding Christ's tomb is found in some apocryphal Gospels, such as MtN, the Gospel of Peter, and the Gospel of Nicodemus. Most likely these all postdate the four Canonicals.

[1652] i.e., if we are willing to consider the possibility that Jesus may have appeared to the Apostles in his astral body.

of the Gospels.[1653] It is a historical theory, thus doing justice to the fossil passages. It does not have the baggage of fundamentalism. It also does not have the baggage of the many strong and valid objections against each of the other four theories. The reburial theory emerges as the true theory by default alone. But we can also see that there is a simplicity and economy to the reburial theory that lends itself to our recommendation. It is the only alternative theory to the resurrection *explicitly* mentioned within the New Testament itself.[1654] It emerged as a suspicion *before* there were any rumors that Simon of Cyrene had been substituted for Jesus.[1655] The only alternative theory that *might conceivably* predate the reburial theory was a survival theory, based upon the use of the Greek word *ptoma* in some manuscripts of Mark's Gospel.[1656] But as we have seen there are at least four very strong and valid objections against the survival theory. However improbable the reburial theory may at first seem, it is in fact the *least* improbable theory, and therefore it must be true on that basis.[1657] Stated otherwise, the reburial theory is the most probable theory, and can be safely accepted as provisionally true. It is a better working model than any of the others.

I have sought to use words as my tools herein, to illustrate historical truth, or at least the most probable truth. I have sought to paint a picture, take a snapshot, sculpt a scenario, tell a story, decode literary texts, and decipher true history, hidden beneath layers of religious legend, myth, and tradition. But what is more important than

---

[1653] In other words, this phenomenon remains a problem for all six theories, but it is less of a problem by far for the reburial theory than for any of the other five. Furthermore we know that one of the six theories *must* be true, so the reburial theory must be true by default.

[1654] Mt 28:13–15.

[1655] This is evident by the fact that both Matthew and Luke mention Simon of Cyrene in their respective narratives; cf Mt 27:32; Lk 23:26 cp Jn 19:17. See discussion on the order of the Gospels above.

[1656] Mk 15:45, Greek. See Nestle-Aland.

[1657] The only possible justification for countenancing a more improbable theory as being true would be the additional assumption that the facts of the case are more complex than what I have stated herein. However I feel that any such assumption is entirely unwarranted; I feel that I have diligently presented all of the relevant evidence herein, albeit circumscribed by the necessity of comparative brevity.

my words are my reasons. The reasons offered are simple and easy to understand. It is easy to make a comparison now between the various theories, and to see clearly which of them is the best and strongest, and therefore the most likely to be true.

One final point I would also like to make or rather reiterate before moving on. My case in favor of the reburial theory as presented herein is not in any way deleterious to the chronological theory presented in my earlier work, and neither is my former chronological theory injurious in the least to a reburial scenario as depicted herein. While each book will have to stand or fall on its own merits, and each theory must be considered discretely, there is no logical prohibition from assuming a reburial scenario in the first century B.C. While neither theory is contingent upon the other, neither is there any necessity to keep them altogether separate; they both could be true.

Occam's Razor & The Movie Script Test

The principle of parsimony, otherwise known as Occam's razor, or simply economy of thought, is essentially that the simplest, most straightforward explanation of a given phenomenon or set of facts is the most likely to be true, all other things being equal. In other words, more complex explanations are less likely to be true, and additional assumptions to any theory inherently weaken it and render it less plausible. The principle of Occam's razor is generally held to be axiomatic, although strictly speaking it is not regarded as an axiom of logic. It is more of a common sense approach to interpreting empirical evidence. It has been pointed out that sometimes the principle has been falsified in terms of earlier scientific theories, but this is acknowledged to be due to an accumulation of previously unknown facts, giving rise, in some cases, to more complex theories to account for the universe or the laws of physics. However, in respect to a historical puzzle or unsolved mystery, Occam's razor seems to be an eminently appropriate criterion to determine the most probable hidden circumstances of a given case. Only if certain previously unknown historical facts come to light could a more simple theory give way to a somewhat more complex explanation.[1658] On the other hand, in some

---

[1658] Note well the use of the conditional "could" rather than the necessary

cases at least, the relevant facts of the case can be isolated in such a way and reduced to such a bare minimum of possible interpretations that no amount of additional evidence can reasonably alter the verdict of the diligent historian. I dare say that the case of Jesus Christ is one perfect example of this. No amount of additional evidence can possibly alter the verdict offered herein, since the essential evidence is something that can never be changed. In the case of Jesus Christ, the essential evidence is the New Testament itself. The New Testament documents are what they are, and no subsequent discovery[1659] can change the essential contents of those texts. For example, nothing can remove the fossil passages from the New Testament; they stand as witnesses to a genuine historical subtext to the narrative. Merely ignoring them is not going to make them disappear or go away. Neither will the various contradictions vanish if a person chooses to turn a blind eye to them. The order of the Gospels can only be further confirmed by diligent literary analysis. In other words, the essential evidence will always remain the same. Various other documents such as the Dead Sea Scrolls and the Nag Hammadi Codices may provide a greater literary and historical context, but they do not radically alter the essential facts of the case. The evidence is what it is, and lends itself to a finite number of possible interpretations. It is a matter of asking the right questions, and maintaining clarity of thought in our inquiry. We have sought to simplify matters by asking a single pointed question: namely, How did belief in Christ's resurrection first arise? We have seen that there are only six possible answers to this question. And by a comparison of the merits of each of the six possible answers we have finally arrived at the correct solution. And there can be very little, if any, reasonable doubt that the reburial scenario is the correct answer to the question. I challenge the reader to refute this statement. From now on, anyone advocating any one of the other five explanations will have to address all of the evidence presented herein, if he or she expects to be taken seriously. The problem for

---

"would" in the sentence above; this is intentional; for in some instances, any number of additional facts may only serve to reinforce a good, sound historical theory.

[1659] Such as the Dead Sea Scrolls, the Damascus Document, the books of Enoch and Jubilees, the Nag Hammadi Codices, or the Gospel of Judas. This is even more the case with respect to certain dubious documents that allegedly claim that Jesus traveled to India, etc.

them is that there is no other theory or paradigm that accounts for all of the relevant evidence as well as the simple reburial paradigm does. The reburial solution is the one with the fewest attendant problems. Furthermore we know that one of the six possible solutions must be true, since there are no other solutions to the paradox of Jesus Christ. Therefore the reburial explanation must be true. It is the most parsimonious explanation, and therefore must be accepted as true. The evidence converges in an unexpected and unsolicited way to prove the truth of the reburial paradigm. It can safely be regarded as a historical fact.

One further thought-experiment may be carried out to confirm the truth of the reburial theory. I call it the movie script test. One can imagine each one of the six theories as the basis for a movie script.[1660] The test involves using all of the available evidence as the basis for the movie script, and then following through with each one of the six possible theories; the final test is whether or not one can come up with a plausible, historically believable theatrical production.[1661] In other words, rather than mere entertainment, we are looking for realism. Does any one of the other five theories even remotely come out looking like something that could have actually happened in real life? I don't think so. Once again, the script cannot blithely ignore

---

[1660] Of course we have had devotional religious movies about Jesus, as well as traditional passion plays. Mel Gibson's *The Passion of the Christ* is a popular example. Another is a movie entitled simply *Jesus,* which was based entirely on the Gospel of Luke. But both of these examples fail the movie-script test miserably, since important key evidence is ignored; for example, by using *only* the Gospel of Luke as a scriptural basis for the latter movie, the fact that the four Gospels are hopelessly contradictory to one another is not addressed, and conveniently swept under the rug. In the case of Mel Gibson's movie, the same principle applies; it is based almost entirely on the Gospel of Matthew; and even if any other Gospel were consulted, any discrepancies between the Gospels is selectively omitted. This is unfair and creates a false impression that the resurrection scenario is plausible, when in fact it is not. Devotional movies based on belief in Christ's corporeal resurrection from the dead should probably instead use the text of the *Diatessaron* as the scriptural basis. It would still be unfair and dishonest, but would give a more comprehensive view. Those with New Age beliefs about Jesus would probably want to use *The Aquarian Age Gospel of Jesus, the Christ of the Piscean Age* as their scriptural basis, or possibly the earlier *Unknown Life of Jesus Christ.*

[1661] i.e., as opposed to the completely surreal *Last Temptation of Christ.*

important pieces of the evidence; everything must be explained in some way. And the explanation has to be *believable*. There is no room for poetic license. Take for example, the survival theory as the basis for the movie script. The movie would have to show how Jesus was able to first of all survive his brutal ordeal, and then also escape detection from both the Romans and the Jewish elders, scribes, chief priests, Pharisees, Sadducees, Herodians, publicans, and their agents, after his recovery. The movie would also have to somehow reconcile the four starkly different Gospel accounts of Jesus' post-crucifixion appearances to his Apostles. The movie would also have to show how the Apostles mistook a Jesus who survived crucifixion for one who rose from the dead. And this would have to be presented in a believable way. Oh yes, the movie is also not supposed to be a comedy, but more of a drama or even a documentary. Even Hollywood could not produce a believable epic meeting all of the above requirements. The same holds true for the impersonation theory, the phantom theory, and any version of the substitution theory. These could be nothing but the most outrageous farces imaginable. Imagine a movie depicting some impostor impersonating Jesus after the crucifixion, and actually convincing the Apostles that he was really Jesus. Even the very actors would not be able to keep a straight face. Or imagine a movie in which a group of men conspire to invent the character of Jesus by writing mutually contradictory Gospels. That doesn't pass the smell test. Or imagine a movie in which Barabbas is crucified in place of Jesus. Superficially it may sound like an interesting plotline, but what about the loose ends? How will the fact that Barabbas was never actually released be accounted for? How could Jesus be depicted as anything but the most villainous con-artist if he sought to perpetrate an outrageous fraud on his own trusted Apostles? And how could those Apostles be depicted as anything but comical dunces if they accepted Jesus as risen from the dead, in the midst of such a charade?[1662] We can clearly see that these

---

[1662] It should be pointed out that, in the case of either a substitution or survival scenario, if Jesus disclosed the truth to his Apostles, then his mere appearance to them after the crucifixion could no longer function as the *explanation* for how belief in his resurrection originated; thus those theories themselves would thereby be rendered superfluous and redundant. If the story of a miraculous resurrection from the dead was merely a historical parable within such a context, the reburial theory is a simpler model in which to frame such an explanation, and it lacks the various problems and objections that these two other theories have as unnecessary baggage.

other theories all fail the movie script test. By contrast, a script based on the reburial scenario would be believable, and could also do justice to all of the available evidence.

So we can see that the reburial scenario is confirmed both by Occam's razor and also by the movie script test.

The Mystery Solved

●

Ｗe sought to unravel the key mystery of Jesus Christ herein, and we succeeded. We used a process of diligent analysis of all the evidence, forensic literary archaeology, and critical reductionism. We first presented a wealth of relevant data in great detail, sobriety and candor. We then proceeded to show that all of the relevant evidence is subject to interpretation. We narrowed the focus of our inquiry by asking the single most pointed and relevant question about Jesus Christ. Namely, How did belief in his resurrection from the dead first originate? We made a conscious decision to maintain clarity of thought and expression throughout our inquiry. We saw that all of the available evidence lends itself to only six possible answers to our question. By a process of comparison, contrast, and sharp analysis, we found that only one theory satisfied all of the evidence, and emerged by default as the true theory. A process of selection through elmination was utilized, producing a coherent result. While the author does not claim to be particularly eloquent or articulate, neither did he seek to obfuscate the issue by unnecessary obscurity or prolixity. Neither did he seek to cloud the question at hand with tedious artifices or contrived erudition. At the same time he realized the gravity and profundity of the subject-matter and treated it accordingly. He did not seek to affect an irreverent or iconoclastic attitude, but rather one of historical inquiry. A veil has been lifted from a great mystery. It is now time to turn the page in Western history, and in the history of the world. Jesus Christ has been dead and buried for two millennia; it is now time to bury him again in our collective *psyche*. This is not to deny that he may live on in a spiritual sense; but the same is equally true of all souls who have passed beyond the gates of death.

JESUS CHRIST
REST IN PEACE

Bibliography

ABINGDON'S STRONG'S EXHAUSTIVE CONCORDANCE
OF THE BIBLE WITH HEBREW, CHALDEE &
GREEK DICTIONARIES. STRONGEST STRONG'S
EXHAUSTIVE CONCORDANCE OF THE BIBLE
[Larger Print Edition] James Strong, LL.D, S.T.D. FULLY
REVISED AND CORRECTED BY John R. Kohlenberger
III & James A. Swanson. © 2001 Zondervan. [including
Hebrew, Aramaic & Greek dictionaries]. Apocrypha: King
James Version. 1611. Bible; Holy Bible: King James Version.
1611. BIBLIA HEBRAICA STUTTGARTENSIA. (©1983
Deutsche Bibelgesellschaft Stuttgart) EDITIO FUNDITAS
RENOVATA. H.P. Ruger & J. Ziegler (ediderunt) K.
ELLIGER & W. RUDOLPH. Textum Masoreticum curavit
G.E. Weil. (Leningrad Codex B19A). BIBLIA SACRA
VULGATA. (©1969 Deutsche Bibelgesellschaft Stuttgart)
IUXTA VULGATAM VERSIONEM.

Allegro, John M., *The Sacred Mushroom and the Cross.* © 1970 John
Allegro.

Allegro, John M., *The Chosen People.* © 1971 John Allegro.

Allegro, John M., *The Dead Sea Scrolls and the Christian Myth.* © 1981
John Allegro.

Anderson, Robert., *DANIEL IN THE CRITICS' DEN*. [public domain].

Andrews, Richard, and Paul Schellenberger., *THE TOMB OF GOD*. © 1996 Pactolus. Warner Books.

Baigent, Michael, with Richard Leigh & Henry Lincoln., *HOLY BLOOD, HOLY GRAIL*. © 1982 Michael Baigent, Richard Leigh & Henry Lincoln. London: Jonathan Cape.

Baigent, Michael, with Richard Leigh & Henry Lincoln., *THE MESSIANIC LEGACY*. © 1986 Michael Baigent, Richard Leigh & Henry Lincoln. Bantam Dell.

Baigent, Michael, with Richard Leigh and Henry Lincoln., *The Dead Sea Scrolls Deception*. © 1991 Michael Baigent, Richard Leigh & Henry Lincoln. London: Jonathan Cape.

Baigent, Michael., *THE JESUS PAPERS*. © 2006 Michael Baigent. HarperCollins Publishers 10 East 53rd Street, New York, NY 10022.

Barker, Margaret., *The Great Angel: A Study of Israel's Second God*. © 1992 Margaret Barker. Westminster/John Knox Press.

Barnwell, F. Aster., *The Meaning of Christ for Our Age*. © 1984 F. Aster Barnwell. Llewellyn Publications.

Budge, E.A. Wallis., *The Book of the Bee*. (the Book of the Bee was first written in Syriac by Solomon of Akhlat in the early thirteenth century; an English translation by E.A.Wallis Budge was first published by Clarendon Press in 1886; reprint available from Gorgias Press ©2006). Gorgias Press 46 Orris Ave., Piscataway, NJ 08854 USA. ISBN: 1-59333-402-8.

Charles, R.H., (translator), *The Book of Jubliees*. (Originally published in 1917 by the Society for Promoting Christian Knowledge, London). Reprint available from The Book Tree. The Book Tree P.O. Box 16476 San Diego, California 92176. http://www.thebooktree.com. ISBN: 1-58509-238-X.

Charles, R.H., (translator & editor), *The Book of Enoch*. (First published in 1917); reprint available from The Book Tree. The Book Tree P.O. Box 724 Escondido, California 92033. ISBN: 1-58509-019-0.

Clay, Albert Tobias., *AMURRU, THE HOME OF THE NORTHERN SEMITES*. [1909].

Cohen, Abraham., *EVERYMAN'S TALMUD.* © 1949 E.P. Dutton. Schocken Books.

Cohn, Haim., *THE TRIAL AND DEATH OF JESUS*. HarperCollins Publishers © 1967.

Del Mar, Alexander., *The Worship of Augustus Caesar*. (1900; reprint available from Kessinger Publishers). http://www.kessinger.net.

d'Olivet, Fabre., *The Hebraic Tongue Restored*. [1921]

Dunlap, S.F., *SOD THE SON OF MAN*. [1877 or earlier; public domain].

Ehrman, Bart D., *Lost Scriptures*. (©2003 Oxford University Press). ISBN: 13-978-0-19-514182-5.

Ehrman, Bart D., *Lost Christianities*. (© 2003 Oxford University Press).

Ehrmman, Bart D., *Forged: Writing in the Name of God*. © 2011 Bart D. Ehrman. New York: HarperOne.

Ehrman, Bart D., *The Orthodox Corruption of Scripture*. © 2011 Bart D. Ehrman. Oxford University Press.

Einhorn, Lena., *THE JESUS MYSTERY*. © 2007 Lena Einhorn. The Lyons Press.

Einhorn, Lena., *A SHIFT IN TIME*. © 2016 Lena Einhorn. Yucca Publishing.

Eisenman, Robert., *The Dead Sea Scrolls and the First Christians*. © 2000 Robert Eisenman. Element Books.

Eisenman, Robert., *James the Brother of Jesus.* © 1997 Robert Eisenman. Penguin Books.

Eisenman, Robert., *The New Testament Code.* © 2006 Robert Eisenman. London: Watkins Publishing.

Eisenman, Robert, & Michael Wise., *The Dead Sea Scrolls Uncovered.* © 1992 Robert Eisenman and Michael Wise. Penguin Books.

Eisler, Robert., *The Messiah Jesus and John the Baptist.* © 1931 Robert Eisler.

Elkington, David & Jennifer., *DISCOVERING THE LEAD CODICES.* © 2014 David & Jennifer Elkington. Watkins.

Eysinga, Gustaaf Adolf van den Bergh van., *RADICAL VIEWS ABOUT THE NEW TESTAMENT.* [1912]

Faber-Kaiser, Andreas., *Jesus Died in Kashmir.* © 1978 Andreas Faber-Kaiser. London: Abacus/Sphere.

Feather, Robert., *THE COPPER SCROLL DECODED.* © 1999 Robert Feather. HarperCollins.

Feather, Robert., *The Secret Initiation of Jesus at Qumran.* © 2005 Robert Feather. Bear & Co.

Feather, Robert., *Black Holes in the Dead Sea Scrolls.* © 2012 Robert Feather. London: Watkins Publishing.

Finkelstein, Israel, with Neil Asher Silberman., *The Bible Unearthed.* (©2001 Israel Finkelstein & Neil Asher Silberman). Touchstone (Simon & Schuster). Rockefeller Center 1230 Avenue of the Americas New York, NY 10020. ISBN: 9780684869131. Business@simonandschuster.com.

Gardner, Laurence., *BLOODLINE OF THE HOLY GRAIL.* © 1996 Laurence Gardner. Barnes & Noble Books [1997 edition]

Gebhardt, Joseph Glen., (ed., trans.), *THE SYRIAC CLEMENTINE RECOGNITIONS AND HOMILIES.* © 2014 Joseph

Glen Gebhardt. Grave Distractions Publications Nashville, Tennessee www.gravedistractions.com.

Goodacre, Marc., *The Case Against Q.* © 2002 Trinity Press International.

Green, Jay. P., Senior., *Interlinear Greek-English New Testament.* (Third Edition). (©1996 by Jay. P. Green, Sr.) Published by Baker Books, a divison of Baker House Company. P.O. Box 6287 Grand Rapids, Michigan 49516-6287. ISBN: 0-8010-2138-3.

Hemphill, Samuel., *THE DIATESSARON OF TATIAN.* [1888]

Hillman, David C.A., *Hermaphrodites, Gynomorphs & Jesus.* © 2013 D.C.A. Hillman. Ronin Publishing, Inc. PO Box 3008 Oakland, CA 94609 www.roninpub.com.

Hone, William., (ed.), *The Lost Books of the Bible & the Forgotten Books of Eden.* (Thomas Nelson); ISBN: 0-529-03385-2. [public domain]

Howard, George., (ed., trans.), *Hebrew Gospel of Matthew.* © 1995 Mercer University Press. Macon, Georgia.

Huller, Stephan., *THE REAL MESSIAH.* © 2009 Stephan Huller. Watkins.

Jacobivici, Simcha, and Barrie Wilson., *THE LOST GOSPEL.* © 2014 Simcha Jacobivici and Barrie Wilson. Pegasus Books LLC.

James, Montague Rhodes., *THE APOCRYPHAL NEW TESTAMENT.* © 1924 Clarendon Press. Currently available from Apocryphile Press. 1700 Shattuck Ave., #81 Berkeley CA, 94709 www.apocryphile.org.

Jonas, Hans., *The Gnostic Religion.* (©1963 by Hans Jonas). Beacon Press Books, published under the auspices of the Unitarian Universalist Association.

Josephus Flavius., *The Complete Works.* (Josephus, late first century). English translation by William Whiston, A.M. (Nashville: Thomas Nelson Publishers).

Kasser, Rodolphe, with Marvin Meyer & Gregor Wurst (editors & translators)., *The Gospel of Judas*. [with additional commentary by Bart D. Ehrman] Published by the National Geographic Society. Washington, D.C. 20036-4688. ISBN: 9781426200427. © 2008 National Geographic Society.

Kersten, Holger., *Jesus Lived in India*. © 1987 Holger Kersten. Element Books.

Kersten, Holger, with E.R. Gruber., *The Jesus Conspiracy*. (©1992 by Albert Langen/Georg Muller Verlag in der F.A. Herbig Verlagbuchhandlung GmbH, Munchen); (English translation ©Holger Kersten & Elmar R. Gruber, 1994) (©Barnes & Noble Books). Published by Barnes & Noble, Inc. by arrangement with Element Books. ISBN: 1-56619-878-X.

King, C.W., *The Gnostics and their Remains*. 1887.

Koestler, Arthur., *The Thirteenth Tribe*. © 1976 Arthur Koestler. GSG & ASSOCIATES PUBLISHERS.

Krosney, Herbert., *The Lost Gospel*. (©2006 Krosney Productions, Ltd.) National Geographic Society Washington D.C. ISBN: 9781426200410.

Laurence, Richard., (translator), *The Book of Enoch*. (first translated by Richard Laurence in 1821; reprint of the 1883 edition available from Adventures Unlimited Press). Adventures Unlimited Press One Adventure Place Kempton, Illinois 60946. ISBN: 0-932813-85-2.

Lumpkin, Joseph., (ed., trans.), *THE APOCRYPHA: Including Books from the Ethiopic Bible*. © 2009 Joseph B. Lumpkin. Fifth Estate Publishers.

Mack, Burton., *THE LOST GOSPEL: The Book of Q & Christian Origins*. © 1993 Burton L. Mack. HarperCollins Publishers.

Martinez, Florentino Garcia., (ed., trans.), *The Dead Sea Scrolls Translated*. © 1996 E.J. Brill, Leiden, the Netherlands. Eerdmans.

Mead, G.R.S., *Did Jesus Live 100 B.C.?* (1903; University Books). Reprint available from Cosimo Classics. Cosimo, P.O. Box 416 Old Chelsea Station New York, NY 10113-0416. http://www. cosimobooks.com.

Meyer, Marvin., (ed.), *THE NAG HAMMADI SCRIPTURES.* © 2007 Marvin Meyer. HarperOne.

Moss, Candida., *The Myth of Persecution.* © 2013 Candida Moss. HarperCollins.

Murdock, D.M., *Christ in Egypt.* © 2009 D.M. Murdock aka Acharya S. Stellar House Publishing.

Murdock, D.M., *WHO WAS JESUS? Fingerprints of the Christ.* © 2011 D.M. Murdock aka Acharya S. Stellar House Publishing.

Nestle-Aland., NOVUM TESTAMENTUM GRAECE. (26th critical edition) (©1979 Deutsche Bibelgesellschaft Stuttgart).

Pagels, Elaine., *The Gnostic Paul.* (©1975 by Elaine Pagels); Trinity Press International 3725 Chestnut Street Philadelphia, Pennsylvania 19104 ISBN: 1-56338-039-0.

Pagels, Elaine, and Karen L. King., *READING JUDAS.* © 2007 Elaine Pagels & Karen L. King. Penguin Books.

Patai, Raphael., *The Hebrew Goddess.* © 1967 Wayne State University Press.

Prophet, Elizabeth Clare, *Forbidden Mysteries of Enoch.* © 1983 Summit University Press.

Robinson, James M., *The Secrets of Judas.* (©2006 James M. Robinson) HarperCollins Publishers 10 East 53rd Street, New York, NY 10022. http://www.harpercollins.com.

Rule, William Harris., *HISTORY OF THE KARAITE JEWS.* [1870] Forgotten Books.

Salibi, Kamal., *Conspiracy in Jerusalem: Who was Jesus?* (©1998 Kamal Salibi) First published in 1988 in hardback as *Conspiracy in*

Jerusalem: The Hidden Origins of Jesus. Paperback edition first published in 1992. Published in 2007 by Tauris Parke Paperbacks, and imprint of I.B.Tauris and Co. Ltd. 6 Salem Road, London W2 4BU. 175 Fifth Avenue, New York NY 10010. Distributed in the United States of America and Canada by Palgrave Macmillan, a division of St. Martin's Press. http://www.ibtauris.com. ISBN: 978-1-84511-314-8.

Schneelmelcher, Wilhelm., *New Testament Apocrypha; Volume One: Gospels & Related Writings.* (©J.C.B Mohr (Paul Siebeck) Tubingen, 1990) (English translation Copyright © James Clarke & Co. Ltd. 1991) Westminster/John Knox Press, Louisville, Kentucky 40202-1396.

Schonfield, Hugh., *The Passover Plot.* © 1965 Hugh Schonfield.

Schonfield, Hugh., *The Essene Odyssey.* © 1984 Hugh Schonfield. Element Books. SEPTUAGINTA. (©1979 Deutsche Bibelgesellschaft Stuttgart). Afred Rahlfs, editor. (Duo volumina in uno). ISBN: 3438051214.

Shanks, Hershel., (editor), *Understanding the Dead Sea Scrolls.* (©1992 Biblical Archaeology Society) Random House: New York. ISBN: 0-679-41448-7.

Smith, George., *THE CHALDEAN ACCOUNT OF GENESIS.* [1876].

Suetonius, *The Lives of the Twelve Caesars.* (Rome; late first or early second century).

Tabor, James D., *PAUL AND JESUS.* © 2012 James D. Tabor. Simon & Schuster 1230 Avenue of the Americas New York, NY 10020.

Temple, Robert K.G., *The Sirius Mystery.* (©1976 Robert K.G. Temple). Destiny Books One Park Street Rochester, Vermont 05767. ISBN: 0-89281-163-3. http://www. InnerTraditions.com.

Thiede, Carsten Peter, with Matthew d'Ancona., *THE JESUS PAPYRUS*. © 1996 Carsten Peter Thiede and Matthew d'Ancona. Bantam Doubleday Dell.

Thiering, Barbara., *Jesus and the Riddle of the Dead Sea Scrolls.* © 1992 Barbara Thiering.

Thomas, Michael., *JESUS 100 B.C.* © 2011 Michael Thomas. AuthorHouse. 1663 Liberty Drive Bloomington, INDIANA 47403. www.authorhouse.com.

Tsedaka, Benyamim., (ed., trans.), *THE ISRAELITE SAMARITAN VERSION OF THE TORAH.* © 2013 Benyamim Tsedaka and Sharon Sullivan. Eerdman's Publishing Co.

Unterbrink, Daniel T., *JUDAS of NAZARETH.* © 2014 Daniel T. Unterbrink. Bear & Co.

Vermes, Geza., *The Complete Dead Sea Scrolls in English.* © 2011 Geza Vermes. Penguin Books.

Voskuilen, Thijs, and Rose Mary Sheldon., *Operation Messiah.* © 2008 Thijs Voskuuilen & Rose Mary Sheldon. Valentine Mitchell. www.vmbooks.com.

Wiebe, Wolfgang., *The Bible Delusion: A Born Again Nightmare.* © 2008 Wolfgang Wiebe. Trafford Publishing. www.trafford.com.

Wise, Michael, with Martin Abegg, Jr. & Edward Cook., *The Dead Sea Scrolls.* (©1996 by Michael Wise, Martin Abegg, Jr., & Edward Cook). HarperCollins Publishers, 10 East 53rd Street, New York, NY 10022. ISBN: 0060692006. http://www.harpercollins.com.

Abegg, Martin Jr., Peter Flint & Eugene Ulrich., *The Dead Sea Scrolls Bible.* © 1999 Martin Abegg Jr., Peter Flint & Eugene Ulrich. HarperCollins. Yonge., (trans.), *The Works of Philo.* © 1993 Hendrickson Publishers Marketing LLC. ISBN: 978-1-56563-809-9.

Addenda

I wrote the original edition of *The Secret Tomb* in 2010 as a sequel [of sorts] to my first book, *JESUS 100 B.C.* {although *Jesus 100 B.C.* was not published until early the following year}. Due to setbacks and preoccupation with more-or-less necessary activities, I didn't have occasion to do much with the manuscript in the interim. But an opportunity presented itself, and I *seized the day,* as it were. Yet with such a massive text as the foregoing, it would have been a truly Herculean task to do any kind of extensive editing, much less rewrite the book from scratch, as it were. Therefore I chose to only do relatively light editing to the text. Nevertheless I still wanted to be sure that it accorded with my own current views. I have sought to do the appropriate editing to the best of my ability, without making my publisher wait an undue length of time. But I thought it would be most economical and ergonomical to simply add these brief *addenda* to my manuscript above. Therefore I crave the reader's indulgence; hopefully the reader will not have lost patience with such a lengthy thesis as the above. But I felt that the gravity of the subject-matter fully justified such an in-depth treatment. I wanted to illustrate just how broad, deep and complex the subject of the origin of Christianity as a religion could be. But I also feel that, after presenting and covering sufficient ground in that respect, I thereafter greatly simplified the relevant subject-matter by asking the single most important question. I trust that I have provided a sufficiently compelling answer above.

Neither do I wish to in any way dilute or weaken what I have written in the foregoing text.

In respect to *Jesus 100 B.C.*, I want to clear up a few possible misconceptions. While I mentioned my mistake about *membranas* and the codex form of books, compared to scrolls, above, my own sense of honesty and intellectual integrity compels me to also be honest about the rest of that work. In this respect I feel that I am eminently more honest and honorable than any number of other authors, who write about these things. Aside from the actual *thesis* of that book, which is ultimately a question of interpretation of the evidence, I still feel that in regard to the factual correctness of what I presented, most of it was correct. One thing I got wrong, aside from the forementioned issue of codices versus scrolls, was that I said that there was no English translation of the actual *biblical* texts of the Dead Sea Scrolls. I was wrong about that: even at the time, there had been an English translation of such documents, known as the *Dead Sea Scrolls Bible*. The text had been edited and translated by Martin Abegg Jr., Peter Flint, and Eugene Ulrich. So, technically I was wrong. Nevertheless I still feel a sense of vindication, since the context in which I had made the statement had to do with the texts of Ezra and Nehemiah, and my contention that those texts are both pseudepigraphal and late. Having since read the requisite book in question, I can now say with even greater confidence that what I had written in the chapter on *Xerxes and Artaxerxes* was essentially correct; the tiny little fragments of what the three editors/translators claimed to be fragments of the biblical text of Ezra–Nehemiah could just as readily be fragments of a Hebrew [or Aramaic] prototype of the apocryphal text known as I Esdras. Furthermore, in either case, there is absolutely no proof that the text in question had been written before 50 B.C. This was essentially all that I was claiming in respect to the "delay of the time" evident after that date, or within three or four years after that date, based upon a supposition that the Decree of Cyrus had been the *terminus a quo* of Daniel's prophecy of the seventy weeks. I pointed out how an apparent "delay of the time" was evident in the Habakkuk pesher. There may have been a few other mistakes in my text, but for the most part, the text I believe will stand up to genuine, honest scholarly scrutiny, rather than biased scholars who allow their own myopic view of the world to cloud their judgement. In terms of quality, my book is not the least bit inferior; in fact, I dare say it generally towers over a plenitude of more popular books written within the same *genre*. But apparently there is an ongoing conspiracy of silence surrounding that work, for whatever reason. Perhaps it is due to a false and superficial conception of political correctness on the part of people whom I expected to be sophisticated enough to know better. Doubtless my theory and much of my material were highly controversial; nevertheless it was hardly written for a gratuitous "shock" value. For me to be accused of being some kind of "National Socialist" simply because I had the temerity to suggest that the historical Jesus may not have been ethnically Jewish is something I might have expected in the immediate aftermath of the Second World War, but not long after the Cold War era had passed. Are these people merely children or juveniles? Obviously, the entirety of the book must be read in context. To take something entirely out of context, and use that as an example of the tenor or tone of my work is eminently unfair. I merely pointed out the rather inconvenient fact that the people of Galilee were for the most part Gentiles, rather than Jews or Hebrew Israelites. This is simply history. Josephus wrote about this. Therefore if Jesus and his family were native to Galilee, as the text of *Luke* implies, they were probably not ethnically Jewish. Period. End of sentence. Full stop. Why am I castigated for pointing this out? These people are like shameless McCarthyites. I was not trying to invent or present a so-called "Aryan" Jesus, like some latter-day Nazi. To me it is no more or less than a mere item of historical curiosity whether the historical Jesus had been ethnically Jewish, Arab, Samaritan, Idumaean, black, Levite, Hebrew Israelite, Greek, Scythian, or any other ethnic or racial identity. But I will not shrink from writing my opinions simply because it may be offensive to some people. In any case that was not the main thrust of my book. It was and is only speculation. But why is Jewish ethnic identity such a taboo topic anyway? The vast majority of people who practice Judaism as their religion in the world today are not lineal descendants of the original twelve tribes of Israel. And most of the peoples descended from nine out of the twelve tribes had apostasized from primordial Judaism even before the time of Jesus and the Apostles. Furthermore, even among the remnant of Jews who survived until the time of the prophet Ezekiel were told by that very prophet that they were descendants of Amorites and Hittites. The relevant passage is as follows:

16   Again the word of the LORD came unto me, saying, Son of man, cause Jerusalem to know her abominations, and say, Thus saith the Lord GOD unto Jerusalem: Thy birth and thy nativity *is* of the land of Canaan; the father *was* an Amorite, and thy mother an Hittite. [Ezekiel 16:1-3; KJV].

According to a literal reading of the passage above, even the Jews of that time would not have been regarded as "Jewish" according to Talmudic standards, since they had a "Hittite" for a mother. According to biblical standards, they would not have been regarded as Jewish or Israelite whatsoever; neither parent being Israelite. Bible fundamentalists cannot easily worm out of this one. Orthodox Rabbis will probably remain silent. But if we are told by apologists for the Bible that the passage in question is not meant to be taken literally, then what exactly are we to take as literal from the Bible? The whole thing might as well be a parable. I don't deserve grief over the whole Jewish question. It is all a left-wing version of fascism. As far as any other parts of my book that might seem to be "anti-Jewish" I can only urge the careful reader to read it in context. The Talmud does say the things that I pointed out, as well as any number of other things that are not too salubrious. And if any Jews are put off by anything written, either in this book, or my former book, they should rather be grateful to me, since I have in these volumes given them powerful ammunition against the Christians.

Moving on, despite what I have written in the last few chapters, I still feel that there is a good chance that the earliest Messianic Hebrews associated with Jesus were very likely *Ebionim*. In fact, I even strongly suspect that the Qumranites were actually *Ebionim*. But I will have to study the Dead Sea Scrolls more to verify this. In fact, Florentino Garcia Martinez, editor and translator of the most complete edition of the sectarian Dead Sea Scrolls, hypothesizes that the Qumranites split off from the other Essenes.[1663] This is interesting, since it necessarily qualifies, to some degree, what I have written in my manuscript above; namely, that Jesus and his group of disciples were a third remove from the Essenes. I would now quaify that by saying, more likely, the original Jesus movement was probably a third remove from Qumranism, as distinct from Essenism; John the Baptist being the

---

[1663]   Martinez, op. cit., pgs. lii-liii.

requisite link between Qumran and Jesus. In general terms, this seems historically probable.

We can certainly learn from any number of authors, even if we disagree with their theories. For example, Hugh Schonfield's book, *The Passover Plot,* may have postulated an untenable theory, but we can still learn a lot from that book, as well as his others. In the same way, John Allegro's controversial book *The Sacred Mushroom and the Cross,* may have postulated an impossible *phantom* theory vis-à-vis Jesus, but there is no doubt that Allegro was a great scholar and philologist. We can learn from all of his books. And while it is clear that I have a few "dry bones" to pick with Robert Eisenman, his scholarship is stratospheric. I also must say that I was incredibly impressed with *The Messiah Jesus and John the Baptist,* by Robert Eisler. I would say that he was probably about 96% correct in that book. I hardly ever would give anywhere near such a high rating as that. But it is worth mentioning that, in his book, Mr. Eisler brought forward evidence that Jesus may have been crucified as early as 21 C.E. This is derived from a dating in the original Latin *Acta Pilati,* which was published by the Roman Emperor Maximin Daia in 311. These original *Acta Pilati* ought not to be confused with the muchlater apocryphal text that sometimes went by the name "Acts of Pilate" in the New Testament Apocrypha. The Latin originals were purportedly the original trial transcript of Jesus Christ. There is a fairly strong presumption that this text may have been genuine, and hence most likely, correct about the date. Since Robert Eisler was such a diligent scholar, and he seems to have been correct about so much, his evidence is weighty. But aginst this Stephan Huller, in his book, *THE REAL MESSIAH,* provides evidence that Jesus was crucified in 36 C.E. Despite these rival claims, I now feel that the evidence presented by Simcha Jacobovici and Barrie Wilson in their book, *THE LOST GOSPEL,* provides the most likely crucifixion date as 32 C.E./E.V. This has to do with a possible political connection between Jesus and Sejanus. Some readers might feel that this possible connection, however tenuous or dubious, might tend to tip the scales in favor of either a substitution scenario or a survival scenario. While to some degree this *might* be true, nevertheless the totality of the evidence presented above superabundantly demonstrates the termination theory as the stongest theory. I still feel this is true. I do want to make a few observations, however. Haim Cohn, in his excellent book, *THE TRIAL AND DEATH OF JESUS,* pointed out that, according to Roman law and custom, men who were crucified were generally not permitted burial; they were apparently otherwise disposed of. While Cohn does admit that, in some rare cases, burial may have been permitted, this was not standard practice. This must have been particularly vexing to the Jews, who were so diligent about burial. But if in the case of Jesus burial had been denied, then his corpse would most likely have been cast in *Gehenna,* the garbage-heap just east of Jerusalem. Does this affect the thesis herein? Well yes and no. If we define the thesis as a reburial theory, then strictly speaking, there was no such reburial in a secret tomb. But as far as the termination theory itself goes, that remains utterly intact. Virgo intacta. But we do not know for certain whether Jesus had actually been buried or not; however it is worth pointing out that, if burial were so unheard-of amongst the peoples of the Roman empire vis-à-vis crucifixion victims, then it would never have been written into the Gospel texts. This does not assure us that Jesus in fact had been buried; but it does assure us that this was at least possible.

I also now want to make a distinction, however fine, between what I have termed above the termination theory or the reburial theory, and a pure Suffering Servant theory. This is because I left unresolved a certain distinction between a termination theory *per se* and a distinct theory I now refer to as the *doppleganger* theory. The latter theory would involve an appearance by an astral double or etheric double of Jesus; in other words, Jesus appeared in his astral body or his etheric body to the Apostles and other disciples, regardless of whether he had been buried or not. But the main problem with the *doppleganger* theory is the same problem we have with the supposition of a corporeal, bodily resurrection from the dead: the contradictory accounts between the Gospels. While to many persons in our society, the concept of survival in an ethereal body is less problematic or objectionable than the reanimation or resurrection of a corpse, based upon the known laws of physics, the problem vis-à-vis a *doppleganger* theory in the case of Jesus is that any paranormal, preternatural, or supernatural explanation for belief in Christ's resurrection from the dead is confronted with the problem of the mutually contradictory accounts, and the fact that, most likely, had there been anything extraordinary behind the proclamation of the resurrection, then we would have expected greater consistency in the accounts. Even an appeal to esotericism is unlikely to be fully satisfying in the regard, since, even the exoteric parabolic shell of an esoteric secret ought to have been more consistent. Appeal could possibly be made to rival factions within the movement; we can really only speculate about the origin of such wide discrepancies. But a pure Suffering Servant theory is essentially that pure faith alone justified belief in Christ's [spiritual] resurrection and ascension to the heavens, on the basis of the supposition that he had prophetically fulfilled the role of the Suffering Servant. From this it was not far for the early disciples to also conclude that Jesus had been the Great Prophet "like unto Moses" and also even the Messiah.

Finally, I have a few words on the Pauline corpus and the Dutch Radical Critics. I had the good pleasure to read *Marcion and the New Testament,* by John Knox.[1664] I learned a great deal from that book, needless to say. I strongly urge the reader to find and read this valuable book. From that book I learned about the Marcionite Prologues to the Pauline epistles. This forced me to rethink my position vis-à-vis the colophons to the Pauline epistles. Needless to say, there is an interesting comparison to be made between the colophons and the Marcionite Prologues. But before moving on, I cannot resist pointing out that, to the best of my knowledge, I am the first and so far only person to appeal to the colophons of the Pauline epistles as evidence of pseudepigraphy. And yet I am confronted with a stone cold silence, without any comment about this innovation. As far as I know, the Dutch Radical Critics never made such an appeal. However, they did have their reasons. Unfortunately for me, however, neither Acharya S. nor G.R.S. Mead actually went so far as to share any of this information; they merely share the bare fact that Van Manen rejected the authenticity of the entire Pauline corpus, but without giving us the benefit of his reasons. This and this alone is the reason why I accused such a person of mere "pontification" in my earlier work; had either G.R.S. Mead or Acharya S. done their due diligence, I would have been better informed. But briefly, Van Manen appealed oto internal evidence, whereas Loman had appealed to external evidence, that the entire Pauline corpus was pseudepigraphal. An excellent summary and introduction to the views of the Dutch Radical Critics can be found in *RADICAL VIEWS ABOUT THE NEW TESTAMENT,* by Gustaaf Adolf van den Bergh van Eysinga. Furthermore there is an excellent article by Hermann Detering available online in the Journal

---

[1664] Not to be confused with the famous Scottish Protestant Reformer.

of Higher Criticism vis-à-vis the pseudepigraphy of the Pauline corpus, as well as the probable original identity of the man who came to be known [to us] as the apostle Paul. See https://vridar.org/wp-content/uploads/2008/04/FabricatedJHC.pdf. The article offers heavy food for thought. Hermann Detering makes it reasonably clear that there must have been both Marcionite and Catholic recensions of the Pauline texts, and that he believes the Marcionite recension is the older of the two. While I partially agree with that, I presonally doubt that Marcion himself wrote such texts. I believe it was probably some proto-Marcionite group or person who wrote the first editions of such texts. The colophons to the epistles may denote such persons. But an alternate possibility, which I now suspect may have a greater probability, is that the colophons denote instead the final redactors of the Catholic versions of those epistles. But it is also worth pointing out that, despite all the evidence of pseudepigraphy and even lateness in the Pauline corpus, the issue is far from settled, at least in my mind. While neither time nor space will permit it, there are nevertheless strong and weighty reasons for supposing that the Pauline texts are authentic. The same is true of the Petrine epistles, or at least first Peter. There should be no fear that this position is somehow a stepping-stone to fundamentalism. There is no danger of that, at least in my case. I've already "been there; done that". But critical biblical scholarship should not feel threatened by possible early dates for biblical texts. Very likely miracles were claimed for Sabbatai Zevi, even before his occultation. The same is true of the Baal Shem Tov.

But a few other points are worth mentioning. Eysinga, in his book, postulates that Matthew was the earliest of the canonical Gospels. In this we are in agreement. He also postulates an earlier Gospel text, written either in Aramaic or Hebrew. But he proposes that the very earliest Gospel text was likely written in Greek. This latter assumption may be related to his acceptance of a *phantom* Christ theory. But this latter supposition, if true, could accord just as readily (or more readily, in my view) with the assumption that Jesus and his family had been Greek-speaking Egyptian Levites, as I speculated in my former book. Eysinga classes the Gospel of Mark as a rationalist or humanist text. There seems to be some truth to that. But to me the evidence seems to suggest that *Mark* was originally a coded anti-Gospel.

I fear I have finally reached the end of a long discourse. Rather than rambling on endlessly, I must finally reach a conclusion. What remains to be said? I certainly hope that, despite the highly controversial nature of my book, the reader has found my message to be uplifting, rather than an act of gratuitous iconoclasm. This book is not for the faint of heart. Hopefully it has been both informative as well as convincing. It is time to put away childish things. Sometimes the sage proves his wisdom by words, and sometimes he proves his wisdom by silence. And here I end.